THE
INTELLECTUAL
TRADITION
OF
THE WEST

Readings in the History of Ideas / Volume I: Hesiod to Calvin

Edited by

MORTON DONNER   *University of Utah*

KENNETH E. EBLE   *University of Utah*

ROBERT E. HELBLING   *University of Utah*

Scott, Foresman and Company

Library of Congress Catalog Card No. 67-25914
Copyright © 1967 by Scott, Foresman and Company, Glenview, Illinois 60025
All rights reserved.
Printed in the United States of America.

Regional offices of Scott, Foresman and Company are located in Atlanta, Dallas, Glenview, Palo Alto, and Oakland, N.J.

Credit lines for the readings in this volume appear with the selections themselves. The authors gratefully acknowledge the following publishers for permission to quote passages from their works among the critical comments:
Jonathan Cape Ltd. for excerpts from *Thomas More* by R. W. Chambers, copyright 1935. Reprinted by permission of the Executors of the R. W. Chambers Estate and Jonathan Cape Ltd.
Clarendon Press for excerpts from *English Literature in the 16th Century* by C. S. Lewis. Reprinted by permission of the Clarendon Press, Oxford.
Harcourt, Brace & World, Inc., for excerpts from *Medieval Culture: An Introduction to Dante and His Times* by Karl Vossler. Reprinted by permission.
Harcourt, Brace & World, Inc., and **George Weidenfeld & Nicolson Ltd.** for excerpts from *A History of Western Morals* by Crane Brinton. Reprinted by permission.
Harper & Row for excerpts from *Freedom in the Ancient World* by Herbert J. Muller, copyright 1961. Reprinted by permission of Harper & Row.
Harper & Row for excerpts from *The Image of Man* by Herschel Baker, copyright 1961. Reprinted by permission of Harper & Row.
Harper & Row for excerpts from *The World of Humanism* by M. P. Gilmore, copyright 1962. Reprinted by permission of Harper & Row.
Harvard University Press (Cambridge, Mass.) for excerpts from *Founders of the Middle Ages* by Edward K. Rand. Copyright, 1928, by the President and Fellows of Harvard College. Copyright 1956, by Belle Palmer Rand. Reprinted by permission of the publishers.
Harvard University Press (Cambridge, Mass.) for excerpts from *Three Philosophical Poets* by George Santayana. Reprinted by permission of the publishers.
Harvard University Press (Cambridge, Mass.) and **Bowes & Bowes Publishers Ltd.** (London) for excerpts from *Machiavelli and the Renaissance* by Federico Chabod. Copyright 1958, by Federico Chabod. Reprinted by permission of the publishers.

Preface

This book springs from the editors' conviction that understanding the ideas which have shaped our cultural heritage is an essential step toward sharing that heritage. A good way to reach that understanding, we believe, is to trace the formation and growth of those ideas as they have manifested themselves in the development of Western culture; and the best way to do this, we are certain, is to read the texts themselves, the primary documents that embody the ideas which have nurtured our culture. This book attempts to provide a representative collection of such texts, arranged in roughly chronological order.

In selecting the readings, we have not limited ourselves to any one intellectual discipline but have drawn from works of history, philosophy, imaginative literature, psychology, political and social theory—on the principle that the diversity in the forms of writing helps to show the breadth of impact created by the ideas. Our main criterion has been that the readings included be truly representative in two senses. First, each work chosen not only has its own individual significance but also stands for a widespread ideological attitude, so that the entire collection represents a reasonably broad survey of the important ideas that have contributed to the development of Western culture. At the same time, we have attempted to emphasize the sequence of development of certain major ideas. Second, since a two-volume survey of this sort could be managed only by printing extracts rather than complete works, each selection was chosen to capture the character of the work as a whole. To this end, rather than piece together disconnected bits from a given work to make up a sampling of the whole, we have usually selected reasonably long, continuous passages that illustrate not only what the whole work is about but how it achieves its distinctive quality.

We have deliberately excluded one kind of text from our collection —important longer works that are readily available in inexpensive complete editions. Our feeling is that works like Homer's epics, the Greek tragedies, Plato's dialogues, the Bible, Dante's *Divine Comedy*, Voltaire's

Candide are important enough to be read in their entirety or, at least, in more substantial extracts than could be printed here. Numerous editions are available, and the individual instructor can assign them in whole or part as he chooses. We have, however, included selections from associated texts that contribute to an understanding of these longer works and that are designed to be read in conjunction with them: Hesiod's *Descent of the Gods,* Aristotle's *Poetics,* Xenophon's *Recollections of Socrates,* Biblical commentaries by Philo Judaeus and Origen, Dante's *Letter to Can Grande,* Pope's *Essay on Man.*

To help stimulate individual reactions to the readings, we have presented at the end of each selection a sampling of critical comments that have been directed toward that particular work. A comprehensive list of the critical sources appears in the back of each volume for the student interested in further pursuing the analysis of any of the critics. These comments have been deliberately selected and arranged in the text to illustrate the differences of opinion among the critics and, very often, among the centuries they represent. We have found that the process of judging the validity of differing critical appraisals of a work helps establish the vitality of the ideas it represents. These comments have been chosen to help demonstrate to each individual student the spirit which has been behind the conception and creation of this entire two-volume endeavor: that the ideas that have solidified into what we call our "intellectual tradition" are still very much alive today.

Morton Donner
Kenneth E. Eble
Robert E. Helbling

Contents

Introduction

The readings in this volume range from the first ideologically significant documents in Western culture to writings that represent the last stages of development preceding the rise of modern civilization. The scene shifts from place to place and from society to society, but a common concern for human values gives continuity to different ways of thinking and establishes a single intellectual tradition throughout.

The beginnings are in ancient Greece almost three thousand years ago. In this civilization, where the small village was the largest social unit and a group of such villages the largest political unit, men felt the urge to formulate and preserve in writing their appraisal of human values and their assessment of man's role in the universe. By the end of the fifth century B.C., Greek civilization had evolved a politically sophisticated system of city-states that dominated the world around the eastern end of the Mediterranean and a culture that produced significant achievements in art, architecture, literature, historiography, science, and speculative philosophy. The main concerns in Greek thought continued to be human values and man's place in the universe, but these were now applied to a great number of specific points of inquiry. On scientific grounds, Greek thinkers set out to explain the workings of natural phenomena from the viewpoints of biology, mathematics, and physics, arriving at fundamental notions about such principles as the atomic composition of matter and its classification into basic elements. On philosophic grounds, they attempted to explain such ideas as the means that produce human knowledge, the qualities that constitute human nature, the relationships that determine human society, the forces that govern human destiny. The scope of Greek thought ran from the physical bases of the operations of the universe to the metaphysical implications of abstract conceptions like truth, knowledge, beauty, virtue, justice, freedom, deity.

Greek political influence, which had reached its peak with the conquests of Alexander the Great in the third quarter of the fourth century B.C., diminished rapidly after his death; but Greek cultural influence remained a potent force throughout the ancient Mediterranean world. When Rome began to emerge as a great power during the second century B.C., it drew upon the Greek heritage for its cultural life. Roman art, architecture, literature, historiography, science, and philosophy were all based on Greek models. The main topics in Roman thought were Greek in inspiration, though distinctly Roman in their practical turn. The Romans were better at engineering aqueducts than at formulating theories to explain gravity, better at devising equitable legal codes than at speculating about justice in the abstract. But the Roman intellectual achievement was still motivated by the same urge to understand man's physical environment and his moral being, the need to find human values in the scheme of things.

As the Roman Empire spread to encompass all the lands surrounding the Mediterranean and most of Europe, the Greek intellectual tradition spread with it. However, in one small corner of the Roman Empire among the Hebrews, there flourished an intellectual tradition which had developed largely independently of Greek culture but which had begun to confront much the same questions about human values at roughly the same time as had the Greeks. Although the Hebrews had little impact, culturally or politically, on the ancient world, they preserved a record of their own ideological development in the Old Testament. The New Testament sprang from these same ideological roots but also drew upon the Greco-Roman philosophical heritage that made up the general intellectual environment in which Christianity had its beginnings. This combination of Greek, Roman, and Hebrew thought spread with Christianity throughout the Roman world. Thus, by the fifth century A.D., when the Roman Empire had disintegrated and the Roman world had ceased to be a political entity, that same world was still very much an ideological entity because of Christianity.

For at least the next thousand years, during the so-called Middle Ages that stand between the ancient and modern worlds, Christianity was the most important single element of Western civilization, and for much of that time, Christian ideological attitudes governed the outlook of Western culture. The tone of thought expressed by St. Augustine during the first third of the fifth century dominated Christian thinking for more than seven centuries to come. Christian ideology still showed the Greco-Roman concern for human values, but the emphasis had shifted: speculative inquiry was directed mainly toward fitting men for life not in this world but in the next, for life in the hereafter rather than in the here-and-now. Social and political achievement during these centuries reflected this attitude, and the shape of Western civilization, with a few exceptions, showed little change from the forms left in the ruins of the Roman Empire.

By the twelfth century, the outlook began to broaden once again. The nation-states of Europe began to assume recognizably modern political identities, society grew more culturally sophisticated, and the scope of intellectual activity ranged over a fuller variety of human experience. The Greco-Roman ideological tradition again began to assert its influence, leading within a few centuries to a renewed emphasis in Western thought on the values that make up human life in human society as well as on man's position in the universal scheme of things. This change in emphasis is a distinctive feature of what has come to be known as the Renaissance, a label marking the overall effect of the widespread changes that took place in Western culture from the fourteenth through the sixteenth centuries.

The Renaissance, by renewing the ideological influence of Greece and Rome, necessarily embodied a change in outlook toward the relationship between Christian ideology and society. By the sixteenth century, an even more striking change began to take place in the nature of Christian ideology itself as a result of the Reformation. The Reformation, by denying the authority of the Roman Catholic Church, fragmented the previously monolithic, authoritative nature of Christian ideology. A variety of competing Christian ideologies developed, and the dominant position long held by Christian thought in Western culture in consequence of its authoritative nature began to give way. Christian ideology became only one among a number of potent ideas that engaged thoughtful men. The Reformation thus laid the foundation for the broad diversity in intellectual outlook that has distinguished the Western tradition in the modern world.

Hesiod
8th century B.C.

At the beginning of those ideas which have shaped Western culture is the ancient Greek conception of man himself, of his place in the universe, and of how he managed to reach that place. Long before philosophers attempted to explain these matters in realistic terms, the ancient Greeks were giving figurative expression to their viewpoint about the nature of man and his relationship to the world around him through their myths and legendary stories, establishing for themselves a sense of their own identity as human beings.

Our first clear insight into this process comes from the writings of Hesiod and Homer. Although it is difficult to determine the exact dates for men, events, and writings this far back in history, scholars believe that these writers lived during the ninth and eighth centuries B.C. and that the events narrated by Homer in the *Iliad* and the *Odyssey* probably took place around 1200 B.C. The mythological world Hesiod describes in the *Theogony (The Descent of the Gods)* is much older, representing the beginning of time as the Greeks conceived it. Still, it is this world which provides the vital background for all subsequent Greek thought, which came to be mixed with Roman mythology and in this form extended its influence into the Christian era.

We know little about either Homer or Hesiod, though Hesiod's *Works and Days* does give an account of his life and times. His *Descent of the Gods* represents an introduction to myth and to the bearing it has upon the great speculations of life. Hesiod's purpose is to reveal the process of development whereby man has arrived at the place he occupies in the scheme of things. That development begins with the first ruler, Heaven (Uranus), extends through his son Cronus, and culminates in the reign of Zeus, son of Cronus and chief figure in Greek mythology. In tracing the genealogy of the gods, Hesiod distinguishes three different patterns: the divine cosmos, in which Zeus and the Olympian gods are the central figures; the physical cosmos, in which everything begins with Chaos and Earth; and the human cosmos—Hesiod's invocation tells us that the Muses will chant of "the race of men and strong giants."

But there is more to Hesiod's poem (like Homer's work, it is in the tradition of oral poetry) than an account of the physical universe, gods, and men. In his acknowledgment of the eternal laws of the universe, he was anticipating in mythical terms two of the great philosophical problems in later Greek thought: how to find unity in diversity, the problem of the one and the many; and how to find permanence in the midst of change, the problem of the eternal and the mutable.

The systematic account of the gods provided by Hesiod gives way to a more dramatic description emphasizing their relationship with the world of men in Homer's *Iliad* and *Odyssey*. These two poems tell of the war in which a group of Greek tribes besiege the city of Troy in Asia Minor. The struggle is both human and cosmic. Although the ostensible cause is the abduction of Helen, the wife of a Greek ruler, Menelaus, by the Trojan prince, Paris, these are no ordinary people: in Greek mythology Helen is the daughter of a mortal woman and Zeus, and Paris was chosen to judge a beauty contest among the goddesses. Throughout the Homeric epic, the gods mingle, often meddle, in the affairs of men.

The conception of religion as we see it in the *Odyssey* displays a number of striking features: it is polytheistic, in that there are many gods; it is anthropomorphic, in that the gods are like men; and it is relatively unconcerned with human morality. Among humans, according to the Homeric conception, the greatest virtues are those that make up the heroic ideal: physical strength combined with mental agility; bravery and fortitude; curiosity and a willingness to expose oneself fully to life; a sense of honor as the guide to conduct; and a strong determination to excel no matter what the undertaking. Throughout the course of classical Greek civilization, this ideal held a high place in men's values.

The emphasis on this ideal in Homer's two poems also contributed to the nature of the epic tradition in Western thought, a tradition whose strength derives from its insistence on man's capabilities despite his limited time on earth. "There are two modes of teaching by example," wrote the Renaissance poet Torquato Tasso: "One that of inciting to good works by showing the reward of the noblest virtue and of well-nigh divine valor; the other that of frightening us from evil with a punishment. The first is that of the epic, the second that of tragedy." Although Aristotle held that tragedy was the superior form, the Homeric epics provide the indispensable background for Greek tragedy and for almost all later Greek literature and thought.

The Descent of the Gods

From the Heliconian Muses let us begin to sing, who hold the great and holy mount of Helicon, and dance on soft feet about the deep-blue spring and the altar of the almighty son of Cronos, and, when

From *Homeric Hymns and Homerica*, translated by H. G. Evelyn-White (Cambridge, Mass.: Harvard University Press). Reprinted by permission of the publishers and The Loeb Classical Library.

they have washed their tender bodies in Permessus or in the Horse's Spring or Olmeius, make their fair, lovely dances upon highest Helicon and move with vigorous feet. Thence they arise and go abroad by night, veiled in thick mist, and utter their song with lovely voice, praising Zeus the aegis-holder and queenly Hera of Argos who walks on golden sandals and the daughter of Zeus the aegis-holder bright-eyed Athene, and Phoebus Apollo, and Artemis who delights in arrows, and Poseidon the earth-holder who shakes the earth, and reverend Themis and quick-glancing Aphrodite, and Hebe with the crown of gold, and fair Dione, Leto, Iapetus, and Cronos the crafty counsellor, Eos and great Helius and bright Selene, Earth too, and great Oceanus, and dark Night, and the holy race of all the other deathless ones that are for ever. And one day they taught Hesiod glorious song while he was shepherding his lambs under holy Helicon, and this word first the goddesses said to me— the Muses of Olympus, daughters of Zeus who holds the aegis:

"Shepherds of the wilderness, wretched things of shame, mere bellies, we know how to speak many false things as though they were true; but we know, when we will, to utter true things."

So said the ready-voiced daughters of great Zeus, and they plucked and gave me a rod, a shoot of sturdy olive, a marvellous thing, and breathed into me a divine voice to celebrate things that shall be and things that were aforetime; and they bade me sing of the race of the blessed gods that are eternally, but ever to sing of themselves both first and last. But why all this about oak or stone?

Come thou, let us begin with the Muses who gladden the great spirit of their father Zeus in Olympus with their songs, telling of things that are and that shall be and that were aforetime with consenting voice. Unwearying flows the sweet sound from their lips, and the house of their father Zeus the loud-thunderer is glad at the lily-like voice of the goddesses as it spreads abroad, and the peaks of snowy Olympus re-sound, and the homes of the immortals. And they uttering their im-mortal voice, celebrate in song first of all the reverend race of the gods from the beginning, those whom Earth and wide Heaven begot, and the gods sprung of these, givers of good things. Then, next, the goddesses sing of Zeus, the father of gods and men, as they begin and end their strain, how much he is the most excellent among the gods and supreme in power. And again, they chant the race of men and strong giants, and gladden the heart of Zeus within Olympus,—the Olympian Muses, daughters of Zeus the aegis-holder. (vv. 1–52)

Hail, children of Zeus! Grant lovely song and celebrate the holy race of the deathless gods who are for ever, those that were born of Earth and starry Heaven and gloomy Night and them that briny Sea did rear. Tell how at the first gods and earth came to be, and rivers, and the boundless sea with its raging swell, and the gleaming stars, and the wide heaven above, and the gods who were born of them, givers of good things, and how they divided their wealth, and how they shared their honours amongst them, and also how at the first they took many-folded

Olympus. These things declare to me from the beginning, ye Muses who dwell in the house of Olympus, and tell me which of them first came to be.

Verily at the first Chaos came to be, but next wide-bosomed Earth, the ever-sure foundation of all the deathless ones who hold the peaks of snowy Olympus, and dim Tartarus in the depth of the wide-pathed Earth, and Eros (Love), fairest among the deathless gods, who unnerves the limbs and overcomes the mind and wise counsels of all gods and all men within them. From Chaos came forth Erebus and black Night; but of Night were born Aether and Day, whom she conceived and bare from union in love with Erebus. And Earth first bare starry Heaven, equal to herself, to cover her on every side, and to be an ever-sure abiding-place for the blessed gods. And she brought forth long Hills, graceful haunts of the goddess-Nymphs who dwell amongst the glens of the hills. She bare also the fruitless deep with his raging swell, Pontus, without sweet union of love. But afterwards she lay with Heaven and bare deep-swirling Oceanus, Coeus and Crius and Hyperion and Iapetus, Theia and Rhea, Themis and Mnemosyne and gold-crowned Phoebe and lovely Tethys. After them was born Cronos the wily, youngest and most terrible of her children, and he hated his lusty sire.

And again, she bare the Cyclopes, overbearing in spirit, Brontes, and Steropes and stubborn-hearted Arges, who gave Zeus the thunder and made the thunderbolt: in all else they were like the gods, but one eye only was set in the midst of their foreheads. And they were surnamed Cyclopes (Orb-eyed) because one orbed eye was set in their foreheads. Strength and might and craft were in their works.

And again, three other sons were born of Earth and Heaven, great and doughty beyond telling, Cottus and Briareos and Gyes, presumptuous children. From their shoulders sprang an hundred arms, not to be approached, and each had fifty heads upon his shoulders on their strong limbs, and irresistible was the stubborn strength that was in their great forms. For of all the children that were born of Earth and Heaven, these were the most terrible, and they were hated by their own father from the first. And he used to hide them all away in a secret place of Earth so soon as each was born, and would not suffer them to come up into the light: and Heaven rejoiced in his evil doing. But vast Earth groaned within, being straitened, and she thought a crafty and an evil wile. Forthwith she made the element of grey flint and shaped a great sickle, and told her plan to her dear sons. And she spoke, cheering them, while she was vexed in her dear heart:

"My children, gotten of a sinful father, if you will obey me, we should punish the vile outrage of your father; for he first thought of doing shameful things."

So she said; but fear seized them all, and none of them uttered a word. But great Cronos the wily took courage and answered his dear mother:

"Mother, I will undertake to do this deed, for I reverence not our father of evil name, for he first thought of doing shameful things."

So he said: and vast Earth rejoiced greatly in spirit, and set and hid him in an ambush, and put in his hands a jagged sickle, and revealed to him the whole plot.

And Heaven came, bringing on night and longing for love, and he lay about Earth spreading himself full upon her. Then the son from his ambush stretched forth his left hand and in his right took the great long sickle with jagged teeth, and swiftly lopped off his own father's members and cast them away to fall behind him. And not vainly did they fall from his hand; for all the bloody drops that gushed forth Earth received, and as the seasons moved round she bare the strong Erinyes and the great Giants with gleaming armour, holding long spears in their hands, and the Nymphs whom they call Meliae all over the boundless earth. And so soon as he had cut off the members with flint and cast them from the land into the surging sea, they were swept away over the main a long time: and a white foam spread around them from the immortal flesh, and in it there grew a maiden. First she drew near holy Cythera, and from there, afterwards, she came to sea-girt Cyprus, and came forth an awful and lovely goddess, and grass grew up about her beneath her shapely feet. Her gods and men call Aphrodite, and the foam-born goddess and rich-crowned Cytherea, because she grew amid the foam, and Cytherea because she reached Cythera, and Cyprogenes because she was born in billowy Cyprus, and Philommedes because she sprang from the members. And with her went Eros, and comely Desire followed her at her birth at the first and as she went into the assembly of the gods. This honour she has from the beginning, and this is the portion allotted to her amongst men and undying gods, —the whisperings of maidens and smiles and deceits with sweet delight and love and graciousness.

But these sons whom he begot himself great Heaven used to call Titans (Strainers) in reproach, for he said that they strained and did presumptuously a fearful deed, and that vengeance for it would come afterwards. (vv. 104−210)

But Rhea was subject in love to Cronos and bare splendid children, Hestia, Demeter, and gold-shod Hera and strong Hades, pitiless in heart, who dwells under the earth, and the loud-crashing Earth-Shaker, and wise Zeus, father of gods and men, by whose thunder the wide earth is shaken. These great Cronos swallowed as each came forth from the womb to his mother's knees with this intent, that no other of the proud sons of Heaven should hold the kingly office amongst the deathless gods. For he learned from Earth and starry Heaven that he was destined to be overcome by his own son, strong though he was, through the contriving of great Zeus. Therefore he kept no blind outlook, but watched and swallowed down his children: and unceasing grief seized Rhea. But when she was about to bear Zeus, the father of gods and men, then she besought her own dear parents, Earth and starry Heaven, to devise some plan with her that the birth of her dear child might be concealed, and that retribution might overtake great, crafty Cronos for his own father and also for the children whom he had swallowed down. And they readily heard and obeyed their dear daughter, and told her all that was destined to happen touching Cronos the king and his stout-hearted son. So they sent her to Lyctus, to the rich land of Crete, when she was ready to bear great Zeus, the youngest of her children. Him did vast Earth receive from Rhea in wide Crete to nourish and to bring up. Thither came Earth carrying him swiftly through the black night to Lyctus first, and took him in her arms and hid him in a remote cave beneath the secret places of the holy earth on thick-wooded Mount Aegeum; but to the mightily ruling son of Heaven, the earlier king of the gods, she gave a great stone wrap'ped in swaddling clothes. Then he took it in his hands and thrust it down into his belly: wretch! he knew not in his heart that in place of the stone his son was left behind, unconquered and untroubled, and that he was soon to overcome him by force and might and drive him from his honours, himself to reign over the deathless gods.

After that, the strength and glorious limbs of the prince increased quickly, and as the years rolled on, great Cronos the wily was beguiled by the deep suggestions of Earth, and brought up again his offspring, vanquished by the arts and might of his own son, and he vomited up first the stone which he had swallowed last. And Zeus set it fast in the wide-pathed earth at goodly Pytho under the glens of Parnassus, to be a sign thenceforth and a marvel to mortal men. And he set free from their deadly bonds the brothers of his father, sons of Heaven whom his father in his foolishness had bound. And they remembered to be grateful to him for his kindness, and gave him thunder and the glowing thunderbolt and lightning: for before that, huge Earth had hidden these. In them he trusts and rules over mortals and immortals.

Now Iapetus took to wife the neat-ankled maid Clymene, daughter of Ocean, and went up with her into one bed. And she bare him a stout-hearted son, Atlas: also she bare very glorious Menoetius and clever Prometheus, full of various wiles, and scatter-brained Epimetheus who from the first was a mischief to men who eat bread; for it was he who first took of Zeus the woman, the maiden whom he had formed. But Menoetius was outrageous, and far-seeing Zeus struck him with a lurid thunderbolt and sent him down to Erebus because of his mad presumption and exceeding pride. And Atlas through hard constraint upholds the wide heaven with unwearying head and arms, standing at the borders of the earth before the clear-voiced Hesperides; for this lot wise Zeus assigned to him. And ready-witted Prometheus he bound with inextricable bonds, cruel chains, and drove a shaft through his middle, and set on him a long-winged eagle, which used to eat his immortal liver; but by night the liver grew as much again everyway as the long-winged bird devoured in the whole day. That bird Heracles, the valiant son of shapely-ankled Alcmene, slew; and delivered the son of Iapetus from the cruel plague, and released him from his affliction—not without the will of Olympian Zeus who reigns on high, that the glory of Heracles the Theban-born might be yet greater than it was before over the plenteous earth. This, then, he regarded, and honoured his famous son; though he was angry, he ceased from the wrath which he had before because Prometheus matched himself in wit with the almighty son of Cronos. For when the gods and mortal men had a dispute at Mecone, even then Prometheus was forward to cut up a great ox and set portions before them, trying to befool the mind of Zeus. Before the rest he set flesh and inner parts thick with fat upon the hide, covering them with an ox paunch; but for Zeus he put the white bones dressed up with cunning art and covered with shining fat. Then the father of men and of gods said to him:

"Son of Iapetus, most glorious of all lords, good sir, how unfairly you have divided the portions!"

So said Zeus whose wisdom is everlasting, rebuking him. But wily Prometheus answered him, smiling softly and not forgetting his cunning trick:

"Zeus, most glorious and greatest of the eternal gods, take which ever of these portions your heart within you bids." So he said, thinking trickery. But Zeus, whose wisdom is everlasting, saw and failed not to perceive the trick, and in his heart he thought mischief against mortal men which also was to be fulfilled. With both hands he took up the white fat and was angry at heart, and wrath came to his spirit when he saw the white ox-bones craftily tricked out: and because of this the tribes of men upon earth burn white bones to the deathless gods upon fragrant altars. But Zeus who drives the clouds was greatly vexed and said to him:

"Son of Iapetus, clever above all! So, sir, you have not yet forgotten your cunning arts!"

So spake Zeus in anger, whose wisdom is everlasting; and from that time he was always mindful of the trick, and would not give the power of unwearying fire to the Melian race of mortal men who live on the earth. But the noble son of Iapetus outwitted him and stole the far-seen gleam of unwearying fire in a hollow fennel stalk. And Zeus who thunders on high was stung in spirit, and his dear heart was angered when he saw amongst men the far-seen ray of fire. Forthwith he made an evil thing for men as the price of fire; for the very famous Limping God formed of earth the likeness of a shy maiden as the son of Cronos willed. And the goddess bright-eyed Athene girded and clothed her with silvery raiment, and down from her head she spread with her hands a broidered veil, a wonder to see; and she, Pallas Athene, put about her head lovely garlands, flowers of new-grown herbs. Also she put upon her head a crown of gold which the very famous Limping God made himself and worked with his own hands as a favour to Zeus his father. On it was much curious work, wonderful to see; for of the many creatures which the land and sea rear up, he put most upon it, wonderful things, like living beings with voices: and great beauty shone out from it.

But when he had made the beautiful evil to be the price for the blessing, he brought her out, delighting in the finery which the bright-eyed daughter of a mighty father had given her, to the place where the other gods and men were. And wonder took hold of the deathless gods and mortal men when they saw that which was sheer guile, not to be withstood by men.

For from her is the race of women and female kind: of her is the deadly race and tribe of women who live amongst mortal men to their great trouble, no helpmeets in hateful poverty, but only in wealth. And as

in thatched hives bees feed the drones whose nature is to do mischief—
by day and throughout the day until the sun goes down the bees are
busy and lay the white combs, while the drones stay at home in the covered skeps and reap the toil of others into their own bellies—even so
Zeus who thunders on high made women to be an evil to mortal men,
with a nature to do evil. And he gave them a second evil to be the price
for the good they had: whoever avoids marriage and the sorrows that
women cause, and will not wed, reaches deadly old age without anyone
to tend his years, and though he at least has no lack of livelihood while
he lives, yet, when he is dead, his kinsfolk divide his possessions amongst
them. And as for the man who chooses the lot of marriage and takes
a good wife suited to his mind, evil continually contends with good;
for whoever happens to have mischievous children, lives always with
unceasing grief in his spirit and heart within him; and this evil cannot
be healed.

So it is not possible to deceive or go beyond the will of Zeus; for
not even the son of Iapetus, kindly Prometheus, escaped his heavy anger,
but of necessity strong bands confined him, although he knew many a
wile. (vv. 453–616)

Now Zeus, king of the gods, made Metis his wife first, and she was
wisest among gods and mortal men. But when she was about to bring
forth the goddess bright-eyed Athene, Zeus craftily deceived her with
cunning words and put her in his own belly, as Earth and starry Heaven
advised. For they advised him so, to the end that no other should hold
royal sway over the eternal gods in place of Zeus; for very wise children
were destined to be born of her, first the maiden bright-eyed Tritogeneia, equal to her father in strength and in wise understanding; but
afterwards she was to bear a son of overbearing spirit, king of gods and
men. But Zeus put her into his own belly first, that the goddess might
devise for him both good and evil.

Next he married bright Themis who bare the Horae (Hours), and
Eunomia (Order), Diké (Justice), and blooming Eirene (Peace), who mind
the works of mortal men, and the Moerae (Fates) to whom wise Zeus
gave the greatest honour, Clotho, and Lachesis, and Atropos who give
mortal men evil and good to have.

And Eurynome, the daughter of Ocean, beautiful in form, bare him
three fair-cheeked Charites (Graces), Aglaea, and Euphrosyne, and lovely
Thaleia, from whose eyes as they glanced flowed love that unnerves the
limbs: and beautiful is their glance beneath their brows.

Also he came to the bed of all-nourishing Demeter, and she bare
white-armed Persephone whom Aïdoneus carried off from her mother;
but wise Zeus gave her to him.

And again, he loved Mnemosyne with the beautiful hair: and of her
the nine gold-crowned Muses were born who delight in feasts and the
pleasures of song.

And Leto was joined in love with Zeus who holds the aegis, and bare
Apollo and Artemis delighting in arrows, children lovely above all
the sons of Heaven.

Lastly, he made Hera his blooming wife: and she was joined in love with the king of gods and men, and brought forth Hebe and Ares and Eileithyia.

But Zeus himself gave birth from his own head to bright-eyed Tritogeneia, the awful, the strife-stirring, the host-leader, the unwearying, the queen, who delights in tumults and wars and battles. But Hera without union with Zeus—for she was very angry and quarrelled with her mate—bare famous Hephaestus, who is skilled in crafts more than all the sons of Heaven. (vv. 886–929)

Comments / on Hesiod and Homer

Hesiod's description of the human cosmos leaves an overwhelming impression of a rich variety of possibilities in human life, between which man is free to choose. Man is even free, as the story of Prometheus shows, to align himself with forces opposed to Zeus.

NORMAN O. BROWN (1953)

The work of Hesiod as a whole is one of the most valiant failures in literature. The confusion and absurdity of it are only equalled by its strange helpless beauty and its extraordinary historical interest. The Hesiodic system when compared with that of Homer is much more explicit, much less expurgated, infinitely less accomplished and tactful. At the back of Homer lay the lordly warrior-gods of the Heroic Age, at the back of Hesiod the crude and tangled superstitions of the peasantry of the mainland.

GILBERT MURRAY (1925)

Hesiod founded this philosophy of life on the eternal laws of the universe, laws which he himself enunciates in the religious language and setting of myths. Even in Homer can be traced the beginnings of an attempt to interpret different myths by one universal philosophy. But it was Hesiod in the *Theogony* or *Descent of the Gods,* who first ventured to arrange all mythology into a comprehensive system. *WERNER JAEGER (1933)*

Of the Homeric heroes most could trace their line up through three generations, then comes a god. With some irreverence this has been suggested as meaning "And who *his* father was, God only knows"; with more reverence, one may suggest alternatively that it represents a claim to divine favor made by the founder of a dynasty.

Homer had no complete philosophic system. Nevertheless, he sees that there is a unity in things, that events have their causes and their results, that certain moral laws exist. This is the framework into which the particular action is seen to fit. The divine background of the epic means ultimately that particular actions are at the same time unique and universal.

H. D. F. KITTO (1951)

Aristotle
384—322 B.C.

Tragedy was a means by which the Greeks of the sixth century, and men in the Western world ever since, expressed in dramatic terms the basic question of man's destiny. It grew out of religious observances celebrating the god Dionysus, who can be regarded as the god of all that gives life its vitality. It embraced the great myths brought forth in Homer and Hesiod to dramatize man's passion for life against the inevitability of death. It grew into civic performances at which the greatest playwrights competed for prizes and public renown. Though we know the names of other writers of tragedy, we have the works of only three—Aeschylus (525-456 B.C.), Sophocles (494?-406 B.C.), and Euripides (480?-406 B.C.).

It is possible to generalize about these three tragedians in a way that suggests the scope and impact of their work. Aeschylus seems to be the most religious of the three, using his mythological material almost in the manner of Homer to pose the universal question of man against the great natural forces. Sophocles seems more social in his concern—for example, in *Antigone* he poses the problem of loyalty to the state versus loyalty to inner conviction. Euripides is the most psychological, treating the myths more symbolically in order to dramatize the psychological conflicts that drive men and women to tragic ends.

It is to Aristotle that we owe most of our knowledge of Greek tragedy. Although he wrote a century after the great flourishing of Greek drama, he knew many plays and was close enough to the sources of their origin to be considered reliable in what he says about their development. He undoubtedly also discussed comedy and the epic in detail, but most of what he wrote about them has not been preserved. Tragedy seemed to him to be the most highly developed form of poetry. Its connection to the mythical past in which philosophic thought was first embodied and its deliberate attempt to dramatize man's most serious problems endowed tragedy with great philosophic importance.

Aristotle's celebrated definition of tragedy has probably been the subject of more literary discussion than any other critical pronouncement. His

beginning statement that tragedy is an imitation of an action that is serious, entire, and of a proper magnitude places the emphasis on *action*
and *form,* both major concerns in Aristotle's total philosophy and, for
that matter, in Greek thought. The most controversial parts of his definition involve the concepts of tragic flaw, *hamartia,* the inner defect of
character responsible for a tragic hero's downfall, and *catharsis,* the
purgation through pity and fear of these and similar emotions in the
audience, which Aristotle regarded as the ultimate effect of tragedy.

Aristotle came from Stagira, a town in Macedonia. He entered Plato's
Academy in Athens when he was about eighteen and remained there
almost twenty years, until Plato's death in 347 B.C. He became a lecturer
and then returned to his native Stagira to tutor Alexander the Great for a
number of years. In 334 B.C. he established his own school, known as
the Lyceum, in Athens. Here he taught and wrote until the death of Alexander in 323 B.C. when a wave of feeling against Alexander's rule caused a
charge of impiety to be brought against him. He left Athens rather than,
as he said, give the Athenians a chance to sin once more against philosophy (as they had by executing Socrates). He died a year later.

Aristotle's interest in poetry probably derives in part from his intention
of being a comprehensive philosopher and in part from the importance
of poetry in Greek life and thought. Further, Plato, with whom Aristotle
disagreed in many respects, had banished poetry from his ideal republic
because it was twice removed from reality and because it was aimed
at man's emotions. Aristotle proceeded with no such bias, but rather
attempted to examine the chief forms of poetry, to analyze their parts,
and to judge them on their merits.

Aristotle came at the end of the great period of Greek culture, about
three hundred years after the beginnings of Greek drama. Like Plato,
he made almost every concern of man the object of his inquiry. But
much more than Plato, he was systematic, marked by common sense,
and lacking in strong religious feeling. He was very much a scholar, at
his best in observing, classifying, and analyzing the subject before him.
An important philosopher in his own time, his influence in the Middle
Ages became so great that he became known as "The Philosopher."

Poetics

---

4. It is clear that the general origin of poetry was due to two causes,
each of them part of human nature. Imitation is natural to man from
childhood, one of his advantages over the lower animals being this,
that he is the most imitative creature in the world, and learns at first

From *The Works of Aristotle, Vol. XI: De Poetica,* translated by Ingram Bywater. Reprinted by permission of the Clarendon Press, Oxford.

by imitation. And it is also natural for all to delight in works of imitation. The truth of this second point is shown by experience: though the objects themselves may be painful to see, we delight to view the most realistic representations of them in art, the forms for example of the lowest animals and of dead bodies. The explanation is to be found in a further fact: to be learning something is the greatest of pleasures not only to the philosopher but also to the rest of mankind, however small their capacity for it; the reason of the delight in seeing the picture is that one is at the same time learning—gathering the meaning of things, e.g. that the man there is so-and-so; for if one has not seen the thing before, one's pleasure will not be in the picture as an imitation of it, but will be due to the execution or colouring or some similar cause. Imitation, then, being natural to us—as also the sense of harmony and rhythm, the metres being obviously species of rhythms—it was through their original aptitude, and by a series of improvements for the most part gradual on their first efforts, that they created poetry out of their improvisations.

Poetry, however, soon broke up into two kinds according to the differences of character in the individual poets; for the graver among them would represent noble actions, and those of noble personages; and the meaner sort the actions of the ignoble. The latter class produced invectives at first, just as others did hymns and panegyrics. We know of no such poem by any of the pre-Homeric poets, though there were probably many such writers among them; instances, however, may be found from Homer downwards, e.g. his *Margites*,[1] and the similar poems of others. In this poetry of invective its natural fitness brought an iambic metre into use; hence our present term 'iambic', because it was the metre of their 'iambs'[2] or invectives against one another. The result was that the old poets became some of them writers of heroic and others of iambic verse. Homer's position, however, is peculiar: just as he was in the serious style the poet of poets, standing alone not only through the literary excellence, but also through the dramatic character of his imitations, so too he was the first to outline for us the general forms of Comedy by producing not a dramatic invective, but a dramatic picture of the Ridiculous; his *Margites* in fact stands in the same relation to our comedies as the *Iliad* and *Odyssey* to our tragedies. As soon, however, as Tragedy and Comedy appeared in the field, those naturally drawn to the one line of poetry became writers of comedies instead of iambs, and those naturally drawn to the other, writers of tragedies instead of epics, because these new modes of art were grander and of more esteem than the old.

If it be asked whether Tragedy is now all that it need be in its formative elements, to consider that, and decide it theoretically and in relation to the theatres, is a matter for another inquiry.

---

[1]A famous lost poem of antiquity, a satirical epic having a fool as its hero. The author and date of the poem are unknown, although Aristotle obviously thought it had been written by Homer.

[2]According to tradition, when the goddess Demeter was mourning the loss of her daughter Persephone, she was first made to smile by the maiden Iambe's jests. The verse form is supposed to have derived its name from this maiden since iambic meter (a foot of verse composed of an unstressed syllable followed by a stressed one) is suited to light or mocking themes. Probably, however, the story of Iambé is of later date than the nomenclature of the verse, the story having been devised to explain the nomenclature.

It certainly began in improvisations—as did also Comedy; the one originating with the authors of the Dithyramb,[3] the other with those of the phallic songs, which still survive as institutions in many of our cities. And its advance after that was little by little, through their improving on whatever they had before them at each stage. It was in fact only after a long series of changes that the movement of Tragedy stopped on its attaining to its natural form. (1) The number of actors was first increased to two by Aeschylus, who curtailed the business of the Chorus, and made the dialogue, or spoken portion, take the leading part in the play. (2) A third actor and scenery were due to Sophocles. (3) Tragedy acquired also its magnitude. Discarding short stories and a ludicrous diction, through its passing out of its satyric[4] stage, it assumed, though only at a late point in its progress, a tone of dignity; and its metre changed then from trochaic to iambic. The reason for their original use of the trochaic tetrameter was that their poetry was satyric and more connected with dancing than it now is. As soon, however, as a spoken part came in, nature herself found the appropriate metre. The iambic, we know, is the most speakable of metres, as is shown by the fact that we very often fall into it in conversation, whereas we rarely talk hexameters, and only when we depart from the speaking tone of voice. (4) Another change was a plurality of episodes or acts. As for the remaining matters, the superadded embellishments and the account of their introduction, these must be taken as said, as it would probably be a long piece of work to go through the details.

5. As for Comedy, it is (as has been observed) an imitation of men worse than the average; worse, however, not as regards any and every sort of fault, but only as regards one particular kind, the Ridiculous, which is a species of the Ugly. The Ridiculous may be defined as a mistake or deformity not productive of pain or harm to others; the mask, for instance, that excites laughter, is something ugly and distorted without causing pain.

Though the successive changes in Tragedy and their authors are not unknown, we cannot say the same of Comedy; its early stages passed unnoticed, because it was not as yet taken up in a serious way. It was only at a late point in its progress that a chorus of comedians was officially granted by the archon;[5] they used to be mere volunteers. It had also already certain definite forms at the time when the record of those termed comic poets begins. Who it was who supplied it with masks, or prologues, or a plurality of actors and the like, has remained unknown. The invented Fable, or Plot, however, originated in Sicily, with Epicharmus and Phormis; of Athenian poets Crates was the first to drop the Comedy of invective and frame stories of a general and non-personal nature, in other words, Fables or Plots.

Epic poetry, then, has been seen to agree with Tragedy to this ex-

---

[3]Ancient Greek choral lyric, originally connected with the worship of the god Dionysus.

[4]In Greek mythology, satyrs were spirits of the woods and hills, especially connected with the idea of fertility. They are represented as grotesque creatures, primarily human but with some bestial part, e.g., the tail of a horse or the legs of a goat. Satyric drama was among the earliest forms of Greek drama. The plays resembled tragedies but dealt with grotesque portions of ancient legends or dealt with the legends grotesquely. The chorus were dressed to represent satyrs and performed with crude and often obscene language and gestures.

[5]An official of the city government who had the performance of dramas under his jurisdiction.

tent, that of being an imitation of serious subjects in a grand kind of verse. It differs from it, however, (1) in that it is in one kind of verse and in narrative form; and (2) in its length—which is due to its action having no fixed limit of time, whereas Tragedy endeavours to keep as far as possible within a single circuit of the sun, or something near that. This, I say, is another point of difference between them, though at first the practice in this respect was just the same in tragedies as in epic poems. They differ also (3) in their constituents, some being common to both and others peculiar to Tragedy—hence a judge of good and bad in Tragedy is a judge of that in epic poetry also. All the parts of an epic are included in Tragedy; but those of Tragedy are not all of them to be found in the Epic.

6. Reserving hexameter poetry and Comedy for consideration here-after, let us proceed now to the discussion of Tragedy; before doing so, however, we must gather up the definition resulting from what has been said. A tragedy, then, is the imitation of an action that is serious and also, as having magnitude, complete in itself; in language with pleasurable accessories, each kind brought in separately in the parts of the work; in a dramatic, not in a narrative form; with incidents arous-ing pity and fear, wherewith to accomplish its catharsis of such emotions. Here by 'language with pleasurable accessories' I mean that with rhythm and harmony or song superadded; and by 'the kinds separately' I mean that some portions are worked out with verse only, and others in turn with song.

As they act the stories, it follows that in the first place the Spectacle (or stage-appearance of the actors) must be some part of the whole; and in the second Melody and Diction, these two being the means of their imitation. Here by 'Diction' I mean merely this, the composition of the verses; and by 'Melody', what is too completely understood to require explanation. But further: the subject represented also is an action; and the action involves agents, who must necessarily have their distinctive qualities both of character and thought, since it is from these that we ascribe certain qualities to their actions. There are in the natural order of things, therefore, two causes, Thought and Character, of their actions, and consequently of their success or failure in their lives. Now the action (that which was done) is represented in the play by the Fable or Plot. The Fable, in our present sense of the term, is simply this, the combination of the incidents, or things done in the story; whereas Char-acter is what makes us ascribe certain moral qualities to the agents; and Thought is shown in all they say when proving a particular point or, it may be, enunciating a general truth. There are six parts consequently of every tragedy, as a whole (that is) of such or such quality, viz. a Fable or Plot, Characters, Diction, Thought, Spectacle, and Melody; two of them arising from the means, one from the manner, and three from the objects of the dramatic imitation; and there is nothing else besides these six. Of these, its formative elements, then, not a few of the dramatists have made due use, as every play, one may say, admits of Spectacle, Character, Fable, Diction, Melody, and Thought.

The most important of the six is the combination of the incidents of the story. Tragedy is essentially an imitation not of persons but of action and life, of happiness and misery. All human happiness or misery takes the form of action; the end for which we live is a certain kind of activity, not a quality. Character gives us qualities, but it is in our actions —what we do—that we are happy or the reverse. In a play accordingly they do not act in order to portray the Characters; they include the Characters for the sake of the action. So that it is the action in it, i.e. its Fable or Plot, that is the end and purpose of the tragedy; and the end is everywhere the chief thing. Besides this, a tragedy is impossible without action, but there may be one without Character. The tragedies of most of the moderns are characterless—a defect common among poets of all kinds, and with its counterpart in painting in Zeuxis as compared with Polygnotus;[6] for whereas the latter is strong in character, the work of Zeuxis is devoid of it. And again: one may string together a series of characteristic speeches of the utmost finish as regards Diction and Thought, and yet fail to produce the true tragic effect; but one will have much better success with a tragedy which, however inferior in these respects, has a Plot, a combination of incidents, in it. And again: the most powerful elements of attraction in Tragedy, the Peripeties and Discoveries,[7] are parts of the Plot. A further proof is in the fact that beginners succeed earlier with the Diction and Characters than with the construction of a story; and the same may be said of nearly all the early dramatists. We maintain, therefore, that the first essential, the life and soul, so to speak, of Tragedy is the Plot; and that the Characters come second—compare the parallel in painting, where the most beautiful colours laid on without order will not give one the same pleasure as a simple black-and-white sketch of a portrait. We maintain that Tragedy is primarily an imitation of action, and that it is mainly for the sake of the action that it imitates the personal agents. Third comes the element of Thought, i.e. the power of saying whatever can be said, or what is appropriate to the occasion. This is what, in the speeches in Tragedy, falls under the arts of Politics and Rhetoric; for the older poets make their personages discourse like statesmen, and the moderns like rhetoricians. One must not confuse it with Character. Character in a play is that which reveals the moral purpose of the agents, i.e. the sort of thing they seek or avoid, where that is not obvious—hence there is no room for Character in a speech on a purely indifferent subject. Thought, on the other hand, is shown in all they say when proving or disproving some particular point, or enunciating some universal proposition. Fourth among the literary elements is the Diction of the personages, i.e., as before explained, the expression of their thoughts in words, which is practically the same thing with verse as with prose. As for the two remaining parts, the Melody is the greatest of the pleasurable accessories of Tragedy. The Spectacle, though an attraction, is the least artistic of all the parts, and has least to do with the art of poetry. The tragic effect is quite possible without a public performance and actors; and besides, the getting-up of the Spectacle is more a matter for the costumier than the poet.

---

[6] Famous Greek painters who flourished toward the end and toward the beginning of fifth century B.C., respectively.

[7] Technical dramaturgic terms which Aristotle discusses in detail in Chapter 11.

7. Having thus distinguished the parts, let us now consider the proper construction of the Fable or Plot, as that is at once the first and the most important thing in Tragedy. We have laid it down that a tragedy is an imitation of an action that is complete in itself, as a whole of some magnitude; for a whole may be of no magnitude to speak of. Now a whole is that which has beginning, middle, and end. A beginning is that which is not itself necessarily after anything else, and which has naturally something else after it; an end is that which is naturally after something itself, either as its necessary or usual consequent, and with nothing else after it, and a middle, that which is by nature after one thing and has also another after it. A well-constructed Plot, therefore, cannot either begin or end at any point one likes; beginning and end in it must be of the forms just described. Again: to be beautiful, a living creature, and every whole made up of parts, must not only present a certain order in its arrangement of parts, but also be of a certain definite magnitude. Beauty is a matter of size and order, and therefore impossible either (1) in a very minute creature, since our perception becomes indistinct as it approaches instantaneity; or (2) in a creature of vast size—one, say, 1,000 miles long—as in that case, instead of the object being seen all at once, the unity and wholeness of it is lost to the beholder. Just in the same way, then, as a beautiful whole made up of parts, or a beautiful living creature, must be of some size, but a size to be taken in by the eye, so a story or Plot must be of some length, but of a length to be taken in by the memory. As for the limit of its length, so far as that is relative to public performances and spectators, it does not fall within the theory of poetry. If they had to perform a hundred tragedies, they would be timed by water-clocks, as they are said to have been at one period. The limit, however, set by the actual nature of the thing is this: the longer the story, consistently with its being comprehensible as a whole, the finer it is by reason of its magnitude. As a rough general formula, 'a length which allows of the hero passing by a series of probable or necessary stages from misfortune to happiness, or from happiness to misfortune', may suffice as a limit for the magnitude of the story.

8. The Unity of a Plot does not consist, as some suppose, in its having one man as its subject. An infinity of things befall that one man, some of which it is impossible to reduce to unity; and in like manner there are many actions of one man which cannot be made to form one action. One sees, therefore, the mistake of all the poets who have written a *Heracleid,* a *Theseid,* or similar poems; they suppose that, because Heracles was one man, the story also of Heracles must be one story. Homer, however, evidently understood this point quite well, whether by art or instinct, just in the same way as he excels the rest in every other respect. In writing an *Odyssey,* he did not make the poem cover all that ever befell his hero—it befell him, for instance, to get wounded on Parnassus and also to feign madness at the time of the call to arms, but the two incidents had no necessary or probable connexion with one another—instead of doing that, he took as the subject of the *Odyssey,* as also of the *Iliad,* an action with a Unity of the kind we are describing. The truth is that, just as in the other imitative arts one imitation is

always of one thing, so in poetry the story, as an imitation of action, must represent one action, a complete whole, with its several incidents so closely connected that the transposal or withdrawal of any one of them will disjoin and dislocate the whole. For that which makes no perceptible difference by its presence or absence is no real part of the whole.

9. From what we have said it will be seen that the poet's function is to describe, not the thing that has happened, but a kind of thing that might happen, i.e. what is possible as being probable or necessary. The distinction between historian and poet is not in the one writing prose and the other verse—you might put the work of Herodotus into verse, and it would still be a species of history; it consists really in this, that the one describes the thing that has been, and the other a kind of thing that might be. Hence poetry is something more philosophic and of graver import than history, since its statements are of the nature rather of universals, whereas those of history are singulars. By a universal statement I mean one as to what such or such a kind of man will probably or necessarily say or do—which is the aim of poetry, though it affixes proper names to the characters; by a singular statement, one as to what, say, Alcibiades did or had done to him. In Comedy this has become clear by this time; it is only when their plot is already made up of probable incidents that they give it a basis of proper names, choosing for the purpose any names that may occur to them, instead of writing like the old iambic poets about particular persons. In Tragedy, however, they still adhere to the historic names; and for this reason: what convinces is the possible; now whereas we are not yet sure as to the possibility of that which has not happened, that which has happened is manifestly possible, else it would not have come to pass. Nevertheless even in Tragedy there are some plays with but one or two known names in them, the rest being inventions; and there are some without a single known name, e.g. Agathon's *Antheus,* in which both incidents and names are of the poet's invention; and it is no less delightful on that account. So that one must not aim at a rigid adherence to the traditional stories on which tragedies are based. It would be absurd, in fact, to do so, as even the known stories are only known to a few, though they are a delight none the less to all.

It is evident from the above that the poet must be more the poet of his stories or Plots than of his verses, inasmuch as he is a poet by virtue of the imitative element in his work, and it is actions that he imitates. And if he should come to take a subject from actual history, he is none the less a poet for that; since some historic occurrences may very well be in the probable and possible order of things; and it is in that aspect of them that he is their poet.

Of simple Plots and actions the episodic are the worst. I call a Plot episodic when there is neither probability nor necessity in the sequence of its episodes. Actions of this sort bad poets construct through their own fault, and good ones on account of the players. His work being for public performance, a good poet often stretches out a Plot beyond its capabilities, and is thus obliged to twist the sequence of incident.

Tragedy, however, is an imitation not only of a complete action, but also of incidents arousing pity and fear. Such incidents have the very greatest effect on the mind when they occur unexpectedly and at the same time in consequence of one another; there is more of the marvellous in them then than if they happened of themselves or by mere chance. Even matters of chance seem most marvellous if there is an appearance of design as it were in them; as for instance the statue of Mitys at Argos killed the author of Mitys' death by falling down on him when a looker-on at a public spectacle; for incidents like that we think to be not without a meaning. A Plot, therefore, of this sort is necessarily finer than others.

10. Plots are either simple or complex, since the actions they represent are naturally of this twofold description. The action, proceeding in the way defined, as one continuous whole, I call simple, when the change in the hero's fortunes takes place without Peripety or Discovery; and complex, when it involves one or the other, or both. These should each of them arise out of the structure of the Plot itself, so as to be the consequence, necessary or probable, of the antecedents. There is a great difference between a thing happening *propter hoc* and *post hoc.*[8]

11. A Peripety is the change of the kind described from one state of things within the play to its opposite, and that too in the way we are saying, in the probable or necessary sequence of events; as it is for instance in *Oedipus:* here the opposite state of things is produced by the Messenger, who, coming to gladden Oedipus and to remove his fears as to his mother, reveals the secret of his birth. And in *Lynceus:* just as he is being led off for execution, with Danaus at his side to put him to death, the incidents preceding this bring it about that he is saved and Danaus put to death. A Discovery is, as the very word implies, a change from ignorance to knowledge, and thus to either love or hate, in the personages marked for good or evil fortune. The finest form of Discovery is one attended by Peripeties, like that which goes with the Discovery in *Oedipus.* There are no doubt other forms of it; what we have said may happen in a way in reference to inanimate things, even things of a very casual kind; and it is also possible to discover whether some one has done or not done something. But the form most directly connected with the Plot and the action of the piece is the first-mentioned. This, with a Peripety, will arouse either pity or fear—actions of that nature being what Tragedy is assumed to represent; and it will also serve to bring about the happy or unhappy ending. The Discovery, then, being of persons, it may be that of one party only to the other, the latter being already known; or both the parties may have to discover themselves. Iphigenia, for instance, was discovered to Orestes by sending the letter; and another Discovery was required to reveal him to Iphigenia.[9]

Two parts of the Plot, then, Peripety and Discovery, are on matters of this sort. A third part is Suffering; which we may define as an action of a destructive or painful nature, such as murders on the stage, tortures, woundings, and the like. The other two have been already explained.

12. The parts of Tragedy to be treated as formative elements in the

---

[8]"Because of this" and "after this." Terms in logic to distinguish between a causal relationship and a simple chronological relationship.

[9]Aristotle is referring to events from the tragedy *Iphigenia in Tauris,* by Euripides.

whole were mentioned in a previous Chapter. From the point of view, however, of its quantity, i.e. the separate sections into which it is divided, a tragedy has the following parts: Prologue, Episode, Exode, and a choral portion, distinguished into Parode and Stasimon; these two are common to all tragedies, whereas songs from the stage and *Commoe* are only found in some. The Prologue is all that precedes the Parode of the chorus; an Episode all that comes in between two whole choral songs; the Exode all that follows after the last choral song. In the choral portion the Parode is the whole first statement of the chorus; a Stasimon, a song of the chorus without anapaests or trochees; a *Commos,* a lamentation sung by chorus and actor in concert. The parts of Tragedy to be used as formative elements in the whole we have already mentioned; the above are its parts from the point of view of its quantity, or the separate sections into which it is divided.

13. The next points after what we have said above will be these: (1) What is the poet to aim at, and what is he to avoid, in constructing his Plots? and (2) What are the conditions on which the tragic effect depends?

We assume that, for the finest form of Tragedy, the Plot must be not simple but complex; and further, that it must imitate actions arousing fear and pity, since that is the distinctive function of this kind of imitation. It follows, therefore, that there are three forms of Plot to be avoided. (1) A good man must not be seen passing from happiness to misery, or (2) a bad man from misery to happiness. The first situation is not fear-inspiring or piteous, but simply odious to us. The second is the most untragic that can be; it has no one of the requisites of Tragedy; it does not appeal either to the human feeling in us, or to our pity, or to our fears. Nor, on the other hand, should (3) an extremely bad man be seen falling from happiness into misery. Such a story may arouse the human feeling in us, but it will not move us to either pity or fear; pity is occasioned by undeserved misfortune, and fear by that of one like ourselves; so that there will be nothing either piteous or fear-inspiring in the situation. There remains, then, the intermediate kind of personage, a man not pre-eminently virtuous and just, whose misfortune, however, is brought upon him not by vice and depravity but by some error of judgement [*hamartia*], of the number of those in the enjoyment of great reputation and prosperity; e.g. Oedipus, Thyestes, and the men of note of similar families. The perfect Plot, accordingly, must have a single, and not (as some tell us) a double issue; the change in the hero's fortunes must be not from misery to happiness, but on the contrary from happiness to misery; and the cause of it must lie not in any depravity, but in some great error on his part; the man himself being either such as we have described, or better, not worse, than that. Fact also confirms our theory. Though the poets began by accepting any tragic story that came to hand, in these days the finest tragedies are always on the story of some few houses, on that of Alcmeon, Oedipus, Orestes, Meleager, Thyestes, Telephus, or any others that may have been involved, as either agents or sufferers, in some deed of horror. The theoretically best tragedy, then, has a Plot of this description. The critics, therefore, are wrong who blame Euripides for taking this line in his tragedies, and giving many of them an unhappy ending. It is, as we have said, the right line to take. The best proof is this: on the stage, and in the public performances, such plays, properly worked out, are seen to be the most truly tragic; and Euripides, even if his execution be faulty in every other point, is seen to be nevertheless the most tragic certainly of the dramatists. After this comes the construction of Plot which some rank first, one with a double story (like the *Odyssey*) and an opposite issue for the good and the bad personages. It is ranked as first only through the weakness of the audiences; the poets merely follow their public, writing as its wishes dictate. But the pleasure here is not that of Tragedy. It belongs rather to Comedy, where the bitterest enemies in the piece (e.g. Orestes and Aegisthus) walk off good friends at the end, with no slaying of any one by any one.

14. The tragic fear and pity may be aroused by the Spectacle; but they may also be aroused by the very structure and incidents of the play —which is the better way and shows the better poet. The Plot in fact should be so framed that, even without seeing the things take place, he who simply hears the account of them shall be filled with horror and pity at the incidents; which is just the effect that the mere recital of the story in *Oedipus* would have on one. To produce this same effect by means of the Spectacle is less artistic, and requires extraneous aid. Those, however, who make use of the Spectacle to put before us that which is merely monstrous and not productive of fear, are wholly out of touch with Tragedy; not every kind of pleasure should be required of a tragedy, but only its own proper pleasure.

The tragic pleasure is that of pity and fear, and the poet has to produce it by a work of imitation; it is clear, therefore, that the causes should be included in the incidents of his story. Let us see, then, what kinds of incident strike one as horrible, or rather as piteous. In a deed of this description the parties must necessarily be either friends, or enemies, or indifferent to one another. Now when enemy does it on enemy, there is nothing to move us to pity either in his doing or in his meditating the deed, except so far as the actual pain of the sufferer is concerned; and the same is true when the parties are indifferent to one another. Whenever the tragic deed, however, is done within the family—when murder or the like is done or meditated by brother on brother, by son on father, by mother on son, or son on mother—these are the situations the poet should seek after. The traditional stories, accordingly, must be kept as they are, e.g. the murder of Clytaemnestra by Orestes and of Eriphyle by Alcmeon. At the same time even with these there is something left to the poet himself; it is for him to devise the right way of treating them. Let us explain more clearly what we mean by 'the right way'. The deed of horror may be done by the doer knowingly and consciously, as in the old poets, and in Medea's murder of her children in Euripides.[10] Or he may do it, but in ignorance of his relationship, and discover that afterwards, as does the Oedipus in Sophocles. Here the deed is outside the play; but it may be within it, like the act of the Alcmeon in Astydamas, or that of the Telegonus in *Ulysses Wounded.*

---

[10] In the tragedy *Medea*.

A third possibility is for one meditating some deadly injury to another, in ignorance of his relationship, to make the discovery in time to draw back. These exhaust the possibilities, since the deed must necessarily be either done or not done, and either knowingly or unknowingly.

The worst situation is when the personage is with full knowledge on the point of doing the deed, and leaves it undone. It is odious and also (through the absence of suffering) untragic; hence it is that no one is made to act thus except in some few instances, e.g. Haemon and Creon in *Antigone*. Next after this comes the actual perpetration of the deed meditated. A better situation than that, however, is for the deed to be done in ignorance, and the relationship discovered afterwards, since there is nothing odious in it, and the Discovery will serve to astound us. But the best of all is the last; what we have in *Cresphontes,* for example, where Merope, on the point of slaying her son, recognizes him in time; in *Iphigenia,* where sister and brother are in a like position; and in *Helle,* where the son recognizes his mother, when on the point of giving her up to her enemy.

This will explain why our tragedies are restricted (as we said just now) to such a small number of families. It was accident rather than art that led the poets in quest of subjects to embody this kind of incident in their Plots. They are still obliged, accordingly, to have recourse to the families in which such horrors have occurred.

On the construction of the Plot, and the kind of Plot required for Tragedy, enough has now been said.

15. In the Characters there are four points to aim at. First and foremost, that they shall be good. There will be an element of character in the play, if (as has been observed) what a personage says or does reveals a certain moral purpose; and a good element of character, if the purpose so revealed is good. Such goodness is possible in every type of personage, even in a woman or a slave, though the one is perhaps an inferior, and the other a wholly worthless being. The second point is to make them appropriate. The Character before us may be, say, manly; but it is not appropriate in a female Character to be manly, or clever. The third is to make them like the reality, which is not the same as their being good and appropriate, in our sense of the term. The fourth is to make them consistent and the same throughout; even if inconsistency be part of the man before one for imitation as presenting that form of character, he should still be consistently inconsistent. We have an instance of baseness of character, not required for the story, in the Menelaus in *Orestes;* of the incongruous and unbefitting in the lamentation of Ulysses in *Scylla,* and in the (clever) speech of Melanippe;[11] and of inconsistency in *Iphigenia at Aulis,* where Iphigenia the suppliant is utterly unlike the later Iphigenia. The right thing, however, is in the Characters just as in the incidents of the play to endeavour always after the necessary or the probable; so that whenever such-and-such a personage says or does such-and-such a thing, it shall be the necessary or probable outcome of his character; and whenever this incident follows on that, it shall be either the necessary or the probable consequence

---

[11] In a lost play by Euripides, *Melanippe the Wise.*

of it. From this one sees (to digress for a moment) that the Dénouement also should arise out of the plot itself, and not depend on a stage-artifice, as in *Medea,* or in the story of the (arrested) departure of the Greeks in the *Iliad.* The artifice must be reserved for matters outside the play—for past events beyond human knowledge, or events yet to come, which require to be foretold or announced; since it is the privilege of the Gods to know everything. There should be nothing improbable among the actual incidents. If it be unavoidable, however, it should be outside the tragedy, like the improbability in the *Oedipus* of Sophocles. But to return to the Characters. As Tragedy is an imitation of personages better than the ordinary man, we in our way should follow the example of good portrait-painters, who reproduce the distinctive features of a man, and at the same time, without losing the likeness, make him handsomer than he is. The poet in like manner, in portraying men quick or slow to anger, or with similar infirmities of character, must know how to represent them as such, and at the same time as good men, as Agathon and Homer have represented Achilles.

All these rules one must keep in mind throughout, and, further, those also for such points of stage-effect as directly depend on the art of the poet, since in these too one may often make mistakes. Enough, however, has been said on the subject in one of our published writings.[12]

Comments / on the *Poetics*
and the Idea of Tragedy

The *Poetics* is therefore far from being a theory of poetry in general, still less a theory of fine art. No complete or even entirely consistent aesthetic theory can be elicited from it. Yet it contains perhaps a greater number of pregnant ideas on art than any other book. It marks the beginning of the deliverance from two mistakes which have over and over again marred aesthetic theory—the tendency to confuse aesthetic with moral judgments, and the tendency to think of art as duplicative or photographic of reality.   *W. D. ROSS (1923)*

Apparently, tragedy always centers in some elemental conflict between man and a destiny he cannot master. At one time that conflict may be interpreted as man's defeat through an error which is moral, which he would have avoided had he been wiser or more virtuous. At another time it may be the defeat of man through forces so arbitrary and so outside his control that in the heroic bearing of his defeat we, who are men as well as he, see the marks of victory. At still another time the defeat of man may

---

[12] In the lost dialogue *On Poets.*

be an unrelieved sorrow with, at best, the text "as flies to wanton boys, are we to the gods, they kill us for their sport."   *DAVID GRENE (1942)*

Tragedy could, it is true, be called pessimistic in its view of the evil in the universe as unremitting and irremediable, the blight man was born for, the necessary condition of existence. It is pessimistic, also, in its view of the overwhelming proportion of evil to good and in its awareness of the mystery of why this should be. . . . But it is optimistic in what might be called its vitalism, which is in some sense mystical, not earth-bound; in its faith in a cosmic good; in its vision, however fleeting, of a world in which all questions could be answered.   *RICHARD B. SEWALL (1954)*

The essential thing which distinguishes real tragedy from those distressing modern works sometimes called by its name is the fact that it is in the former alone that the artist has found himself capable of considering and of making us consider that his people and his actions have that amplitude and importance which make them noble. Tragedy arises then when, as in Periclean Greece or Elizabethan England, a people fully aware of the calamities of life is nevertheless serenely confident of the greatness of man, whose mighty passions and supreme fortitude are revealed when one of these calamities overtakes him.

JOSEPH WOOD KRUTCH (1929)

A far more active solvent was rationalism. While treating with forbearance the myths that formed the tragic poet's stock in trade and the background of his country's history, Euripides makes it plain that many supernatural powers, traditionally assumed, have no real existence. Homer made the gods responsible for the good and evil acts of men. Euripides rejects the whole theory and lays the responsibility for conduct upon the individual; while the eminent comic poet, Aristophanes, in other ways conservative, ridicules the gods and their weaknesses. The drama thus introduced advanced ideas to a large audience.   *C. A. ROBINSON, JR. (1956)*

Herodotus
484?–425? B.C.

A striking characteristic of Greek culture in the fifth century B.C. was the intensified effort among thoughtful men to reach an objective and rational basis for their understanding of life and reality. By applying this way of thinking to the circumstances of men's relationship to their own past, Herodotus, the "Father of History," originated the conception of history as a scientific type of knowledge that would in itself help men better comprehend their place in the scheme of things. He was interested not in myths and legends dealing with gods and goddesses in some dateless past, but in the actions of men in the present and immediate past. Although he did include some myths and legends in his work, for him they remained obscure attempts to fathom baffling mysteries.

Herodotus was born at Halicarnassus in Asia Minor, then under the rule of the Persians. Political unrest in his native city prompted him to set out on travels which took him throughout the Near East, the Grecian Islands, and Egypt before he settled down in an Athenian colony in his later years. A highly literate man, thoroughly familiar with the Greek intellectual heritage, Herodotus reported the historical lore of the various countries he visited. His emphasis, however, was primarily on the wars between the Greeks and the barbarians, especially the long struggle between Greece and Persia which was still fresh in everybody's mind. Although he does not present a fully integrated or "universal" history of the Mediterranean world of his day, he does record a great number of important events, giving us illuminating glimpses of the world the Greeks lived in.

Herodotus' *History* is remarkable for both the method of investigation which produced it and the philosophy of life which animates it. He set out to ask questions about how and why things happened, actually interrogating eyewitnesses and the children of eyewitnesses about events in the Persian Wars. In this sense, his *History* is a thoroughgoing "investigation," the original meaning of the Greek word *historia*. Such a method has obvious limitations: it is only as reliable as eyewitness reports can be, and it cannot reach into the distant past. But it has the virtue of being immediate and vivid, especially in dealing with the recent past. As might be expected, Herodotus' work displays less of this quality and becomes more legendary the further back in time he extends his "investigations." Still, his *History* remains largely humanistic and scientific. In contrast to the writer of legends who merely recorded what he already knew, Herodotus deliberately set out to discover what he did not yet know. Further, he asked questions about things done by men in a determinate past, thus indicating what man is and can do through the actual record of what he has been and has done.

The philosophy of life in Herodotus' *History* reflects the outlook of fifth-century Greece, the same outlook that gave rise to the spirit and idea of Greek tragedy. The world, including human life, is subject to catastrophic change. Earthquakes and erosion violate the face of the earth just as for no apparent reason sudden misfortune destroys happiness in human life. Men can best cope with this kind of world by recognizing it for precisely what it is. From Herodotus' point of view, while history might not be able to explain why man lived in a world given to catastrophe, it could be useful to men simply because the rhythm of its changes was likely to repeat itself forever.

In one sense, however, Herodotus' attempt to derive from history something close to certain knowledge about human affairs seems to run against the prevailing current of Greek philosophy. Many Greek thinkers in his time—and even more later, under the influence of Socrates and Plato—expected to find certitude only in a world of permanent things that could be grasped only by the mind, such as the objects of mathematical knowledge. If everything in the visible world changes, they insisted, how could there be certain knowledge about the world? They may well have searched so intensely for the eternal and immutable precisely because they had such a vivid awareness of the temporal and changeable, the kind of awareness that Herodotus himself demonstrates. Even Herodotus did not pretend to formulate eternal truths or convey certain knowledge, but he was at least in quest of useful principles for human action. In this sense he stands both as historian and as moral philosopher.

History

Book 1

These are the researches of Herodotus of Halicarnassus, which he publishes, in the hope of thereby preserving from decay the remem-

From *History*, Vol. I, translated by George Rawlinson (New York: The Tandy-Thomas Co., 1909).

brance of what men have done, and of preventing the great and wonderful actions of the Greeks and the Barbarians[1] from losing their due meed of glory; and withal to put on record what were their grounds of feud.

1. According to the Persians best informed in history, the Phœnicians began the quarrel.[2] This people, who had formerly dwelt on the shores of the Erythræan Sea, having migrated to the Mediterranean and settled in the parts which they now inhabit,[3] began at once, they say, to adventure on long voyages, freighting their vessels with the wares of Egypt and Assyria. They landed at many places on the coast, and among the rest at Argos, which was then pre-eminent above all the states included now under the common name of Hellas. Here they exposed their merchandise, and traded with the natives for five or six days; at the end of which time, when almost everything was sold, there came down to the beach a number of women, and among them the daughter of the king, who was, they say, agreeing in this with the Greeks, Io, the child of Inachus. The women were standing by the stern of the ship intent upon their purchases, when the Phœnicians, with a general shout, rushed upon them. The greater part made their escape, but some were seized and carried off. Io herself was among the captives. The Phœnicians put the women on board their vessel and set sail for Egypt. Thus did Io pass into Egypt, according to the Persian story, which differs widely from the Phœnician; and thus commenced, according to their authors, the series of outrages.

2. At a later period, certain Greeks, with whose name they are unacquainted, but who would probably be Cretans, made a landing at Tyre, on the Phœnician coast, and bore off the king's daughter, Europé. In this they only retaliated; but afterwards the Greeks, they say, were guilty of a second violence. They manned a ship of war, and sailed to Æa, a city of Colchis,[4] on the river Phasis; from whence, after despatching the rest of the business on which they had come, they carried off Medea, the daughter of the king of the land. The monarch sent a herald into Greece to demand reparation of the wrong, and the restitution of his child; but the Greeks made answer, that having received no reparation of the wrong done them in the seizure of Io the Argive, they should give none in this instance.

3. In the next generation afterwards, according to the same authorities, Alexander the son of Priam,[5] bearing these events in mind, resolved to procure himself a wife out of Greece by violence, fully persuaded, that as the Greeks had not given satisfaction for their outrages, so neither would he be forced to make any for his. Accordingly he made prize of Helen; upon which the Greeks decided that, before resorting to other measures, they would send envoys to reclaim the princess and require reparation of the wrong. Their demands were met by a

---

[1]*Barbarian* is a Greek word which originally signified anyone who was not a Greek.

[2]Herodotus is referring to what has come to be known as the Trojan War, taking that as the beginning of significant events in the history of the Greek peoples.

[3]At the eastern end of the Mediterranean.

[4]Ancient country in Asia occupying the area on the eastern shores of what is now the Black Sea.

[5]King of Troy, a Phoenician city-state in the northwestern section of Asia Minor on the eastern shore of what is now called the Dardanelles, the narrow body of water running northward out of the Aegean Sea and separating Europe from Asia.

reference to the violence which had been offered to Medea, and they were asked with what face they could now require satisfaction, when they had formerly rejected all demands for either reparation or restitution addressed to them.

4. Hitherto the injuries on either side had been mere acts of common violence; but in what followed the Persians consider that the Greeks were greatly to blame, since before any attack had been made on Europé, they led an army into Asia. Now as for the carrying off of women, it is the deed, they say, of a rogue; but to make a stir about such as are carried off, argues a man a fool. Men of sense care nothing for such women, since it is plain that without their own consent they would never be forced away. The Asiatics, when the Greeks ran off with their women, never troubled themselves about the matter; but the Greeks, for the sake of a single Lacedæmonian⁶ girl, collected a vast armament, invaded Asia, and destroyed the kingdom of Priam. Henceforth they ever looked upon the Greeks as their open enemies. For Asia, with all the various tribes of barbarians that inhabit it, is regarded by the Persians as their own; but Europe and the Greek race they look on as distinct and separate.

5. Such is the account which the Persians give of these matters. They trace to the attack upon Troy their ancient enmity towards the Greeks. The Phœnicians, however, as regards Io, vary from the Persian statements. They deny that they used any violence to remove her into Egypt; she herself, they say, having formed an intimacy with the captain, while his vessel lay at Argos, and perceiving herself to be with child, of her own freewill accompanied the Phœnicians on their leaving the shore, to escape the shame of detection and the reproaches of her parents. Whether this latter account be true, or whether the matter happened otherwise, I shall not discuss further. I shall proceed at once to point out the person who first within my own knowledge inflicted injury on the Greeks, after which I shall go forward with my history, describing equally the greater and the lesser cities. For the cities which were formerly great, have most of them become insignificant; and such as are at present powerful, were weak in the olden time. I shall therefore discourse equally of both, convinced that human happiness never continues long in one stay.

6. Crœsus, son of Alyattes, by birth a Lydian,⁷ was lord of all the nations to the west of the river Halys.⁸ This stream, which separates Syria from Paphlagonia, runs with a course from south to north, and finally falls into the Euxine.⁹ So far as our knowledge goes, he was the first of the barbarians who had dealings with the Greeks, forcing some of them to become his tributaries, and entering into alliance with others. He conquered the Æolians, Ionians, and Dorians¹⁰ of Asia, and made a

---

⁶Helen's husband, Menelaus, was king of the Greek city-state of Sparta, which was also known in ancient times as Lacedaemonia.

⁷Lydia was a region in the central part of the western portion of Asia Minor. Croesus reigned 560–546 B.C.

⁸The modern "Red River" running northward into the Black Sea through the central part of Turkey. In ancient times it marked a rough boundary between the Indo-European peoples to the west of it and the Semitic peoples to the east.

⁹The modern Black Sea.

¹⁰Greek tribes inhabiting Asia Minor.

treaty with the Lacedæmonians. Up to that time all Greeks had been free. For the Cimmerian[11] attack upon Ionia, which was earlier than Crœsus, was not a conquest of the cities, but only an inroad for plundering.

25. Having brought the war with the Milesians[12] to a close, and reigned over the land of Lydia for fifty-seven years, Alyattes died. He was the second prince of his house who made offerings at Delphi.[13] His gifts, which he sent on recovering from his sickness, were a great bowl of pure silver, with a salver in steel curiously inlaid, a work among all the offerings at Delphi the best worth looking at. Glaucus, the Chian, made it, the man who first invented the art of inlaying steel.

26. On the death of Alyattes, Crœsus, his son, who was thirty-five years old, succeeded to the throne. Of the Greek cities, Ephesus[14] was the first that he attacked. The Ephesians, when he laid siege to the place, made an offering of their city to Diana, by stretching a rope from the town wall to the temple of the goddess, which was distant from the ancient city, then besieged by Crœsus, a space of seven furlongs. They were, as I said, the first Greeks whom he attacked. Afterwards, on some pretext or other, he made war in turn upon every Ionian and Æolian state, bringing forward, where he could, a substantial ground of complaint; where such failed him, advancing some poor excuse.

27. In this way he made himself master of all the Greek cities in Asia, and forced them to become his tributaries; after which he began to think of building ships, and attacking the islanders. Everything had been got ready for this purpose, when Bias of Priêné[15] (or, as some say, Pittacus the Mytilenean[16]) put a stop to the project. The king had made inquiry of this person, who was lately arrived at Sardis,[17] if there were any news from Greece; to which he answered, "Yes, sire, the islanders are gathering ten thousand horse, designing an expedition against you and against your capital." Crœsus, thinking he spake seriously, broke out, "Ah, might the gods put such a thought into their minds as to attack the sons of the Lydians with cavalry!" "It seems, oh! king," rejoined the other, "that you desire earnestly to catch the islanders on horseback upon the mainland,—you know well what would come of it. But what think you the islanders desire better, now that they hear you are about to build ships and sail against them, than to catch the Lydians at sea, and there revenge on them the wrongs of their brothers upon the mainland, whom you hold in slavery?" Crœsus was charmed with the turn of the speech; and thinking there was reason in what

---

[11]An Asiatic people from above the northeast portion of the Black Sea who descended into Asia Minor and drove through almost to the Mediterranean during the seventh century B.C.

[12]The citizens of Miletus, a city in Ionia, which was a region along the west coast of Asia Minor inhabited by Greek peoples.

[13]The site of a shrine dedicated to the god Apollo, situated on Mt. Parnassus in the north-central region of Greece. It was probably the most famous shrine in the ancient Greek world, where people worshiped Apollo in order to obtain prophecies from the oracle there. The prophecies were delivered by the priestess who served the shrine.

[14]An Ionian city on the coast of the Aegean Sea.

[15]An Ionian city.

[16]Mytilene was the chief city on Lesbos, an island inhabited by Greek peoples near the eastern shore of the Aegean Sea off the coast of Asia Minor.

[17]The capital city of Croesus.

was said, gave up his ship-building and concluded a league of amity with the Ionians of the isles.

28. Crœsus, afterwards, in the course of many years, brought under his sway almost all the nations to the west of the Halys. The Lycians and Cilicians alone continued free; all the other tribes he reduced and held in subjection. They were the following: the Lydians, Phrygians, Mysians, Mariandynians, Chalybians, Paphlagonians, Thynian and Bithynian Thracians, Carians, Ionians, Dorians, Æolians, and Pamphylians.

29. When all these conquests had been added to the Lydian empire, and the prosperity of Sardis was now at its height, there came thither one after another, all the sages of Greece living at the time, and among them Solon, the Athenian. He was on his travels, having left Athens to be absent ten years, under the pretence of wishing to see the world, but really to avoid being forced to repeal any of the laws which, at the request of the Athenians, he had made for them. Without his sanction the Athenians could not repeal them, as they had bound themselves under a heavy curse to be governed for ten years by the laws which should be imposed on them by Solon.[18]

30. On this account, as well as to see the world, Solon set out upon his travels, in the course of which he went to Egypt to the court of Amasis, and also came on a visit to Crœsus at Sardis. Crœsus received him as his guest, and lodged him in the royal palace. On the third or fourth day after, he bade his servants conduct Solon over his treasuries, and show him all their greatness and magnificence. When he had seen them all, and, so far as time allowed, inspected them, Crœsus addressed this question to him: "Stranger of Athens, we have heard much of your wisdom and of your travels through many lands, from love of knowledge and a wish to see the world. I am curious therefore to inquire of you, whom, of all the men that you have seen, you deem the most happy?" This he asked because he thought himself the happiest of mortals: but Solon answered him without flattery, according to his true sentiments, "Tellus of Athens, sire." Full of astonishment at what he heard, Crœsus demanded sharply, "And wherefore do you deem Tellus happiest?" To which the other replied, "First, because his country was flourishing in his days, and he himself had sons both beautiful and good, and he lived to see children born to each of them, and these children all grew up; and further because, after a life spent in what our people look upon as comfort, his end was surpassingly glorious. In a battle between the Athenians and their neighbours near Eleusis, he came to the assistance of his countrymen, routed the foe, and died upon the field most gallantly. The Athenians gave him a public funeral on the spot where he fell, and paid him the highest honours."

31. Thus did Solon admonish Crœsus by the example of Tellus, enumerating the manifold particulars of his happiness. When he had ended, Crœsus inquired a second time, who after Tellus seemed to him the happiest, expecting that at any rate, he would be given the second

---

[18]Solon (640?–558? B.C.] was famous for instituting legal, political, economic, and social reforms in the government of Athens. Herodotus' account of his visit to Croesus was rejected as fabulous even before the time of the first century A.D. historian Plutarch, because of the chronological difficulties.

place. "Cleobis and Bito," Solon answered; "they were of Argive[19] race;
their fortune was enough for their wants, and they were besides endowed
with so much bodily strength that they had both gained prizes at the
Games.[20] Also this tale is told of them:—There was a great festival in
honour of the goddess Juno at Argos, to which their mother must needs
be taken in a car. Now the oxen did not come home from the field in
time; so the youths, fearful of being too late, put the yoke on their own
necks, and themselves drew the car in which their mother rode. Five and
forty furlongs did they draw her, and stopped before the temple. This
deed of theirs was witnessed by the whole assembly of worshippers, and
then their life closed in the best possible way. Herein, too, God showed
forth most evidently, how much better a thing for man death is than life.
For the Argive men, who stood around the car, extolled the vast strength
of the youths; and the Argive women extolled the mother who was
blessed with such a pair of sons; and the mother herself, overjoyed at
the deed and at the praises it had won, standing straight before the
image, besought the goddess to bestow on Cleobis and Bito, the sons
who had so mightily honoured her, the highest blessing to which mortals
can attain. Her prayer ended, they offered sacrifice and partook of the
holy banquet, after which the two youths fell asleep in the temple. They
never woke more, but so passed from the earth. The Argives, looking
on them as among the best of men, caused statues of them to be made,
which they gave to the shrine at Delphi."

32. When Solon had thus assigned these youths the second place,
Crœsus broke in angrily, "What, stranger of Athens, is my happiness,
then, so utterly set at nought by you, that you do not even put me on
a level with private men?"

"Oh! Crœsus," replied the other, "you asked a question concerning
the condition of man, of one who knows that the power above us is
full of jealousy, and fond of troubling our lot. A long life gives one to
witness much, and experience much oneself, that one would not choose.
Seventy years I regard as the limit of the life of man. In these seventy
years are contained, without reckoning intercalary months, twenty-
five thousand and two hundred days. Add an intercalary month to every
other year, that the seasons may come round at the right time, and there
will be, besides the seventy years, thirty-five such months, making an
addition of one thousand and fifty days. The whole number of the days
contained in the seventy years will thus be twenty-six thousand two hundred and fifty, whereof not one but will produce events unlike the rest.
Hence man is wholly accident. For yourself, oh! Crœsus, I see that you
are wonderfully rich, and are the lord of many nations; but with respect
to that whereon you question me, I have no answer to give, until I
hear that you have closed your life happily. For assuredly he who possesses great store of riches is no nearer happiness than he who has what
suffices for his daily needs, unless it so hap that luck attend upon him,
and so he continue in the enjoyment of all his good things to the end

---

[19]Argos was one of the major Greek city-states.
[20]The Olympic Games, traditionally of great antiquity, as part of a festival in honor of Zeus, had a formal,
recorded existence from 776 B.C. Within a century they were attracting competitors from city-states throughout the Greek world.

of life. For many of the wealthiest men have been unfavoured of fortune, and many whose means were moderate have had excellent luck. Men of the former class excel those of the latter but in two respects; these last excel the former in many. The wealthy man is better able to content his desires, and to bear up against a sudden buffet of calamity. The other has less ability to withstand these evils (from which, however, his good luck keeps him clear), but he enjoys all these following blessings: he is whole of limb, a stranger to disease, free from misfortune, happy in his children, and comely to look upon. If, in addition to all this, he end his life well, he is of a truth the man of whom you are in search, the man who may rightly be termed happy. Call him, however, until he die, not happy but fortunate. Scarcely, indeed, can any man unite all these advantages: as there is no country which contains within it all that it needs, but each, while it possesses some things, lacks others, and the best country is that which contains the most; so no single human being is complete in every respect—something is always lacking. He who unites the greatest number of advantages, and retaining them to the day of his death, then dies peaceably, that man alone, sire, is, in my judgment, entitled to bear the name of 'happy.' But in every matter it behoves us to mark well the end: for oftentimes God gives men a gleam of happiness, and then plunges them into ruin."

33. Such was the speech which Solon addressed to Crœsus, a speech which brought him neither largess nor honour. The king saw him depart with much indifference, since he thought that a man must be an arrant fool who made no account of present good, but bade men always wait and mark the end.

34. After Solon had gone away a dreadful vengeance, sent of God, came upon Crœsus, to punish him, it is likely, for deeming himself the happiest of men. First he had a dream in the night, which foreshowed him truly the evils that were about to befall him in the person of his son. For Crœsus had two sons, one blasted by a natural defect, being deaf and dumb; the other, distinguished far above all his co-mates in every pursuit. The name of the last was Atys. It was this son concerning whom he dreamt a dream, that he would die by the blow of an iron weapon. When he woke, he considered earnestly with himself, and, greatly alarmed at the dream, instantly made his son take a wife, and whereas in former years the youth had been wont to command the Lydian forces in the field, he now would not suffer him to accompany them. All the spears and javelins, and weapons used in the wars, he removed out of the male apartments, and laid them in heaps in the chambers of the women, fearing lest perhaps one of the weapons that hung against the wall might fall and strike him.

35. Now it chanced that while he was making arrangements for the wedding, there came to Sardis a man under a misfortune, who had upon him the stain of blood. He was by race a Phrygian,[21] and belonged to the family of the king. Presenting himself at the palace of Crœsus, he prayed to be admitted to purification according to the customs of the country. Now the Lydian method of purifying is very nearly the same as the

---

[21]A people inhabiting the northwest region of Asia Minor.

Greek. Crœsus granted the request, and went through all the customary rites, after which he asked the suppliant of his birth and country, addressing him as follows:—"Who are you, stranger, and from what part of Phrygia fled you to take refuge at my hearth? And whom, moreover, what man or what woman, have you slain?" "Oh! king," replied the Phrygian, "I am the son of Gordias, son of Midas. I am named Adrastus. The man I unintentionally slew was my own brother. For this my father drove me from the land, and I lost all. Then fled I here to you." "You are the offspring," Crœsus rejoined, "of a house friendly to mine, and you have come to friends. You shall want for nothing so long as you abide in my dominions. Bear your misfortune as easily as you may, so will it go best with you." Thenceforth Adrastus lived in the palace of the king.

36. It chanced that at this very same time there was in the Mysian Olympus[22] a huge monster of a boar, which went forth often from this mountain-country, and wasted the corn-fields of the Mysians. Many a time had the Mysians collected to hunt the beast, but instead of doing him any hurt, they came off always with some loss to themselves. At length they sent ambassadors to Crœsus, who delivered their message to him in these words: "Oh! king, a mighty monster of a boar has appeared in our parts, and destroys the labour of our hands. We do our best to take him, but in vain. Now therefore we beseech you to let your son accompany us back, with some chosen youths and hounds, that we may rid our country of the animal." Such was the tenor of their prayer.

But Crœsus bethought him of his dream, and answered, "Say no more of my son going with you; that may not be in any wise. He is but just joined in wedlock, and is busy enough with that. I will grant you a picked band of Lydians, and all my huntsmen and hounds; and I will charge those whom I send to use all zeal in aiding you to rid your country of the brute."

37. With this reply the Mysians were content; but the king's son, hearing what the prayer of the Mysians was, came suddenly in, and on the refusal of Crœsus to let him go with them, thus addressed his father: "Formerly, my father, it was deemed the noblest and most suitable thing for me to frequent the wars and hunting-parties, and win myself glory in them; but now you keep me away from both, although you have never beheld in me either cowardice or lack of spirit. What face meanwhile must I wear as I walk to the forum or return from it? What must the citizens, what must my young bride think of me? What sort of man will she suppose her husband to be? Either, therefore, let me go to the chase of this boar, or give me a reason why it is best for me to do according to your wishes."

38. Then Crœsus answered, "My son, it is not because I have seen in you either cowardice or aught else which has displeased me that I keep you back; but because a vision which came before me in a dream as I slept, warned me that you were doomed to die young, pierced by an iron weapon. It was this which first led me to hasten on your wedding,

---

[22]Mysia was a large area of northwestern Asia Minor. Although *the* Mt. Olympus was in northern Greece, Mysia also contained a mountain so named.

and now it hinders me from sending you upon this enterprise. Fain would I keep watch over you, if by any means I may cheat fate of you during my own lifetime. For you are the one and only son that I possess; the other, whose hearing is destroyed, I regard as if he were not."

39. "Ah! father," returned the youth, "I blame you not for keeping watch over me after a dream so terrible; but if you mistake, if you do not apprehend the dream aright, 'tis no blame for me to show you wherein you err. Now the dream, you said yourself foretold that I should die stricken by an iron weapon. But what hands has a boar to strike with? What iron weapon does he wield? Yet this is what you fear for me. Had the dream said that I should die pierced by a tusk, then you had done well to keep me away; but it said a weapon. Now here we do not combat men, but a wild animal. I pray you, therefore, let me go with them."

40. "There you have me, my son," said Crœsus, "your interpretation is better than mine. I yield to it, and change my mind, and consent to let you go."

41. Then the king sent for Adrastus, the Phrygian, and said to him, "Adrastus, when you were smitten with the rod of affliction—no reproach, my friend—I purified you, and have taken you to live with me in my palace, and have been at every charge. Now, therefore, it behoves you to requite the good offices which you have received at my hands by consenting to go with my son on this hunting party, and to watch over him, if perchance you should be attacked upon the road by some band of daring robbers. Even apart from this, it were right for you to go where you may make yourself famous by noble deeds. They are the heritage of your family, and you too are so stalwart and strong."

42. Adrastus answered, "Except for your request, oh! king, I would rather have kept away from this hunt; for methinks it ill beseems a man under a misfortune such as mine to consort with his happier compeers; and besides, I have no heart to it. On many grounds I had stayed behind; but, as you urge it, and I am bound to pleasure you (for truly it does behove me to requite your good offices), I am content to do as you wish. For your son, whom you give into my charge, be sure you shall receive him back safe and sound, so far as depends upon a guardian's carefulness."

43. Thus assured, Crœsus let them depart accompanied by a band of picked youths, and well provided with dogs of chase. When they reached Olympus, they scattered in quest of the animal; he was soon found, and the hunters, drawing round him in a circle, hurled their weapons at him. Then the stranger, the man who had been purified of blood, whose name was Adrastus, he also hurled his spear at the boar, but missed his aim, and struck Atys. Thus was the son of Crœsus slain by the point of an iron weapon, and the warning of the vision was fulfilled. Then one ran to Sardis to bear the tidings to the king, and he came and informed him of the combat and of the fate that had befallen his son.

44. If it was a heavy blow to the father to learn that his child was dead, it yet more strongly affected him to think that the very man whom he himself once purified had done the deed. In the violence of his grief

he called aloud on Jupiter Catharsius, to be a witness of what he had suffered at the stranger's hands. Afterwards he invoked the same god as Jupiter Ephistus and Hetæreus—using the one term because he had unwittingly harboured in his house the man who had now slain his son; and the other, because the stranger, who had been sent as his child's guardian, had turned out his most cruel enemy.

45. Presently the Lydians arrived, bearing the body of the youth, and behind them followed the homicide. He took his stand in front of the corse, and, stretching forth his hand to Crœsus, delivered himself unto his power with earnest entreaties that he would sacrifice him upon the body of his son—"his former misfortune was burden enough; now that he had added to it a second, and had brought ruin on the man who purified him, he could not bear to live." Then Crœsus, when he heard these words, was moved with pity towards Adrastus, notwithstanding the bitterness of his own calamity; and so he answered, "Enough, my friend; I have all the revenge that I require, since you give sentence of death against yourself. But in sooth it is not you who has injured me, except so far as you have unwittingly dealt the blow. Some god is the author of my misfortune, and I was forewarned of it a long time ago." Crœsus after this buried the body of his son, with such honours as befitted the occasion. Adrastus, son of Gordias, son of Midas, the destroyer of his brother in time past, the destroyer now of his purifier, regarding himself as the most unfortunate wretch whom he had ever known, so soon as all was quiet about the place, slew himself upon the tomb. Crœsus, bereft of his son, gave himself up to mourning for two full years.

46. At the end of this time the grief of Crœsus was interrupted by intelligence from abroad. He learnt that Cyrus,[23] the son of Cambyses, had destroyed the empire of Astyages,[24] the son of Cyaxares; and that the Persians were becoming daily more powerful. This led him to consider with himself whether it were possible to check the growing power of that people before it came to a head. With this design he resolved to make instant trial of the several oracles in Greece, and of the one in Libya.[25] So he sent his messengers in different directions, some to Delphi, some to Abæ in Phocis, and some to Dodôna; others to the oracle of Amphiaraüs; others to that of Trophonius; others again, to Branchidæ in Milesia. These were the Greek oracles which he consulted. To Libya he sent another embassy, to consult the oracle of Ammon. These messengers were sent to test the knowledge of the oracles, that, if they were found really to return true answers, he might send a second time, and inquire if he ought to attack the Persians.

47. The messengers who were despatched to make trial of the oracles were given the following instructions: they were to keep count of the days from the time of their leaving Sardis, and, reckoning from that date, on the hundredth day they were to consult the oracles, and to in-

---

[23]King of Persia and founder of the Persian Empire. He reigned 550?–529 B.C.

[24]Last king of Media, an important country on the northern boundary of Persia. He reigned 584?–550 B.C. Cyrus' conquest of Media marked the beginning of his creation of the Persian Empire.

[25]The Greek name for the continent of Africa in general, as well as for the region of northern Africa west of Egypt.

quire of them what Crœsus, the son of Alyattes, king of Lydia, was doing at that moment. The answers given them were to be taken down in writing, and brought back to him. None of the replies remain on record except that of the oracle at Delphi. There, the moment that the Lydians entered the sanctuary, and before they put their questions, the Pythoness thus answered them in hexameter verse:

"I can count the sands, and I can measure the ocean;
I have ears for the silent, and know what the dumb man meaneth;
Lo! on my sense there striketh the smell of a shell-covered tortoise,
Boiling now on the fire, with the flesh of a lamb, in a cauldron,—
Brass is the vessel below, and brass the cover above it."

48. These words the Lydians wrote down at the mouth of the Pythoness as she prophesied, and then set off on their return to Sardis. When all the messengers had come back with the answers which they had received, Crœsus undid the rolls, and read what was written in each. Only one approved itself to him, that of the Delphic oracle. This he had no sooner heard than he instantly made an act of adoration, and accepted it as true, declaring that the Delphic was the only really oracular shrine, the only one that had discovered in what way he was in fact employed. For on the departure of his messengers he had set himself to think what was most impossible for any one to conceive of his doing, and then, waiting till the day agreed on came, he acted as he had determined. He took a tortoise and a lamb, and cutting them in pieces with his own hands, boiled them both together in a brazen cauldron, covered over with a lid which was also of brass.

49. Such then was the answer returned to Crœsus from Delphi. What the answer was which the Lydians who went to the shrine of Amphiaraüs and performed the customary rites, obtained of the oracle there, I have it not in my power to mention, for there is no record of it. All that is known is that Crœsus believed himself to have found there also an oracle which spoke the truth.

50. After this Crœsus, having resolved to propitiate the Delphic god with a magnificent sacrifice, offered up three thousand of every kind of sacrificial beast, and besides made a huge pile, and placed upon it couches coated with silver and with gold, and golden goblets, and robes and vests of purple; all which he burnt in the hope of thereby making himself more secure of the favour of the god. Further, he issued his orders to all the people of the land to offer a sacrifice according to their means. When the sacrifice was ended, the king melted down a vast quantity of gold, and ran it into ingots, making them six palms long, three palms broad, and one palm in thickness. The number of ingots was a hundred and seventeen, four being of refined gold, in weight two talents[26] and a half; the others of pale gold, and in weight two talents. He also caused a statue of a lion to be made in refined gold, the weight of which was ten

---

[26]The talent (literally, "the thing weighed") was the heaviest unit of measurement of weight. The actual weight of a talent varied at different times and places in Greece, but in general it can be considered as about equivalent to seventy-five pounds.

talents. At the time when the temple of Delphi was burnt to the ground, this lion fell from the ingots on which it was placed; it now stands in the Corinthian treasury, and weighs only six talents and a half, having lost three talents and a half by the fire.

51. On the completion of these works, Crœsus sent them away to Delphi, and with them two bowls of an enormous size, one of gold, the other of silver, which used to stand, the latter upon the right, the former upon the left, as one entered the temple. They, too, were moved at the time of the fire; and now the golden one is in the Clazomenian treasury, and weighs eight talents and forty-two minæ;[27] the silver one stands in the corner of the ante-chapel, and holds six hundred amphoræ.[28] This is known, because the Delphians fill it at the time of the Theophania. It is said by the Delphians to be a work of Theodore the Samian, and I think that they say true, for assuredly it is the work of no common artist. Crœsus sent also four silver casks, which are in the Corinthian treasury, and two lustral vases,[29] a golden and a silver one. On the former is inscribed the name of the Lacedæmonians, and they claim it as a gift of theirs, but wrongly, since it was really given by Crœsus. The inscription upon it was cut by a Delphian, who wished to pleasure the Lacedæmonians. His name is known to me, but I forbear to mention it. The boy, through whose hand the water runs, is (I confess) a Lacedæmonian gift, but they did not give either of the lustral vases. Besides these various offerings, Crœsus sent to Delphi many others of less account, among the rest a number of round silver basins. Also he dedicated a female figure in gold, three cubits[30] high, which is said by the Delphians to be the statue of his baking-woman; and further, he presented the necklace and the girdles of his wife.

52. These were the offerings sent by Crœsus to Delphi. To the shrine of Amphiaraüs, with whose valour and misfortune he was acquainted, he sent a shield entirely of gold, and a spear, also of solid gold, both head and shaft. They were still existing in my day at Thebes, laid up in the temple of Ismenian Apollo.

53. The messengers who had the charge of conveying these treasures to the shrines, received instructions to ask the oracles whether Crœsus should go to war with the Persians, and if so, whether he should strengthen himself by the forces of an ally. Accordingly, when they had reached their destinations and presented the gifts, they proceeded to consult the oracles in the following terms: "Crœsus, king of Lydia and other countries, believing that these are the only real oracles in all the world, has sent you such presents as your discoveries deserved, and now inquires of you whether he shall go to war with the Persians, and if so, whether he shall strengthen himself by the forces of a confederate." Both the oracles agreed in the tenor of their reply, which was in each case a prophecy that if Crœsus attacked the Persians, he would destroy a mighty empire, and a recommendation to him to look and see who were the most powerful of the Greeks, and to make alliance with them.

---

[27]A mina was a unit of measurement of weight computed as one-sixtieth of a talent.
[28]An amphora was a unit of liquid measure equivalent to about nine gallons.
[29]Vessels to be used in purification rites.
[30]A cubit was a measure of length originally computed as the length of the human arm from the elbow to the tip of the middle finger but later standardized to represent the equivalent of about eighteen inches.

54. At the receipt of these oracular replies Crœsus was overjoyed, and feeling sure now that he would destroy the empire of the Persians, he sent once more to Pytho,[31] and presented to the Delphians, the number of whom he had ascertained, two gold staters[32] apiece. In return for this the Delphians granted to Crœsus and the Lydians the privilege of precedency in consulting the oracle, exemption from all charges, the most honourable seat at the festivals, and the perpetual right of becoming at pleasure citizens of their town.

55. After sending these presents to the Delphians, Crœsus a third time consulted the oracle, for having once proved its truthfulness, he wished to make constant use of it. The question whereto he now desired an answer was—"Whether his kingdom would be of long duration?" The following was the reply of the Pythoness:

"Wait till the time shall come when a mule is monarch of Media;
Then, thou delicate Lydian, away to the pebbles of Hermus;[33]
Haste, oh! haste thee away, nor blush to behave like a coward."

56. Of all the answers that had reached him, this pleased him far the best, for it seemed incredible that a mule should ever come to be king of the Medes, and so he concluded that the sovereignty would never depart from himself or his seed after him. Afterwards he turned his thoughts to the alliance which he had been recommended to contract, and sought to ascertain by inquiry which was the most powerful of the Grecian states. His inquiries pointed out to him two states as pre-eminent above the rest. These were the Lacedæmonians and the Athenians, the former of Doric, the latter of Ionic blood. And indeed these two nations had held from very early times the most distinguished place in Greece, the one being a Pelasgic, the other a Hellenic[34] people, and the one having never quitted its original seats, while the other had been excessively migratory; for during the reign of Deucalion, Phthiôtis was the country in which the Hellenes dwelt, but under Dorus, the son of Hellen, they moved to the tract at the base of Ossa and Olympus, which is called Histiæôtis; forced to retire from that region by the Cadmeians, they settled, under the name of Macedni, in the chain of Pindus. Hence they once more removed and came to Dryopis; and from Dryopis, having entered the Peloponnese in this way, they became known as Dorians.

85. With respect to Crœsus himself, this is what befell him at the taking of the town.[35] He had a son, of whom I made mention above, a worthy youth, whose only defect was that he was deaf and dumb. In

---

[31]The more ancient name of Delphi, presumably from the serpent Python, which Apollo was supposed to have slain. Herodotus often calls the priestess of Delphi the Pythoness.

[32]The principal gold coin of Greece, weighing two drachmae. The drachma was one-hundredth of a mina. Units of weight like minae also designated units of monetary value, so that the term *mina* also represented the sum of coined money weighing one mina.

[33]A large river in Asia Minor, flowing near the city of Sardis.

[34]Herodotus draws a distinction between the Pelasgians, whom he considers to be the original prehistoric inhabitants of Greece, and the Hellenes, peoples who settled Greece as a result of migrations in historic times. He describes this movement in the remainder of the chapter.

[35]Herodotus, in Chapters 57–85, has been describing Croesus' wars against the Persians, which culminated in his defeat and in the capture of his capital city of Sardis.

the days of his prosperity Crœsus had done the utmost that he could for him, and among other plans which he had devised, had sent to Delphi to consult the oracle on his behalf. The answer which he had received from the Pythoness ran thus:

> "Lydian, wide-ruling monarch, thou wondrous simple Crœsus,
> Wish not ever to hear in thy palace the voice thou has prayed for,
> Uttering intelligent sounds. Far better thy son should be silent!
> Ah! woe worth the day when thine ear shall first list to his accents."

When the town was taken, one of the Persians was just going to kill Crœsus, not knowing who he was. Crœsus saw the man coming, but under the pressure of his affliction, did not care to avoid the blow, not minding whether or no he died beneath the stroke. Then this son of his, who was voiceless, beholding the Persian as he rushed towards Crœsus, in the agony of his fear and grief burst into speech, and said, "Man, do not kill Crœsus." This was the first time that he had ever spoken a word, but afterwards he retained the power of speech for the remainder of his life.

86. Thus was Sardis taken by the Persians, and Crœsus himself fell into their hands, after having reigned fourteen years, and been besieged in his capital fourteen days; thus, too, did Crœsus fulfil the oracle, which said that he should destroy a mighty empire,—by destroying his own. Then the Persians who had made Crœsus prisoner brought him before Cyrus. Now, a vast pile had been raised by his orders, and Crœsus, laden with fetters, was placed upon it, and with him twice seven of the sons of the Lydians. I know not whether Cyrus was minded to make an offering of the first-fruits to some god or other, or whether he had vowed a vow and was performing it, or whether, as may well be, he had heard that Crœsus was a holy man, and so wished to see if any of the heavenly powers would appear to save him from being burnt alive. However it might be, Cyrus was thus engaged, and Crœsus was already on the pile, when it entered his mind in the depth of his woe that there was a divine warning in the words which had come to him from the lips of Solon, "No one while he lives is happy." When this thought smote him he fetched a long breath, and breaking his deep silence, groaned out aloud, thrice uttering the name of Solon. Cyrus caught the sounds, and bade the interpreters inquire of Crœsus who it was he called on. They drew near and asked him, but he held his peace, and for a long time made no answer to their questionings, until at length, forced to say something, he exclaimed, "One I would give much to see converse with every monarch." Not knowing what he meant by this reply, the interpreters begged him to explain himself; and as they pressed for an answer, and grew to be troublesome, he told them how, a long time before, Solon, an Athenian, had come and seen all his splendour, and made light of it; and how whatever he had said to him had fallen out exactly as he foreshowed, although it was nothing that especially concerned him, but applied to all mankind alike, and most to those who seemed to themselves happy. Meanwhile, as he thus spoke, the pile was lighted, and the outer portion began to blaze. Then Cyrus, hearing from the interpreters what Crœsus had said, relented, bethinking himself that he too was a

man, and that it was a fellow-man, and one who had once been as blessed by fortune as himself, that he was burning alive; afraid, moreover, of retribution, and full of the thought that whatever is human is insecure. So he bade them quench the blazing fire as quickly as they could, and take down Crœsus and the other Lydians, which they tried to do, but the flames were not to be mastered.

87. Then, the Lydians say that Crœsus, perceiving by the efforts made to quench the fire that Cyrus had relented, and seeing also that all was in vain, and that the men could not get the fire under, called with a loud voice upon the god Apollo, and prayed him, if he had ever received at his hands any acceptable gift, to come to his aid, and deliver him from his present danger. As thus with tears he besought the god, suddenly, though up to that time the sky had been clear and the day without a breath of wind, dark clouds gathered, and the storm burst over their heads with rain of such violence that the flames were speedily extinguished. Cyrus, convinced by this that Crœsus was a good man and a favourite of heaven, asked him after he was taken off the pile, "Who it was that persuaded him to lead an army into his country, and so become his foe rather than continue his friend?" to which Crœsus made answer as follows: "What I did, oh! king, was to your advantage and to my own loss. If there be blame, it rests with the god of the Greeks, who encouraged me to begin the war. No one is so foolish as to prefer to peace war, in which, instead of sons burying their fathers, fathers bury their sons. But the gods willed it so."

88. Thus did Crœsus speak. Cyrus then ordered his fetters to be taken off, and made him sit down near himself, and paid him much respect, looking upon him, as did also the courtiers, with a sort of wonder. Crœsus, wrapped in thought, uttered no word. After a while, happening to turn and perceive the Persian soldiers engaged in plundering the town, he said to Cyrus, "May I now tell you, oh! king, what I have in my mind, or is silence best?" Cyrus bade him speak his mind boldly. Then he put this question: "What is it, oh, Cyrus, which those men yonder are doing so busily?" "Plundering your city," Cyrus answered, "and carrying off your riches." "Not my city," rejoined the other, "nor my riches. They are not mine any more. It is your wealth which they are pillaging."

89. Cyrus, struck by what Crœsus had said, bade all the court to withdraw, and then asked Crœsus what he thought it best for him to do as regarded the plundering. Crœsus answered, "Now that the gods have made me your slave, oh, Cyrus, it seems to me that it is my part, if I see anything to your advantage, to show it to you. Your subjects, the Persians, are a poor people with a proud spirit. If then you let them pillage and possess themselves of great wealth, I will tell you what you have to expect at their hands. The man who gets the most, look to having him rebel against you. Now, then, if my words please you, do thus, oh! king: Let some of your body-guards be placed as sentinels at each of the city gates, and let them take their booty from the soldiers as they leave the town, and tell them that they do so because the tenths are due to Jupiter. So will you escape the hatred they would feel if the plunder were taken away from them by force; and they, seeing that what is proposed is just, will do it willingly."

90. Cyrus was beyond measure pleased with this advice, so excellent

did it seem to him. He praised Crœsus highly, and gave orders to his body-guard to do as he had suggested. Then, turning to Crœsus, he said, "Oh! Crœsus, I see that you are resolved both in speech and act to show yourself a virtuous prince: ask me, therefore, whatever you will as a gift at this moment." Crœsus replied, "Oh! my lord, if you will suffer me to send these fetters to the god of the Greeks, whom I once honoured above all other gods, and ask him if it is his wont to deceive his bene-factors,—that will be the highest favour you can confer on me." Cyrus upon this inquired what charge he had to make against the god. Then Crœsus gave him a full account of all his projects, and of the answers of the oracle, and of the offerings which he had sent, on which he dwelt especially, and told him how it was the encouragement given him by the oracle which had led him to make war upon Persia. All this he related, and at the end again besought permission to reproach the god with his behaviour. Cyrus answered with a laugh, "This I readily grant you, and whatever else you shall at any time ask at my hands." Crœsus, finding his request allowed, sent certain Lydians to Delphi, enjoining them to lay his fetters upon the threshold of the temple, and ask the god, "If he were not ashamed of having encouraged him, as the destined destroyer of the empire of Cyrus, to begin a war with Persia, of which such were the first-fruits?" As they said this they were to point to the fetters; and further they were to inquire, "if it was the wont of the Greek gods to be ungrateful?"

91. The Lydians went to Delphi and delivered their message, on which the Pythoness is said to have replied: "It is not possible even for a god to escape the decree of destiny. Crœsus has been punished for the sin of his fifth ancestor, who, when he was one of the body-guard of the Heraclides,[36] joined in a woman's fraud, and, slaying his master, wrong-fully seized the throne. Apollo was anxious that the fall of Sardis should not happen in the lifetime of Crœsus, but be delayed to his son's days; he could not, however, persuade the Fates. All that they were willing to allow he took and gave to Crœsus. Let Crœsus know that Apollo delayed the taking of Sardis three full years, and that he is thus a prisoner three years later than was his destiny. Moreover, it was Apollo who saved him from the burning pile. Nor has Crœsus any right to complain with respect to the oracular answer which he received. For when the god told him that, if he attacked the Persians, he would destroy a mighty empire, he ought, if he had been wise, to have sent again and inquired which empire was meant, that of Cyrus or his own; but if he neither un-derstood what was said, nor took the trouble to seek for enlightenment, he has only himself to blame for the result. Besides, he had misunder-stood the last answer which had been given him about the mule. Cyrus was that mule. For the parents of Cyrus were of different races, and of different conditions,—his mother a Median princess, daughter of King Astyages, and his father a Persian and a subject, who, though so far be-neath her in all respects, had married his royal mistress."

---

[36]A legendary family, supposedly descended from the god Hercules, which had ruled Lydia before being overthrown by one of Croesus' ancestors, who was supposed to have been a member of their court. Herodotus recounts the legend in Chapters 7–14.

Such was the answer of the Pythoness. The Lydians returned to Sardis and communicated it to Crœsus, who confessed, on hearing it, that the fault was his, not the god's. Such was the way in which Ionia was first conquered, and so was the empire of Crœsus brought to a close.

Comments / on Herodotus

The conversion of legend-writing into the science of history was a fifth-century invention, and Herodotus was the man who invented it. It is equally clear that history for Herodotus is humanistic as distinct from either mythical or theocratic. As he says in his preface, his purpose is to describe the deeds of men.   *R. G. COLLINGWOOD (1946)*

Herodotus too was much impressed by the jealousy of the gods, who seemed bent on destroying great men just because they were great: yet he treated history essentially as an affair of, by, and for men. Most unusual, he set about inquiring into the manifold stories not only of the Greeks but of other peoples as well. He was still far from being a profound analyst of causes and consequences, or of the means and ends of Greek freedom, the central theme of his *Persian Wars*. . . . Herodotus was a remarkable pioneer. He was the first to profit fully from the stimulus of diversity in the many little city-states, and especially from their commerce with the greater world of the ancient East. He traveled all over the known world "for the sake of learning, for the sake of inquiry." With his lively intelligence, eager curiosity, and breadth of interest he had a still more exceptional dispassionate spirit, which enabled him to be fair to the "barbarians." In this respect no philosopher was wiser than he, no religious prophet freer from tribalism. He was perhaps a better educator in history because he had no preconceived standards, knew no laws, and so tampered with the evidence less than some modern systematizers of history do.   *HERBERT J. MULLER (1961)*

The history of Herodotus has an epic character, not only from the equable and uninterrupted flow of the narrative, but also from certain pervading ideas, which give an uniform tone to the whole. The principal of these is the idea of a fixed destiny, of a wise arrangement of the world, which has prescribed to every being his path and which allots ruin and destruction, not only to crime and violence, but to excessive power and riches, and the overweening pride which is their companion.

                                              K. O. MÜLLER (1840)

Herodotus was able to keep before his reader the sense that Greece, the centre of his interest, was still only one country in an immense and diverse world which it was yet to dominate by virtue of certain qualities which that world lacked, above all by that passion for independence and self-determination which was both her glory and her bane; to be aware of the past, not only the immediate but the most remote, as a living element in the present; and to find—unlike most historians writing today —a continuing moral pattern in the vicissitudes of human fortune all the world over.   *AUBREY DE SÉLINCOURT (1962)*

The last and most serious charge that is brought against the work of Herodotus is his weakness in tracing the real relation of events; he continually confuses the mere occasion and the cause. . . . Hence Herodotus is always laying stress on personal activity and motive, and understands little of the great movements of which persons are only the expression.
                                    W. W. HOW, J. WELLS (1912)

Thucydides

460?—400? B.C.

The clash of those ideas that brought about both the rise and fall of ancient Greek civilization is embodied in the conflict between Athens and Sparta known as the Peloponnesian War (431-404 B.C.). This bitter power struggle ended in the defeat of Athens and the short-lived supremacy of Sparta over Greece and all but exhausted both cities in the process. The record of that war compiled by the historian Thucydides has long fascinated men both because of its description of political and military actions and because of its illumination of the competing ideas responsible for those actions.

Thucydides had stronger reasons than most historians to probe for the causes of the events he describes, since he was himself an Athenian leader deeply involved in them. Although he was a historian scrupulously concerned about gathering reliable evidence, he was even more a political scientist and psychologist bent upon fathoming the hidden forces, motives, and interests which impel men to violence and intrigue as political action. Symptomatic of his concern with the pathology of war and politics are the many speeches he reports, through which he attempts to reconstruct the reasons behind particular events and for which his *History* is justly famous. The chief purpose of these speeches is to show how general psychological laws operate in the workings of political forces and in the process to provide a lesson for the future. They also show Thucydides himself as a tough-minded, disabused observer of human nature whose trenchant analysis of political action seems no less valid in our time than it was in his.

This quality of mind, combined with his literary skill, enabled Thucydides to report men for what they were—to reproduce in turn the elevation of Pericles' orations, the cynicism of the Athenians in the Melian debate, and the casuistry of the brilliant but wily Alcibiades who looms in the background of the trial of Socrates. A comparison of Pericles' Funeral Oration with the Melian Dialogue offers some measure of the scope of Thucydides' mind. He knew the ideals of freedom and beauty which had made Pericles' Athens great, and he also knew how little these ideals counted in a foreign policy animated by imperialist power politics.

Thucydides mentions himself only sparingly in his *History,* and information about him from other sources is scanty. We do know that he was born in Athens, undertook his writing at the outbreak of the war, but left it unfinished at the time of his death, probably a few years after Athens' downfall. In 424 B.C. he was one of two generals in charge of an important naval operation which, through no fault of his, failed to achieve its objective. Exiled from Athens for over twenty years because of this failure, he was received by Spartan leaders and thus had the advantage of familiarity with both belligerent parties, which may account for the general objectivity of his history.

But more than his objectivity, Thucydides' vivid sense of deriving from the experience of a whole generation new insights into the relationships between man and society, freedom and authority, material progress and social decay—these give his *History* its power and enduring value. In this sense, even more than Herodotus, Thucydides turned the writing of history into a thoroughly humanistic and scientific discipline which reveals to man what he may do by carefully observing and interpreting what he has done.

History

Book I

1. Thucydides, an Athenian, wrote the history of the war in which the Peloponnesians and the Athenians fought against one another. He began to write when they first took up arms, believing that it would be great and memorable above any previous war. For he argued that both states were then at the full height of their military power, and he saw the rest of the Hellenes either siding or intending to side with one or other of them. No movement ever stirred Hellas more deeply than this; it was shared by many of the Barbarians, and might be said even to affect the world at large. The character of the events which preceded, whether immediately or in more remote antiquity, owing to the lapse of time cannot be made out with certainty. But, judging from the evidence which I am able to trust after most careful enquiry, I should imagine that former ages were not great either in their wars or anything else.

From *History*, Vols. I-III, translated by Benjamin Jowett (New York: The Tandy-Thomas Co., 1909).

22. As to the speeches which were made either before or during the war, it is hard for me, and for others who reported them to me, to recollect the exact words. I have therefore put into the mouth of each speaker the sentiments proper to the occasion, expressed as I thought he would be likely to express them, while at the same time I endeavoured, as nearly as I could, to give the general purport of what was actually said. Of the events of the war I have not ventured to speak from any chance information, nor according to any notion of my own; I have described nothing but what I either saw myself, or learned from others of whom I made the most careful and particular enquiry. The task was a laborious one, because eye-witnesses of the same occurrences gave different accounts of them, as they remembered or were interested in the actions of one side or the other. And very likely the strictly historical character of my narrative may be disappointing to the ear. But if he who desires to have before his eyes a true picture of the events which have happened, and of the like events which may be expected to happen hereafter in the order of human things, shall pronounce what I have written to be useful, then I shall be satisfied. My history is an everlasting possession, not a prize composition which is heard and forgotten.

Book II

34. During the same winter,[1] in accordance with an old national custom, the funeral of those who first fell in this war was celebrated by the Athenians at the public charge. The ceremony is as follows: Three days before the celebration they erect a tent in which the bones of the dead are laid out, and every one brings to his own dead any offering which he pleases. At the time of the funeral the bones are placed in chests of cypress wood, which are conveyed on hearses; there is one chest for each tribe. They also carry a single empty litter decked with a pall for all whose bodies are missing, and cannot be recovered after the battle. The procession is accompanied by any one who chooses, whether citizen or stranger, and the female relatives of the deceased are present at the place of interment and make lamentation. The public sepulchre is situated in the most beautiful spot outside the walls; there they always bury those who fall in war; only after the battle of Marathon[2] the dead, in recognition of their pre-eminent valour, were interred on the field. When the remains have been laid in the earth, some man of known ability and high reputation, chosen by the city, delivers a suitable oration over them; after which the people depart. Such is the manner of interment; and the ceremony was repeated from time to time throughout the war. Over those who were the first buried Pericles was chosen to speak. At the fitting moment he advanced from the sepulchre to a lofty stage, which had been erected in order that he might be heard as far as possible by the multitude, and spoke as follows:

---

[1] 431 B.C.

[2] A town some twenty-six miles from Athens where, in 490 B.C., a relatively small army of Athenians defeated and inflicted enormous casualties on an overwhelmingly larger army of invading Persians.

35. "Most of those who have spoken here before me have commended the lawgiver who added this oration to our other funeral customs; it seemed to them a worthy thing that such an honour should be given at their burial to the dead who have fallen on the field of battle. But I should have preferred that, when men's deeds have been brave, they should be honoured in deed only, and with such an honour as this public funeral, which you are now witnessing. Then the reputation of many would not have been imperilled on the eloquence or want of eloquence of one, and their virtues believed or not as he spoke well or ill. For it is difficult to say neither too little nor too much; and even moderation is apt not to give the impression of truthfulness. The friend of the dead who knows the facts is likely to think that the words of the speaker fall short of his knowledge and of his wishes; another who is not so well informed, when he hears of anything which surpasses his own powers, will be envious and will suspect exaggeration. Mankind are tolerant of the praises of others so long as each hearer thinks that he can do as well or nearly as well himself but, when the speaker rises above him, jealousy is aroused and he begins to be incredulous. However, since our ancestors have set the seal of their approval upon the practice, I must obey, and to the utmost of my power shall endeavour to satisfy the wishes and beliefs of all who hear me.

36. "I will speak first of our ancestors, for it is right and seemly that now, when we are lamenting the dead, a tribute should be paid to their memory. There has never been a time when they did not inhabit this land, which by their valour they have handed down from generation to generation, and we have received from them a free state. But if they were worthy of praise, still more were our fathers, who added to their inheritance, and after many a struggle transmitted to us their sons this great empire. And we ourselves assembled here to-day, who are still most of us in the vigour of life, have carried the work of improvement further, and have richly endowed our city with all things, so that she is sufficient for herself both in peace and war. Of the military exploits by which our various possessions were acquired, or of the energy with which we or our fathers drove back the tide of war, Hellenic or Barbarian, I will not speak; for the tale would be long and is familiar to you. But before I praise the dead, I should like to point out by what principles of action we rose to power, and under what institutions and through what manner of life our empire became great. For I conceive that such thoughts are not unsuited to the occasion, and that this numerous assembly of citizens and strangers may profitably listen to them.

37. "Our form of government does not enter into rivalry with the institutions of others. We do not copy our neighbours, but are an example to them. It is true that we are called a democracy, for the administration is in the hands of the many and not of the few. But while the law secures equal justice to all alike in their private disputes, the claim of excellence is also recognised; and when a citizen is in any way distinguished, he is preferred to the public service, not as a matter of privilege, but as the reward of merit. Neither is poverty a bar, but a man may benefit his country whatever be the obscurity of his condition. There is no exclusiveness in our public life, and in our private intercourse we

are not suspicious of one another, nor angry with our neighbour if he does what he likes; we do not put on sour looks at him which, though harmless, are not pleasant. While we are thus unconstrained in our private intercourse, a spirit of reverence pervades our public acts; we are prevented from doing wrong by respect for the authorities and for the laws, having an especial regard to those which are ordained for the protection of the injured as well as to those unwritten laws which bring upon the transgressor of them the reprobation of the general sentiment.

38. "And we have not forgotten to provide for our weary spirits many relaxations from toil; we have regular games and sacrifices throughout the year; our homes are beautiful and elegant; and the delight which we daily feel in all these things helps to banish melancholy. Because of the greatness of our city the fruits of the whole earth flow in upon us; so that we enjoy the goods of other countries as freely as of our own.

39. "Then, again, our military training is in many respects superior to that of our adversaries. Our city is thrown open to the world, and we never expel a foreigner or prevent him from seeing or learning anything of which the secret if revealed to an enemy might profit him. We rely not upon management or trickery, but upon our own hearts and hands. And in the matter of education, whereas they[3] from early youth are always undergoing laborious exercises which are to make them brave, we live at ease, and yet are equally ready to face the perils which they face. And here is the proof. The Lacedæmonians come into Attica not by themselves, but with their whole confederacy following; we go alone into a neighbour's country; and although our opponents are fighting for their homes and we on a foreign soil, we have seldom any difficulty in overcoming them. Our enemies have never yet felt our united strength; the care of a navy divides our attention, and on land we are obliged to send our own citizens everywhere. But they, if they meet and defeat a part of our army, are as proud as if they had routed us all, and when defeated they pretend to have been vanquished by us all.

40. "If then we prefer to meet danger with a light heart but without laborious training, and with a courage which is gained by habit and not enforced by law, are we not greatly the gainers? Since we do not anticipate the pain, although, when the hour comes, we can be as brave as those who never allow themselves to rest; and thus too our city is equally admirable in peace and in war. For we are lovers of the beautiful, yet simple in our tastes, and we cultivate the mind without loss of manliness. Wealth we employ, not for talk and ostentation, but when there is a real use for it. To avow poverty with us is no disgrace; the true disgrace is in doing nothing to avoid it. An Athenian citizen does not neglect the state because he takes care of his own household; and even those of us who are engaged in business have a very fair idea of politics. We alone regard a man who takes no interest in public affairs, not as a harmless, but as a useless character; and if few of us are originators, we are all sound judges of policy. The great impediment to action is, in our opinion, not discussion, but the want of that knowledge which is gained

---

[3]The Lacedaemonians (Spartans).

by discussion preparatory to action. For we have a peculiar power of thinking before we act and of acting too, whereas other men are courageous from ignorance but hesitate upon reflection. And they are surely to be esteemed the bravest spirits who, having the clearest sense both of the pains and pleasures of life, do not on that account shrink from danger. In doing good, again, we are unlike others; we make our friends by conferring, not by receiving favours. Now he who confers a favour is the firmer friend, because he would fain by kindness keep alive the memory of an obligation; but the recipient is colder in his feelings, because he knows that in requiting another's generosity he will not be winning gratitude but only paying a debt. We alone do good to our neighbours, not upon a calculation of interest, but in the confidence of freedom and in a frank and fearless spirit.

41. "To sum up: I say that Athens is the school of Hellas, and that the individual Athenian in his own person seems to have the power of adapting himself to the most varied forms of action with the utmost versatility and grace. This is no passing and idle word, but truth and fact; and the assertion is verified by the position to which these qualities have raised the state. For in the hour of trial Athens alone among her contemporaries is superior to the report of her. No enemy who comes against her is indignant at the reverses which he sustains at the hands of such a city; no subject complains that his masters are unworthy of him. And we shall assuredly not be without witnesses; there are mighty monuments of our power which will make us the wonder of this and of succeeding ages; we shall not need the praises of Homer or of any other panegyrist whose poetry may please for the moment, although his representation of the facts will not bear the light of day. For we have compelled every land and every sea to open a path for our valour, and have everywhere planted eternal memorials of our friendship and of our enmity. Such is the city for whose sake these men nobly fought and died; they could not bear the thought that she might be taken from them; and every one of us who survive should gladly toil on her behalf.

42. "I have dwelt upon the greatness of Athens because I want to show you that we are contending for a higher prize than those who enjoy none of these privileges, and to establish by manifest proof the merit of these men whom I am now commemorating. Their loftiest praise has been already spoken. For in magnifying the city I have magnified them, and men like them whose virtues made her glorious. And of how few Hellenes can it be said as of them, that their deeds when weighed in the balance have been found equal to their fame! Methinks that a death such as theirs has been gives the true measure of a man's worth; it may be the first revelation of his virtues, but is at any rate their final seal. For even those who come short in other ways may justly plead the valour with which they have fought for their country; they have blotted out the evil with the good, and have benefited the state more by their public services than they have injured her by their private actions. None of these men were enervated by wealth or hesitated to resign the pleasures of life; none of them put off the evil day in the hope, natural to poverty, that a man, though poor, may one day become rich. But, deeming that the punishment of their enemies was sweeter

than any of these things, and that they could fall in no nobler cause, they determined at the hazard of their lives to be honourably avenged, and to leave the rest. They resigned to hope their unknown chance of happiness; but in the face of death they resolved to rely upon themselves alone. And when the moment came they were minded to resist and suffer, rather than to fly and save their lives; they ran away from the word of dishonour, but on the battlefield their feet stood fast, and in an instant, at the height of their fortune, they passed away from the scene, not of their fear, but of their glory.

43. "Such was the end of these men; they were worthy of Athens, and the living need not desire to have a more heroic spirit, although they may pray for a less fatal issue. The value of such a spirit is not to be expressed in words. Any one can discourse to you for ever about the advantages of a brave defence, which you know already. But instead of listening to him I would have you day by day fix your eyes upon the greatness of Athens, until you become filled with the love of her; and when you are impressed by the spectacle of her glory, reflect that this empire has been acquired by men who knew their duty and had the courage to do it, who in the hour of conflict had the fear of dishonour always present to them, and who, if ever they failed in an enterprise, would not allow their virtues to be lost to their country, but freely gave their lives to her as the fairest offering which they could present at her feast. The sacrifice which they collectively made was individually repaid to them; for they received again each one for himself a praise which grows not old, and the noblest of all sepulchres—I speak not of that in which their remains are laid, but of that in which their glory survives, and is proclaimed always and on every fitting occasion both in word and deed. For the whole earth is the sepulchre of famous men; not only are they commemorated by columns and inscriptions in their own country, but in foreign lands there dwells also an unwritten memorial of them, graven not on stone but in the hearts of men. Make them your examples, and, esteeming courage to be freedom and freedom to be happiness, do not weigh too nicely the perils of war. The unfortunate who has no hope of a change for the better has less reason to throw away his life than the prosperous who, if he survive, is always liable to a change for the worse, and to whom any accidental fall makes the most serious difference. To a man of spirit, cowardice and disaster coming together are far more bitter than death striking him unperceived at a time when he is full of courage and animated by the general hope.

44. "Wherefore I do not now commiserate the parents of the dead who stand here; I would rather comfort them. You know that your life has been passed amid manifold vicissitudes; and that they may be deemed fortunate who have gained most honour, whether an honourable death like theirs, or an honourable sorrow like yours, and whose days have been so ordered that the term of their happiness is likewise the term of their life. I know how hard it is to make you feel this, when the good fortune of others will too often remind you of the gladness which once lightened your hearts. And sorrow is felt at the want of those blessings, not which a man never knew, but which were a part of his life before they were taken from him. Some of you are of an age at

which they may hope to have other children, and they ought to bear their sorrow better; not only will the children who may hereafter be born make them forget their own lost ones, but the city will be doubly a gainer. She will not be left desolate, and she will be safer. For a man's counsel cannot have equal weight or worth, when he alone has no children to risk in the general danger. To those of you who have passed their prime, I say: 'Congratulate yourselves that you have been happy during the greater part of your days; remember that your life of sorrow will not last long, and be comforted by the glory of those who are gone. For the love of honour alone is ever young, and not riches, as some say, but honour is the delight of men when they are old and useless.'

45. "To you who are the sons and brothers of the departed, I see that the struggle to emulate them will be an arduous one. For all men praise the dead, and, however pre-eminent your virtue may be, hardly will you be thought, I do not say to equal, but even to approach them. The living have their rivals and detractors, but when a man is out of the way, the honour and good-will which he receives is unalloyed. And, if I am to speak of womanly virtues to those of you who will henceforth be widows, let me sum them up in one short admonition: To a woman not to show more weakness than is natural to her sex is a great glory, and not to be talked about for good or for evil among men.

46. "I have paid the required tribute, in obedience to the law, making use of such fitting words as I had. The tribute of deeds has been paid in part; for the dead have been honourably interred, and it remains only that their children should be maintained at the public charge until they are grown up: this is the solid prize with which, as with a garland, Athens crowns her sons living and dead, after a struggle like theirs. For where the rewards of virtue are greatest, there the noblest citizens are enlisted in the service of the state. And now, when you have duly lamented, every one his own dead, you may depart."

Book V

84. In the ensuing summer,[4] Alcibiades sailed to Argos with twenty ships, and seized any of the Argives who were still suspected to be of the Lacedæmonian faction, to the number of three hundred; and the Athenians deposited them in the subject islands near at hand. The Athenians next made an expedition against the island of Melos[5] with thirty ships of their own, six Chian, and two Lesbian,[6] twelve hundred hoplites[7] and three hundred archers besides twenty mounted archers of their own, and about fifteen hundred hoplites furnished by their allies in the islands. The Melians are colonists of the Lacedæmonians who would not submit to Athens like the other islanders. At first they were neutral and took no part. But when the Athenians tried to coerce them by ravaging their lands, they were driven into open hostilities.

---

[4]416 B.C.
[5]An island in the Aegean Sea.
[6]The governments on the Aegean islands of Chios and Lesbos were allied with Athens at this time of the war.
[7]Heavily armed infantry soldiers.

The generals, Cleomedes the son of Lycomedes and Tisias the son of Tisimachus, encamped with the Athenian forces on the island. But before they did the country any harm they sent envoys to negotiate with the Melians. Instead of bringing these envoys before the people, the Melians desired them to explain their errand to the magistrates and to the dominant class. They spoke as follows:

85. "Since we are not allowed to speak to the people, lest, forsooth, a multitude should be deceived by seductive and unanswerable arguments which they would hear set forth in a single uninterrupted oration (for we are perfectly aware that this is what you mean in bringing us before a select few), you who are sitting here may as well make assurance yet surer. Let us have no set speeches at all, but do you reply to each several statement of which you disapprove, and criticise it at once. Say first of all how you like this mode of proceeding."

86. The Melian representatives answered: "The quiet interchanging of explanations is a reasonable thing, and we do not object to that. But your warlike movements, which are present not only to our fears but to our eyes, seem to belie your words. We see that, although you may reason with us, you mean to be our judges; and that at the end of the discussion, if the justice of our cause prevail and we therefore refuse to yield, we may expect war; if we are convinced by you, slavery."

87. ATH: "Nay, but if you are only going to argue from fancies about the future, or if you meet us with any other purpose than that of looking your circumstances in the face and saving your city, we have done; but if this is your intention we will proceed."

88. MEL: "It is an excusable and natural thing that men in our position should neglect no argument and no view which may avail. But we admit that this conference has met to consider the question of our preservation; and therefore let the argument proceed in the manner which you propose."

89. ATH: "Well, then, we Athenians will use no fine words; we will not go out of our way to prove at length that we have a right to rule, because we overthrew the Persians; or that we attack you now because we are suffering any injury at your hands. We should not convince you if we did; nor must you expect to convince us by arguing that, although a colony of the Lacedæmonians, you have taken no part in their expeditions, or that you have never done us any wrong. But you and we should say what we really think, and aim only at what is possible, for we both alike know that into the discussion of human affairs the question of justice only enters where there is equal power to enforce it, and that the powerful exact what they can, and the weak grant what they must."

90. MEL: "Well, then, since you set aside justice and invite us to speak of expediency, in our judgment it is certainly expedient that you should respect a principle which is for the common good; that to every man when in peril a reasonable claim should be accounted a claim of right, and that any plea which he is disposed to urge, even if failing of the point a little, should help his cause. Your interest in this principle is quite as great as ours, inasmuch as you, if you fall, will incur the heaviest vengeance, and will be the most terrible example to mankind."

91. ATH: "The fall of our empire, if it should fall, is not an event to which we look forward with dismay; for ruling states such as Lacedæmon are not cruel to their vanquished enemies. With the Lacedæmonians, however, we are not now contending; the real danger is from our many subject states, who may of their own motion rise up and overcome their masters. But this is a danger which you may leave to us. And we will now endeavour to show that we have come in the interests of our empire, and that in what we are about to say we are only seeking the preservation of your city. For we want to make you ours with the least trouble to ourselves, and it is for the interests of us both that you should not be destroyed."

92. MEL: "It may be your interest to be our masters, but how can it be ours to be your slaves?"

93. ATH: "To you the gain will be that by submission you will avert the worst; and we shall be all the richer for your preservation."

94. MEL: "But must we be your enemies? Will you not receive us as friends if we are neutral and remain at peace with you?"

95. ATH: "No, your enmity is not half so mischievous to us as your friendship; for the one is in the eyes of our subjects an argument of our power, the other of our weakness."

96. MEL: "But are your subjects really unable to distinguish between states in which you have no concern, and those which are chiefly your own colonies, and in some cases have revolted and been subdued by you?"

97. ATH: "Why, they do not doubt that both of them have a good deal to say for themselves on the score of justice, but they think that states like yours are left free because they are able to defend themselves, and that we do not attack them because we dare not. So that your subjection will give us an increase of security, as well as an extension of empire. For we are masters of the sea, and you who are islanders, and insignificant islanders too, must not be allowed to escape us."

98. MEL: "But do you not recognise another danger? For once more, since you drive us from the plea of justice and press upon us your doctrine of expediency, we must show you what is for our interest, and, if it be for yours also, may hope to convince you: Will you not be making enemies of all who are now neutrals? When they see how you are treating us they will expect you some day to turn against them; and if so, are you not strengthening the enemies whom you already have, and bringing upon you others who, if they could help, would never dream of being your enemies at all?"

99. ATH: "We do not consider our really dangerous enemies to be any of the peoples inhabiting the mainland who, secure in their freedom, may defer indefinitely any measures of precaution which they take against us, but islanders who, like you, happen to be under no control, and all who may be already irritated by the necessity of submission to our empire—these are our real enemies, for they are the most reckless and most likely to bring themselves as well as us into a danger which they cannot but foresee."

100. MEL: "Surely then, if you and your subjects will brave all this risk, you to preserve your empire and they to be quit of it, how base and

cowardly would it be in us who retain our freedom, not to do and suffer anything rather than be your slaves."

101. ATH: "Not so, if you calmly reflect: for you are not fighting against equals to whom you cannot yield without disgrace, but you are taking counsel whether or no you shall resist an overwhelming force. The question is not one of honour but of prudence."

102. MEL: "But we know that the fortune of war is sometimes impartial, and not always on the side of numbers. If we yield now, all is over; but if we fight, there is yet a hope that we may stand upright."

103. ATH: "Hope is a good comforter in the hour of danger, and when men have something else to depend upon, although hurtful, she is not ruinous. But when her spendthrift nature has induced them to stake their all, they see her as she is in the moment of their fall, and not till then. While the knowledge of her might enable them to be aware of her, she never fails. You are weak and a single turn of the scale might be your ruin. Do not you be thus deluded; avoid the error of which so many are guilty, who, although they might still be saved if they would take the natural means, when visible grounds of confidence forsake them, have recourse to the invisible, to prophecies and oracles and the like, which ruin men by the hopes which they inspire in them."

104. MEL: "We know only too well how hard the struggle must be against your power, and against fortune, if she does not mean to be impartial. Nevertheless we do not despair of fortune; for we hope to stand as high as you in the favour of heaven, because we are righteous, and you against whom we contend are unrighteous; and we are satisfied that our deficiency in power will be compensated by the aid of our allies the Lacedæmonians; they cannot refuse to help us, if only because we are their kinsmen, and for the sake of their own honour. And therefore our confidence is not so utterly blind as you suppose."

105. ATH: "As for the gods, we expect to have quite as much of their favour as you: for we are not doing or claiming anything which goes beyond common opinion about divine or men's desires about human things. For of the gods we believe, and of men we know, that by a law of their nature wherever they can rule they will. This law was not made by us, and we are not the first who have acted upon it; we did but inherit it, and shall bequeath it to all time, and we know that you and all mankind, if you were as strong as we are, would do as we do. So much for the gods; we have told you why we expect to stand as high in their opinion as you. And then as to the Lacedæmonians—when you imagine that out of very shame they will assist you, we admire the innocence of your idea, but we do not envy you the folly of it. The Lacedæmonians are exceedingly virtuous among themselves, and according to their national standard of morality. But, in respect of their dealings with others, although many things might be said, they can be described in few words—of all men whom we know they are the most notorious for identifying what is pleasant with what is honourable, and what is expedient with what is just. But how inconsistent is such a character with your present blind hope of deliverance!"

106. MEL: "That is the very reason why we trust them; they will look to their interest, and therefore will not be willing to betray the Me-

lians, who are their own colonists, lest they should be distrusted by their friends in Hellas and play into the hands of their enemies."

107. ATH: "But do you not see that the path of expediency is safe, whereas justice and honour involve danger in practice, and such dangers the Lacedæmonians seldom care to face?"

108. MEL: "On the other hand, we think that whatever perils there may be, they will be ready to face them for our sakes, and will consider danger less dangerous where we are concerned. For if they need our aid we are close at hand, and they can better trust our loyal feeling because we are their kinsmen."

109. ATH: "Yes, but what encourages men who are invited to join in a conflict is clearly not the good-will of those who summon them to their side, but a decided superiority in real power. To this no men look more keenly than the Lacedæmonians; so little confidence have they in their own resources, that they only attack their neighbours when they have numerous allies, and therefore they are not likely to find their way by themselves to an island, when we are masters of the sea."

110. MEL: "But they may send their allies: the Cretan sea is a large place; and the masters of the sea will have more difficulty in overtaking vessels which want to escape than the pursued in escaping. If the attempt should fail they may invade Attica itself, and find their way to allies of yours whom Brasidas[8] did not reach: and then you will have to fight, not for the conquest of a land in which you have no concern, but nearer home, for the preservation of your confederacy and of your own territory."

111. ATH: "Help may come from Lacedæmon to you as it has come to others, and should you ever have actual experience of it, then you will know that never once have the Athenians retired from a siege through fear of a foe elsewhere. You told us that the safety of your city would be your first care, but we remark that, in this long discussion, not a word has been uttered by you which would give a reasonable man expectation of deliverance. Your strongest grounds are hopes deferred, and what power you have is not to be compared with that which is already arrayed against you. Unless after we have withdrawn you mean to come, as even now you may, to a wiser conclusion, you are showing a great want of sense. For surely you cannot dream of flying to that false sense of honour which has been the ruin of so many when danger and dishonour were staring them in the face. Many men with their eyes still open to the consequences have found the word 'honour' too much for them, and have suffered a mere name to lure them on, until it has drawn down upon them real and irretrievable calamities; through their own folly they have incurred a worse dishonour than fortune would have inflicted upon them. If you are wise you will not run this risk; you ought to see that there can be no disgrace in yielding to a great city which invites you to become her ally on reasonable terms, keeping your own land, and merely paying tribute; and that you will certainly gain no

---

[8]A Spartan general who had been successful at converting some of the smaller Greek states to the Spartan cause.

honour if, having to choose between two alternatives, safety and war, you obstinately prefer the worse. To maintain our rights against equals, to be politic with superiors, and to be moderate towards inferiors is the path of safety. Reflect once more when we have withdrawn, and say to yourselves over and over again that you are deliberating about your one and only country, which may be saved or may be destroyed by a single decision."

112. The Athenians left the conference: the Melians, after consulting among themselves, resolved to persevere in their refusal, and made answer as follows: "Men of Athens, our resolution is unchanged; and we will not in a moment surrender that liberty which our city, founded seven hundred years ago, still enjoys; we will trust to the good fortune which, by the favour of the gods, has hitherto preserved us, and for human help to the Lacedæmonians, and endeavour to save ourselves. We are ready however to be your friends, and the enemies neither of you nor of the Lacedæmonians, and we ask you to leave our country when you have made such a peace as may appear to be in the interest of both parties."

113. Such was the answer of the Melians; the Athenians, as they quitted the conference, spoke as follows: "Well, we must say, judging from the decision at which you have arrived, that you are the only men who deem the future to be more certain than the present, and regard things unseen as already realised in your fond anticipation, and that the more you cast yourselves upon the Lacedæmonians and fortune and hope, and trust them, the more complete will be your ruin."

114. The Athenian envoys returned to the army; and the generals, when they found that the Melians would not yield, immediately commenced hostilities. They surrounded the town of Melos with a wall, dividing the work among the several contingents. They then left troops of their own and of their allies to keep guard both by land and by sea, and retired with the greater part of their army; the remainder carried on the blockade.

115. ... The Melians took that part of the Athenian wall which looked towards the agora[9] by a night assault, killed a few men, and brought in as much corn and other necessaries as they could; they then retreated and remained inactive. After this the Athenians set a better watch. So the summer ended.

116. In the following winter the Lacedæmonians had intended to make an expedition into the Argive territory, but finding that the sacrifices which they offered at the frontier were unfavourable they returned home. The Argives, suspecting that the threatened invasion was instigated by citizens of their own, apprehended some of them; others however escaped.

About the same time the Melians took another part of the Athenian wall; for the fortifications were insufficiently guarded. Whereupon the Athenians sent fresh troops, under the command of Philocrates the son of Demeas. The place was now closely invested, and there was treachery

---

[9]The place within a Greek city where the citizens were accustomed to hold their assemblies.

among the citizens themselves. So the Melians were induced to surrender at discretion. The Athenians thereupon put to death all who were of military age, and made slaves of the women and children. They then colonised the island, sending thither five hundred settlers of their own.

Book VI

15. Such were the words of Nicias.[10] Most of the Athenians who came forward to speak were in favour of war, and reluctant to rescind the vote which had been already passed, although a few took the other side. The most enthusiastic supporter of the expedition was Alcibiades the son of Cleinias; he was determined to oppose Nicias, who was always his political enemy and had just now spoken of him in disparaging terms; but the desire to command was even a stronger motive with him.[11] He was hoping that he might be the conqueror of Sicily and Carthage; and that success would repair his private fortunes, and gain him money as well as glory. He had a great position among the citizens and was devoted to horse-racing and other pleasures which outran his means. And in the end his wild courses went far to ruin the Athenian state. For the people feared the extremes to which he carried the lawlessness of his personal habits, and the far-reaching purposes which invariably animated him in all his actions. They thought that he was aiming at a tyranny and set themselves against him. And therefore, although his talents as a military commander were unrivalled, they entrusted the administration of the war to others, because they personally objected to his private habits; and so they speedily shipwrecked the state. He now came forward and spoke as follows:

16. "I have a better right to command, men of Athens, than another; for as Nicias has attacked me, I must begin by praising myself; and I consider that I am worthy. Those doings of mine for which I am so much cried out against are an honour to myself and to my ancestors, and a solid advantage to my country. In consequence of the distinguished manner in which I represented the state at Olympia, the other Hellenes formed an idea of our power which even exceeded the reality, although they had previously imagined that we were exhausted by war. I sent into the lists seven chariots,—no other private man ever did the like; I was victor, and also won the second and fourth prize; and I ordered everything in a style worthy of my victory. Apart from the conventional honour paid to such successes, the energy which is shown by them creates an impression of power. At home, again, whenever I gain distinction by providing choruses or by the performance of some other public duty, although the citizens are naturally jealous of me, to strangers these acts of munificence are a new argument of our strength. There is some use in the folly of a man who at his own cost benefits not only himself,

---

[10]Thucydides has been describing a debate that occurred among the Athenians during 415 B.C. concerning whether or not they should undertake an expedition against Sicily. Nicias was one of the generals chosen to lead the expedition, but he doubted its wisdom and spoke against it. As it happened, the expedition proved disastrous for the Athenians.
[11]Alcibiades had also been appointed one of the commanders of the expedition.

but the state. And where is the injustice, if I or any one who feels his own superiority to another refuses to be on a level with him? The unfortunate keep their misfortunes to themselves. We do not expect to be recognised by our acquaintance when we are down in the world; and on the same principle why should any one complain when treated with disdain by the more fortunate? He who would have proper respect shown to him should himself show it towards others. I know that men of this lofty spirit, and all who have been in any way illustrious, are hated while they are alive, by their equals especially, and in a lesser degree by others who have to do with them; but that they leave behind them to after-ages a reputation which leads even those who are not of their family to claim kindred with them, and that they are the glory of their country, which regards them, not as aliens or as evil-doers, but as her own children, of whose character she is proud. These are my own aspirations, and this is the reason why my private life is assailed; but let me ask you, whether in the management of public affairs any man surpasses me. Did I not, without involving you in any great danger or expense, combine the most powerful states of Peloponnesus against the Lacedæmonians, whom I compelled to stake at Mantinea[12] all that they had upon the fortune of one day? And even to this hour, although they were victorious in the battle, they have hardly recovered courage.

17. "These were the achievements of my youth, and of what is supposed to be my monstrous folly; thus did I by winning words conciliate the Peloponnesian powers, and my heartiness made them believe in me and follow me. And now do not be afraid of me because I am young, but while I am in the flower of my days and Nicias enjoys the reputation of success, use the services of us both. Having determined to sail, do not change your minds under the impression that Sicily is a great power. For although the Sicilian cities are populous, their inhabitants are a mixed multitude, and they readily give up old forms of government and receive new ones from without. No one really feels that he has a city of his own; and so the individual is ill provided with arms, and the country has no regular means of defence. A man looks only to what he can win from the common stock by arts of speech or by party violence; hoping, if he is overthrown, at any rate to carry off his prize and enjoy it elsewhere. They are a motley crew, who are never of one mind in counsel, and are incapable of any concert in action. Every man is for himself, and will readily come over to any one who makes an attractive offer; the more readily if, as report says, they are in a state of internal discord. They boast of their hoplites, but, as has proved to be the case in all Hellenic states, the number of them is grossly exaggerated. Hellas has been singularly mistaken about her heavy infantry; and even in this war it was as much as she could do to collect enough of them. The obstacles then which will meet us in Sicily, judging of them from the information which I have received, are not great; indeed, I have overrated them, for there will be many barbarians who, through fear of the Syracusans,[13] will join us in attacking them. And at home there

---

[12]A great battle fought some three years earlier.
[13]Syracuse was the chief city of Sicily.

is nothing which, viewed rightly, need interfere with the expedition. Our forefathers had the same enemies whom we are now told that we are leaving behind us, and the Persian besides; but their strength lay in the greatness of their navy, and by that and that alone they gained their empire. Never were the Peloponnesians more hopeless of success than at the present moment; and let them be ever so confident, they will only invade us by land, which they can equally do whether we go to Sicily or not. But on the sea they cannot hurt us, for we shall leave behind us a navy equal to theirs.

18. "What reason can we give to ourselves for hesitation? what excuse can we make to our allies for denying them aid? We have sworn to them, and have no right to argue that they never assisted us. In seeking their alliance we did not intend that they should come and help us here, but that they should harass our enemies in Sicily, and prevent them from coming hither. Like all other imperial powers, we have acquired our dominion by our readiness to assist any one, whether Barbarian or Hellene, who may have invoked our aid. If we are all to sit and do nothing, or to draw distinctions of race when our help is requested, we shall add little to our empire, and run a great risk of losing it altogether. For mankind do not await the attack of a superior power, they anticipate it. We cannot cut down an empire as we might a household; but having once gained our present position, we must, while keeping a firm hold upon some, contrive occasion against others; for if we are not rulers we shall be subjects. You cannot afford to regard inaction in the same light as others might, unless you impose a corresponding restriction on your practice. Convinced then that we shall be most likely to increase our power here if we attack our enemies there, let us sail. We shall humble the pride of the Peloponnesians when they see that, scorning the delights of repose, we have attacked Sicily. By the help of our acquisitions there, we shall probably become masters of all Hellas; at any rate we shall injure the Syracusans, and at the same time benefit ourselves and our allies. Whether we succeed and remain, or depart, in either case our navy will ensure our safety; for at sea we shall be more than a match for all Sicily. Nicias must not divert you from your purpose by preaching indolence, and by trying to set the young against the old; rather in your accustomed order, old and young taking counsel together, after the manner of your fathers who raised Athens to this height of greatness, strive to rise yet higher. Consider that youth and age have no power unless united; but that the shallower and the more exact and the middle sort of judgment, when duly attempered, are likely to be most efficient. The state, if at rest, like everything else will wear herself out by internal friction. Every pursuit which requires skill will tend to decay, whereas by conflict the city will always be gaining fresh experience and learning to defend herself, not in theory, but in practice. My opinion in short is, that a state used to activity will quickly be ruined by the change to inaction; and that they of all men enjoy the greatest security who are truest to themselves and their institutions even when they are not the best."

Comments / on Thucydides

If there is one historian who busies himself incessantly with the "ultimate laws" which are behind the "observed facts," that historian is Thucydides. . . . The [various] speeches [or] the Melian Dialogue, in whichever way they are construed, whether as Thucydides' personal exegesis of the spirit of Athenian imperialism or as the dramatic expression of speeches actually delivered, are full of evidence of a theory of "ultimate law behind the observed facts." DAVID GRENE (1950)

The dominant influence on Thucydides is the influence of Hippocratic medicine. Hippocrates was not only the father of medicine, he was also the father of psychology, and his influence is evident not only in such things as the Thucydidean description of the plague, but in such studies in morbid psychology as the description of war-neurosis in general and the special instances of it in. . .the Melian dialogue. Herodotus may be the father of history, but Thucydides is the father of psychological history. R. G. COLLINGWOOD (1946)

One would never guess from Thucydides' history that throughout the fateful war, sometimes with the enemy camped outside their walls, the Athenians carried on the rich cultural life that made their city the school of Hellas. They kept on adorning their acropolis, attending the plays of Sophocles, Euripides, and Aristophanes, listening to Socrates and the Sophists, speculating about everything under the sun. They even put on *The Trojan Women*—an impassioned denunciation of Athenian atrocities. (It was produced after their brutal assault on the neutral island of Melos, described by Thucydides.) They might have fared better had they devoted all their thought, energy, and wealth to the life-and-death struggle with Sparta. As it was, the glory and the tragedy were inseparably linked to the end. HERBERT J. MULLER (1961)

[The] competition [between Athens and Sparta] was far more ferocious than it appears to most modern lovers of ancient Greece to have been. It was at its most intense in the constant wars that culminated in the great Peloponnesian War at the end of the fifth century. Actual fighting among human beings is clearly never a gentle pursuit, but there is, nevertheless, a remarkable range between the extremes of stylized and not very murderous fighting, as in the knightly combats of the later Middle Ages, and all-out fighting like that of our own wars and those of the Greeks of the Great Age. It does not become us, whose culture has produced Auschwitz, Katyn, and Hiroshima, to reproach the Greeks of the Great Age with Melos and Corcyra. But read—and no one concerned at all with public affairs today should fail to read—the pages of Thucydides in which he describes what went on at Melos and Corcyra. Here, certainly, that ambiguous and perhaps meaningless commonplace that a sufficiently great difference in degree can be a difference in kind does not hold. In numbers of victims, our outrages exceed those of the Greeks a thousand to one; morally they are identical. CRANE BRINTON (1959)

Pre-Socratic Philosophers

Philosophy before Plato comes to us largely as a collection of fragments and scattered observations, many of them cryptic, many of them bold and arresting. They are concerned chiefly with the universe but also to some extent with man's place in it. If one common purpose can be seen amidst the diversity of opinions voiced by pre-Socratic philosophers, it is probably the search for order based on the premise that there is some unifying explanation for the many natural objects that surround man. These early thinkers all seem to possess the extraordinary curiosity for which the Greeks were noted. They seem also to share the belief that if a man put his mind to it, he could find reasonable answers to most puzzling questions.

The pre-Socratic philosophers include other philosophers than the ones sampled in this text: Anaximander and Anaximenes, Milesian philosophers (named after Miletus, an important Ionian city); Anaxagorus, who introduced philosophy to the Athenians; Empedocles, whom legend regarded as a magician and prophet; and the atomist Leucippus, predecessor of Democritus. These philosophers were active from the beginning of the sixth century B.C. to the time of Socrates. Their philosophy is sometimes called Ionic philosophy for its place of origin, Ionia in Asia Minor.

Thales *(fl.* 585 B.C.*)* is foremost among the Milesian philosophers, who were known for a skeptical turn of mind and for a practical, rational, observational outlook that can be called scientific. Thales' most important contribution was not that he proposed that everything was made of water but that he sought to prove that the world was not really made of many things but of one. Leucippus *(fl.* 440 B.C.*)*, the latest of the Milesians, arrived at an indivisible basic unit, the atom, as the basic substance. He is a very shadowy figure, but his follower, Democritus *(fl.* 420 B.C.*)*, is known not only for passing on the belief in atoms but for being a thoroughgoing materialist. He believed that the soul was composed of atoms, that thought itself was a physical process, and that the universe had no divine purpose. The attempt by the Milesian philosophers and Democritus to find simple, material, rational explanations for the multiplicity of physical things is closely related to our modern understanding of the physical world.

Somewhat opposed to the scientific bent of the Milesians are those philosophers whose mystic tendencies may have helped them arrive at ideas extremely important to later Greek philosophy. Pythagoras (*fl.* 525 B.C.) established the fundamental importance of mathematics to knowledge, though he also believed that numbers had magical properties. In addition, he taught that the soul was immortal and believed that living beings were transformed into other kinds of living beings after death. Both beliefs appear as important aspects of Plato's philosophy. Pythagoras is the most influential of the pre-Socratic philosophers, introducing the combination of mathematics and theology, the blending of religion and reasoning, the belief in the presence of an eternal world beyond the senses, which have all played a large part in Western thought.

Heraclitus (*fl.* 500 B.C.) thought fire was the basic physical element. But more important than that theory, which is but a reflection of the Milesian philosophers' search for the primal substance, was Heraclitus' belief that everything was in a state of flux, that change was the basic certainty of the universe. A belief of this sort, contradicting one of man's most deeply felt convictions, inevitably produced philosophic controversy. For ordinary men as well as for philosophers, the search for something permanent seems to be a necessary part of being. The eternal nature of God and of the spiritual world is probably the most widely held answer to this search in Western thought. Among the pre-Socratics, both Parmenides (*fl.* 475? B.C.) and Zeno, his disciple (*b.* 490? B.C.), opposed Heraclitus' changing world with the assertion that nothing changes. Parmenides based his belief on the argument that since our thoughts and our words are about real substances which have to exist, which still exist, and which will go on existing, all things must be unchanging. Zeno, slightly younger than Parmenides, opposed the idea of change by creating his famous paradoxes in which motion itself—the flight of an arrow, for instance—is regarded as being simply a succession of static moments. Further, since an arrow aimed at a target must pass through a series of infinitely divisible distances, it will never reach its target.

The philosopher Xenophanes (*fl.* 510 B.C.), who lived between the time of Pythagoras and Heraclitus, belongs with the Ionian rationalistic philosophers, and the fragments we have show a skeptical freethinker willing to challenge the religious beliefs of Homer and Hesiod as well as those of Pythagoras.

Briefly represented in the following selections are the Sophists, a group of philosopher-teachers whose original writings are almost all lost but much of whose thought is preserved in various dialogues of Plato. Plato, however, offers a biased view of them, since both he and Socrates had a low opinion of the Sophists (even though Socrates himself was often identified with them by his contemporaries). The opening section of *Protagoras* shows Socrates confronting one of the most eminent Sophists, from whom the dialogue takes its name (*fl.* 450 B.C.). Although the picture of Protagoras here reflects Plato's bias, it does offer a clear idea of the characteristic Sophist way of thinking. Unlike the pre-Socratic philosophers who were mainly concerned with nature, the Sophists focused upon man and his culture. They were skeptical, shrewd observers of men's ways and emphasized the usefulness of knowledge in the practical affairs of life. They were preeminently teachers; one reason for Socrates' distrust of them was that they taught for money. Sophism is important for turning Greek philosophy toward a consideration of man himself and for its genuine concern for educating the young. Perhaps the most just criticism of it is that in serving practical ends it lost sight of the higher purposes of philosophy, which appear so strikingly in Platonism.

Thales

ARISTOTLE, *Metaphysics*

i. 3; 983 b 6. Most of the early students of philosophy thought that first principles in the form of matter, and only these, are the sources of all things; for that of which all things consist, the antecedent from which they have sprung, and into which they are finally resolved (in so far as being underlies them and is changed with their changes), this they say is the element and first principle of things. 983 b 18. As to the quantity and form of this first principle, there is a difference of opinion; but Thales, the founder of this sort of philosophy, says that it is water (accordingly he declares that the earth rests on water), getting the idea, I suppose, because he saw that the nourishment of all beings is moist, and that warmth itself is generated from moisture and persists in it (for that from which all things spring is the first principle of them); and getting the idea also from the fact that the germs of all beings are of a moist nature, while water is the first principle of the nature of what is moist. And there are some who think that the ancients, and they who lived long before the present generation, and the first students of the gods, had a similar idea in regard to nature; for in their poems Okeanos and Tethys were the parents of generation,[1] and that by which the gods swore was water,—the poets themselves called it Styx;[2] for that which is most ancient is most highly esteemed, and that which is most highly esteemed is an object to swear by. Whether there is any such ancient and early opinion concerning nature would be an obscure question; but Thales is said to have expressed this opinion in regard to the first cause.

ARISTOTLE, *de Anima*

i. 2; 405 a 19. And Thales, according to what is related of him, seems to have regarded the soul as something endowed with the power of

---

From *The First Philosophers of Greece*, edited by Arthur Fairbanks. Copyright 1898. Reprinted by permission of Routledge & Kegan Paul Ltd.
[1]In early Greek cosmology, Oceanus was the river supposed to encircle the plain of the earth. He was also personified as one of the giants, called Titans, who first inhabited the earth and, with his consort Tethys, as the progenitor of the gods and parent of the rivers of the world and the ocean nymphs.
[2]The name of the principal river of the underworld in early Greek cosmology.

motion, if indeed he said that the loadstone has a soul because it moves iron. i. 5; 411 a 7. Some say that soul is diffused throughout the whole universe; and it may have been this which led Thales to think that all things are full of gods.

Democritus

DIOGENES LAERTIUS,[3] *Lives and Opinions of Eminent Philosophers*

IX, 44-45. His opinions are these. The first principles of the universe are atoms and empty space; everything else is merely thought to exist. The worlds are unlimited; they come into being and perish. Nothing can come into being from that which is not nor pass away into that which is not. Further, the atoms are unlimited in size and number, and they are borne along in the whole universe in a vortex, and thereby generate all composite things—fire, water, air, earth; for even these are conglomerations of given atoms. And it is because of their solidity that these atoms are impassive and unalterable. The sun and the moon have been composed of such smooth and spherical masses [i.e., atoms], and so also the soul, which is identical with reason. We see by virtue of the impact of images upon our eyes.

All things happen by virtue of necessity, the vortex being the cause of the creation of all things, and this he calls necessity. The end of action is tranquillity, which is not identical with pleasure, as some by a false interpretation have understood, but a state in which the soul continues calm and strong, undisturbed by any fear or superstition or any other emotion. This he calls well-being and many other names. The qualities of things exist merely by convention; in nature there is nothing but atoms and void space. These, then, are his opinions.

Pythagoras

HIPPOLYTUS,[4] *Philosophical Problems*

2. There is a second philosophy not far distant from the same time, of which Pythagoras, whom some call a Samian, was the first repre-

---

From *Lives of Eminent Philosophers*, Vol. II, by Diogenes Laertius, translated by R. D. Hicks (Cambridge, Mass.: Harvard University Press). Reprinted by permission of the publishers and The Loeb Classical Library.

From *The First Philosophers of Greece*, edited by Arthur Fairbanks. Copyright 1898. Reprinted by permission of Routledge & Kegan Paul Ltd.

[3]A Greek biographer and historian of philosophy of the third century A.D.

[4]A Christian ecclesiastical writer of the third century A.D. His *Philosophumena* consists of a refutation of various heresies, so that he concerns himself with examining the theories of ancient Greek philosophers.

sentative. And this they call the Italian philosophy because Pythagoras fled the rule of Polykrates over the Samians and settled in a city of Italy where he spent his life. The successive leaders of this sect shared the same spirit. And he in his studies of nature mingled astronomy and geometry and music and arithmetic. And thus he asserted that god is a monad, and examining the nature of number with especial care, he said that the universe produces melody and is put together with harmony, and he first proved the motion of the seven stars to be rhythm and melody. And in wonder at the structure of the universe, he decreed that at first his disciples should be silent, as it were [mystics] who were coming into the order of the all; then when he thought they had sufficient education in the principles of truth, and had sought wisdom sufficiently in regard to stars and in regard to nature, he pronounced them pure and then bade them speak. He separated his disciples into two groups, and called one esoteric, and the other exoteric. To the former he entrusted the more perfect sciences, to the latter the more moderate. And he dealt with magic, as they say, and himself discovered the art of physiognomy. Postulating both numbers and measures he was wont to say that the first principle of arithmetic embraced philosophy by combination. . . .

He said that the soul is immortal, and that it changes from one body to another; so he was wont to say that he himself had been born before the Trojan war as Aethalides, and at the time of the Trojan war as Euphorbos,[5] and after that as Hermotimos of Samos, then as Pyrrhos of Delos, fifth as Pythagoras. And Diodoros of Eretria and Aristoxenos the musician[6] say that Pythagoras had come into Zaratas of Chaldaea;[7] and he set forth that in his view there were from the beginning two causes of things, father and mother; and the father is light and the mother darkness; and the parts of light are warm, dry, light, swift; and of darkness are cold, moist, heavy, slow; and of these all the universe is composed, of male and female. And he says that the universe exists in accordance with musical harmony, so the sun also makes an harmonious period. And concerning the things that arise from the earth and the universe they say that Zaratas spoke as follows: There are two divinities, one of the heavens and the other of the earth; the one of the earth produces things from the earth, and it is water; and the divinity of the heavens is fire with a portion of air, warm, and cold; wherefore he says that none of these things will destroy or even pollute the soul, for these are the essence of all things. And it is said that Zaratas forbade men to eat beans because he said that at the beginning and composition of all things when the earth was still a whole, the bean arose. And he says that the proof of this is that if one chews a bean to a pulp and exposes it to the sun for a certain time (for the sun will affect it quickly), it gives out the odour of human seed. And he says that there is another and clearer proof: if when a bean is in flower we were to take the bean and its flower,

---

[5]Legendary figures in ancient Greek tradition. Aethalides was the son of the god Hermes, Euphorbos a renowned Trojan warrior.
[6]Greek philosophers of the fourth century B.C.
[7]This figure probably represents a confusion of traditions that Pythagoras was influenced by teachers influenced by the ancient Persian religion of Zoroastrianism, whose founder, Zoroaster (Zarathustra) flourished during the first half of the sixth century B.C.

and putting it into a pitcher moisten it and then bury it in the earth, and after a few days dig it up again, we should see in the first place that it had the form of a womb, and examining it closely we should find the head of a child growing with it. . . .

Heraclitus

FRAGMENTS

1. Not on my authority, but on that of truth, it is wise for you to accept the fact that all things are one.

4. Eyes and ears are bad witnesses for men, since their souls lack understanding.

5. Most men do not understand such things as they are wont to meet with; nor by learning do they come to know them, though they think they do.

10. Nature loves to hide.

18. No one of all whose discourses I have heard has arrived at this result: the recognition that wisdom is apart from all other things.

19. Wisdom is one thing: to understand the intelligence by which all things are steered through all things; it is willing and it is unwilling to be called by the name of Zeus.

20. This order, the same for all things, no one of gods or men has made, but it always was, and is, and ever shall be, an ever-living fire, kindling according to fixed measure, and extinguished according to fixed measure.

25. Fire lives in the death of earth, and air lives in the death of fire; water lives in the death of air, and earth in that of water.

29. The sun will not overstep his bounds; if he does, the Erinnyes,[8] allies of justice, will find him out.

36. God is day and night, winter and summer, war and peace, satiety and hunger; but he assumes different forms, just as when incense is mingled with incense; every one gives him the name he pleases.

41-42. You could not step twice in the same river; for other and yet other waters are ever flowing on.

59. You should unite things whole and things not whole, that which tends to unite and that which tends to separate, the harmonious and the discordant; from all things arises the one, and from the one all things.

60. They would not have known the name of justice, were it not for these things.

61. God, ordering things as they ought to be, perfects all things in

From *The First Philosophers of Greece,* edited by Arthur Fairbanks. Copyright 1898. Reprinted by permission of Routledge & Kegan Paul Ltd.
[8]In Greek mythology, three sister goddesses whose function was to avenge crime.

the harmony of the whole. For god all things are fair and good and just, but men suppose that some are unjust and others just.

78. Life and death, and waking and sleeping, and youth and old age, are the same; for the latter change and are the former, and the former change back to the latter.

91. Understanding is common to all. It is necessary for those who speak with intelligence to hold fast to the common element of all, as a city holds fast to law, and much more strongly. For all human laws are nourished by one which is divine, and it has power so much as it will; and it suffices for all things and more than suffices.

92. And though reason is common, most people live as though they had an understanding peculiar to themselves.

98. And does not Heraclitus, whom you bring forward, say this very thing, that the wisest of men will appear as an ape before God, both in wisdom and in beauty and in all other respects?

104. It is not good for men to have whatever they want. Disease makes health sweet and good; hunger, satiety; toil, rest.

105. It is hard to contend with passion; for whatever it desires to get it buys at the cost of soul.

106. It is the part of all men to know themselves and to be temperate.

107. To be temperate is the greatest virtue; and it is wisdom to speak the truth and to act according to nature with understanding.

Parmenides

CONCERNING TRUTH

Come now I will tell thee—and do thou hear my word and heed it— what are the only ways of enquiry that lead to knowledge. The one way, assuming that being is and that it is impossible for it not to be, is the trustworthy path, for truth attends it. The other, that not-being is and that it necessarily is, I call a wholly incredible course, since thou canst not recognise not-being (for this is impossible), nor couldst thou speak of it, for thought and being are the same thing.

It makes no difference to me at what point I begin, for I shall always come back again to this.

It is necessary both to say and to think that being is; for it is possible that being is, and it is impossible that not-being is; this is what I bid thee ponder. I restrain thee from this first course of investigation; and from that course also along which mortals knowing nothing wander aimlessly, since helplessness directs the roaming thought in their bosoms, and they are borne on deaf and likewise blind, amazed, headstrong races, they who consider being and not-being as the same and not the same; and that all things follow a back-turning course.

That things which are not are, shall never prevail, she said, but do thou restrain thy mind from this course of investigation.

And let not long-practised habit compel thee along this path, thine eye careless, thine ear and thy tongue overpowered by noise; but do thou weigh the much contested refutation of their words, which I have uttered.

There is left but this single path to tell thee of: namely, that being is. And on this path there are many proofs that being is without beginning and indestructible; it is universal, existing alone, immovable and without end; nor ever was it nor will it be, since it now *is*, all together, one, and continuous. For what generating of it wilt thou seek out? From what did it grow, and how? I will not permit thee to say or to think that it came from not-being; for it is impossible to think or to say that not-being is. What thing would then have stirred it into activity that it should arise from not-being later rather than earlier? So it is necessary that being either is absolutely or is not. Nor will the force of the argument permit that anything spring from being except being itself. Therefore justice does not slacken her fetters to permit generation or destruction, but holds being firm. . . .

Either being exists or it does not exist. It has been decided in accordance with necessity to leave the unthinkable, unspeakable path, as this is not the true path, but that the other path exists and is true. How then should being suffer destruction? How come into existence? If it came into existence, it is not being, nor will it be if it ever is to come into existence. . . . So its generation is extinguished, and its destruction is proved incredible.

Nor is it subject to division, for it is all alike; nor is anything more in it, so as to prevent its cohesion, nor anything less, but all is full of being; therefore the all is continuous, for being is contiguous to being.

Farther it is unmoved, in the hold of great chains, without beginning or end, since generation and destruction have completely disappeared and true belief has rejected them. It lies the same, abiding in the same state and by itself; accordingly it abides fixed in the same spot. For powerful necessity holds it in confining bonds, which restrain it on all sides. Therefore divine right does not permit being to have any end; but it is lacking in nothing, for if it lacked anything it would lack everything.

Nevertheless, behold steadfastly all absent things as present to thy mind; for thou canst not separate being in one place from contact with being in another place; it is not scattered here and there through the universe, nor is it compounded of parts.

Therefore thinking and that by reason of which thought exists are one and the same thing, for thou wilt not find thinking without the *being* from which it receives its name. Nor is there nor will there be anything apart from being; for fate has linked it together, so that it is a whole and immovable. Wherefore all these things will be but a name, all these things which mortals determined in the belief that they were true, viz. that things arise and perish, that they are and are not, that they change their position and vary in colour.

But since there is a final limit, it is perfected on every side, like the mass of a rounded sphere, equally distant from the centre at every point. For it is necessary that it should neither be greater at all nor less anywhere, since there is no not-being which can prevent it from arriving at equality, nor is being such that there may ever be more than what is in one part and less in another, since the whole is inviolate. For if it is equal on all sides, it abides in equality within its limits.

Zeno the Eleatic

ARISTOTLE, *Physics*

vi. 9; 239 b 5. And Zeno's reasoning is fallacious. For if, he says, everything is at rest or in motion when it is in a space equal to itself, and the moving body is always in the present moment in a space equal to itself, then the moving arrow is still. This is false; for time is not composed of present moments that are indivisible, nor indeed is any other quantity. Zeno presents four arguments concerning motion which involve puzzles to be solved, and the first of these shows that motion does not exist because the moving body must go half the distance before it goes the whole distance; of this we have spoken before (viii. 8; 263 a 5). And the second is called the Achilles argument;[9] it is this:—The slow runner will never be overtaken by the swiftest, for it is necessary that the pursuer should first reach the point from which the pursued started, so that necessarily the slower is always somewhat in advance. This argument is the same as the preceding, the only difference being that the distance is not divided each time into halves. . . . His opinion is false that the one in advance is not overtaken; he is not indeed overtaken while he is in advance; but nevertheless he is overtaken, if you will grant that he passes through the limited space. These are the first two arguments, and the third is the one that has been alluded to, that the arrow in its flight is stationary. This depends on the assumption that time is composed of present moments; there will be no syllogism if this is not granted. And the fourth argument is with reference to equal bodies moving in opposite directions past equal bodies in the stadium with equal speed, some from the end of the stadium, others from the middle; in which case he thinks half the time equal to twice the time. The fallacy lies in the fact that while he postulates that bodies of equal size move forward with equal speed for an equal time, he compares the one with something in motion, the other with something at rest.

From *The First Philosophers of Greece*, edited by Arthur Fairbanks. Copyright 1898. Reprinted by permission of Routledge & Kegan Paul Ltd.
[9]Because Zeno uses Achilles as an example of a swift runner.

Xenophanes

FRAGMENTS

1. God is one, supreme among gods and men, and not like mortals in body or in mind.

2. The whole [of god] sees, the whole perceives, the whole hears.

3. But without effort he sets in motion all things by mind and thought.

4. It [i.e., being] always abides in the same place, not moved at all, nor is it fitting that it should move from one place to another.

5. But mortals suppose that the gods are born (as they themselves are), and that they wear man's clothing and have human voice and body.

6. But if cattle or lions had hands, so as to paint with their hands and produce works of art as men do, they would paint their gods and give them bodies in form like their own—horses like horses, cattle like cattle.

7. Homer and Hesiod attributed to the gods all things which are disreputable and worthy of blame when done by men; and they told of them many lawless deeds, stealing, adultery, and deception of each other.

8. For all things come from earth, and all things end by becoming earth.

9. For we are all sprung from earth and water.

10. All things that come into being and grow are earth and water.

16. In the beginning the gods did not at all reveal all things clearly to mortals, but by searching men in the course of time find them out better.

Protagoras

PLATO, *Protagoras*

• • •

When we were all seated, Protagoras said: Now that the company are assembled, Socrates, you might repeat what you said to me just now on behalf of this young man.

I replied: I will begin again at the same point, Protagoras, and tell you once more the purport of my visit: this is my friend Hippocrates, who is desirous of your society; he would like to know what will happen to him if he associates with you. I have no more to say.

Protagoras answered: Young man, if you associate with me, on the

From *The First Philosophers of Greece,* edited by Arthur Fairbanks. Copyright 1898. Reprinted by permission of Routledge & Kegan Paul Ltd.

From *The Dialogues of Plato,* 1953 edition, Vol. I, translated by B. Jowett. Reprinted by permission of the Clarendon Press, Oxford.

very first day you will return home a better man than you came, and better on the second day than on the first, and better every day than you were on the day before.

When I heard this, I said: Protagoras, I do not at all wonder at hearing you say this; even at your age, and with all your wisdom, if anyone were to teach you what you did not know before, you would become better no doubt: but please to answer in a different way—I will explain how by an example. Let me suppose that Hippocrates, instead of desiring your society, were suddenly to desire that of the young man Zeuxippus of Heraclea, who has lately arrived on a visit to Athens, and he had come to him as he has come to you, and had heard him say, as he has heard you say, that every day he would grow and become better if he associated with him: and then suppose that he were to ask him, 'In what shall I become better, and in what shall I grow?'—Zeuxippus would answer, 'In painting.' And suppose that he went to Orthagoras the Theban, and heard him say the same thing, and asked him, 'In what shall I become better day by day?' he would reply, 'In flute-playing.' Now I want you to make the same sort of answer to this young man and to me, who am asking questions on his account. When you say that on the first day on which he associates with you he will return home a better man, and on every day will grow in like manner,—in what, Protagoras, will he be better? and about what?

When Protagoras heard me say this, he replied: You ask questions fairly, and I like to answer a question which is fairly put. If Hippocrates comes to me he will not experience the sort of drudgery with which other sophists are in the habit of insulting their pupils; who, when they have just escaped from the arts, are taken against their will and driven back into them by these teachers, and made to learn calculation, and astronomy, and geometry, and music (he gave a look at Hippias as he said this); but if he comes to me, he will learn that which he comes to learn. And this is prudence in affairs private as well as public; he will learn to order his own house in the best manner, and he will be fully qualified to speak and act in the affairs of the state.

Do I understand you, I said; and is your meaning that you teach the art of politics, and that you promise to make men good citizens?

That, Socrates, is exactly the profession which I make.

Then, I said, you possess a truly noble art, if there is no mistake about this; for to you, Protagoras, I will speak with entire candour, and admit that I used to think that this art is incapable of being taught, and yet I know not how to disbelieve your assertion. And I ought to tell you why I am of opinion that this art cannot be taught or communicated by man to man. I say that the Athenians are an understanding people, and indeed they are esteemed to be such by the other Hellenes. Now I observe that when we are met together in the assembly, and the matter in hand relates to building, the builders are summoned as advisers; when the question is one of ship-building, then the ship-wrights; and the like of other arts which they think capable of being taught and learned. And if some person offers to give them advice who is not supposed by them to have any skill in the art, even though he be good-looking and rich and noble, they will not listen to him; but laugh and hoot at him, until either he is clamoured down and retires of himself, or he is dragged away or put out by the constables at the command of the prytanes. This is their way of behaving about that which they deem to be the subject of an art. But when the question is an affair of state, then everybody is free to have a say—carpenter, tinker, cobbler, merchant, sea-captain; rich and poor, high and low—anyone who likes gets up, and no one reproaches him, as in the former case, with not having learned, and having no teacher, and yet giving advice; evidently because they are under the impression that this sort of knowledge cannot be taught. And not only is this true of the state, but of individuals; the best and wisest of our citizens are unable to impart their own excellence to others; as for example, Pericles, the father of these young men, who provided them with admirable instruction in all that could be learned from masters, in his own department of politics neither taught them, nor gave them teachers; but they were allowed to wander at their own free will in a sort of hope that they would light upon virtue of their own accord. Or take another example: there was Cleinias the younger brother of our friend Alcibiades, of whom this very same Pericles was the guardian; and he being in fact under the apprehension that Cleinias would be corrupted by Alcibiades snatched him away from his brother, and placed him in the house of Ariphron to be educated; but before six months had elapsed, Pericles sent him back to Alcibiades, not knowing what to do with him. And I could mention numberless other instances of persons who were good themselves, and never yet made any one else good, whether friend or stranger. Now I, Protagoras, when I contemplate these examples, am of opinion that virtue cannot be taught. But then again, when I listen to your words, I waver; and am disposed to think that there must be something in what you say, because I know that you have great experience, and learning, and invention. And I wish that you would, if possible, show me a little more clearly that virtue can be taught. Will you be so good?

That I will, Socrates, and gladly. But what would you like? Shall I, as an elder, speak to you as younger men in an apologue or myth, or shall I argue out the question?

To this several of the company answered that he should choose for himself.

Well, then, he said, I think that the myth will be more interesting.

Once upon a time there were gods only, and no mortal creatures. But when the appointed time came that these also should be created, the gods fashioned them out of earth and fire and various mixtures of both elements in the interior of the earth; and when they were about to bring them into the light of day, they ordered Prometheus and Epimetheus to equip them, and to distribute to them severally their proper qualities. Epimetheus said to Prometheus: 'Let me distribute, and do you inspect.' This was agreed, and Epimetheus made the distribution. There were some to whom he gave strength without swiftness, while he equipped the weaker with swiftness; some he armed, and others he left unarmed; and devised for the latter some other means of preservation. Upon those whom he clothed in diminutive bodies, he bestowed winged flight or subterranean habitation: those which he aggrandized with magnitude, he protected by their very size: and similarly with the rest of his distribution, always compensating. These devices he used as precautions that no race should be destroyed. And when he had provided against their destruction by one another, he contrived also a means of protecting them against the seasons of heaven; clothing them with close hair and thick skins sufficient to defend them against the winter cold, yet able to resist the summer heat, and serving also as a natural bed of their own when they wanted to rest; also he furnished them with hoofs and hair and hard and callous skins under their feet. Then he gave them varieties of food,—herb of the soil to some, to others fruits of trees, and to others roots, and to some again he gave other animals as food. And some he made to have few young ones, while those who were their prey were very prolific; and in this manner the race was preserved. Thus did Epimetheus, who, not being very wise, forgot that he had distributed among the brute animals all the qualities which he had to give,—and when he came to man, who was still un-provided, he was terribly perplexed. Now while he was in this perplexity, Prometheus came to inspect the distribution, and he found that the other animals were quite suitably furnished, but that man was naked and shoe-less, and had neither bed nor arms of defence. The appointed hour was approaching when man in his turn was to emerge from earth into the light of day; and Prometheus, not knowing how he could devise his salvation, stole the mechanical arts of Hephaestus and Athene, and fire with them (they could neither have been acquired nor used without fire), and gave them to man. Thus man had the wisdom necessary to the support of life, but political wisdom he had not; for that was in the keeping of Zeus, and the power of Prometheus no longer extended to entering into the citadel of heaven, where Zeus dwelt, who moreover had terrible sentinels; but he did enter by stealth into the common workshop of Athene and Hephaestus, in which they used to practise their favourite arts, and carried off Hephaestus' art of working by fire, and also the art of Athene, and gave them to man. And in this way man was supplied with the means of life. But Prometheus is said to have been afterwards prosecuted for theft, owing to the blunder of Epimetheus.

Now man, having a share of the divine attributes, was at first the only one of the animals who had any gods, because he alone was of their kindred; and he would raise altars and images of them. He was not long in inventing articulate speech and names; and he also constructed houses and clothes and shoes and beds, and drew sustenance from the earth. Thus provided, mankind at first lived dispersed, and there were no cities. But the consequence was that they were destroyed by the wild beasts, for they were utterly weak in comparison of them, and their practical attainments were only sufficient to provide them with the means of life, and did not enable them to carry on war against the animals: food they had, but not as yet the art of government, of which the art of war is a part. After a while the desire of self-preservation gathered them into cities; but when they were gathered together, having no art of government, they evil entreated one another, and were again in proc-ess of dispersion and destruction. Zeus feared that the entire race would be exterminated, and so he sent Hermes to them, bearing reverence and justice to be the ordering principles of cities and the bonds of friendship and conciliation. Hermes asked Zeus how he should impart justice and reverence among men:—Should he distribute them as the arts are distributed; that is to say,—to a favoured few only, one skilled individual having enough of medicine or of any other art for many unskilled ones? 'Shall this be the manner in which I am to distribute justice and reverence among men, or shall I give them to all?' 'To all,' said Zeus; 'I should like them all to have a share; for cities cannot exist, if a few only share in the virtues, as in the arts. And further, make a law by my order, that he who has no part in reverence and justice shall be put to death, for he is a plague of the state.'

And this is the reason, Socrates, why the Athenians and mankind in general, when the question relates to carpentering or any other mechanical art, allow but a few to share in their deliberations; and when anyone else interferes, then, as you say, they object, if he be not of the favoured few; which, as I reply, is very natural. But when they meet to deliberate about political virtue, which proceeds only by way of justice and wisdom, they are patient enough of any man who speaks of them, as is also natural, because they think that every man ought to share in this sort of virtue, and that states could not exist if this were otherwise. Such, Socrates, is the reason of this phenomenon.

And that you may not suppose yourself to be deceived in thinking that all men regard every man as having a share of justice or honesty and of every other political virtue, let me give you a further proof. In other cases, as you are aware, if a man says that he is a good flute-player, or skilful in any other art in which he has no skill, people either laugh at him or are angry with him, and his relations think that he is mad and go and admonish him; but when honesty is in question, or some other political virtue, even if they know that he is dishonest, yet, if the man comes forward publicly and tells the truth against himself, then, what in the other case was held by them to be good sense, viz., telling the truth, they now deem to be madness. They say that all men ought to profess honesty whether they are honest or not, and that a man is out of his mind who makes no claim to that virtue. Their notion is, that every man must have it in some degree, or else he ought not to be in the world.

I have been showing that they are right in admitting every man as a counsellor about this sort of virtue, as they are of opinion that every man is a partaker of it. And I will now endeavour to show further that they do not conceive this virtue to be given by nature, or to grow spontaneously, but to be a thing which may be taught; and which comes to those to whom it does come, by taking pains. No one would instruct, no one would rebuke or be angry with those whose calamities they suppose to be due to nature or chance; they do not try to punish or to prevent them from being what they are; they do but pity them. Who is so foolish as to chastise or instruct the ugly, or the diminutive, or the feeble? And for this reason. Because, I take it, everyone knows that good and evil of this kind is the work of nature and of chance; whereas if a man is wanting in those good qualities which are held to be attainable by study and exercise and teaching, and has only the contrary evil qualities, other men are angry with him, and punish and reprove him

—of these evil qualities one is impiety, another injustice, and they may be described generally as the very opposite of political virtue. In such cases any man will be angry with another, and reprimand him,— clearly because he thinks that by study and learning the virtue may be acquired. If you think, Socrates, of the effect of punishment upon the wrong-doer, you will see at once that in the opinion of mankind virtue may be acquired; no one punishes the evil-doer under the notion, or for the reason, that he has done wrong,—only the unreasonable fury of a beast acts in that manner. But he who desires to inflict rational punishment does not retaliate for a past wrong, for what has been done cannot be undone; he has regard to the future, and is desirous that the man who is punished, and he who sees him punished, may be deterred from doing wrong again. Now if this is his conception, then he also conceives that virtue may be taught; since it is for the sake of deterrence that he punishes. This is the notion of all who retaliate upon others either privately or publicly. And the Athenians, too, your own citizens, like other men, punish and take vengeance on all whom they regard as evil doers; and hence we may infer them to be of the number of those who think that virtue may be acquired and taught. Thus far, Socrates, I have shown you clearly enough, if I am not mistaken, that your countrymen are right in admitting the tinker and the cobbler to advise about politics, and also that they deem virtue to be capable of being taught and acquired.

There yet remains one difficulty which has been raised by you about good men. What is the reason why good men teach their sons the knowledge which can be gained from teachers, and make them wise in that, but make them no better than anyone else in the virtues which distinguish themselves? And here, Socrates, I will leave the apologue and resume the argument. Please to consider: Is there or is there not some one quality of which all the citizens must be partakers, if there is to be a city at all? In the answer to this question is contained the only solution of your difficulty; there is no other. For if there be any such quality, and this quality or unity is not the art of the carpenter, or the smith, or the potter, but justice and temperance and holiness and, in a word, manly virtue—if this is the quality of which all men must be partakers, and which is the very condition of their learning or doing anything else, and if he who is wanting in this, whether he be a child only or a grown-up man or woman, must be taught and punished, until by punishment he becomes better, and he who rebels against instruction and punishment must be either exiled or condemned to death as incurable—if what I am saying be true, and yet good men have their sons taught other things and not this, do consider what a strange thing their goodness has become. For we have shown that they think virtue capable of being taught and cultivated both in private and public; and, notwithstanding, they have their sons taught lesser matters, ignorance of which does not involve the punishment of death: but greater things, of which the ignorance may cause death and exile to their own children, if they have no knowledge of virtue or encouragement toward it—aye, and confiscation as well as death, and, in a word, may be the ruin of families—those things, I say, they are supposed not to have them taught,—not to take the utmost care that they should learn. How improbable is this, Socrates!

Education and admonition commence in the first years of childhood, and last to the very end of life. Mother and nurse and father and tutor are vying with one another about the improvement of the child as soon as ever he is able to understand what is being said to him: he cannot say or do anything without their teaching him and setting forth to him that this is just and that is unjust; this is honourable, that is dishonourable; this is holy, that is unholy; do this and abstain from that. And if he obeys, well and good; if not, he is straightened by threats and blows, like a piece of bent or warped wood. At a later stage they send him to teachers, and enjoin them to see to his good behaviour even more than to his reading and music; and the teachers do as they are desired. And when the boy has learned his letters and is beginning to understand what is written, as before he understood only what was spoken, they put on his desk the works of great poets for him to read; in these are contained many admonitions, and many tales and praises and encomia of famous men of old, which he is required to learn by heart, in order that he may imitate or emulate them and desire to become like them. Then, again, the teachers of the lyre take similar care that their young disciple is temperate and gets into no mischief; and when they have taught him the use of the lyre, they introduce him to the poems of other excellent poets, who are the lyric poets; and these they set to music, and make their harmonies and rhythms quite familiar to the children's souls, in order that they may learn to be more gentle, and harmonious, and rhythmical, and so more fitted for speech and action; for the life of man in every part has need of harmony and rhythm. Then they send them to the master of gymnastic, in order that the improvement of their bodies may better minister to the virtuous mind, and that they may not be compelled through bodily weakness to play the coward in war or on any other occasion. This is principally done by those who have the means, and those who have the means are the rich; their children begin to go to school soonest and leave off latest. When they have done with masters, the state again compels them to learn the laws, and live after the pattern which they furnish, and not after their own fancies; and just as the writing-master first traces outlines with a style for the use of the young beginner who is not yet able to write, then gives him the tablet and makes him write along those lines, so the city outlines the laws, which were the invention of good lawgivers living in the olden time, and compels us to exercise and to obey authority in accordance with those; and he who transgresses them is to be corrected, or, in other words, called to account, which is a term used not only in your country, but also in many others, seeing that justice calls men to account. Now when there is all this care about virtue private and public, why, Socrates, do you still wonder and doubt whether virtue can be taught? Cease to wonder, for the opposite would be far more surprising.

But why then do the sons of good fathers often turn out ill? Learn now the cause of this. There is nothing very wonderful in it, if what I said before was true, that the existence of a state implies that no man is unskilled in virtue. If so—and nothing can be truer—then I will further ask you to take as an illustration some other pursuit or branch of knowledge, and reflect upon that. Suppose that there could be no state unless we were all flute-players, as far as each had the capacity, and everybody was freely teaching everybody the art, both in private and public, and reproving the bad player as freely and openly as every man now teaches justice and the laws, not concealing them as he would conceal the other arts, but imparting them—for all of us have a mutual interest in the justice and virtue of one another, and this is the reason why everyone is so ready to propagate and teach justice and the laws;—suppose, I say, that there were the same readiness and liberality among us in teaching one another flute-playing, do you imagine, Socrates, that the sons of good flute-players would be more likely to be good than the sons of bad ones? I think not. Would not their sons grow up to be distinguished or undistinguished according to their own natural capacities as flute-players, and the son of a good player would often turn out to be a bad one, and the son of a bad player to be a good one; but at least they would all play the flute reasonably well in comparison of those who were ignorant and unacquainted with the art of flute-playing? In like manner I would have you consider that he who appears to you to be the worst of those who have been brought up in laws and human society, would appear to be a just man and an artificer of justice if he were to be compared with men who had no education, or courts of justice, or laws, or any constraints forcing them incessantly to the practice of virtue—with savages like those whom the poet Pherecrates exhibited on the stage at last year's Lenaean festival. If you were living among such as the man-haters of his Chorus, you would be only too glad to meet with Eurybates and Phrynondas, and you would sorrowfully long to revisit the rascality of this part of the world. Now you, Socrates, are being fastidious, and why? Because all men are teachers of virtue, each one according to his ability; and you say Where are the teachers? You might as well ask, Who teaches Greek? For of that too there will not be any teachers found. Or you might ask, Who is to teach the sons of our artisans this same art which they have learned of their fathers? He and his fellow workmen have taught them to the best of their ability,—but who will carry them farther in their arts? You would certainly have a difficulty, Socrates, in finding a teacher of them, but there would be no difficulty whatever in finding a teacher of those who are ignorant; this is true of virtue or of anything else. But if there is anyone better able than we are to promote virtue ever so little, we must be content with the result. A teacher of this sort I believe myself to be, excelling all other human beings in the power to raise a man towards nobility and goodness; and I give my pupils their money's-worth, and even more, as they themselves confess. And therefore I have introduced the following mode of payment:—When a man is my pupil, if he likes he pays my fee; if he does not like, he has only to go into a temple and take an oath of the value of the instruction, and he pays no more than that.

Such is my apologue, Socrates, and such is the argument by which I endeavour to show that virtue may be taught, and that this is the opinion of the Athenians. . . .

Comments / on Pre-Socratic Philosophers

But most significant of all is the fact that he [Thales] assumed, in spite of appearances, that the world consists not of many things but of one. Here we meet a permanent feature of Greek thought: the universe, both the physical and the moral universe, must be not only rational, and therefore knowable, but also simple; the apparent multiplicity of physical things is only superficial.   *H. D. F. KITTO (1951)*

Ionic philosophy in its first representatives, considered from a methodological point of view, is pure dogmatism. Without first making any sort of inquiry into the possibilities of human knowledge, they made an immediate attack on the ultimate problems of the origin of the universe. Their philosophy is rightly called "natural philosophy" after the chief object of their inquiries. They first raised the question of the basic substance underlying all things, to which the three Milesians gave different answers. From this supposition of a uniform basic substance the problem of change and, together with it, of being and not being, becoming and passing away, rest and motion followed as a logical consequence.
                                                      EDUARD ZELLER (1883)

Learning had been acquired and knowledge gathered before the origin of philosophy in Miletus: Hesiod had arranged an hierarchy of gods; Homer had aided in establishing the gods of Olympus. To the Milesians, Thales, Anaximander and Anaximenes, the primary question is not merely, "What do we know?" but "How do we know and what evidence do we have to corroborate the explanation offered?"
                                                      MILTON C. NAHM (1934)

It was natural that the inquisitive nature of the Ionians, the great explorers and observers, should make them push their investigations to the point where the ultimate problems arise; and equally natural that, once they had asked what the universe was and how it came into existence, they should find themselves impelled to extend their knowledge of facts and to explain individual phenomena.   *WERNER JAEGER (1933)*

Socrates
469?—399 B.C.

Socrates is probably the most memorable of the many great figures Greek civilization gave to the world. So powerful was the impress of his personality and teachings on the young men who became his followers that a new literary form, the dialogue, was created to capture both the man and his teachings. He taught by question and answer, the dialectic method, aimed at making men think and providing a means by which the participants might come to a common agreement. Socrates himself left no written word; his aim was to work with living men, to call them to a consideration of virtue and an examination of their own lives. Faithful to his own principles, he accepted death rather than compromise or repudiate that to which he had devoted his life.

Socrates' place in philosophy is difficult to describe. Since what we know of his philosophy comes largely through his disciple Plato, we cannot be sure what is Socratic and what Platonic. Since Socrates created no philosophic system but, as Cicero said, brought philosophy down from heaven into the cities and homes of men, we cannot set forth a systematic outline of his teachings. Since what he said was so much a matter of how he said it and of his own powerful personality, his philosophy is largely a matter of exposure to Socrates himself and to the world he occupied.

Primarily, Socrates was a moralist, interested in how men lived their lives. In Plato's *Apology,* Socrates describes his "philosophizing" thus: "For all that I do is go round and persuade young and old among you not to give so much of your attention to your bodies and your money as to the perfection of your souls." The statement suggests two of the great contributions Socrates made: his method of rigorous examination through dialogue of the great questions of human life aimed at reaching an agreement valid to everyone; and his emphasis upon the spiritual world, man's inner life, as being superior to the material world, mere physical existence.

From this last attitude, it is not far to the Platonic Theory of Ideas, to the knowledge of the Good as the aim for man, to the examination of Justice in Plato's *Republic*.

Socrates is an elusive figure, revealed most in dialogues like the *Symposium* where the conversation is as natural, as earthy, as men have always been. Yet out of the banter and good fellowship develops a profound discussion of the power of love to animate men to the loftiest heights. The dialogue is illuminated by Socratic irony, which is best illustrated by Socrates' insistence that he is the wisest of men because he knows that he does not know. Surrounded by brilliant and powerful men of Athens, Socrates lets himself be seen as the humble, ugly figure he must have been. Yet at the end of the *Symposium,* he has captured the entire group with his conversation, and it is he alone who remains awake, still talking, when morning comes.

We do know that Socrates was born in Athens, that his wife was named Xanthippe, and that he had three sons. He was actively involved in the Peloponnesian War and in the political turmoil in the years before Athens finally fell to Sparta. Most of his life was spent in Athens, where he gained a devoted circle of followers and a reputation as a great teacher. In 399 B.C., he was arrested, convicted, and executed.

Plato (429?–347 B.C.) is the most famous of Socrates' followers. He was probably closely associated with Socrates during the ten years before the latter's death. After that time he spent a period in travel, returning to Athens in 386 to found a school called the Academy. Here he remained, devoting himself to philosophy and mathematics, the chief studies in the Academy, and to his writing. All of his writings take the form of dialogues in which two or more persons argue philosophic questions. Although it is possible to make informed conjectures about Plato's philosophy as distinct from the Socratic philosophy recorded in the dialogues, such distinctions are unnecessary for a first look at a philosophy which can be called either Platonic or Socratic.

Plato's philosophic inquiries were not specialized as the search for knowledge is today. Physics, metaphysics, ethics, politics, religion, art, literature, mathematics—especially mathematics—are all part of Plato's concern, and all blend together in his dialogues. In view of the range and depth of his inquiries, appearing so early in the development of Western thought, Plato's impact on our culture comes close to justifying the famous exaggeration voiced by a noted modern philosopher, "All philosophy is but a footnote to Plato."

Xenophon (431?–354? B.C.), a minor Greek historian as compared with Herodotus or Thucydides, furnishes the most extensive account of Socrates' life and teachings aside from that of Plato. He was born at almost the same time as Plato and doubtless had some association with Socrates, even though he is never mentioned by Plato, who referred to all the important men in the Socratic circle. His writings have provoked controversy as to whether his or Plato's account comes closest to capturing the real Socrates, but both men's works are valuable in acquainting us with a figure who must have been puzzling even to his own contemporaries.

Recollections of Socrates

Book I

1. I have often wondered by what arguments those who indicted Socrates could have persuaded the Athenians that his life was justly forfeit to the state. The indictment was to this effect: "Socrates is guilty of crime in refusing to recognise the gods acknowledged by the state, and importing strange divinities of his own; he is further guilty of corrupting the young."

In the first place, what evidence did they produce that Socrates refused to recognise the gods acknowledged by the state? Was it that he did not sacrifice? or that he dispensed with divination? On the contrary he was often to be seen engaged in sacrifice, at home or at the common altars of the state. Nor was his dependence on divination less manifest. Indeed that saying of his, "A divinity gives me a sign," was on everybody's lips. So much so that, if I am not mistaken, it lay at the root of the imputation that he imported novel divinities; though there was no greater novelty in his case than in that of other believers in oracular help, who commonly rely on omens of all sorts: the flight or cry of birds, the utterances of man, chance meetings, or a victim's entrails. Even according to the popular conception, it is not the mere fowl, it is not the chance individual one meets, who knows what things are profitable for a man, but it is the gods who vouchsafe by such instruments to signify the same. This was also the tenet of Socrates. Only, whereas men ordinarily speak of being turned aside, or urged onwards by birds, or other creatures encountered on the path, Socrates suited his language to his conviction. "The divinity," said he, "gives me a sign." Further, he would constantly advise his associates to do this, or beware of doing that, upon the authority of this same divine voice; and, as a matter of fact, those who listened to his warnings prospered, whilst he who turned a deaf ear to them repented afterwards. Yet it will be readily conceded, he would hardly desire to present himself to his everyday companions in the character of either knave or fool. Whereas he would have appeared to be both, supposing the God-given revelations had but revealed his own proneness to deception. It is plain he would not have ventured on forecast at all, but for his belief that the words he spoke would in fact be verified. Then on whom, or what, was the assurance rooted, if not upon God? And if he had faith in the gods, how could he fail to recognise them?

But his mode of dealing with his intimates has another aspect. As regards the ordinary necessities of life, his advice was, "Act as you believe these things may best be done." But in the case of those darker problems, the issues of which are incalculable, he directed his friends to

From *History*, Vols. III-IV, by Xenophon, translated by Henry Graham Dakyns (New York: Tandy-Thomas Co., 1909).

consult the oracle, whether the business should be undertaken or not. "No one," he would say, "who wishes to manage a house or city with success: no one aspiring to guide the helm of state aright, can afford to dispense with aid from above. Doubtless, skill in carpentering, building, smithying, farming, or the art of governing men, together with the theory of these processes, and the sciences of arithmetic, economy, strategy, are affairs of study, and within the grasp of human intelligence. Yet there is a side even of these, and that not the least important, which the gods reserve to themselves, the bearing of which is hidden from mortal vision. Thus, let a man sow field or plant farm never so well, yet he cannot foretell who will gather in the fruits: another may build him a house of fairest proportion, yet he knows not who will inhabit it. Neither can a general foresee whether it will profit him to conduct a campaign, nor a politician be certain whether his leadership will turn to evil or to good. Nor can the man who weds a fair wife, looking forward to joy, know whether through her he shall not reap sorrow. Neither can he who has built up a powerful connection in the state know whether he shall not by means of it be cast out of his city. To suppose that all these matters lay within the scope of human judgment to the exclusion of the preternatural, was preternatural folly. Nor was it less extravagant to go and consult the will of Heaven on questions which it is given to us to decide by dint of learning. As though a man should inquire, 'Am I to choose an expert driver as my coachman, or one who has never handled the reins?' 'Shall I appoint a mariner to be skipper of my vessel, or a landsman?' And so with respect to all we may know by numbering, weighing, and measuring. To seek advice from Heaven on such points was a sort of profanity. Our duty is plain," he would observe; "where we are permitted to work through our natural faculties, there let us by all means apply them. But in things which are hidden, let us seek to gain knowledge from above by divination; for the gods," he added, "grant signs to those to whom they will be gracious."

Again, Socrates ever lived in the public eye; at early morning he was to be seen betaking himself to one of the promenades, or wrestling-grounds; at noon he would appear with the crowds in the market-place; and as day declined, wherever the largest throng might be encountered, there was he to be found, talking for the most part, while any one who chose might stop and listen. Yet no one ever heard him say, or saw him do anything impious or irreverent. Indeed, in contrast to others he set his face against all discussion of such high matters as the nature of the Universe; how the "kosmos," as the [sophists] phrase it, came into being; or by what forces the celestial phenomena arise. To trouble one's brain about such matters was, he argued, to play the fool. He would ask first: Did these investigators feel their knowledge of things human so complete that they betook themselves to these lofty speculations? Or did they maintain that they were playing their proper parts in thus neglecting the affairs of man to speculate on the concerns of God? He was astonished they did not see how far these problems lay beyond mortal ken; since even those who pride themselves most on their discussion of these points differ from each other, as madmen do. For just as some madmen, he said, have no apprehension of what is truly terrible, others fear where no fear is; some are ready to say and do anything in public without the slightest symptom of shame; others think they ought not so much as to set foot among their fellow-men; some honour neither temple, nor altar, nor aught else sacred to the name of God; others bow down to stocks and stones and worship the very beasts: so is it with those thinkers whose minds are cumbered with cares concerning the Universal Nature. One sect has discovered that Being is one and indivisible. Another that it is infinite in number. If one proclaims that all things are in a continual flux, another replies that nothing can possibly be moved at any time. The theory of the universe as a process of birth and death is met by the counter theory, that nothing ever could be born or ever will die.

But the questioning of Socrates on the merits of these speculators sometimes took another form. The student of human learning expects, he said, to make something of his studies for the benefit of himself or others, as he likes. Do these explorers into the divine operations hope that when they have discovered by what forces the various phenomena occur, they will create winds and waters at will and fruitful seasons? Will they manipulate these and the like to suit their needs? or has no such notion perhaps ever entered their heads, and will they be content simply to know how such things come into existence? But if this was his mode of describing those who meddle with such matters as these, he himself never wearied of discussing human topics. What is piety? what is impiety? What is the beautiful? what the ugly? What the noble? what the base? What are meant by just and unjust? what by sobriety and madness? what by courage and cowardice? What is a state? what is a statesman? what is a ruler over men? what is a ruling character? and other like problems, the knowledge of which, as he put it, conferred a patent of nobility on the possessor, whereas those who lacked the knowledge might deservedly be stigmatised as slaves.

Now, in so far as the opinions of Socrates were unknown to the world at large, it is not surprising that the court should draw false conclusions respecting them; but that facts patent to all should have been ignored is indeed astonishing.

At one time Socrates was a member of the Council,[1] he had taken the senatorial oath, and sworn "as a member of that house to act in conformity with the laws." It was thus he chanced to be President of the Popular Assembly,[2] when that body was seized with a desire to put the nine generals, Thrasyllus, Erasinides, and the rest, to death by a single inclusive vote.[3] Whereupon, in spite of the bitter resentment of the people, and the menaces of several influential citizens, he refused to put the question, esteeming it of greater importance faithfully to abide by

[1]The chief administrative agency of Athenian representative democracy. It was composed of five hundred citizens responsible for conducting the affairs of government for the whole city-state.

[2]The supreme authority in Athenian democracy; the meeting of all male citizens at which each one could vote.

[3]Xenophon is referring to events that occurred just after the conclusion of the Peloponnesian War, during the years 404–403 B.C. A group of Athenian conservatives, with the help of the victorious Spartans, seized control of the machinery of government and substituted a short-lived tyrannical oligarchy for democracy. During the time they were in power, they instituted a reign of terror against democratic sympathizers, especially against the former leaders of Athens.

the oath which he had taken, than to gratify the people wrongfully, or to screen himself from the menaces of the mighty. The fact being, that with regard to the care bestowed by the gods upon men, his belief differed widely from that of the multitude. Whereas most people seem to imagine that the gods know in part, and are ignorant in part, Socrates believed firmly that the gods know all things—both the things that are said and the things that are done, and the things that are counselled in the silent chambers of the heart. Moreover, they are present everywhere, and bestow signs upon man concerning all the things of man.

I can, therefore, but repeat my former words. It is a marvel to me how the Athenians came to be persuaded that Socrates fell short of sobermindedness as touching the gods. A man who never ventured one impious word or deed against the gods we worship, but whose whole language concerning them, and his every act, closely coincided, word for word, and deed for deed, with all we deem distinctive of devoutest piety.

2. No less surprising to my mind is the belief that Socrates corrupted the young. This man, who, beyond what has been already stated, kept his appetites and passions under strict control, who was pre-eminently capable of enduring winter's cold and summer's heat and every kind of toil, who was so schooled to curtail his needs that with the scantiest of means he never lacked sufficiency,—is it credible that such a man could have made others irreverent or lawless, or licentious, or effeminate in face of toil? Was he not rather the saving of many through the passion for virtue which he roused in them, and the hope he infused that through careful management of themselves they might grow to be truly beautiful and good,—not indeed that he ever undertook to be a teacher of virtue, but being evidently virtuous himself he made those who associated with him hope that by imitating they might at last resemble him.

But let it not be inferred that he was negligent of his own body or approved of those who neglected theirs. If excess of eating, counteracted by excess of toil, was a dietary of which he disapproved, to gratify the natural claim of appetite in conjunction with moderate exercise was a system he favoured, as tending to a healthy condition of the body without trammelling the cultivation of the spirit. On the other hand, there was nothing dandified or pretentious about him; he indulged in no foppery of shawl or shoes, or other effeminacy of living.

Least of all did he tend to make his companions greedy of money. He would not, while restraining passion generally, make capital out of the one passion which attached others to himself; and by this abstinence, he believed, he was best consulting his own freedom; in so much that he stigmatised those who condescended to take wages for their society as vendors of their own persons, because they were compelled to discuss for the benefit of their paymasters.[4] What surprised him was that any one possessing virtue should deign to ask money as its price instead of simply finding his reward in the acquisition of an honest friend, as if the new-fledged soul of honour could forget her debt of gratitude to her greatest benefactor.

---

[4]Xenophon is referring here to the Sophists.

For himself, without making any such profession, he was content to believe that those who accepted his views would play their parts as good and true friends to himself and one another their lives long. Once more then: how should a man of this character corrupt the young? unless the careful cultivation of virtue be corruption.

But, says the accuser, by all that's sacred! did not Socrates cause his associates to despise the established laws when he dwelt on the folly of appointing state officers by ballot? a principle which, he said, no one would care to apply in selecting a pilot or a flute-player or in any similar case, where a mistake would be far less disastrous than in matters political. Words like these, according to the accuser, tended to incite the young to contemn the established constitution, rendering them violent and headstrong. . . .

3. It may serve to illustrate the assertion that he benefited his associates partly by the display of his own virtue and partly by verbal discourse and argument, if I set down my various recollections on these heads. And first with regard to religion and the concerns of heaven. In conduct and language his behaviour conformed to the rule laid down by the Pythia[5] in reply to the question, "How shall we act?" as touching a sacrifice or the worship of ancestors, or any similar point. Her answer is: "Act according to the law and custom of your state, and you will act piously." After this pattern Socrates behaved himself, and so he exhorted others to behave, holding them to be but busybodies and vain fellows who acted on any different principle.

His formula of prayer was simple: "Give me that which is best for me," for, said he, the gods know best what good things are—to pray for gold or silver or despotic power were no better than to make some particular throw at dice or stake in battle or any such thing the subject of prayer, of which the future consequences are manifestly uncertain.

If with scant means he offered but small sacrifices he believed that he was in no wise inferior to others who make frequent and large sacrifices from an ampler store. It were ill surely for the very gods themselves, could they take delight in large sacrifices rather than in small, else oftentimes must the offerings of bad men be found acceptable rather than of good; nor from the point of view of men themselves would life be worth living if the offerings of a villain rather than of a righteous man found favour in the sight of Heaven. His belief was that the joy of the gods is greater in proportion to the holiness of the giver, and he was ever an admirer of that line of Hesiod which says:

"According to thine ability do sacrifice to the immortal gods."

"Yes," he would say, "in our dealings with friends and strangers alike, and in reference to the demands of life in general, there is no better motto for a man than that: 'let a man do according to his ability.'"

Or to take another point. If it appeared to him that a sign from heaven had been given him, nothing would have induced him to go against the heavenly warning: he would as soon have been persuaded

---

to accept the guidance of a blind man ignorant of the path to lead him on a journey in place of one who knew the road and could see; and so he denounced the folly of others who do things contrary to the warnings of God in order to avoid some disrepute among men. For himself he despised all human aids by comparison with counsel from above. . . .

6. . . . Returning to the charge at another time, this same Antiphon[6] engaged Socrates in conversation thus.

ANT: Socrates, for my part, I believe you to be a good and upright man; but for your wisdom I cannot say much. I fancy you would hardly dispute the verdict yourself, since, as I remark, you do not ask a money payment for your society; and yet if it were your cloak now, or your house, or any other of your possessions, you would set some value upon it, and never dream, I will not say of parting with it gratis, but of exchanging it for less than its worth. A plain proof, to my mind, that if you thought your society worth anything, you would ask for it not less than its equivalent in gold. Hence the conclusion to which I have come, as already stated: good and upright you may be, since you do not cheat people from pure selfishness; but wise you cannot be since your knowledge is not worth a cent.

To this onslaught Socrates: Antiphon, it is a tenet which we cling to that beauty and wisdom have this in common, that there is a fair way and a foul way in which to dispose of them. The vendor of beauty purchases an evil name, but supposing the same person have discerned a soul of beauty in his lover and makes that man his friend, we regard his choice as sensible. So is it with wisdom; he who sells it for money to the first bidder we name a sophist, as though one should say a man who prostitutes his wisdom; but if the same man, discerning the noble nature of another, shall teach that other every good thing, and make him his friend, of such an one we say he does that which it is the duty of every good citizen of gentle soul to do. In accordance with this theory, I too, Antiphon, having my tastes, even as another finds pleasure in his horse and his hounds, and another in his fighting cocks, so I too take my pleasure in good friends; and if I have any good thing myself I teach it them, or I commend them to others by whom I think they will be helped forwards in the path of virtue. The treasures also of the wise of old, written and bequeathed in their books, I unfold and peruse in common with my friends. If our eye light upon any good thing we cull it eagerly, and regard it as great gain if we may but grow in friendship with one another.

As I listened to this talk I could not but reflect that he, the master, was a person to be envied, and that we, his hearers, were being led by him to beauty and nobility of soul. . . .

Book III

9. Being again asked by some one: could courage be taught, or did it come by nature? he answered: I imagine that just as one body is by

---

[6]A Sophist. Xenophon has been describing a series of arguments between him and Socrates.

nature stronger than another body to encounter toils, so one soul by nature grows more robust than another soul in face of dangers. Certainly I do note that people brought up under the same condition of laws and customs differ greatly in respect of daring. Still my belief is that by learning and practice the natural aptitude may always be strengthened towards courage. It is clear, for instance, that Scythians or Thracians would not venture to take shield and spear and contend with Lacedæmonians; and it is equally evident that Lacedæmonians would demur to entering the lists of battle against Thracians if limited to their light shields and javelins, or against Scythians without some weapon more familiar than their bows and arrows. And as far as I can see, this principle holds generally: the natural differences of one man from another may be compensated by artificial progress, the result of care and attention. All which proves clearly that whether nature has endowed us with keener or blunter sensibilities, the duty of all alike is to learn and practise those things in which we would fain achieve distinction.

Between wisdom and sobriety of soul (which is temperance) he drew no distinction. Was a man able on the one hand to recognise things beautiful and good sufficiently to live in them? Had he, on the other hand, knowledge of the "base and foul" so as to beware of them? If so, Socrates judged him to be wise at once and sound of soul (or temperate).

And being further questioned whether "he considered those who have the knowledge of right action, but do not apply it, to be wise and self-controlled?"—"Not a whit more," he answered, "than I consider them to be unwise and intemperate. Every one, I conceive, deliberately chooses what, within the limits open to him, he considers most conducive to his interest, and acts accordingly. I must hold therefore that those who act against rule and crookedly are neither wise nor self-controlled."

He said that justice, moreover, and all other virtue is wisdom. That is to say, things just, and all things else that are done with virtue, are "beautiful and good"; and neither will those who know these things deliberately choose aught else in their stead; nor will he who lacks the special knowledge of them be able to do them, but even if he makes the attempt he will miss the mark and fail. So the wise alone can perform the things which are "beautiful and good"; they that are unwise cannot, but even if they try they fail. Therefore, since all things just, and generally all things "beautiful and good," are wrought with virtue, it is clear that justice and all other virtue is wisdom.

On the other hand, madness (he maintained) was the opposite to wisdom; not that he regarded simple ignorance as madness, but he put it thus: for a man to be ignorant of himself, to imagine and suppose that he knows what he knows not, was (he argued), if not madness itself, yet something very like it. The mass of men no doubt hold a different language: if a man is all abroad on some matter of which the mass of mankind are ignorant, they do not pronounce him "mad"; but a like aberration of mind, if only it be about matters within the scope of ordinary knowledge, they call madness. For instance, any one who imagined himself too tall to pass under a gateway of the Long Wall[7] without stooping, or so strong as to try to lift a house, or to attempt any other obvious impossibility, is a madman according to them; but in the popular sense he is not mad, if his obliquity is confined to small matters. In fact, just as strong desire goes by the name of passion in popular parlance, so mental obliquity on a grand scale is entitled madness.

In answer to the question: what is envy? he discovered it to be a certain kind of pain; not certainly the sorrow felt at the misfortunes of a friend or the good fortune of an enemy—that is not envy; but, as he said, "envy is felt by those alone who are annoyed at the successes of their friends." And when some one or other expressed astonishment that any one friendlily disposed to another should be pained at his well-doing, he reminded him of a common tendency in people: when any one is faring ill their sympathies are touched, they rush to the aid of the unfortunate; but when fortune smiles on others, they are somehow pained. "I do not say," he added, "this could happen to a thoughtful person; but it is no uncommon condition of a silly mind."

In answer to the question: what is leisure? I discover (he said) that most men do something: for instance, the dice player, the gambler, the buffoon, do something, but these have leisure; they can, if they like, turn and do something better; but nobody has leisure to turn from the better to the worse, and if he does so turn, when he has no leisure, he does but ill in that.

(To pass to another definition.) They are not kings or rulers (he said) who hold the sceptre merely, or are chosen by fellows out of the street, or are appointed by lot, or have stepped into office by violence or by fraud; but those who have the special knowledge how to rule. Thus having won the admission that it is the function of a ruler to enjoin what ought to be done, and of those who are ruled to obey, he proceeded to point out by instances that in a ship the ruler or captain is the man of special knowledge, to whom, as an expert, the shipowner himself and all the others on board obey. So likewise, in the matter of husbandry, the proprietor of an estate; in that of sickness, the patient; in that of physical training of the body, the youthful athlete going through a course; and, in general, every one directly concerned in any matter needing attention and care will either attend to this matter personally, if he thinks he has the special knowledge; or, if he mistrusts his own science, will be eager to obey any expert on the spot, or will even send and fetch one from a distance. The guidance of this expert he will follow, and do what he has to do at his dictation.

And thus, in the art of spinning wool, he liked to point out that women are the rulers of men—and why? because they have the knowledge of the art, and men have not.

And if any one raised the objection that a tyrant has it in his power not to obey good and correct advice, he would retort: "Pray, how has he the option not to obey, considering the penalty hanging over him

---

[7]The Long Walls joining Athens and Piraeus, a town five miles away which served as the chief seaport of Athens.

who disobeys the words of wisdom? for whatever the matter be in which he disobeys the word of good advice, he will fall into error, I presume, and falling into error, be punished." And to the suggestion that the tyrant could, if he liked, cut off the head of the man of wisdom, his answer was: "Do you think that he who destroys his best ally will go scot free, or suffer a mere slight and passing loss? Is he more likely to secure his salvation that way, think you, or to compass his own swift destruction?"

When some one asked him: "What he regarded as the best pursuit or business for a man?" he answered: "Successful conduct;" and to a second question: "Did he then regard good fortune as an end to be pursued?"—"On the contrary," he answered, "for myself, I consider fortune and conduct to be diametrically opposed. For instance, to succeed in some desirable course of action without seeking to do so, I hold to be good fortune; but to do a thing well by dint of learning and practice, that according to my creed is successful conduct, and those who make this the serious business of their life seem to me to do well."

They are at once the best and dearest in the sight of God (he went on to say) who for instance in husbandry do well the things of farming, or in the art of healing all that belongs to healing, or in statecraft the affairs of state; whereas the man who does nothing well—nor well in anything—is (he added) neither good for anything nor dear to God.

Book IV

8. Now if any one should be disposed to set the statement of Socrates touching the divinity which warned him what he ought to do or not to do, against the fact that he was sentenced to death by the board of judges, and argue that thereby Socrates stood convicted of lying and delusion in respect of this "divinity" of his, I would have him to note in the first place that, at the date of his trial, Socrates was already so far advanced in years that had he not died then his life would have reached its natural term soon afterwards; and secondly, as matters went, he escaped life's bitterest load in escaping those years which bring diminution of intellectual force to all,—instead of which he was called upon to exhibit the full robustness of his soul and acquire glory in addition, partly by the style of his defence—felicitous alike in its truthfulness, its freedom, and its rectitude—and partly by the manner in which he bore the sentence of condemnation with infinite gentleness and manliness. Since no one within the memory of man, it is admitted, ever bowed his head to death more nobly. After the sentence he must needs live for thirty days, since it was the month of the "Delia,"[8] and the law does not suffer any man to die by the hand of the public executioner until the sacred embassy return from Delos. During the whole of that period (as his acquaintances without exception can testify) his life proceeded as usual. There was nothing to mark a difference between now and formerly in the even

---

[8]An annual festival of great antiquity dedicated to the god Apollo. The solemnities were held at Delos, an island in the Aegean Sea.

tenour of its courage; and it was a life which at all times had been a marvel of cheerfulness and calm content.

Let us pause and ask how could man die more nobly and more beautifully than in the way described? or put it thus: dying so, then was his death most noble and most beautiful; and being the most beautiful, then was it also the most fortunate and heaven-blest; and being most blessed of heaven, then was it also most precious in the sight of God.

And now I will mention further certain things which I have heard from Hermogenes,[9] the son of Hipponicus, concerning him. He said that even after Melêtus had drawn up the indictment, he himself used to hear Socrates conversing and discussing everything rather than the suit impending, and had ventured to suggest that he ought to be considering the line of his defence, to which, in the first instance the master answered: "Do I not seem to you to have been practising that my whole life long?" And upon asking "How?" added in explanation that he had passed his days in nothing else save in distinguishing between what is just and what is unjust (right and wrong), and in doing what is right and abstaining from what is wrong; "which conduct" (he added) "I hold to be the finest possible practice for my defence"; and when he (Hermogenes), returning to the point again, pleaded with Socrates: "Do you not see, Socrates, how commonly it happens that an Athenian jury, under the influence of argument, condemns innocent people to death, and acquits real criminals?"—Socrates replied, "I assure you, Hermogenes, that each time I have essayed to give my thoughts to the defence which I am to make before the court, the divinity has opposed me." And when he (Hermogenes) exclaimed, "How strange!"—"Do you find it strange" (he continued), "that to the Godhead it should appear better for me to close my life at once? Do you not know that up to the present moment there is no man whom I can admit to have spent a better or happier life than mine. Since theirs I regard as the best of lives who study best to become as good as may be, and theirs the happiest who have the liveliest sense of growth in goodness; and such, hitherto, is the happy fortune which I perceive to have fallen to my lot. To such conclusion I have come, not only in accidental intercourse with others, but by a strict comparison drawn between myself and others, and in this faith I continue to this day; and not I only, but my friends continue in a like persuasion with regard to me, not for the lame reason that they are my friends and love me (or else would others have been in like case as regards their friends), but because they are persuaded that by being with me they will attain to their full height of goodness. But, if I am destined to prolong my days, maybe I shall be enforced to pay in full the penalties of old age—to see and hear less keenly, to fail in intellectual force, and to leave school, as it were, more of a dunce than when I came, less learned and more forgetful,—in a word, I shall fall from my high estate, and daily grow worse in that wherein aforetime I excelled. But indeed, were it possible to remain unconscious of the change, the life left would scarcely be worth living; but given that there is a conscious-

---

[9] A friend and disciple of Socrates.

ness of the change, then must the existence left to live be found by comparison insipid, joyless, a death in life, devoid of life's charm. . . .

Such are the words which he spoke in conversation with Hermogenes and the rest. But amongst those who knew Socrates and recognised what manner of man he was, all who make virtue and perfection their pursuit still to this day cease not to lament his loss with bitterest regret, as for one who helped them in the pursuit of virtue as none else could.

To me, personally, he was what I have myself endeavoured to describe: so pious and devoutly religious that he would take no step apart from the will of heaven; so just and upright that he never did even a trifling injury to any living soul; so self-controlled, so temperate, that he never at any time chose the sweeter in place of the better; so sensible, and wise, and prudent that in distinguishing the better from the worse he never erred; nor had he need of any helper, but for the knowledge of these matters, his judgment was at once infallible and self-sufficing. Capable of reasonably setting forth and defining moral questions, he was also able to test others, and where they erred, to cross-examine and convict them, and so to impel and guide them in the path of virtue and noble manhood. With these characteristics, he seemed to be the very impersonation of human perfection and happiness.

Such is our estimate. If the verdict fail to satisfy, I would ask those who disagree with it to place the character of any other side by side with this delineation, and then pass sentence.

Defense of Socrates

. . .

More than this of course was said both by Socrates himself and by the friends who joined in his defence. But I have not made it a point to report the whole trial; rather I am satisfied to make it clear that while Socrates' whole concern was to keep free from any act of impiety toward the gods or any appearance of wrong-doing toward man, he did not think it meet to beseech the jury to let him escape death; instead, he believed that the time had now come for him to die. This conviction of his became more evident than ever after the adverse issue of the trial. For, first of all, when he was bidden to name his penalty,[1] he refused personally and forbade his friends to name one, but said that naming the penalty in itself implied an acknowledgment of guilt. Then, when

From *Anabasis, Symposium, Apology IV-VIII*, by Xenophon, translated by O. J. Todd (Cambridge, Mass.: Harvard University Press). Reprinted by permission of the publishers and The Loeb Classical Library.
    [1]There was no penalty prescribed by Athenian law for Socrates' offense. When he was adjudged guilty, the law required him to propose his own penalty as an alternative to the death penalty proposed by Meletus.

his companions wished to remove him clandestinely from prison, he would not accompany them, but seemed actually to banter them, asking them whether they knew of any spot outside of Attica that was inaccessible to death.

When the trial was over, Socrates (according to Hermogenes) remarked: "Well, gentlemen, those who instructed the witnesses that they must bear false witness against me, perjuring themselves to do so, and those who were won over to do this must feel in their hearts a guilty consciousness of great impiety and iniquity; but as for me, why should my spirit be any less exalted now than before my condemnation, since I have not been proved guilty of having done any of the acts mentioned in the indictment? For it has not been shown that I have sacrificed to new deities in the stead of Zeus and Hera and the gods of their company, or that I have invoked in oaths or mentioned other gods. And how could I be corrupting the young by habituating them to fortitude and frugality? Now of all the acts for which the laws have prescribed the death-penalty —temple robbery, burglary, enslavement, treason to the state—not even my adversaries themselves charge me with having committed any of these. And so it seems astonishing to me how you could ever have been convinced that I had committed an act meriting death. But further, my spirit need not be less exalted because I am to be executed unjustly; for the ignominy of that attaches not to me but to those who condemned me. And I get comfort from the case of Palamedes, also, who died in circumstances similar to mine; for even yet he affords us far more noble themes for song than does Odysseus, the man who unjustly put him to death.[2] And I know that time to come as well as time past will attest that I, too, far from ever doing any man a wrong or rendering him more wicked, have rather profited those who conversed with me by teaching them, without reward, every good thing that lay in my power."

With these words he departed, blithe in glance, in mien, in gait, as comported well indeed with the words he had just uttered. When he noticed that those who accompanied him were in tears, "What is this?" Hermogenes reports him as asking. "Are you just now beginning to weep? Have you not known all along that from the moment of my birth nature had condemned me to death? Verily, if I am being destroyed before my time while blessings are still pouring in upon me, clearly that should bring grief to me and to my well-wishers; but if I am ending my life when only troubles are in view, my own opinion is that you ought all to feel cheered, in the assurance that my state is happy."

A man named Apollodorus, who was there with him, a very ardent disciple of Socrates, but otherwise simple, exclaimed, "But, Socrates, what I find it hardest to bear is that I see you being put to death unjustly!" The other, stroking Apollodorus' head, is said to have replied, "My beloved Apollodorus, was it your preference to see me put to death justly?" and smiled as he asked the question.

---

[2]According to Greek mythology, Palamedes was one of the Greek heroes of the Trojan War. When Odysseus tried to avoid his obligation to join in the expedition to Troy by feigning madness, Palamedes exposed his deceit. Thereafter Odysseus, to avenge himself, forged a letter purporting to come from the Trojan king, Priam, offering gold to Palamedes to betray the Greeks; and the gold, by the contrivance of Odysseus, was found in Palamedes' tent. Palamedes was consequently stoned to death.

It is said also that he remarked as he saw Anytus[3] passing by: "There goes a man who is filled with pride at the thought that he has accomplished some great and noble end in putting me to death, because, seeing him honoured by the state with the highest offices, I said that he ought not to confine his son's education to hides.[4] What a vicious fellow," he continued, "not to know, apparently, that whichever one of us has wrought the more beneficial and noble deeds for all time, *he* is the real victor. But," he is reported to have added, "Homer has attributed to some of his heroes at the moment of dissolution the power to foresee the future; and so I too wish to utter a prophecy. At one time I had a brief association with the son of Anytus, and I thought him not lacking in firmness of spirit; and so I predict that he will not continue in the servile occupation that his father has provided for him; but through want of a worthy adviser he will fall into some disgraceful propensity and will surely go far in the career of vice." In saying this he was not mistaken; the young man, delighting in wine, never left off drinking night or day, and at last turned out worth nothing to his city, his friends, or himself. So Anytus, even though dead, still enjoys an evil repute for his own hard-heartedness. And as for Socrates, by exalting himself before the court, he brought ill-will upon himself and made his conviction by the jury all the more certain. Now to me he seems to have met a fate that the gods love; for he escaped the hardest part of life and met the easiest sort of death. And he displayed the stalwart nature of his heart; for having once decided that to die was better for him than to live longer, he did not weaken in the presence of death (just as he had never set his face against any other thing, either, that was for his good), but was cheerful not only in the expectation of death but in meeting it.

And so, in contemplating the man's wisdom and nobility of character, I find it beyond my power to forget him or, in remembering him, to refrain from praising him. And if among those who make virtue their aim any one has ever been brought into contact with a person more helpful than Socrates, I count that man worthy to be called most blessed.

Comments / on Socrates and Plato

Socrates, however, was busying himself about ethical matters and neglecting the world of nature as a whole but seeking the universal in these ethical matters, and fixed thought for the first time on definitions; Plato accepted his teaching, but held that the problem applied not to sensible things but to entities of another kind—for this reason, that the common

---

[3]One of the men who had joined with Meletus in placing formal charges against Socrates.
[4]Anytus owned a tannery.

definition could not be a definition of any sensible thing, as they were always changing. Things of this other sort, then, he called Ideas, and sensible things, he said, were all named after these, and in virtue of a relation to these; for the many existed by participation in the Ideas that have the same name as they. *ARISTOTLE (334—322* B.C.*)*

The chief value of Plato's writings lies in the powerful impetus they give to the intellectual life of the reader. In brief, it is not the knowledge discovered by Plato, but his belief in spiritual realities, his aspiration to the beautiful, the good, and the true, his conception of the vast heights attainable by man, that place him among the most powerful intellectual and moral forces that operate upon the human race.

C. A. ROBINSON, Jr. (1954)

CHORUS: Blessed the man who has perfected wisdom! Everything is happiness for him. Behold Aeschylus; thanks to the talent, to the cleverness he has shown, he returns to his country; and his fellow citizens, his relations, his friends will all hail his return with joy. Let us beware of jabbering with Socrates and of disdaining the sublime notes of the tragic Muse. To pass an idle life reeling off grandiloquent speeches and foolish quibbles is the part of a madman. *ARISTOPHANES (405* B.C.*)*

Socrates had from the first turned his back on natural science. Plato, too, was the less disposed to devote any attention to this study because for him the only world accessible to true knowledge and thought was of a supersensual, mental nature, while of nature, the realm of the corporeal, there could be only an untrustworthy vague idea transmitted to us through the senses. All his efforts and thoughts had been directed to educating mankind into an understanding of the supersensual, mental world of the ideas which could provide the only basis for human society.

EDUARD ZELLER (1883)

To take an example: The physical philosophers had sketched each his theory of the world; the theory of atoms, of fire, of flux, of spirit; theories mechanical and chemical in their genius. Plato, a master of mathematics, studious of all natural laws and causes, feels these, as second causes, to be no theories of the world but bare inventories and lists. To the study of nature he therefore prefixes the dogma—"Let us declare the cause which led the Supreme Ordainer to produce and compose the universe. He was good; and he who is good has no kind of envy. Exempt from envy, he wished that all things should be as much as possible like himself. Whosoever, taught by wise men, shall admit this as the prime cause of the origin and foundation of the world, will be in the truth." "All things are for the sake of the good, and it is the cause of every thing beautiful." This dogma animates and impersonates his philosophy.

RALPH WALDO EMERSON (1850)

The Platonic Socrates anticipates both the Stoics and the Cynics. The Stoics held that the supreme good is virtue, and that a man cannot be deprived of virtue by outside causes; this doctrine is implicit in the contention of Socrates that his judges cannot harm him. The Cynics despised worldly goods, and showed their contempt by eschewing the comforts of civilization; this is the same point of view that led Socrates to go barefoot and ill-clad. *BERTRAND RUSSELL (1945)*

Socrates was a very wise man. He went around giving people advice. They poisoned him.
AN ESSAY ON GREEK HISTORY WRITTEN BY A LITTLE GIRL
AND QUOTED BY HENRY H. FOWLER

Aristotle

Basically, Aristotle's philosophy was shaped by his interest in the phenomena of growth and change in things. While Plato's Theory of Ideal Forms might appeal to the mathematician's desire to perceive an immutable order behind changing things, Aristotle's view of reality reflected his training as a biologist. How can the concepts and forms stored up in Plato's intelligible world partake of matter, Aristotle asks. How can they impart motion and change in things? Plato, in order to explain the relationship between matter and form, resorted to the notion of "imitation": the visible world of matter is an imperfect reflection or imitation of the intelligible world of Ideal Forms. In Aristotle's view, however, both matter and form are present in a substance; more precisely, form is a dynamic principle of motion operative in matter. The Aristotelian concept of motion is all-encompassing: it denotes not only mechanical motion but also change in physical appearance as well as biological growth.

At times, Aristotle expresses his doctrine with the aid of the two notions of *potentiality* and *actuality*. Matter is conceived of as a potentiality of form; all that exists yearns to actualize an innate potential. In modern terms, this inborn tendency to achieve a certain end may be called "intrinsic purposiveness." However, the purposive drive which inheres in the world, as Aristotle sees it, can be equated with "evolution" only in the sense that after a certain change has occurred, a thing has more "form" than before. God, for instance, is pure form or pure actuality. In Him, therefore, there can be no change. He is an Unmoved Mover and as such instills a "teleological yearning" in things to become what they ought to become or to be where they ought to be.

From these premises it follows that actuality or form is in a sense "prior" to matter. If the potential form of a blade of grass, for instance, were not embedded in its seed, it could never become a blade of grass. Similarly, the state could never be actualized by the human species if the form of the political animal were not inborn in man. Further, to define the essence or nature of a thing, it is necessary to look at its actualized form since, according to Aristotle, "the nature of a thing is its end."

Aristotle's *Ethics* is conditioned by his teleological and activist outlook on the nature of things. It stresses the necessity to determine, through observation of the actual behavior of men, the end, "final cause," or ultimate good of man. This good should itself be an end which can be reached only through the complete unfolding of man's potential both as a rational and as a political animal, since for Aristotle, virtue and happiness are not conceivable outside of man's potential as a rational creature living in a city-state, or *polis.* In this sense, ethics is to Aristotle a branch of politics.

But Aristotle also knew that for a reflective being such as man the process of maturing was not automatic but required conscious effort. Thus he is concerned with gaining insight not only into the potential nature of man but also into the principles of action or "habituation" that would allow man to actualize his essence. Simply to know the good is not enough; it must be put into practice. Though Aristotle concedes, in almost Platonic fashion, that "intellectual virtue"—contemplation or pure mental activity—is the highest virtue, he never loses sight of the importance of moral judgments and principles of right conduct.

In this respect, Aristotle's *Ethics* is genuinely concerned with *ethos,* the Greek word for "character"; while Plato was more absorbed, even when mapping out his ideal republic, with *episteme,* the Greek word for "knowledge." Although Aristotle's speculative theories in some places turn out to be as esoteric and abstract as Plato's, their most marked characteristic, throughout the body of Aristotle's work, is the practical and empirical qualities evident in the *Ethics* and *Politics.*

Ethics

Book I

1. Every art and every inquiry, and similarly every action and pursuit, is thought to aim at some good; and for this reason the good has rightly been declared to be that at which all things aim. But a certain difference is found among ends; some are activities, others are products apart from the activities that produce them. Where there are ends apart from the actions, it is the nature of the products to be better than the activities. Now, as there are many actions, arts, and sciences, their ends also are many; the end of the medical art is health, that of shipbuilding a vessel, that of strategy victory, that of economics wealth. But where such arts

From *The Works of Aristotle, Vol. IX: Ethica Nichomachea,* translated by W. D. Ross. Reprinted by permission of the Clarendon Press, Oxford.

fall under a single capacity—as bridle-making and the other arts concerned with the equipment of horses fall under the art of riding, and this and every military action under strategy, in the same way other arts fall under yet others—in all of these the ends of the master arts are to be preferred to all the subordinate ends; for it is for the sake of the former that the latter are pursued. It makes no difference whether the activities themselves are the ends of the actions, or something else apart from the activities, as in the case of the sciences just mentioned.

2. If, then, there is some end of the things we do, which we desire for its own sake (everything else being desired for the sake of this), and if we do not choose everything for the sake of something else (for at that rate the process would go on to infinity, so that our desire would be empty and vain), clearly this must be the good and the chief good. Will not the knowledge of it, then, have a great influence on life? Shall we not, like archers who have a mark to aim at, be more likely to hit upon what is right? If so, we must try, in outline at least, to determine what it is, and of which of the sciences or capacities it is the object. It would seem to belong to the most authoritative art and that which is most truly the master art. And politics appears to be of this nature; for it is this that ordains which of the sciences should be studied in a state, and which each class of citizens should learn and up to what point they should learn them; and we see even the most highly esteemed of capacities to fall under this, e.g. strategy, economics, rhetoric; now, since politics uses the rest of the sciences, and since, again, it legislates as to what we are to do and what we are to abstain from, the end of this science must include those of the others, so that this end must be the good for man. For even if the end is the same for a single man and for a state, that of the state seems at all events something greater and more complete whether to attain or to preserve; though it is worth while to attain the end merely for one man, it is finer and more godlike to attain it for a nation or for city-states. These, then, are the ends at which our inquiry aims, since it is political science, in one sense of that term.

4. Let us resume our inquiry and state, in view of the fact that all knowledge and every pursuit aims at some good, what it is that we say political science aims at and what is the highest of all goods achievable by action. Verbally there is very general agreement; for both the general run of men and people of superior refinement say that it is happiness, and identify living well and doing well with being happy; but with regard to what happiness is they differ, and the many do not give the same account as the wise. For the former think it is some plain and obvious thing, like pleasure, wealth, or honour; they differ, however, from one another—and often even the same man identifies it with different things, with health when he is ill, with wealth when he is poor; but, conscious of their ignorance, they admire those who proclaim some great ideal that is above their comprehension. Now some[1] thought that apart from these many goods there is another which is self-subsistent and causes the goodness of all these as well. To examine all the opinions

---

[1] The Platonic school.

that have been held were perhaps somewhat fruitless; enough to examine those that are most prevalent or that seem to be arguable. . . .

5. . . . To judge from the lives that men lead, most men, and men of the most vulgar type, seem (not without some ground) to identify the good, or happiness, with pleasure; which is the reason why they love the life of enjoyment. For there are, we may say, three prominent types of life—that just mentioned, the political, and thirdly the contemplative life. Now the mass of mankind are evidently quite slavish in their tastes, preferring a life suitable to beasts, but they get some ground for their view from the fact that many of those in high places share the tastes of Sardanapallus.[2] A consideration of the prominent types of life shows that people of superior refinement and of active disposition identify happiness with honour; for this is, roughly speaking, the end of the political life. But it seems too superficial to be what we are looking for, since it is thought to depend on those who bestow honour rather than on him who receives it, but the good we divine to be something proper to a man and not easily taken from him. Further, men seem to pursue honour in order that they may be assured of their goodness; at least it is by men of practical wisdom that they seek to be honoured, and among those who know them, and on the ground of their virtue; clearly, then, according to them, at any rate, virtue is better. And perhaps one might even suppose this to be, rather than honour, the end of the political life. But even this appears somewhat incomplete; for possession of virtue seems actually compatible with being asleep, or with lifelong inactivity, and, further, with the greatest sufferings and misfortunes; but a man who was living so no one would call happy, unless he were maintaining a thesis at all costs. But enough of this; for the subject has been sufficiently treated even in the current discussions. Third comes the contemplative life, which we shall consider later.

The life of money-making is one undertaken under compulsion, and wealth is evidently not the good we are seeking; for it is merely useful and for the sake of something else. And so one might rather take the aforenamed objects to be ends; for they are loved for themselves. But it is evident that not even these are ends; yet many arguments have been thrown away in support of them. Let us leave this subject, then.

6. We had perhaps better consider the universal good and discuss thoroughly what is meant by it, although such an inquiry is made an uphill one by the fact that the Forms have been introduced by friends of our own. Yet it would perhaps be thought to be better, indeed to be our duty, for the sake of maintaining the truth even to destroy what touches us closely, especially as we are philosophers or lovers of wisdom; for, while both are dear, piety requires us to honour truth above our friends.

The men who introduced this doctrine did not posit Ideas of classes within which they recognized priority and posteriority (which is the reason why they did not maintain the existence of an Idea embracing all numbers); but the term 'good' is used both in the category of substance and in that of quality and in that of relation, and that which is

---

[2]The last king who reigned over the Assyrian Empire of Nineveh, in the seventh century B.C. He was notorious for his hedonistic way of life.

per se, i.e. substance, is prior in nature to the relative (for the latter is like an offshoot and accident of being); so that there could not be a common Idea set over all these goods. Further, since 'good' has as many senses as 'being' (for it is predicated both in the category of substance, as of God and of reason, and in quality, i.e. of the virtues, and in quantity, i.e. of that which is moderate, and in relation, i.e. of the useful, and in time, i.e. of the right opportunity, and in place, i.e. of the right locality and the like), clearly it cannot be something universally present in all cases and single; for then it could not have been predicated in all the categories but in one only. Further, since of the things answering to one Idea there is one science, there would have been one science of all the goods; but as it is there are many sciences even of the things that fall under one category, e.g. of opportunity, for opportunity in war is studied by strategics and in disease by medicine, and the moderate in food is studied by medicine and in exercise by the science of gymnastics. And one might ask the question, what in the world they *mean* by 'a thing itself', if (as is the case) in 'man himself' and in a particular man the account of man is one and the same. For in so far as they are man, they will in no respect differ; and if this is so, neither will 'good itself' and particular goods, in so far as they are good. But again it will not be good any the more for being eternal, since that which lasts long is no whiter than that which perishes in a day. The Pythagoreans seem to give a more plausible account of the good, when they place the one in the column of goods; and it is they that Speusippus[3] seems to have followed.

But let us discuss these matters elsewhere; an objection to what we have said, however, may be discerned in the fact that the Platonists have not been speaking about *all* goods, and that the goods that are pursued and loved for themselves are called good by reference to a single Form, while those which tend to produce or to preserve these somehow or to prevent their contraries are called so by reference to these, and in secondary sense. Clearly, then, goods must be spoken of in two ways, and some must be good in themselves, the others by reason of these. Let us separate, then, things good in themselves from things useful, and consider whether the former are called good by reference to a single Idea. What sort of goods would one call good in themselves? Is it those that are pursued even when isolated from others, such as intelligence, sight, and certain pleasures and honours? Certainly, if we pursue these also for the sake of something else, yet one would place them among things good in themselves. Or is nothing other than the Idea of good good in itself? In that case the Form will be empty. But if the things we have named are also things good in themselves, the account of the good will have to appear as something identical in them all, as that of whiteness is identical in snow and in white lead. But of honour, wisdom, and pleasure, just in respect of their goodness, the accounts are distinct and diverse. The good, therefore, is not some common element answering to one Idea.

But what then do we mean by the good? It is surely not like the things

---

[3]An Athenian philosopher of the fourth century B.C., Plato's nephew and his successor as head of the Academy.

that only chance to have the same name. Are goods one, then, by being derived from one good or by all contributing to one good, or are they rather one by analogy? Certainly as sight is in the body, so is reason in the soul, and so on in other cases. But perhaps these subjects had better be dismissed for the present; for perfect precision about them would be more appropriate to another branch of philosophy. And similarly with regard to the Idea; even if there is some one good which is universally predicable of goods or is capable of separate and independent existence, clearly it could not be achieved or attained by man; but we are now seeking something attainable. Perhaps, however, some one might think it worth while to recognize this with a view to the goods that *are* attainable and achievable; for having this as a sort of pattern we shall know better the goods that are good for us, and if we know them shall attain them. This argument has some plausibility, but seems to clash with the procedure of the sciences; for all of these, though they aim at some good and seek to supply the deficiency of it, leave on one side the knowledge of *the* good. Yet that all the exponents of the arts should be ignorant of, and should not even seek, so great an aid is not probable. It is hard, too, to see how a weaver or a carpenter will be benefited in regard to his own craft by knowing this 'good itself', or how the man who has viewed the Idea itself will be a better doctor or general thereby. For a doctor seems not even to study health in this way, but the health of man, or perhaps rather the health of a particular man; it is individuals that he is healing. But enough of these topics.

7. Let us again return to the good we are seeking, and ask what it can be. It seems different in different actions and arts; it is different in medicine, in strategy, and in the other arts likewise. What then is the good of each? Surely that for whose sake everything else is done. In medicine this is health, in strategy victory, in architecture a house, in any other sphere something else, and in every action and pursuit the end; for it is for the sake of this that all men do whatever else they do. Therefore, if there is an end for all that we do, this will be the good achievable by action, and if there are more than one, these will be the goods achievable by action.

So the argument has by a different course reached the same point; but we must try to state this even more clearly. Since there are evidently more than one end, and we choose some of these (e.g. wealth, flutes, and in general instruments) for the sake of something else, clearly not all ends are final ends; but the chief good is evidently something final. Therefore, if there is only one final end, this will be what we are seeking, and if there are more than one, the most final of these will be what we are seeking. Now we call that which is in itself worthy of pursuit more final than that which is worthy of pursuit for the sake of something else, and that which is never desirable for the sake of something else more final than the things that are desirable both in themselves and for the sake of that other thing, and therefore we call final without qualification that which is always desirable in itself and never for the sake of something else.

Now such a thing happiness, above all else, is held to be; for this we choose always for itself and never for the sake of something else, but honour, pleasure, reason, and every virtue we choose indeed for themselves (for if nothing resulted from them we should still choose each of them), but we choose them also for the sake of happiness, judging that by means of them we shall be happy. Happiness, on the other hand, no one chooses for the sake of these, nor, in general, for anything other than itself.

From the point of view of self-sufficiency the same result seems to follow; for the final good is thought to be self-sufficient. Now by self-sufficient we do not mean that which is sufficient for a man by himself, for one who lives a solitary life, but also for parents, children, wife, and in general for his friends and fellow citizens, since man is born for citizenship. But some limit must be set to this; for if we extend our requirement to ancestors and descendants and friends' friends we are in for an infinite series. Let us examine this question, however, on another occasion; the self-sufficient we now define as that which when isolated makes life desirable and lacking in nothing; and such we think happiness to be; and further we think it most desirable of all things, without being counted as one good thing among others—if it were so counted it would clearly be made more desirable by the addition of even the least of goods; for that which is added becomes an excess of goods, and of goods the greater is always more desirable. Happiness, then, is something final and self-sufficient, and is the end of action.

Presumably, however, to say that happiness is the chief good seems a platitude, and a clearer account of what it is is still desired. This might perhaps be given, if we could first ascertain the function of man. For just as for a flute-player, a sculptor, or any artist, and, in general, for all things that have a function or activity, the good and the 'well' is thought to reside in the function, so would it seem to be for man, if he has a function. Have the carpenter, then, and the tanner certain functions or activities, and has man none? Is he born without a function? Or as eye, hand, foot, and in general each of the parts evidently has a function, may one lay it down that man similarly has a function apart from all these? What then can this be? Life seems to be common even to plants, but we are seeking what is peculiar to man. Let us exclude, therefore, the life of nutrition and growth. Next there would be a life of perception, but *it* also seems to be common even to the horse, the ox, and every animal. There remains, then, an active life of the element that has a rational principle; of this, one part has such a principle in the sense of being obedient to one, the other in the sense of possessing one and exercising thought. And, as 'life of the rational element' also has two meanings, we must state that life in the sense of activity is what we mean; for this seems to be the more proper sense of the term. Now if the function of man is an activity of soul which follows or implies a rational principle, and if we say 'a so-and-so' and 'a good so-and-so' have a function which is the same in kind, e.g. a lyre-player and a good lyre-player, and so without qualification in all cases, eminence in respect of goodness being added to the name of the function (for the function of a lyre-player is to play the lyre, and that of a good lyre-player is to do so well): if this is the case, and we state the function of man to be a certain kind of life, and this to be an activity or actions of the soul implying a rational principle, and the function of a good man to be the good and noble performance of these, and if any action is well performed when it is performed in accordance with the appropriate excellence: if this is the case, human good turns out to be activity of soul in accordance with virtue, and if there are more than one virtue, in accordance with the best and most complete.

But we must add 'in a complete life'. For one swallow does not make a summer, nor does one day; and so too one day, or a short time, does not make a man blessed and happy. . . .

Book II

1. Virtue, then, being of two kinds, intellectual and moral, intellectual virtue in the main owes both its birth and its growth to teaching (for which reason it requires experience and time), while moral virtue comes about as a result of habit, whence also its name (*ethike*) is one that is formed by a slight variation from the word *ethos* (habit). From this it is also plain that none of the moral virtues arises in us by nature; for nothing that exists by nature can form a habit contrary to its nature. For instance the stone which by nature moves downwards cannot be habituated to move upwards, not even if one tries to train it by throwing it up ten thousand times; nor can fire be habituated to move downwards, nor can anything else that by nature behaves in one way be trained to behave in another. Neither by nature, then, nor contrary to nature do the virtues arise in us; rather we are adapted by nature to receive them, and are made perfect by habit.

Again, of all the things that come to us by nature we first acquire the potentiality and later exhibit the activity (this is plain in the case of the senses; for it was not by often seeing or often hearing that we got these senses, but on the contrary we had them before we used them, and did not come to have them by using them); but the virtues we get by first exercising them, as also happens in the case of the arts as well. For the things we have to learn before we can do them, we learn by doing them, e.g. men become builders by building and lyre-players by playing the lyre; so too we become just by doing just acts, temperate by doing temperate acts, brave by doing brave acts.

This is confirmed by what happens in states; for legislators make the citizens good by forming habits in them, and this is the wish of every legislator, and those who do not effect it miss their mark, and it is in this that a good constitution differs from a bad one.

Again, it is from the same causes and by the same means that every virtue is both produced and destroyed, and similarly every art; for it is from playing the lyre that both good and bad lyre-players are produced. And the corresponding statement is true of builders and of all the rest; men will be good or bad builders as a result of building well or badly. For if this were not so, there would have been no need of a teacher, but all men would have been born good or bad at their craft. This, then, is the case with the virtues also; by doing the acts that we do in our transactions with other men we become just or unjust, and by doing the acts that we do in the presence of danger, and being habituated to feel fear or confidence, we become brave or cowardly. The same is true of appetites and feelings of anger; some men become temperate and good-tempered, others self-indulgent and irascible, by behaving in one way or the other in the appropriate circumstances. Thus, in one word, states of character arise out of like activities. This is why the activities we exhibit must be of a certain kind; it is because the states of character correspond to the differences between these. It makes no small difference, then, whether we form habits of one kind or of another from our very youth; it makes a very great difference, or rather *all* the difference.

2. Since, then, the present inquiry does not aim at theoretical knowledge like the others (for we are inquiring not in order to know what virtue is, but in order to become good, since otherwise our inquiry would have been of no use), we must examine the nature of actions, namely how we ought to do them; for these determine also the nature of the states of character that are produced, as we have said. Now, that we must act according to the right rule is a common principle and must be assumed—it will be discussed later, i.e. both what the right rule is, and how it is related to the other virtues. But this must be agreed upon beforehand, that the whole account of matters of conduct must be given in outline and not precisely, as we said at the very beginning that the accounts we demand must be in accordance with the subject-matter; matters concerned with conduct and questions of what is good for us have no fixity, any more than matters of health. The general account being of this nature, the account of particular cases is yet more lacking in exactness; for they do not fall under any art or precept but the agents themselves must in each case consider what is appropriate to the occasion, as happens also in the art of medicine or of navigation.

But though our present account is of this nature we must give what help we can. First, then, let us consider this, that it is the nature of such things to be destroyed by defect and excess, as we see in the case of strength and of health (for to gain light on things imperceptible we must use the evidence of sensible things); both excessive and defective exercise destroys the strength, and similarly drink or food which is above or below a certain amount destroys the health, while that which is proportionate both produces and increases and preserves it. So too is it, then, in the case of temperance and courage and the other virtues. For the man who flies from and fears everything and does not stand his ground against anything becomes a coward, and the man who fears nothing at all but goes to meet every danger becomes rash; and similarly the man who indulges in every pleasure and abstains from none becomes self-indulgent, while the man who shuns every pleasure, as boors do, becomes in a way insensible; temperance and courage, then, are destroyed by excess and defect, and preserved by the mean.

But not only are the sources and causes of their origination and growth the same as those of their destruction, but also the sphere of their actualization will be the same; for this is also true of the things which are more evident to sense, e.g. of strength; it is produced by taking much food and undergoing much exertion, and it is the strong

man that will be most able to do these things. So too is it with the virtues;
by abstaining from pleasures we become temperate, and it is when we
have become so that we are most able to abstain from them; and similarly
too in the case of courage; for by being habituated to despise things
that are terrible and to stand our ground against them we become brave,
and it is when we have become so that we shall be most able to stand
our ground against them.

3. We must take as a sign of states of character the pleasure or pain
that ensues on acts; for the man who abstains from bodily pleasures
and delights in this very fact is temperate, while the man who is annoyed
at it is self-indulgent, and he who stands his ground against things that
are terrible and delights in this or at least is not pained is brave, while
the man who is pained is a coward. For moral excellence is concerned
with pleasures and pains; it is on account of the pleasure that we do
bad things, and on account of the pain that we abstain from noble ones.
Hence we ought to have been brought up in a particular way from our
very youth, as Plato says, so as both to delight in and to be pained by
the things that we ought; for this is the right education.

Again, if the virtues are concerned with actions and passions, and
every passion and every action is accompanied by pleasure and pain,
for this reason also virtue will be concerned with pleasures and pains.
This is indicated also by the fact that punishment is inflicted by these
means; for it is a kind of cure, and it is the nature of cures to be effected
by contraries.

Again, as we said but lately, every state of soul has a nature relative
to and concerned with the kind of things by which it tends to be made
worse or better; but it is by reason of pleasures and pains that men
become bad, by pursuing and avoiding these—either the pleasures
and pains they ought not or when they ought not or as they ought not,
or by going wrong in one of the other similar ways that may be distinguished. Hence men even define the virtues as certain states of impas-
sivity and rest; not well, however, because they speak absolutely, and
do not say 'as one ought' and 'as one ought not' and 'when one ought
or ought not', and the other things that may be added. We assume, then,
that this kind of excellence tends to do what is best with regard to
pleasures and pains, and vice does the contrary.

The following facts also may show us that virtue and vice are concerned with these same things. There being three objects of choice
and three of avoidance, the noble, the advantageous, the pleasant, and
their contraries, the base, the injurious, the painful, about all of these
the good man tends to go right and the bad man to go wrong, and especially about pleasure; for this is common to the animals, and also
it accompanies all objects of choice; for even the noble and the advantageous appear pleasant.

Again, it has grown up with us all from our infancy; this is why it
is difficult to rub off this passion, engrained as it is in our life. And we
measure even our actions, some of us more and others less, by the rule
of pleasure and pain. For this reason, then, our whole inquiry must be
about these; for to feel delight and pain rightly or wrongly has no small
effect on our actions.

Again, it is harder to fight with pleasure than with anger, to use Heraclitus' phrase, but both art and virtue are always concerned with what is harder; for even the good is better when it is harder. Therefore for this reason also the whole concern both of virtue and of political science is with pleasures and pains; for the man who uses these well will be good, he who uses them badly bad.

That virtue, then, is concerned with pleasures and pains, and that by the acts from which it arises it is both increased and, if they are done differently, destroyed, and that the acts from which it arose are those in which it actualizes itself—let this be taken as said.

4. The question might be asked, what we mean by saying that we must become just by doing just acts, and temperate by doing temperate acts; for if men do just and temperate acts, they are already just and temperate, exactly as, if they do what is in accordance with the laws of grammar and of music, they are grammarians and musicians.

Or is this not true even of the arts? It is possible to do something that is in accordance with the laws of grammar, either by chance or at the suggestion of another. A man will be a grammarian, then, only when he has both done something grammatical and done it grammatically; and this means doing it in accordance with the grammatical knowledge in himself.

Again, the case of the arts and that of the virtues are not similar; for the products of the arts have their goodness in themselves, so that it is enough that they should have a certain character, but if the acts that are in accordance with the virtues have themselves a certain character it does not follow that they are done justly or temperately. The agent also must be in a certain condition when he does them; in the first place he must have knowledge, secondly he must choose the acts, and choose them for their own sakes, and thirdly his action must proceed from a firm and unchangeable character. These are not reckoned in as conditions of the possession of the arts, except the bare knowledge; but as a condition of the possession of the virtues knowledge has little or no weight, while the other conditions count not for a little but for everything, i.e. the very conditions which result from often doing just and temperate acts.

Actions, then, are called just and temperate when they are such as the just or the temperate man would do; but it is not the man who does these that is just and temperate, but the man who also does them *as* just and temperate men do them. It is well said, then, that it is by doing just acts that the just man is produced, and by doing temperate acts the temperate man; without doing these no one would have even a prospect of becoming good.

But most people do not do these, but take refuge in theory and think they are being philosophers and will become good in this way, behaving somewhat like patients who listen attentively to their doctors, but do none of the things they are ordered to do. As the latter will not be made well in body by such a course of treatment, the former will not be made well in soul by such a course of philosophy.

5. Next we must consider what virtue is. Since things that are found in the soul are of three kinds—passions, faculties, states of character,

virtue must be one of these. By passions I mean appetite, anger, fear, confidence, envy, joy, friendly feeling, hatred, longing, emulation, pity, and in general the feelings that are accompanied by pleasure or pain; by faculties the things in virtue of which we are said to be capable of feeling these, e.g. of becoming angry or being pained or feeling pity; by states of character the things in virtue of which we stand well or badly with reference to the passions, e.g. with reference to anger we stand badly if we feel it violently or too weakly, and well if we feel it moderately; and similarly with reference to the other passions.

Now neither the virtues nor the vices are *passions,* because we are not called good or bad on the ground of our passions, but are so called on the ground of our virtues and our vices, and because we are neither praised nor blamed for our passions (for the man who feels fear or anger is not praised, nor is the man who simply feels anger blamed, but the man who feels it in a certain way), but for our virtues and our vices we *are* praised or blamed.

Again, we feel anger and fear without choice, but the virtues are modes of choice or involve choice. Further, in respect of the passions we are said to be moved, but in respect of the virtues and the vices we are said not to be moved but to be disposed in a particular way.

For these reasons also they are not *faculties;* for we are neither called good nor bad, nor praised nor blamed, for the simple capacity of feeling the passions; again, we have the faculties by nature, but we are not made good or bad by nature; we have spoken of this before.

If, then, the virtues are neither passions nor faculties, all that remains is that they should be *states of character.*

Thus we have stated what virtue is in respect of its genus.

6. We must, however, not only describe virtue as a state of character, but also say what sort of state it is. We may remark, then, that every virtue or excellence both brings into good condition the thing of which it is the excellence and makes the work of that thing be done well; e.g. the excellence of the eye makes both the eye and its work good; for it is by the excellence of the eye that we see well. Similarly the excellence of the horse makes a horse both good in itself and good at running and at carrying its rider and at awaiting the attack of the enemy. Therefore, if this is true in every case, the virtue of man also will be the state of character which makes a man good and which makes him do his own work well.

How this is to happen we have stated already, but it will be made plain also by the following consideration of the specific nature of virtue. In everything that is continuous and divisible it is possible to take more, less, or an equal amount, and that either in terms of the thing itself or relatively to us; and the equal is an intermediate between excess and defect. By the intermediate in the object I mean that which is equidistant from each of the extremes, which is one and the same for all men; by the intermediate relatively to us that which is neither too much nor too little—and this is not one, nor the same for all. For instance, if ten is many and two is few, six is the intermediate, taken in terms of the object; for it exceeds and is exceeded by an equal amount; this is intermediate according to arithmetical proportion. But the intermediate relatively to us is not to be taken so; if ten pounds are too much for a particular person to eat and two too little, it does not follow that the trainer will order six pounds; for this also is perhaps too much for the person who is to take it, or too little—too little for Milo,[4] too much for the beginner in athletic exercises. The same is true of running and wrestling. Thus a master of any art avoids excess and defect, but seeks the intermediate and chooses this—the intermediate not in the object but relatively to us.

If it is thus, then, that every art does its work well—by looking to the intermediate and judging its works by this standard (so that we often say of good works of art that it is not possible either to take away or to add anything, implying that excess and defect destroy the goodness of works of art, while the mean preserves it; and good artists, as we say, look to this in their work), and if, further, virtue is more exact and better than any art, as nature also is, then virtue must have the quality of aiming at the intermediate. I mean moral virtue; for it is this that is concerned with passions and actions, and in these there is excess, defect, and the intermediate. For instance, both fear and confidence and appetite and anger and pity and in general pleasure and pain may be felt both too much and too little, and in both cases not well; but to feel them at the right times, with reference to the right objects, towards the right people, with the right motive, and in the right way, is what is both intermediate and best, and this is characteristic of virtue. Similarly with regard to actions also there is excess, defect, and the intermediate. Now virtue is concerned with passions and actions, in which excess is a form of failure and so is defect, while the intermediate is praised and is a form of success; and being praised and being successful are both characteristics of virtue. Therefore virtue is a kind of mean, since, as we have seen, it aims at what is intermediate.

Again, it is possible to fail in many ways (for evil belongs to the class of the unlimited, as the Pythagoreans conjectured, and good to that of the limited), while to succeed is possible only in one way (for which reason also one is easy and the other difficult—to miss the mark easy, to hit it difficult); for these reasons also, then, excess and defect are characteristic of vice, and the mean of virtue;

For men are good in but one way, but bad in many.

Virtue, then, is a state of character concerned with choice, lying in a mean, i.e. the mean relative to us, this being determined by a rational principle, and by that principle by which the man of practical wisdom would determine it. Now it is a mean between two vices, that which depends on excess and that which depends on defect; and again it is a mean because the vices respectively fall short of or exceed what is right in both passions and actions, while virtue both finds and chooses that which is intermediate. Hence in respect of its substance and the definition which states its essence virtue is a mean, with regard to what is best and right an extreme.

---

[4]A famous Greek wrestler.

But not every action nor every passion admits of a mean; for some have names that already imply badness, e.g. spite, shamelessness, envy, and in the case of actions adultery, theft, murder; for all of these and suchlike things imply by their names that they are themselves bad, and not the excesses or deficiencies of them. It is not possible, then, ever to be right with regard to them; one must always be wrong. Nor does goodness or badness with regard to such things depend on committing adultery with the right woman, at the right time, and in the right way, but simply to do any of them is to go wrong. It would be equally absurd, then, to expect that in unjust, cowardly, and voluptuous action there should be a mean, an excess, and a deficiency; for at that rate there would be a mean of excess and of deficiency, and excess of excess, and a deficiency of deficiency. But as there is no excess and deficiency of temperance and courage because what is intermediate is in a sense an extreme, so too of the actions we have mentioned there is no mean nor any excess and deficiency, but however they are done they are wrong; for in general there is neither a mean of excess and deficiency, nor excess and deficiency of a mean.

Book X

7. If happiness is activity in accordance with virtue, it is reasonable that it should be in accordance with the highest virtue; and this will be that of the best thing in us. Whether it be reason or something else that is this element which is thought to be our natural ruler and guide and to take thought of things noble and divine, whether it be itself also divine or only the most divine element in us, the activity of this in accordance with its proper virtue will be perfect happiness. That this activity is contemplative we have already said.

Now this would seem to be in agreement both with what we said before and with the truth. For, firstly, this activity is the best (since not only is reason the best thing in us, but the objects of reason are the best of knowable objects); and, secondly, it is the most continuous, since we can contemplate truth more continuously than we can *do* anything. And we think happiness has pleasure mingled with it, but the activity of philosophic wisdom is admittedly the pleasantest of virtuous activities; at all events the pursuit of it is thought to offer pleasures marvellous for their purity and their enduringness, and it is to be expected that those who know will pass their time more pleasantly than those who inquire. And the self-sufficiency that is spoken of must belong most to the contemplative activity. For while a philosopher, as well as a just man or one possessing any other virtue, needs the necessaries of life, when they are sufficiently equipped with things of that sort the just man needs people towards whom and with whom he shall act justly, and the temperate man, the brave man, and each of the others is in the same case, but the philosopher, even when by himself, can contemplate truth, and the better the wiser he is; he can perhaps do so better if he has fellow-workers, but still he is the most self-sufficient. And this activity alone would seem to be loved for its own sake; for nothing arises from it apart from the contemplating, while from practical activities we gain more or less apart from the action. And happiness is thought to depend on leisure; for we are busy that we may have leisure, and make war that we may live in peace. Now the activity of the practical virtues is exhibited in political or military affairs, but the actions concerned with these seem to be unleisurely. Warlike actions are completely so (for no one chooses to be at war, or provokes war, for the sake of being at war; any one would seem absolutely murderous if he were to make enemies of his friends in order to bring about battle and slaughter); but the action of the statesman is also unleisurely, and—apart from the political action itself—aims at despotic power and honours, or at all events happiness, for him and his fellow citizens—a happiness different from political action, and evidently sought as being different. So if among virtuous actions political and military actions are distinguished by nobility and greatness, and these are unleisurely and aim at an end and are not desirable for their own sake, but the activity of reason, which is contemplative, seems both to be superior in serious worth and to aim at no end beyond itself, and to have its pleasure proper to itself (and this augments the activity), and the self-sufficiency, leisureliness, unweariedness (so far as this is possible for man), and all the other attributes ascribed to the supremely happy man are evidently those connected with this activity, it follows that this will be the complete happiness of man, if it be allowed a complete term of life (for none of the attributes of happiness is *in*complete).

But such a life would be too high for man; for it is not in so far as he is man that he will live so, but in so far as something divine is present in him; and by so much as this is superior to our composite nature is its activity superior to that which is the exercise of the other kind of virtue. If reason is divine, then, in comparison with man, the life according to it is divine in comparison with human life. But we must not follow those who advise us, being men, to think of human things, and, being mortal, of mortal things, but must, so far as we can, make ourselves immortal, and strain every nerve to live in accordance with the best thing in us; for even if it be small in bulk, much more does it in power and worth surpass everything. This would seem, too, to be each man himself, since it is the authoritative and better part of him. It would be strange, then, if he were to choose not the life of his self but that of something else. And what we said before will apply now; that which is proper to each thing is by nature best and most pleasant for each thing; for man, therefore, the life according to reason is best and pleasantest, since reason more than anything else *is* man. This life therefore is also the happiest.

8. But in a secondary degree the life in accordance with the other kind of virtue is happy; for the activities in accordance with this befit our human estate. Just and brave acts, and other virtuous acts, we do in relation to each other, observing our respective duties with regard to contracts and services and all manner of actions and with regard to passions; and all of these seem to be typically human. Some of them seem even to arise from the body, and virtue of character to be in many ways bound up with the passions. Practical wisdom, too, is linked to virtue

of character, and this to practical wisdom, since the principles of practical wisdom are in accordance with the moral virtues and rightness in morals is in accordance with practical wisdom. Being connected with the passions also, the moral virtues must belong to our composite nature; and the virtues of our composite nature are human; so, therefore, are the life and the happiness which correspond to these. The excellence of the reason is a thing apart; we must be content to say this much about it, for to describe it precisely is a task greater than our purpose requires. It would seem, however, also to need external equipment but little, or less than moral virtue does. Grant that both need the necessaries, and do so equally, even if the statesman's work is the more concerned with the body and things of that sort; for there will be little difference there; but in what they need for the exercise of their activities there will be much difference. The liberal man will need money for the doing of his liberal deeds, and the just man too will need it for the returning of services (for wishes are hard to discern, and even people who are not just pretend to wish to act justly); and the brave man will need power if he is to accomplish any of the acts that correspond to his virtue, and the temperate man will need opportunity; for how else is either he or any of the others to be recognized? It is debated, too, whether the will or the deed is more essential to virtue, which is assumed to involve both; it is surely clear that its perfection involves both; but for deeds many things are needed, and more, the greater and nobler the deeds are. But the man who is contemplating the truth needs no such thing, at least with a view to the exercise of his activity; indeed they are, one may say, even hindrances, at all events to his contemplation; but in so far as he is a man and lives with a number of people, he chooses to do virtuous acts; he will therefore need such aids to living a human life.

But that perfect happiness is a contemplative activity will appear from the following consideration as well. We assume the gods to be above all other beings blessed and happy; but what sort of actions must we assign to them? Acts of justice? Will not the gods seem absurd if they make contracts and return deposits, and so on? Acts of a brave man, then, confronting dangers and running risks because it is noble to do so? Or liberal acts? To whom will they give? It will be strange if they are really to have money or anything of the kind. And what would their temperate acts be? Is not such praise tasteless, since they have no bad appetites? If we were to run through them all, the circumstances of action would be found trivial and unworthy of gods. Still, every one supposes that they *live* and therefore that they are active; we cannot suppose them to sleep like Endymion.[5] Now if you take away from a living being action, and still more production, what is left but contemplation? Therefore the activity of God, which surpasses all others in blessedness, must be contemplative; and of human activities, therefore, that which is most akin to this must be most of the nature of happiness.

This is indicated, too, by the fact that the other animals have no share in happiness, being completely deprived of such activity. For while the

---

[5]In Greek mythology, Endymion was a mortal, the most beautiful of men, who was loved by the goddess Selene (the Moon). By her contrivance he was thrown into a perpetual sleep, and the moon descended every night to embrace him.

whole life of the gods is blessed, and that of men too in so far as some likeness of such activity belongs to them, none of the other animals is happy, since they in no way share in contemplation. Happiness extends, then, just so far as contemplation does, and those to whom contemplation more fully belongs are more truly happy, not as a mere concomitant but in virtue of the contemplation; for this is in itself precious. Happiness, therefore, must be some form of contemplation.

But, being a man, one will also need external prosperity; for our nature is not self-sufficient for the purpose of contemplation, but our body also must be healthy and must have food and other attention. Still, we must not think that the man who is to be happy will need many things or great things, merely because he cannot be supremely happy without external goods; for self-sufficiency and action do not involve excess, and we can do noble acts without ruling earth and sea; for even with moderate advantages one can act virtuously (this is manifest enough; for private persons are thought to do worthy acts no less than despots —indeed even more); and it is enough that we should have so much as that; for the life of the man who is active in accordance with virtue will be happy. Solon, too, was perhaps sketching well the happy man when he described him as moderately furnished with externals but as having done (as Solon thought) the noblest acts, and lived temperately;[6] for one can with but moderate possessions do what one ought. Anaxagoras[7] also seems to have supposed the happy man not to be rich nor a despot, when he said that he would not be surprised if the happy man were to seem to most people a strange person; for they judge by externals, since these are all they perceive. The opinions of the wise seem, then, to harmonize with our arguments. But while even such things carry some conviction, the truth in practical matters is discerned from the facts of life; for these are the decisive factor. We must therefore survey what we have already said, bringing it to the test of the facts of life, and if it harmonizes with the facts we must accept it, but if it clashes with them we must suppose it to be mere theory. Now he who exercises his reason and cultivates it seems to be both in the best state of mind and most dear to the gods. For if the gods have any care for human affairs, as they are thought to have, it would be reasonable both that they should delight in that which was best and most akin to them (i.e. reason) and that they should reward those who love and honour this most, as caring for the things that are dear to them and acting both rightly and nobly. And that all these attributes belong most of all to the philosopher is manifest. He, therefore, is the dearest to the gods. And he who is that will presumably be also the happiest; so that in this way too the philosopher will more than any other be happy.

9. If these matters and the virtues, and also friendship and pleasure, have been dealt with sufficiently in outline, are we to suppose that our programme has reached its end? Surely, as the saying goes, where there are things to be done the end is not to survey and recognize the various things, but rather to do them; with regard to virtue, then, it is not enough

---

[6]See Herodotus, I, 30.
[7]Greek philosopher of the fifth century B.C.

to know, but we must try to have and use it, or try any other way there may be of becoming good. Now if arguments were in themselves enough to make men good, they would justly, as Theognis[8] says, have won very great rewards, and such rewards should have been provided; but as things are, while they seem to have power to encourage and stimulate the generous-minded among our youth, and to make a character which is gently born, and a true lover of what is noble, ready to be possessed by virtue, they are not able to encourage the many to nobility and goodness. For these do not by nature obey the sense of shame, but only fear, and do not abstain from bad acts because of their baseness but through fear of punishment; living by passion they pursue their own pleasures and the means to them, and avoid the opposite pains, and have not even a conception of what is noble and truly pleasant, since they have never tasted it. What argument would remould such people? It is hard, if not impossible, to remove by argument the traits that have long since been incorporated in the character; and perhaps we must be content if, when all the influences by which we are thought to become good are present, we get some tincture of virtue.

Now some think that we are made good by nature, others by habituation, others by teaching. Nature's part evidently does not depend on us, but as a result of some divine causes is present in those who are truly fortunate; while argument and teaching, we may suspect, are not powerful with all men, but the soul of the student must first have been cultivated by means of habits for noble joy and noble hatred, like earth which is to nourish the seed. For he who lives as passion directs will not hear argument that dissuades him, nor understand it if he does; and how can we persuade one in such a state to change his ways? And in general passion seems to yield not to argument but to force. The character, then, must somehow be there already with a kinship to virtue, loving what is noble and hating what is base.

But it is difficult to get from youth up a right training for virtue if one has not been brought up under right laws; for to live temperately and hardily is not pleasant to most people, especially when they are young. For this reason their nurture and occupations should be fixed by law; for they will not be painful when they have become customary. But it is surely not enough that when they are young they should get the right nurture and attention; since they must, even when they are grown up, practise and be habituated to them, we shall need laws for this as well, and generally speaking to cover the whole of life; for most people obey necessity rather than argument, and punishments rather than the sense of what is noble.

This is why some think that legislators ought to stimulate men to virtue and urge them forward by the motive of the noble, on the assumption that those who have been well advanced by the formation of habits will attend to such influences; and that punishments and penalties should be imposed on those who disobey and are of inferior nature, while the incurably bad should be completely banished. A good man (they think), since he lives with his mind fixed on what is noble, will submit to argu-

---

[8]Greek lyric poet of the sixth century B.C.

ment, while a bad man, whose desire is for pleasure, is corrected by pain like a beast of burden. This is, too, why they say the pains inflicted should be those that are most opposed to the pleasures such men love.

However that may be, if (as we have said) the man who is to be good must be well trained and habituated, and go on to spend his time in worthy occupations and neither willingly nor unwillingly do bad actions, and if this can be brought about if men live in accordance with a sort of reason and right order, provided this has force,—if this be so, the paternal command indeed has not the required force or compulsive power (nor in general has the command of one man, unless he be a king or something similar), but the law *has* compulsive power, while it is at the same time a rule proceeding from a sort of practical wisdom and reason. And while people hate *men* who oppose their impulses, even if they oppose them rightly, the law in its ordaining of what is good is not burdensome. . . .

Politics

Book I

1. Every state is a community of some kind, and every community is established with a view to some good: for mankind always act in order to obtain that which they think good. But, if all communities aim at some good, the state or political community, which is the highest of all, and which embraces all the rest, aims at good in a greater degree than any other, and at the highest good.

Some people think that the qualifications of a statesman, king, householder, and master are the same, and that they differ, not in kind, but only in the number of their subjects. For example, the ruler over a few is called a master; over more, the manager of a household; over a still larger number, a statesman or king as if there were no difference between a great household and a small state. The distinction which is made between the king and the statesman is as follows: When the government is personal, the ruler is a king; when, according to the rules of the political science, the citizens rule and are ruled in turn, then he is called a statesman.

But all this is a mistake; for governments differ in kind, as will be evident to any one who considers the matter according to the method which has hitherto guided us. As in other departments of science, so in

From the *Works of Aristotle, Vol. X: Politica,* translated by Benjamin Jowett. Reprinted by permission of the Clarendon Press, Oxford.

politics, the compound should always be resolved into the simple elements or least parts of the whole. We must therefore look at the elements of which the state is composed, in order that we may see in what the different kinds of rule differ from one another, and whether any scientific result can be attained about each one of them.

2. He who thus considers things in their first growth and origin, whether a state or anything else, will obtain the clearest view of them. In the first place there must be a union of those who cannot exist without each other; namely, of male and female, that the race may continue (and this is a union which is formed, not of deliberate purpose, but because in common with other animals and with plants, mankind have a natural desire to leave behind them an image of themselves), and of natural ruler and subject, that both may be preserved. For that which can foresee by the exercise of mind is by nature intended to be lord and master, and that which can with its body give effect to such foresight is a subject, and by nature a slave; hence master and slave have the same interest. Now nature has distinguished between the female and the slave. For she is not niggardly, like the smith who fashions the Delphian knife for many uses; she makes each thing for a single use, and every instrument is best made when intended for one and not for many uses. But among barbarians no distinction is made between women and slaves, because there is no natural ruler among them: they are a community of slaves, male and female. Wherefore the poets say,—

'It is meet that Hellenes should rule over barbarians';

as if they thought that the barbarian and the slave were by nature one.

Out of these two relationships between man and woman, master and slave, the first thing to arise is the family, and Hesiod is right when he says,—

'First house and wife and an ox for the plough',

for the ox is the poor man's slave. The family is the association established by nature for the supply of men's everyday wants, and the members of it are called by Charondas[1] 'companions of the cupboard', and by Epimenides the Cretan,[2] 'companions of the manger'. But when several families are united, and the association aims at something more than the supply of daily needs, the first society to be formed is the village. And the most natural form of the village appears to be that of a colony from the family, composed of the children and grandchildren, who are said to be 'suckled with the same milk'. And this is the reason why Hellenic states were originally governed by kings; because the Hellenes were under royal rule before they came together, as the barbarians still are. Every family is ruled by the eldest, and therefore in the colonies of the family the kingly form of government prevailed because they were of the same blood. As Homer says:

[1] A Sicilian legislator of the seventh century B.C.
[2] A semilegendary poet and prophet of the seventh century B.C.

'Each one gives law to his children and to his wives.'

For they lived dispersedly, as was the manner in ancient times. Where-fore men say that the Gods have a king, because they themselves either are or were in ancient times under the rule of a king. For they imagine, not only the forms of the Gods, but their ways of life to be like their own.

When several villages are united in a single complete community, large enough to be nearly or quite self-sufficing, the state comes into existence, originating in the bare needs of life, and continuing in exist-ence for the sake of a good life. And therefore, if the earlier forms of society are natural, so is the state, for it is the end of them, and the nature of a thing is its end. For what each thing is when fully developed, we call its nature, whether we are speaking of a man, a horse, or a family. Besides, the final cause and end of a thing is the best, and to be self-sufficing is the end and the best.

Hence it is evident that the state is a creation of nature, and that man is by nature a political animal. And he who by nature and not by mere accident is without a state, is either a bad man or above humanity; he is like the

'Tribeless, lawless, hearthless one,'

whom Homer denounces—the natural outcast is forthwith a lover of war; he may be compared to an isolated piece at draughts.

Now, that man is more of a political animal than bees or any other gregarious animals is evident. Nature, as we often say, makes nothing in vain, and man is the only animal whom she has endowed with the gift of speech. And whereas mere voice is but an indication of pleasure or pain, and is therefore found in other animals (for their nature attains to the perception of pleasure and pain and the intimation of them to one another, and no further), the power of speech is intended to set forth the expedient and inexpedient, and therefore likewise the just and the unjust. And it is a characteristic of man that he alone has any sense of good and evil, of just and unjust, and the like, and the association of living beings who have this sense makes a family and a state.

Further, the state is by nature clearly prior to the family and to the individual, since the whole is of necessity prior to the part; for example, if the whole body be destroyed, there will be no foot or hand, except in an equivocal sense, as we might speak of a stone hand; for when destroyed the hand will be no better than that. But things are defined by their working and power; and we ought not to say that they are the same when they no longer have their proper quality, but only that they have the same name. The proof that the state is a creation of nature and prior to the individual is that the individual, when isolated, is not self-sufficing; and therefore he is like a part in relation to the whole. But he who is unable to live in society, or who has no need because he is sufficient for himself, must be either a beast or a god: he is no part of a state. A social instinct is implanted in all men by nature, and yet he who first founded the state was the greatest of benefactors. For man, when perfected, is the best of animals, but, when separated from law and justice, he is the worst of all; since armed injustice is the more dangerous, and he is equipped at birth with arms, meant to be used by intelligence and virtue, which he may use for the worst ends. Wherefore, if he have not virtue, he is the most unholy and the most savage of animals, and the most full of lust and gluttony. But justice is the bond of men in states, for the administration of justice, which is the determination of what is just, is the principle of order in political society.

Book II

1. Our purpose is to consider what form of political community is best of all for those who are most able to realize their ideal of life. We must therefore examine not only this but other constitutions, both such as actually exist in well-governed states, and any theoretical forms which are held in esteem; that what is good and useful may be brought to light. And let no one suppose that in seeking for something beyond them we are anxious to make a sophistical display at any cost; we only undertake this inquiry because all the constitutions with which we are acquainted are faulty.

We will begin with the natural beginning of the subject. Three alternatives are conceivable: The members of a state must either have (1) all things or (2) nothing in common, or (3) some things in common and some not. That they should have nothing in common is clearly impossible, for the constitution is a community, and must at any rate have a common place—one city will be in one place, and the citizens are those who share in that one city. But should a well-ordered state have all things, as far as may be, in common, or some only and not others? For the citizens might conceivably have wives and children and property in common, as Socrates proposes in the *Republic* of Plato. Which is better, our present condition, or the proposed new order of society?

2. There are many difficulties in the community of women. And the principle on which Socrates rests the necessity of such an institution evidently is not established by his arguments. Further, as a means to the end which he ascribes to the state, the scheme, taken literally, is impracticable, and how we are to interpret it is nowhere precisely stated. I am speaking of the premiss from which the argument of Socrates proceeds, 'that the greater the unity of the state the better'. Is it not obvious that a state may at length attain such a degree of unity as to be no longer a state?—since the nature of a state is to be a plurality, and in tending to greater unity, from being a state, it becomes a family, and from being a family, an individual; for the family may be said to be more one than the state, and the individual than the family. So that we ought not to attain this greatest unity even if we could, for it would be the destruction of the state. Again, a state is not made up only of so many men, but of different kinds of men; for similars do not constitute a state. It is not like a military alliance. The usefulness of the latter depends upon its quantity even where there is no difference in quality (for mutual

protection is the end aimed at), just as a greater weight of anything is more useful than a less (in like manner, a state differs from a nation, when the nation has not its population organized in villages, but lives an Arcadian sort of life); but the elements out of which a unity is to be formed differ in kind. Wherefore the principle of compensation ... is the salvation of states. Even among freemen and equals this is a principle which must be maintained, for they cannot all rule together, but must change at the end of a year or some other period of time or in some order of succession. The result is that upon this plan they all govern; just as if shoemakers and carpenters were to exchange their occupations, and the same persons did not always continue shoemakers and carpenters. And since it is better that this should be so in politics as well, it is clear that while there should be continuance of the same persons in power where this is possible, yet where this is not possible by reason of the natural equality of the citizens, and at the same time it is just that all should share in the government (whether to govern be a good thing or a bad), an approximation to this is that equals should in turn retire from office, and should, apart from official position, be treated alike. Thus the one party rule and the others are ruled in turn, as if they were no longer the same persons. In like manner when they hold office there is a variety in the offices held. Hence it is evident that a city is not by nature one in that sense which some persons affirm; and that what is said to be the greatest good of cities is in reality their destruction; but surely the good of things must be that which preserves them. Again, in another point of view, this extreme unification of the state is clearly not good; for a family is more self-sufficing than an individual, and a city than a family, and a city only comes into being when the community is large enough to be self-sufficing. If then self-sufficiency is to be desired, the lesser degree of unity is more desirable than the greater.

5. ... The error of Socrates must be attributed to the false notion of unity from which he starts. Unity there should be, both of the family and of the state, but in some respects only. For there is a point at which a state may attain such a degree of unity as to be no longer a state, or at which, without actually ceasing to exist, it will become an inferior state, like harmony passing into unison, or rhythm which has been reduced to a single foot. The state, as I was saying, is a plurality, which should be united and made into a community by education; and it is strange that the author of a system of education which he thinks will make the state virtuous, should expect to improve his citizens by regulations of this sort, and not by philosophy or by customs and laws, like those which prevail at Sparta and Crete respecting common meals, whereby the legislator has made property common. Let us remember that we should not disregard the experience of ages; in the multitude of years these things, if they were good, would certainly not have been unknown; for almost everything has been found out, although sometimes they are not put together; in other cases men do not use the knowledge which they have. Great light would be thrown on this subject if we could see such a form of government in the actual process of construction; for the legislator could not form a state at all without distributing and dividing its constituents into associations for common meals, and into

phratries³ and tribes. But all this legislation ends only in forbidding agriculture to the guardians, a prohibition which the Lacedaemonians try to enforce already.

But, indeed, Socrates has not said, nor is it easy to decide, what in such a community will be the general form of the state. The citizens who are not guardians are the majority, and about them nothing has been determined: are the husbandmen, too, to have their property in common? Or is each individual to have his own? and are their wives and children to be individual or common? If, like the guardians, they are to have all things in common, in what do they differ from them, or what will they gain by submitting to their government? Or, upon what principle would they submit, unless indeed the governing class adopt the ingenious policy of the Cretans, who give their slaves the same institutions as their own, but forbid them gymnastic exercises and the possession of arms. If, on the other hand, the inferior classes are to be like other cities in respect of marriage and property, what will be the form of the community? Must it not contain two states in one, each hostile to the other? He makes the guardians into a mere occupying garrison, while the husbandmen and artisans and the rest are the real citizens. But if so the suits and quarrels, and all the evils which Socrates affirms to exist in other states, will exist equally among them. He says indeed that, having so good an education, the citizens will not need many laws, for example laws about the city or about the markets; but then he confines his education to the guardians. Again, he makes the husbandmen owners of the property upon condition of their paying a tribute. But in that case they are likely to be much more unmanageable and conceited than the Helots, or Penestae,⁴ or slaves in general. And whether community of wives and property be necessary for the lower equally with the higher class or not, and the questions akin to this, what will be the education, form of government, laws of the lower class, Socrates has nowhere determined: neither is it easy to discover this, nor is their character of small importance if the common life of the guardians is to be maintained.

Again, if Socrates makes the women common, and retains private property, the men will see to the fields, but who will see to the house? And who will do so if the agricultural class have both their property and their wives in common? Once more: it is absurd to argue, from the analogy of the animals, that men and women should follow the same pursuits, for animals have not to manage a household. The government, too, as constituted by Socrates, contains elements of danger; for he makes the same persons always rule. And if this is often a cause of disturbance among the meaner sort, how much more among high-spirited warriors? But that the persons whom he makes rulers must be the same is evident; for the gold which the God mingles in the souls of men is not at one time given to one, at another time to another, but always to the same: as he says, 'God mingles gold in some, and silver in others, from their very

---

³At Athens, in primitive times, a clan consisting of a noble family and its dependents, who shared in the family religious cult. Later, the *phratria* (brotherhoods) were religious organizations.
⁴The terms applied, respectively, to the slave classes in Sparta and in Thessaly.

birth; but brass and iron in those who are meant to be artisans and husbandmen.' Again, he deprives the guardians even of happiness, and says that the legislator ought to make the whole state happy. But the whole cannot be happy unless most, or all, or some of its parts enjoy happiness. In this respect happiness is not like the even principle in numbers, which may exist only in the whole, but in neither of the parts; not so happiness. And if the guardians are not happy, who are? Surely not the artisans, or the common people. The Republic of which Socrates discourses has all these difficulties, and others quite as great.

Comments / on Aristotle

Aristotle's ethics is, at all points, consistent with his metaphysics. Indeed, his metaphysical theories are themselves the expression of an ethical optimism. He believes in the scientific importance of final causes, and this implies the belief that purpose governs the course of development in the universe. He thinks that changes are, in the main, such as embody an increase of organization or "form," and at bottom virtuous actions are those that favour this tendency. It is true that a great deal of his practical ethics is not particularly philosophical, but merely the result of observation of human affairs; but this part of his doctrine, though it may be independent of his metaphysics, is not inconsistent with it.

BERTRAND RUSSELL (1945)

His thought, no less than Plato's, is governed by the idea of aspiration, inherited by his master from Socrates—the idea that the true cause or explanation of things is to be sought, not in the beginning, but in the end. Aristotelian philosophy remains a philosophy of final causes. . . . Aristotle's thought is at its best in the biological treatises and in the *Ethics*. The reason is that a philosophy of final causes is most illuminating in the study of animal life and of the moral nature of man. . . . But when he passes beyond biology to the whole range of physical science, he cannot dispense with a God; and this God is precisely the ultimate goal of aspiration. So deeply is this idea rooted in Aristotle's mind that it is invoked to account for all motion and change in Nature.

F. M. CORNFORD (1932)

Aristotle accepts from "the many" the view that the end is *eudaemonia*. The corresponding adjective originally meant "watched over by a good genius," but in ordinary Greek usage the word means just good fortune, often with special reference to external prosperity. The conventional translation "happiness" is unsuitable in the *Ethics;* for whereas "happiness" means a state of feeling, differing from "pleasure" only by its suggestion of permanence, depth, and serenity, Aristotle insists that *eudaemonia* is a kind of activity; that it is not any kind of pleasure, though pleasure naturally accompanies it. The more non-committal translation "well-being" is therefore better. If the question be asked whether Aristotle was a hedonist, it is better to go by his repeated and deliberate statement that the end of life is activity rather than by his use, for want of a better word, of one which suggests not action but feeling.

W. D. ROSS (1923)

When Aristotle speaks of virtue as a mean, he is not thinking of a mean that has to be calculated arithmetically: that is why he says in his definition "relatively to us." We cannot determine what is excess, what mean, and what defect by hard-and-fast, mathematical rules: so much depends on the character of the feeling or action in question: in some cases it may be preferable to err on the side of excess rather than on that of defect, while in other cases the reverse may be true. Nor, of course, should the Aristotelian doctrine of the mean be taken as equivalent to an exaltation of mediocrity in the moral life, for as far as excellence is concerned virtue is an extreme: it is in respect of its essence and its definition that it is a mean.

FREDERICK COPLESTON (1946)

The excellence or virtue of a man will be to live efficiently, but since life can be manifested at different levels, if we would know what man's work is we must ask whether there is not some form of life which can only be lived by man. Now the life which consists in merely feeding and growing belongs to all organisms and can be lived with equal vigour by them all. There is, however, a kind of life which can only be lived by man—the life which consists in conscious direction of one's actions by a rule. It is the work of man to live this kind of life, and his happiness consists in living it efficiently and well.

A. E. TAYLOR (1919)

Aristotle rejects the conception of freedom as self-realization through being able to do as one pleases. He also makes plain in many passages that democracy, even in moderation, is far from his conception of the ideal form of government. But while he does not think that all freeborn men are equally qualified for citizenship, or that the freedom of the citizen consists in doing as he pleases, Aristotle's remark to the effect that citizens should regard the constitution as their salvation does indicate that, in his own view, the status of citizenship under constitutional government is one of political liberty.

MORTIMER J. ADLER (1958)

Lucretius
96?—55? B.C.

The Greek world before the conquests of Alexander the Great had been largely self-contained. Secure in their belief that Greek men were superior to other peoples and that the Greek city-states were superior to other forms of civilization and convinced that the ideals of Greek culture in themselves provided the answers to the problems of daily living, philosophers like Plato, and Aristotle after him, had primarily concerned themselves with the large, abstract questions of philosophy. Devoting their best efforts to the discovery of the nature of knowledge, of reason, and of experience itself, pre-Alexandrian Greek philosophers had aimed mainly at helping men understand their universe, not at making them feel at home in it.

But in the expanded Hellenistic world (the term applied to the regions under the influence of Greek culture after the conquests of Alexander), a world that soon became chaotic after Alexander's death, thoughtful men were less certain of themselves and of the inherent superiority of their culture. The circumstances of life and civilization itself offered less grounds for certitude about the purpose and functions of human existence. Hellenistic philosophers devoted their energies to more practical matters than their predecessors; they were concerned not so much with explaining the bases underlying human experience as with equipping men to cope with it. Epistemology and metaphysics gave way to ethics as the prime concern of philosophers, who concentrated their powers on devising sets of principles that would enable men to confront successfully the uncertainties posed by Hellenistic civilization.

The two most important branches of Hellenistic philosophy were Epicureanism and Stoicism. Both developed schools of knowledge based on the disciplines of logic, physics, and ethics, but the systems of logic and physics in both were designed mainly to support a system of ethics that would make man at home in an unfriendly, uncertain world. To reach this end, the Stoics emphasized the internal resources inherent in man himself, aiming in this way at a state of individual self-reliance that would make the external world seem immaterial. The Epicureans, in almost direct contrast, emphasized the complete materialism of everything external to man—and of man himself—on the principle that since anything objective is knowable, then when everything is objective, everything is knowable. In a world containing only concrete objects, a world composed of matter and space alone, it was possible for men to have certain knowledge about the circumstances of their existence.

Epicureanism takes its name from its founder, Epicurus (341—270 B.C.), a native of the Greek Aegean island of Samos who established a philosophical school in Athens toward the end of the fourth century B.C. and soon acquired a large and devoted following. The physical basis of his system was derived from the work of the Ionian philosophers Leucippus and Democritus, whose theories about the atomic structure of the universe provided Epicurus with a scientific justification for his philosophical materialism. In an atomic universe, only atoms could be eternal; spiritual conceptions had no intrinsic, and therefore no permanent, reality. Man had only one life to live—and this amidst only material things—and he could best live it by recognizing things for what they are—just things. Epicurean ethics had the practical aim, in its simplest form, of showing men that a happy life consisted of seeking those things that brought pleasure and avoiding those that brought pain. In this form, Epicureanism has often been mistaken for outright hedonism, the unthinking pursuit of pleasure. But in the fully developed exposition of his philosophic system, Epicurus carefully attempted to demonstrate that in the long run only ethically good things actually bring lasting pleasure. His main point is that there is nothing mysterious about life or the circumstances of human existence, that man's ability to control things is the measure of his ability to control those circumstances.

Although we know that Epicurus wrote voluminously, only a few fragments of his original work have survived. The only extensive, systematic exposition of Epicurean philosophy remaining from classical times is the work of the Roman poet Lucretius. Almost nothing is known about Lucretius other than that during the first half of the first century B.C. he wrote *De Natura Rerum (The Nature of the Universe),* a long poem running to well over seven thousand lines in which he tried to demonstrate the validity of the principal beliefs of Epicureanism. He arranged his work into six books, describing the nature of matter and space; the movements and shapes of atoms; the characteristics of mind and spirit; the operation of sense perceptions, thought, and emotions; the formation of the universe and the development of human society; and the operations of natural phenomena in the heavens and on earth. Lucretius' choice of poetry as his medium for expounding a system of philosophical beliefs probably reflects his own intense, personal reaction to them. He writes impassioned, highly charged verse, perhaps trying to show that Epicureanism embodies poetic as well as philosophic truth—that it produces not only intellectual certitude but emotional conviction as well. For Lucretius, philosophy does not simply replace religion; it becomes religion.

The Nature of the Universe

Book I

Matter and Space

When human life lay grovelling in all men's sight, crushed to the earth under the dead weight of superstition whose grim features loured menacingly upon mortals from the four quarters of the sky, a man of Greece[1] was first to raise mortal eyes in defiance, first to stand erect and brave the challenge. Fables of the gods did not crush him, nor the lightning flash and the growling menace of the sky. Rather, they quickened his manhood, so that he, first of all men, longed to smash the constraining locks of nature's doors. The vital vigour of his mind prevailed. He ventured far out beyond the flaming ramparts of the world and voyaged in mind throughout infinity. Returning victorious, he proclaimed to us what can be and what cannot: how a limit is fixed to the power of everything and an immovable frontier post. Therefore superstition in its turn lies crushed beneath his feet, and we by his triumph are lifted level with the skies.

One thing that worries me is the fear that you[2] may fancy yourself embarking on an impious course, setting your feet on the path of sin. Far from it. More often it is this very superstition that is the mother of sinful and impious deeds. Remember how at Aulis the altar of the Virgin Goddess was foully stained with the blood of Iphigeneia by the leaders of the Greeks, the patterns of chivalry.[3] The headband was bound about her virgin tresses and hung down evenly over both her cheeks. Suddenly she caught sight of her father standing sadly in front of the altar, the attendants beside him hiding the knife and her people bursting into tears when they saw her. Struck dumb with terror, she sank on her knees to the ground. Poor girl, at such a moment it did not help her that she had been first to give the name of father to a king. Raised by the hands of men, she was led trembling to the altar. Not for her the sacrament of marriage and the loud chant of Hymen. It was her fate in the very hour of marriage to fall a sinless victim to a sinful rite, slaughtered to her greater grief by a father's hand, so that a fleet might sail under happy auspices. Such are the heights of wickedness to which men are driven by superstition.

You yourself, if you surrender your judgment at any time to the bloodcurdling declamations of the prophets, will want to desert our ranks. Only think what phantoms they can conjure up to overturn the tenor

---

From *Lucretius: On the Nature of the Universe,* translated by Ronald Latham, 1951, reproduced by permission of the publishers Penguin Books Ltd., England.

[1]Epicurus.

[2]Memmius, an eminent Roman statesman to whom Lucretius addressed his poem.

[3]Lucretius here refers to one of the legends connected with the Trojan War. Agamemnon supposedly offered his own daughter Iphigeneia as a human sacrifice in order to appease the gods, who had becalmed the Greeks at Aulis while they were on their way to Troy.

of your life and wreck your happiness with fear. And not without cause. For, if men saw that a term was set to their troubles, they would find strength in some way to withstand the hocus-pocus and intimidations of the prophets. As it is, they have no power of resistance, because they are haunted by the fear of eternal punishment after death. They know nothing of the nature of the spirit. Is it born, or is it implanted in us at birth? Does it perish with us, dissolved by death, or does it visit the murky depths and dreary sloughs of Hades? Or is it transplanted by divine power into other creatures, as described in the poems of our own Ennius, who first gathered on the delectable slopes of Helicon an evergreen garland destined to win renown among the nations of Italy? Ennius indeed in his immortal verses proclaims that there is also a Hell, which is peopled not by our actual spirits or bodies but only by shadowy images, ghastly pale. It is from this realm that he pictures the ghost of Homer, of unfading memory, as appearing to him, shedding salt tears and revealing the nature of the universe.

I must therefore give an account of celestial phenomena, explaining the movements of sun and moon and also the forces that determine events on earth. Next, and no less important, we must look with keen insight into the makeup of spirit and mind: we must consider those alarming phantasms that strike upon our minds when they are awake but disordered by sickness, or when they are buried in slumber, so that we seem to see and hear before us men whose dead bones lie in the embraces of earth.

I am well aware that it is not easy to elucidate in Latin verse the obscure discoveries of the Greeks. The poverty of our language and the novelty of the theme compel me often to coin new words for the purpose. But your merit and the joy I hope to derive from our delightful friendship encourage me to face any task however hard. This it is that leads me to stay awake through the quiet of the night, studying how by choice of words and the poet's art I can display before your mind a clear light by which you can gaze into the heart of hidden things.

This dread and darkness of the mind cannot be dispelled by the sunbeams, the shining shafts of day, but only by an understanding of the outward form and inner workings of nature. In tackling this theme, our starting-point will be this principle: *Nothing can ever be created by divine power out of nothing.* The reason why all mortals are so gripped by fear is that they see all sorts of things happening on the earth and in the sky with no discernible cause, and these they attribute to the will of a god. Accordingly, when we have seen that nothing can be created out of nothing, we shall then have a clearer picture of the path ahead, the problem of how things are created and occasioned without the aid of the gods.

First then, if things were made out of nothing, any species could spring from any source and nothing would require seed. Men could arise from the sea and scaly fish from the earth, and birds could be hatched out of the sky. Cattle and other domestic animals and every kind of wild beast, multiplying indiscriminately, would occupy cultivated and waste lands alike. The same fruits would not grow constantly on the same trees, but they would keep changing: any tree might bear any fruit. If each species were not composed of its own generative bodies, why should each be born always of the same kind of mother? Actually, since each is formed out of specific seeds, it is born and emerges into the sunlit world only from a place where there exists the right material, the right kind of atoms. This is why everything cannot be born of everything, but a specific power of generation inheres in specific objects.

Again, why do we see roses appear in spring, grain in summer's heat, grapes under the spell of autumn? Surely, because it is only after specific seeds have drifted together at their own proper time that every created thing stands revealed, when the season is favourable and the life-giving earth can safely deliver delicate growths into the sunlit world. If they were made out of nothing, they would spring up suddenly after varying lapses of time and at abnormal seasons, since there would of course be no primary bodies which could be prevented by the harshness of the season from entering into generative unions. Similarly, in order that things might grow, there would be no need of any lapse of time for the accumulation of seed. Tiny tots would turn suddenly into grown men, and trees would shoot up spontaneously out of the earth. But it is obvious that none of these things happens, since everything grows gradually, as is natural, from a specific seed and retains its specific character. It is a fair inference that each is increased and nourished by its own raw material.

Here is a further point. Without seasonable showers the earth cannot send up gladdening growths. Lacking food, animals cannot reproduce their kind or sustain life. This points to the conclusion that many elements are common to many things, as letters are to words, rather than to the theory that anything can come into existence without atoms.

Or again, why has not nature been able to produce men on such a scale that they could ford the ocean on foot or demolish high mountains with their hands or prolong their lives over many generations? Surely, because each thing requires for its birth a particular material which determines what can be produced. It must therefore be admitted that nothing can be made out of nothing, because everything must be generated from a seed before it can emerge into the unresisting air.

Lastly, we see that tilled plots are superior to untilled, and their fruits are improved by cultivation. This is because the earth contains certain atoms which we rouse to productivity by turning the fruitful clods with the ploughshare and stirring up the soil. But for these, you would see great improvements arising spontaneously without any aid from our labours.

The second great principle is this: *nature resolves everything into its component atoms and never reduces anything to nothing.* If anything were perishable in all its parts, anything might perish all of a sudden and vanish from sight. There would be no need of any force to separate its parts and loosen their links. In actual fact, since everything is composed of indestructible seeds, nature obviously does not allow anything to perish till it has encountered a force that shatters it with a blow or creeps into chinks and unknits it.

If the things that are banished from the scene by age are annihilated through the exhaustion of their material, from what source does Venus bring back the several races of animals into the light of life? And, when they are brought back, where does the inventive earth find for each the special food required for its sustenance and growth? From what fount is the sea replenished by its native springs and the streams that flow into it from afar? Whence does the ether draw nutriment for the stars? For everything consisting of a mortal body must have been exhausted by the long day of time, the illimitable past. If throughout this bygone eternity there have persisted bodies from which the universe has been perpetually renewed, they must certainly be possessed of immortality. Therefore things cannot be reduced to nothing.

Again, all objects would regularly be destroyed by the same force and the same cause, were it not that they are sustained by imperishable matter more or less tightly fastened together. Why, a mere touch would be enough to bring about destruction supposing there were no imperishable bodies whose union could be dissolved only by the appropriate force. Actually, because the fastenings of the atoms are of various kinds while their matter is imperishable, compound objects remain intact until one of them encounters a force that proves strong enough to break up its particular constitution. Therefore nothing returns to nothing, but everything is resolved into its constituent bodies.

Lastly, showers perish when father ether has flung them down into the lap of mother earth. But the crops spring up fresh and gay; the branches on the trees burst into leaf; the trees themselves grow and are weighed down with fruit. Hence in turn man and brute draw nourishment. Hence we see flourishing cities blest with children and every leafy thicket loud with new broods of songsters. Hence in lush pastures cattle wearied by their bulk fling down their bodies, and the white milky juice oozes from their swollen udders. Hence a new generation frolic friskily on wobbly legs through the fresh grass, their young minds tipsy with undiluted milk. Visible objects therefore do not perish utterly, since nature repairs one thing from another and allows nothing to be born without the aid of another's death.

Well, Memmius, I have taught you that things cannot be created out of nothing nor, once born, be summoned back to nothing. Perhaps, however, you are becoming mistrustful of my words, because these atoms of mine are not visible to the eye. Consider, therefore, this further evidence of *bodies whose existence you must acknowledge though they cannot be seen.* First, wind, when its force is roused, whips up waves, founders tall ships and scatters cloud-rack. Sometimes scouring plains with hurricane force it strews them with huge trees and batters mountain peaks with blasts that hew down forests. Such is wind in its fury, when it whoops aloud with a mad menace in its shouting. Without question, therefore, there must be invisible particles of wind which sweep sea and land and the clouds in the sky, swooping upon them and whirling them along in a headlong hurricane. In the way they flow and the havoc they spread they are no different from a torrential flood of water when it rushes down in a sudden spate from the mountain heights, swollen by heavy rains, and heaps together wreckage from the forest and entire trees. Soft though it is by nature, the sudden shock of oncoming water is more than even stout bridges can withstand, so furious is the force with which the turbid, storm-flushed torrent surges against their piers. With a mighty roar it lays them low, rolling huge rocks under its waves and brushing aside every obstacle from its course. Such, therefore, must be the movement of blasts of wind also. When they have come surging along some course like a rushing river, they push obstacles before them and buffet them with repeated blows; and sometimes, eddying round and round, they snatch them up and carry them along in a swiftly circling vortex. Here then is proof upon proof that winds have invisible bodies, since in their actions and behaviour they are found to rival great rivers, whose bodies are plain to see.

Then again, we smell the various scents of things though we never see them approaching our nostrils. Similarly, heat and cold cannot be detected by our eyes, and we do not see sounds. Yet all these must be composed of bodies, since they are able to impinge upon our senses. For nothing can touch or be touched except body.

Again, clothes hung out on a surf-beaten shore grow moist. Spread in the sun they grow dry. But we do not see how the moisture has soaked into them, nor again how it has been dispelled by the heat. It follows that the moisture is split up into minute parts which the eye cannot possibly see.

Again, in the course of many annual revolutions of the sun a ring is worn thin next to the finger with continual rubbing. Dripping water hollows a stone. A curved ploughshare, iron though it is, dwindles imperceptibly in the furrow. We see the cobble-stones of the highway worn by the feet of many wayfarers. The bronze statues by the city gates show their right hands worn thin by the touch of travellers who have greeted them in passing. We see that all these are being diminished, since they are worn away. But to perceive what particles drop off at any particular time is a power grudged to us by our ungenerous sense of sight.

To sum up, whatever is added to things gradually by nature and the passage of days, causing a cumulative increase, eludes the most attentive scrutiny of our eyes. Conversely, you cannot see what objects lose by the wastage of age—sheer sea-cliffs, for instance, exposed to prolonged erosion by the mordant brine—or at what time the loss occurs. It follows that nature works through the agency of invisible bodies.

On the other hand, things are not hemmed in by the pressure of solid bodies in a tight mass. This is because *there is vacuity in things.* A grasp of this fact will be helpful to you in many respects and will save you from much bewildered doubting and questioning about the universe and from mistrust of my teaching. Well then, by vacuity I mean intangible and empty space. If it did not exist, things could not move at all. For the distinctive action of matter, which is counteraction and obstruction, would be in force always and everywhere. Nothing could proceed, because nothing would give it a starting-point by receding. As it is, we see with our own eyes at sea and on land and high up in the sky that all sorts of things in all sorts of ways are on the move. If there were no empty space, these things would be denied the power of restless movement—or rather, they could not possibly have come into existence, embedded as they would have been in motionless matter.

Besides, there are clear indications that things that pass for solid are in fact porous. Even in rocks a trickle of water seeps through into caves, and copious drops ooze from every surface. Food percolates to every part of an animal's body. Trees grow and bring forth their fruit in season, because their food is distributed throughout their length from the tips of the roots through the trunk and along every branch. Noises pass through walls and fly into closed buildings. Freezing cold penetrates to the bones. If there were no vacancies through which the various bodies could make their way, none of these phenomena would be possible.

Again, why do we find some things outweigh others of equal volume? If there is as much matter in a ball of wool as in one of lead, it is natural that it should weigh as heavily, since it is the function of matter to press everything downwards, while it is the function of space on the other hand to remain weightless. Accordingly, when one thing is not less bulky than another but obviously lighter, it plainly declares that there is more vacuum in it, while the heavier object proclaims that there is more matter in it and much less empty space. We have therefore reached the goal of our diligent enquiry: there is in things an admixture of what we call vacuity.

In case you should be misled on this question by the idle imagining of certain theorists, I must anticipate their argument. They maintain that water yields and opens a penetrable path to the scaly bodies of fish that push against it, because they leave spaces behind them into which the yielding water can flow together. In the same way, they suppose, other things can move by mutually changing places, although every place remains filled. This theory has been adopted utterly without warrant. For how can the fish advance till the water has given way? And how can the water retire when the fish cannot move? There are thus only two alternatives: either all bodies are devoid of movement, or you must admit that things contain an admixture of vacuity whereby each is enabled to make the first move.

Lastly, if two bodies suddenly spring apart from contact on a broad surface, all the intervening space must be void until it is occupied by air. However quickly the air rushes in all round, the entire space cannot be filled instantaneously. The air must occupy one spot after another until it has taken possession of the whole space. If anyone supposes that this consequence of such springing apart is made possible by the condensation of air, he is mistaken. For condensation implies that something that was full becomes empty, or *vice versā*. And I contend that air could not condense so as to produce this effect; or at any rate, if there were no vacuum, it could not thus shrink into itself and draw its parts together.

However many pleas you may advance to prolong the argument, you must end by admitting that there is vacuity in things. There are many other proofs I could add to the pile in order to strengthen conviction; but for an acute intelligence these small clues should suffice to enable you to discover the rest for yourself. As hounds that range the hills often smell out the lairs of wild beasts screened in thickets, when once they have got on to the right trail, so in such questions one thing will lead on to another, till you can succeed by yourself in tracking down the truth to its lurking-places and dragging it forth. If you grow weary and relax from the chase, there is one thing, Memmius, that I can safely promise you: my honeyed tongue will pour from the treasury of my breast such generous draughts, drawn from inexhaustible springs, that I am afraid slow-plodding age may creep through my limbs and unbolt the bars of my life before the full flood of my arguments on any single point has flowed in verse through your ears.

To pick up the thread of my discourse, all nature as it is in itself consists of two things—bodies and the vacant space in which the bodies are situated and through which they move in different directions. The existence of bodies is vouched for by the agreement of the senses. If a belief resting directly on this foundation is not valid, there will be no standard to which we can refer any doubt on obscure questions for rational confirmation. If there were no place and space, which we call vacuity, these bodies could not be situated anywhere or move in any direction whatever. This I have just demonstrated. It remains to show that *nothing exists that is distinct both from body and from vacuity* and could be ranked with the others as a third substance. For whatever *is* must also be something. If it offers resistance to touch, however light and slight, it will increase the mass of body by such amount, great or small, as it may amount to, and will rank with it. If, on the other hand, it is intangible, so that it offers no resistance whatever to anything passing through it, then it will be that empty space which we call vacuity. Besides, whatever it may be in itself, either it will act in some way, or react to other things acting upon it, or else it will be such that things can be and happen in it. But without body nothing can act or react; and nothing can afford a place except emptiness and vacancy. Therefore, besides matter and vacuity, we cannot include in the number of things any third substance that can either affect our senses at any time or be grasped by the reasoning of our minds.

You will find that anything that can be named is either a property or an accident of these two. A *property* is something that cannot be detached or separated from a thing without destroying it, as weight is a property of rocks, heat of fire, fluidity of water, tangibility of all bodies, intangibility of vacuum. On the other hand, servitude and liberty, poverty and riches, war and peace, and all other things whose advent or departure leaves the essence of a thing intact, all these it is our practice to call by their appropriate name, *accidents*.

Similarly, time by itself does not exist; but from things themselves there results a sense of what has already taken place, what is now going on and what is to ensue. It must not be claimed that anyone can sense time by itself apart from the movement of things or their restful immobility.

Again, when men say it *is* a fact that Helen was ravished or the Trojans were conquered, do not let anyone drive you to the admission that any such event *is* independently of any object, on the ground that the generations of men of whom these events were accidents have been swept away by the irrevocable lapse of time. For we could put it that whatever has taken place is an accident of a particular tract of earth or of the space it occupied. If there had been no matter and no space or place in which things could happen, no spark of love kindled by the beauty of Tyndareus' daughter would ever have stolen into the breast of Phrygian Paris to light that dazzling blaze of pitiless war;[4] no Wooden Horse, unmarked by the sons of Troy, would have set the towers of Ilium aflame through the midnight issue of Greeks from its womb. So you may see that events cannot be said to *be* by themselves like matter or in the same sense as space. Rather, you should describe them as accidents of matter, or of the place in which things happen.

Material objects are of two kinds, atoms and compounds of atoms. The atoms themselves cannot be swamped by any force, for they are preserved indefinitely by their absolute solidity. Admittedly, it is hard to believe that anything can exist that is absolutely solid. The lightning stroke from the sky penetrates closed buildings, as do shouts and other noises. Iron glows molten in the fire, and hot rocks are cracked by untempered scorching. Hard gold is softened and melted by heat; and bronze, ice-like, is liquefied by flame. Both heat and piercing cold seep through silver, since we feel both alike when a cooling shower of water is poured into a goblet that we hold ceremonially in our hands. All these facts point to the conclusion that nothing is really solid. But sound reasoning and nature itself drive us to the opposite conclusion. Pay attention, therefore, while I demonstrate in a few lines that there exist certain bodies that are absolutely solid and indestructible, namely those atoms which according to our teaching are the seeds or prime units of things from which the whole universe is built up.

In the first place, we have found that nature is twofold, consisting of two totally different things, matter and the space in which things happen. Hence each of these must exist by itself without admixture of the other. For, where there is empty space (what we call vacuity), there matter is not; where matter exists, there cannot be a vacuum. Therefore the prime units of matter are solid and free from vacuity.

Again, since composite things contain some vacuum, the surrounding matter must be solid. For you cannot reasonably maintain that anything can hide vacuity and hold it within its body unless you allow that the container itself is solid. And what contains the vacuum in things can only be an accumulation of matter. Hence matter, which possesses absolute solidity, can be everlasting when other things are decomposed.

Again, if there were no empty space, everything would be one solid mass; if there were no material objects with the property of filling the space they occupy, all existing space would be utterly void. It is clear, then, that there is an alternation of matter and vacuity, mutually distinct, since the whole is neither completely full nor completely empty. There are therefore solid bodies, causing the distinction between empty space and full. And these, as I have just shown, can be neither decomposed by blows from without nor invaded and unknit from within nor destroyed by any other form of assault. For it seems that a thing without vacuum can be neither knocked to bits nor snapped nor chopped in

---

[4]Tyndareus was a legendary king of Sparta, the father of Helen, whose abduction by Paris was the cause of the Trojan War.

two by cutting; nor can it let in moisture or seeping cold or piercing fire, the universal agents of destruction. The more vacuum a thing contains within it, the more readily it yields to these assailants. Hence, if the units of matter are solid and without vacuity, as I have shown, they must be everlasting.

Yet again, if the matter in things had not been everlasting, everything by now would have gone back to nothing, and the things we see would be the product of rebirth out of nothing. But, since I have already shown that nothing can be created out of nothing nor any existing thing be summoned back to nothing, the atoms must be made of imperishable stuff into which everything can be resolved in the end, so that there may be a stock of matter for building the world anew. The atoms, therefore, are absolutely solid and unalloyed. In no other way could they have survived throughout infinite time to keep the world in being.

Furthermore, if nature had set no limit to the breaking of things, the particles of matter in the course of ages would have been ground so small that nothing could be generated from them so as to attain in the fullness of time to the summit of its growth. For we see that anything can be more speedily disintegrated than put together again. Hence, what the long day of time, the bygone eternity, has already shaken and loosened to fragments could never in the residue of time be reconstructed. As it is, there is evidently a limit set to breaking, since we see that everything is renewed and each according to its kind has a fixed period in which to grow to its prime.

Here is a further argument. Granted that the particles of matter are absolutely solid, we can still explain the composition and behaviour of soft things—air, water, earth, fire—by their intermixture with empty space. On the other hand, supposing the atoms to be soft, we cannot account for the origin of hard flint and iron. For there would be no foundation for nature to build on. Therefore there must be bodies strong in their unalloyed solidity by whose closer clustering things can be knit together and display unyielding toughness.

If we suppose that there is no limit set to the breaking of matter, we must still admit that material objects consist of particles which throughout eternity have resisted the forces of destruction. To say that these are breakable does not square with the fact that they have survived throughout eternity under a perpetual bombardment of innumerable blows.

Again, there is laid down for each thing a specific limit to its growth and its tenure of life, and the laws of nature ordain what each can do and what it cannot. No species is ever changed, but each remains so much itself that every kind of bird displays on its body its own specific markings. This is a further proof that their bodies are composed of changeless matter. For, if the atoms could yield in any way to change, there would be no certainty as to what could arise and what could not, at what point the power of everything was limited by an immovable frontierpost; nor could successive generations so regularly repeat the nature, behaviour, habits and movements of their parents.

To proceed with our argument, there is an ultimate point in visible objects which represents the smallest thing that can be seen. So also there must be an ultimate point in objects that lie below the limit of perception by our senses. This point is without parts and is the smallest thing that can exist. It never has been and never will be able to exist by itself, but only as one primary part of something else. It is with a mass of such parts, solidly jammed together in order, that matter is filled up. Since they cannot exist by themselves, they must needs stick together in a mass from which they cannot by any means be prized loose. The atoms therefore are absolutely solid and unalloyed, consisting of a mass of least parts tightly packed together. They are not compounds formed by the coalescence of their parts, but bodies of absolute and ever-lasting solidity. To these nature allows no loss or diminution, but guards them as seeds for things. If there are no such least parts, even the smallest bodies will consist of an infinite number of parts, since they can always be halved and their halves halved again without limit. On this showing, what difference will there be between the whole universe and the very least of things? None at all. For, however endlessly infinite the universe may be, yet the smallest things will equally consist of an infinite number of parts. Since true reason cries out against this and denies that the mind can believe it, you must needs give in and admit that there are least parts which themselves are partless. Granted that these parts exist, you must needs admit that the atoms they compose are also solid and ever-lasting. But, if all things were compelled by all-creating nature to be broken up into these least parts, nature would lack the power to rebuild anything out of them. For partless objects cannot have the essential properties of generative matter—those varieties of attachment, weight, impetus, impact and movement on which everything depends. (vv. 62 – 634)

And now pay special attention to what follows and listen more in-tently. I am well aware how full it is of obscurity. But high hope of fame has struck my heart with its sharp goad and in so doing has implanted in my breast the sweet love of the Muses.[5] That is the spur that lends my spirit strength to pioneer through pathless tracts of their Pierian realm where no foot has ever trod before. What joy it is to light upon virgin springs and drink their waters. What joy to pluck new flowers and gather for my brow a glorious garland from fields whose blossoms were never yet wreathed by the Muses round any head. This is my reward for teaching on these lofty topics, for struggling to loose men's minds from the tight knots of superstition and shedding on dark corners the bright beams of my song that irradiate everything with the sparkle of the Muses. My art is not without a purpose. Physicians, when they wish to treat children with a nasty dose of wormwood, first smear the rim of the cup with a sweet coat of yellow honey. The children, too young as yet for foresight, are lured by the sweetness at their lips into swallowing the bitter draught. So they are tricked but not trapped, for the treatment restores them to health. In the same way our doctrine often seems unpalatable to those who have not sampled it, and the multitude shrink from it. That is why I have tried to administer it to you in the dulcet strains of poesy, coated with the sweet honey of the Muses. My object has been to engage your mind with my verses while

---

[5]In Greek mythology, the nine sisters who were the goddesses of literature and the arts.

you gain insight into the nature of the universe and the pattern of its architecture.

Well then, since I have shown that there are completely solid indestructible particles of matter flying about through all eternity, let us elucidate whether or not there is any limit to their number. Similarly, as we have found that there is a vacuum, the place or space in which things happen, let us see whether its whole extent is limited or whether it stretches far and wide into immeasurable depths.

Learn, therefore, that *the universe is not bounded in any direction.* If it were, it would necessarily have a limit somewhere. But clearly a thing cannot have a limit unless there is something outside to limit it, so that the eye can follow it up to a certain point but not beyond. Since you must admit that there is nothing outside the universe, it can have no limit and is accordingly without end or measure. It makes no odds in which part of it you may take your stand: whatever spot anyone may occupy, the universe stretches away from him just the same in all directions without limit. Suppose for a moment that the whole of space were bounded and that someone made his way to its uttermost boundary and threw a flying dart. Do you choose to suppose that the missile, hurled with might and main, would speed along the course on which it was aimed? Or do you think something would block the way and stop it? You must assume one alternative or the other. But neither of them leaves you a loophole. Both force you to admit that the universe continues without end. Whether there is some obstacle lying on the boundary line that prevents the dart from going farther on its course or whether it flies on beyond, it cannot in fact have started from the boundary. With this argument I will pursue you. Wherever you may place the ultimate limit of things, I will ask you: 'Well then, what does happen to the dart?' The upshot is that the boundary cannot stand firm anywhere, and final escape from this conclusion is precluded by the limitless possibility of running away from it.

It is a matter of observation that one thing is limited by another. The hills are demarcated by air, and air by the hills. Land sets bounds to sea, and sea to every land. But the universe has nothing outside to limit it.

Further, if all the space in the universe were shut in and confined on every side by definite boundaries, the supply of matter would already have accumulated by its own weight at the bottom, and nothing could happen under the dome of the sky—indeed, there would be no sky and no sunlight, since all the available matter would have settled down and would be lying in a heap throughout eternity. As it is, no rest is given to the atoms, because there is no bottom where they can accumulate and take up their abode. Things go on happening all the time through ceaseless movement in every direction; and atoms of matter bouncing up from below are supplied out of the infinite. There is therefore a limitless abyss of space, such that even the dazzling flashes of the lightning cannot traverse it in their course, racing through an interminable tract of time, nor can they even shorten the distance still to be covered. So vast is the scope that lies open to things far and wide without limit in any dimension.

The universe is restrained from setting any limit to itself by nature, which compels body to be bounded by vacuum and vacuum by body. Thus nature either makes them both infinite in alternation, or else one of them, if it is not bounded by the other, must extend in a pure state without limit. Space, however, being infinite, so must matter be. Otherwise neither sea nor land nor the bright zones of the sky nor mortal beings nor the holy bodies of the gods could endure for one brief hour of time. The supply of matter would be shaken loose from combination and swept through the vastness of the void in isolated particles; or rather, it would never have coalesced to form anything, since its scattered particles could never have been driven into union.

Certainly the atoms did not post themselves purposefully in due order by an act of intelligence, nor did they stipulate what movements each should perform. As they have been rushing everlastingly throughout all space in their myriads, undergoing a myriad changes under the disturbing impact of collisions, they have experienced every variety of movement and conjunction till they have fallen into the particular pattern by which this world of ours is constituted. This world has persisted many a long year, having once been set going in the appropriate motions. From these everything else follows. The rivers replenish the thirsty sea with profuse streams of water. Incubated by the sun's heat, the earth renews its fruits, and the brood of animals that springs from it grows lustily. The gliding fires of ether sustain their life. None of these results would be possible if there were not an ample supply of matter to bounce up out of infinite space in replacement of all that is lost. Just as animals deprived of food waste away through loss of body, so everything must decay as soon as its supply of matter goes astray and is cut off.

Whatever world the atoms have combined to form, impacts from without cannot preserve it at every point. By continual battering they can hold back part of it till others come along to make good the deficiency. But they are compelled now and then to bounce back and in so doing to leave space and time for the atoms to break loose from combination. It is thus essential that there should be great numbers of atoms coming up. Indeed, the impacts themselves could not be maintained without an unlimited supply of matter from all quarters.

There is one belief, Memmius, that you must beware of entertaining —*the theory that everything tends towards what they call 'the centre of the world'*. On this theory, the world stands fast without any impacts from without, and top and bottom cannot be parted in any direction, because everything has been tending towards the centre—if you can believe that anything rests upon itself. Whatever heavy bodies there may be under the earth must then tend upwards and rest against the surface upside down, like the images of things which we now see reflected in water. In the same way they would have it that animals walk about topsy-turvy and cannot fall off the earth into the nether quarters of the sky any more than our bodies can soar up spontaneously into the heavenly regions. When they are looking at the sun, we see the stars of night; so they share the hours with us alternately and experience nights corresponding to our days. But this is an idle fancy of fools who have got hold of the wrong end of the stick. There can be no centre in infinity. And, even if there were, nothing could stand fast there rather than flee from it. For all place or space, at the centre no less than elsewhere, must give way to heavy bodies, no matter in what direction they are moving. There is no place to which bodies can come where they lose the property of weight and stand still in the void. And vacuum cannot stand in the way of anything so as not to allow it free passage, as its own nature demands. Therefore things cannot be held in combination by this means through surrender to a craving for the centre.

Besides, they do not claim that all bodies have this tendency towards the centre, but only those of moisture and earth—the waters of the deep and the floods that pour down from the hills and in general whatever is composed of a more or less earthy body. But according to their teaching the light breaths of air and hot fires are simultaneously wafted outwards away from the centre. The reason why the encircling ether twinkles with stars and the sun feeds its flames in the blue pastures of the sky is supposed to be that fire all congregates there in its flight from the centre. Similarly, the topmost branches of trees could not break into leaf unless their food had this same upward urge. But, if you allow matter to escape from the world in this way, you are leaving the ramparts of the world at liberty to crumble of a sudden and take flight with the speed of flame into the boundless void. The rest will follow. The thunder-breeding quarters of the sky will rush down from aloft. The ground will fall away from our feet, its particles dissolved amid the mingled wreckage of heaven and earth. The whole world will vanish into the abyss, and in the twinkling of an eye no remnant will be left but empty space and invisible atoms. At whatever point you first allow matter to fall short, this will be the gateway to perdition. Through this gate the whole concourse of matter will come streaming out.

If you take a little trouble, you will attain to a thorough understanding of these truths. For one thing will be illumined by another, and eyeless night will not rob you of your road till you have looked into the heart of nature's darkest mysteries. So surely will facts throw light upon facts. (vv. 921 – 1117)

Book II

Movements and Shapes of Atoms

What joy it is, when out at sea the stormwinds are lashing the waters, to gaze from the shore at the heavy stress some other man is enduring! Not that anyone's afflictions are in themselves a source of delight; but to realize from what troubles you yourself are free is joy indeed. What joy, again, to watch opposing hosts marshalled on the field of battle when you have yourself no part in their peril! But this is the greatest joy of all: to stand aloof in a quiet citadel, stoutly fortified by the teaching of the wise, and to gaze down from that elevation on others wandering aimlessly in a vain search for the way of life, pitting their wits one against another, disputing for precedence, struggling night and day with unstinted effort to scale the pinnacles of wealth and power. O joyless hearts of men! O minds without vision! How dark and dangerous the life in which this tiny span is lived away! Do you not see that nature is clamouring for two things only, a body free from pain, a mind released from worry and fear for the enjoyment of pleasurable sensations?

So we find that the requirements of our bodily nature are few indeed, no more than is necessary to banish pain. To heap pleasure upon pleasure may heighten men's enjoyment at times. But what matter if there are no golden images of youths about the house, holding flaming torches in their right hands to illumine banquets prolonged into the night? What matter if the hall does not sparkle with silver and gleam with gold, and no carved and gilded rafters ring to the music of the lute? Nature does not miss these luxuries when men recline in company on the soft grass by a running stream under the branches of a tall tree and refresh their bodies pleasurably at small expense. Better still if the weather smiles upon them and the season of the year stipples the green herbage with flowers. Burning fevers flee no swifter from your body if you toss under figured counterpanes and coverlets of crimson than if you must lie in rude homespun.

If our bodies are not profited by treasures or titles or the majesty of kingship, we must go on to admit that neither are our minds. Or tell me, Memmius, when you see your legions thronging the Campus Martius in the ardour of mimic warfare, supported by ample auxiliaries, magnificently armed and fired by a common purpose, does that sight scare the terrors of superstition from your mind? Does the fear of death retire from your breast and leave it carefree at the moment when you sight your warships ranging far and wide? Or do we not find such resources absurdly ineffective? The fears and anxieties that dog the human breast do not shrink from the clash of arms or the fierce rain of missiles. They stalk unabashed among princes and potentates. They are not awe-struck by the gleam of gold or the bright sheen of purple robes.

Can you doubt then that this power rests with reason alone? All life is a struggle in the dark. As children in blank darkness tremble and start at everything, so we in broad daylight are oppressed at times by fears as baseless as those horrors which children imagine coming upon them in the dark. This dread and darkness of the mind cannot be dispelled by the sunbeams, the shining shafts of day, but only by an understanding of the outward form and inner workings of nature.

And now to business. I will explain *the motion by which the generative bodies of matter give birth to various things,* and, after they are born, dissolve them once more; the force that compels them to do this; and the power of movement through the boundless void with which they are endowed. It is for you to devote yourself attentively to my words.

Be sure that matter does not stick together in a solid mass. For we see that everything grows less and seems to melt away with the lapse of time and withdraw its old age from our eyes. And yet we see no diminution in the sum of things. This is because the bodies that are shed by one thing lessen it by their departure but enlarge another by their coming; here they bring decay, there full bloom, but they do not linger there. So the sum of things is perpetually renewed. Mortals live by mutual interchange. One race increases by another's decrease. The generations of living things pass in swift succession and like runners hand on the torch of life.

If you think that the atoms can stop and by their stopping generate new motions in things, you are wandering far from the path of truth. Since the atoms are moving freely through the void, they must all be kept in motion either by their own weight or on occasion by the impact of another atom. For it must often happen that two of them in their course knock together and immediately bounce apart in opposite directions, a natural consequence of their hardness and solidity and the absence of anything behind to stop them. As a further indication that all particles of matter are on the move, remember that the universe is bottomless: there is no place where the atoms could come to rest. As I have already shown by various arguments and proved conclusively, space is without end or limit and spreads out immeasurably in all directions alike.

It clearly follows that no rest is given to the atoms in their course through the depths of space. Driven along in an incessant but variable movement, some of them bounce far apart after a collision while others recoil only a short distance from the impact. From those that do not recoil far, being driven into a closer union and held there by the entanglement of their own interlocking shapes, are composed firmly rooted rock, the stubborn strength of steel and the like. Those others that move freely through larger tracts of space, springing far apart and carried far by the rebound—these provide for us thin air and blazing sunlight. Besides these, there are many other atoms at large in empty space which have been thrown out of compound bodies and have nowhere even been granted admittance so as to bring their motions into harmony.

This process, as I might point out, is illustrated by an image of it that is continually taking place before our very eyes. Observe what happens when sunbeams are admitted into a building and shed light on its shadowy places. You will see a multitude of tiny particles mingling in a multitude of ways in the empty space within the light of the beam, as though contending in everlasting conflict, rushing into battle rank upon rank with never a moment's pause in a rapid sequence of unions and disunions. From this you may picture what it is for the atoms to be perpetually tossed about in the illimitable void. To some extent a small thing may afford an illustration and an imperfect image of great things. Besides, there is a further reason why you should give your mind to these particles that are seen dancing in a sunbeam: their dancing is an actual indication of underlying movements of matter that are hidden from our sight. There you will see many particles under the impact of invisible blows changing their course and driven back upon their tracks, this way and that, in all directions. You must understand that they all derive this restlessness from the atoms. It originates with the atoms, which move of themselves. Then those small compound bodies that are least removed from the impetus of the atoms are set in motion by the impact of their invisible blows and in turn cannon against slightly larger bodies. So the movement mounts up from the atoms and gradually emerges to the level of our senses, so that those bodies are in motion that we see in sunbeams, moved by blows that remain invisible.

And now, Memmius, as to the rate at which the atoms move, you may gauge this readily from these few indications. First, when dawn sprays the earth with new-born light and the birds, flitting through pathless thickets, fill the neighbourhood according to their kind with liquid notes that glide through the thin air, it is plain and palpable for all to see how suddenly the sun at the moment of his rising drenches and clothes the world with his radiance. But the heat and the bright light which the sun emits do not travel through empty space. Therefore they are forced to move more slowly, cleaving their way as it were through waves of air. And the atoms that compose this radiance do not travel as isolated individuals but linked and massed together. Thus their pace is retarded by one dragging back another as well as by external obstacles. But, when separate atoms are travelling in solitary solidity through empty space, they encounter no obstruction from without and move as single units on the course on which they have embarked. Obviously therefore they must far outstrip the sunlight in speed of movement and traverse an extent of space many times as great in the time it takes for the sun's rays to flash across the sky. No wonder that men cannot follow the individual atoms, so as to discern the agency by which everything is brought about.

In the face of these truths, some people who know nothing of matter believe that nature without the guidance of the gods could not bring round the changing seasons in such perfect conformity to human needs, creating the crops and those other blessings that mortals are led to enjoy by the guide of life, divine pleasure, which coaxes them through the arts of Venus to reproduce their kind, lest the human race should perish. Obviously, in imagining that the gods established everything for the sake of men, they have stumbled in all respects far from the path of truth. Even if I knew nothing of the atoms, I would venture to assert on the evidence of the celestial phenomena themselves, supported by many other arguments, that the universe was certainly not created for us by divine power: it is so full of imperfections. All this, Memmius, I will elucidate for you at a later stage. Now let me complete my account of atomic movements.

Now, I should judge, is the place to insert a demonstration that *no material thing can be uplifted or travel upwards by its own power.* Do not be misled by the particles that compose flame. The fact that all weights taken by themselves tend downwards does not prevent lusty crops and trees from being born with an upward thrust and from growing and increasing upwards. Similarly, when fires leap up to the house-tops and devour beams and rafters with rapid flame, it must not be supposed that they do this of their own accord with no force to fling them up. Their behaviour is like that of blood released from our body when it spouts forth and springs aloft in a gory fountain. Observe also with what force beams and rafters are heaved up by water. The more we have shoved them down into the depths, many of us struggling strenuously together to push them under, the more eagerly the water spews and ejects them back again, so that more than half their bulk shoots up above the surface. And yet, I should judge, we have no doubt that all these, taken by themselves, would move downwards through empty space. It must be just the same with flames: under pressure they can shoot up through the gusty air, although their weight, taken by itself, strives to tug them down. Observe how the nocturnal torches of the sky in their lofty flight draw in their wake long trails of flame in whatever direction nature has set their course. See how stars and meteors fall upon the earth. The sun from the summit of the sky scatters heat in all directions and sows the fields with light. The sun's radiance therefore tends also towards the earth. Note again how the lightning flies through the rain-storms aslant. The fires that break out of the clouds rush together, now this way, now that; often enough the fiery force falls upon the earth.

In this connexion there is another fact that I want you to grasp. *When the atoms are travelling straight down through empty space by their own weight, at quite indeterminate times and places they swerve ever so little from their course,* just so much that you can call it a change of direction. If it were not for this swerve, everything would fall downwards like rain-drops through the abyss of space. No collision would take place and no impact of atom on atom would be created. Thus nature would never have created anything.

If anyone supposes that heavier atoms on a straight course through empty space could outstrip lighter ones and fall on them from above, thus causing impacts that might give rise to generative motions, he is going far astray from the path of truth. The reason why objects falling through water or thin air vary in speed according to their weight is simply that the matter composing water or air cannot obstruct all objects equally, but is forced to give way more speedily to heavier ones. But empty space can offer no resistance to any object in any quarter at any time, so as not to yield free passage as its own nature demands. Therefore, through undisturbed vacuum all bodies must travel at equal speed though impelled by unequal weights. The heavier will never be able to fall on the lighter from above or generate of themselves impacts leading to that variety of motions out of which nature can produce things. We are thus forced back to the conclusion that the atoms swerve a little —but only a very little, or we shall be caught imagining slantwise movements, and the facts will prove us wrong. For we see plainly and palpably that weights, when they come tumbling down, have no power of their own to move aslant, so far as meets the eye. But who can possibly perceive that they do not diverge in the very least from a vertical course?

Again, if all movement is always interconnected, the new arising from the old in a determinate order—if the atoms never swerve so as to originate some new movement that will snap the bonds of fate, the ever-lasting sequence of cause and effect—what is the source of the free will possessed by living things throughout the earth? What, I repeat, is the source of that will-power snatched from the fates, whereby we follow the path along which we are severally led by pleasure, swerving from our course at no set time or place but at the bidding of our own hearts? There is no doubt that on these occasions the will of the individual originates the movements that trickle through his limbs. Observe, when the starting barriers are flung back, how the race-horses in the eagerness of their strength cannot break away as suddenly as their hearts desire. For the whole supply of matter must first be mobilized throughout every member of the body: only then, when it is mustered in a continuous array, can it respond to the prompting of the heart. So you may see that the beginning of movement is generated by the heart; starting from the voluntary action of the mind, it is then transmitted throughout the body and the limbs. Quite different is our experience when we are shoved along by a blow inflicted with compulsive force by someone else. In that case it is obvious that all the matter of our body is set going and pushed along involuntarily, till a check is imposed through the limbs by the will. Do you see the difference? Although many men are driven by an external force and often constrained involuntarily to advance or to rush headlong, yet there is within the human breast something that can fight against this force and resist it. At its command the supply of matter is forced to take a new course through our limbs and joints or is checked in its course and brought once more to a halt. So also in the atoms you must recognize the same possibility: besides weight and impact there must be a third cause of movement, the source of this inborn power of ours, since we see that nothing can come out of nothing. For the weight of an atom prevents its movements from being completely determined by the impact of other atoms. But the fact that the mind itself has no internal necessity to determine its every act and compel it to suffer in helpless passivity —this is due to the slight swerve of the atoms at no determinate time or place. (vv. 1—293)

Book III

Life and Mind

First, I maintain that *the mind,* which we often call the intellect, the seat of the guidance and control of life, *is part of a man,* no less than hand or foot or eyes are parts of a whole living creature. There are some who argue that the sentience of the mind is not lodged in any particular part, but is a vital condition of the body, what the Greeks call a *harmony,* which makes us live as sentient beings without having any locally determined mind. Just as good health may be said to belong to the healthy body without being any specific part of it, so they do not station the sentience of the mind in any specific part. In this they seem to me very wide of the mark. Often enough the visible body is obviously ill, while in some other unseen part we are enjoying ourselves. No less often the reverse happens: one who is sick at heart enjoys bodily well-being. This is no different from the experience of a invalid whose foot is hurting while his head is in no pain.

Or consider what happens when we have surrendered our limbs to soothing slumber and our body, replete and relaxed, lies insensible. At that very time there is something else in us that is awake to all sorts of stimuli—something that gives free admittance to all the motions of joy and to heart-burnings void of substance.

Next, you must understand that *there is also a vital spirit in our limbs* and the body does not derive its sentience from harmony. In the first place, life often lingers in our limbs after a large part of the body has been cut off. On the other hand, when a few particles of heat have dispersed and some air has been let out through the mouth, life forsakes the veins forthwith and abandons the bones. Hence you may infer that all the elements do not hold equal portions of vitality or sustain it equally, but it is chiefly thanks to the atoms of wind and heat that life lingers in the limbs. There is therefore in the body itself a vital breath and heat which forsakes our limbs at death.

Now that we have discovered the nature of the mind and of the vital spirit as a part of the man, drop this name harmony which was passed down to the musicians from the heights of Helicon—or else perhaps they fetched it themselves from some other source and applied it to the matter of their art, which had then no name of its own. Whatever it be, let them keep it. And give your attention now to the rest of my discourse.

Next, I maintain that *mind and spirit are interconnected* and compose between them a single substance. But what I may call the head and the dominant force in the whole body is that guiding principle which we term mind or intellect. This is firmly lodged in the mid-region of the breast. Here is the place where fear and alarm pulsate. Here is felt the caressing touch of joy. Here, then, is the seat of intellect and mind. The rest of the vital spirit, diffused throughout the body, obeys the mind and moves under its direction and impulse. The mind by itself experiences thought and joy of its own at a time when nothing moves either the body or the spirit.

When our head or eye suffers from an attack of pain, our whole body does not share in its aching. Just so the mind sometimes suffers by itself or jumps for joy when the rest of the spirit, diffused through every limb and member, is not stirred by any new impulse. But, when the mind is upset by some more overwhelming fear, we see all the spirit in every limb upset in sympathy. Sweat and pallor break out all over the body. Speech grows inarticulate; the voice fails; the eyes swim; the ears buzz; the limbs totter. Often we see men actually drop down because of the terror that has gripped their minds. Hence you may readily infer a connexion between the mind and the spirit which, when shaken by the impact of the mind, immediately jostles and propels the body.

The same reasoning proves that *mind and spirit are both composed of matter.* We see them propelling the limbs, rousing the body from sleep, changing the expression of the face and guiding and steering the whole man—activities that all clearly involve touch, as touch in turn involves matter. How then can we deny their material nature? You see the mind sharing in the body's experiences and sympathizing with it. When the nerve-racking impact of a spear gashes bones and sinews, even if it does not penetrate to the seat of life, there ensues faintness and a tempting inclination earthwards and on the ground a turmoil in the mind and an intermittent faltering impulse to stand up again. The substance of the mind must therefore be material, since it is affected by the impact of material weapons.

My next task will be to demonstrate to you what sort of matter it is of which this mind is composed and how it was formed. First, I affirm that *it is of very fine texture and composed of exceptionally minute particles.* If you will mark my words, you will be able to infer this from the following facts. It is evident that nothing happens as quickly as the mind represents and sketches the happening to itself. Therefore the mind sets itself in motion more swiftly than any of those things whose substance is visible to our eyes. But what is so mobile must consist of exceptionally minute and spherical atoms, so that it can be set going by a slight push. The reason why water is set going and flowing by such a slight push is of course the smallness of its atoms and their readiness to roll. The stickier consistency of honey—its relatively sluggish flow and dilatory progress—is due to the closer coherence of the component matter, consisting, as it obviously does, of particles not so smooth or so fine or so round. A high pile of poppy seed can be disturbed by a light puff of breeze, so that it trickles down from the top, whereas a heap of stones or corn ears remains immovable. In proportion as objects are smaller and smoother, so much the more do they enjoy mobility; the greater their weight and roughness, the more firmly are they anchored. Since, therefore, the substance of the mind has been found to be extraordinarily mobile, it must consist of particles exceptionally small and smooth and round. This discovery, my dear fellow, will prove a timely aid to you in many problems.

Here is a further indication how flimsy is the texture of the vital spirit and in how small a space it could be contained if it could be massed together. At the instant when a man is mastered by the care-free calm of death and forsaken by mind and spirit, you cannot tell either by sight or by weight that any part of the whole has been filched away from his body. Death leaves everything there, except vital sentience and warmth. Therefore the vital spirit as a whole must consist of very tiny atoms, linked together throughout veins, flesh and sinews—atoms so small that, when all the spirit has escaped from the whole body, the outermost contour of the limbs appears intact and there is no loss of weight. The same thing happens when the bouquet has evaporated from the juice of Bacchus, or the sweet perfume of an ointment has escaped into the air, or some substance has lost its savour. The substance itself is not visibly diminished by the loss, and its weight is not lessened, obviously because savour and scent are caused by many minute atoms distributed throughout the mass. On every ground, therefore, it may be inferred that mind and spirit are composed of exceptionally diminutive atoms, since their departure is not accompanied by any loss of weight.

It must not be supposed that the stuff of mind or spirit is a single element. The body at death is abandoned by a sort of rarefied wind mixed with warmth, while the warmth carries with it also air. Indeed, heat never occurs without an intermixture of air: because it is naturally sparse, it must have many atoms of air moving in its interstices.

The composition of mind is thus found to be *at least three-fold.* But all these three components together are not enough to create sentience, since the mind does not admit that any of these can create the sensory motions that originate the meditations revolved in the mind. *We must* accordingly *add to these a fourth component,* which is quite nameless. Than this there is nothing more mobile or more tenuous—nothing whose component atoms are smaller or smoother. This it is that first sets the sensory motions coursing through the limbs. Owing to the minuteness of its atoms, it is first to be stirred. Then the motions are caught up by warmth and the unseen energy of wind, then by air. Then everything is roused to movement: the blood is quickened; the impulse spreads throughout the flesh; last of all, bones and marrow are thrilled with pleasure or the opposite excitement. To this extremity pain cannot lightly penetrate, or the pangs of anguish win through. If they do, then everything is so confounded that no room is left for life, and the components of the vital spirit escape through all the pores of the body. But usually a stop is put to these movements as near as may be at the surface of the body. Thanks to this stoppage we contrive to cling on to life.

At this point I should like to demonstrate *how these components are intermixed* and from what mode of combination they derive their powers. Reluctantly I am thwarted in my purpose by the poverty of our native tongue. But, so far as I can touch upon the surface of this topic, I will tackle it.

The atoms rush in and out amongst one another on atomic trajectories, so that no one of them can be segregated nor its distinctive power isolated by intervening space. They co-exist like the many properties of a single body. In the flesh of any living thing there are regularly scent and colour and taste; and yet from all these there is formed only one corporeal bulk. Just so, warmth and air and the unseen energy of wind create in combination a single substance, together with that mobile force which imparts to them from itself the initial impetus from which the sensory motion takes its rise throughout the flesh. This basic substance lurks at our very core. There is nothing in our bodies more fundamental than this, the most vital element of their whole vital spirit. Just as in our limbs and body as a whole mind and spirit with their interconnected powers are latent, because their component atoms are small and sparse, so this nameless element composed of minute atoms is latent in the vital spirit and is in turn its vital element and controls the whole body.

In the same way, wind and air and warmth commingled through the limbs must interact, one being relatively latent, another prominent. In appearance a single stuff is formed by them all: warmth and wind and air do not display their powers separately so as to blot out sentience and dissolve it by their disunion. First, there is at the mind's disposal that element of heat which it brings into play when it boils with rage and passion blazes more fiercely from the eyes. There is likewise no lack of that chill wind, associated with fear, which sets the limbs atremble and impels them to flight. There is lastly that calm and steady air which prevails in a tranquil breast and unruffled mien.

In those creatures whose passionate hearts and choleric dispositions easily boil up in anger, there is a surplus of the hot element. An outstanding example is the truculent temper of lions, who often roar till they burst their chests with bellowing and cannot keep the torrents of their rage pent within. But the cold hearts of deer are of a windier blend: they are quicker to set chill breezes blowing through the flesh, provoking a shuddering movement in the limbs. Cattle, again, have in their vital composition a bigger portion of calm air. They are never too hotly fired by a touch of that smoky torch of anger which clouds the mind with its black and blinding shadow. They are never transfixed and benumbed by the icy shaft of fear. Their nature is a mean between the timidity of the deer and the lion's ferocity.

So it is with men. Though education may apply a similar polish to various individuals, it still leaves fundamental traces of their several temperaments. It must not be supposed that innate vices can be completely eradicated: one man will still incline more readily to outbursts of rage; another will give way a little sooner to fear; a third will accept some contingencies too impassively. And in a host of other ways men must differ one from another in temperament and so also in the resultant behaviour. To unfold here the secret causes of these differences is beyond my power. I cannot even find names for the multiplicity of atomic shapes that give rise to this variety of types. But I am clear that there is one relevant fact I can affirm: the lingering traces of inborn temperament that cannot be eliminated by philosophy are so slight that there is nothing to prevent men from leading a life worthy of the gods.

This *vital spirit,* then, *is present in the whole body.* It is the body's guardian and preserver. For the two are interlocked by common roots and cannot be torn apart without manifest disaster. As easily could the scent be torn out of lumps of incense without destroying their nature as mind and spirit could be abstracted from the whole body without total dissolution. So from their earliest origin the two are charged with a communal life by the intertangled atoms that compose them. It is clear that neither body nor mind by itself without the other's aid possesses the power of sensation: it is by the interacting motions of the two combined that the flame of sentience is kindled in our flesh.

Again, body by itself never experiences birth or growth, and we see that it does not persist after death. Water, we know, often gives up the heat imparted to it without being disrupted in the process, and survives intact. Not so can the derelict limbs outlast the departure of the vital spirit: they are utterly demolished by internal decomposition and decay. So from the very beginning, even when they are at rest in the mother's womb, body and spirit in mutual contact acquire the motions that generate life. They cannot be wrenched apart without hurt and havoc. So you may see, since their very existence depends upon conjunction, that their nature must likewise be conjoint.

If anyone still denies that the body is sentient, and believes it is the spirit interfused throughout the body that assumes this motion which we term sensation, he is fighting against manifest facts. Who can explain what bodily sensation really is, if it is not such as it is palpably presented to us by experience? Admittedly, when the spirit is banished, the body is quite insensible. That is because what it loses was never one of its permanent properties, but one of many attributes which it loses at death.

Again, it is awkward to maintain that the eyes can see nothing, but the mind peeps out through them as though through open doors. The sense of sight itself leads us the other way, dragging and tugging us right to the eyeballs. Often, for instance, we cannot see bright objects, because our eyes are dazzled by light. This is an experience unknown to doors: the doorways through which we gaze suffer no distress by being flung open. Besides, if our eyes are equivalent to doors, then when the eyes are removed the mind obviously ought to see things better now that the doors are away, doorposts and all.

Another error to be avoided, and one that is sanctioned by the revered authority of the great Democritus, is the belief that the limbs are knit together by atoms of body and mind arranged alternately, first one and then the other. In fact, *the atoms of spirit are not only much less in magnitude than those composing our body and flesh; they are also correspondingly inferior in number* and scattered but sparsely through our limbs. Observe what are the smallest objects whose impact serves to excite sensory motions in our bodies: these will give you the measure of the gaps between the atoms of spirit. Sometimes we are unaware that dust is sticking to our bodies or a cloud of chalk has settled on our limbs; we do not feel the night mist, or the slight threads of gossamer in our path that enmesh us as we walk, or the fall of a flimsy cobweb on our heads, or plumes of birds or flying thistledown, which from their very lightness do not lightly descend. We do not mark the path of every creeping thing that crawls across our body or every separate footfall planted by a gnat or midge. So quite a considerable commotion must be made in our bodies before the atomic disturbance is felt by the atoms of spirit interspersed through our limbs and before these can knock together across the intervening gaps and clash and combine and again bounce apart.

Note also that *it is mind, far more than spirit, that keeps life under lock and key*—mind that has the greater mastery over life. Without mind and intellect no scrap of vital spirit can linger one instant in our limbs. Spirit follows smoothly in the wake of mind and scatters into the air, leaving the limbs cold with the chill of death. While mind remains, life remains. One whose limbs are all lopped from the mangled trunk, despite the loss of vital spirit released from the limbs, yet lives and inhales the life-giving gusts of air. Though robbed, if not of all, at least of a large proportion of his spirit, he lingers still in life and clings fast to it. Just so, though the eye is lacerated all round, so long as the pupil remains intact, the faculty of vision remains alive, provided always that you do not hack away the whole encircling orb and leave the eyeball detached and isolated; for that cannot be done without total destruction. But tamper with that tiny bit in the middle of the eye, and out goes the light there and then and darkness falls, although the shining orb is otherwise unscathed. It is on just such terms that spirit and mind are everlastingly linked together.

My next point is this: you must understand that the *minds of living things and the light fabric of their spirits are neither birthless nor deathless.* To this end I have long been mustering and inventing verses with a labour that is also a joy. Now I will try to set them out in a style worthy of your career.

Please note that both objects are to be embraced under one name.

When, for instance, I proceed to demonstrate that 'spirit' is mortal, you must understand that this applies equally to 'mind', since the two are so conjoined as to constitute a single substance.

First of all, then, I have shown that spirit is flimsy stuff composed of tiny particles. Its atoms are obviously far smaller than those of swift-flowing water or mist or smoke, since it far outstrips them in mobility and is moved by a far slighter impetus. Indeed, it is actually moved by images of smoke and mist. So, for instance, when we are sunk in sleep, we may see altars sending up clouds of steam and giving off smoke; and we cannot doubt that we are here dealing with images. Now, we see that water flows out in all directions from a broken vessel and the moisture is dissipated, and mist and smoke vanish into thin air. Be assured, therefore, that spirit is similarly dispelled and vanishes far more speedily and is sooner dissolved into its component atoms once it has been let loose from the human frame. When the body, which served as a vessel for it, is by some means broken and attenuated by loss of blood from the veins, so as to be no longer able to contain it, how can you suppose that it can be contained by any kind of air, which must be far more tenuous than our bodily frame?

Again, we are conscious that mind and body are born together, grow up together and together decay. With the weak and delicate frame of wavering childhood goes a like infirmity of judgement. The robust vigour of ripening years is accompanied by a steadier resolve and a maturer strength of mind. Later, when the body is palsied by the potent forces of age and the limbs begin to droop with blunted vigour, the understanding limps, the tongue falters and the mind totters: everything weakens and gives way at the same time. It is thus natural that the vital spirit should all evaporate like smoke, soaring into the gusty air, since we have seen that it shares the body's birth and growth and wearies with the weariness of age. (vv. 94—458)

From all this it follows that *death is nothing to us* and no concern of ours, since our tenure of the mind is mortal. In days of old, we felt no disquiet when the hosts of Carthage poured in to battle on every side—when the whole earth, dizzied by the convulsive shock of war, reeled sickeningly under the high ethereal vault, and between realm and realm the empire of mankind by land and sea trembled in the balance. So, when we shall be no more—when the union of body and spirit that engenders us has been disrupted—to us, who shall then be nothing, nothing by any hazard will happen any more at all. Nothing will have power to stir our senses, not though earth be fused with sea and with sky.

If any feeling remains in mind or spirit after it has been torn from our body, that is nothing to us, who are brought into being by the wedlock of body and spirit, conjoined and coalesced. Or even if the matter that composes us should be reassembled by time after our death and brought back into its present state—if the light of life were given to us anew—even that contingency would still be no concern of ours once the chain of our identity had been snapped. We who are now are not concerned with ourselves in any previous existence: the sufferings of those selves do not touch us. When you look at the immeasurable extent of time gone by and the multiform movements of matter, you will readily credit that these same atoms that compose us now must many a time before have entered into the self-same combinations as now. But our mind cannot recall this to remembrance. For between then and now is interposed a breach in life, and all the atomic motions have been wandering far astray from sentience.

If the future holds travail and anguish in store, the self must be in existence, when that time comes, in order to experience it. But from this fate we are redeemed by death, which denies existence to the self that might have suffered these tribulations. Rest assured, therefore, that we have nothing to fear in death. One who no longer is cannot suffer, or differ in any way from one who has never been born, when once this mortal life has been usurped by death the immortal.

When you find a man treating it as a grievance that after death he will either moulder in the grave or fall a prey to flames or to the jaws of predatory beasts, be sure that his utterance does not ring true. Subconsciously his heart is stabbed by a secret dread, however loudly the man himself may disavow the belief that after death he will still experience sensation. I am convinced that he does not grant the admission he professes, nor the grounds of it; he does not oust and pluck himself root and branch out of life, but all unwittingly makes something of himself linger on. When a living man confronts the thought that after death his body will be mauled by birds and beasts of prey, he is filled with self-pity. He does not banish himself from the scene nor distinguish sharply enough between himself and that abandoned carcass. He visualizes that object as himself and infects it with his own feelings as an onlooker. That is why he is aggrieved at having been created mortal. He does not see that in real death there will be no other self alive to mourn his own decease—no other self standing by to flinch at the agony he suffers lying there being mangled, or indeed being cremated. For if it is really a bad thing after death to be mauled and crunched by ravening jaws, I cannot see why it should not be disagreeable to roast in the scorching flames of a funeral pyre, or to lie embalmed in honey, stifled and stiff with cold, on the surface of a chilly slab, or to be squashed under a crushing weight of earth.

'Now it is all over. Now the happy home and the best of wives will welcome you no more, nor winsome children rush to snatch the first kiss at your coming and touch your heart with speechless joy. No chance now to further your fortune or safeguard your family. Unhappy man,' they cry, 'unhappily cheated by one treacherous day out of all the uncounted blessings of life!' But they do not go on to say: 'And now no repining for these lost joys will oppress you any more.' If they perceived this clearly with their minds and acted according to the words, they would free their breasts from a great load of grief and dread.

'Ah yes! *You* are at peace now in the sleep of death, and so you will stay to the end of time. Pain and sorrow will never touch you again. But to *us,* who stood weeping inconsolably while you were consumed to ashes on the dreadful pyre—to us no day will come that will lift the undying sorrow from our hearts.' Ask the speaker, then, what is so heart-rending about this. If something returns to sleep and peace, what reason is that for pining in inconsolable grief?

Here, again, is the way men often talk from the bottom of their hearts when they recline at a banquet, goblet in hand and brows decked with garlands: 'How all too short are these good times that come to us poor creatures! Soon they will be past and gone, and there will be no recalling them.' You would think the crowning calamity in store for them after death was to be parched and shrivelled by a tormenting thirst or oppressed by some other vain desire. But even in sleep, when mind and body alike are at rest, no one misses himself or sighs for life. If such sleep were prolonged to eternity, no longing for ourselves would trouble us. And yet the vital atoms in our limbs cannot be far removed from their sensory motions at a time when a mere jolt out of sleep enables a man to pull himself together. Death, therefore, must be regarded, so far as we are concerned, as having much less existence than sleep, if anything can have less existence than what we perceive to be nothing. For death is followed by a far greater dispersal of the seething mass of matter: once that icy breach in life has intervened, there is no more waking.

Suppose that Nature herself were suddenly to find a voice and round upon one of us in these terms: 'What is your grievance, mortal, that you give yourself up to this whining and repining? Why do you weep and wail over death? If the life you have lived till now has been a pleasant thing—if all its blessings have not leaked away like water poured into a cracked pot and run to waste unrelished—why then, you silly creature, do you not retire as a guest who has had his fill of life and take your care-free rest with a quiet mind? Or, if all your gains have been poured profitless away and life has grown distasteful, why do you seek to swell the total? The new can but turn out as badly as the old and perish as unprofitably. Why not rather make an end of life and labour? Do you expect me to invent some new contrivance for your pleasure? I tell you, there is none. All things are always the same. If your body is not yet withered with age, nor your limbs decrepit and flagging, even so there is nothing new to look forward to—not though you should out-live all living creatures, or even though you should never die at all.' What are we to answer, except that Nature's rebuttal is justified and the plea she puts forward is a true one?

But suppose it is some man of riper years who complains—some dismal greybeard who frets unconscionably at his approaching end. Would she not have every right to protest more vehemently and repulse him in stern tones: 'Away with your tears, old reprobate! Have done with your grumbling! You are withering now after tasting all the joys of life. But, because you are always pining for what is not and unappreciative of the things at hand, your life has slipped away unfulfilled and unprized. Death has stolen upon you unawares, before you are ready to retire from life's banquet filled and satisfied. Come now, put away all that is unbecoming to your years and compose your mind to make way for others. You have no choice.' I cannot question but she would have right on her side; her censure and rebuke would be well merited. The old is always thrust aside to make way for the new, and one thing must be built out of the wreck of another. There is no murky pit of Hell awaiting anyone. There is need of matter, so that later generations may arise; when they have lived out their span, they will all follow you. Bygone generations have taken your road, and those to come will take it no less. So one thing will never cease to spring from another. To none is life given in freehold; to all on lease. Look back at the eternity that passed before we were born, and mark how utterly it counts to us as nothing. This is a mirror that Nature holds up to us, in which we may see the time that shall be after we are dead. Is there anything terrifying in the sight—anything depressing—anything that is not more restful than the soundest sleep?

As for those torments that are said to take place in the depths of Hell, they are actually present here and now, in our own lives.

There is no wretched Tantalus,[6] as the myth relates, transfixed with groundless terror at the huge boulder poised above him in the air. But in this life there really are mortals oppressed by unfounded fear of the gods and trembling at the impending doom that may fall upon any of them at the whim of chance.

There is no Tityos[7] lying in Hell for ever probed by birds of prey. Assuredly they cannot find food by groping under those giant ribs to glut them throughout eternity. No matter to what length that titanic frame may lie outstretched, so that he covers not a paltry nine acres with his spread-eagled limbs but the whole extent of earth, he will not be able to suffer an eternity of pain nor furnish food from his body for evermore. But Tityos is here in our midst—that poor devil prostrated by love, torn indeed by birds of prey, devoured by gnawing jealousy or rent by the fangs of some other passion.

Sisyphus[8] too is alive for all to see, bent on winning the insignia of office, its rods and ruthless axes,[9] by the people's vote and embittered by perpetual defeat. To strive for this profitless and never-granted prize, and in striving toil and moil incessantly, this truly is to push a boulder laboriously up a steep hill, only to see it, once the top is reached, rolling and bounding down again to the flat levels of the plain.

By the same token, to be for ever feeding a malcontent mind, filling it with good things but never satisfying it—the fate we suffer when the circling seasons enrich us with their products and their ever-changing charms but we are never filled with the fruits of life—this surely exemplifies the story of those maidens in the flower of life for ever pouring water into a leaking vessel which can never by any sleight be filled.

As for Cerberus[10] and the Furies and the pitchy darkness and the jaws of Hell belching abominable fumes, these are not and cannot be anywhere at all. But life is darkened by the fear of retribution for our misdeeds, a fear enormous in proportion to their enormity, and by the penalties imposed for crime—imprisonment and ghastly precipitation from Tarpeia's Crag, the lash, the block, the rack, the boiling pitch, the

---

[6]In Greek mythology, a man whose punishment in Hades consisted of having a great stone suspended over his head, threatening to overwhelm him, so that he was prevented from enjoying the banquet set before him.

[7]In Greek mythology, a giant punished in Hades by having to lie bound while two vultures tore at his liver. His body covered nine acres as he lay.

[8]In Greek mythology, a man punished in Hades by being condemned eternally to roll a large stone to the top of a hill, from which it immediately rolled down and had to be rolled up again.

[9]In Rome the symbol of royal, and then of consular, authority were the *fasces*, a bundle of rods fastened together with a red strap and enclosing an axe.

[10]In Greek mythology, a monstrous dog with three heads, the watchdog of Hades.

firebrand and the branding iron. Even though these horrors are not physically present, yet the conscience-ridden mind in terrified anticipation torments itself with its own goads and whips. It does not see what term there can be to its suffering nor where its punishment can have an end. It is afraid that death may serve merely to intensify pain. So at length the life of misguided mortals becomes a Hell on earth.

Here is something that you might well say to yourself from time to time: 'Even good king Ancus[11] looked his last on the daylight—a better man than you, my presumptuous friend, by a long reckoning. Death has come to many another monarch and potentate, who lorded it over mighty nations. Even that King of Kings who once built a highway across the great deep—who gave his legions a path to tread among the waves and taught them to march on foot over the briny gulfs and with his chargers trampled scornfully upon the ocean's roar—even he was robbed of the light and poured out the spirit from a dying frame. Scipio,[12] that thunderbolt of war, the terror of Carthage, gave his bones to the earth as if he had been the meanest of serfs. Add to this company the discoverers of truth and beauty. Add the attendants of the Muses, among them Homer who in solitary glory bore the sceptre but has sunk into the same slumber as the rest. Democritus, when ripe age warned him that the mindful motions of his intellect were running down, made his unbowed head a willing sacrifice to death. And the Master himself, when his daylit race was run, Epicurus himself died, whose genius outshone the race of men and dimmed them all, as the stars are dimmed by the rising of the fiery sun. And will *you* kick and protest against your sentence? You, whose life is next-door to death while you are still alive and looking on the light. You, who waste the major part of your time in sleep and, when you are awake, are snoring still and dreaming. You, who bear a mind hag-ridden by baseless fear and cannot find the commonest cause of your distress, hounded as you are, poor creature, by a pack of troubles and drifting in a drunken stupor upon a wavering tide of fantasy.'

Men feel plainly enough within their minds, a heavy burden, whose weight depresses them. If only they perceived with equal clearness the causes of this depression, the origin of this lump of evil within their breasts, they would not lead such a life as we now see all too commonly —no one knowing what he really wants and everyone for ever trying to get away from where he is, as though mere locomotion could throw off the load. Often the owner of some stately mansion, bored stiff by staying at home, takes his departure, only to return as speedily when he feels himself no better off out of doors. Off he goes to his country seat, driving his carriage and pair hot-foot, as though in haste to save a house on fire. No sooner has he crossed its doorstep than he starts yawning or retires moodily to sleep and courts oblivion, or else rushes back to revisit the city. In so doing the individual is really running away from himself. Since he remains reluctantly wedded to the self whom he cannot of course escape, he grows to hate him, because he is a sick man ignorant of the cause of his malady. If he did but see this, he would cast

---

[11] A semilegendary king of Rome, supposed to have reigned during the second half of the seventh century B.C.
[12] A distinguished Roman statesman and general of the second century B.C.

other thoughts aside and devote himself first to studying the nature of the universe. It is not the fortune of an hour that is in question, but of all time—the lot in store for mortals throughout the eternity that awaits them after death.

What is this deplorable lust of life that holds us trembling in bondage to such uncertainties and dangers? A fixed term is set to the life of mortals, and there is no way of dodging death. In any case the setting of our lives remains the same throughout, and by going on living we do not mint any new coin of pleasure. So long as the object of our craving is unattained, it seems more precious than anything besides. Once it is ours, we crave for something else. So an unquenchable thirst for life keeps us always on the gasp. There is no telling what fortune the future may bring—what chance may throw in our way, or what upshot lies in waiting. By prolonging life, we cannot subtract or whittle away one jot from the duration of our death. The time after our taking off remains constant. However many generations you may add to your store by living, there waits for you none the less the same eternal death. The time of not-being will be no less for him who made an end of life with yesterday's daylight than for him who perished many a moon and many a year before. (vv. 830—1094)

Comments / on Lucretius

Lucretius was arguing counter to the cherished beliefs of the Graeco-Roman world and an instinctive longing of the human race. . . . While it might seem true that there is no Hell for sinners because of soul-mortality, of course, there could be no Heaven, either, for the virtuous; that gave readers pause.   *G. D. HADZITS (1937)*

In one particular Epicurus indulged in a metaphysical subtlety foreign to the spirit of his materialist doctrine. As a moralist, he believed in free will. If the movements of the atoms were absolutely determined, as Democritus had taught, it seemed to him that all human actions must be equally determinate. Therefore the atoms must swerve, very rarely and very little, from the paths ordained for them by nature. To contemporaries this seemed an absurd notion. We may doubt whether it was really relevant to the moral question at issue.   *R. E. LATHAM (1951)*

. . . Lucretius, a poet of powerful and original genius, whose passion it was to discredit religion and whose achievement to display perhaps the most sincere religious enthusiasm in the whole of Roman literature.   *R. H. BARROW (1949)*

No poem is more deeply, more madly, penetrated by paradox. No sooner are two of its contradictions suggested than two others suggest themselves. The *De Rerum Natura* is a passionate attack upon passion. And it is a poem whose purpose is to kill poetry. . . . Lucretius makes his poem out of the death of poetries—of fear, of love, of superstition, of error, of myth, of custom, of tale and tradition—and nothing leaves him more ecstatic than the bleakness he discovers, the hues he sees dissolving. The perfect hue for him is now the cold grey he finds in his atoms. The perfect mystery is the lack of mystery underlying death and change, birth and corruption, loveliness and decay. The perfect song is the silence of what is because it is. The clamor of tragedy comes no longer to his ears: the cries of heroes lost between irreconcilable necessities. There is only one necessity, that things should be what they are.

MARK VAN DOREN (1946)

Lucretius was unique [among philosophical poets] for two reasons which go together, his real scientific ardor for close reasoning and for truth, and the deep poetic emotion which impelled him to seek in science that union between the mind and the outer world for which all poetry contends.   *W. F. J. KNIGHT (1944)*

Stoicism

The Stoic response to the uncertainties posed by the circumstances of life in Hellenistic civilization was not to insist upon the material reality of all existence, as the Epicureans did, but to deny the importance of such reality. Stoic thought turned man in upon himself, ignoring the external world. The basic principle was that if a man's will were rightly instructed, he could attain a self-reliance that rendered all things outside himself insignificant. Although other features of the Stoic ethical system were modified, this attitude remained the most distinctive characteristic of Stoic thought from Zeno of Citium, who founded the Stoic school in Athens in the third century B.C., to Marcus Aurelius, who in the second century A.D. was the last significant spokesman of explicitly Stoic philosophy in the ancient world. It is this concept of self-reliance that remains the greatest contribution of Stoic thought to the Western world.

Stoic self-reliance was founded on the belief that man lives in an ordered universe that obeys natural laws because it is governed by a divine principle. This principle could be equated with Zeus, with the idea of fate or destiny, or with the idea of reason itself; but in any case, it permeated the universe and affected all its operations. The role of man was to conform to these natural laws, to live, as the Stoics expressed it, a life in accordance with nature. Whether this role implied a call to reform society, as in the writings of the early Stoics, or a call to ignore society, as in the writings of the later Stoics, it was based on the idea that men should distinguish between those things which reason showed to be necessary parts of existence and those which were "things indifferent"—activities, such as the pursuit of fame or wealth, which originated in the emotions rather than in reason and which were subject to forces outside the individual himself. If a man relied only on what were natural parts of the conditions of human existence, he would not be disappointed.

Zeno the Stoic
335?—263? B.C.

Zeno was born in Citium, on the island of Cyprus, but went to Athens as a young man and by the turn of the century had begun to acquire a reputation as a teacher and writer of philosophy. Many of his ideas came from earlier philosophical schools, but his synthesis, modification, and development of them resulted in the creation of a unified system that as a whole represented a new branch of philosophy. The name applied to it derives from his habit of giving lectures expounding his system from the *stoa* (porch) of one of the public buildings in Athens; his followers thus came to be called Stoics. Although Zeno's writings were considerable, none of them have survived in their original form. Our knowledge of Zeno's thought is based on summaries, paraphrases, and fragmentary quotations found in the work of his successors, where the distinction between his own ideas and later modifications of them is often obscured. One of the main sources of information about Zeno is the work of a third-century A.D. Greek named Diogenes Laertius, whose *Lives and Opinions of Eminent Philosophers* is an indispensable, if unskillful, treatment of its subject. Diogenes tends to be gossipy and naïve in his handling of biography and unsophisticated and uncritical in dealing with philosophical doctrines. But since he apparently had access to a great many texts no longer extant, his book is invaluable in reconstructing the principles of a system, like Early Stoicism, the original works of which have not survived. Diogenes' "Life of Zeno" contains a detailed exposition of the main outlines of early Stoic thought as it appeared to a student of philosophy some five centuries after the time of Zeno. The selection from the "Life of Zeno" printed below presents Diogenes' account of Stoic ethics.

Life of Zeno

. . .

The ethical branch of philosophy they [the Stoics] divide as follows: (1) the topic of impulse; (2) the topic of things good and evil; (3) that of the passions; (4) that of virtue; (5) that of the end; (6) that of primary value and of actions; (7) that of duties or the befitting; and (8) of inducements to act or refrain from acting. The foregoing is the subdivision adopted by Chrysippus, Archedemus, Zeno of Tarsus, Apollodorus, Diogenes, Antipater, and Posidonius, and their disciples.[1] Zeno of Citium and Cleanthes treated the subject somewhat less elaborately,

---

From *Lives of Eminent Philosophers*, Vol. II, by Diogenes Laertius, translated by R. D. Hicks (Cambridge, Mass.: Harvard University Press). Reprinted by permission of the publishers and The Loeb Classical Library.
[1]These are all Stoic philosophers of the third and second centuries B.C.

as might be expected in an older generation. They, however, did sub-divide Logic and Physics as well as Ethics.

An animal's first impulse, say the Stoics, is to self-preservation, be-cause nature from the outset endears it to itself, as Chrysippus affirms in the first book of his work *On Ends:* his words are, "The dearest thing to every animal is its own constitution and its consciousness thereof"; for it was not likely that nature should estrange the living thing from itself or that she should leave the creature she has made without either estrangement from or affection for its own constitution. We are forced then to conclude that nature in constituting the animal made it near and dear to itself; for so it comes to repel all that is injurious and give free access to all that is serviceable or akin to it.

As for the assertion made by some people that pleasure is the object to which the first impulse of animals is directed, it is shown by the Stoics to be false. For pleasure, if it is really felt, they declare to be a by-product, which never comes until nature by itself has sought and found the means suitable to the animal's existence or constitution; it is an after-math comparable to the condition of animals thriving and plants in full bloom. And nature, they say, made no difference originally between plants and animals, for she regulates the life of plants too, in their case without impulse and sensation, just as also certain processes go on of a vegetative kind in us. But when in the case of animals impulse has been superadded, whereby they are enabled to go in quest of their proper aliment, for them, say the Stoics, Nature's rule is to follow the direction of impulse. But when reason by way of a more perfect leader-ship has been bestowed on the beings we call rational, for them life according to reason rightly becomes the natural life. For reason super-venes to shape impulse scientifically.

This is why Zeno was the first (in his treatise *On the Nature of Man*) to designate as the end "life in agreement with nature" (or living agreeably to nature), which is the same as a virtuous life, virtue being the goal towards which nature guides us. So too Cleanthes in his treatise *On Pleasure,* as also Posidonius, and Hecato[2] in his work *On Ends.* Again, living virtuously is equivalent to living in accordance with experience of the actual course of nature, as Chrysippus says in the first book of his *De finibus;* for our individual natures are parts of the nature of the whole universe. And this is why the end may be defined as life in accord-ance with nature, or, in other words, in accordance with our own human nature as well as that of the universe, a life in which we refrain from every action forbidden by the law common to all things, that is to say, the right reason which pervades all things, and is identical with this Zeus, lord and ruler of all that is. And this very thing constitutes the virtue of the happy man and the smooth current of life, when all actions promote the har-mony of the spirit dwelling in the individual man with the will of him who orders the universe. Diogenes then expressly declares the end to be to act with good reason in the selection of what is natural. Arche-demus says the end is to live in the performance of all befitting actions.

By the nature with which our life ought to be in accord, Chrysippus

---

[2]Stoic philosophers of the third and second centuries B.C.

understands both universal nature and more particularly the nature of man, whereas Cleanthes takes the nature of the universe alone as that which should be followed, without adding the nature of the individual.

And virtue, he holds, is a harmonious disposition, choice-worthy for its own sake and not from hope or fear or any external motive. Moreover, it is in virtue that happiness consists; for virtue is the state of mind which tends to make the whole of life harmonious. When a rational being is perverted, this is due to the deceptiveness of external pursuits or sometimes to the influence of associates. For the starting-points of nature are never perverse.

Virtue, in the first place, is in one sense the perfection of anything in general, say of a statue; again, it may be non-intellectual, like health, or intellectual, like prudence. For Hecato says in his first book *On the Virtues* that some are scientific and based upon theory, namely, those which have a structure of theoretical principles, such as prudence and justice; others are non-intellectual, those that are regarded as co-extensive and parallel with the former, like health and strength. For health is found to attend upon and be co-extensive with the intellectual virtue of temperance, just as strength is a result of the building of an arch. These are called non-intellectual, because they do not require the mind's assent; they supervene and they occur even in bad men: for instance, health, courage. The proof, says Posidonius in the first book of his treatise on *Ethics,* that virtue really exists is the fact that Socrates, Diogenes, and Antisthenes[3] and their followers made moral progress. And for the existence of vice as a fundamental fact the proof is that it is the opposite of virtue. That it, virtue, can be taught is laid down by Chrysippus in the first book of his work *On the End,* by Cleanthes, by Posidonius in his *Protreptica,* and by Hecato; that it can be taught is clear from the case of bad men becoming good.

Panaetius,[4] however, divides virtue into two kinds, theoretical and practical; others make a threefold division of it into logical, physical, and ethical; while by the school of Posidonius four types are recognized, and more than four by Cleanthes, Chrysippus, Antipater, and their followers. Apollophanes for his part counts but one, namely, practical wisdom.

Amongst the virtues some are primary, some are subordinate to these. The following are the primary: wisdom, courage, justice, temperance. Particular virtues are magnanimity, continence, endurance, presence of mind, good counsel. And wisdom they define as the knowledge of things good and evil and of what is neither good nor evil; wisdom as knowledge of what we ought to choose, what we ought to beware of, and what is indifferent; justice . . . ; magnanimity as the knowledge or habit of mind which makes one superior to anything that happens, whether good or evil equally; continence as a disposition never overcome in that which concerns right reason, or a habit which no pleasures can get the better of; endurance as a knowledge or habit which suggests

---

[3]Diogenes and Antisthenes, philosophers influenced by Socrates, were the originators of the Cynic school of philosophy, which in turn helped shape Zeno's thought.

[4]A second-century B.C. Stoic philosopher who played an important part in influencing the development of Stoic thought among the Romans.

what we are to hold fast to, what not, and what is indifferent; presence of mind as a habit prompt to find out what is meet to be done at any moment; good counsel as knowledge by which we see what to do and how to do it if we would consult our own interests.

Similarly, of vices some are primary, others subordinate: *e.g.* folly, cowardice, injustice, profligacy are accounted primary; but incontinence, stupidity, ill-advisedness subordinate. Further, they hold that the vices are forms of ignorance of those things whereof the corresponding virtues are the knowledge.

Good in general is that from which some advantage comes, and more particularly what is either identical with or not distinct from benefit. Whence it follows that virtue itself and whatever partakes of virtue is called good in these three senses—viz. as being (1) the source from which benefit results; or (2) that in respect of which benefit results, *e.g.* the virtuous act; or (3) that by the agency of which benefit results, *e.g.* the good man who partakes in virtue.

Another particular definition of good which they give is "the natural perfection of a rational being *qua* rational." To this answers virtue and, as being partakers in virtue, virtuous acts and good men; as also its supervening accessories, joy and gladness and the like. So with evils: either they are vices, folly, cowardice, injustice, and the like; or things which partake of vice, including vicious acts and wicked persons as well as their accompaniments, despair, moroseness, and the like.

Again, some goods are goods of the mind and others external, while some are neither mental nor external. The former include the virtues and virtuous acts; external goods are such as having a good country or a good friend, and the prosperity of such. Whereas to be good and happy oneself is of the class of goods neither mental nor external. Similarly of things evil some are mental evils, namely, vices and vicious actions; others are outward evils, as to have a foolish country or a foolish friend and the unhappiness of such; other evils again are neither mental nor outward, *e.g.* to be yourself bad and unhappy.

Again, goods are either of the nature of ends or they are the means to these ends, or they are at the same time end and means. A friend and the advantages derived from him are means to good, whereas confidence, high-spirit, liberty, delight, gladness, freedom from pain, and every virtuous act are of the nature of ends.

The virtues (they say) are goods of the nature at once of ends and of means. On the one hand, in so far as they cause happiness they are means, and on the other hand, in so far as they make it complete, and so are themselves part of it, they are ends. Similarly of evils some are of the nature of ends and some of means, while others are at once both means and ends. Your enemy and the harm he does you are means; consternation, abasement, slavery, gloom, despair, excess of grief, and every vicious action are of the nature of ends. Vices are evils both as ends and as means, since in so far as they cause misery they are means, but in so far as they make it complete, so that they become part of it, they are ends.

Of mental goods some are habits, others are dispositions, while others again are neither the one nor the other. The virtues are dispositions, while accomplishments or avocations are matters of habit, and activities as such or exercise of faculty neither the one nor the other. And in general there are some mixed goods: *e.g.* to be happy in one's children or in one's old age. But knowledge is a pure good. Again, some goods are permanent like the virtues, others transitory like joy and walking-exercise.

All good (they say) is expedient, binding, profitable, useful, service-able, beautiful, beneficial, desirable, and just or right. It is expedient, because it brings about things of such a kind that by their occurrence we are benefited. It is binding, because it causes unity where unity is needed; profitable, because it defrays what is expended on it, so that the return yields a balance of benefit on the transaction. It is useful, because it secures the use of benefit; it is serviceable, because the utility it affords is worthy of all praise. It is beautiful, because the good is pro-portionate to the use made of it; beneficial, because by its inherent nature it benefits; choiceworthy, because it is such that to choose it is reason-able. It is also just or right, inasmuch as it is in harmony with law and tends to draw men together.

The reason why they characterize the perfect good as beautiful is that it has in full all the "factors" required by nature or has perfect pro-portion. Of the beautiful there are (say they) four species, namely, what is just, courageous, orderly and wise; for it is under these forms that fair deeds are accomplished. Similarly there are four species of the base or ugly, namely, what is unjust, cowardly, disorderly, and unwise. By the beautiful is meant properly and in an unique sense that good which renders its possessors praiseworthy, or briefly, good which is worthy of praise; though in another sense it signifies a good aptitude for one's proper function; while in yet another sense the beautiful is that which lends new grace to anything, as when we say of the wise man that he alone is good and beautiful.

And they say that only the morally beautiful is good. So Hecato in his treatise *On Goods,* book iii., and Chrysippus in his work *On the Morally Beautiful.* They hold, that is, that virtue and whatever partakes of virtue consists in this: which is equivalent to saying that all that is good is beautiful, or that the term "good" has equal force with the term "beauti-ful," which comes to the same thing. "Since a thing is good, it is beauti-ful; now it is beautiful, therefore it is good." They hold that all goods are equal and that all good is desirable in the highest degree and admits of no lowering or heightening of intensity. Of things that are, some, they say, are good, some are evil, and some neither good nor evil (that is, morally indifferent).

Goods comprise the virtues of prudence, justice, courage, temper-ance, and the rest; while the opposites of these are evils, namely, folly, injustice, and the rest. Neutral (neither good nor evil, that is) are all those things which neither benefit nor harm a man: such as life, health, pleasure, beauty, strength, wealth, fair fame and noble birth, and their opposites, death, disease, pain, ugliness, weakness, poverty, ignominy, low birth, and the like. This Hecato affirms in his *De fine,* book vii., and also Apollodorus in his *Ethics,* and Chrysippus. For, say they, such things (as life, health, and pleasure) are not in themselves goods, but are morally indifferent, though falling under the species or subdivision "things preferred." For as the property of hot is to warm, not to cool, so the property of good is to benefit, not to injure; but wealth and health do no more benefit than injury, therefore neither wealth nor health is good. Further, they say that that is not good of which both good and bad use can be made; but of wealth and health both good and bad use can be made; therefore wealth and health are not goods. On the other hand, Posidonius maintains that these things too are among goods. Hecato in the ninth book of his treatise *On Goods,* and Chrysippus in his work *On Pleasure,* deny that pleasure is a good either; for some pleasures are disgraceful, and nothing disgraceful is good. To benefit is to set in motion or sustain in accordance with virtue; whereas to harm is to set in motion or sustain in accordance with vice.

The term "indifferent" has two meanings: in the first it denotes the things which do not contribute either to happiness or to misery, as wealth, fame, health, strength, and the like; for it is possible to be happy without having these, although, if they are used in a certain way, such use of them tends to happiness or misery. In quite another sense those things are said to be indifferent which are without the power of stirring inclination or aversion; *e.g.* the fact that the number of hairs on one's head is odd or even or whether you hold out your finger straight or bent. But it was not in this sense that the things mentioned above were termed indifferent, they being quite capable of exciting inclination or aversion. Hence of these latter some are taken by preference, others are rejected, whereas indifference in the other sense affords no gound for either choosing or avoiding.

Of things indifferent, as they express it, some are "preferred," others "rejected." Such as have value, they say, are "preferred," while such as have negative, instead of positive, value are "rejected." Value they define as, first, any contribution to harmonious living, such as attaches to every good; secondly, some faculty or use which indirectly contributes to the life according to nature: which is as much as to say "any assistance brought by wealth or health towards living a natural life"; thirdly, value is the full equivalent of an appraiser, as fixed by an expert acquainted with the facts—as when it is said that wheat exchanges for so much barley with a mule thrown in.

Thus things of the preferred class are those which have positive value, *e.g.* amongst mental qualities, natural ability, skill, moral improvement, and the like; among bodily qualities, life, health, strength, good condition, soundness of organs, beauty, and so forth; and in the sphere of external things, wealth, fame, noble birth, and the like. To the class of things "rejected" belong, of mental qualities, lack of ability, want of skill, and the like; among bodily qualities, death, disease, weakness, being out of condition, mutilation, ugliness, and the like; in the sphere of external things, poverty, ignominy, low birth, and so forth. But again there are things belonging to neither class; such are not preferred, neither are they rejected.

Again, of things preferred some are preferred for their own sake, some for the sake of something else, and others again both for their own sake and for the sake of something else. To the first of these classes belong natural ability, moral improvement, and the like; to the second wealth, noble birth, and the like; to the last strength, perfect faculties, soundness of bodily organs. Things are preferred for their own sake because they accord with nature; not for their own sake, but for the sake of something else, because they secure not a few utilities. And similarly with the class of things rejected under the contrary heads.

Furthermore, the term Duty is applied to that for which, when done, a reasonable defence can be adduced, *e.g.* harmony in the tenor of life's process, which indeed pervades the growth of plants and animals. For even in plants and animals, they hold, you may discern fitness of behaviour.

Zeno was the first to use this term *kathekon* of conduct. Etymologically it is derived from *kata tinas hekein, i.e.* reaching as far as, being up to, or incumbent on so and so. And it is an action in itself adapted to nature's arrangements. For of the acts done at the prompting of impulse some, they observe, are fit and meet, others the reverse, while there is a third class which is neither the one nor the other.

Befitting acts are all those which reason prevails with us to do; and this is the case with honouring one's parents, brothers and country, and intercourse with friends. Unbefitting, or contrary to duty, are all acts that reason deprecates, *e.g.* to neglect one's parents, to be indifferent to one's brothers, not to agree with friends, to disregard the interests of one's country, and so forth. Acts which fall under neither of the foregoing classes are those which reason neither urges us to do nor forbids, such as picking up a twig, holding a style or a scraper, and the like.

Again, some duties are incumbent unconditionally, others in certain circumstances. Unconditional duties are the following: to take proper care of health and one's organs of sense, and things of that sort. Duties imposed by circumstances are such as maiming oneself and sacrifice of property. And so likewise with acts which are violations of duty. Another division is into duties which are always incumbent and those which are not. To live in accordance with virtue is always a duty, whereas dialectic by question and answer or walking-exercise and the like are not at all times incumbent. The same may be said of the violations of duty. And in things intermediate also there are duties; as that boys should obey the attendants who have charge of them.

According to the Stoics there is an eight-fold division of the soul: the five senses, the faculty of speech, the intellectual faculty, which is the mind itself, and the generative faculty, being all parts of the soul. Now from falsehood there results perversion, which extends to the mind; and from this perversion arise many passions or emotions, which are causes of instability. Passion, or emotion, is defined by Zeno as an irrational and unnatural movement in the soul, or again as impulse in excess.

The main, or most universal, emotions, according to Hecato in his treatise *On the Passions,* book ii., and Zeno in his treatise with the same title, constitute four great classes, grief, fear, desire or craving, pleasure. They hold the emotions to be judgements, as is stated by Chrysippus in his treatise *On the Passions:* avarice being a supposition that money is a good, while the case is similar with drunkenness and profligacy and all the other emotions.

And grief or pain they hold to be an irrational mental contraction. Its species are pity, envy, jealousy, rivalry, heaviness, annoyance, distress, anguish, distraction. Pity is grief felt at undeserved suffering; envy, grief at others' prosperity; jealousy, grief at the possession by another of that which one desires for oneself; rivalry, pain at the possession by another of what one has oneself. Heaviness or vexation is grief which weighs us down, annoyance that which coops us up and straitens us for want of room, distress a pain brought on by anxious thought that lasts and increases, anguish painful grief, distraction irrational grief, rasping and hindering us from viewing the situation as a whole.

Fear is an expectation of evil. Under fear are ranged the following emotions: terror, nervous shrinking, shame, consternation, panic, mental agony. Terror is a fear which produces fright; shame is fear of disgrace; nervous shrinking is a fear that one will have to act; consternation is fear due to a presentation of some unusual occurrence; panic is fear with pressure exercised by sound; mental agony is fear felt when some issue is still in suspense.

Desire or craving is irrational appetency, and under it are ranged the following states: want, hatred, contentiousness, anger, love, wrath, resentment. Want, then, is a craving when it is baulked and, as it were, cut off from its object, but kept at full stretch and attracted towards it in vain. Hatred is a growing and lasting desire or craving that it should go ill with somebody. Contentiousness is a craving or desire connected with partisanship; anger a craving or desire to punish one who is thought to have done you an undeserved injury. The passion of love is a craving from which good men are free; for it is an effort to win affection due to the visible presence of beauty. Wrath is anger which has long rankled and has become malicious, waiting for its opportunity, as is illustrated by the lines:

Even though for the one day he swallow his anger, yet doth he still keep his displeasure thereafter in his heart, till he accomplish it.[5]

Resentment is anger in an early stage.

Pleasure is an irrational elation at the accruing of what seems to be choiceworthy; and under it are ranged ravishment, malevolent joy, delight, transport. Ravishment is pleasure which charms the ear. Malevolent joy is pleasure at another's ills. Delight is the mind's propulsion to weakness, its name in Greek (*terpsis*) being akin to *trepsis* or turning. To be in transports of delight is the melting away of virtue.

And as there are said to be certain infirmities in the body, as for instance gout and arthritic disorders, so too there is in the soul love of fame, love of pleasure, and the like. By infirmity is meant disease accompanied by weakness; and by disease is meant a fond imagining of something that seems desirable. And as in the body there are tendencies to certain maladies such as colds and diarrhoea, so it is with the soul, there are tendencies like enviousness, pitifulness, quarrelsomeness, and the like.

---

[5] *Iliad*, I, 81 f.

Also they say that there are three emotional states which are good, namely, joy, caution, and wishing. Joy, the counterpart of pleasure, is rational elation; caution, the counterpart of fear, rational avoidance; for though the wise man will never feel fear, he will yet use caution. And they make wishing the counterpart of desire (or craving), inasmuch as it is rational appetency. And accordingly, as under the primary passions are classed certain others subordinate to them, so too is it with the primary eupathies or good emotional states. Thus under wishing they bring well-wishing or benevolence, friendliness, respect, affection; under caution, reverence and modesty; under joy, delight, mirth, cheerfulness.

Now they say that the wise man is passionless, because he is not prone to fall into such infirmity. But they add that in another sense the term apathy is applied to the bad man, when, that is, it means that he is callous and relentless. Further, the wise man is said to be free from vanity; for he is indifferent to good or evil report. However, he is not alone in this, there being another who is also free from vanity, he who is ranged among the rash, and that is the bad man. Again, they tell us that all good men are austere or harsh, because they neither have dealings with pleasure themselves nor tolerate those who have. The term harsh is applied, however, to others as well, and in much the same sense as a wine is said to be harsh when it is employed medicinally and not for drinking at all.

Again, the good are genuinely in earnest and vigilant for their own improvement, using a manner of life which banishes evil out of sight and makes what good there is in things appear. At the same time they are free from pretence; for they have stripped off all pretence or "make-up" whether in voice or in look. Free too are they from all business cares, declining to do anything which conflicts with duty. They will take wine, but not get drunk. Nay more, they will not be liable to madness either; not but what there will at times occur to the good man strange impressions due to melancholy or delirium, ideas not determined by the principle of what is choiceworthy but contrary to nature. Nor indeed will the wise man ever feel grief; seeing that grief is irrational contraction of the soul, as Apollodorus says in his *Ethics*.

They are also, it is declared, godlike; for they have a something divine within them; whereas the bad man is godless. And yet of this word—godless or ungodly—there are two senses, one in which it is the opposite of the term "godly," the other denoting the man who ignores the divine altogether: in this latter sense, as they note, the term does not apply to every bad man. The good, it is added, are also worshippers of God; for they have acquaintance with the rites of the gods, and piety is the knowledge of how to serve the gods. Further, they will sacrifice to the gods and they keep themselves pure; for they avoid all acts that are offences against the gods, and the gods think highly of them: for they are holy and just in what concerns the gods. The wise too are the only priests; for they have made sacrifices their study, as also the building of temples, purifications, and all the other matters appertaining to the gods.

The Stoics approve also of honouring parents and brothers in the second place next after the gods. They further maintain that parental affection for children is natural to the good, but not to the bad. It is one of their tenets that sins are all equal: so Chrysippus in the fourth book of his *Ethical Questions,* as well as Persaeus and Zeno. For if one truth is not more true than another, neither is one falsehood more false than another, and in the same way one deceit is not more so than another, nor sin than sin. For he who is a hundred furlongs from Canopus and he who is only one furlong away are equally not in Canopus, and so too he who commits the greater sin and he who commits the less are equally not in the path of right conduct. But Heraclides of Tarsus, who was the disciple of Antipater of Tarsus, and Athenodorus both assert that sins are not equal.

Again, the Stoics say that the wise man will take part in politics, if nothing hinders him—so, for instance, Chrysippus in the first book of his work *On Various Types of Life*—since thus he will restrain vice and promote virtue. Also (they maintain) he will marry, as Zeno says in his *Republic,* and beget children. Moreover, they say that the wise man will never form mere opinions, that is to say, he will never give assent to anything that is false; that he will also play the Cynic, Cynicism being a short cut to virtue, as Apollodorus calls it in his *Ethics;* that he will even turn cannibal under stress of circumstances. They declare that he alone is free and bad men are slaves, freedom being power of independent action, whereas slavery is privation of the same: though indeed there is also a second form of slavery consisting in subordination, and a third which implies possession of the slave as well as his subordination; the correlative of such servitude being lordship; and this too is evil. Moreover, according to them not only are the wise free, they are also kings; kingship being irresponsible rule, which none but the wise can maintain: so Chrysippus in his treatise vindicating Zeno's use of terminology. For he holds that knowledge of good and evil is a necessary attribute of the ruler, and that no bad man is acquainted with this science. Similarly the wise and good alone are fit to be magistrates, judges, or orators, whereas among the bad there is not one so qualified. Furthermore, the wise are infallible, not being liable to error. They are also without offence; for they do no hurt to others or to themselves. At the same time they are not pitiful and make no allowance for anyone; they never relax the penalties fixed by the laws, since indulgence and pity and even equitable consideration are marks of a weak mind, which affects kindness in place of chastizing. Nor do they deem punishments too severe. Again, they say that the wise man never wonders at any of the things which appear extraordinary, such as Charon's mephitic caverns,[6] ebbings of the tide, hot springs or fiery eruptions. Nor yet, they go on to say, will the wise man live in solitude; for he is naturally made for society and action. He will, however, submit to training to augment his powers of bodily endurance.

And the wise man, they say, will offer prayers, and ask for good things from the gods: so Posidonius in the first book of his treatise *On Duties,* and Hecato in his third book *On Paradoxes.* Friendship, they declare,

---

[6]In Greek mythology, Charon was the boatman who ferried the dead across the River Styx into Hades. His caverns were the passages down into the underworld.

exists only between the wise and good, by reason of their likeness to one another. And by friendship they mean a common use of all that has to do with life, wherein we treat our friends as we should ourselves. They argue that a friend is worth having for his own sake and that it is a good thing to have many friends. But among the bad there is, they hold, no such thing as friendship, and thus no bad man has a friend. Another of their tenets is that the unwise are all mad, inasmuch as they are not wise but do what they do from that madness which is the equivalent of their folly.

Furthermore, the wise man does all things well, just as we say that Ismenias plays all airs on the flute well. Also everything belongs to the wise. For the law, they say, has conferred upon them a perfect right to all things. It is true that certain things are said to belong to the bad, just as what has been dishonestly acquired may be said, in one sense, to belong to the state, in another sense to those who are enjoying it.

They hold that the virtues involve one another, and that the possessor of one is the possessor of all, inasmuch as they have common principles, as Chrysippus says in the first book of his work *On Virtues,* Apollodorus in his *Physics according to the Early School,* and Hecato in the third book of his treatise *On Virtues.* For if a man be possessed of virtue, he is at once able to discover and to put into practice what he ought to do. Now such rules of conduct comprise rules for choosing, enduring, staying, and distributing; so that if a man does some things by intelligent choice, some things with fortitude, some things by way of just distribution, and some steadily, he is at once wise, courageous, just, and temperate. And each of the virtues has a particular subject with which it deals, as, for instance, courage is concerned with things that must be endured, practical wisdom with acts to be done, acts from which one must abstain, and those which fall under neither head. Similarly each of the other virtues is concerned with its own proper sphere. To wisdom are subordinate good counsel and understanding; to temperance, good discipline and orderliness; to justice, equality and fair-mindedness; to courage, constancy and vigour.

It is a tenet of theirs that between virtue and vice there is nothing intermediate, whereas according to the Peripatetics[7] there is, namely, the state of moral improvement. For, say the Stoics, just as a stick must be either straight or crooked, so a man must be either just or unjust. Nor again are there degrees of justice and injustice; and the same rule applies to the other virtues. Further, while Chrysippus holds that virtue can be lost, Cleanthes maintains that it cannot. According to the former it may be lost in consequence of drunkenness or melancholy; the latter takes it to be inalienable owing to the certainty of our mental apprehension. And virtue in itself they hold to be worthy of choice for its own sake. At all events we are ashamed of bad conduct as if we knew that nothing is really good but the morally beautiful. Moreover, they hold that

---

[7]*Peripatetics* literally means "persons in the habit of walking about." The name was applied to followers of Aristotle's philosophy because of Aristotle's habit of walking along pleasant shaded paths with his disciples while discussing philosophy.

it is in itself sufficient to ensure well-being: thus Zeno, and Chrysippus in the first book of his treatise *On Virtues,* and Hecato in the second book of his treatise *On Goods:* "For if magnanimity by itself alone can raise us far above everything, and if magnanimity is but a part of virtue, then too virtue as a whole will be sufficient in itself for well-being—despising all things that seem troublesome." Panaetius, however, and Posidonius deny that virtue is self-sufficing: on the contrary, health is necessary, and some means of living and strength.

Another tenet of theirs is the perpetual exercise of virtue, as held by Cleanthes and his followers. For virtue can never be lost, and the good man is always exercising his mind, which is perfect. Again, they say that justice, as well as law and right reason, exists by nature and not by convention: so Chrysippus in his work *On the Morally Beautiful.* Neither do they think that the divergence of opinion between philosophers is any reason for abandoning the study of philosophy, since at that rate we should have to give up life altogether: so Posidonius in his *Exhortations.* Chrysippus allows that the ordinary Greek education is serviceable.

It is their doctrine that there can be no question of right as between man and the lower animals, because of their unlikeness. Thus Chrysippus in the first book of his treatise *On Justice,* and Posidonius in the first book of his *De officio.* Further, they say that the wise man will feel affection for the youths who by their countenance show a natural endowment for virtue. So Zeno in his *Republic,* Chrysippus in book i. of his work *On Modes of Life,* and Apollodorus in his *Ethics.*

Their definition of love is an effort toward friendliness due to visible beauty appearing, its sole end being friendship, not bodily enjoyment. At all events, they allege that Thrasonides, although he had his mistress in his power, abstained from her because she hated him. By which it is shown, they think, that love depends upon regard, as Chrysippus says in his treatise *Of Love,* and is not sent by the gods. And beauty they describe as the bloom or flower of virtue.

Of the three kinds of life, the contemplative, the practical, and the rational, they declare that we ought to choose the last, for that a rational being is expressly produced by nature for contemplation and for action. They tell us that the wise man will for reasonable cause make his own exit from life, on his country's behalf or for the sake of his friends, or if he suffer intolerable pain, mutilation, or incurable disease.

It is also their doctrine that amongst the wise there should be a community of wives with free choice of partners, as Zeno says in his *Republic* and Chrysippus in his treatise *On Government* and not only they, but also Diogenes the Cynic and Plato. Under such circumstances we shall feel paternal affection for all the children alike, and there will be an end of the jealousies arising from adultery. The best form of government they hold to be a mixture of democracy, kingship, and aristocracy (or the rule of the best).

Such, then, are the statements they make in their ethical doctrines, with much more besides, together with their proper proofs: let this, however, suffice for a statement of them in a summary and elementary form. . . .

Comments / on Zeno the Stoic

[T]he ethics of Stoicism are originally and essentially, not a doctrine of virtue, but merely a guide to a rational life, the end and aim of which is happiness through peace of mind. Virtuous conduct appears in it as it were merely by accident, as the means, not the end. Therefore the ethical theory of Stoicism is in its whole nature and point of view fundamentally different from the ethical systems which lay stress directly upon virtue, such as the doctrines of the Vedas, of Plato, of Christianity, and of Kant.   *ARTHUR SCHOPENHAUER (1818)*

The Stoic School, whose founder, Zeno, was a disciple of Antisthenes, gradually built up a theory of moral life which has on the whole weathered the storms of time with great success. It largely dominated later antiquity by its imaginative and emotional power. It gave form to the aspirations of early Christianity. It lasts now as the nearest approach to an acceptable system of conduct for those who do not accept revelation, but still keep some faith in the Purpose of Things.   *GILBERT MURRAY (1925)*

It should be insisted that the greatest practical inheritance the Greeks left in philosophy was not the splendour of Plato, or the vast erudition of Aristotle, but the practical systems of Zeno and Epicurus, and the scepticism of Pyrrho. In our own day every man is either a Stoic, an Epicurean, or a Sceptic.   *J. P. MAHAFFY (1896)*

When Stoicism, led by its founder Zeno, argued that nothing matters but virtue and that it is to be found in following the purposes of the Cosmos, he eliminated the emotions, even pity, because they disturb the rational calm which should be the end of life. Stoicism might produce its martyrs to duty, but it hardly produced full human beings.
                              C. M. BOWRA (1957)

[T]he literature of the first Stoics is a mere wreck, and we are thrown back upon indirect evidence, which may or may not do justice in detail. At the same time, two decisive facts are apparent. The Stoics attempted to frame a theory of the physical universe of the individual man as he finds himself under compulsion in this universe, and, combining the two, to formulate a rule of life in conformity with Reason. Approaching these problems in a new humanistic spirit, they suffused them with fresh and general interest. On the other hand, the several aspects of their teaching revert to previous philosophy, and although it would be unfair to allege that a mosaic resulted, the various elements lay side by side imperfectly unified. Like eclectics always, they forced contradictions to the point of paradox, and were inclined to save the day by appeal to practical consideration.   *R. M. WENLEY (1924)*

Cleanthes
331?—232? B.C.

Cleanthes was Zeno's successor as head of the Stoic school in Athens. Aside from some poetry versifying Stoic beliefs, very little of his writing has survived. However, we do know that he devoted a good deal of energy to showing how Heraclitus' theories about physics, adapted by Zeno to provide a scientific basis for the Stoic ethical system, could be used to demonstrate the validity of the Stoic idea of deity. His main contribution to Stoicism, which was not so much philosophical as theological, was his emphasis on the religious implications of the Stoic conception of the divine principle that governed the universe. Cleanthes, so far as we can tell, was chiefly responsible for combining the Stoic conceptions of "creative fire," adapted by Zeno from Heraclitus' conception of fire as one of the primary elements of the universe, and of *logos,* the idea of reason itself, into the single broader conception of "spirit," the divine force in the universe and in man. This idea had a striking impact on the development not only of Stoicism but of all subsequent Western thought. Cleanthes' ways of thinking are revealed in his "Hymn to Zeus," a short poem but the most important work of his extant. It is characteristic of the religious temper he imparted to Stoicism as well as of his ardent attempts to resolve philosophy, physics, and theology into one harmonious whole.

Hymn to Zeus

O God most glorious, called by many a name,
Nature's great King, through endless years the same;
Omnipotence, who by thy just decree
Controllest all, hail, Zeus, for unto thee
Behooves thy creatures in all lands to call.
We are thy children, we alone, of all
On earth's broad ways that wander to and fro,
Bearing thine image wheresoe'er we go.
Wherefore with songs of praise thy power I will forth show.
Lo! yonder heaven, that round the earth is wheeled,
Follows thy guidance, still to thee doth yield
Glad homage; thine unconquerable hand
Such flaming minister, the levin-brand,
Wieldeth, a sword two-edged, whose deathless might
Pulsates through all that Nature brings to light;

Essential Works of Stoicism; edited by Moses Hadas; © Copyright, 1961, by Bantam Books, Inc. Reprinted by permission of Bantam Books, Inc.

Vehicle of the universal Word, that flows
Through all, and in the light celestial glows
Of stars both great and small. O King of Kings
Through ceaseless ages, God, whose purpose brings
To birth, whate'er on land or in the sea
Is wrought, or in high heaven's immensity;
Save what the sinner works infatuate.
Nay, but thou knowest to make crooked straight:
Chaos to thee is order: in thine eyes
The unloved is lovely, who did'st harmonize
Things evil with things good, that there should be
One Word through all things everlastingly.
One Word—whose voice alas! the wicked spurn;
Insatiate for the good their spirits yearn:
Yet seeing see not, neither hearing hear
God's universal law, which those revere,
By reason guided, happiness who win.
The rest, unreasoning, diverse shapes of sin
Self-prompted follow: for an idle name
Vainly they wrestle in the lists of fame:
Others inordinately Riches woo,
Or dissolute, the joys of flesh pursue.
Now here, now there they wander, fruitless still,
For ever seeking good and finding ill.
Zeus the all-bountiful, whom darkness shrouds,
Whose lightning lightens in the thunder clouds;
Thy children save from error's deadly sway:
Turn thou the darkness from their souls away:
Vouchsafe that unto knowledge they attain;
For thou by knowledge art made strong to reign
O'er all, and all things rulest righteously.
So by thee honoured, we will honour thee,
Praising thy works continually with songs,
As mortals should; nor higher meed belongs
E'en to the gods, than justly to adore
The Universal law for evermore.

Comments / on Cleanthes

The universe he [Cleanthes] considered a living being, with God as its soul. . . .   *MOSES HADAS (1961)*

The belief in the deity, which in the fragments of Zeno's teaching appears merely formal and argumentative, becomes in the verse of Cleanthes ardent and dominating.   *E. V. ARNOLD (1911)*

Stoicism, while seeking to construct a natural ethic for the intellectual classes, sought to preserve the old supernatural aids for the morality of the common man, and, as time went on, gave a more and more religious color to its own metaphysical and ethical thought. . . . Cleanthes identifies God with Zeus in a monotheistic hymn worthy of Ikhnaton or Isaiah. *WILL DURANT (1939)*

Cicero
106 – 43 B.C.

During the second century B.C., Rome became the leading power in the Western world and provided one of the striking paradoxes in the history of Western culture as it assumed political domination over Greece but fell under the intellectual domination of Greek thought. Of all the Greek philosophical systems, Stoicism was most suited to the Roman temperament, because it emphasized practical ethics rather than abstract speculative inquiry. Also, the Stoic idea of a single guiding destiny ruling the universe could easily be fitted into the Roman imperialistic idea of world dominion, giving the Romans philosophic justification for doing what they did anyhow. From early in the second century B.C., the intellectual life of Rome was strongly influenced by Stoic philosophy, which formed an important part of the education of the leaders of Roman society. Roman Stoicism, though indebted to Zeno and his followers, acquired its own distinctive characteristics and modified many of the ideas of the early Stoics. Thus, it is customary to consider this period in the development of Stoic thought as Middle Stoicism, as distinguished from the Early Stoicism of Zeno and Cleanthes and from the Late Stoicism of the Roman Empire during the Christian centuries.

The philosophers most instrumental in introducing Stoicism into Roman culture were Panaetius of Rhodes (180? – 110 B.C.) and his pupil, Posidonius of Apamea (135? – 50 B.C.), men of Greek heritage whose ideas were adopted by influential Romans. The most important changes they introduced into Stoic thought were the identification of divine destiny with Roman imperialism and the modification of the absolute quality of virtue Zeno had envisioned. According to Zeno, men were either virtuous or not and the man who tried to achieve virtue but fell short was no better than the man who made no effort at all. Roman Stoicism, in line with the realistic Roman view of human affairs, allowed for gradations of virtue—just as Roman law, with its distinction between felony and misdemeanor, allowed for gradations of evil. Roman Stoicism was, above all, practical.

The impact of a philosophic system on a society is seldom measurable, since the ideas of that system tend to blend into the overall pattern of assumptions, ideals, attitudes, and viewpoints—conscious and unconscious—which shape that society. One of the major insights we have of this process in the case of Stoicism and Roman society is contained in Virgil's *Aeneid*. With this poem, Virgil (70—19 B.C.) initiated the tradition of the "secondary" epic: that is, he not only conceptualized the human ideals of his society in a hero (which was the main purpose of the "primary" epic as established by Homer), but he modified these ideals in accord with philosophical considerations of the nature, function, and purpose of the society itself. Virgil uses a legendary story of the founding of Rome by Aeneas, a Trojan briefly mentioned by Homer but credited in later tradition with escaping from Troy, wandering about the Mediterranean world, and eventually establishing a kingdom in Italy which ultimately became Rome. But as Virgil tells it, Aeneas does not simply wander aimlessly, he is destined to reach Italy; he does not set up a kingdom haphazardly, he establishes a dominion suitable for its destiny as ruler of the world. Virgil has combined the Stoic conception of destiny, of a purposeful orderly design in the operations of the universe, with the Roman sense of national greatness—illustrating the identification which the Romans made between the Stoic idea of world order and their own attempt to impose order, namely, Roman rule, upon the world. Aeneas embodies the Stoic virtues appropriate to an ideal Roman as Virgil saw them; but even more, he is, as Virgil calls him, "destiny's darling," the agent of divine forces working to establish the universal supremacy of Rome.

Most of what we know about Middle Stoicism as a philosophical system has come down to us secondhand. Very little of Panaetius' or Posidonius' original work has survived; but in the writings of Marcus Tullius Cicero we do have an account of their ideas, closer to them in time than Diogenes Laertius to Zeno and much superior in style. Cicero is one of the great figures in Roman history—a statesman, orator, philosopher, and writer who had considerable influence on his own time and enormous impact on the subsequent development of Western culture. He stands as a classic representative of the Roman republican spirit, and his writing has served for centuries as *the* model of Latin prose style. His reputation during the Renaissance cast him as the embodiment of the ideal of classical civilization: a statesman concerned with legitimacy in government, a moral philosopher concerned with men's fulfilling their potential as members of society, a writer concerned with clarity of thought and cogency of expression. In our own time Cicero's reputation as a philosopher has been somewhat modified. He is recognized not as an original thinker but as a skillful expositor of Greek thought, the first significant Roman spokesman for the philosophic attitudes that characterized Roman civilization. Although some of his work has been lost, a considerable amount of it is still extant, including enough of his philosophical writings to present a reasonably full exposition of Stoic philosophy as it was understood by a thoughtful, aristocratic Roman man of affairs during the first century B.C.

This quality of his thinking is well illustrated in his essay *On Old Age,* a philosophic dialogue examining the practical applications of Stoic objectivity in creating a full, satisfactory life. Cicero conceived the dialogue as taking place among three eminent Romans of the preceding century, in the year 150 B.C., when Cato, the chief speaker, was eighty-four years old and Laelius and Scipio, the other two speakers, were both in early middle age. The ideas voiced by Cato are based on Stoic thought, but the practical achievements of Stoicism are demonstrated in the person of Cato himself—in the serene detachment with which a well-stocked and perceptive mind can view the circumstances of human existence.

On Old Age

2. SCIPIO: Many a time have I in conversation with my friend Gaius Laelius here expressed my admiration, Marcus Cato, of the eminent, nay perfect, wisdom displayed by you indeed at all points, but above everything because I have noticed that old age never seemed a burden to you, while to most old men it is so hateful that they declare themselves under a weight heavier than Aetna.

CATO: Your admiration is easily excited, it seems, my dear Scipio and Laelius. Men, of course, who have no resources in themselves for securing a good and happy life find every age burdensome. But those who look for all happiness from within can never think anything bad which nature makes inevitable. In that category before anything else comes old age, to which all wish to attain, and at which all grumble when attained. Such is Folly's inconsistency and unreasonableness! They say that it is stealing upon them faster than they expected. In the first place, who compelled them to hug an illusion? For in what respect did old age steal upon manhood faster than manhood upon childhood? In the next place, in what way would old age have been less disagreeable to them if they were in their eight-hundredth year than in their eightieth? For their past, however long, when once it was past, would have no consolation for a stupid old age. Wherefore, if it is your wont to admire my wisdom—and I would that it were worthy of your good opinion and of my own surname of Sapiens[1] it really consists in the fact that I follow Nature, the best of guides, as I would a god, and am loyal to her commands. It is not likely, if she has written the rest of the play well, that she has been careless about the last act like some idle poet. But after all some "last" was inevitable, just as to the berries of a tree and the fruits of the earth there comes in the fulness of time a period of decay and fall. A wise man will not make a grievance of this. To rebel against nature—is not that to fight like the giants with the gods?

LAELIUS: And yet, Cato, you will do us a very great favour (I venture to speak for Scipio as for myself) if—since we all hope, or at least wish, to become old men—you would allow us to learn from you in good time before it arrives, by what methods we may most easily acquire the strength to support the burden of advancing age.

From *Letters and Treatises*, translated by E. S. Shuckburgh. This material reprinted with the kind permission of Crowell Collier and Macmillan, Inc.
    [1]"The wise."

CATO: I will do so without doubt, Laelius, especially if, as you say, it will be agreeable to you both.

LAELIUS: We do wish very much, Cato, if it is no trouble to you, to be allowed to see the nature of the bourne which you have reached after completing a long journey, as it were, upon which we too are bound to embark.

3. CATO: I will do the best I can, Laelius. It has often been my fortune to hear the complaints of my contemporaries—like will to like, you know, according to the old proverb—complaints to which men like C. Salinator and Sp. Albinus, who were of consular rank and about my time, used to give vent. They were, first, that they had lost the pleasures of the senses, without which they did not regard life as life at all; and, secondly, that they were neglected by those from whom they had been used to receive attentions. Such men appear to me to lay the blame on the wrong thing. For if it had been the fault of old age, then these same misfortunes would have befallen me and all other men of advanced years. But I have known many of them who never said a word of complaint against old age; for they were only too glad to be freed from the bondage of passion, and were not at all looked down upon by their friends. The fact is that the blame for all complaints of that kind is to be charged to character, not to a particular time of life. For old men who are reasonable and neither cross-grained nor churlish find old age tolerable enough: whereas unreason and churlishness cause uneasiness at every time of life.

LAELIUS: It is as you say, Cato. But perhaps some one may suggest that it is your large means, wealth, and high position that make you think old age tolerable: whereas such good fortune only falls to few.

CATO: There is something in that, Laelius, but by no means all. For instance, the story is told of the answer of Themistocles[2] in a wrangle with a certain Seriphian, who asserted that he owed his brilliant position to the reputation of his country, not to his own. "If I had been a Seriphian," said he, "even I should never have been famous, nor would you if you had been an Athenian." Something like this may be said of old age. For the philosopher himself could not find old age easy to bear in the depths of poverty, nor the fool feel it anything but a burden though he were a millionaire. You may be sure, my dear Scipio and Laelius, that the arms best adapted to old age are culture and the active exercise of the virtues. For if they have been maintained at every period—if one has lived much as well as long—the harvest they produce is wonderful, not only because they never fail us even in our last days (though that in itself is supremely important), but also because the consciousness of a well-spent life and the recollection of many virtuous actions are exceedingly delightful.

5. ... Yet it is after all true that everybody cannot be a Scipio or a Maximus,[3] with stormings of cities, with battles by land and sea, with wars in which they themselves commanded, and with triumphs to recall.

---

[2]Athenian statesman of the early fifth century B.C. who commanded the Athenian forces in their victory over the Persians in the great naval battle of Salamis.
[3]Famous Roman generals of the third century B.C.

Besides this there is a quiet, pure, and cultivated life which produces a calm and gentle old age, such as we have been told Plato's was, who died at his writing-desk in his eighty-first year; or like that of Isocrates,[4] who says that he wrote the book called *The Panegyric* in his ninety-fourth year, and who lived for five years afterwards; while his master Gorgias of Leontini completed a hundred and seven years without ever relaxing his diligence or giving up work. When some one asked him why he consented to remain so long alive—"I have no fault," said he, "to find with old age." That was a noble answer, and worthy of a scholar. For fools impute their own frailties and guilt to old age, contrary to the practice of Ennius[5]. . . . In the lines—

Like some brave steed that oft before
The Olympic wreath of victory bore,
Now by the weight of years oppressed,
Forgets the race, and takes his rest—

he compares his own old age to that of a high-spirited and successful race-horse. And him indeed you may very well remember. . . .

The fact is that when I come to think it over, I find that there are four reasons for old age being thought unhappy: First, that it withdraws us from active employments; second, that it enfeebles the body; third, that it deprives us of nearly all physical pleasures; fourth, that it is the next step to death. Of each of these reasons, if you will allow me, let us examine the force and justice separately.

6. *Old age withdraws us from active employments.* From which of them? Do you mean from those carried on by youth and bodily strength? Are there then no old men's employments to be after all conducted by the intellect, even when bodies are weak? So then Q. Maximus did nothing; nor L. Aemilius—your father, Scipio, and my excellent son's father-in-law! So with other old men—the Fabricii, the Curii and Coruncanii—when they were supporting the State by their advice and influence, they were doing nothing! To old age Appius Claudius[6] had the additional disadvantage of being blind; yet it was he who, when the Senate was inclining towards a peace with Pyrrhus and was for making a treaty, did not hesitate to say what Ennius has embalmed in the verses:

Whither have swerved the souls so firm of yore?
Is sense grown senseless? Can feet stand no more?

And so on in a tone of the most passionate vehemence. You know the poem, and the speech of Appius himself is extant. Now, he delivered it seventeen years after his second consulship, there having been an interval of ten years between the two consulships, and he having been censor before his previous consulship. This will show you that at the

---

[4]Athenian orator and rhetorician, 436—338 B.C.
[5]The first great Roman poet, 239—169 B.C.
[6]Roman statesman who flourished around the end of the fourth and beginning of the third centuries B.C.

time of the war with Pyrrhus he was a very old man. Yet this is the story handed down to us.

There is therefore nothing in the arguments of those who say that old age takes no part in public business. They are like men who would say that a steersman does nothing in sailing a ship, because, while some of the crew are climbing the masts, others hurrying up and down the gangways, others pumping out the bilge water, he sits quietly in the stern holding the tiller. He does not do what young men do; nevertheless he does what is much more important and better. The great affairs of life are not performed by physical strength, or activity, or nimbleness of body, but by deliberation, character, expression of opinion. Of these old age is not only not deprived, but, as a rule, has them in a greater degree. Unless by any chance I, who as a soldier in the ranks, as military tribune, as legate, and as consul have been employed in various kinds of war, now appear to you to be idle because not actively engaged in war. But I enjoin upon the Senate what is to be done, and how. Carthage has long been harbouring evil designs, and I accordingly proclaim war against her in good time. I shall never cease to entertain fears about her till I hear of her having been levelled with the ground. . . . And if those qualities had not resided in us *seniors,* our ancestors would never have called their supreme council a *Senate.*[7] At Sparta, indeed, those who hold the highest magistracies are in accordance with the fact actually called "elders." But if you will take the trouble to read or listen to foreign history, you will find that the mightiest States have been brought into peril by young men, have been supported and restored by old. The question occurs in the poet Naevius's[8] *Sport:*

> Pray, who are those who brought your State
> With such despatch to meet its fate?

There is a long answer, but this is the chief point:

> A crop of brand-new orators we grew,
> And foolish, paltry lads who thought they knew.

For of course rashness is the note of youth, prudence of old age.

7. But, it is said, memory dwindles. No doubt, unless you keep it in practice, or if you happen to be somewhat dull by nature. Themistocles had the names of all his fellow-citizens by heart. Do you imagine that in his old age he used to address Aristides as Lysimachus? For my part, I know not only the present generation, but their fathers also, and their grandfathers. Nor have I any fear of losing my memory by reading tombstones, according to the vulgar superstition. On the contrary, by reading them I renew my memory of those who are dead and gone. Nor, in point of fact, have I ever heard of any old man forgetting where he had hidden his money. They remember everything that interests them: when to answer to their bail, business appointments, who owes them money,

---

[7]Both words are formed from the root *sen-*, meaning "old."
[8]Roman poet of the third century B.C.

and to whom they owe it. What about lawyers, pontiffs, augurs, philosophers, when old? What a multitude of things they remember! Old men retain their intellects well enough, if only they keep their minds active and fully employed. Nor is that the case only with men of high position and great office: it applies equally to private life and peaceful pursuits. Sophocles composed tragedies to extreme old age; and being believed to neglect the care of his property owing to his devotion to his art, his sons brought him into court to get a judicial decision depriving him of the management of his property on the ground of weak intellect —just as in our law it is customary to deprive a paterfamilias of the management of his property if he is squandering it. Thereupon the old poet is said to have read to the judges the play he had on hand and had just composed—the *Oedipus Coloneus*—and to have asked them whether they thought that the work of a man of weak intellect. After the reading he was acquitted by the jury. Did old age then compel this man to become silent in his particular art, or Homer, Hesiod, Simonides, or Isocrates and Gorgias whom I mentioned before, or the founders of schools of philosophy, Pythagoras, Democritus, Plato, Xenocrates, or later Zeno and Cleanthes, or Diogenes the Stoic, whom you too saw at Rome? Is it not rather the case with all these that the active pursuit of study only ended with life?

But, to pass over these sublime studies, I can name some rustic Romans from the Sabine district, neighbours and friends of my own, without whose presence farm work of importance is scarcely ever performed—whether sowing, or harvesting or storing crops. And yet in other things this is less surprising; for no one is so old as to think that he may not live a year. But they bestow their labour on what they know does not affect them in any case:

He plants his trees to serve a race to come,

as our poet Statius[9] says in his *Comrades*. Nor indeed would a farmer, however old, hesitate to answer any one who asked him for whom he was planting: "For the immortal gods, whose will it was that I should not merely receive these things from my ancestors, but should also hand them on to the next generation."

8. That remark about the old man is better than the following:

If age brought nothing worse than this,
It were enough to mar our bliss,
That he who bides for many years
Sees much to shun and much for tears.

Yes, and perhaps much that gives him pleasure too. Besides, as to subjects for tears, he often comes upon them in youth as well.

A still more questionable sentiment in the same Caecilius is:

No greater misery can of age be told
Than this: be sure, the young dislike the old.

---

[9]Caecilius Statius, a comic playwright contemporary with Cato.

Delight in them is nearer the mark than dislike. For just as old men, if they are wise, take pleasure in the society of young men of good parts, and as old age is rendered less dreary for those who are courted and liked by the youth, so also do young men find pleasure in the maxims of the old, by which they are drawn to the pursuit of excellence. Nor do I perceive that you find my society less pleasant than I do yours. But this is enough to show you how, so far from being listless and sluggish, old age is even a busy time, always doing and attempting something, of course of the same nature as each man's taste had been in the previous part of his life. Nay, do not some even add to their stock of learning? We see Solon, for instance, boasting in his poems that he grows old "daily learning something new." Or again in my own case, it was only when an old man that I became acquainted with Greek literature, which in fact I absorbed with such avidity—in my yearning to quench, as it were, a long-continued thirst—that I became acquainted with the very facts which you see me now using as precedents. When I heard what Socrates had done about the lyre I should have liked for my part to have done that too, for the ancients used to learn the lyre but, at any rate, I worked hard at literature.

9. Nor, again, do I now *miss the bodily strength of a young man* (for that was the second point as to the disadvantages of old age) any more than as a young man I missed the strength of a bull or an elephant. You should use what you have, and whatever you may chance to be doing, do it with all your might. What could be weaker than Milo of Croton's[10] exclamation? When in his old age he was watching some athletes practising in the course, he is said to have looked at his arms and to have exclaimed with tears in his eyes: "Ah well! these are now as good as dead." Not a bit more so than yourself, you trifler! For at no time were you made famous by your real self, but by chest and biceps. Sext. Aelius never gave vent to such a remark, nor, many years before him, Titus Coruneanius, nor, more recently, P. Crassus—all of them learned juris-consults in active practice, whose knowledge of their profession was maintained to their last breath. I am afraid an orator does lose vigour by old age, for his art is not a matter of the intellect alone, but of lungs and bodily strength. Though as a rule that musical ring in the voice even gains in brilliance in a certain way as one grows old—certainly I have not yet lost it, and you see my years. Yet after all the style of speech suitable to an old man is the quiet and unemotional, and it often happens that the chastened and calm delivery of an old man eloquent secures a hearing. If you cannot attain to that yourself, you might still instruct a Scipio and a Laelius. For what is more charming than old age surrounded by the enthusiasm of youth? Shall we not allow old age even the strength to teach the young, to train and equip them for all the duties of life? And what can be a nobler employment? For my part, I used to think Publius and Gnaeus Scipio and your two grandfathers, L. Aemilius and P. Africanus, fortunate men when I saw them with a company of young nobles about them. Nor should we think any teachers of the fine arts otherwise than happy, however much their bodily forces

---

[10] A famous Greek athlete of the late sixth century B.C.

may have decayed and failed. And yet that same failure of the bodily forces is more often brought about by the vices of youth than of old age; for a dissolute and intemperate youth hands down the body to old age in a worn-out state. . . . Don't you see in Homer how frequently Nestor talks of his own good qualities? For he was living through a third generation; nor had he any reason to fear that upon saying what was true about himself he should appear either over vain or talkative. For, as Homer says, "from his lips flowed discourse sweeter than honey," for which sweet breath he wanted no bodily strength. And yet, after all, the famous leader of the Greeks nowhere wishes to have ten men like Ajax, but like Nestor: if he could get them, he feels no doubt of Troy shortly falling.

10. But to return to my own case: I am in my eighty-fourth year. I could wish that I had been able to make the same boast as Cyrus;[11] but, after all, I can say this: I am not indeed as vigorous as I was as a private soldier in the Punic war, or as quaestor in the same war, or as consul in Spain, and four years later when as a military tribune I took part in the engagement at Thermopylae under the consul Manius Acilius Glabrio; but yet, as you see, old age has not entirely destroyed my muscles, has not quite brought me to the ground. The Senate-house does not find all my vigour gone, nor the rostra, nor my friends, nor my clients, nor my foreign guests. For I have never given in to that ancient and much-praised proverb:

Old when young
Is old for long.

For myself, I had rather be an old man a somewhat shorter time than an old man *before* my time. Accordingly, no one up to the present has wished to see me, to whom I have been denied as engaged. But, it may be said, I have less strength than either of you. Neither have you the strength of the centurion T. Pontius: is he the more eminent man on that account? Let there be only a proper husbanding of strength, and let each man proportion his efforts to his powers. Such an one will assuredly not be possessed with any great regret for his loss of strength. At Olympia Milo is said to have stepped into the course carrying a live ox on his shoulders. Which then of the two would you prefer to have given to you—bodily strength like that, or intellectual strength like that of Pythagoras? In fine, enjoy that blessing when you have it; when it is gone, don't wish it back—unless we are to think that young men should wish their childhood back, and those somewhat older their youth! The course of life is fixed, and nature admits of its being run but in one way, and only once; and to each part of our life there is something specially seasonable; so that the feebleness of children, as well as the high spirit of youth, the soberness of maturer years, and the ripe wisdom of old age—all have a certain natural advantage which should be

---

[11]Persian prince of the late fifth century B.C., whom Xenophon served as a general and later described in his historical writings. On his deathbed, at a very advanced age, Cyrus claimed that he never perceived his old age to have become weaker than his youth.

secured in its proper season. I think you are informed, Scipio, what your grandfather's foreign friend Masinissa does to this day, though ninety years old. When he has once begun a journey on foot he does not mount his horse at all; when on horseback he never gets off his horse. By no rain or cold can he be induced to cover his head. His body is absolutely free from unhealthy humours, and so he still performs all the duties and functions of a king. Active exercise, therefore, and temperance can preserve some part of one's former strength even in old age.

11. Bodily strength is wanting to old age; but neither is bodily strength demanded from old men. Therefore, both by law and custom, men of my time of life are exempt from those duties which cannot be supported without bodily strength. Accordingly not only are we not forced to do what we cannot do; we are not even obliged to do as much as we can. But, it will be said, many old men are so feeble that they cannot perform any duty in life of any sort or kind. That is not a weakness to be set down as peculiar to old age: it is one shared by ill health. How feeble was the son of P. Africanus, who adopted you! What weak health he had, or rather no health at all! If that had not been the case, we should have had in him a second brilliant light in the political horizon; for he had added a wider cultivation to his father's greatness of spirit. What wonder, then, that old men are eventually feeble, when even young men cannot escape it? My dear Laelius and Scipio, we must stand up against old age and make up for its drawbacks by taking pains. We must fight it as we should an illness. We must look after our health, use moderate exercise, take just enough food and drink to recruit, but not to overload, our strength. Nor is it the body alone that must be supported, but the intellect and soul much more. For they are like lamps: unless you feed them with oil, they too go out from old age. Again, the body is apt to get gross from exercise; but the intellect becomes nimbler by exercising itself. For what Caecilius means by "old dotards of the comic stage" are the credulous, the forgetful, and the slipshod. These are faults that do not attach to old age as such, but to a sluggish, spiritless, and sleepy old age. Young men are more frequently wanton and dissolute than old men; but yet, as it is not all young men that are so, but the bad set among them, even so senile folly—usually called imbecility—applies to old men of unsound character, not to all. Appius governed four sturdy sons, five daughters, that great establishment, and all those clients, though he was both old and blind. For he kept his mind at full stretch like a bow, and never gave in to old age by growing slack. He maintained not merely an influence, but an absolute command over his family: his slaves feared him, his sons were in awe of him, all loved him. In that family, indeed, ancestral custom and discipline were in full vigour. The fact is that old age is respectable just as long as it asserts itself, maintains its proper rights, and is not enslaved to any one. For as I admire a young man who has something of the old man in him, so do I an old one who has something of a young man. The man who aims at this may possibly become old in body—in mind he never will. I am now engaged in composing the seventh book of my *Origins*. I collect all the records of antiquity. The speeches delivered in all the celebrated cases which I have defended I am at this particular time getting into shape for pub-

lication. I am writing treatises on augural, pontifical, and civil law. I am, besides, studying hard at Greek, and after the manner of the Pythagoreans—to keep my memory in working order—I repeat in the evening whatever I have said, heard, or done in the course of each day. These are the exercises of the intellect, these the training grounds of the mind; while I sweat and labour on these I don't much feel the loss of bodily strength. I appear in court for my friends; I frequently attend the Senate and bring motions before it on my own responsibility, prepared after deep and long reflection. And these I support by my intellectual, not my bodily forces. And if I were not strong enough to do these things, yet I should enjoy my sofa—imagining the very operations which I was now unable to perform. But what makes me capable of doing this is my past life. For a man who is always living in the midst of these studies and labours does not perceive when old age creeps upon him. Thus, by slow and imperceptible degrees life draws to its end. There is no sudden breakage; it just slowly goes out.

12. The third charge against old age is that it *lacks sensual pleasures.* What a splendid service does old age render, if it takes from us the greatest blot of youth! Listen, my dear young friends, to a speech of Archytas of Tarentum,[12] among the greatest and most illustrious of men, which was put into my hands when as a young man I was at Tarentum with Q. Maximus. "No more deadly curse than sensual pleasure has been inflicted on mankind by nature, to gratify which our wanton appetites are roused beyond all prudence or restraint. It is a fruitful source of treasons, revolutions, secret communications with the enemy. In fact, there is no crime, no evil deed, to which the appetite for sensual pleasures does not impel us. Fornications and adulteries, and every abomination of that kind are brought about by the enticements of pleasure and by them alone. Intellect is the best gift of nature or God: to this divine gift and endowment there is nothing so inimical as pleasure. For when appetite is our master, there is no place for self-control; nor where pleasure reigns supreme can virtue hold its ground. To see this more vividly, imagine a man excited to the highest conceivable pitch of sensual pleasure. It can be doubtful to no one that such a person, so long as he is under the influence of such excitation of the senses, will be unable to use to any purpose either intellect, reason, or thought. Therefore nothing can be so execrable and so fatal as pleasure; since, when more than ordinarily violent and lasting, it darkens all the light of the soul.". . .

What is the point of all this? It is to show you that, if we were unable to scorn pleasure by the aid of reason and philosophy, we ought to have been very grateful to old age for depriving us of all inclination for that which it was wrong to do. For pleasure hinders thought, is a foe to reason, and, so to speak, blinds the eyes of the mind. It is, moreover, entirely alien to virtue. . . .

13. . . . But, you will say, it is deprived of the pleasures of the table, the heaped up board, the rapid passing of the wine-cup. Well, then, it is also free from headache, disordered digestion, broken sleep. But

---

[12]A Greek Pythagorean philosopher of the early fourth century B.C.

if we must grant pleasure something, since we do not find it easy to
resist its charms,—for Plato, with happy inspiration, calls pleasure
"vice's bait," because of course men are caught by it as fish by a hook,
—yet, although old age has to abstain from extravagant banquets, it
is still capable of enjoying modest festivities. . . . To begin with, I
have always remained a member of a "club"—clubs, you know, were
established in my quaestorship on the reception of the Magna Mater
from Ida.[13] So I used to dine at their feast with the members of my
club—on the whole with moderation, though there was a certain warmth
of temperament natural to my time of life; but as that advances there
is a daily decrease of all excitement. Nor was I, in fact, ever wont to
measure my enjoyment even of these banquets by the physical pleasures
they gave more than by the gathering and conversation of friends. For
it was a good idea of our ancestors to style the presence of guests at
a dinner-table—seeing that it implied a community of enjoyment—a
convivium, "a living together." It is a better term than the Greek words
which mean "a drinking together," or, "an eating together." For they
would seem to give the preference to what is really the least important
part of it.

14. For myself, owing to the pleasure I take in conversation, I enjoy
even banquets that begin early in the afternoon, and not only in company
with my contemporaries—of whom very few survive—but also with
men of your age and with yourselves. I am thankful to old age, which
has increased my avidity for conversation, while it has removed that
for eating and drinking. But if anyone does enjoy these—not to seem
to have proclaimed war against all pleasure without exception, which
is perhaps a feeling inspired by nature—I fail to perceive even in these
very pleasures that old age is entirely without the power of appreciation.
For myself, I take delight even in the old-fashioned appointment of
master of the feast; and in the arrangement of the conversation, which
according to ancestral custom is begun from the last place on the left-
hand couch when the wine is brought in; as also in the cups which, as
in Xenophon's banquet, are small and filled by driblets; and in the contrivance for cooling in summer, and for warming by the winter sun
or winter fire. These things I keep up even among my Sabine countrymen, and every day have a full dinner-party of neighbours, which we
prolong as far into the night as we can with varied conversation.

But you may urge—there is not the same tingling sensation of pleasure in old men. No doubt; but neither do they miss it so much. For
nothing gives you uneasiness which you do not miss. That was a fine
answer of Sophocles to a man who asked him, when in extreme old
age, whether he was still a lover. "Heaven forbid!" he replied; "I was
only too glad to escape from that, as though from a boorish and insane
master." To men indeed who are keen after such things it may possibly
appear disagreeable and uncomfortable to be without them; but to jaded
appetites it is pleasanter to lack than to enjoy. However, he cannot be

---

[13]The establishment in Roman religious rites of the worship of the Great Mother, corresponding to the
worship of Rhea, a Greek goddess who represented the fruitfulness of nature and whose main shrine was on
Mt. Ida.

said to lack who does not want: my contention is that not to want is the pleasanter thing.

But even granting that youth enjoys these pleasures with more zest; in the first place, they are insignificant things to enjoy, as I have said; and in the second place, such as age is not entirely without, if it does not possess them in profusion. Just as a man gets greater pleasure from Ambivius Turpio[14] if seated in the front row at the theatre than if he was in the last, yet, after all, the man in the last row does get pleasure; so youth, because it looks at pleasures at closer quarters, perhaps enjoys itself more, yet even old age, looking at them from a distance, does enjoy itself well enough. Why, what blessings are these—that the soul, having served its time, so to speak, in the campaigns of desire and ambition, rivalry and hatred, and all the passions, should live in its own thoughts, and, as the expression goes, should dwell apart! Indeed, if it has in store any of what I may call the food of study and philosophy, nothing can be pleasanter than an old age of leisure. . . .

17. . . . For the crowning grace of old age is influence. How great was that of L. Caecilius Metellus! How great that of Atilius Calatinus,[15] over whom the famous epitaph was placed, "Very many classes agree in deeming this to have been the very first man of the nation"! The line cut on his tomb is well known. It is natural, then, that a man should have had influence, in whose praise the verdict of history is unanimous. Again, in recent times, what a great man was Publius Crassus, Pontifex Maximus, and his successor in the same office, M. Lepidus! I need scarcely mention Paulus or Africanus, or, as I did before, Maximus. It was not only their senatorial utterances that had weight: their least gesture had it also. In fact, old age, especially when it has enjoyed honours, has an influence worth all the pleasures of youth put together.

18. But throughout my discourse remember that my panegyric applies to an old age that has been established on foundations laid by youth. From which may be deduced what I once said with universal applause, that it was a wretched old age that had to defend itself by speech. Neither white hairs nor wrinkles can at once claim influence in themselves: it is the honourable conduct of earlier days that is rewarded by possessing influence at the last. Even things generally regarded as trifling and matters of course—being saluted, being courted, having way made for one, people rising when one approaches, being escorted to and from the forum, being referred to for advice—all these are marks of respect, observed among us and in other States—always most sedulously where the moral tone is highest. . . .

There are many excellent rules in our augural college,[16] but among the best one which affects our subject—that precedence in speech goes by seniority; and augurs who are older are preferred not only to those who have held higher office, but even to those who are actually in possession of *imperium*.[17] What then are the physical pleasures to

---

[14]A famous actor of Cato's time.

[15]Metellus and Calatinus were both prominent Roman statesmen of the third century B.C.

[16]The augural college was a group of priestly officials, usually distinguished citizens, who were charged with interpreting divine signs, the "auspices," in regard to any official public undertaking.

[17]"Political power."

be compared with the reward of influence? Those who have employed it with distinction appear to me to have played the drama of life to its end, and not to have broken down in the last act like unpractised players.

But, it will be said, old men are fretful, fidgety, ill-tempered, and disagreeable. If you come to that, they are also avaricious. But these are faults of character, not of the time of life. And, after all, fretfulness and the other faults I mentioned admit of some excuse—not, indeed, a complete one, but one that may possibly pass muster: they think themselves neglected, looked down upon, mocked. Besides, with bodily weakness every rub is a source of pain. Yet all these faults are softened both by good character and good education. Illustrations of this may be found in real life, as also on the stage in the case of the brothers in the *Adelphi*.[18] What harshness in the one, what gracious manners in the other! The fact is that, just as it is not every wine, so it is not every life, that turns sour from keeping. Serious gravity I approve of in old age, but, as in other things, it must be within due limits: bitterness I can in no case approve. What the object of senile avarice may be I cannot conceive. For can there be anything more absurd than to seek more journey money, the less there remains of the journey?

19. There remains the fourth reason, which more than anything else appears to torment men of my age and keep them in a flutter—*the nearness of death,* which, it must be allowed, cannot be far from an old man. But what a poor dotard must he be who has not learnt in the course of so long a life that death is not a thing to be feared? Death, that is either to be totally disregarded, if it entirely extinguishes the soul, or is even to be desired, if it brings him where he is to exist forever. A third alternative, at any rate, cannot possibly be discovered. Why then should I be afraid if I am destined either not to be miserable after death or even to be happy? After all, who is such a fool as to feel certain —however young he may be—that he will be alive in the evening? Nay, that time of life has many more chances of death than ours. Young men more easily contract diseases; their illnesses are more serious; their treatment has to be more severe. Accordingly, only a few arrive at old age. If that were not so, life would be conducted better and more wisely; for it is in old men that thought, reason, and prudence are to be found; and if there had been no old men, States would never have existed at all. But I return to the subject of the imminence of death. What sort of charge is this against old age, when you see that it is shared by youth? I had reason in the case of my excellent son—as you had, Scipio, in that of your brothers, who were expected to attain the highest honours—to realise that death is common to every time of life. Yes, you will say; but a young man expects to live long; an old man cannot expect to do so. Well, he is a fool to expect it. For what can be more foolish than to regard the uncertain as certain, the false as true? "An old man has nothing even to hope." Ah, but it is just there that he is in a better position than a young man, since what the latter only hopes he has obtained. The one wishes to live long; the other has lived long.

---

[18]A comedy by Terence, a Roman comic playwright contemporary with Cato.

And yet, good heaven! what is "long" in a man's life? For grant the utmost limit: let us expect an age like that of the King of the Tartessi. For there was, as I find recorded, a certain Agathonius at Gades who reigned eighty years and lived a hundred and twenty. But to my mind nothing seems even long in which there is any "last," for when that arrives, then all the past has slipped away—only that remains to which you have attained by virtue and righteous actions. Hours indeed, and days and months and years depart, nor does past time ever return, nor can the future be known. Whatever time each is granted for life, with that he is bound to be content. An actor, in order to earn approval, is not bound to perform the play from beginning to end; let him only satisfy the audience in whatever act he appears. Nor need a wise man go on to the concluding "plaudite." For a short term of life is long enough for living well and honourably. But if you go farther, you have no more right to grumble than farmers do because the charm of the spring season is past and the summer and autumn have come. For the word "spring" in a way suggests youth, and points to the harvest to be: the other seasons are suited for the reaping and storing of the crops. Now the harvest of old age is, as I have often said, the memory and rich store of blessings laid up in earlier life. Again, all things that accord with nature are to be counted as good. But what can be more in accordance with nature than for old men to die? A thing, indeed, which also befalls young men, though nature revolts and fights against it. Accordingly, the death of young men seems to me like putting out a great fire with a deluge of water; but old men die like a fire going out because it has burnt down of its own nature without artificial means. Again, just as apples when unripe are torn from trees, but when ripe and mellow drop down, so it is violence that takes life from young men, ripeness from old. This ripeness is so delightful to me, that, as I approach nearer to death, I seem as it were to be sighting land, and to be coming to port at last after a long voyage.

20. Again, there is no fixed borderline for old age, and you are making a good and proper use of it as long as you can satisfy the call of duty and disregard death. The result of this is, that old age is even more confident and courageous than youth. That is the meaning of Solon's answer to the tyrant Pisistratus. When the latter asked him what he relied upon in opposing him with such boldness, he is said to have replied, "On my old age." But that end of life is the best, when, without the intellect or senses being impaired, Nature herself takes to pieces her own handiwork which she also put together. Just as the builder of a ship or a house can break them up more easily than any one else, so the nature that knit together the human frame can also best unfasten it. Moreover, a thing freshly glued together is always difficult to pull asunder; if old, this is easily done.

The result is that the short time of life left to them is not to be grasped at by old men with greedy eagerness, or abandoned without cause. Pythagoras forbids us, without an order from our commander, that is God, to desert life's fortress and outpost. Solon's epitaph, indeed, is that of a wise man, in which he says that he does not wish his death to be unaccompanied by the sorrow and lamentations of his friends.

He wants, I suppose, to be beloved by them. But I rather think Ennius says better:

> None grace me with their tears, nor weeping loud
> Make sad my funeral rites!

He holds that a death is not a subject for mourning when it is followed by immortality.

Again, there may possibly be some sensation of dying—and that only for a short time, especially in the case of an old man: *after* death, indeed, sensation is either what one would desire, or it disappears altogether. But to disregard death is a lesson which must be studied from our youth up; for unless that is learnt, no one can have a quiet mind. For die we certainly must, and that too without being certain whether it may not be this very day. As death, therefore, is hanging over our head every hour, how can a man ever be unshaken in soul if he fears it?

. . . As a general truth, as it seems to me, it is weariness of all pursuits that creates weariness of life. There are certain pursuits adapted to childhood: do young men miss them? There are others suited to early manhood: does that settled time of life called "middle age" ask for them? There are others, again, suited to that age, but not looked for in old age. There are, finally, some which belong to old age. Therefore, as the pursuits of the earlier ages have their time for disappearing, so also have those of old age. And when that takes place, a satiety of life brings on the ripe time for death.

21. For I do not see why I should not venture to tell you my personal opinion as to death, of which I seem to myself to have a clearer vision in proportion as I am nearer to it. I believe, Scipio and Laelius, that your fathers—those illustrious men and my dearest friends—are still alive, and that too with a life which alone deserves the name. For as long as we are imprisoned in this framework of the body, we perform a certain function and laborious work assigned us by fate. The soul, in fact, is of heavenly origin, forced down from its home in the highest, and, so to speak, buried in earth, a place quite opposed to its divine nature and its immortality. But I suppose the immortal gods to have sown souls broadcast in human bodies, that there might be some to survey the world, and while contemplating the order of the heavenly bodies to imitate it in the unvarying regularity of their life. Nor is it only reason and arguments that have brought me to this belief, but the great fame and authority of the most distinguished philosophers. I used to be told that Pythagoras and the Pythagoreans—almost natives of our country, who in old times had been called the Italian school of philosophers—never doubted that we had souls drafted from the universal Divine intelligence. I used besides to have pointed out to me the discourse delivered by Socrates on the last day of his life upon the immortality of the soul—Socrates who was pronounced by the oracle at Delphi to be the wisest of men. I need say no more. I have convinced myself, and I hold—in view of the rapid movement of the soul, its vivid memory of the past and its prophetic knowledge of the future, its many accomplishments, its vast range of knowledge, its numerous discoveries

—that a nature embracing such varied gifts cannot itself be mortal. And since the soul is always in motion and yet has no external source of motion, for it is self-moved, I conclude that it will also have no end to its motion, because it is not likely ever to abandon itself. Again, since the nature of the soul is not composite, nor has in it any admixture that is not homogeneous and similar, I conclude that it is indivisible, and, if indivisible, that it cannot perish. It is again a strong proof of men knowing most things before birth, that when mere children they grasp innumerable facts with such speed as to show that they are not then taking them in for the first time, but remembering and recalling them. This is roughly Plato's argument.

22. Once more in Xenophon we have the elder Cyrus on his death-bed speaking as follows:—

"Do not suppose, my dearest sons, that when I have left you I shall be nowhere and no one. Even when I was with you, you did not see my soul, but knew that it was in this body of mine from what I did. Believe then that it is still the same, even though you see it not. The honours paid to illustrious men had not continued to exist after their death, had the souls of these very men not done something to make us retain our recollection of them beyond the ordinary time. For myself, I never could be persuaded that souls while in mortal bodies were alive, and died directly they left them; nor, in fact, that the soul only lost all intelligence when it left the unintelligent body. I believe rather that when, by being liberated from all corporeal admixture, it has begun to be pure and undefiled, it is then that it becomes wise. And again, when man's natural frame is resolved into its elements by death, it is clearly seen whither each of the other elements departs: for they all go to the place from which they came: but the soul alone is invisible alike when present and when departing. Once more, you see that nothing is so like death as sleep. And yet it is in sleepers that souls most clearly reveal their divine nature; for they foresee many events when they are allowed to escape and are left free. This shows what they are likely to be when they have completely freed themselves from the fetters of the body. Wherefore, if these things are so, obey me as a god. But if my soul is to perish with my body, nevertheless do you from awe of the gods, who guard and govern this fair universe, preserve my memory by the loyalty and piety of your lives."

23. Such are the words of the dying Cyrus. I will now, with your good leave, look at home. No one, my dear Scipio, shall ever persuade me that your father Paulus and your two grandfathers Paulus and Africanus, or the father of Africanus, or his uncle, or many other illustrious men not necessary to mention, would have attempted such lofty deeds as to be remembered by posterity, had they not seen in their minds that future ages concerned them. Do you suppose—to take an old man's privilege of a little self-praise—that I should have been likely to undertake such heavy labours by day and night, at home and abroad, if I had been destined to have the same limit to my glory as to my life? Had it not been much better to pass an age of ease and repose without any labour or exertion? But my soul, I know not how, refusing to be kept down, ever fixed its eyes upon future ages, as though from a con-

viction that it would begin to live only when it had left the body. But had it not been the case that souls were immortal, it would not have been the souls of all the best men that made the greatest efforts after an immortality of fame.

Again, is there not the fact that the wisest man ever dies with the greatest cheerfulness, the most unwise with the least? Don't you think that the soul which has the clearer and longer sight sees that it is starting for better things, while the soul whose vision is dimmer does not see it? For my part, I am transported with the desire to see your fathers, who were the object of my reverence and affection. Nor is it only those whom I knew that I long to see; it is those also of whom I have been told and have read, whom I have myself recorded in my history. When I am setting out for that, there is certainly no one who will find it easy to draw me back, or boil me up again like second Pelios. Nay, if some god should grant me to renew my childhood from my present age and once more to be crying in my cradle, I would firmly refuse; nor should I in truth be willing, after having, as it were, run the full course, to be recalled from the winning-crease to the barriers. For what blessings has life to offer? Should we not rather say what labour? But granting that it has, at any rate it has after all a limit to enjoyment or to existence. I don't wish to depreciate life, as many men and good philosophers have often done; nor do I regret having lived, for I have done so in a way that lets me think that I was not born in vain. But I quit life as I would an inn, not as I would a home. For nature has given us a place of entertainment, not of residence.

Oh glorious day when I shall set out to join that heavenly conclave and company of souls, and depart from the turmoil and impurities of this world! For I shall not go to join only those whom I have before mentioned, but also my son Cato, than whom no better man was ever born, nor one more conspicuous for piety. His body was burnt by me, though mine ought, on the contrary, to have been burnt by him; but his spirit, not abandoning, but ever looking back upon me, has certainly gone whither he saw that I too must come. I was thought to bear that loss heroically, not that I really bore it without distress, but I found my own consolation in the thought that the parting and separation between us was not to be for long.

It is by these means, my dear Scipio,—for you said that you and Laelius were wont to express surprise on this point,—that my old age stis lightly on me, and is not only not oppressive but even delightful. But if I am wrong in thinking the human soul immortal, I am glad to be wrong; nor will I allow the mistake which gives me so much pleasure to be wrested from me as long as I live. But if when dead, as some insignificant philosophers think, I am to be without sensation, I am not afraid of dead philosophers deriding my errors. Again, if we are not to be immortal, it is nevertheless what a man must wish—to have his life end at its proper time. For nature puts a limit to living as to everything else. Now, old age is as it were the playing out of the drama, the full fatigue of which we should shun, especially when we also feel that we have had more than enough of it.

This is all I had to say on old age. I pray that you may arrive at it, that you may put my words to a practical test.

Comments / on Cicero

To me the composition of this book [*On Old Age*] has been so delightful that it has not only wiped away all the annoyances of old age, but has even made it an easy and happy state.   *CICERO (44* B.C.*)*

He [Cicero] enthusiastically accepted the belief of the Greek Stoics that high moral standards, the determination to live up to them, and the emotional self-restraint needed to do so . . . were the most important things in the world—probably the only important things. . . . In general Cicero may be inscribed as an acute reader of a wide range of Greek philosophers, well equipped to extract from them what suited him, adding shifts of emphasis appropriate to his character, nation, and environment. In his capacity to do this, and to transform his conclusions into words, he is very much a figure for the twentieth century, the effective popularizer of knowledge and doctrine. . . .   *MICHAEL GRANT (1960)*

Estimates of Cicero as a philosophical writer have varied. . . . At the present moment he is derided as a mere middle-man of no great intelligence. . . . Moreover, even if Cicero's works are derivative, they select what they derive and present it in such form that there is probably no better introduction to moral philosophy—not excepting Plato himself. Of originality there is none—except in style, language, and presentation. . . .
          R. H. BARROW (1949)

To run through the most famous of them [Cicero's writings] now, the essay on Old Age, is to feel the impatience a perpetual mental "Of course" always awakens, but once these truisms were strangely new and it was Cicero who made them common.   *EDITH HAMILTON (1932)*

Epictetus
55?—134? A.D.

Stoicism as represented by Cicero's Cato tended to be an aristocratic philosophy, aimed not at the mass of society but at men who already had well-developed intellectual resources. The change from Middle to Late Stoicism in the first century A.D. is marked by its development into a popular philosophy, attractive to the ordinary unlettered citizen as a guide for living. Late Stoicism demonstrates ways of thinking by which any individual can reconcile himself to the circumstances of human existence.

   This popular appeal characteristic of late Stoic thought is illustrated in the work of Epictetus, a Greek slave in Rome whose master allowed him to study under Stoic teachers and who became an eminent philosopher himself. Epictetus' fame rested on his ability as a teacher, for he left no writings; but his lectures had great popularity among people from many different classes of society. One devoted listener was the historian Arrian, who, in his *Discourses of Epictetus,* has provided us with what amounts to a stenographic record of the philosopher's teachings. The *Discourses* have the rambling, discursive, repetitive quality of material delivered orally. However, from his lecture notes, Arrian also prepared a *Manual,* a concise summary of the essence of Epictetus' doctrines, which provides a compact but comprehensive survey of late Stoic thought as voiced by Epictetus.

Manual

1. Of things some are in our power, and others are not. In our power are opinion, movement towards a thing, desire, aversion (turning from a thing); and in a word, whatever are our own acts: not in our power are the body, property, reputation, offices (magisterial power), and in a word, whatever are not our own acts. And the things in our power are by nature free, not subject to restraint nor hindrance: but the things not in our power are weak, slavish, subject to restraint, in the power of others. Remember then that if you think the things which are by nature slavish to be free, and the things which are in the power of others to be your own, you will be hindered, you will lament, you will be disturbed, you will blame both gods and men: but if you think that only which is your own to be your own, and if you think that what is another's, as it really is, belongs to another, no man will ever compel you, no man will hinder you, you will never blame any man, you will accuse no man, you will do nothing against your will, no man will harm you, you will have no enemy, for you will not suffer any harm.

If then you aim at such great things, remember that you must not attempt to lay hold of them with a small effort; but you must leave alone some things entirely, and postpone others for the present. But if you wish for these great things, and also power and wealth, perhaps you will not gain even these because you aim also at the former: certainly you will fail in those things through which alone happiness and freedom are secured. Straightway then practice saying to every harsh appearance, "You are an appearance, and in no manner what you appear to be." Then examine it by the rules which you possess, and by this first and chiefly, whether it relates to the things which are in our power or to the things which are not in our power: and if it relates to anything which is not in our power, be ready to say, that it does not concern you.

From *Discourses,* translated by George Long (Chicago: Donahue Brothers, n.d.).

2. Remember that desire contains in it the hope of obtaining that which you desire; and the hope in aversion is that you will not fall into that which you attempt to avoid: and he who fails in his desire is unfortunate; and he who falls into that which he would avoid is unhappy. If then you attempt to avoid only the things contrary to nature which are within your power, you will not be involved in any of the things which you would avoid. But if you attempt to avoid disease or death or poverty, you will be unhappy. Take away then aversion from all things which are not in our power, and transfer it to the things contrary to nature which are in our power. But destroy desire completely for the present. For if you desire anything which is not in our power, you must be unfortunate: but of the things in our power, and which it would be good to desire, nothing yet is before you. But employ the power of moving toward an object and retiring from it; and these powers indeed only slightly and with exceptions and with remission.

3. In everything which pleases the soul, or supplies a want, or is loved, remember to add this: what is the nature of each thing, beginning from the smallest? If you love an earthen vessel, say it is an earthen vessel which you love; for when it has been broken, you will not be disturbed. If you are kissing your child or wife, say that it is a human being whom you are kissing, for when the wife or child dies, you will not be disturbed.

4. When you are going to take in hand any act, remind yourself what kind of an act it is. If you are going to bathe, place before yourself what happens in the bath: some splashing the water, others pushing against one another, others abusing one another, and some stealing: and thus with more safety you will undertake the matter, if you say to yourself, "I now intend to bathe, and to maintain my will in a manner conformable to nature." And so you will do in every act: for thus if any hindrance to bathing shall happen, let this thought be ready: "It was not this only that I intended, but I intended also to maintain my will in a way conformable to nature; but I shall not maintain it so, if I am vexed at what happens."

5. Men are disturbed not by the things which happen, but by the opinions about the things: for example, death is nothing terrible, for if it were, it would have seemed so to Socrates. The opinion about death, that it is terrible, is the terrible thing. When then we are impeded or disturbed or grieved, let us never blame others, but ourselves, that is, our opinions. It is the act of an ill-instructed man to blame others for his own bad condition; it is the act of one who has begun to be instructed, to lay the blame on himself; and of one whose intruction is completed, neither to blame another, nor himself.

6. Be not elated at any excellence which belongs to another. If a horse when he is elated should say, "I am beautiful," one might endure it. But when you are elated, and say, "I have a beautiful horse," you must know that you are elated at having a good horse. What then is your own? The use of appearances. Consequently when in the use of appearances you are conformable to nature, then be elated, for then you will be elated at something good which is your own.

7. As on a voyage when the vessel has reached a port, if you go out to get water, it is an amusement by the way to pick up a shell-fish or some bulb, but your thoughts ought to be directed to the ship, and you ought to be constantly watching if the captain should call, and then you must throw away all those things, that you may not be bound and pitched into the ship like sheep: so in life also, if there be given to you instead of a little bulb and a shell a wife and child, there will be nothing to prevent you from taking them. But if the captain should call, run to the ship, and leave all those things without regard to them. But if you are old, do not even go far from the ship, lest when you are called you make default.

8. Seek not that the things which happen should happen as you wish; but wish the things which happen to be as they are, and you will have a tranquil flow of life.

9. Disease is an impediment to the body, but not to the will, unless the will itself chooses. Lameness is an impediment to the leg, but not to the will. And add this reflection on the occasion of everything that happens; for you will find it an impediment to something else, but not to yourself.

10. On the occasion of every accidental event that befalls you, re-member to turn to yourself and inquire what power you have for turning it to use. If you see a fair man or a fair woman, you will find that the power to resist is continence. If pain be presented to you, you will find that it is endurance. If it be abusive words, you will find it to be patience. And if you have been thus formed to the proper habit, the appearances will not carry you along with them.

11. Never say about anything, "I have lost it," but say "I have restored it." Is your child dead? It has been restored. Is your wife dead? She has been restored. Has your estate been taken from you? Has not then this also been restored? "But he who has taken it from me is a bad man." But what is it to you, by whose hands the giver demanded it back? So long as he may allow you, take care of it as a thing which belongs to another, as travelers do with their inn.

12. If you intend to improve, throw away such thoughts as these: "If I neglect my affairs, I shall not have the means of living; unless I chastise my slave, he will be bad." For it is better to die of hunger and so to be released from grief and fear than to live in abundance with perturbation; and it is better for your slave to be bad than for you to be unhappy. Begin then from little things. Is the oil spilled? Is a little wine stolen? Say on the occasion, "At such price is sold freedom from perturbation; at such price is sold tranquillity, but nothing is got for nothing." And when you call your slave, consider that it is possible that he does not hear; and if he does hear, that he will do nothing which you wish. But matters are not so well with him, that it should be in his power for you to be not disturbed.

13. If you would improve, submit to be considered without sense and foolish with respect to externals. Wish to be considered to know nothing: and if you shall seem to some to be a person of importance, distrust yourself. For you should know that it is not easy both to keep

your will in a condition conformable to nature and to secure external things: but if a man is careful about the one, it is an absolute necessity that he will neglect the other.

14. If you would have your children and your wife and your friends live forever, you are silly; for you would have the things which are not in your power to be in your power, and the things which belong to others to be yours. So if you would have your slave to be free from faults, you are a fool; for you would have badness not to be badness, but something else. But if you wish not to fail in your desires, you are able to do that. Practice then this which you are able to do. He is the master of every man who has the power over the things which another person wishes or does not wish, the power to confer them on him or to take them away. Whoever then wishes to be free, let him neither wish for anything nor avoid anything which depends on others; if he does not observe this rule, he must be a slave.

15. Remember that in life you ought to behave as at a banquet. Suppose that something is carried round and is opposite to you. Stretch out your hand and take a portion with decency. Suppose that it passes by you. Do not detain it. Suppose that it is not yet come to you. Do not send your desire forward to it, but wait till it is opposite to you. Do so with respect to children, with respect to a wife, with respect to magisterial offices, with respect to wealth, and you will be some time a worthy partner of the banquets of the gods. But if you take none of the things which are set before you, and even despise them, then you will be not only a fellow-banqueter with the gods, but also a partner with them in power. For by acting thus Diogenes and Heracleitus[1] and those like them were deservedly divine, and were so called.

16. When you see a person weeping in sorrow either when a child goes abroad or when he is dead, or when the man has lost his property, take care that the appearance do not hurry you away with it, as if he were suffering in external things. But straightway make a distinction in your own mind, and be in readiness to say, "It is not that which has happened that afflicts this man, for it does not afflict another, but it is the opinion about this thing which afflicts the man." So far as words then do not be unwilling to show him sympathy, and even if it happens so, to lament with him. But take care that you do not lament internally also.

17. Remember that you are an actor in a play of such a kind as the author may choose; if short, of a short one; if long, of a long one: if he wishes you to act the part of a poor man, see that you act the part naturally; if the part of a lame man, of a magistrate, of a private person, do the same. For this is your duty, to act well the part that is given to you; but to select the part, belongs to another.

18. When a raven has croaked inauspiciously, let not the appearance hurry you away with it; but straightway make a distinction in your mind and say, "None of these things is signified to me, but either to my poor body, or to my small property, or to my reputation, or to my children or to my wife: but to me all significations are auspicious if I choose.

---

[1] Greek philosophers of the fourth century B.C.

For whatever of these things results, it is in my power to derive benefit from it."

19. You can be invincible, if you enter into no contest in which it is not in your power to conquer. Take care then when you observe a man honored before others or possessed of great power or highly esteemed for any reason, not to suppose him happy, and be not carried away by the appearance. For if the nature of the good is in our power, neither envy nor jealousy will have a place in us. But you yourself will not wish to be a general or senator or consul, but a free man: and there is only one way to this, to despise the things which are not in our power.

20. Remember that it is not he who reviles you or strikes you who insults you, but it is your opinion about these things as being insulting. When then a man irritates you, you must know that it is your own opinion which has irritated you. Therefore especially try not to be carried away by the appearance. For if you once gain time and delay, you will more easily master yourself.

21. Let death and exile and every other thing which appears dreadful be daily before your eyes; but most of all death: and you will never think of anything mean nor will you desire anything extravagantly.

22. If you desire philosophy, prepare yourself from the beginning to be ridiculed, to expect that many will sneer at you, and say, "He has all at once returned to us as a philosopher; and whence does he get this supercilious look for us?" Do you not show a supercilious look; but hold on to the things which seem to you best as one appointed by God to this station. And remember that if you abide in the same principles, these men who first ridiculed will afterward admire you; but if you shall have been overpowered by them, you will bring on yourself double ridicule.

23. If it should ever happen to you to be turned to externals in order to please some person, you must know that you have lost your purpose in life. Be satisfied then in everything with being a philosopher; and if you wish to seem also to any person to be a philosopher, appear so to yourself, and you will be able to do this.

24. Let not these thoughts afflict you: "I shall live unhonored and be nobody nowhere." For if want of honor is an evil, you cannot be in evil through the means of another any more than you can be involved in anything base. Is it then your business to obtain the rank of a magistrate, or to be received at a banquet? By no means. How then can this be want of honor? And how will you be nobody nowhere, when you ought to be somebody in those things only which are in your power, in which indeed it is permitted to you to be a man of the greatest worth?

But your friends will be without assistance! What do you mean by being without assistance? They will not receive money from you, nor will you make them Roman citizens. Who then told you that these are among the things which are in our power, and not in the power of others? And who can give to another what he has not himself?

"Acquire money then," your friends say, "that we also may have something." "If I can acquire money and also keep myself modest, and faithful and magnanimous, point out the way, and I will acquire it. But if you ask me to lose the things which are good and my own, in order that you may gain the things which are not good, see how unfair and silly you are. Besides, which would you rather have, money or a faithful and modest friend? For this end then rather help me to be such a man, and do not ask me to do this by which I shall lose that character."

"But my country," you say, "as far as it depends on me, will be without my help." I ask again, what help do you mean? It will not have porticoes or baths through you. And what does this mean? For it is not furnished with shoes by means of a smith, nor with arms by means of a shoemaker. But it is enough if every man fully discharges the work that is his own: and if you provided it with another citizen faithful and modest, would you not be useful to it? Yes. Then you also cannot be useless to it. "What place then," you say, "shall I hold in the city?" Whatever you can, if you maintain at the same time your fidelity and modesty. But if when you wish to be useful to the state, you lose these qualities, what profit could you be to it, if you were made shameless and faithless?

25. Has any man been preferred before you at a banquet, or in being saluted, or in being invited to a consultation? If these things are good, you ought to rejoice that he has obtained them: but if bad, be not grieved because you have not obtained them; and remember that you cannot, if you do not do the same as they in order to obtain what is not in our power, be considered worthy of the same things. For how can a man obtain an equal share with another when he does not visit a man's doors as that other man does, when he does not attend him when he goes abroad, as the other man does; when he does not flatter him as another does? You will be unjust then and insatiable, if you do not part with the price for which those things are sold, and if you wish to obtain them for nothing. Well, what is the price of lettuces? An obolus[2] perhaps. If then a man gives up the obolus, and receives the lettuces, and if you do not give up the obolus and do not obtain the lettuces, do not suppose that you receive less than he who has got the lettuces; for as he has the lettuces, so you have the obolus which you did not give. In the same way then in the other matter also you have not been invited to a man's feast, for you did not give to the host the price at which the supper is sold; but he sells it for flattery, he sells it for personal attention. Give then the price, if it is for your interest. But if you wish both not to give the price and to obtain the things, you are insatiable and silly. Have you nothing then in place of the supper? You have indeed, you have the not-flattering of him whom you did not choose to flatter; you have the not-enduring of the man when he enters the room.

26. We may learn the will of nature from the things in which we do not differ from one another; for instance, when your neighbor's slave has broken his cup, or anything else, we are ready to say forthwith, "It is one of the things which happen." You must know then that when your cup also is broken, you ought to think as you did when your neighbor's cup was broken. Transfer this reflection to greater things also. Is another man's child or wife dead? There is no one who would

---

[2]A coin of small denomination. Epictetus is making a point that would be conveyed today by mentioning a dime or a quarter.

not say, "This is an event incident to man." But when a man's own child or wife is dead, forthwith he calls out, "Woe to me, how wretched I am." But we ought to remember how we feel when we hear that it has happened to others.

27. As a mark is not set up for the purpose of missing the aim, so neither does the nature of evil exist in the world.

28. If any person was intending to put your body in the power of any man whom you fell in with on the way, you would be vexed: but that you put your understanding in the power of any man whom you meet, so that if he should revile you, it is disturbed and troubled, are you not ashamed at this?

29. In every act observe the things which come first, and those which follow it; and so proceed to the act. If you do not, at first you will approach it with alacrity, without having thought of the things which will follow; but afterward, when certain ugly things have shown themselves, you will be ashamed. A man wishes to conquer at the Olympic games. I also wish indeed, for it is a fine thing. But observe both the things which come first, and the things which follow; and then begin the act. You must do everything according to rule, eat according to strict orders, abstain from delicacies, exercise yourself as you are bid at appointed times, in heat, in cold; you must not drink cold water, nor wine as you choose; in a word, you must deliver yourself up to the exercise master as you do to the physician, and then proceed to the contest. And sometimes you will strain the hand, put the ankle out of joint, swallow much dust, sometimes be flogged, and after all this be defeated. When you have considered all this, if you still choose, go to the contest. If you do not, you will behave like children, who at one time play at wrestlers, another time at flute players, again as gladiators, then as trumpeters, then as tragic actors; so you also will be at one time an athlete, at another a gladiator, then a rhetorician, then a philosopher, but with your whole soul you will be nothing at all; but like an ape you imitate everything that you see, and one thing after another pleases you. For you have not undertaken anything with consideration, nor have you surveyed it well; but carelessly and with cold desire. Thus some who have seen a philosopher and having heard one speak, as Euphrates[3] speaks—and who can speak as he does?—they wish to be philosophers themselves also. My man, first of all consider what kind of thing it is; and then examine your own nature to see if you are able to sustain the character. Do you wish to be a pentathlete or a wrestler? Look at your arms, your thighs, examine your loins. For different men are formed by nature for different things. Do you think that if you do these things, you can eat in the same manner, drink in the same manner, and in the same manner loathe certain things? You must pass sleepless nights, endure toil, go away from your kinsmen, be despised by a slave, in everything have the inferior part, in honor, in office, in the courts of justice, in every little matter. Consider these things, if you would exchange for them freedom from passions, liberty, tranquillity. If not, take care that, like little children, you be not now a philosopher, then a servant of the publicans,

---

[3] A notable Stoic philosopher who flourished early in the second century A.D.

then a rhetorician, then a procurator for Caesar. These things are not consistent. You must be one man, either good or bad. You must either cultivate your own ruling faculty, or external things; you must either exercise your skill on internal things or on external things; that is, you must either maintain the position of a philosopher or that of a common person.

30. Duties are universally measured by relations. Is a man a father? The precept is to take care of him, to yield to him in all things, to submit when he is reproachful, when he inflicts blows. But suppose that he is a bad father. Were you then by nature made akin to a good father? No; only to a father. Does a brother wrong you? Maintain then your own position toward him, and examine not what he is doing, but what you must do so that your will shall be conformable to nature. For another will not damage you, unless you choose; but you will be damaged only then when you shall think that you are damaged. In this way then you will discover your duty in relation to a neighbor, to a citizen, to a general, if you become accustomed to contemplate these relationships.

31. As to piety toward the Gods you must know that this is the chief thing: to have right opinions about them, to think that they exist, and that they administer the Universe well and justly. And you must fix yourself in this principle: to obey them, and yield to them in everything which happens, and voluntarily to follow it as being accomplished by the wisest intelligence. For if you do so, you will never either blame the Gods, nor will you accuse them of neglecting you. And it is not possible for this to be done in any other way than by withdrawing from the things which are not in our power, and by placing the good and the evil only in those things which are in our power. For if you think that any of the things which are not in our power is good or bad, it is absolutely necessary that when you do not obtain what you wish and fall into those things which you do not wish, you will find fault and hate those who are the cause of them; for every animal is formed by nature to fly from the things which appear harmful and the things which are the cause of the harm, but to follow and admire the things which are useful and the causes of the useful. It is impossible then for a person who thinks that he is harmed to be delighted with that which he thinks to be the cause of the harm, as it is also impossible to be pleased with the harm itself. For this reason also a father is reviled by his son, when he gives no part to his son of the things which are considered to be good: and it was this which made Polynices and Eteocles[4] enemies, the opinion that royal power was a good. It is for this reason that the cultivator of the earth reviles the gods, for this reason the sailor does, and the merchant, and for this reason those who lose their wives and their children. For where the useful is, there also piety is. Consequently he who takes care to desire as he ought and to avoid as he ought, at the same time also cares after piety. But to make libations and to sacrifice and to offer first fruits according to the custom of our fathers, purely and not meanly nor carelessly nor scantily nor above our ability, is a thing which belongs to all to do.

---

[4]In ancient Greek tradition, the sons of Oedipus, who killed each other during a quarrel over their inheritance of the kingship of Thebes.

Comments / on Epictetus

A novice or one unacquainted with true philosophy he [Epictetus] will hardly stir or affect, but when a man has made some progress or is already far advanced, it is amazing how Epictetus stirs him up, and though he is always touching some tender spot, yet he gives delight also. . . .
                                                    JUSTUS LIPSIUS (1605)

Like the religions of the time, though they were so different in their conclusions, [Epictetus'] emphasis on choice and purpose represents a move away from Greek rationalism, a shift of emphasis from knowledge to nonintellectual qualities. Although the world was in Stoic theory well ordered, its actual appearance presented a complexity so many-sided as to appear meaningless, and in this uncongenial confusion Epictetus—though in tougher, less easily consoling vein than the religions—helped men maintain their self-respect.
                                                    MICHAEL GRANT (1960)

[T]he Stoics perfected the theory of equanimity and independence at the cost of the practice, for they reduced everything to a mental process, and by arguments, such as are presented in the first chapter of Epictetus, sophisticated themselves into all the amenities of life. But in doing so they left out of account that everything to which one is accustomed becomes a need, and therefore can only be given up with pain; that the will does not allow itself to be played with, cannot enjoy without loving the pleasures; that a dog does not remain indifferent if one draws a piece of meat through its mouth, and neither does a wise man if he is hungry; and that there is no middle path between desiring and renouncing.
                                                    ARTHUR SCHOPENHAUER (1818)

Epictetus was a man of warm feelings and clear head; his addresses . . . serve admirably to stimulate the domestic virtues and to keep alive the religious spirit; but his teaching lacks the force which befits the training of a statesman or a king. . . . [H]e makes it clear that the true philosopher is not (as many believe the Stoics to hold) a man devoid of natural feeling, but on the contrary affectionate and considerate in all the relations of life.   *E. V. ARNOLD (1911)*

Of all pagan teachers his [Epictetus'] doctrine stands closest to the teachings of Jesus. . . .   *MOSES HADAS (1954)*

Marcus Aurelius
121 – 180 A.D.

The development of Late Stoicism into a medium for personal edification, which is evident in the teachings of Epictetus, reaches its culmination in the writings of Marcus Aurelius, a nobleman who was the Roman emperor for the last two decades of his life. As historians of philosophy like to point out, the universal attraction and individualistic quality of late Stoic thought are probably best demonstrated by the fact that of its two foremost exponents one was a slave at Rome and the other was the ruler of the Roman Empire.

The very nature of Marcus Aurelius' writings testify to the personal quality of his work: they consist of twelve books of philosophic meditations not intended for publication but addressed simply *To Himself.* They constitute a sort of spiritual diary in which he expressed the ideas that helped shape his inner life, ideas derived from Stoic philosophy but tempered by his own personality. In this form they have always struck a responsive chord in men likewise concerned with the development of their inner life. The strength that these ideas exerted in Marcus Aurelius is evident from the external circumstances under which he wrote these books, circumstances that are nowhere mentioned or even hinted at in them. At the same time that he was examining his private existence, writing to himself about the abiding truths of human experience as he understood them, he was, in his public capacity as emperor of Rome, leading his troops against wild Germanic tribes in the harsh winter of northern Europe. The only recognition he gives to these circumstances in his books is an occasional indication of where one of them was written. As a Roman emperor, he led troops and fought wars; as a Stoic philosopher, he apparently classed such matters among "things indifferent" and simply ignored them when considering the nature of his spiritual being.

To Himself

Book XII

1. All those things at which you wish to arrive by a circuitous road you can have now, if you do not refuse them to yourself. And this means, if you will take no notice of all the past, and trust the future to providence, and direct the present only conformably to piety and justice. Conformably to piety, that you may be content with the lot which is assigned to you, for nature designed it for you and you for it. Conformably to justice, that you may always speak the truth freely and without disguise, and do the things which are agreeable to law and according to the worth of each. And let neither another man's wickedness hinder you, nor opinion nor voice, nor yet the sensations of the poor flesh

Marcus Aurelius, *Meditations,* (George Long, translator), Great Books of the Western World, 1952, Vol. 12, published by Encyclopaedia Britannica, Inc., Chicago, Illinois.

which has grown about you; for the passive part will look to this. If then, whatever the time may be when you shall be near to your departure, neglecting everything else you shall respect only your ruling faculty and the divinity within you, and if you shall be afraid not because you must some time cease to live, but if you shall fear never to have begun to live according to nature—then you will be a man worthy of the universe which has produced you, and you will cease to be a stranger in your native land, and to wonder at things which happen daily as if they were something unexpected, and to be dependent on this or that.

2. God sees the ruling principles of all men bared of the material vesture and rind and impurities. For with his intellectual part alone he touches the intelligence only which has flowed and been derived from himself into these bodies. And if you also use yourself to do this, you will rid yourself of much trouble. For he who regards not the poor flesh which envelops him, surely will not trouble himself by looking after raiment and dwelling and fame and such like externals and show.

3. The things are three of which you are composed—a little body, a little breath, intelligence. Of these the first two are yours, so far as it is your duty to take care of them; but the third alone is properly yours. Therefore if you shall separate from yourself, that is, from your understanding, whatever others do or say, and whatever you have done or said yourself, and whatever future things trouble you because they may happen, and whatever in the body which envelops you or in the breath which is by nature associated with the body and attached to you independent of your will, and whatever the external circumfluent vortex whirls round, so that the intellectual power exempt from the things of fate can live pure and free by itself, doing what is just and accepting what happens and saying the truth: if you will separate, I say, from this ruling faculty the things which are attached to it by the impressions of sense, and the things of time to come and of time that is past, and will make yourself like Empedocles' sphere,[1]

All round, and in its joyous rest reposing;

and if you shall strive to live only what is really your life, that is, the present—then you will be able to pass that portion of life which remains for you up to the time of your death, free from perturbations, nobly, and obedient to your own daemon.

4. I have often wondered how it is that every man loves himself more than all the rest of men, but yet sets less value on his own opinion of himself than on the opinion of others. If then a god or a wise teacher should present himself to man and bid him to think of nothing and to design nothing which he would not express as soon as he conceived it, he could not endure it even for a single day. So much more respect

---

[1] Philosopher and scientist of the fifth century B.C. whose conceptions included the idea of a spherical universe.

have we to what our neighbors shall think of us than to what we shall think of ourselves.

5. How can it be that the gods after having arranged all things well and benevolently for mankind, have overlooked this alone, that some men and very good men, and men who, as we may say, have had most communion with the divinity, and through pious acts and religious observances have been most intimate with the divinity, when they have once died should never exist again, but should be completely extinguished?

But if this is so, be assured that if it ought to have been otherwise, the gods would have done it. For if it were just, it would also be possible; and if it were according to nature, nature would have had it so. But because it is not so, if in fact it is not so, be convinced that it ought not to have been so. You see even of yourself that in this inquiry you are disputing with the deity; and we should not thus dispute with the gods, unless they were most excellent and most just; but if this is so, they would not have allowed anything in the ordering of the universe to be neglected unjustly and irrationally.

6. Practice even the things which you despair of accomplishing. For even the left hand, which is ineffectual for all other things for want of practice, holds the bridle more vigorously than the right hand; for it has been practiced in this.

7. Consider in what condition both in body and soul a man should be when he is overtaken by death; and consider the shortness of life, the boundless abyss of time past and future, the feebleness of all matter.

8. Contemplate the formative principles of things bare of their coverings; the purposes of actions; consider what pain is, what pleasure is, and death, and fame; who is to himself the cause of his uneasiness; how no man is hindered by another; that everything is opinion.

9. In the application of your principles you must be like the pancratiast, not like the gladiator,[2] for the gladiator lets fall the sword which he uses and is killed; but the other always has his hand, and needs to do nothing else than use it.

10. See what things are in themselves, dividing them into matter, form, and purpose.

11. What a power man has to do nothing except what God will approve, and to accept all that God may give him.

12. With respect to that which happens conformably to nature, we ought to blame neither gods, for they do nothing wrong either voluntarily or involuntarily, nor men, for they do nothing wrong except involuntarily. Consequently we should blame nobody.

13. How ridiculous and what a stranger he is who is surprised at anything which happens in life.

14. Either there is a fatal necessity and invincible order, or a kind Providence, or a confusion without a purpose and without a director.

---

[2] Two of the many different kinds of professional fighters who performed in Roman arenas. The pancratiasts fought bareheaded, using a combination of boxing and wrestling skills; the gladiators fought with swords.

If then there is an invincible necessity, why do you resist? But if there is a Providence which allows itself to be propitiated, make yourself worthy of the help of the divinity. But if there is a confusion without a governor, be content that in such a tempest you have in yourself a certain ruling intelligence. And even if the tempest carry you away, let it carry away the poor flesh, the poor breath, everything else; for the intelligence at least it will not carry away.

15. Does the light of the lamp shine without losing its splendor until it is extinguished; and shall the truth which is in you and justice and temperance be extinguished?

16. When a man has presented the appearance of having done wrong, say, "How then do I know if this is a wrongful act? And even if he has done wrong, how do I know that he has not condemned himself? and so this is like tearing his own face. Consider that he who would not have the bad man do wrong, is like the man who would not have the fig tree to bear juice in the figs and infants to cry and the horse to neigh, and whatever else must of necessity be. For what must a man do who has such a character?" If then you are irritable, cure this man's disposition.

17. If it is not right, do not do it: if it is not true, do not say it.

18. In everything always observe what the thing is which produces for you an appearance, and resolve it by dividing it into the formal, the material, the purpose, and the time within which it must end.

19. Perceive at last that you have in you something better and more divine than the things which cause the various affects, and as it were pull you by the strings. What is there now in my mind? Is it fear, or suspicion, or desire, or anything of the kind?

20. First, do nothing inconsiderately, nor without a purpose. Second, make your acts refer to nothing else than to a social end.

21. Consider that before long you will be nobody and nowhere, nor will any of the things exist which you now see, nor any of those who are now living. For all things are formed by nature to change and be turned and to perish in order that other things in continuous succession may exist.

22. Consider that everything is opinion, and opinion is in your power. Take away then, when you choose, your opinion, and like a mariner, who has doubled the promontory, you will find calm, everything stable, and a waveless bay.

23. Any one activity whatever it may be, when it has ceased at its proper time, suffers no evil because it has ceased; nor does he who has done this act suffer any evil for this reason that the act has ceased. In like manner then the whole which consists of all the acts, which is our life, if it cease at its proper time, suffers no evil for the reason that it has ceased; nor has he who has terminated this series at the proper time been ill dealt with. But the proper time and the limit nature fixes, sometimes as in old age the peculiar nature of man, but always the universal nature, by the change of whose parts the whole universe continues ever young and perfect. And everything which is useful to the universal is always good and in season. Therefore the termination of life for every man is no evil, because it is not shameful, since it is both independent of the will and not opposed to the general interest, but good, since it

is seasonable and profitable to and congruent with the universal. He is moved by the deity who is moved in the same manner with the deity and moved toward the same things in his mind.

24. These three principles you must have in readiness. In the things which you do, do nothing either inconsiderately or otherwise than as justice herself would act; but with respect to what may happen to you from without, consider that it happens either by chance or according to Providence, and you must neither blame chance nor accuse Providence. Second, consider what every being is from the seed to the time of its receiving a soul, and from the reception of a soul to the giving back of the same, and of what things every being is compounded and into what things it is resolved. Third, if you should suddenly be raised up above the earth, and should look down on human things, and observe how great the variety is, and at the same time also should see at a glance how great is the number of beings who dwell all around in the air and the ether, consider that as often as you should be raised up, you would see the same things, sameness of form and shortness of duration. Are these things to be proud of?

25. Cast away opinion: you are saved. Who then hinders you from casting it away?

26. When you are troubled about anything, you have forgotten this: that all things happen according to the universal nature; and forgotten this: that a man's wrongful act is nothing to you. And further you have forgotten this: that everything which happens, always happened so and will happen so, and now happens so everywhere; forgotten this too, how close is the kinship between a man and the whole human race, for it is a community, not of a little blood or seed, but of intelligence. And you have forgotten this too: that every man's intelligence is a god, and is an efflux of the deity; and forgotten this: that nothing is a man's own, but that his child and his body and his very soul came from the deity; forgotten this: that everything is opinion; and lastly you have forgotten that every man lives the present time only, and loses only this.

27. Constantly bring to your recollection those who have complained greatly about anything, those who have been most conspicuous by the greatest fame or misfortunes or enmities or fortunes of any kind: then think where are they all now? Smoke and ash and a tale, or not even a tale. And let there be present on your mind also everything of this sort, how Fabius Catullinus lived in the country, and Lucius Lupus in his gardens, and Stertinius at Baiae, and Tiberius at Capri and Rufus at Velia; and in fine think of the eager pursuit of anything conjoined with pride; and how worthless everything is after which men violently strain; and how much more philosophical it is for a man in the opportunities presented to him to show himself just, temperate, obedient to the gods, and to do this with all simplicity: for the pride which is proud of its want of pride is the most intolerable of all.

28. To those who ask, Where have you seen the gods or how do you comprehend that they exist and so worship them, I answer, in the first place, they may be seen even with the eyes; in the second place neither have I seen even my own soul and yet I honor it. Thus then with respect to the gods, from what I constantly experience of their power I comprehend that they exist and I venerate them.

29. The safety of life is this, to examine everything all through, what it is itself, what is its material, what the formal part; with all your soul to do justice and to say the truth. What remains except to enjoy life by joining one good thing to another so as not to leave even the smallest intervals between?

30. There is one light of sun, though it is interrupted by walls, mountains, and other things infinite. There is one common substance, though it is distributed among countless bodies which have their several qualities. There is one soul, though it is distributed among infinite natures and individual limitations. There is one intelligent soul, though it seems to be divided. Now in the things which have been mentioned all the other parts, such as those which are air and matter, are without sensation and have no fellowhsip: and yet even these parts the intelligent principle holds together and the gravitation toward the same. But intellect in a peculiar manner tends to that which is of the same kin, and combines with it, and the feeling for communion is not interrupted.

31. What do you wish? To continue to exist? Well, do you wish to have sensation? movement? growth? and then again to grow? to use your speech? to think? What is there of all these things which seems to you worth desiring? But if it is easy to set little value on all these things, turn to that which remains, which is to follow reason and God. But it is inconsistent with honoring reason and God to be troubled because by death a man will be deprived of the other things.

32. How small a part of boundless and unfathomable time is assigned to every man? for it is very soon swallowed up in the eternal. And how small a part of the whole substance? and how small a part of the universal soul? and on what a small clod of the whole earth you creep? Reflecting on all this consider nothing to be great, except to act as your nature leads you, and to endure that which the common nature brings.

33. How does the ruling faculty make use of itself? for all lies in this. But everything else, whether it is in the power of your will or not, is only lifeless ashes and smoke.

34. This reflection is most adapted to move us to contempt of death —that even those who think pleasure to be a good and pain an evil still have despised it.

35. The man to whom the only good is that which comes in due season, and to whom it is the same thing whether he has done more or fewer acts conformable to right reason, and to whom it makes no difference whether he contemplates the world for a longer or a shorter time—for this man neither is death a terrible thing.

36. Man, you have been a citizen in this great world state: what difference does it make to you whether for five years or three? for that which is conformable to the laws is just for all. Where is the hardship then, if no tyrant nor yet an unjust judge sends you away from the state, but nature who brought you into it? the same as if a praetor who has employed an actor dismisses him from the stage. "But I have not finished the five acts, but only three of them." You say well, but in life the three acts are the whole drama; for what shall be a complete drama is determined by him who was once the cause of its composition, and now of its dissolution: but you are the cause of neither. Depart then satisfied, for he also who releases you is satisfied.

Comments / on Marcus Aurelius

We do not go to Aurelius to learn what Stoic doctrine was; this is taken for granted throughout the book; but we can see how it affected a man in whom the intellectual outlook was after all foreshortened by sympathies and yearnings which had grown up in his nature. The traditional criticism of the school as being harsh, unsympathetic, unfeeling, breaks to pieces as we read these "thoughts"; rather we find an excess of emotion, a surrender to human weakness. A study of Stoicism based on the work of Aurelius alone would indeed give us but a one-sided picture; but a study in which they were omitted would certainly lack completeness.

E. V. ARNOLD (1911)

All readers of Marcus Aurelius' *To Himself* have been impressed by the author's saintliness. . . . Countless moderns have cherished Marcus' book, but it is notable that men of action—Frederick the Great, Maximilian of Bavaria, Captain John Smith of Virginia, and "Chinese" Gordon —have been particularly attached to it. *MOSES HADAS (1954)*

Marcus Aurelius has always shattered derogatory criticism, because his appeal to the resources of pure, selfless conscience is at once so sublime and so infinitely pathetic. *R. M. WENLEY (1924)*

Some critics account *To Himself* . . . [as] merely the morbid haverings of a priggish mind torturing itself by its own introspective irresolution.

R. H. BARROW (1949)

Stoicism preached as a duty the taking of an active part in public affairs if opportunity arose. . . . Despite the part, judicious and otherwise, which they thus played from time to time in the affairs of the State (their most famous public man was of course Marcus Aurelius), Stoicism was a strongly individual philosophy, and its chief aim was the good of the individual's soul. *H. J. ROSE (1948)*

Philo Judaeus
20? B.C. — 50? A.D.

Hebrew and Hellenistic Thought

Old Testament Philosophy: Unlike Greek philosophy, the Old Testament never becomes engrossed in abstract speculations about the nature of ultimate reality. The Hebrews were not in search of a cosmic law; their thought did not incorporate natural science or physics. Even the creation story of the Hebrews is not a speculative cosmogony but is rather a confession of faith in God as the true creator of the world, one who transcends and at the same imposes his will on that world. The Old Testament thus attests to the presence and activity of God in the midst of the Israelite community.

The Old Testament writers scrutinized the history of their people to discover God's purposes and moral demands and to determine how men should be related to their God. The foremost concern of the Hebrews was to be justified in the eyes of Yahweh, the god of the Israelites and supreme ruler of the universe. That one should be justified before his Maker was a foregone conclusion for the Old Testament writers, but they differed a good deal about *how* one should reach this end.

The Old Testament extols in different places the holiness of sacrificial rites and temple worship, the strict adherence to a rigid system of laws, the inward ethics of purity of heart coupled with a concern for social justice, and the mere blind faith in the boundless power of God. Historically, a nearly uninterrupted string of national disasters, attributed by many prophets to the tendency of the Chosen People to forget their covenant with God, render the search for the just way of life more poignant. How could God's justice be operative in a wayward world in which even the chosen ones had gone astray? As national calamities intensified, the Hebrews looked increasingly toward the future when divine justice would be consummated and the People of God restored.

The diversity of injunctions and the various forms of writings found in the Old Testament are due not so much to dispassionate debate as to an anxious effort to satisfy the stern demands of God in times of extreme stress and great suffering. Thus Hebrew writers voiced their concerns and anguish through books of law, prophecy, prayer, praise, wisdom literature, and apocalyptic messages.

It is rather difficult to divide the development of Hebrew thought into historic stages, especially since many books of the Old Testament are of uncertain date and are not arranged in strict chronological sequence. However, there are certain prominent ideological trends evident to most biblical scholars.

According to available evidence, the Hebrew religion of Mosaic times (twelfth to ninth century B.C.) must have been essentially materialistic and worldly, promising rich earthly rewards—many children, large flocks, prosperity—for unquestioning obedience to Yahweh. At this stage, though, it was hardly monotheism, but rather monolatry. The Israelites worshiped Yahweh as their tribal god, but they recognized the existence of other gods who were of no concern to Israel.

It is mainly in the teaching of the prophets (eighth to fifth century B.C.) such as Amos that a lofty message of ethical monotheism is heard. In these writings, Yahweh is a "jealous god" who tolerates no other gods beside him and who affects other nations as well as his Covenant People. Further, as the creator and sole ruler of the world he is less interested in the peculiar sacrificial rites of one people than in personal righteousness and universal justice among all men. The parable of Jonah, who grows angry at the Lord when he sees His mercy bestowed on the people of Nineveh, reiterates by implication the prophetic message.

This sublime conception of divine justice became increasingly difficult to uphold as the destiny of the Hebrew people grew progressively worse. The prophets who flourished immediately before and during the Babylonian Exile, such as Isaiah, Jeremiah, and Ezekiel, had to reconcile the suffering that befell the Israelites with the notion of God's justice. Their method was to show how the Hebrews, through their own iniquity, had broken their covenant with God. An endless stream of forewarnings, chastisements, threats, and promises pours from their teachings. If Israel will return to Yahweh, then the whole people can and will be restored. Otherwise, further collective or individual retribution for their transgressions will lie in store for all Hebrews.

On the other hand, certain portions of the Jewish wisdom literature, such as the Book of Job and Ecclesiastes, attempt to explain the fact of undeserved suffering and injustice in human life without any overt reference to national misfortunes. The author of Job, writing most likely in Exilic times, seems to find an answer of sorts in the power and scope of blind faith in God's omnipotence and omniscience. The author of Ecclesiastes, writing in the late fourth or the third century B.C., remains a spokesman of an earthy sort of wisdom tinged with philosophic skepticism.

In their attempts to understand God's justice, the Hebrew writers of Exilic and post-Exilic times came more and more under the influence of foreign religious thought. The Book of Job, for example, shows a good deal of Babylonian fatalism. Under Persian influence, a body of literature developed within post-Exilic Israel which may be called "apocalyptic." Here, the world is sharply divided into the forces of good and evil, the hosts of light and darkness; the two powers are about to be joined in decisive conflict, after which the triumphant forces of light will reign supreme on a regenerated earth. It is the duty, then, of the faithful community to wait in confidence for the advent of the Day of the Lord. The later portions of the Book of Isaiah are symptomatic of these beliefs.

In the Book of Daniel, written in the second century B.C., the Jewish faith in a divine future reached the stage of a full-fledged messianism. A savior-god or messiah is prophesied who will lead the Jews to new national greatness and restore the Kingdom of God on earth. Coupled with these messianic hopes are assertions about a future life in another world. The appearance of such eschatological beliefs in late Jewish thought may have been due to the influence of the salvationist creed disseminated by a host of mystery religions flourishing in the Near East in Hellenistic times (third century B.C. to first century A.D.). Otherwise the Old Testament shows little evidence of a full-grown belief in those tenets which were to become the core of the Christian dogma: immortality of the soul, resurrection of the body, and redemption from an innate defilement of human nature—all achieved through the ministry and atonement of a savior-god.

Hellenistic Judaism and the New Testament: Philo Judaeus was the most eminent spokesman of Hellenistic Judaism, a philosophic movement centered in the city of Alexandria, which attempted to bring about a fusion of Jewish and Greek thought. The speculative synthesis which it produced foreshadowed Christian theology and found its way into the Gospel of St. John.

Founded by Alexander the Great in the fourth century B.C. and developed by his successors, Alexandria soon became the cultural and intellectual center of the Near Eastern world. It was here that many Jews of great intellectual abilities came into touch with the best of Greek culture and philosophy. In post-Exilic times a large number of Jews left their native Palestine, continually threatened or overrun by foreign conquerors, to settle in the various parts of the Mediterranean world where they formed the so-called *Diaspora* (literally "dispersion," a term applied specifically to the dispersion of the Jews after the Babylonian captivity).

Alexandria had a large Jewish community. The translation of the Old Testament into Greek—the Septuagint—in the second century B.C. fostered a literary activity among Hellenistic Jews which was devoted primarily to the interpretation of Scripture in the light of Greek thought. Thus Philo's basic intention was to demonstrate that Judaism is a religion compatible with Greek philosophy. This he hoped to achieve by means of an allegorical method of interpretation designed to explain away anthropomorphisms in the biblical text and through the use of Platonic and Stoic materials in the exegesis of Hebrew ethics and cosmology.

While Philo did not elaborate a complete philosophic system, he nevertheless advanced a theory of the Logos, or Supreme Idea, which impressed later Christian theologians but was largely ignored by the more orthodox Jewish thinkers. According to Philo, the world is permeated and sustained by "ideas" or forces emanating from and contained in the Logos (Word), or the Reason of God. The Logos, not unlike God the Son in the Christian Trinity, is a mediator between God and the world. The Gospel of St. John, written some fifty to seventy years after Philo, is filled with such Platonic-Stoic speculations as: "In the beginning was the Word, and the Word was with God and the Word was God" (1:1); or even more explicitly, Christ is the Word that "was made flesh" (1:4).

It was natural enough for Philo and the writer of the Gospel of St. John to come so much under the spell of Greek philosophy. They thought, spoke, and wrote in Greek. Some scholars maintain that Philo knew both Aramaic and Hebrew imperfectly, if at all. To the Jews living in the Diaspora, Greek had become a universal language, used to convey both mundane and esoteric matters, and it carried with it an immense cultural and intellectual patrimony.

St. Paul is another example of a man whose credo, although growing out of Judaism, is conditioned by Hellenistic factors. In his case, however, it is not so much the cosmological theories of Greek philosophers which left an indelible mark on his thought but rather the salvationist creed of the mystery religions. More than any of the other Christian disciples, St. Paul stresses Christ as the redeemer and savior of mankind, which leads him ultimately to propagate a stark predestinarian doctrine anchored in the notion of absolute faith in Christ.

From its very outset, Christianity was a syncretistic phenomenon: a religion composed of elements from Judaism, Greek philosophy, and Hellenistic beliefs and held together in due time by a church whose structure was to a significant extent modeled on the administrative system of the Roman Empire.

On the Creation of the World

II. There are some people who, having the world in admiration rather than the Maker of the world, pronounce it to be without beginning and everlasting, while with impious falsehood they postulate in God a vast inactivity; whereas we ought on the contrary to be astonied at His powers as Maker and Father, and not to assign to the world a disproportionate majesty. Moses, both because he had attained the very summit of philosophy, and because he had been divinely instructed in the greater and most essential part of Nature's lore, could not fail to recognize that the universal must consist of two parts, one part active Cause and the other passive object; and that the active Cause is the perfectly pure and unsullied Mind of the universe, transcending virtue, transcending knowledge, transcending the good itself and the beautiful itself; while the passive part is in itself incapable of life and motion, but, when set in motion and shaped and quickened by Mind, changes into the most perfect masterpiece, namely this world. Those who assert that this

From *Works*, translated by F. H. Colson and G. H. Whitaker (Cambridge, Mass.: Harvard University Press). Reprinted by permission of the publishers and The Loeb Classical Library.

world is unoriginate unconsciously eliminate that which of all incentives to piety is the most beneficial, and the most indispensable, namely providence.[1] For it stands to reason that what has been brought into existence should be cared for by its Father and Maker. For, as we know, it is a father's aim in regard of his offspring and an artificer's in regard of his handiwork to preserve them, and by every means to fend off from them aught that may entail loss or harm. He keenly desires to provide for them in every way all that is beneficial and to their advantage: but between that which has never been brought into being and one who is not its Maker no such tie is formed. It is a worthless and baleful doctrine, setting up anarchy in the well-ordered realm of the world, leaving it without protector, arbitrator, or judge, without anyone whose office it is to administer and direct all its affairs. Not so Moses. That great master, holding the unoriginate to be of a different order from that which is visible, since everything that is an object of sensible perception is subject to becoming and to constant change, never abiding in the same state,[2] assigned to that which is invisible and an object of intellectual apprehension the infinite and undefinable as united with it by closest tie; but on that which is an object of the senses he bestowed "genesis," "becoming," as its appropriate name. Seeing then that this world is both visible and perceived by the senses, it follows that it must also have had an origin. Whence it was entirely to the point that he put on record that origin, setting forth in its true grandeur the work of God.

IV. . . . To speak of or conceive that world which consists of ideas as being in some place is illegitimate; how it consists of these ideas we shall know if we carefully attend to some image supplied by the things of our world. When a city is being founded to satisfy the soaring ambition of some king or governor, who lays claim to despotic power and being magnificent in his ideas would fain add a fresh lustre to his good fortune, there comes forward now and again some trained architect who, observing the favourable climate and convenient position of the site, first sketches in his own mind wellnigh all the parts of the city that is to be wrought out, temples, gymnasia, town-halls, market-places, harbours, docks, streets, walls to be built, dwelling-houses as well as public buildings to be set up. Thus after having received in his own soul, as it were in wax, the figures of these objects severally, he carried about the image of a city which is the creation of his mind. Then by his innate power of memory, he recalls the images of the various parts of this city, and imprints their types yet more distinctly in it: and like a good craftsman he begins to build the city of stones and timber, keeping his eye upon his pattern and making the visible and tangible objects correspond in each case to the incorporeal ideas.

Just such must be our thoughts about God. We must suppose that, when He was minded to found the one great city, He conceived beforehand the models of its parts, and that out of these He constituted and brought to completion a world discernible only by the mind, and then, with that for a pattern, the world which our senses can perceive.

VI. Now God, with no counsellor to help Him (who was there beside

---

[1] The notion of providence plays a vital role in Stoic metaphysics.
[2] The Platonic influence is easily discernible throughout Philo's treatise on the creation.

Him?) determined that it was meet to confer rich and unrestricted benefits upon that nature which apart from Divine bounty could obtain of itself no good thing. But not in proportion to the greatest of His own bounties does He confer benefits—for these are without end or limit —but in proportion to the capacities of the recipients. For it is not the nature of creation to receive good treatment in like manner as it is the nature of God to bestow it, seeing that the powers of God are overwhelmingly vast, whereas creation, being too feeble to entertain their abundance, would have broken down under the effort to do so, had not God with appropriate adjustment dealt out to each his due portion. Should a man desire to use words in a more simple and direct way, he would say that the world discerned only by the intellect is nothing else than the Word of God[3] when He was already engaged in the act of creation. For (to revert to our illustration) the city discernible by the intellect alone is nothing else than the reasoning faculty of the architect in the act of planning to found the city. It is Moses who lays down this, not I. Witness his express acknowledgement in the sequel, when setting on record the creation of man, that he was moulded after the image of God (Gen. i. 27). Now if the part is an image of an image, it is manifest that the whole is so too, and if the whole creation, this entire world perceived by our senses (seeing that it is greater than any human image) is a copy of the Divine image, it is manifest that the archetypal seal also, which we aver to be the world descried by the mind, would be the very Word of God.

VII. Then he says that "in the beginning God made the heaven and the earth," taking "beginning" not, as some think, in a chronological sense, for time there was not before there was a world. Time began either simultaneously with the world or after it. For since time is a measured space determined by the world's movement, and since movement could not be prior to the object moving, but must of necessity arise either after it or simultaneously with it, it follows of necessity that time also is either coeval with or later born than the world.[4] To venture to affirm that it is elder born would be to do violence to philosophic sense. And since the word "beginning" is not here taken as the chronological beginning, it would seem likely that the numerical order is indicated, so that "in the beginning He made" is equivalent to "He made the heaven first": for it is indeed reasonable that it should come into existence first, being both best of created things and made from the purest of all that is, seeing that it was destined to be the most holy dwelling-place of manifest and visible gods. For, even if the Maker made all things simultaneously, order was none the less an attribute of all that came into existence in fair beauty, for beauty is absent where there is disorder. Now order is a series of things going on before and following after, in due sequence, a sequence which, though not seen in the finished productions, yet exists in the designs of the contrivers; for only so could these things be fashioned with perfect accuracy, and work without leaving their path or clashing with each other.

---

[3]Here Philo associates the intelligible world of Platonism with the *Logos* of the Stoics.
[4]Among later Christian theologians, St. Augustine (354–430 A.D.) especially espoused Philo's concept of time.

First, then, the Maker made an incorporeal heaven, and an invisible earth, and the essential form of air and void. To the one he gave the name of "Darkness," since the air when left to itself, is black. The other he named "abyss," for the void is a region of immensity and vast depths. Next He made the incorporeal essence of water and of life-breath[5] and, to crown all, of light. This again, the seventh in order, was an incorporeal pattern, discernible only by the mind, of the sun and of all luminaries which were to come into existence throughout heaven.

VIII. Special distinction is accorded by Moses to life-breath and to light. The one he entitles the "breath" of God, because breath is most life-giving, and of life God is the author, while of light he says that it is beautiful pre-eminently (Gen. i. 4): for the intelligible as far surpasses the visible in the brilliancy of its radiance, as sunlight assuredly surpasses darkness and day night, and mind, the ruler of the entire soul, the bodily eyes. Now that invisible light perceptible only by mind has come into being as an image of the Divine Word Who brought it within our ken: it is a supercelestial constellation, fount of the constellations obvious to sense. It would not be amiss to term it "all-brightness," to signify that from which sun and moon, as well as fixed stars and planets draw, in proportion to their several capacity, the light befitting each of them: for that pure and undiluted radiance is bedimmed so soon as it begins to undergo the change that is entailed by the passage from the intelligible to the sensibly discerned, for no object of sense is free from dimness.

XVII. . . . Knowing that of all things light is best, He made it the indispensable means of sight, the best of the senses; for what the intellect is in the soul, this the eye is in the body; for each of them sees, one the things of the mind, the other the things of sense; and they have need, the mind of knowledge, that it may become cognizant of incorporeal objects, the eye of light, for the apprehending of bodily forms. Light has proved itself the source of many other boons to mankind, but pre-eminently of philosophy, the greatest boon of all. For man's faculty of vision, led upwards by light, discerned the nature of the heavenly bodies and their harmonious movement. He saw the well-ordered circuits of fixed stars and planets, how the former moved in unchanging orbit and all alike, while the latter sped round in two revolutions out of harmony with each other. He marked the rhythmic dances of all these, how they were marshalled by the laws of a perfect music,[6] and the sight produced in his soul an ineffable delight and pleasure. Banqueting on sights displayed to it one after another, his soul was insatiate in beholding. And then, as usually happens, it went on to busy itself with questionings, asking What is the essence of these visible objects? Are they in nature unoriginate, or had they a beginning of existence? What is the method of their movement? And what are the principles by which each is governed? It was out of the investigation of these problems that philosophy grew, than which no more perfect good has come into the life of mankind.

---

[5]In Greek, *pneuma*, a word used by Stoics and Gnostics to denote the spark of divine "spirit" dwelling in man.

[6]In Pythagoreanism the heavenly spheres are said to emit an ethereal music as they rotate on their axes, the so-called "harmony of the spheres."

XXIII. After all the rest, as I have said, Moses tells us that man was created after the image of God and after His likeness (Gen. i. 26). Right well does he say this, for nothing earth-born is more like God than man. Let no one represent the likeness as one to a bodily form; for neither is God in human form, nor is the human body God-like. No, it is in respect of the Mind, the sovereign element of the soul, that the word "image" is used; for after the pattern of a single Mind, even the Mind of the Universe as an archetype, the mind in each of those who successively came into being was moulded. It is in a fashion a god to him who carries and enshrines it as an object of reverence; for the human mind evidently occupies a position in men precisely answering to that which the great Ruler occupies in all the world. It is invisible while itself seeing all things, and while comprehending the substances of others, it is as to its own substance unperceived; and while it opens by arts and sciences roads branching in many directions, all of them great highways, it comes through land and sea investigating what either element contains. Again, when on soaring wing it has contemplated the atmosphere and all its phases, it is borne yet higher to the ether and the circuit of heaven, and is whirled round with the dances of planets and fixed stars, in accordance with the laws of perfect music, following that love of wisdom which guides its steps. And so, carrying its gaze beyond the confines of all substance discernible by sense, it comes to a point at which it reaches out after the intelligible world, and on descrying in that world sights of surpassing loveliness, even the patterns and the originals of the things of sense which it saw here, it is seized by a sober intoxication, like those filled with Corybantic frenzy, and is inspired, possessed by a longing far other than theirs and a nobler desire. Wafted by this to the topmost arch of the things perceptible to mind, it seems to be on its way to the Great King Himself; but, amid its longing to see Him, pure and untempered rays of concentrated light stream forth like a torrent, so that by its gleams the eye of the understanding is dazzled. And, since images do not always correspond to their archetype and pattern, but are in many instances unlike it, the writer further brought out his meaning by adding "after the likeness" to the words "after the image," thus showing that an accurate cast, bearing a clear impression, was intended.

XXIV. One may not unfitly raise the question what reason there could be for his ascribing the creation in the case of man only not to one Creator as in the case of the rest but, as the words would suggest, to several. For he represents the Father of the universe as speaking thus, "Let us make man after our image and likeness." 'Can it be,' I would ask, 'that He to whom all things are subject, is in need of anyone whatever? Or can it be that when He made the heaven and the earth and the seas, he required no one to be his fellow-worker, yet was unable apart from the co-operation of others by His own unaided power to fashion a creature so puny and perishable as man?' The full truth about the cause of this it must needs be that God alone knows, but the cause which by probable conjecture seems plausible and reasonable we must not conceal. It is this. Among existences some partake neither of virtue nor of vice, like plants and animals devoid of reason; the one sort because they are without animal life and furnished with a nature incapable of consciously receiving impressions; the other sort because from them mind and reason have been eliminated: for mind and reason are as it were the dwelling-place of vice and virtue, which are by nature constituted to make their abode in them. Others again have partnership with virtue only, and have no part or lot in vice. Such are the heavenly bodies; for these are said to be not only living creatures but living creatures endowed with mind, or rather each of them a mind in itself, excellent through and through and unsusceptible of any evil. Others are of mixed nature, as man, who is liable to contraries, wisdom and folly, self-mastery and licentiousness, courage and cowardice, justice and injustice, and (in a word) to things good and evil, fair and foul, to virtue and vice. Now it was most proper to God the universal Father to make those excellent things by Himself alone, because of their kinship to Him. To make those which are neither good nor bad was not alien to Him, since those too are free from vice which is hateful to Him. To make those of mixed nature was in one respect proper to Him, in another not so; proper, so far as the better principle which forms an ingredient in them is concerned, alien, in virtue of the contrary and worse principle. So we see why it is only in the instance of man's creation that we are told by Moses that God said "Let us make," an expression which plainly shows the taking with Him of others as fellow-workers. It is to the end that, when man orders his course aright, when his thoughts and deeds are blameless, God the universal Ruler may be owned as their Source; while others from the number of His subordinates are held responsible for thoughts and deeds of a contrary sort: for it could not be that the Father should be the cause of an evil thing to His offspring: and vice and vicious activities are an evil thing. . . .

Moses

Book I

XII. . . . Now, as [Moses] was leading the flock to a place where the water and the grass were abundant,[1] and where there happened to be plentiful growth of herbage for the sheep, he found himself at a glen where he saw a most astonishing sight. There was a bramble-bush, a thorny sort of plant, and of the most weakly kind, which, without anyone's setting it alight, suddenly took fire; and, though enveloped from

From *Works*, translated by F. H. Colson and G. H. Whitaker (Cambridge, Mass.: Harvard University Press). Reprinted by permission of the publishers and The Loeb Classical Library.
[1]This is an allegorical interpretation of Exodus, Chapter 3.

root to twigs in a mass of fire, which looked as though it were spouted up from a fountain, yet remained whole, and, instead of being consumed, seemed to be a substance impervious to attack, and, instead of serving as fuel to the fire, actually fed on it. In the midst of the flame was a form of the fairest beauty, unlike any visible object, an image supremely divine in appearance, refulgent with a light brighter than the light of fire. It might be supposed that this was the image of Him that is; but let us rather call it an angel or herald, since, with a silence that spoke more clearly than speech, it employed as it were the miracle of sight to herald future events. For the burning bramble was a symbol of those who suffered wrong, as the flaming fire of those who did it. Yet that which burned was not burnt up, and this was a sign that the sufferers would not be destroyed by their aggressors, who would find that the aggression was vain and profitless while the victims of malice escaped unharmed. The angel was a symbol of God's providence, which all silently brings relief to the greatest dangers, exceeding every hope.

XIII. But the details of the comparison must be considered. The bramble, as I have said, is a very weakly plant, yet it is prickly and will wound if one do but touch it. Again, though fire is naturally destructive, the bramble was not devoured thereby, but on the contrary was guarded by it, and remained just as it was before it took fire, lost nothing at all but gained an additional brightness. All this is a description of the nation's condition as it then stood, and we may think of it as a voice proclaiming to the sufferers: "Do not lose heart; your weakness is your strength, which can prick, and thousands will suffer from its wounds. Those who desire to consume you will be your unwilling saviours instead of your destroyers. Your ills will work you no ill. Nay, just when the enemy is surest of ravaging you, your fame will shine forth most gloriously." Again fire, the element which works destruction, convicts the cruel-hearted. "Exult not in your own strength" it says. "Behold your invincible might brought low, and learn wisdom. The property of flame is to consume, yet it is consumed, like wood. The nature of wood is to be consumed yet it is manifested as the consumer, as though it were the fire."

The Special Laws:
The Existence and Nature of God

VII. As for the divine essence, though in fact it is hard to track and hard to apprehend, it still calls for all the inquiry possible. For nothing

From *Works*, translated by F. H. Colson and G. H. Whitaker (Cambridge, Mass.: Harvard University Press). Reprinted by permission of the publishers and The Loeb Classical Library.

is better than to search for the true God, even if the discovery of Him eludes human capacity, since the very wish to learn, if earnestly entertained, produces untold joys and pleasures. We have the testimony of those who have not taken a mere sip of philosophy but have feasted more abundantly on its reasonings and conclusions. For with them the reason soars away from earth into the heights, travels through the upper air and accompanies the revolutions of the sun and moon and the whole heaven and in its desire to see all that is there finds its powers of sight blurred, for so pure and vast is the radiance that pours therefrom that the soul's eye is dizzied by the flashing of the rays. Yet it does not therefore faintheartedly give up the task, but with purpose unsubdued presses onwards to such contemplation as is possible, like the athlete who strives for the second prize since he has been disappointed of the first. Now second to the true vision stands conjecture and theorizing and all that can be brought into the category of reasonable probability. So then just as, though we do not know and cannot with certainty determine what each of the stars is in the purity of its essence, we eagerly persist in the search because our natural love of learning makes us delight in what seems probable, so too, though the clear vision of God as He really is is denied us, we ought not to relinquish the quest. For the very seeking, even without finding, is felicity in itself, just as no one blames the eyes of the body because when unable to see the sun itself they see the emanation of its rays as it reaches the earth, which is but the extremity of the brightness which the beams of the sun give forth.

VIII. It was this which Moses the sacred guide, most dearly beloved of God, had before his eyes when he besought God with the words, "Reveal Thyself to me."[1] In these words we may almost hear plainly the inspired cry "This universe has been my teacher, to bring me to the knowledge that Thou art and dost subsist. As Thy son, it has told me of its Father, as Thy work of its contriver. But what Thou art in Thy essence I desire to understand, yet find in no part of the All any to guide me to this knowledge. Therefore I pray and beseech Thee to accept the supplication of a suppliant, a lover of God, one whose mind is set to serve Thee alone; for as knowledge of the light does not come by any other source but what itself supplies, so too Thou alone canst tell me of Thyself. Wherefore I crave pardon if, for lack of a teacher, I venture to appeal to Thee in my desire to learn of Thee." He replies, "Thy zeal I approve as praiseworthy, but the request cannot fitly be granted to any that are brought into being by creation. I freely bestow what is in accordance with the recipient; for not all that I can give with ease is within man's power to take, and therefore to him that is worthy of My grace I extend all the boons which he is capable of receiving. But the apprehension of Me is something more than human nature, yea even the whole heaven and universe will be able to contain. Know thyself, then, and do not be led away by impulses and desires beyond thy capacity, nor let yearning for the unattainable uplift and carry thee off thy feet, for of the obtainable nothing shall be denied thee." When Moses heard this, he addressed to Him a second petition and said,

---

[1] What follows is a meditation on Exodus 33:13-23.

"I bow before Thy admonitions, that I never could have received the vision of Thee clearly manifested, but I beseech Thee that I may at least see the glory that surrounds Thee, and by Thy glory I understand the powers that keep guard around Thee, of whom I would fain gain apprehension, for though hitherto that has escaped me, the thought of it creates in me a mighty longing to have knowledge of them." To this He answers, "The powers which thou seekest to know are discerned not by sight but by mind even as I, Whose they are, am discerned by mind and not by sight, and when I say 'they are discerned by mind' I speak not of those which are now actually apprehended by mind but mean that if these other powers could be apprehended it would not be by sense but by mind at its purest. But while in their essence they are beyond your apprehension, they nevertheless present to your sight a sort of impress and copy of their active working.[2] You men have for your use seals which when brought into contact with wax or similar material stamp on them any number of impressions while they themselves are not docked in any part thereby but remain as they were. Such you must conceive My powers to be, supplying quality and shape to things which lack either and yet changing or lessening nothing of their eternal nature. Some among you call them not inaptly 'forms' or 'ideas,' since they bring form into everything that is, giving order to the disordered, limit to the unlimited, bounds to the unbounded, shape to the shapeless, and in general changing the worse to something better. Do not, then, hope to be ever able to apprehend Me or any of My powers in Our essence. But I readily and with right goodwill will admit you to a share of what is attainable. That means that I bid you come and contemplate the universe and its contents, a spectacle apprehended not by the eye of the body but by the unsleeping eyes of the mind. Only let there be the constant and profound longing for wisdom which fills its scholars and disciples with verities glorious in their exceeding loveliness." When Moses heard this, he did not cease from his desire but kept the yearning for the invisible aflame in his heart.

Comments / on Philo

Greek philosophy helped prepare the way for the coming of the Christian religion; for twelve hundred years creative thinkers had sought to solve the prolems of man and the universe. Through the use of reason in the attainment of truth, the Greek philosophers made a unique contribution to civilization and to religion. . . . Christianity originated as an oriental religion, in which the revelation of the divine will to the prophets was of supreme importance; but before a half century of its history had passed,

---

[2]Philo explains here, within a Platonic framework, the concept of a *Deus absconditus* (a hidden, unknowable God) found, for instance, in the Book of Job.

the Christian religion had to meet all the aspects of Hellenistic culture, including its philosophy. In the second century, leadership in the Christian church passed to men who knew Greek philosophy and who knew how to combine creatively the best in Hebrew thought with the best in Greek thought.   *MEREDITH F. ELLER (1958)*

In Philo we meet the greatest mind Hellenistic Judaism produced. To what extent he influenced his fellow religionists is uncertain; the influence he exerted upon Christian theology through the famous Alexandrian school cannot be overemphasized. . . . For Philo, Greek philosophy and biblical revelation were identical in scope and content. He thus, perhaps in a unique degree, stood as the bridge between Judaism and Hellenism over which Christian theology was to cross.
MORTON S. ENSLIN (1938)

The question of contact between deity—pure spirituality—and impure matter is for a monotheistic Jew a more difficult question than it is for a Greek philosopher, whose monotheism is a theoretical principle of existence and not a principle of life (a "living God"—fashioner and creator, "the first and the last"—the God of society and the God of history). On this account, Philo was forced to come to the conclusion that there are mediators or intermediate causes between deity and the world, between absolute spirit and matter mixed with spirit. By means of these, then, there is formed a bridge or passageway from absolutely good deity to the corporeal world, where good and bad lie together in confusion.   *JOSEPH KLAUSNER (1944)*

Philo's conception of the Logos was totally alien to Judaism. The God of the Bible is a living God, not the impersonal being of Greek metaphysics. He does employ intermediaries to execute His Will, but is certainly not inactive Himself. Furthermore, the conception of the Logos as a second God seemed to impair the absolute monotheism of the Jewish religion. Nor was his allegorical method which reduced the scriptures to a mere textbook of Greek metaphysics acceptable to Judaism.
ISIDORE EPSTEIN (1959)

As well as Stoicism, Platonism, or rather Neo-Platonism, had an effect on Hellenistic Judaism. In some ways this provided still more serviceable instruments than Stoicism for the expression of certain Old Testament ideas. For Philo, Plato is the greatest of the saints, the unsurpassed ally of Moses. Platonic idealism with its antithesis between the eternal world of ideas the phenomenal world of becoming and decaying seemed to provide a suitable terminology for describing God's transcendence over the world. But, inevitably, the result was a new version of transcendence: it was now thought of in terms of the contrariety between spirit and matter. Like the earlier Wisdom of Solomon, Philo combines Stoic theology with ideas derived from Platonism. The Logos is not only the rational law pervading and controlling the universe, but also the sum of the transcendent world of ideas, the 'spiritual world', at the head of which stands God himself, the perfect Being devoid of all quality.
RUDOLF BULTMANN (1956)

Justin Martyr
110?—165? A.D.

The Fathers of the Church were ecclesiastical writers of the first few Christian centuries whose works helped establish the foundations of Christian belief. For the first century or so, the Fathers continued in the Apostolic tradition, simply preaching the word of Christ and the tenets of Christianity. They professed to be disciples of either the Apostles themselves or their immediate disciples. But by the second century, this sense of direct contact with the origins of Christianity was necessarily lost, and the writings of the Fathers began to turn toward theological speculation, attempting to make the doctrinal bases of Christianity intellectually comprehensible. One practical reason for this development, aside from the Fathers' interest in theology for its own sake, was the need to defend Christians from persecution by the Roman emperors. If Roman officials fully understood the nature of Christian beliefs, so the theory went, then they would see that Christianity offered no real threat to Roman institutions and would stop persecuting Christians. With this purpose in mind, many of the early Fathers wrote apologies, a term then in use to describe a formal statement made before a judge on behalf of a defendant. The Christian apologies are actually formal claims put to the Roman emperors in order to gain official recognition of the rights of Christians to practice their religion.

Justin Martyr was one of the earliest apologists. Born in Syria, of Gentile origin, he devoted himself to philosophy early in life, seeking intellectual certitude among the various systems of Greek philosophy. But all of these left him unsatisfied, and he became a convert to Christianity by the time he was twenty. From then on he spent his life propagating Christian belief as the only true philosophy and was ultimately beheaded by the Romans, thus becoming a martyr to the Christian faith.

Justin's *First Apology* is of particular interest because it marks one of the earliest attempts to effect some kind of systematic harmony between the doctrines of Christianity and the principles of Greek philosophy. Justin was a man of Greek culture for whom philosophical training, according to the practices current in the second century, was training in a distinctive profession. The philosopher did not talk, think, or even dress like other men; but, clothed in his philosopher's robes, he pursued knowledge of divine things as his most important business. It was natural for Justin, who throughout his life considered himself a philosopher in this traditional sense, to try to adapt the fruits of his philosophic training into the framework of Christianity. A reasonable man himself, he wanted reasonable men to see that Christianity was a reasonable religion; as a result, much of his *Apology* is devoted to demonstrating the connections between Christian beliefs and the Greco-Roman intellectual heritage.

The First Apology

1. To the Emperor Titus Ælius Adrianus Antoninus Pius Augustus Cæsar,[1] and to his son Verissimus the Philosopher, and to Lucius the Philosopher, the natural son of Cæsar, and the adopted son of Pius, a lover of learning, and to the sacred Senate, with the whole People of the Romans, I, Justin, the son of Priscus and grandson of Bacchius, natives of Flavia Neapolis in Palestine, present this address and petition in behalf of those of all nations who are unjustly hated and wantonly abused, myself being one of them.

2. Reason directs those who are truly pious and philosophical to honour and love only what is true, declining to follow traditional opinions, if these be worthless. For not only does sound reason direct us to refuse the guidance of those who did or taught anything wrong, but it is incumbent on the lover of truth, by all means, and if death be threatened, even before his own life, to choose to do and say what is right. Do you, then, since ye are called pious and philosophers, guardians of justice and lovers of learning, give good heed, and hearken to my address; and if ye are indeed such, it will be manifested. For we have come, not to flatter you by this writing, nor please you by our address, but to beg that you pass judgment, after an accurate and searching investigation, not flattered by prejudice or by a desire of pleasing superstitious men, nor induced by irrational impulse or evil rumours which have long been prevalent, to give a decision which will prove to be against yourselves. For as for us, we reckon that no evil can be done us, unless we be convicted as evil-doers, or be proved to be wicked men; and you, you can kill, but not hurt us.

From *The Ante-Nicene Fathers*, Vol. I, edited by Alexander Roberts and James Donaldson. Reprinted by permission of Wm. B. Eerdmans Publishing Co., Grand Rapids, Michigan.
[1]Reigned 138–161 A.D.

3. But lest any one think that this is an unreasonable and reckless utterance, we demand that the charges against the Christians be investigated, and that, if these be substantiated, they be punished as they deserve; or rather, indeed, we ourselves will punish them. But if no one can convict us of anything, true reason forbids you, for the sake of a wicked rumour, to wrong blameless men, and indeed rather yourselves, who think fit to direct affairs, not by judgment, but by passion. And every sober-minded person will declare this to be the only fair and equitable adjustment, namely, that the subjects render an unexceptional account of their own life and doctrine; and that, on the other hand, the rulers should give their decision in obedience, not to violence and tyranny, but to piety and philosophy. For thus would both rulers and ruled reap benefit. For even one of the ancients somewhere said, "Unless both rulers and ruled philosophize, it is impossible to make states blessed."[2] It is our task, therefore, to afford to all an opportunity of inspecting our life and teachings, lest, on account of those who are accustomed to be ignorant of our affairs, we should incur the penalty due to them for mental blindness; and it is your business, when you hear us, to be found, as reason demands, good judges. For if, when ye have learned the truth, you do not what is just, you will be before God without excuse.

4. By the mere application of a name, nothing is decided, either good or evil, apart from the actions implied in the name; and indeed, so far at least as one may judge from the name we are accused of, we are most excellent people.[3] But as we do not think it just to beg to be acquitted on account of the name, if we be convicted as evil-doers, so, on the other hand, if we be found to have committed no offence, either in the matter of thus naming ourselves, or of our conduct as citizens, it is your part very earnestly to guard against incurring just punishment, by unjustly punishing those who are not convicted. For from a name neither praise nor punishment could reasonably spring, unless something excellent or base in action be proved. And those among yourselves who are accused you do not punish before they are convicted; but in our case you receive the name as proof against us, and this although, so far as the name goes, you ought rather to punish our accusers. For we are accused of being Christians, and to hate what is excellent *(Chrestian)* is unjust. Again, if any of the accused deny the name, and say that he is not a Christian, you acquit him, as having no evidence against him as a wrong-doer; but if any one acknowledge that he is a Christian, you punish him on account of this acknowledgment. Justice requires that you inquire into the life both of him who confesses and of him who denies, that by his deeds it may be apparent what kind of man each is. For as some who have been taught by the Master, Christ, not to deny Him, give encouragement to others when they are put to the question, so in all probability do those who lead wicked lives give occasion to those who, without consideration, take upon them to accuse all the Christians of impiety

---

[2]Plato, *Republic*, Book V.

[3]Justin is making a play on words based on the similarity in sound of the two Greek words, *Christos* (Christ) and *chrestos* (good, worthy, excellent). He continues to do this throughout the chapter.

and wickedness. And this also is not right. For of philosophy, too, some assume the name and the garb who do nothing worthy of their profession; and you are well aware, that those of the ancients whose opinions and teachings were quite diverse, are yet all called by the one name of philosophers. And of these some taught atheism; and the poets who have flourished among you raise a laugh out of the uncleanness of Jupiter with his own children. And those who now adopt such instruction are not restrained by you; but, on the contrary, you bestow prizes and honours upon those who euphoniously insult the gods.

5. Why, then, should this be? In our case, who pledge ourselves to do no wickedness, nor to hold these atheistic opinions, you do not examine the charges made against us; but, yielding to unreasoning passion, and to the instigation of evil demons, you punish us without consideration or judgment. For the truth shall be spoken; since of old these evil demons, effecting apparitions of themselves, both defiled women and corrupted boys, and showed such fearful sights to men, that those who did not use their reason in judging of the actions that were done, were struck with terror; and being carried away by fear, and not knowing that these were demons, they called them gods, and gave to each the name which each of the demons chose for himself. And when Socrates endeavoured, by true reason and examination, to bring these things to light, and deliver men from the demons, then the demons themselves, by means of men who rejoiced in iniquity, compassed his death, as an atheist and a profane person, on the charge that "he was introducing new divinities;" and in our case they display a similar activity. For not only among the Greeks did reason *(Logos)* prevail to condemn these things through Socrates, but also among the Barbarians were they condemned by Reason (or the Word, the *Logos*) Himself, who took shape, and became man, and was called Jesus Christ,[4] and in obedience to Him, we not only deny that they who did such things as these are gods, but assert that they are wicked and impious demons, whose actions will not bear comparison with those even of men desirous of virtue.

6. Hence are we called atheists. And we confess that we are atheists, so far as gods of this sort are concerned, but not with respect to the most true God, the Father of righteousness and temperance and the other virtues, who is free from all impurity. But both Him, and the Son (who came forth from Him and taught us these things, and the host of the other good angels who follow and are made like to Him), and the prophetic Spirit, we worship and adore, knowing them in reason and truth, and declaring without grudging to every one who wishes to learn, as we have been taught.

7. But some one will say, Some have ere now been arrested and convicted as evil-doers. For you condemn many, many a time, after inquiring into the life of each of the accused severally, but not on account of those of whom we have been speaking. And this we acknowledge, that as among the Greeks those who teach such theories as please themselves

---

[4]*Logos,* a Greek word whose root meaning is "word," also acquired in Greek philosophy the meanings of reason, spirit, the divine essence, God. In early Christian thought, *Logos* was adapted to stand for Christ, the Holy Spirit, God.

are all called by the one name "Philosopher," though their doctrines be diverse, so also among the Barbarians this name on which accusations are accumulated is the common property of those who are and those who seem wise. For all are called Christians. Wherefore we demand that the deeds of all those who are accused to you be judged, in order that each one who is convicted may be punished as an evil-doer, and not as a Christian; and if it is clear that any one is blameless, that he may be acquitted, since by the mere fact of his being a Christian he does no wrong. For we will not require that you punish our accusers; they being sufficiently punished by their present wickedness and ignorance of what is right.

8. And reckon ye that it is for your sakes we have been saying these things; for it is in our power, when we are examined, to deny that we are Christians; but we would not live by telling a lie. For, impelled by the desire of the eternal and pure life, we seek the abode that is with God, the Father and Creator of all, and hasten to confess our faith, persuaded and convinced as we are that they who have proved to God by their works that they followed Him, and loved to abide with Him where there is no sin to cause disturbance, can obtain these things. This, then, to speak shortly, is what we expect and have learned from Christ, and teach. And Plato, in like manner, used to say that Rhadamanthus and Minos would punish the wicked who came before them; and we say that the same thing will be done, but at the hand of Christ, and upon the wicked in the same bodies united again to their spirits which are now to undergo everlasting punishment; and not only, as Plato said, for a period of a thousand years. And if any one say that this is incredible or impossible, this error of ours is one which concerns ourselves only, and no other person, so long as you cannot convict us of doing any harm.

[Chapters 9 — 10: Justin denounces the folly of idol worship and expounds the Christian belief that man serves God best by leading a virtuous life.]

11. And when you hear that we look for a kingdom, you suppose, without making any inquiry, that we speak of a human kingdom; whereas we speak of that which is with God, as appears also from the confession of their faith made by those who are charged with being Christians, though they know that death is the punishment awarded to him who so confesses. For if we looked for a human kingdom, we should also deny our Christ, that we might not be slain; and we should strive to escape detection, that we might obtain what we expect. But since our thoughts are not fixed on the present, we are not concerned when men cut us off; since also death is a debt which must at all events be paid.

12. And more than all other men are we your helpers and allies in promoting peace, seeing that we hold this view, that it is alike impossible for the wicked, the covetous, the conspirator, and for the virtuous, to escape the notice of God, and that each man goes to everlasting punishment or salvation according to the value of his actions. For if all men knew this, no one would choose wickedness even for a little, knowing that he goes to the everlasting punishment of fire; but would by all

means restrain himself, and adorn himself with virtue, that he might obtain the good gifts of God, and escape the punishments. For those who, on account of the laws and punishments you impose, endeavour to escape detection when they offend (and they offend, too, under the impression that it is quite possible to escape your detection, since you are but men), those persons, if they learned and were convinced that nothing, whether actually done or only intended, can escape the knowledge of God, would by all means live decently on account of the penalties threatened, as even you yourselves will admit. But you seem to fear lest all men become righteous, and you no longer have any to punish. Such would be the concern of public executioners, but not of good princes. But, as we before said, we are persuaded that these things are prompted by evil spirits, who demand sacrifices and service even from those who live unreasonably; but as for you, we presume that you who aim at a reputation for piety and philosophy will do nothing unreasonable. But if you also, like the foolish, prefer custom to truth, do what you have power to do. But just so much power have rulers who esteem opinion more than truth, as robbers have in a desert. And that you will not succeed is declared by the Word, than whom, after God who begat Him, we know there is no ruler more kingly and just. For as all shrink from succeeding to the poverty or sufferings or obscurity of their fathers, so whatever the Word forbids us to choose, the sensible man will not choose. That all these things should come to pass, I say, our Teacher foretold, He who is both Son and Apostle of God the Father of all and the Ruler, Jesus Christ; from whom also we have the name of Christians. Whence we become more assured of all the things He taught us, since whatever He beforehand foretold should come to pass, is seen in fact coming to pass; and this is the work of God, to tell of a thing before it happens, and as it was foretold so to show it happening. It were possible to pause here and add no more, reckoning that we demand what is just and true; but because we are well aware that it is not easy suddenly to change a mind possessed by ignorance, we intend to add a few things, for the sake of persuading those who love the truth, knowing that it is not impossible to put ignorance to flight by presenting the truth.

13. What sober-minded man, then, will not acknowledge that we are not atheists, worshipping as we do the Maker of this universe, and declaring, as we have been taught, that He has no need of streams of blood and libations and incense; whom we praise to the utmost of our power by the exercise of prayer and thanksgiving for all things wherewith we are supplied, as we have been taught that the only honour that is worthy of Him is not to consume by fire what He has brought into being for our sustenance, but to use it for ourselves and those who need, and with gratitude to Him to offer thanks by invocations and hymns for our creation, and for all the means of health, and for the various qualities of the different kinds of things, and for the changes of the seasons; and to present before Him petitions for our existing again in incorruption through faith in Him. Our teacher of these things is Jesus Christ, who also was born for this purpose, and was crucified under Pontius Pilate, procurator of Judæa, in the times of Tiberius Cæsar; and that we reasonably worship Him, having learned that He is the Son of the

true God Himself, and holding Him in the second place, and the prophetic Spirit in the third, we will prove. For they proclaim our madness to consist in this, that we give to a crucified man a place second to the unchangeable and eternal God, the Creator of all; for they do not discern the mystery that is herein, to which, as we make it plain to you, we pray you to give heed.

[Chapters 14 — 19: Justin argues that heathen critics misrepresent Christian doctrine. He goes on to describe briefly Christian doctrine regarding chastity, poverty, tolerance, oaths, civil obedience, the immortality of the soul, and the resurrection of the flesh.]

20. And the Sibyl and Hystaspes[5] said that there should be a dissolution by God of things corruptible. And the philosophers called Stoics teach that even God Himself shall be resolved into fire, and they say that the world is to be formed anew by this revolution; but we understand that God, the Creator of all things, is superior to the things that are to be changed. If, therefore, on some points we teach the same things as the poets and philosophers whom you honour, and on other points are fuller and more divine in our teaching, and if we alone afford proof of what we assert, why are we unjustly hated more than all others? For while we say that all things have been produced and arranged into a world by God, we shall seem to utter the doctrine of Plato; and while we say that there will be a burning up of all, we shall seem to utter the doctrine of the Stoics;[6] and while we affirm that the souls of the wicked, being endowed with sensation even after death, are punished, and that those of the good being delivered from punishment spend a blessed existence, we shall seem to say the same things as the poets and philosophers; and while we maintain that men ought not to worship the works of their hands, we say the very things which have been said by the comic poet Menander,[7] and other similar writers, for they have declared that the workman is greater than the work.

21. And when we say also that the Word, who is the first-birth of God, was produced without sexual union, and that He, Jesus Christ, our Teacher, was crucified and died, and rose again, and ascended into heaven, we propound nothing different from what you believe regarding those whom you esteem sons of Jupiter.[8] For you know how many sons your esteemed writers ascribed to Jupiter: Mercury, the interpreting word and teacher of all; Æsculapius, who, though he was a great physician, was struck by a thunderbolt, and so ascended to heaven; and Bacchus too, after he had been torn limb from limb; and Hercules, when he had committed himself to the flames to escape his toils; and the sons of Leda, and Dioscuri; and Perseus, son of Danae; and Bel-

---

[5]The Sibyl was a legendary prophetess supposed to have flourished in Greece in Homeric times and to have composed a number of prophetic books. Hystaspes was a legendary Persian king who was supposed to have lived about 1000 B.C. and to have helped promulgate the religious doctrines of the prophet Zoroaster.

[6]According to the Stoic theory of the universe, all things were permeated by the divine spirit, which they considered a sort of celestial fire. They believed that all matter eventually tended to change into spirit, into celestial fire.

[7]A Greek playwright (342—291 B.C.) who wrote more than one hundred comedies.

[8]Justin alludes to a number of extravagant stories out of ancient Greek mythology in the references which follow.

lerophon, who, though sprung from mortals, rose to heaven on the horse Pegasus. For what shall I say of Ariadne, and those who, like her, have been declared to be set among the stars? And what of the emperors who die among yourselves, whom you deem worthy of deification, and in whose behalf you produce some one who swears he has seen the burning Cæsar rise to heaven from the funeral pyre? And what kind of deeds are recorded of each of these reputed sons of Jupiter, it is needless to tell to those who already know. This only shall be said, that they are written for the advantage and encouragement of youthful scholars; for all reckon it an honourable thing to imitate the gods. But far be such a thought concerning the gods from every well-conditioned soul, as to believe that Jupiter himself, the governor and creator of all things, was both a parricide and the son of a parricide, and that being overcome by the love of base and shameful pleasures, he came in to Ganymede and those many women whom he had violated and that his sons did like actions. But, as we said above, wicked devils perpetrated these things. And we have learned that those only are deified who have lived near to God in holiness and virtue; and we believe that those who live wickedly and do not repent are punished in everlasting fire.

22. Moreover, the Son of God called Jesus, even if only a man by ordinary generation, yet, on account of His wisdom, is worthy to be called the Son of God; for all writers call God the Father of men and gods. And if we assert that the Word of God was born of God in a peculiar manner, different from ordinary generation, let this, as said above, be no extraordinary thing to you, who say that Mercury is the angelic word of God. But if any one objects that He was crucified, in this also He is on a par with those reputed sons of Jupiter of yours, who suffered as we have now enumerated. For their sufferings at death are recorded to have been not all alike, but diverse; so that not even by the peculiarity of His sufferings does He seem to be inferior to them; but, on the contrary, as we promised in the preceding part of this discourse, we will now prove Him superior—or rather have already proved Him to be so—for the superior is revealed by His actions. And if we even affirm that He was born of a virgin, accept this in common with what you accept of Perseus. And in that we say that He made whole the lame, the paralytic, and those born blind, we seem to say what is very similar to the deeds said to have been done by Æsculapius.

[Chapters 23 – 42: Justin argues that Christian doctrines alone are true and are to be believed on their own account, not merely because of any resemblance they bear to the sentiments of the poets and philosophers. He asserts the divinity of Christ, arguing from the prophecies about divine incarnation in the Old Testament.]

43. But lest some suppose, from what has been said by us, that we say that whatever happens, happens by a fatal necessity, because it is foretold as known beforehand, this too we explain. We have learned from the prophets, and we hold it to be true, that punishments, and chastisements, and good rewards, are rendered according to the merit

of each man's actions. Since if it be not so, but all things happen by fate, neither is anything at all in our own power. For if it be fated that this man, e.g., be good, and this other evil, neither is the former meritorious nor the latter to be blamed. And again, unless the human race have the power of avoiding evil and choosing good by free choice, they are not accountable for their actions, of whatever kind they be. But that it is by free choice they both walk uprightly and stumble, we thus demonstrate. We see the same man making a transition to opposite things. Now, if it had been fated that he were to be either good or bad, he could never have been capable of both the opposites, nor of so many transitions. But not even would some be good and others bad, since we thus make fate the cause of evil, and exhibit her as acting in opposition to herself; or that which has been already stated would seem to be true, that neither virtue nor vice is anything, but that things are only reckoned good or evil by opinion; which, as the true word shows, is the greatest impiety and wickedness. But this we assert is inevitable fate, that they who choose the good have worthy rewards, and they who choose the opposite have their merited awards. For not like other things, as trees and quadrupeds, which cannot act by choice, did God make man: for neither would he be worthy of reward or praise did he not of himself choose the good, but were created for this end; nor, if he were evil, would he be worthy of punishment, not being evil of himself, but being able to be nothing else than what he was made.

44. And the holy Spirit of prophecy taught us this, telling us by Moses that God spoke thus to the man first created: "Behold, before thy face are good and evil: choose the good." And again, by the other prophet Isaiah, that the following utterance was made as if from God the Father and Lord of all: "Wash you, make you clean; put away evils from your souls; learn to do well; judge the orphan, and plead for the widow; and come and let us reason together, saith the Lord: And if your sins be as scarlet, I will make them white as wool; and if they be red like as crimson, I will make them white as snow. And if ye be willing and obey Me, ye shall eat the good of the land; but if ye do not obey Me, the sword shall devour you: for the mouth of the Lord hath spoken it." And that expression, "The sword shall devour you," does not mean that the disobedient shall be slain by the sword, but the sword of God is fire, of which they who choose to do wickedly become the fuel. Wherefore He says, "The sword shall devour you: for the mouth of the Lord hath spoken it." And if He had spoken concerning a sword that cuts and at once despatches, He would not have said, shall *devour*. And so, too, Plato, when he says, "The blame is his who chooses, and God is blameless," took this from the prophet Moses and uttered it. For Moses is more ancient than all the Greek writers. And whatever both philosophers and poets have said concerning the immortality of the soul, or punishments after death, or contemplation of things heavenly, or doctrines of the like kind, they have received such suggestions from the prophets as have enabled them to understand and interpret these things. And hence there seem to be seeds of truth among all men; but they are charged with not accurately understanding the truth when they assert contradictories. So that what we say about future events being

foretold, we do not say it as if they came about by a fatal necessity; but God foreknowing all that shall be done by all men, and it being His decree that the future actions of men shall all be recompensed according to their several value, He foretells by the Spirit of prophecy that He will bestow meet rewards according to the merit of the actions done, always urging the human race to effort and recollection, showing that He cares and provides for men. But by the agency of the devils death has been decreed against those who read the books of Hystaspes, or of the Sibyl, or of the prophets, that through fear they may prevent men who read them from receiving the knowledge of the good, and may retain them in slavery to themselves; which, however, they could not always effect. For not only do we fearlessly read them, but, as you see, bring them for your inspection, knowing that their contents will be pleasing to all. And if we persuade even a few, our gain will be very great; for, as good husbandmen, we shall receive the reward from the Master.

45. And that God the Father of all would bring Christ to heaven after He had raised Him from the dead, and would keep Him there until He has subdued His enemies the devils, and until the number of those who are foreknown by Him as good and virtuous is complete, on whose account He has still delayed the consummation—hear what was said by the prophet David. These are his words: "The Lord said unto My Lord, Sit Thou at My right hand, until I make Thine enemies Thy footstool. The Lord shall send to Thee the rod of power out of Jerusalem; and rule Thou in the midst of Thine enemies. With Thee is the government in the day of Thy power, in the beauties of Thy saints: from the womb of morning have I begotten Thee." That which he says, "He shall send to Thee the rod of power out of Jerusalem," is predictive of the mighty word, which His apostles, going forth from Jerusalem, preached everywhere; and though death is decreed against those who teach or at all confess the name of Christ, we everywhere both embrace and teach it. And if you also read these words in a hostile spirit, ye can do no more, as I said before, than kill us; which indeed does no harm to us, but to you and all who unjustly hate us, and do not repent, brings eternal punishment by fire.

46. But lest some should, without reason, and for the perversion of what we teach, maintain that we say that Christ was born one hundred and fifty years ago under Cyrenius, and subsequently, in the time of Pontius Pilate, taught what we say He taught; and should cry out against us as though all men who were born before Him were irresponsible —let us anticipate and solve the difficulty. We have been taught that Christ is the first-born of God, and we have declared above that He is the Word of whom every race of men were partakers; and those who lived reasonably are Christians, even though they have been thought atheists; as, among the Greeks, Socrates and Heraclitus, and men like them; and among the barbarians,[9] Abraham, and Ananias, and Azarias, and Misael, and Elias, and many others whose actions and names we now

---

[9]The ancient Greeks used the term *barbarian* simply to designate anyone who was not a Greek. Justin uses the word in this sense to refer to figures from the Old Testament.

decline to recount, because we know it would be tedious. So that even they who lived before Christ, and lived without reason, were wicked and hostile to Christ, and slew those who lived reasonably. But who, through the power of the Word, according to the will of God the Father and Lord of all, He was born of a virgin as a man, and was named Jesus, and was crucified, and died, and rose again, and ascended into heaven, an intelligent man will be able to comprehend from what has been already so largely said. And we, since the proof of this subject is less needful now, will pass for the present to the proof of those things which are urgent.

[Chapters 47 – 58: Justin continues his argument that prophecies testify to the divinity of Christ. He then goes on to show that the heathens, who also have some prophetic knowledge of Christ, though in a distorted form, were able to anticipate in their religious ideas some of the facts of the incarnation, although these were also in distorted form.]

59. And that you may learn that it was from our teachers—we mean the account given through the prophets—that Plato borrowed his statement that God, having altered matter which was shapeless, made the world, hear the very words spoken through Moses, who, as above shown, was the first prophet, and of greater antiquity than the Greek writers; and through whom the Spirit of prophecy, signifying how and from what materials God at first formed the world, spake thus: "In the beginning God created the heaven and the earth. And the earth was invisible and unfurnished, and darkness was upon the face of the deep; and the Spirit of God moved over the waters. And God said, Let there be light; and it was so." So that both Plato and they who agree with him, and we ourselves, have learned, and you also can be convinced, that by the word of God the whole world was made out of the substance spoken of before by Moses. And that which the poets call Etebus, we know was spoken of formerly by Moses.[10]

60. And the physiological discussion concerning the Son of God in the *Timæus* of Plato, where he says, "He placed him crosswise in the universe," he borrowed in like manner from Moses; for in the writings of Moses it is related how at that time, when the Israelites went out of Egypt and were in the wilderness, they fell in with poisonous beasts, both vipers and asps, and every kind of serpent, which slew the people; and that Moses, by the inspiration and influence of God, took brass, and made it into the figure of a cross, and set it in the holy tabernacle, and said to the people, "If ye look to this figure, and believe, ye shall be saved thereby." And when this was done, it is recorded that the serpents died, and it is handed down that the people thus escaped death. Which things Plato reading, and not accurately understanding, and not apprehending that it was the figure of the cross, but taking it to be a placing crosswise, he said that the power next to the first God was placed crosswise in the universe. And as to his speaking of a third, he did this

---

[10]Erebus, according to Greek mythology, was the gloomy space through which souls passed on the way to Hades. The Old Testament reference is to Deuteronomy 32:22.

because he read, as we said above, that which was spoken by Moses, "that the Spirit of God moved over the waters." For he gives the second place to the Logos which is with God, who he said was placed cross-wise in the universe; and the third place to the Spirit who was said to be borne upon the water, saying, "And the third around the third." And hear how the Spirit of prophecy signified through Moses that there should be a conflagration. He spoke thus: "Everlasting fire shall descend, and shall devour to the pit beneath." It is not, then, that we hold the same opinions as others, but that all speak in imitation of ours. Among us these things can be heard and learned from persons who do not even know the forms of the letters, who are uneducated and barbarous in speech, though wise and believing in mind; some, indeed, even maimed and deprived of eyesight; so that you may understand that these things are not the effect of human wisdom, but are uttered by the power of God.

[Chapters 61 — 68: Justin concludes his apology with a description of the Christian sacraments and an appeal to the Emperor's sense of reason that Christians should be dealt with justly.]

Comments / on Justin

[A]s soon as men of Greek culture became Christians, they initiated between Christianity and philosophy a dialogue which has not yet come to an end. . . .

Since a doctrine founded upon the teaching of inspired men and prophets was answering philosophical questions better than any philosopher had ever done, its followers felt justified in claiming for it the title of philosophy and in calling themselves philosophers. Such, at least, was the case of Justin: he had achieved philosophical wisdom on the very day when he became a Christian. . . . Justin was quite in earnest when he presented the Christian faith as a divinely inspired answer to the questions of the philosophers. . . . From [Justin's] point of view, Greek philosophy and Christian revelation appear as two moments of one and the same revelation of the divine Word. . . .   *ETIENNE GILSON (1955)*

[The Apologists felt that] the content of revelation should be rational; but does that which is rational require a revelation?

ADOLF HARNACK (1894)

Origen

185?—254?

One of the chief obstacles to the acceptance of Christianity in the Roman world was that much of the material in its sacred texts hardly seemed credible. The Scriptures were full of miraculous narratives, many of them dealing with what seemed to be petty events, which rational men found unworthy of belief and incongruous with the exalted claims that Christians made on behalf of their religion. One way to overcome this difficulty was to assume that not everything in the Scriptures need be understood as literal fact but could rather be taken figuratively as allegorical narrative having some symbolic meaning essential to the tenets of the religion. The tendency to allegorize in matters of religion was firmly established in Greek intellectual tradition. From as early as the sixth century B.C., it had been customary to apply allegorical interpretations to the Homeric gods as a means of making Greek religious beliefs more credible. A few centuries later, Hebrew theologians, with the same purpose in mind for their own religion but in accord with their own philosophical conceptions, had applied the same kind of process to the Old Testament. And during the first century of the Christian era, Hebrew thinkers exposed to Greek culture had undertaken to allegorize the Old Testament in accord with Greek philosophical principles. It was almost inevitable, as Christianity sought to make headway in the ancient world, that both Greek and Hebrew traditions of religious allegory should influence Christian intellectuals to interpret the sacred writings of the Christian faith allegorically as a means of making them seem reasonable.

Origen is the founder of systematic Christian allegory. He grew up in the Egyptian city of Alexandria, which during the second and third centuries was the most important center of both Greek and Christian thought in the Roman world. His parents were intensely pious Christians, and his father was eventually martyred during one of the sporadic official persecutions of Christians. Even though Origen was brought up as a devout Christian trained in the painstaking study of the Scriptures, it was also possible for him in a place like Alexandria to receive a thorough education in Greek philosophy. A brilliant student, he was chosen to conduct the Christian school at Alexandria when he was only eighteen, thus beginning a career as a teacher which he followed with great success and fame for the rest of his life.

Origen was a prolific writer with an exceptionally imaginative mind, especially as applied to Biblical commentary. His work exerted a profound influence on the development of Christian theology by stimulating philosophic awareness in the early Church. In his *De Principiis (Concerning First Principles),* he made the first attempt to formulate a systematic theology of the Christian religion by articulating and expounding what he considered to be the fundamental principles of Christian belief. Although many of the ideas contained in this treatise were rejected by later theologians, it expresses a conception of the nature of allegorical interpretation of Scripture which lies at the foundation of all subsequent Christian endeavor to find figurative truth in the Bible.

Concerning First Principles

Book IV / Chapter 1

9. Now the cause, in all the points previously enumerated, of the false opinions, and of the impious statements or ignorant assertions about God, appears to be nothing else than the not understanding the Scripture according to its spiritual meaning, but the interpretation of it agreeably to the mere letter. And therefore, to those who believe that the sacred books are not the compositions of men, but that they were composed by inspiration of the Holy Spirit, agreeably to the will of the Father of all things through Jesus Christ, and that they have come down to us, we must point out the ways of interpreting them which appear correct to us, who cling to the standard of the heavenly Church of Jesus Christ according to the succession of the apostles. Now, that there are certain mystical economies made known by the holy Scriptures, all—even the most simple of those who adhere to the word—have believed; but what these are, candid and modest individuals confess that they know not. If, then, one were to be perplexed about the intercourse of Lot with his daughters, and about the two wives of Abraham, and the two sisters married to Jacob, and the two handmaids who bore him children, they can return no other answer than this, that these are mysteries not understood by us. Nay, also, when the description of the fitting out of

From *The Ante-Nicene Fathers,* Vol. IV, edited by Alexander Roberts and James Donaldson. Reprinted by permission of Wm. B. Eerdmans Publishing Co., Grand Rapids, Michigan.

the tabernacle is read, believing that what is written is a type, they seek to adapt what they can to each particular related about the tabernacle, —not being wrong so far as regards their belief that the tabernacle is a type of *something,* but erring sometimes in adapting the description of that of which the tabernacle is a type, to some special thing in a manner worthy of Scripture. And all the history that is considered to tell of marriages, or the begetting of children, or of wars, or any histories whatever that are in circulation among the multitude, they declare to be types; but of what in each individual instance, partly owing to their habits not being thoroughly exercised—partly, too, owing to their precipitation —sometimes, even when an individual does happen to be well trained and clear-sighted, owing to the excessive difficulty of discovering things on the part of men,—the nature of each particular regarding these types is not clearly ascertained.

10. And what need is there to speak of the prophecies, which we all know to be filled with enigmas and dark sayings? And if we come to the Gospels, the exact understanding of these also, as being the mind of Christ, requires the grace that was given to him who said, "But we have the mind of Christ, that we might know the things freely given to us by God. Which things also we speak, not in the words which man's wisdom teacheth, but which the Spirit teacheth." And who, on reading the revelations made to John, would not be amazed at the unspeakable mysteries therein concealed, and which are evident even to him who does not comprehend what is written? And to what person, skilful in investigating words, would the Epistles of the Apostles seem to be clear and easy of understanding, since even in them there are countless numbers of most profound ideas, which, issuing forth as by an aperture, admit of no rapid comprehension? And therefore, since these things are so, and since innumerable individuals fall into mistakes, it is not safe in reading the Scriptures to declare that one easily understands what needs the key of knowledge, which the Saviour declares is with the lawyers. And let those answer who will not allow that the truth was with these before the advent of Christ, how the key of knowledge is said by our Lord Jesus Christ to be with those who, as they allege, had not the books which contain the secrets of knowledge, and perfect mysteries. For His words run thus: "Woe unto you, ye lawyers! for ye have taken away the key of knowledge: ye have not entered in yourselves, and them that were entering in ye hindered."

11. The way, then, as it appears to us, in which we ought to deal with the Scriptures, and extract from them their meaning, is the following, which has been ascertained from the Scriptures themselves. By Solomon in the Proverbs we find some such rule as this enjoined respecting the divine doctrines of Scripture: "And do thou portray them in a threefold manner, in counsel and knowledge, to answer words of truth to them who propose them to thee." The individual ought, then, to portray the ideas of holy Scripture in a threefold manner upon his own soul; in order that the simple man may be edified by the "flesh," as it were, of the Scripture, for so we name the obvious sense; while he who has ascended a certain way may be edified by the "soul," as it were. The perfect man, again, and he who resembles those spoken of by the

apostle, when he says, "We speak wisdom among them that are perfect but not the wisdom of the world, nor of the rulers of this world, who come to nought; but we speak the wisdom of God in a mystery, the hidden wisdom, which God hath ordained before the ages, unto our glory," may receive edification from the spiritual law, which has a shadow of good things to come. For as man consists of body, and soul, and spirit, so in the same way does Scripture, which has been arranged to be given by God for the salvation of men. And therefore we deduce this also from a book which is despised by some—*The Shepherd*—in respect of the command given to Hermas to write two books, and after so doing to announce to the presbyters of the Church what he had learned from the Spirit. The words are as follows: "You will write two books, and give one to Clement, and one to Grapte. And Grapte shall admonish the widows and the orphans, and Clement will send to the cities abroad, while you will announce to the presbyters of the Church." Now Grapte, who admonishes the widows and the orphans, is the mere letter of Scripture, which admonishes those who are yet children in soul, and not able to call God their Father, and who are on that account styled orphans, —admonishing, moreover, those who no longer have an unlawful bridegroom, but who remain widows, because they have not yet become worthy of the heavenly Bridegroom; while Clement, who is already beyond the letter, is said to send what is written to the cities abroad, as if we were to call these the "souls," who are above the influence of bodily affections and degraded ideas,—the disciple of the Spirit himself being enjoined to make known, no longer by letters, but by living words, to the presbyters of the whole Church of God, who have become grey through wisdom.

12. But as there are certain passages of Scripture which do not at all contain the "corporeal" sense, as we shall show in the following paragraphs, there are also places where we must seek only for the "soul," as it were, and "spirit" of Scripture. And perhaps on this account the water-vessels containing two or three firkins a-piece are said to lie for the purification of the Jews, as we read in the Gospel according to John: the expression darkly intimating, with respect to those who are called by the apostle "Jews" secretly, that they are purified by the word of Scripture, receiving sometimes two firkins, i.e., so to speak, the "psychical" and "spiritual" sense; and sometimes three firkins, since some have, in addition to those already mentioned, also the "corporeal" sense, which is capable of producing edification. And six water-vessels are reasonably appropriate to those who are purified in the world, which was made in six days—the perfect number. That the first "sense," then, is profitable in this respect, that it is capable of imparting edification, is testified by the multitudes of genuine and simple believers; while of that interpretation which is referred back to the "soul," there is an illustration in Paul's first Epistle to the Corinthians. The expression is, "Thou shalt not muzzle the mouth of the ox that treadeth out the corn;" to which he adds, "Doth God take care of oxen? or saith He it altogether for our sakes? For our sakes, no doubt, this was written: that he that plougheth should plough in hope, and that he who thresheth, in hope of partaking." And there are numerous interpretations adapted to

the multitude which are in circulation, and which edify those who are unable to understand profounder meanings, and which have somewhat the same character.

13. But the interpretation is "spiritual," when one is able to show of what heavenly things the Jews "according to the flesh" served as an example and a shadow, and of what future blessings the law contains a shadow. And, generally, we must investigate, according to the apostolic promise, "the wisdom in a mystery, the hidden wisdom which God ordained before the world for the glory" of the just, which "none of the princes of this world knew." And the same apostle says somewhere, after referring to certain events mentioned as occurring in Exodus and Numbers, "that these things happened to them figuratively, but that they were written on our account, on whom the ends of the world are come." And he gives an opportunity for ascertaining of what things these were patterns, when he says: "For they drank of the spiritual Rock that followed them, and that Rock was Christ." And in another Epistle, when sketching the various matters relating to the tabernacle, he used the words: "Thou shalt make everything according to the pattern showed thee in the mount." Moreover, in the Epistle to the Galatians, as if upbraiding those who think that they read the law, and yet do not understand it, judging that those do not understand it who do not reflect that allegories are contained under what is written, he says: "Tell me, ye that desire to be under the law, do ye not hear the law? For it is written, Abraham had two sons; the one by the bond-maid, the other by the free woman. But he who was by the bond-maid was born according to the flesh; but he of the free woman was by promise. Which things are an allegory: for these are the two covenants," and so on. Now we must carefully observe each word employed by him. He says: "Ye who desire to be under the law," not "Ye that are under the law;" and, "Do ye not *hear* the law?"—"hearing" being understood to mean *"comprehending"* and *"knowing."* And in the Epistle to the Colossians, briefly abridging the meaning of the whole legislation, he says: "Let no man therefore judge you in meat, or in drink, or in respect of a festival, or of a new moon, or of Sabbaths, which are a shadow of things to come." Moreover, in the Epistle to the Hebrews, discoursing of those who belong to the circumcision, he writes: "who serve for an ensample and shadow of heavenly things." Now it is probable that, from these illustrations, those will entertain no doubt with respect to the five books of Moses, who have once given in their adhesion to the apostle, as divinely inspired; but do you wish to know, with regard to the rest of the history, if it also happened as a pattern? We must note, then, the expression in the Epistle to the Romans, "I have left to myself seven thousand men, who have not bowed the knee to Baal," quoted from the third book of Kings, which Paul has understood as equivalent in meaning to those who are Israelites according to election, because not only were the Gentiles benefited by the advent of Christ, but also certain of the race of God.

14. This being the state of the case, we have to sketch what seem to us to be the marks of the true understanding of Scriptures. And, in the first place, this must be pointed out, that the object of the Spirit, which

by the providence of God, through the Word who was in the beginning with God, illuminated the ministers of truth, the prophets and apostles, was especially the communication of ineffable mysteries regarding the affairs of men (now by men I mean those souls that make use of bodies), in order that he who is capable of instruction may by investigation, and by devoting himself to the study of the profundities of meaning contained in the words, become a participator of all the doctrines of his counsel. And among those matters which relate to souls who cannot otherwise obtain perfection apart from the rich and wise truth of God, the doctrines belonging to God and His only-begotten Son are necessarily laid down as primary, viz., of what nature He is, and in what manner He is the Son of God, and what are the causes of His descending even to the assumption of human flesh, and of complete humanity; and what, also, is the operation of this Son, and upon whom and when exercised. And it was necessary also that the subject of kindred beings, and other rational creatures, both those who are divine and those who have fallen from blessedness, together with the reasons of their fall, should be contained in the divine teaching; and also that of the diversities of souls, and of the origin of these diversities, and of the nature of the world, and the cause of its existence. We must learn also the origin of the great and terrible wickedness which overspreads the earth, and whether it is confined to this earth only, or prevails elsewhere. Now, while these and similar objects were present to the Spirit, who enlightened the souls of the holy ministers of the truth, there was a second object, for the sake of those who were unable to endure the fatigue of investigating matters so important, viz., to conceal the doctrine relating to the previously mentioned subjects, in expressions containing a narrative which conveyed an announcement regarding the things of the visible creation, the creation of man, and the successive descendants of the first men until they became numerous; and other histories relating the acts of just men, and the sins occasionally committed by these same men as being human beings, and the wicked deeds, both of unchastity and vice, committed by sinful and ungodly men. And what is most remarkable, by the history of wars, and of the victors, and the vanquished, certain mysteries are indicated to those who are able to test these statements. And more wonderful still, the laws of truth are predicted by the written legislation;—all these being described in a connected series, with a power which is truly in keeping with the wisdom of God. For it was intended that the covering also of the spiritual truths—I mean the "bodily" part of Scripture—should not be without profit in many cases, but should be capable of improving the multitude, according to their capacity.

15. But since, if the usefulness of the legislation, and the sequence and beauty of the history, were universally evident of itself, we should not believe that any other thing could be understood in the Scriptures save what was obvious, the word of God has arranged that certain stumbling-blocks, as it were, and offences, and impossibilities, should be introduced into the midst of the law and the history, in order that we may not, through being drawn away in all directions by the merely attractive nature of the language, either altogether fall away from the

true doctrines, as learning nothing worthy of God, or, by not departing from the letter, come to the knowledge of nothing more divine. And this also we must know, that the principal aim being to announce the "spiritual" connection in those things that are done, and that ought to be done, where the Word found that things done according to the history could be adapted to these mystical senses, He made use of them, concealing from the multitude the deeper meaning; but where, in the narrative of the development of super-sensual things, there did not follow the performance of those certain events, which was already indicated by the mystical meaning, the Scripture interwove in the history the account of some event that did not take place, sometimes what could not have happened; sometimes what could, but did not. And sometimes a few words are interpolated which are not true in their literal acceptation, and sometimes a larger number. And a similar practice also is to be noticed with regard to the legislation, in which is often to be found what is useful in itself, and appropriate to the times of the legislation; and sometimes also what does not appear to be of utility; and at other times impossibilities are recorded for the sake of the more skilful and inquisitive, in order that they may give themselves to the toil of investigating what is written, and thus attain to a becoming conviction of the manner in which a meaning worthy of God must be sought out in such subjects.

16. It was not only, however, with the Scriptures composed before the advent of Christ that the Spirit thus dealt; but as being the same Spirit, and proceeding from the one God, He did the same thing both with the evangelists and the apostles,—as even these do not contain throughout a pure history of events, which are interwoven indeed according to the letter, but which did not actually occur. Nor even do the law and the commandments wholly convey what is agreeable to reason. For who that has understanding will suppose that the first, and second, and third day, and the evening and the morning, existed without a sun, and moon, and stars? and that the first day was, as it were, also without a sky? And who is so foolish as to suppose that God, after the manner of a husbandman, planted a paradise in Eden, towards the east, and placed in it a tree of life, visible and palpable, so that one tasting of the fruit by the bodily teeth obtained life? and again, that one was a partaker of good and evil by masticating what was taken from the tree? And if God is said to walk in the paradise in the evening, and Adam to hide himself under a tree, I do not suppose that any one doubts that these things figuratively indicate certain mysteries, the history having taken place in appearance, and not literally. Cain also, when going forth from the presence of God, certainly appears to thoughtful men as likely to lead the reader to inquire what is the presence of God, and what is the meaning of going out from Him. And what need is there to say more, since those who are not altogether blind can collect countless instances of a similar kind recorded as having occurred, but which did not literally take place? Nay, the Gospels themselves are filled with the same kind of narratives; e.g., the devil leading Jesus up into a high mountain, in order to show him from thence the kingdoms of the whole world, and the glory of them. For who is there among those who do not read such accounts carelessly, that would not condemn those who think that with

the eye of the body—which requires a lofty height in order that the parts lying immediately under and adjacent may be seen—the kingdoms of the Persians, and Scythians, and Indians, and Parthians, were beheld, and the manner in which their princes are glorified among men? And the attentive reader may notice in the Gospels innumerable other passages like these, so that he will be convinced that in the histories that are literally recorded, circumstances that did not occur are inserted.

17. And if we come to the legislation of Moses, many of the laws manifest the irrationality, and others the impossibility, of their literal observance. The irrationality in this, that the people are forbidden to eat vultures, although no one even in the direst famines was ever driven by want to have recourse to this bird; and that children eight days old, which are uncircumcised, are ordered to be exterminated from among their people, it being necessary, if the law were to be carried out at all literally with regard to these, that their fathers, or those with whom they are brought up, should be commanded to be put to death. Now the Scripture says: "Every male that is uncircumcised who shall not be circumcised on the eighth day, shall be cut off from among his people." And if you wish to see impossibilities contained in the legislation, let us observe that the goat-stag is one of those animals that cannot exist, and yet Moses commands us to offer it as being a clean beast; whereas a griffin, which is not recorded ever to have been subdued by man, the lawgiver forbids to be eaten. Nay, he who carefully considers the famous injunction relating to the Sabbath, "Ye shall sit each one in your dwellings: let no one go out from his place on the seventh day," will deem it impossible to be literally observed: for no living being is able to sit throughout a whole day, and remain without moving from a sitting position. And therefore those who belong to the circumcision, and all who desire that no meaning should be exhibited, save the literal one, do not investigate at all such subjects as those of the goat-stag and griffin and vulture, but indulge in foolish talk on certain points, multiplying words and adducing tasteless traditions; as, for example, with regard to the Sabbath, saying that two thousand cubits is each one's limit. Others, again, among whom is Dositheus the Samaritan, condemning such an interpretation, think that in the position in which a man is found on the Sabbath-day, he is to remain until evening. Moreover, the not carrying of a burden on the Sabbath-day is an impossibility; and therefore the Jewish teachers have fallen into countless absurdities, saying that a shoe of such a kind was a burden, but not one of another kind; and that a sandal which had nails was a burden, but not one that was without them; and in like manner what was borne on one shoulder was a load, but not that which was carried on both.

18. And if we go to the Gospel and institute a similar examination, what would be more irrational than to take literally the injunction, "Salute no man by the way," which simple persons think the Saviour enjoined on the apostles? The command, moreover, that the right cheek should be smitten, is most incredible, since every one who strikes, unless he happen to have some bodily defect, smites the *left* cheek with his *right* hand. And it is impossible to take literally, the statement in the Gospel about the "offending" of the right eye. For, to grant the

possibility of one being "offended" by the sense of sight, how, when there are two eyes that see, should the blame be laid upon the right eye? And who is there that, condemning himself for having looked upon a women to lust after her, would rationally transfer the blame to the right eye alone, and throw *it* away? The apostle, moreover, lays down the law, saying, "Is any man called, being circumcised? Let him not become uncircumcised." In the first place, any one will see that he does not utter these words in connection with the subject before him. For, when laying down precepts on marriage and purity, how will it not appear that he has introduced these words at random? But, in the second place, who will say that a man does wrong who endeavours to become uncircumcised, if that be possible, on account of the disgrace that is considered by the multitude to attach to circumcision.

All these statements have been made by us, in order to show that the design of that divine power which gave us the sacred Scriptures is, that we should not receive what is presented by the letter alone (such things being sometimes not true in their literal acceptation, but absurd and impossible), but that certain things have been introduced into the actual history and into the legislation that are useful in their literal sense.

19. But that no one may suppose that we assert respecting the whole that no history is real because a certain one is not; and that no law is to be literally observed, because a certain one, understood according to the letter, is absurd or impossible; or that the statements regarding the Saviour are not true in a manner perceptible to the senses; or that no commandment and precept of His ought to be obeyed;—we have to answer that, with regard to certain things, it is perfectly clear to us that the historical account is true; as that Abraham was buried in the double cave at Hebron, as also Isaac and Jacob, and the wives of each of them; and that Shechem was given as a portion to Joseph; and that Jerusalem is the metropolis of Judea, in which the temple of God was built by Solomon; and innumerable other statements. For the passages that are true in their historical meaning are much more numerous than those which are interspersed with a purely spiritual signification. And again, who would not say that the command which enjoins to "honour thy father and thy mother, that it may be well with thee," is useful, apart from all allegorical meaning, and ought to be observed, the Apostle Paul also having employed these very same words? And what need is there to speak of the prohibitions, "Thou shalt not commit adultery," "Thou shalt not kill," "Thou shalt not steal," "Thou shalt not bear false witness?" And again, there are commandments contained in the Gospel which admit of no doubt whether they are to be observed according to the letter or not; e.g., that which says, "But I say unto you, Whoever is angry with his brother," and so on. And again, "But I say unto you, Swear not at all." And in the writings of the apostle the literal sense is to be retained: "Warn them that are unruly, comfort the feeble-minded, support the weak, be patient towards all men;" although it is possible for those ambitious of a deeper meaning to retain the profundities of the wisdom of God, without setting aside the commandment in its literal meaning. The careful reader, however, will be in doubt as to certain

points, being unable to show without long investigation whether this history so deemed literally occurred or not, and whether the literal meaning of this law is to be observed or not. And therefore the exact reader must, in obedience to the Saviour's injunction to "search the Scriptures," carefully ascertain in how far the literal meaning is true, and in how far impossible; and so far as he can, trace out, by means of similar statements, the meaning everywhere scattered through Scripture of that which cannot be understood in a literal signification.

20. Since, therefore, as will be clear to those who read, the connection taken literally is impossible, while the sense preferred is not impossible, but even the true one, it must be our object to grasp the whole meaning, which connects the account of what is literally impossible in an intelligible manner with what is not only not impossible, but also historically true, and which is allegorically understood, in respect of its not having literally occurred. For, with respect to holy Scripture, our opinion is that the whole of it has a "spiritual," but not the whole a "bodily" meaning, because the bodily meaning is in many places proved to be impossible. And therefore great attention must be bestowed by the cautious reader on the divine books, as being divine writings; the manner of understanding which appears to us to be as follows:—The Scriptures relate that God chose a certain nation upon the earth, which they call by several names. For the whole of this nation is termed Israel, and also Jacob. And when it was divided in the times of Jeroboam the son of Nebat, the ten tribes related as being subject to him were called Israel; and the remaining two, along with the tribe of Levi, being ruled over by the descendants of David, were named Judah. And the whole of the territory which the people of this nation inhabited, being given them by God, receives the name of Judah, the metropolis of which is Jerusalem, —a metropolis, namely, of numerous cities, the names of which lie scattered about in many other passages of Scripture, but are enumerated together in the book of Joshua the son of Nun.

21. Such, then, being the state of the case, the apostle, elevating our power of discernment above the letter, says somewhere, "Behold Israel after the flesh," as if there were an Israel "according to the Spirit." And in another place he says, "For they who are the children of the flesh are not the children of God;" nor are "they all Israel who are of Israel;" nor is "he a Jew who is one outwardly, nor is that 'circumcision' which is outward in the flesh: but he is a Jew who is one 'inwardly;' and circumcision is that of the heart, in the spirit, and not in the letter." For if the judgment respecting the "Jew inwardly" be adopted, we must understand that, as there is a "bodily" race of Jews, so also is there a race of "Jews inwardly," the soul having acquired this nobility for certain mysterious reasons. Moreover, there are many prophecies which predict regarding Israel and Judah what is about to befall them. And do not such promises as are written concerning them, in respect of their being mean in expression, and manifesting no elevation of thought, nor anything worthy of the promise of God, need a mystical interpretation? And if the "spiritual" promises are announced by visible signs, then they to whom the promises are made are not "corporeal." And not to linger over the point of the Jew who is a Jew "inwardly," nor over that of the

Israelite according to the "inner man"—these statements being sufficient for those who are not devoid of understanding—we return to
our subject, and say that Jacob is the father of the twelve patriarchs,
and they of the rulers of the people; and these, again, of the other
Israelites. Do not, then, the "corporeal" Israelites refer their descent
to the rulers of the people, and the rulers of the people to the patriarchs,
and the patriarchs to Jacob, and those still higher up; while are not the
"spiritual" Israelites, of whom the "corporeal" Israelites were the type,
sprung from the families, and the families from the tribes, and the tribes
from some one individual whose descent is not of a "corporeal" but of
a better kind,—he, too, being born of Isaac, and he of Abraham,—all
going back to Adam, whom the apostle declares to be Christ? For every
beginning of those families which have relation to God as to the Father
of all, took its commencement lower down with Christ, who is next to
the God and Father of all, being thus the Father of every soul, as Adam
is the father of all men. And if Eve also is intended by the apostle to
refer to the Church, it is not surprising that Cain, who was born of Eve,
and all after him, whose descent goes back to Eve, should be types of
the Church, inasmuch as in a pre-eminent sense they are all descended
from the Church.

22. Now, if the statements made to us regarding Israel, and its tribes
and its families, are calculated to impress us, when the Saviour says,
"I was not sent but to the lost sheep of the house of Israel," we do not
understand the expression as the Ebionites do, who are poor in understanding (deriving their name from the poverty of their intellect—
"Ebion" signifying "poor" in Hebrew), so as to suppose that the Saviour
came specially to the "carnal" Israelites; for "they who are the children
of the flesh are not the children of God." Again, the apostle teaches
regarding Jerusalem as follows: "The Jerusalem which is above is free,
which is the mother of us all." And in another Epistle: "But ye are come
unto mount Zion, and to the city of the living God, to the heavenly
Jerusalem, and to an innumerable company of angels, to the general
assembly and to the Church of the first-born which are written in heaven."
If, then, Israel is among the race of souls, and if there is in heaven a city
of Jerusalem, it follows that the cities of Israel have for their metropolis
the heavenly Jerusalem, and it consequently is the metropolis of all
Judea. Whatever, therefore, is predicted of Jerusalem, and spoken of
it, if we listen to the words of Paul as those of God, and of one who utters
wisdom, we must understand the Scriptures as speaking of the heavenly
city, and of the whole territory included within the cities of the holy
land. For perhaps it is to these cities that the Saviour refers us, when to
those who have gained credit by having managed their "pounds" well,
He assigns the presidency over five or ten cities. If, therefore, the
prophecies relating to Judea, and Jerusalem, and Israel, and Judah, and
Jacob, not being understood by us in a "carnal" sense, indicate some such
mysteries as already mentioned, it will follow also that the predictions
concerning Egypt and the Egyptians, Babylon and the Babylonians,
Tyre and the Tyrians, Sidon and the Sidonians, or the other nations,
are spoken not only of these "bodily" Egyptians, and Babylonians, and
Tyrians, and Sidonians, but also of their "spiritual" counterparts. For

if there be "spiritual" Israelites, it follows that there are also "spiritual" Egyptians and Babylonians. For what is related in Ezekiel concerning Pharaoh king of Egypt does not at all apply to the case of a certain man who ruled or was said to rule over Egypt, as will be evident to those who give it careful consideration. Similarly, what is said about the ruler of Tyre cannot be understood of a certain man who ruled over Tyre. And what is said in many places, and especially in Isaiah, of Nebuchadnezzar, cannot be explained of that individual. For the man Nebuchadnezzar neither fell from heaven, nor was he the morning star, nor did he arise upon the earth in the morning. Nor would any man of understanding interpret what is said in Ezekiel about Egypt—viz., that in forty years it should be laid desolate, so that the footstep of man should not be found thereon, and that the ravages of war should be so great that the blood should run throughout the whole of it, and rise to the knees—of that Egypt which is situated beside the Ethiopians whose bodies are blackened by the sun.

Comments / on Origen

Of all men now living, I have never heard of one who had meditated as he [Origen] had on the pure and luminous words [of Scripture] and had become so expert at fathoming their meaning and teaching them to others. I do not think he could have done that unless he had the Spirit of God in him, for the same grace is needed for understanding the prophecies as for making them. . . . Origen possessed the sovereign gift, which he got from God, of being the interpreter of God's words to men. He had the power to listen to God and understand what he said, and then to explain it to men that they too might understand.
ST. GREGORY THAUMATURGUS (260?)

Withdraw, dearly beloved, from the heresy of Origen . . . he tampers with the true meaning of the [Scriptural] narrative by a false use of allegory, multiplying words without limit; and undermines the faith of the simple by the most varied arguments . . . by distorting the sense of the Scriptures and making them mean what they do not mean at all. . . . This way of acting is common to . . . the votaries of heresies, all of whom draw their proofs from the pure well of the Scriptures, not, however, interpreting it in the sense in which it is written, but trying to make the simple language of the Church's writers accord with their own wishes.
ST. JEROME (394)

Origen's views . . . are that . . . the Bible is one vast allegory, a tremendous sacrament in which every detail is symbolic. But the symbolism is extremely difficult to probe into. Some of it is clear, some of it obscure . . . there is something true in his theory, i.e., the principle that in many of the obscure passages in Scripture the exegete ought to look for a spiritual meaning. But he endangers the principle by declaring that *everything* in Scripture has a figurative meaning. This assertion is the starting-point of all the exaggerations of the medieval allegorizers.

JEAN DANIELOU (1948)

A sure path to mysticism is through allegory. . . . It had flourished vigorously among the Eastern writers, Justin and Clement and Origen. . . . The allegorical habit is absolutely alien to the modern mind, which tosses it over as so much rubbish; but whatever its validity, something may be said for the impulses behind it. St. Hilary . . . declared that the Old Testament proclaimed Christ, in order that posterity might contemplate the present in the past and venerate the past in the present. This is a view of history fatal to the idea of development; but it makes for the solidity of human experience and encourages man to feel at home in any age.

E. K. RAND (1928)

Tertullian
160?—240?

The earliest Fathers of the Church had been men of Greek cultural heritage. Their writings had been in Greek, like the Scriptures themselves. Even in Rome the language of the Church was Greek until well into the third century, and it was not until the beginning of the fifth century that St. Jerome rendered a complete translation of the Scriptures into Latin. As a result, Greek thought had strongly influenced Christianity during its first few centuries. But by the early part of the third century this influence began to be challenged. The Christian faith had by then spread widely through the western part of the Roman world; and as it became a more universal faith, it required a more universal language and the need to rationalize its doctrines into harmony with Greek philosophy became less compelling. When men of Latin cultural heritage began to write about ecclesiastical matters in Latin, they started a new era in the development of Christianity, which eventually culminated in the split of the Church into Roman Catholic and Greek Orthodox branches.

Tertullian was the earliest of the Latin Fathers and the first of a long series of distinguished Christian writers born in North Africa. Until the fifth century, the finest minds in the Roman Church originated not in Rome, or even in Italy, but in the Roman colonies on the southern shores of the Mediterranean. Tertullian's father, a Roman military official and a pagan, provided his son with a good education, and as a young man Tertullian was at Rome engaged in the practice of law. Converted to Christianity there, he returned to Carthage as a priest to begin a long career as an exponent of the Christian faith. Early in the third century he joined the Montanists, a severely ascetic sect that called upon Christians to emulate the simple, unworldly life led by the Apostles, to disregard secular concerns and devote their time wholly to acts of piety, and even to seek martyrdom by flaunting their religion against Roman authority. Montanism was considered heretical by most Church officials, so within a few years Tertullian broke with the Roman Church. Later he left the Montanists and founded his own short-lived sect of Tertullianists.

Tertullian wrote voluminously and vividly on almost every conceivable subject pertaining to Christian life and belief, from the proper attire for Christian women to the metaphysical implications of the doctrine of the resurrection of the flesh. One notable feature of his achievement was his success in devising Latin expressions to convey the ideas of Christian theology, thus creating what was to become the language of the Roman Church, preparing the way for the translation of the Scriptures into Latin, and raising the Western Church into a position of intellectual equality with the Eastern. An intellectual himself, Tertullian paradoxically is the foremost early proponent of the anti-intellectual strain in Christianity. Although he never wrote in just those words the celebrated phrase often attributed to him, *credo quia absurdum,* "I believe because it is absurd," it stands as a valid indication of his attitude. For him, the mystical rather than the rational elements in Christianity provided the most convincing grounds for belief. His *Apology,* in most respects a conventional though brilliantly written example of apologetic writing, demonstrates in the criticism he voices against Greek philosophy a decidedly unconventional attitude which later did become conventional among many Christian theologians.

Apology

---

17. The object of our worship is the One God, He who by His commanding word, His arranging wisdom, His mighty power, brought forth from nothing this entire mass of our world, with all its array of elements, bodies, spirits, for the glory of His majesty; whence also the Greeks have bestowed on it the name of cosmos. The eye cannot see Him, though He is spiritually visible. He is incomprehensible, though in grace He is manifested. He is beyond our utmost thought, though our human faculties conceive of Him. He is therefore equally real and great. But that which, in the ordinary sense, can be seen and handled and conceived, is inferior to the eyes by which it is taken in, and the hands by which it is tainted, and the faculties by which it is discovered; but that which is infinite is known only to itself. This it is which gives some notion of God, while yet beyond all our conceptions—our very incapacity of fully grasping Him affords us the idea of what He really is. He is presented to our minds in His transcendent greatness, as at once known and unknown. And this is the crowning guilt of men, that they will not recognize One, of whom they cannot possibly be ignorant. Would you have the proof from the works of His hands, so numerous

From *The Ante-Nicene Fathers,* Vol. III, edited by Alexander Roberts and James Donaldson. Reprinted by permission of Wm. B. Eerdmans Publishing Co., Grand Rapids, Michigan.

and so great, which both contain you and sustain you, which minister at once to your enjoyment, and strike you with awe; or would you rather have it from the testimony of the soul itself? Though under the oppressive bondage of the body, though led astray by depraving customs, though enervated by lusts and passions, though in slavery to false gods; yet, whenever the soul comes to itself, as out of a surfeit, or a sleep, or a sickness, and attains something of its natural soundness, it speaks of God; using no other word, because this is the peculiar name of the true God. "God is great and good"—"Which may God give," are the words on every lip. It bears witness, too, that God is judge, exclaiming, "God sees," and, "I commend myself to God," and, "God will repay me." O noble testimony of the soul by nature Christian! Then, too, in using such words as these, it looks not to the Capitol, but to the heavens. It knows that there is the throne of the living God, as from Him and from thence itself came down.

46. We have sufficiently met, as I think, the accusation of the various crimes on the ground of which these fierce demands are made for Christian blood. We have made a full exhibition of our case; and we have shown you how we are able to prove that our statement is correct, from the trustworthiness, I mean, and antiquity of our sacred writings, and from the confession likewise of the powers of spiritual wickedness themselves. Who will venture to undertake our refutation; not with skill of words, but, as we have managed our demonstration, on the basis of reality? But while the truth we hold is made clear to all, unbelief meanwhile, at the very time it is convinced of the worth of Christianity, which has now become well known for its benefits as well as from the intercourse of life, takes up the notion that it is not really a thing divine, but rather a kind of philosophy. These are the very things, it says, the philosophers counsel and profess—innocence, justice, patience, sobriety, chastity. Why, then, are we not permitted an equal liberty and impunity for our doctrines as they have, with whom, in respect of what we teach, we are compared? or why are not they, as so like us, not pressed to the same offices, for declining which our lives are imperilled? For who compels a philosopher to sacrifice or take an oath, or put out useless lamps at midday? Nay, they openly overthrow your gods, and in their writings they attack your superstitions; and you applaud them for it. Many of them even, with your countenance, bark out against your rulers, and are rewarded with statues and salaries, instead of being given to the wild beasts. And very right it should be so. For they are called philosophers, not Christians. This name of philosopher has no power to put demons to the rout. Why are they not able to do that too? since philosophers count demons inferior to gods. Socrates used to say, "If the demon grant permission." Yet he, too, though in denying the existence of your divinities he had a glimpse of the truth, at his dying ordered a cock to be sacrificed to Æsculapius, I believe in honour of his father, for Apollo pronounced Socrates the wisest of men. Thoughtless Apollo! testifying to the wisdom of the man who denied the existence of his race. In proportion to the enmity the truth awakens, you give offence by faithfully standing by it; but the man who corrupts and makes a mere pretence of it precisely

on this ground gains favour with its persecutors. The truth which philosophers, these mockers and corrupters of it, with hostile ends merely affect to hold, and in doing so deprave, caring for nought but glory, Christians both intensely and intimately long for and maintain in its integrity, as those who have a real concern about their salvation. So that we are like each other neither in our knowledge nor our ways, as you imagine. For what certain information did Thales, the first of natural philosophers, give in reply to the inquiry of Crœsus regarding Deity, the delay for further thought so often proving in vain? There is not a Christian workman but finds out God, and manifests Him, and hence assigns to Him all those attributes which go to constitute a divine being, though Plato affirms that it is far from easy to discover the Maker of the universe; and when He is found, it is difficult to make Him known to all. But if we challenge you to comparison in the virtue of chastity, I turn to a part of the sentence passed by the Athenians against Socrates, who was pronounced a corrupter of youth. The Christian confines himself to the female sex. I have read also how the harlot Phryne kindled in Diogenes[1] the fires of lust, and how a certain Speusippus, of Plato's school, perished in the adulterous act. The Christian husband has nothing to do with any but his own wife. Democritus, in putting out his eyes, because he could not look on women without lusting after them, and was pained if his passion was not satisfied, owns plainly, by the punishment he inflicts, his incontinence. But a Christian with grace-healed eyes is sightless in this matter; he is mentally blind against the assaults of passion. If I maintain our superior modesty of behaviour, there at once occurs to me Diogenes with filth-covered feet trampling on the proud couches of Plato, under the influence of another pride: the Christian does not even play the proud man to the pauper. If sobriety of spirit be the virtue in debate, why, there are Pythagoras at Thurii, and Zeno at Priene, ambitious of the supreme power: the Christian does not aspire to the ædileship.[2] If equanimity be the contention, you have Lycurgus choosing death by self-starvation, because the Lacons had made some emendation of his laws: the Christian, even when he is condemned, gives thanks. If the comparison be made in regard to trustworthiness, Anaxagoras[3] denied the deposit of his enemies: the Christian is noted for his fidelity even among those who are not of his religion. If the matter of sincerity is to be brought to trial, Aristotle basely thrust his friend Hermias from his place: the Christian does no harm even to his foe. With equal baseness does Aristotle play the sycophant to Alexander, instead of exercising to keep him in the right way, and Plato allows himself to be bought by Dionysius[4] for his belly's sake. Aristippus[5] in the purple, with all his great show of gravity, gives way to extravagance; and Hippias[6] is put to death laying plots against

---

[1]Greek philosopher (412?–324 B.C.).
[2]An important office in the Roman system of government.
[3]Greek philosopher (500?–428 B.C.).
[4]Ruler of Syracuse, a Greek colony in Sicily. Plato spent a couple of years at Dionysius' court instructing him in philosophy.
[5]Greek philosopher (435?–356? B.C.). The allusion to "purple" refers to his distinctive philosopher's garb.
[6]Probably the Greek philosopher Hippias of Elis (late fifth century B.C.), who was interested in political theory. Tertullian's reference to the manner of his death is not verified elsewhere.

the state: no Christian ever attempted such a thing in behalf of his brethren, even when persecution was scattering them abroad with every atrocity. But it will be said that some of us, too, depart from the rules of our discipline. In that case, however, we count them no longer Christians; but the philosophers who do such things retain still the name and the honour of wisdom. So, then, where is there any likeness between the Christian and the philosopher? between the disciple of Greece and of heaven? between the man whose object is fame, and whose object is life? between the talker and the doer? between the man who builds up and the man who pulls down? between the friend and the foe of error? between one who corrupts the truth, and one who restores and teaches it? between its chief and its custodier?

47. Unless I am utterly mistaken, there is nothing so old as the truth; and the already proved antiquity of the divine writings is so far of use to me, that it leads men more easily to take it in that they are the treasure-source whence all later wisdom has been taken. And were it not necessary to keep my work to a moderate size, I might launch forth also into the proof of this. What poet or sophist has not drunk at the fountain of the prophets? Thence, accordingly, the philosophers watered their arid minds, so that it is the things they have from us which bring us into comparison with them. For this reason, I imagine, philosophy was banished by certain states—I mean by the Thebans, by the Spartans also, and the Argives—its disciples sought to imitate our doctrines; and ambitious, as I have said, of glory and eloquence alone, if they fell upon anything in the collection of sacred Scriptures which displeased them, in their own peculiar style of research, they perverted it to serve their purpose: for they had no adequate faith in their divinity to keep them from changing them, nor had they any sufficient understanding of them, either, as being still at the time under veil—even obscure to the Jews themselves, whose peculiar possession they seemed to be. For so, too, if the truth was distinguished by its simplicity, the more on that account the fastidiousness of man, too proud to believe, set to altering it; so that even what they found certain they made uncertain by their admixtures. Finding a simple revelation of God, they proceeded to dispute about Him, not as He had revealed to them, but turned aside to debate about His properties, His nature, His abode. Some assert Him to be incorporeal; others maintain He has a body,—the Platonists teaching the one doctrine, and the Stoics the other. Some think that He is composed of atoms, others of numbers: such are the different views of Epicurus and Pythagoras. One thinks He is made of fire; so it appeared to Heraclitus. The Platonists, again, hold that He administers the affairs of the world; the Epicureans, on the contrary, that He is idle and inactive, and, so to speak, a nobody in human things. Then the Stoics represent Him as placed outside the world, and whirling round this huge mass from without like a potter; while the Platonists place Him within the world, as a pilot is in the ship he steers. So, in like manner, they differ in their views about the world itself, whether it is created or uncreated, whether it is destined to pass away or to remain for ever. So again it is debated concerning the nature of the soul, which some contend is divine and eternal, while others hold that it is dissoluble. According to each one's fancy, He has introduced either something new,

or refashioned the old. Nor need we wonder if the speculations of philosophers have perverted the older Scriptures. Some of their brood, with their opinions, have even adulterated our new-given Christian revelation, and corrupted it into a system of philosophic doctrines, and from the one path have struck off many and inexplicable by-roads. And I have alluded to this, lest any one becoming acquainted with the variety of parties among us, this might seem to him to put us on a level with the philosophers, and he might condemn the truth from the different ways in which it is defended. But we at once put in a plea in bar against these tainters of our purity, asserting that this is the rule of truth which comes down from Christ by transmission through His companions, to whom we shall prove that those devisers of different doctrines are all posterior. Everything opposed to the truth has been got up from the truth itself, the spirits of error carrying on this system of opposition. By them all corruptions of wholesome discipline have been secretly instigated; by them, too, certain fables have been introduced, that, by their resemblance to the truth, they might impair its credibility, or vindicate their own higher claims to faith; so that people might think Christians unworthy of credit because the poets or philosophers are so, or might regard the poets and philosophers as worthier of confidence from their not being followers of Christ. Accordingly, we get ourselves laughed at for proclaiming that God will one day judge the world. For, like us, the poets and philosophers set up a judgment-seat in the realms below. And if we threaten Gehenna, which is a reservoir of secret fire under the earth for purposes of punishment, we have in the same way derision heaped on us. For so, too, they have their Pyriphlegethon, a river of flame in the regions of the dead. And if we speak of Paradise, the place of heavenly bliss appointed to receive the spirits of the saints, severed from the knowledge of this world by that fiery zone as by a sort of enclosure, the Elysian plains have taken possession of their faith. Whence is it, I pray, you have all this, so like us, in the poets and philosophers? The reason simply is, that they have been taken from our religion. But if they are taken from our sacred things, as being of earlier date, then ours are the truer, and have higher claims upon belief, since even their imitations find faith among you. If they maintain their sacred mysteries to have sprung from their own minds, in that case ours will be reflections of what are later than themselves, which by the nature of things is impossible, for never does the shadow precede the body which casts it, or the image the reality.

48. Come now, if some philosopher affirms, as Laberius[7] holds, following an opinion of Pythagoras, that a man may have his origin from a mule, a serpent from a woman, and with skill of speech twists every argument to prove his view, will he not gain acceptance for it, and work in some the conviction that, on account of this, they should even abstain from eating animal food? May any one have the persuasion that he should so abstain, lest by chance in his beef he eats of some ancestor of his? But if a Christian promises the return of a man from a man, and the very actual Gaius[8] from Gaius, the cry of the people will be to have him

---

[7]Roman poet (105?—43 B.C.).
[8]The Roman equivalent of our John Doe.

stoned; they will not even so much as grant him a hearing. If there is any ground for the moving to and fro of human souls into different bodies, why may they not return into the very substance they have left, seeing this is to be restored, to be that which had been? They are no longer the very things they had been; for they could not be what they were not, without first ceasing to be what they had been. If we were inclined to give all rein upon this point, discussing into what various beasts one and another might probably be changed, we would need at our leisure to take up many points. But this we would do chiefly in our own defence, as setting forth what is greatly worthier of belief, that a man will come back from a man—any given person from any given person, still retaining his humanity; so that the soul, with its qualities unchanged, may be restored to the same condition, though not to the same outward framework. Assuredly, as the reason why restoration takes place at all is the appointed judgment, every man must needs come forth the very same who had once existed, that he may receive at God's hands a judgment, whether of good desert or the opposite. And therefore the body too will appear; for the soul is not capable of suffering without the solid substance, that is, the flesh; and for this reason, also, that it is not right that souls should have all the wrath of God to bear: they did not sin without the body, within which all was done by them. But how, you say, can a substance which has been dissolved be made to reappear again? Consider thyself, O man, and thou wilt believe in it! Reflect on what you were before you came into existence. Nothing. For if you had been anything, you would have remembered it. You, then, who were nothing before you existed, reduced to nothing also when you cease to be, why may you not come into being again out of nothing, at the will of the same Creator whose will created you out of nothing at the first? Will it be anything new in your case? You who were not, *were* made; when you cease to be again, you *shall* be made. Explain, if you can, your original creation, and then demand to know how you shall be re-created. Indeed, it will be still easier surely to make you what you were once, when the very same creative power made you without difficulty what you never were before. There will be doubts, perhaps, as to the power of God, of Him who hung in its place this huge body of our world, made out of what had never existed, as from a death of emptiness and inanity, animated by the Spirit who quickens all living things, its very self the unmistakable type of the resurrection, that it might be to you a witness—nay, the exact image of the resurrection. Light, every day extinguished, shines out again; and, with like alternation, darkness succeeds light's outgoing. The defunct stars re-live; the seasons, as soon as they are finished, renew their course; the fruits are brought to maturity, and then are reproduced. The seeds do not spring up with abundant produce, save as they rot and dissolve away;—all things are preserved by perishing, all things are refashioned out of death. Thou, man of nature so exalted, if thou understandest thyself, taught even by the Pythian words,[9] lord of all these

---

[9]Pythia was the name adopted by the priestess who delivered the oracles at the shrine of Apollo at Delphi, famous throughout the ancient world as a place to seek oracles. Tertullian refers to her most famous oracular saying, "Know thyself."

things that die and rise,—shalt thou die to perish evermore? Wherever your dissolution shall have taken place, whatever material agent has destroyed you, or swallowed you up, or swept you away, or reduced you to nothingness, it shall again restore you. Even nothingness is His who is Lord of *all*. You ask, Shall we then be always dying, and rising up from death? If so the Lord of all things had appointed, you would have to submit, though unwillingly, to the law of your creation. But, in fact, He has no other purpose than that of which He has informed us. The Reason which made the universe out of diverse elements, so that all things might be composed of opposite substances in unity—of void and solid, of animate and inanimate, of comprehensible and incomprehensible, of light and darkness, of life itself and death—has also disposed time into order, by fixing and distinguishing its mode, according to which this first portion of it, which we inhabit from the beginning of the world, flows down by a temporal course to a close; but the portion which succeeds, and to which we look forward continues forever. When, therefore, the boundary and limit, that millennial interspace, has been passed, when even the outward fashion of the world itself—which has been spread like a veil over the eternal economy, equally a thing of time —passes away, then the whole human race shall be raised again, to have its dues meted out according as it has merited in the period of good or evil, and thereafter to have these paid out through the immeasurable ages of eternity. Therefore after this there is neither death nor repeated resurrections, but we shall be the same that we are now, and still unchanged—the servants of God, ever with God, clothed upon with the proper substance of eternity; but the profane, and all who are not true worshippers of God, in like manner shall be consigned to the punishment of everlasting fire—that fire which, from its very nature indeed, directly ministers to their incorruptibility. The philosophers are familiar as well as we with the distinction between a common and a secret fire. Thus that which is in common use is far different from that which we see in divine judgments, whether striking as thunderbolts from heaven, or bursting up out of the earth through mountain-tops; for it does not consume what it scorches, but while it burns it repairs. So the mountains continue ever burning; and a person struck by lightning is even now kept safe from any destroying flame. A notable proof this of the fire eternal! a notable example of the endless judgment which still supplies punishment with fuel! The mountains burn, and last. How will it be with the wicked and the enemies of God?

49. These are what are called presumptuous speculations in our case alone; in the philosophers and poets they are regarded as sublime speculations and illustrious discoveries. They are men of wisdom, we are fools. They are worthy of all honour, we are folk to have the finger pointed at; nay, besides that, we are even to have punishments inflicted on us. But let things which are the defence of virtue, if you will, have no foundation, and give them duly the name of fancies, yet still they are necessary; let them be absurd if you will, yet they are of use: they make all who believe them better men and women, under the fear of never-ending punishment and the hope of never-ending bliss. It is not, then, wise to brand as false, nor to regard as absurd, things the truth of which it is expedient to presume. On no ground is it right posi-

tively to condemn as bad what beyond all doubt is profitable. Thus, in fact, you are guilty of the very presumption of which you accuse us, in condemning what is useful. It is equally out of the question to regard them as nonsensical; at any rate, if they are false and foolish, they hurt nobody. For they are just in that case like many other things on which you inflict no penalties—foolish and fabulous things, I mean, which, as quite innocuous, are never charged as crimes or punished. But in a thing of the kind, if this be so indeed, we should be adjudged to ridicule, not to swords, and flames, and crosses, and wild beasts, in which iniquitous cruelty not only the blinded populace exults and insults over us, but in which some of you too glory, not scrupling to gain the popular favour by your injustice. As though all you can do to us did not depend upon our pleasure. It is assuredly a matter of my own inclination, being a Christian. Your condemnation, then, will only reach me in that case, if I wish to be condemned; but when all you can do to me, you can do only at my will, all you can do is dependent on my will, and is not in your power. The joy of the people in our trouble is therefore utterly reasonless. For it is our joy they appropriate to themselves, since we would far rather be condemned than apostatize from God; on the contrary, our haters should be sorry rather than rejoice, as we have obtained the very thing of our own choice.

Comments / on Tertullian

Tertullian, among the Latins, without controversy is the chief of all our writers. For who was more learned than he? Who in divinity or humanity more practised? For, by a certain wonderful capacity of mind, he attained to and understood all philosophy, all the sects of the philosophers, all their founders and supporters, all their systems, all sorts of histories and studies. And for his wit, was he not so excellent, so grave, so forcible, that he scarce ever undertook the overthrow of any position, but either by quickness of wit he undermined, or by weight of reason he crushed it?
                                    ST. VINCENTIUS LIRINENSIS (435?)

. . . Tertullian, a priest of Carthage, a vehement, irate, witty, tender, hater of shams and culture, cultured himself, learned in letters and the law, scorner of rhetoric and master of its devices, original in thought and style, champion of the Catholic faith and self-constituted prosecuting attorney against all heretics, devotee of a sect so strict and so peculiar that it landed him in heresy.   *E. K. RAND (1928)*

[Tertullian's] sentiments . . . are inspired by a passionate fear of the dangers to be apprehended from . . . the development of speculative activity among theologians in a way which seemed to obscure, if not to undermine, the foundations of the faith.   *C. N. COCHRANE (1940)*

This absolute conviction in the self-sufficiency of Christian revelation has always found decided supporters. We find it represented in all the significant periods of the history of Christian thought; its representatives are always there, but it becomes vocal chiefly during such times when philosophy is threatening to invade the field of Revelation. As early as the second century, Tertullian found forceful formulas to stress what he held to be an irreconcilable antagonism between Christianity and philosophy. . . . I have quoted Tertullian at some length because of the very perfection with which he exemplifies this typical attitude. All its essential features are already there, and I do not think we could find a single one of these sentences that was not quoted again and again from the second century until the end of the Middle Ages, or even later. Let us call this family the Tertullian family, and I am sure you will never fail to identify its members when you meet them. . . . [Among their attributes are] unqualified condemnation of Greek philosophy, as though no Greek philosopher had ever said anything true concerning the nature of God, of man and of our destiny; bitter hatred, and vicious attacks especially directed against Dialectics, as if it were possible even to condemn Dialectics without making use of it . . . the crude statement of an absolute opposition between religious faith in the word of God and the use of natural reason in matters pertaining to revelation.   *ETIENNE GILSON (1938)*

St. Jerome
340?—420

From its very beginnings, Christianity tended to foster ascetic practices among its adherents. By demanding total and constant religious devotion, by deprecating material possessions, and by discouraging earthly emotional attachments, the Christian ideal in its purest form inspired men to withdraw from the world of affairs and commit themselves to a life of pious solitude. By the end of the fourth century this impulse was already creating profound changes in the structure of society as more and more Christians isolated themselves from the ordinary life of men. Contemporary conditions helped accelerate this trend. The collapse and decay of Roman social institutions was everywhere visible, so that Christians, faced by the moral corruption evident in the life of the cities, came to the conclusion that a truly devout life could best be lived only by turning away from conventional society. They went off as solitary hermits or as members of monastic communities and devoted their lives to pious activity, thus removing from society a force that might have helped check the decline of Roman civilization. As it was, the civic consciousness characteristic of the Greco-Roman world continued to disintegrate, and monasticism became the outstanding feature of Christian civilization for the better part of the next thousand years.

St. Jerome, famous in his own time as a great Christian scholar and as the translator of both the Old and New Testaments into Latin, exerted a strong influence on the development of monasticism by his own inclination toward ascetic practices. As a young man, even though he had been trained as a scholar, he had lived five years as a hermit in the Syrian Desert with a group of like-minded Christian ascetics. He later spent a few years as a priest at Rome, where he began his translations of the Bible at the request of the pope. But finding the worldliness of ecclesiastical life at Rome uncongenial, he returned to the East. In the year 386 he settled permanently at Bethlehem in a monastery built for him by a wealthy group of pious women who had followed him there and established themselves in a convent nearby.

St. Jerome had already achieved a reputation as an ecclesiastical writer
before settling at Bethlehem, but he added immensely to his output during
his years there. He completed his translation of the Scriptures, which
became known as the Vulgate since it was in the vulgar, i.e., vernacular,
language of fifth-century Europe and which served as the official version
of the Bible in the Roman Catholic Church throughout the Middle Ages.
He also provided lengthy commentaries for many of the Scriptural books,
composed a variety of theological treatises, and carried on a voluminous
correspondence with both the great and the humble throughout the
Christian world. His fame was such that his letters were treasured by
their recipients and were often transcribed for wider circulation, so that
more than one hundred fifty have been preserved. Many of them, letters
of advice to disciples who had sought his counsel, read like, and indeed
were meant to be taken as, sermons. In them he repeatedly emphasizes
the ascetic viewpoint which colored all his theological writings. The
letter to Laeta is characteristic: she was the daughter-in-law of Paula,
his chief benefactress at Bethlehem, and had written to him from Rome
for instructions in raising her own newborn daughter, whom she had
vowed to the service of Christ. St. Jerome's reply demonstrates the kind
of thinking that was to dominate the Christian world for a long time to
come.

Letter CVII (To Laeta)

1. The apostle Paul writing to the Corinthians and instructing in
sacred discipline a church still untaught in Christ has among other commandments laid down also this: "The woman which hath an husband that
believeth not, and if he be pleased to dwell with her, let her not leave
him. For the unbelieving husband is sanctified by the believing wife,
and the unbelieving wife is sanctified by the believing husband; else
were your children unclean but now are they holy." Should any person
have supposed hitherto that the bonds of discipline are too far relaxed
and that too great indulgence is conceded by the teacher, let him look
at the house of your father, a man of the highest distinction and learning,
but one still walking in darkness; and he will perceive as the result
of the apostle's counsel sweet fruit growing from a bitter stock and
precious balsams exhaled from common canes. You yourself are the
offspring of a mixed marriage; but the parents of Paula—you and my
friend Toxotius—are both Christians. Who could have believed that to
the heathen pontiff Albinus should be born—in answer to a mother's

vows—a Christian granddaughter,[1] that a delighted grandfather should hear from the little one's faltering lips Christ's Alleluia, and that in his old age he should nurse in his bosom one of God's own virgins? Our expectations have been fully gratified. The one unbeliever is sanctified by his holy and believing family. For, when a man is surrounded by a believing crowd of children and grandchildren, he is as good as a candidate for the faith. I for my part think that, had he possessed so many Christian kinsfolk when he was a young man, he might then have been brought to believe in Christ. For though he may spit upon my letter and laugh at it, and though he may call me a fool or a madman, his son-in-law did the same before he came to believe. Christians are not born but made. For all its gilding the Capitol is beginning to look dingy. Every temple in Rome is covered with soot and cobwebs. The city is stirred to its depths and the people pour past their half-ruined shrines to visit the tombs of the martyrs. The belief which has not been accorded to conviction may come to be extorted by very shame.

2. I speak thus to you, Laeta my most devout daughter in Christ, to teach you not to despair of your father's salvation. My hope is that the same faith which has gained you your daughter may win your father too, and that so you may be able to rejoice over blessings bestowed upon your entire family. You know the Lord's promise: "The things which are impossible with men are possible with God." It is never too late to mend. The robber passed even from the cross to paradise. Nebuchadnezzar also, the king of Babylon, recovered his reason, even after he had been made like the beasts in body and in heart and had been compelled to live with the brutes in the wilderness. And to pass over such old stories which to unbelievers may well seem incredible, did not your own kinsman Gracchus whose name betokens his patrician origin, when a few years back he held the prefecture of the City, overthrow, break in pieces, and shake to pieces the grotto of Mithras[2] and all the dreadful images therein? Those I mean by which the worshippers were initiated as Raven, Bridegroom, Soldier, Lion, Perseus, Sun, Crab, and Father? Did he not, I repeat, destroy these and then, sending them before him as hostages, obtain for himself Christian baptism?

Even in Rome itself paganism is left in solitude. They who once were the gods of the nations remain under their lonely roofs with horned-owls and birds of night. The standards of the military are emblazoned with the sign of the Cross. The emperor's robes of purple and his diadem sparkling with jewels are ornamented with representations of the shameful yet saving gibbet. Already the Egyptian Serapis has been made a Christian;[3] while at Gaza Marnas mourns in confinement and every moment expects to see his temple overturned.[4] From India, from Persia,

---

[1] The relationships that St. Jerome is referring to in this passage are as follows: Laeta, the recipient of the letter, is the wife of Toxotius, a Christian. Laeta's mother, Paula, was also a Christian but had married the pagan Albinus, who held a priestly status in the Roman religion. Laeta named her daughter Paula, after her own mother.

[2] The Persian sun god, at this time one of the most popular deities in the Roman pantheistic religion.

[3] In 389 A.D. the temple of the Egyptian god Serapis at Alexandria had been torn down and a Christian church built on its site.

[4] Marnas is the name of a heathen god worshiped in the Near East at that time. St. Jerome elsewhere tells a story in which a Christian's prayers enabled him unexpectedly to win a chariot race from a pagan who had prayed to Marnas, with the result that many worshipers of Marnas became converted to Christianity.

from Ethiopia we daily welcome monks in crowds. The Armenian bow-
man has laid aside his quiver, the Huns learn the psalter, the chilly
Scythians are warmed with the glow of the faith. The Getæ, ruddy and
yellow-haired, carry tent-churches about with their armies: and perhaps
their success in fighting against us may be due to the fact that they
believe in the same religion.

3. I have nearly wandered into a new subject, and while I have kept
my wheel going, my hands have been moulding a flagon when it has been
my object to frame an ewer. For, in answer to your prayers and those of
the saintly Marcella,[5] I wish to address you as a mother and to instruct
you how to bring up our dear Paula, who has been consecrated to Christ
before her birth and vowed to His service before her conception. Thus
in our own day we have seen repeated the story told us in the Prophets,
of Hannah, who though at first barren afterwards became fruitful. You
have exchanged a fertility bound up with sorrow for offspring which
shall never die. For I am confident that having given to the Lord your
first-born you will be the mother of sons. It is the first-born that is
offered under the Law. Samuel and Samson are both instances of this,
as is also John the Baptist who when Mary came in leaped for joy.
For he heard the Lord speaking by the mouth of the Virgin and desired
to break from his mother's womb to meet Him. As then Paula has been
born in answer to a promise, her parents should give her a training suitable to her birth. Samuel, as you know, was nurtured in the Temple,
and John was trained in the wilderness. The first as a Nazarite wore
his hair long, drank neither wine nor strong drink, and even in his
childhood talked with God. The second shunned cities, wore a leathern
girdle, and had for his meat locusts and wild honey. Moreover, to typify
that penitence which he was to preach, he was clothed in the spoils of
the hump-backed camel.

4. Thus must a soul be educated which is to be a temple of God. It
must learn to hear nothing and to say nothing but what belongs to the
fear of God. It must have no understanding of unclean words, and no
knowledge of the world's songs. Its tongue must be steeped while still
tender in the sweetness of the psalms. Boys with their wanton thoughts
must be kept from Paula: even her maids and female attendants must
be separated from worldly associates. For if they have learned some
mischief they may teach more. Get for her a set of letters made of box-
wood or of ivory and called each by its proper name. Let her play with
these, so that even her play may teach her something. And not only
make her grasp the right order of the letters and see that she forms
their names into a rhyme, but constantly disarrange their order and put
the last letters in the middle and the middle ones at the beginning that
she may know them all by sight as well as by sound. Moreover, so soon
as she begins to use the style upon the wax, and her hand is still faltering, either guide her soft fingers by laying your hand upon hers, or else
have simple copies cut upon a tablet; so that her efforts confined within
these limits may keep to the lines traced out for her and not stray out-

---

[5]One of the patrician Roman ladies who had followed St. Jerome to Bethlehem. She was a close friend of
Laeta's mother, Paula.

side of these. Offer prizes for good spelling and draw her onwards with little gifts such as children of her age delight in. And let her have companions in her lessons to excite emulation in her, that she may be stimulated when she sees them praised. You must not scold her if she is slow to learn but must employ praise to excite her mind, so that she may be glad when she excels others and sorry when she is excelled by them. Above all you must take care not to make her lessons distasteful to her lest a dislike for them conceived in childhood may continue into her maturer years. The very words which she tries bit by bit to put together and to pronounce ought not to be chance ones, but names specially fixed upon and heaped together for the purpose, those for example of the prophets or the apostles or the list of patriarchs from Adam downwards as it is given by Matthew and Luke. In this way while her tongue will be well-trained, her memory will be likewise developed. Again, you must choose for her a master of approved years, life, and learning. A man of culture will not, I think, blush to do for a kinswoman or a highborn virgin what Aristotle did for Philip's son when, descending to the level of an usher, he consented to teach him his letters.[6] Things must not be despised as of small account in the absence of which great results cannot be achieved. The very rudiments and first beginnings of knowledge sound differently in the mouth of an educated man and of an uneducated. Accordingly you must see that the child is not led away by the silly coaxing of women to form a habit of shortening long words or of decking herself with gold and purple. Of these habits one will spoil her conversation and the other her character. She must not therefore learn as a child what afterwards she will have to unlearn. The eloquence of the Gracchi[7] is said to have been largely due to the way in which from their earliest years their mother spoke to them. Hortensius[8] became an orator while still on his father's lap. Early impressions are hard to eradicate from the mind. When once wool has been dyed purple who can restore it to its previous whiteness? An unused jar long retains the taste and smell of that with which it is first filled. Grecian history tells us that the imperious Alexander who was lord of the whole world could not rid himself of the tricks of manner and gait which in his childhood he had caught from his governor Leonides. We are always ready to imitate what is evil; and faults are quickly copied where virtues appear inattainable. Paula's nurse must not be intemperate, or loose, or given to gossip. Her bearer must be respectable, and her fosterfather of grave demeanour. When she sees her grandfather, she must leap upon his breast, put her arms round his neck, and, whether he likes it or not, sing Alleluia in his ears. She may be fondled by her grandmother, may smile at her father to shew that she recognizes him, and may so endear herself to everyone, as to make the whole family rejoice in the possession of such a rosebud. She should be told at once whom she has for her other grandmother and whom for her aunt; and she ought also to learn in what army it is that she is enrolled as a recruit, and what

---

[6]King Philip of Macedonia appointed Aristotle as tutor to his son, who was to become known as Alexander the Great.
[7]Two brothers who were famous Roman political leaders during the second century B.C.
[8]A Roman orator during the first century B.C. whose reputation rivaled that of Cicero.

Captain it is under whose banner she is called to serve. Let her long to be with the absent ones and encourage her to make playful threats of leaving you for them.

5. Let her very dress and garb remind her to Whom she is promised. Do not pierce her ears or paint her face consecrated to Christ with white lead or rouge. Do not hang gold or pearls about her neck or load her head with jewels, or by reddening her hair make it suggest the fires of gehenna. Let her pearls be of another kind and such that she may sell them hereafter and buy in their place the pearl that is "of great price." In days gone by a lady of rank, Praetextata by name, at the bidding of her husband Hymettius, the uncle of Eustochium,[9] altered that virgin's dress and appearance and arranged her neglected hair after the manner of the world, desiring to overcome the resolution of the virgin herself and the expressed wishes of her mother. But lo in the same night it befell her that an angel came to her in her dreams. With terrible looks he menaced punishment and broke silence with these words, 'Have you presumed to put your husband's commands before those of Christ? Have you presumed to lay sacrilegious hands upon the head of one who is God's virgin? Those hands shall forthwith wither that you may know by torment what you have done, and at the end of five months you shall be carried off to hell. And farther, if you persist still in your wickedness, you shall be bereaved both of your husband and of your children.' All of which came to pass in due time, a speedy death marking the penitence too long delayed of the unhappy woman. So terribly does Christ punish those who violate His temple, and so jealously does He defend His precious jewels. I have related this story here not from any desire to exult over the misfortunes of the unhappy, but to warn you that you must with much fear and carefulness keep the vow which you have made to God.

6. We read of Eli the priest that he became displeasing to God on account of the sins of his children; and we are told that a man may not be made a bishop if his sons are loose and disorderly. On the other hand it is written of the woman that "she shall be saved in childbearing, if they continue in faith and charity and holiness with chastity." If then parents are responsible for their children when these are of ripe age and independent; how much more must they be responsible for them when, still unweaned and weak, they cannot, in the Lord's words, "discern between their right hand and their left:"—when, that is to say, they cannot yet distinguish good from evil? If you take precautions to save your daughter from the bite of a viper, why are you not equally careful to shield her from "the hammer of the whole earth"?[10] to prevent her from drinking of the golden cup of Babylon? to keep her from going out with Dinah to see the daughters of a strange land? to save her from the tripping dance and from the trailing robe? No one administers drugs till he has rubbed the rim of the cup with honey; so, the better to deceive us, vice puts on the mien and the semblance of virtue. Why

---

[9]Laeta's sister, who had followed Jerome to Bethlehem together with her mother.

[10]Babylon. St. Jerome is referring to the fame of the Babylonian Empire as a world power. He uses it as a symbol of the sinfulness to which earthly luxuries lead.

then, you will say, do we read:—"the son shall not bear the iniquity of the father, neither shall the father bear the iniquity of the son," but "the soul that sinneth it shall die"? The passage, I answer, refers to those who have discretion, such as he of whom his parents said in the gospel:—"he is of age . . . he shall speak for himself." While the son is a child and thinks as a child and until he comes to years of discretion to choose between the two roads to which the letter of Pythagoras points,[11] his parents are responsible for his actions whether these be good or bad. But perhaps you imagine that, if they are not baptized, the children of Christians are liable for their own sins; and that no guilt attaches to parents who withhold from baptism those who by reason of their tender age can offer no objection to it. The truth is that, as baptism ensures the salvation of the child, this in turn brings advantage to the parents. Whether you would offer your child or not lay within your choice, but now that you have offered her, you neglect her at your peril. I speak generally for in your case you have no discretion, having offered your child even before her conception. He who offers a victim that is lame or maimed or marked with any blemish is held guilty of sacrilege. How much more then shall she be punished who makes ready for the embraces of the king a portion of her own body and the purity of a stainless soul, and then proves negligent of this her offering?

7. When Paula comes to be a little older and to increase like her Spouse in wisdom and stature and in favour with God and man, let her go with her parents to the temple of her true Father but let her not come out of the temple with them. Let them seek her upon the world's highway amid the crowds and the throng of their kinsfolk, and let them find her nowhere but in the shrine of the scriptures, questioning the prophets and the apostles on the meaning of that spiritual marriage to which she is vowed. Let her imitate the retirement of Mary whom Gabriel found alone in her chamber and who was frightened, it would appear, by seeing a man there. Let the child emulate her of whom it is written that "the king's daughter is all glorious within." Wounded with love's arrow let her say to her beloved, "the king hath brought me into his chambers." At no time let her go abroad, lest the watchmen find her that go about the city, and lest they smite and wound her and take away from her the veil of her chastity, and leave her naked in her blood. Nay rather when one knocketh at her door let her say: "I am a wall and my breasts like towers. I have washed my feet; how shall I defile them?"

8. Let her not take her food with others, that is, at her parents' table; lest she see dishes she may long for. Some, I know, hold it a greater virtue to disdain a pleasure which is actually before them, but I think it a safer self-restraint to shun what must needs attract you. Once as a boy at school I met the words: 'It is ill blaming what you allow to become a habit.' Let her learn even now not to drink wine "wherein is excess." But as, before children come to a robust age, abstinence is dangerous and trying to their tender frames, let her have baths if she require them,

---

[11]The letter Y used by the ancient Greek philosopher Pythagoras to symbolize the diverging paths of good and evil.

and let her take a little wine for her stomach's sake. Let her also be supported on a flesh diet, lest her feet fail her before they commence to run their course. But I say this by way of concession not by way of command; because I fear to weaken her, not because I wish to teach her self-indulgence. Besides why should not a Christian virgin do wholly what others do in part? The superstitious Jews reject certain animals and products as articles of food, while among the Indians the Brahmans[12] and among the Egyptians the Gymnosophists[13] subsist altogether on porridge, rice, and apples. If mere glass repays so much labour, must not a pearl be worth more labour still? Paula has been born in response to a vow. Let her life be as the lives of those who were born under the same conditions. If the grace accorded is in both cases the same, the pains bestowed ought to be so too. Let her be deaf to the sound of the organ, and not know even the uses of the pipe, the lyre, and the cithern.

9. And let it be her task daily to bring to you the flowers which she has culled from scripture. Let her learn by heart so many verses in the Greek, but let her be instructed in the Latin also. For, if the tender lips are not from the first shaped to this, the tongue is spoiled by a foreign accent and its native speech debased by alien elements. You must yourself be her mistress, a model on which she may form her childish conduct. Never either in you nor in her father let her see what she cannot imitate without sin. Remember both of you that you are the parents of a consecrated virgin, and that your example will teach her more than your precepts. Flowers are quick to fade and a baleful wind soon withers the violet, the lily, and the crocus. Let her never appear in public unless accompanied by you. Let her never visit a church or a martyr's shrine unless with her mother. Let no young man greet her with smiles; no dandy with curled hair pay compliments to her. If our little virgin goes to keep solemn eves and all-night vigils, let her not stir a hair's breadth from her mother's side. She must not single out one of her maids to make her a special favourite or a confidante. What she says to one all ought to know. Let her choose for a companion not a handsome well-dressed girl, able to warble a song with liquid notes but one pale and serious, sombrely attired and with the hue of melancholy. Let her take as her model some aged virgin of approved faith, character, and chastity, apt to instruct her by word and by example. She ought to rise at night to recite prayers and psalms; to sing hymns in the morning; at the third, sixth, and ninth hours to take her place in the line to do battle for Christ; and, lastly, to kindle her lamp and to offer her evening sacrifice. In these occupations let her pass the day, and when night comes let it find her still engaged in them. Let reading follow prayer with her, and prayer again succeed to reading. Time will seem short when employed on tasks so many and so varied.

10. Let her learn too how to spin wool, to hold the distaff, to put the basket in her lap, to turn the spinning wheel and to shape the yarn with her thumb. Let her put away with disdain silken fabrics, Chinese fleeces, and gold brocades: the clothing which she makes for herself

---

[12]The priestly caste in the Hindu religion.
[13]A class of Hindu religious ascetics, who were actually found in India rather than in Egypt.

should keep out the cold and not expose the body which it professes to cover. Let her food be herbs and wheaten bread with now and then one or two small fishes. And that I may not waste more time in giving precepts for the regulation of appetite (a subject I have treated more at length elsewhere) let her meals always leave her hungry and able on the moment to begin reading or chanting. I strongly disapprove—especially for those of tender years—of long and immoderate fasts in which week is added to week and even oil and apples are forbidden as food. I have learned by experience that the ass toiling along the high way makes for an inn when it is weary. Our abstinence may turn to glutting, like that of the worshippers of Isis and of Cybele who gobble up pheasants and turtle-doves piping hot that their teeth may not violate the gifts of Ceres.[14] If perpetual fasting is allowed, it must be so regulated that those who have a long journey before them may hold out all through; and we must take care that we do not, after starting well, fall halfway. However in Lent, as I have written before now, those who practise self-denial should spread every stitch of canvas, and the chari-oteer should for once slacken the reins and increase the speed of his horses. Yet there will be one rule for those who live in the world and another for virgins and monks. The layman in Lent consumes the coats of his stomach, and living like a snail on his own juices makes ready a paunch for rich foods and feasting to come. But with the virgin and the monk the case is different; for, when these give the rein to their steeds, they have to remember that for them the race knows of no intermission. An effort made only for a limited time may well be severe, but one that has no such limit must be more moderate. For whereas in the first case we can recover our breath when the race is over, in the last we have to go on continually and without stopping.

11. When you go a short way into the country, do not leave your daughter behind you. Leave her no power or capacity of living without you, and let her feel frightened when she is left to herself. Let her not converse with people of the world or associate with virgins in-different to their vows. Let her not be present at the weddings of your slaves and let her take no part in the noisy games of the household. As regards the use of the bath, I know that some are content with saying that a Christian virgin should not bathe along with eunuchs or with married women, with the former because they are still men at all events in mind, and with the latter because women with child offer a revolting spectacle.[15] For myself, however, I wholly disapprove of baths for a virgin of full age. Such an one should blush and feel overcome at the idea of seeing herself undressed. By vigils and fasts she mortifies her body and brings it into subjection. By a cold chastity she seeks to put out the flame of lust and to quench the hot desires of youth. And by a de-liberate squalor she makes haste to spoil her natural good looks. Why, then, should she add fuel to a sleeping fire by taking baths?

12. Let her treasures be not silks or gems but manuscripts of the holy

---

[14]Isis in Egyptian mythology, Cybele in Greek, and Ceres in Roman were all goddesses representing the fruitfulness of the earth. St. Jerome is referring to people who, having vowed to abstain from bread, make up for it by eating meat.

[15]A striking feature of Roman civilization was the construction of large, elaborate public bathhouses.

scriptures; and in these let her think less of gilding, and Babylonian parchment, and arabesque patterns, than of correctness and accurate punctuation. Let her begin by learning the psalter, and then let her gather rules of life out of the proverbs of Solomon. From the Preacher let her gain the habit of despising the world and its vanities. Let her follow the example set in Job of virtue and of patience. Then let her pass on to the gospels never to be laid aside when once they have been taken in hand. Let her also drink in with a willing heart the Acts of the Apostles and the Epistles. As soon as she has enriched the storehouse of her mind with these treasures, let her commit to memory the prophets, the heptateuch, the books of Kings and of Chronicles, the rolls also of Ezra and Esther. When she has done all these she may safely read the Song of Songs but not before: for, were she to read it at the beginning, she would fail to perceive that, though it is written in fleshly words, it is a marriage song of a spiritual bridal. And not understanding this she would suffer hurt from it. Let her avoid all apocryphal writings, and if she is led to read such not by the truth of the doctrines which they contain but out of respect for the miracles contained in them; let her understand that they are not really written by those to whom they are ascribed, that many faulty elements have been introduced into them, and that it requires infinite discretion to look for gold in the midst of dirt. Cyprian's[16] writings let her have always in her hands. The letters of Athanasius[17] and the treatises of Hilary[18] she may go through without fear of stumbling. Let her take pleasure in the works and wits of all in whose books a due regard for the faith is not neglected. But if she reads the works of others let it be rather to judge them than to follow them.

13. You will answer, 'How shall I, a woman of the world, living at Rome, surrounded by a crowd, be able to observe all these injunctions?' In that case do not undertake a burthen to which you are not equal. When you have weaned Paula as Isaac was weaned and when you have clothed her as Samuel was clothed, send her to her grandmother and aunt; give up this most precious of gems, to be placed in Mary's chamber and to rest in the cradle where the infant Jesus cried. Let her be brought up in a monastery, let her be one amid companies of virgins, let her learn to avoid swearing, let her regard lying as sacrilege, let her be ignorant of the world, let her live the angelic life, while in the flesh let her be without the flesh, and let her suppose that all human beings are like herself. To say nothing of its other advantages this course will free you from the difficult task of minding her, and from the responsibility of guardianship. It is better to regret her absence than to be for ever trembling for her. For you cannot but tremble as you watch what she says and to whom she says it, to whom she bows and whom she likes best to see. Hand her over to Eustochium while she is still but an infant and her every cry is a prayer for you. She will thus become her companion in holiness now as well as her successor hereafter. Let her gaze upon and love, let her "from her earliest years admire" one whose

---

[16]A Father of the Church (200?–258).
[17]A Father of the Church (293?–373).
[18]A Father of the Church (?–367?).

language and gait and dress are an education in virtue. Let her sit in the lap of her grandmother, and let this latter repeat to her granddaughter the lessons that she once bestowed upon her own child. Long experience has shewn Paula how to rear, to preserve, and to instruct virgins; and daily inwoven in her crown is the mystic century which betokens the highest chastity. O happy virgin! happy Paula, daughter of Toxotius, who through the virtues of her grandmother and aunt is nobler in holiness than she is in lineage! Yes, Laeta: were it possible for you with your own eyes to see your mother-in-law and your sister, and to realize the mighty souls which animate their small bodies; such is your innate thirst for chastity that I cannot doubt but that you would go to them even before your daughter, and would emancipate yourself from God's first decree of the Law to put yourself under His second dispensation of the Gospel. You would count as nothing your desire for other off-spring and would offer up yourself to the service of God. But because "there is a time to embrace, and a time to refrain from embracing," and because "the wife hath not power of her own body," and because the apostle says "Let every man abide in the same calling wherein he was called" in the Lord, and because he that is under the yoke ought so to run as not to leave his companion in the mire, I counsel you to pay back to the full in your offspring what meantime you defer paying in your own person. When Hannah had once offered in the tabernacle the son whom she had vowed to God she never took him back; for she thought it unbecoming that one who was to be a prophet should grow up in the same house with her who still desired to have other children. Accordingly after she had conceived him and given him birth, she did not venture to come to the temple alone or to appear before the Lord empty, but first paid to Him what she owed; and then, when she had offered up that great sacrifice, she returned home and because she had borne her firstborn for God, she was given five children for herself. Do you marvel at the happiness of that holy woman? Imitate her faith. Moreover, if you will only send Paula, I promise to be myself both a tutor and a fosterfather to her. Old as I am I will carry her on my shoulders and train her stammering lips; and my charge will be a far grander one than that of the worldly philosopher;[19] for while he only taught a King of Macedon who was one day to die of Babylonian poison, I shall instruct the handmaid and spouse of Christ who must one day be offered to her Lord in heaven.

Comments / on St. Jerome

No doctor of the church did more than St. Jerome to impose the rule of celibacy on its members. . . . His contempt for marriage, indeed, was so

---

[19]Aristotle.

extreme that in spite of the recognized primacy of St. Peter, he considered that apostle as decidedly inferior to St. John, because the one had a wife and the other was a virgin—apparently not observing that, as he denied the marriage of all the apostles save Peter, he was thus relegating the head of the Church to the last place among the holy twelve.

H. C. LEA (1907)

The aversion from the obvious and deplorable fact of sex was one of the fundamental motives in the monastic movement. The emotional quality of Christian asceticism is nowhere seen more clearly than in the letters of Jerome. *HERSCHEL BAKER (1947)*

St. Jerome was also a born teacher. He had ideas on pedagogy that may seem very modern—to one who knows not the ancients. One of his letters is devoted to the subject of the proper education of a little girl [Letter CVII]. . . . St. Jerome has shown in this chance letter that humanism and humanitarianism are sometimes one. *E. K. RAND (1928)*

St. Augustine
354—430

The most striking characteristic of early Christianity was the diversity of religious doctrines and practices among its followers, and the greatest problem confronting the Church, aside from its sheer survival, was the creation of a universally accepted orthodoxy in belief and ritual among the varied peoples who professed themselves Christians. Even as early as Apostolic times, St. Paul's epistles show him grappling with this problem. And the next few centuries saw the rise of a great many sects agreeing on very little in matters of religion other than belief in the divinity of Christ and in the sanctity of the New Testament. Nor was there really complete agreement even about the New Testament, since an authoritative canon of what books should and should not be included in it was not officially established until the fourth century. The Church attempted to promote a more uniform Christianity by occasionally convoking General Councils, assemblages of theologians and ecclesiastical authorities from all over Christendom, who tried to reach agreements about matters of doctrine which might then be promulgated as the basis for orthodox belief among all Christians. Despite these efforts, however, the desired uniformity in belief was still far from being achieved by the end of the fourth century, even within Roman Catholic Christianity. What was needed was a man with sufficient power of mind to impose order on diversity by formulating a systematic, comprehensive, convincingly reasoned exposition of the entire body of the Christian religion—to describe the basic Christian philosophical and theological principles with such judgment as to represent the mainstream of Christian thought and practice and with such force of intellect as to compel acceptance of his work as the basis for Christian orthodoxy.

St. Augustine was this man. His father was a pagan, a minor Roman official in the little North African town of Tagaste, but his mother was an intensely pious Christian. He showed signs of brilliance early and went to nearby Carthage to complete his classical education. He became a professor of rhetoric there and later moved to Rome and then to Milan, where he further advanced his teaching career and enjoyed considerable success. Due to his mother's influence, he had always been attracted to Christianity; but he had been unable to reconcile its ascetic demands and mystic beliefs with his love of earthly pleasures and devotion to classical learning. At Milan, in the year 387, he finally became a Christian. He returned to Africa the next year, spent some time in a monastery, was then ordained as a priest in the city of Hippo, and served as bishop there for the last thirty-five years of his life.

St. Augustine combined prodigious energy with genius of mind. He managed the administration of his diocese; was a vigorous preacher; carried on an enormous correspondence throughout the Christian world; concerned himself deeply with the general affairs of the Church, especially as a spokesman against heresies; and produced the largest and most influential body of ecclesiastical writings among all the Fathers of the Church. His work synthesized the most generally accepted achievements of Christian thought and harmonized them as far as possible with the achievements of pagan philosophy. As St. Thomas Aquinas put it: "Whenever Augustine, who was imbued with the doctrines of the Platonists, found in their teaching anything consistent with faith, he adopted it; and those things which he found contrary to faith he amended." Imposing his own theological conceptions on this body of thought, St. Augustine created a system of Christian doctrine that was to stand as the unquestioned foundation of Christian orthodoxy for a good many centuries.

The fullest expressions of St. Augustine's thought are contained in the two monumental treatises, *On the Trinity* and *The City of God,* which together took more than a quarter century to write. Among the shorter treatises, the *Enchiridion (Manual),* composed in 421 to satisfy a request for a brief handbook presenting the essence of his views on Christian belief, is remarkable for providing a compact summary of his thought on every important tenet of Christian theology. It constitutes his own mature opinion of what he considered essential in his system and, consequently, became a widely read, authoritative doctrinal guide for later ages.

The *Confessions* are St. Augustine's own account of his life up until the time he became a Christian, written some dozen years after his conversion. They constitute a spiritual rather than a literal autobiography, emphasizing not so much the actual events of his life as the emotional experiences which eventually brought him to God. They are, naturally, of prime importance in understanding St. Augustine's thought, and they represent, especially in the description of his actual conversion, one of the finest expressions of the mystical strain in Christianity. Perhaps their greatest distinction is their value to anyone interested in seeing how a great mind appraises its own development.

Confessions

Book II

1. I wish now to review in memory my past wickedness and the carnal corruptions of my soul—not because I still love them, but that I may love thee, O my God. For love of thy love I do this, recalling in the bitterness of self-examination my wicked ways, that thou mayest grow sweet to me, thou sweetness without deception! Thou sweetness happy and assured! Thus thou mayest gather me up out of those fragments in which I was torn to pieces, while I turned away from thee, O Unity, and lost myself among "the many." For as I became a youth, I longed to be satisfied with worldly things, and I dared to grow wild in a succession of various and shadowy loves. My form wasted away, and I became corrupt in thy eyes, yet I was still pleasing to my own eyes—and eager to please the eyes of men.

2. But what was it that delighted me save to love and to be loved? Still I did not keep the moderate way of the love of mind to mind—the bright path of friendship. Instead, the mists of passion steamed up out of the puddly concupiscence of the flesh, and the hot imagination of puberty, and they so obscured and overcast my heart that I was unable to distinguish pure affection from unholy desire. Both boiled confusedly within me, and dragged my unstable youth down over the cliffs of unchaste desires and plunged me into a gulf of infamy. Thy anger had come upon me, and I knew it not. I had been deafened by the clanking of the chains of my mortality, the punishment for my soul's pride, and I wandered farther from thee, and thou didst permit me to do so. I was tossed to and fro, and wasted, and poured out, and I boiled over in my fornications—and yet thou didst hold thy peace, O my tardy Joy! Thou didst still hold thy peace, and I wandered still farther from thee into more and yet more barren fields of sorrow, in proud dejection and restless lassitude.

3. If only there had been someone to regulate my disorder and turn to my profit the fleeting beauties of the things around me, and to fix a bound to their sweetness, so that the tides of my youth might have spent themselves upon the shore of marriage! Then they might have been tranquilized and satisfied with having children, as thy law prescribes, O Lord—O thou who dost form the offspring of our death and art able also with a tender hand to blunt the thorns which were excluded from thy paradise! For thy omnipotence is not far from us even when we are far from thee. Now, on the other hand, I might have given more vigilant heed to the voice from the clouds: "Nevertheless, such shall have trouble in the flesh, but I spare you," and, "It is good for a man not to touch a woman," and, "He that is unmarried cares for the things that belong to the Lord, how he may please the Lord; but he that is married cares for the things that are of the world, how he may please his wife." I

From *Augustine: Confessions and Enchiridion*, LCC, Vol. VII, ed. Albert C. Outler. Published 1955, The Westminster Press. Used by permission of The Westminster Press and Student Christian Movement Press Limited.

should have listened more attentively to these words, and, thus having been "made a eunuch for the Kingdom of Heaven's sake," I would have with greater happiness expected thy embraces.

4. But, fool that I was, I foamed in my wickedness as the sea and, forsaking thee, followed the rushing of my own tide, and burst out of all thy bounds. But I did not escape thy scourges. For what mortal can do so? Thou wast always by me, mercifully angry and flavoring all my unlawful pleasures with bitter discontent, in order that I might seek pleasures free from discontent. But where could I find such pleasure save in thee, O Lord—save in thee, who dost teach us by sorrow, who woundest us to heal us, and dost kill us that we may not die apart from thee. Where was I, and how far was I exiled from the delights of thy house, in that sixteenth year of the age of my flesh, when the madness of lust held full sway in me—that madness which grants indulgence to human shamelessness, even though it is forbidden by thy laws—and I gave myself entirely to it? Meanwhile, my family took no care to save me from ruin by marriage, for their sole care was that I should learn how to make a powerful speech and become a persuasive orator.

5. Now, in that year my studies were interrupted. I had come back from Madaura, a neighboring city where I had gone to study grammar and rhetoric; and the money for a further term at Carthage was being got together for me. This project was more a matter of my father's ambition than of his means, for he was only a poor citizen of Tagaste.

To whom am I narrating all this? Not to thee, O my God, but to my own kind in thy presence—to that small part of the human race who may chance to come upon these writings. And to what end? That I and all who read them may understand what depths there are from which we are to cry unto thee. For what is more surely heard in thy ear than a confessing heart and a faithful life?

Who did not extol and praise my father, because he went quite beyond his means to supply his son with the necessary expenses for a far journey in the interest of his education? For many far richer citizens did not do so much for their children. Still, this same father troubled himself not at all as to how I was progressing toward thee nor how chaste I was, just so long as I was skillful in speaking—no matter how barren I was to thy tillage, O God, who art the one true and good Lord of my heart, which is thy field.

6. During that sixteenth year of my age, I lived with my parents, having a holiday from school for a time—this idleness imposed upon me by my parents' straitened finances. The thornbushes of lust grew about my head, and there was no hand to root them out. Indeed, when my father saw me one day at the baths and perceived that I was becoming a man, and was showing the signs of adolescence, he joyfully told my mother about it as if already looking forward to grandchildren, rejoicing in that sort of inebriation in which the world so often forgets thee, its Creator, and falls in love with thy creature instead of thee—the inebriation of that invisible wine of a perverted will which turns and bows down to infamy. But in my mother's breast thou hadst already begun to build thy temple and the foundation of thy holy habitation—whereas my father was only a catechumen, and that but recently. She was, therefore, startled with a holy fear and trembling: for though I had not yet

been baptized, she feared those crooked ways in which they walk who turn their backs to thee and not their faces.

7. Woe is me! Do I dare affirm that thou didst hold thy peace, O my God, while I wandered farther away from thee? Didst thou really then hold thy peace? Then whose words were they but thine which by my mother, thy faithful handmaid, thou didst pour into my ears? None of them, however, sank into my heart to make me do anything. She deplored and, as I remember, warned me privately with great solicitude, "not to commit fornication; but above all things never to defile another man's wife." These appeared to me but womanish counsels, which I would have blushed to obey. Yet they were from thee, and I knew it not. I thought that thou wast silent and that it was only she who spoke. Yet it was through her that thou didst not keep silence toward me; and in rejecting her counsel I was rejecting thee—I, her son, "the son of thy handmaid, thy servant." But I did not realize this, and rushed on headlong with such blindness that, among my friends, I was ashamed to be less shameless than they, when I heard them boasting of their disgraceful exploits—yes, and glorying all the more the worse their baseness was. What is worse, I took pleasure in such exploits, not for the pleasure's sake only but mostly for praise. What is worthy of vituperation except vice itself? Yet I made myself out worse than I was, in order that I might not go lacking for praise. And when in anything I had not sinned as the worst ones in the group, I would still say that I had done what I had not done, in order not to appear contemptible because I was more innocent than they; and not to drop in their esteem because I was more chaste.

8. Behold with what companions I walked the streets of Babylon! I rolled in its mire and lolled about on it, as if on a bed of spices and precious ointments. And, drawing me more closely to the very center of that city, my invisible enemy trod me down and seduced me, for I was easy to seduce. My mother had already fled out of the midst of Babylon and was progressing, albeit slowly, toward its outskirts. For in counseling me to chastity, she did not bear in mind what her husband had told her about me. And although she knew that my passions were destructive even then and dangerous for the future, she did not think they should be restrained by the bonds of conjugal affection—if, indeed, they could not be cut away to the quick. She took no heed of this, for she was afraid lest a wife should prove a hindrance and a burden to my hopes. These were not her hopes of the world to come, which my mother had in thee, but the hope of learning, which both my parents were too anxious that I should acquire—my father, because he had little or no thought of thee, and only vain thoughts for me; my mother, because she thought that the usual course of study would not only be no hindrance but actually a furtherance toward my eventual return to thee. This much I conjecture, recalling as well as I can the temperaments of my parents. Meantime, the reins of discipline were slackened on me, so that without the restraint of due severity, I might play at whatsoever I fancied, even to the point of dissoluteness. And in all this there was that mist which shut out from my sight the brightness of thy truth, O my God; and my iniquity bulged out, as it were, with fatness!

9. Theft is punished by the law, O Lord, and by the law written in men's hearts, which not even ingrained wickedness can erase. For what thief will tolerate another thief stealing from him? Even a rich thief will not tolerate a poor thief who is driven to theft by want. Yet I had a desire to commit robbery, and did so, compelled to it by neither hunger nor poverty, but through a contempt for well-doing and a strong impulse to iniquity. For I pilfered something which I already had in sufficient measure, and of much better quality. I did not desire to enjoy what I stole, but only the theft and the sin itself.

There was a pear tree close to our own vineyard, heavily laden with fruit, which was not tempting either for its color or for its flavor. Late one night—having prolonged our games in the streets until then, as our bad habit was—a group of young scoundrels, and I among them, went to shake and rob this tree. We carried off a huge load of pears, not to eat ourselves, but to dump out to the hogs, after barely tasting some of them ourselves. Doing this pleased us all the more because it was forbidden. Such was my heart, O God, such was my heart—which thou didst pity even in that bottomless pit. Behold, now let my heart confess to thee what it was seeking there, when I was being gratuitously wanton, having no inducement to evil but the evil itself. It was foul, and I loved it. I loved my own undoing. I loved my error—not that for which I erred but the error itself. A depraved soul, falling away from security in thee to destruction in itself, seeking nothing from the shameful deed but shame itself.

10. Now there is a comeliness in all beautiful bodies, and in gold and silver and all things. The sense of touch has its own power to please and the other senses find their proper objects in physical sensation. Worldly honor also has its own glory, and so do the powers to command and to overcome: and from these there springs up the desire for revenge. Yet, in seeking these pleasures, we must not depart from thee, O Lord, nor deviate from thy law. The life which we live here has its own peculiar attractiveness because it has a certain measure of comeliness of its own and a harmony with all these inferior values. The bond of human friendship has a sweetness of its own, binding many souls together as one. Yet because of these values, sin is committed, because we have an inordinate preference for these goods of a lower order and neglect the better and the higher good—neglecting thee, O our Lord God, and thy truth and thy law. For these inferior values have their delights, but not at all equal to my God, who hath made them all. For in him do the righteous delight and he is the sweetness of the upright in heart.

11. When, therefore, we inquire why a crime was committed, we do not accept the explanation unless it appears that there was the desire to obtain some of those values which we designate inferior, or else a fear of losing them. For truly they are beautiful and comely, though in comparison with the superior and celestial goods they are abject and contemptible. A man has murdered another man—what was his motive? Either he desired his wife or his property or else he would steal to support himself; or else he was afraid of losing something to him; or else, having been injured, he was burning to be revenged. Would a man commit murder without a motive, taking delight simply in the act

of murder? Who would believe such a thing? Even for that savage and brutal man,[1] of whom it was said that he was gratuitously wicked and cruel, there is still a motive assigned to his deeds. "Lest through idleness," he says, "hand or heart should grow inactive." And to what purpose? Why, even this: that, having once got possession of the city through his practice of his wicked ways, he might gain honors, empire, and wealth, and thus be exempt from the fear of the laws and from financial difficulties in supplying the needs of his family—and from the consciousness of his own wickedness. So it seems that even Catiline himself loved not his own villainies, but something else, and it was this that gave him the motive for his crimes.

12. What was it in you, O theft of mine, that I, poor wretch, doted on—you deed of darkness—in that sixteenth year of my age? Beautiful you were not, for you were a theft. But are you anything at all, so that I could analyze the case with you? Those pears that we stole were fair to the sight because they were thy creation, O Beauty beyond compare, O Creator of all, O thou good God—God the highest good and my true good. Those pears were truly pleasant to the sight, but it was not for them that my miserable soul lusted, for I had an abundance of better pears. I stole those simply that I might steal, for, having stolen them, I threw them away. My sole gratification in them was my own sin, which I was pleased to enjoy; for, if any one of these pears entered my mouth, the only good flavour it had was my sin in eating it. And now, O Lord my God, I ask what it was in that theft of mine that caused me such delight; for behold it had no beauty of its own—certainly not the sort of beauty that exists in justice and wisdom, nor such as is in the mind, memory senses, and the animal life of man; nor yet the kind that is the glory and beauty of the stars in their courses; nor the beauty of the earth, or the sea—teeming with spawning life, replacing in birth that which dies and decays. Indeed, it did not have that false and shadowy beauty which attends the deceptions of vice.

13. For thus we see pride wearing the mask of high-spiritedness, although only thou, O God, art high above all. Ambition seeks honor and glory, whereas only thou shouldst be honored above all, and glorified forever. The powerful man seeks to be feared, because of his cruelty; but who ought really to be feared but God only? What can be forced away or withdrawn out of his power—when or where or whither or by whom? The enticements of the wanton claim the name of love; and yet nothing is more enticing than thy love, nor is anything loved more healthfully than thy truth, bright and beautiful above all. Curiosity prompts a desire for knowledge, whereas it is only thou who knowest all things supremely. Indeed, ignorance and foolishness themselves go masked under the names of simplicity and innocence; yet there is no being that has true simplicity like thine, and none is innocent as thou art. Thus it is that by a sinner's own deeds he is himself harmed. Human sloth pretends to long for rest, but what sure rest is there save in the Lord? Luxury would fain be called plenty and abundance; but thou art the fullness and unfailing abundance of unfading joy. Prodigality pre-

---

[1]Catiline, a Roman politician who led a conspiracy to overthrow the Roman Republic in 63 B.C.

sents a show of liberality; but thou art the most lavish giver of all good things. Covetousness desires to possess much; but thou art already the possessor of all things. Envy contends that its aim is for excellence; but what is so excellent as thou? Anger seeks revenge; but who avenges more justly than thou? Fear recoils at the unfamiliar and the sudden changes which threaten things beloved, and is wary for its own security; but what can happen that is unfamiliar or sudden to thee? Or who can deprive thee of what thou lovest? Where, really, is there unshaken security save with thee? Grief languishes for things lost in which desire had taken delight, because it wills to have nothing taken from it, just as nothing can be taken from thee.

14. Thus the soul commits fornication when she is turned from thee, and seeks apart from thee what she cannot find pure and untainted until she returns to thee. All things thus imitate thee—but pervertedly—when they separate themselves far from thee and raise themselves up against thee. But, even in this act of perverse imitation, they acknowledge thee to be the Creator of all nature, and recognize that there is no place whither they can altogether separate themselves from thee. What was it, then, that I loved in that theft? And wherein was I imitating my Lord, even in a corrupted and perverted way? Did I wish, if only by gesture, to rebel against thy law, even though I had no power to do so actually—so that, even as a captive, I might produce a sort of counterfeit liberty, by doing with impunity deeds that were forbidden, in a deluded sense of omnipotence? Behold this servant of thine, fleeing from his Lord and following a shadow! O rottenness! O monstrousness of life and abyss of death! Could I find pleasure only in what was unlawful, and only because it was unlawful?

15. "What shall I render unto the Lord" for the fact that while my memory recalls these things my soul no longer fears them? I will love thee, O Lord, and thank thee, and confess to thy name, because thou hast put away from me such wicked and evil deeds. To thy grace I attribute it and to thy mercy, that thou hast melted away my sin as if it were ice. To thy grace also I attribute whatsoever of evil I did *not* commit—for what might I not have done, loving sin as I did, just for the sake of sinning? Yea, all the sins that I confess now to have been forgiven me, both those which I committed willfully and those which, by thy providence, I did not commit. What man is there who, when reflecting upon his own infirmity, dares to ascribe his chastity and innocence to his own powers, so that he should love thee less—as if he were in less need of thy mercy in which thou forgivest the transgressions of those that return to thee? As for that man who, when called by thee, obeyed thy voice and shunned those things which he here reads of me as I recall and confess them of myself, let him not despise me—for I, who was sick, have been healed by the same Physician by whose aid it was that he did not fall sick, or rather was less sick than I. And for this let him love thee just as much—indeed, all the more—since he sees me restored from such a great weakness of sin by the selfsame Saviour by whom he sees himself preserved from such a weakness.

16. What profit did I, a wretched one, receive from those things which, when I remember them now, cause me shame—above all, from that

theft, which I loved only for the theft's sake? And, as the theft itself was nothing, I was all the more wretched in that I loved it so. Yet by myself alone I would not have done it—I still recall how I felt about this then—I could not have done it alone. I loved it then because of the companionship of my accomplices with whom I did it. I did not, therefore, love the theft alone—yet, indeed, it was only the theft that I loved, for the companionship was nothing. What is this paradox? Who is it that can explain it to me but God, who illumines my heart and searches out the dark corners thereof? What is it that has prompted my mind to inquire about it, to discuss and to reflect upon all this? For had I at that time loved the pears that I stole and wished to enjoy them, I might have done so alone, if I could have been satisfied with the mere act of theft by which my pleasure was served. Nor did I need to have that itching of my own passions inflamed by the encouragement of my accomplices. But since the pleasure I got was not from the pears, it was in the crime itself, enhanced by the companionship of my fellow sinners.

17. By what passion, then, was I animated? It was undoubtedly depraved and a great misfortune for me to feel it. But still, what was it? "Who can understand his errors?"

We laughed because our hearts were tickled at the thought of deceiving the owners, who had no idea of what we were doing and would have strenuously objected. Yet, again, why did I find such delight in doing this which I would not have done alone? Is it that no one readily laughs alone? No one does so readily; but still sometimes, when men are by themselves and no one else is about, a fit of laughter will overcome them when something very droll presents itself to their sense or mind. Yet alone I would not have done it—alone I could not have done it at all.

Behold, my God, the lively review of my soul's career is laid bare before thee. I would not have committed that theft alone. My pleasure in it was not what I stole but, rather, the act of stealing. Nor would I have enjoyed doing it alone—indeed I would not have done it! O friendship all unfriendly! You strange seducer of the soul, who hungers for mischief from impulses of mirth and wantonness, who craves another's loss without any desire for one's own profit or revenge—so that, when they say, "Let's go, let's do it," we are ashamed not to be shameless.

18. Who can unravel such a twisted and tangled knottiness? It is unclean. I hate to reflect upon it. I hate to look on it. But I do long for thee, O Righteousness and Innocence, so beautiful and comely to all virtuous eyes—I long for thee with an insatiable satiety. With thee is perfect rest, and life unchanging. He who enters into thee enters into the joy of his Lord, and shall have no fear and shall achieve excellence in the Excellent. I fell away from thee, O my God, and in my youth I wandered too far from thee, my true support. And I became to myself a wasteland.

Book VIII

1. O my God, let me remember with gratitude and confess to thee thy mercies toward me. Let my bones be bathed in thy love, and let

them say: "Lord, who is like unto thee? Thou hast broken my bonds in sunder, I will offer unto thee the sacrifice of thanksgiving." And how thou didst break them I will declare, and all who worship thee shall say, when they hear these things: "Blessed be the Lord in heaven and earth, great and wonderful is his name."

Thy words had stuck fast in my breast, and I was hedged round about by thee on every side. Of thy eternal life I was now certain, although I had seen it "through a glass darkly." And I had been relieved of all doubt that there is an incorruptible substance and that it is the source of every other substance. Nor did I any longer crave greater certainty about thee, but rather greater steadfastness in thee.

But as for my temporal life, everything was uncertain, and my heart had to be purged of the old leaven. "The Way"—the Saviour himself —pleased me well, but as yet I was reluctant to pass through the strait gate.

And thou didst put it into my mind, and it seemed good in my own sight, to go to Simplicianus,[2] who appeared to me a faithful servant of thine, and thy grace shone forth in him. I had also been told that from his youth up he had lived in entire devotion to thee. He was already an old man, and because of his great age, which he had passed in such a zealous discipleship in thy way, he appeared to me likely to have gained much wisdom—and, indeed, he had. From all his experience, I desired him to tell me—setting before him all my agitations—which would be the most fitting way for one who felt as I did to walk in thy way.

2. For I saw the Church full; and one man was going this way and another that. Still, I could not be satisfied with the life I was living in the world. Now, indeed, my passions had ceased to excite me as of old with hopes of honor and wealth, and it was a grievous burden to go on in such servitude. For, compared with thy sweetness and the beauty of thy house—which I loved—those things delighted me no longer. But I was still tightly bound by the love of women; nor did the apostle forbid me to marry, although he exhorted me to something better, wishing earnestly that all men were as he himself was.[3]

But I was weak and chose the easier way, and for this single reason my whole life was one of inner turbulence and listless indecision, because from so many influences I was compelled—even though unwilling—to agree to a married life which bound me hand and foot.[4] I had heard from the mouth of Truth that "there are eunuchs who have made themselves eunuchs for the Kingdom of Heaven's sake" but, said he, "He that is able to receive it, let him receive it." Of a certainty, all men are vain who do not have the knowledge of God, or have not been able, from the good things that are seen, to find him who is good. But I was no longer fettered in that vanity. I had surmounted it, and from the united testimony of thy whole creation had found thee, our Creator, and thy Word—God with thee, and together with thee and the Holy

---

[2]At the time, adviser to Ambrose, Bishop of Milan; later, Bishop of Milan himself.

[3]St. Paul, I Corinthians 7:7.

[4]St. Augustine's mother had followed him to Milan and had busied herself arranging a suitable marriage for him to a young girl of wealthy family. The marriage was supposed to have taken place two years later, when his fiancée reached marriageable age.

Spirit, one God—by whom thou hast created all things. There is still another sort of wicked men, who "when they knew God, they glorified him not as God, neither were thankful." Into this also I had fallen, but thy right hand held me up and bore me away, and thou didst place me where I might recover. For thou hast said to men, "Behold the fear of the Lord, this is wisdom," and, "Be not wise in your own eyes," because "they that profess themselves to be wise become fools." But I had now found the goodly pearl; and I ought to have sold all that I had and bought it—yet I hesitated.

3. I went, therefore, to Simplicianus, the spiritual father of Ambrose (then a bishop), whom Ambrose truly loved as a father. I recounted to him all the mazes of my wanderings, but when I mentioned to him that I had read certain books of the Platonists which Victorinus—formerly professor of rhetoric at Rome, who died a Christian, as I had been told—had translated into Latin, Simplicianus congratulated me that I had not fallen upon the writings of other philosophers, which were full of fallacies and deceit, "after the beggarly elements of this world," whereas in the Platonists, at every turn, the pathway led to belief in God and his Word.

Then, to encourage me to copy the humility of Christ, which is hidden from the wise and revealed to babes, he told me about Victorinus himself, whom he had known intimately at Rome.

[Augustine repeats the story of the conversion of Victorinus, an influential Roman scholar and statesman. He had been a pagan until an advanced age, became secretly sympathetic to Christianity through his own study, and finally made a public confession of his faith. The story leads Augustine to rejoice in the value to God of a lost soul which is "found."]

10. Now when this man of thine, Simplicianus, told me the story of Victorinus, I was eager to imitate him. Indeed, this was Simplicianus' purpose in telling it to me. But when he went on to tell how, in the reign of the Emperor Julian, there was a law passed by which Christians were forbidden to teach literature and rhetoric; and how Victorinus, in ready obedience to the law, chose to abandon his "school of words" rather than thy Word, by which thou makest eloquent the tongues of the dumb —he appeared to me not so much brave as happy, because he had found a reason for giving his time wholly to thee. For this was what I was longing to do; but as yet I was bound by the iron chain of my own will. The enemy held fast my will, and had made of it a chain, and had bound me tight with it. For out of the perverse will came lust, and the service of lust ended in habit, and habit, not resisted, became necessity. By these links, as it were, forged together—which is why I called it "a chain" —a hard bondage held me in slavery. But that new will which had begun to spring up in me freely to worship thee and to enjoy thee, O my God, the only certain Joy, was not able as yet to overcome my former willfulness, made strong by long indulgence. Thus my two wills—the old and the new, the carnal and the spiritual—were in conflict within me; and by their discord they tore my soul apart.

11. Thus I came to understand from my own experience what I had read, how "the flesh lusts against the Spirit, and the Spirit against the flesh." I truly lusted both ways, yet more in that which I approved in myself than in that which I disapproved in myself. For in the latter it was not now really I that was involved, because here I was rather an unwilling sufferer than a willing actor. And yet it was through me that habit had become an armed enemy against me, because I had willingly come to be what I unwillingly found myself to be.

Who, then, can with any justice speak against it, when just punishment follows the sinner? I had now no longer my accustomed excuse that, as yet, I hesitated to forsake the world and serve thee because my perception of the truth was uncertain. For now it was certain. But, still bound to the earth, I refused to be thy soldier; and was as much afraid of being freed from all entanglements as we ought to fear to be entangled.

12. Thus with the baggage of the world I was sweetly burdened, as one in slumber, and my musings on thee were like the efforts of those who desire to awake, but who are still overpowered with drowsiness and fall back into deep slumber. And as no one wishes to sleep forever (for all men rightly count waking better)—yet a man will usually defer shaking off his drowsiness when there is a heavy lethargy in his limbs; and he is glad to sleep on even when his reason disapproves, and the hour for rising has struck—so was I assured that it was much better for me to give myself up to thy love than to go on yielding myself to my own lust. Thy love satisfied and vanquished me; my lust pleased and fettered me. I had no answer to thy calling to me, "Awake, you who sleep, and arise from the dead, and Christ shall give you light." On all sides, thou didst show me that thy words are true, and I, convicted by the truth, had nothing at all to reply but the drawling and drowsy words: "Presently; see, presently. Leave me alone a little while." But "presently, presently," had no present; and my "leave me alone a little while" went on for a long while. In vain did I "delight in thy law in the inner man" while "another law in my members warred against the law of my mind and brought me into captivity to the law of sin which is in my members." For the law of sin is the tyranny of habit, by which the mind is drawn and held, even against its will. Yet it deserves to be so held because it so willingly falls into the habit. "O wretched man that I am! Who shall deliver me from the body of this death" but thy grace alone, through Jesus Christ our Lord?

13. And now I will tell and confess unto thy name, O Lord, my helper and my redeemer, how thou didst deliver me from the chain of sexual desire by which I was so tightly held, and from the slavery of worldly business. With increasing anxiety I was going about my usual affairs, and daily sighing to thee. I attended thy church as frequently as my business, under the burden of which I groaned, left me free to do so. Alypius[5] was with me, disengaged at last from his legal post, after a third term as assessor, and now waiting for private clients to whom he might sell his legal advice as I sold the power of speaking (as if it could be supplied

---

[5]A friend of Augustine's since his boyhood in Tagaste who had joined him in Milan.

by teaching). But Nebridius[6] had consented, for the sake of our friendship, to teach under Verecundus—a citizen of Milan and professor of grammar, and a very intimate friend of us all—who ardently desired, and by right of friendship demanded from us, the faithful aid he greatly needed. Nebridius was not drawn to this by any desire of gain—for he could have made much more out of his learning had he been so inclined —but as he was a most sweet and kindly friend, he was unwilling, out of respect for the duties of friendship, to slight our request. But in this he acted very discreetly, taking care not to become known to those persons who had great reputations in the world. Thus he avoided all distractions of mind, and reserved as many hours as possible to pursue or read or listen to discussions about wisdom.

[Augustine repeats a story told to him by a friend, Ponticianus, about the conversion of several officers in the emperor's court. They were converted suddenly and totally upon the reading of the life of Anthony (the first Christian monk, c. 250 – 350).]

16. Such was the story Ponticianus told. But while he was speaking, thou, O Lord, turned me toward myself, taking me from behind my back, where I had put myself while unwilling to exercise self-scrutiny. And now thou didst set me face to face with myself, that I might see how ugly I was, and how crooked and sordid, bespotted and ulcerous. And I looked and I loathed myself; but whither to fly from myself I could not discover. And if I sought to turn my gaze away from myself, he would continue his narrative, and thou wouldst oppose me to myself and thrust me before my own eyes that I might discover my iniquity and hate it. I had known it, but acted as though I knew it not—I winked at it and forgot it.

17. But now, the more ardently I loved those whose wholesome affections I heard reported—that they had given themselves up wholly to thee to be cured—the more did I abhor myself when compared with them. For many of my years—perhaps twelve—had passed away since my nineteenth, when, upon the reading of Cicero's *Hortensius*,[7] I was roused to a desire for wisdom. And here I was, still postponing the abandonment of this world's happiness to devote myself to the search. For not just the finding alone, but also the bare search for it, ought to have been preferred above the treasures and kingdoms of this world; better than all bodily pleasures, though they were to be had for the taking. But, wretched youth that I was—supremely wretched even in the very outset of my youth—I had entreated chastity of thee and had prayed, "Grant me chastity and continence, but not yet." For I was afraid lest thou shouldst hear me too soon, and too soon cure me of my disease of lust which I desired to have satisfied rather than extinguished. And I had wandered through perverse ways of godless superstition—not really sure of it, either, but preferring it to the other, which I did not seek in piety, but opposed in malice.

18. And I had thought that I delayed from day to day in rejecting

---

[6]Another boyhood friend of Augustine's who had joined him in Milan.
[7]A treatise no longer extant, in praise of the study of philosophy.

those worldly hopes and following thee alone because there did not appear anything certain by which I could direct my course. And now the day had arrived in which I was laid bare to myself and my conscience was to chide me: "Where are you, O my tongue? You said indeed that you were not willing to cast off the baggage of vanity for uncertain truth. But behold now it is certain, and still that burden oppresses you. At the same time those who have not worn themselves out with searching for it as you have, nor spent ten years and more in thinking about it, have had their shoulders unburdened and have received wings to fly away." Thus was I inwardly confused, and mightily confounded with a horrible shame, while Ponticianus went ahead speaking such things. And when he had finished his story and the business he came for, he went his way. And then what did I not say to myself, within myself? With what scourges of rebuke did I not lash my soul to make it follow me, as I was struggling to go after thee? Yet it drew back. It refused. It would not make an effort. All its arguments were exhausted and confuted. Yet it resisted in sullen disquiet, fearing the cutting off of that habit by which it was being wasted to death, as if that were death itself.

19. Then, as this vehement quarrel, which I waged with my soul in the chamber of my heart, was raging inside my inner dwelling, agitated both in mind and countenance, I seized upon Alypius and exclaimed: "What is the matter with us? What is this? What did you hear? The uninstructed start up and take heaven, and we—with all our learning but so little heart—see where we wallow in flesh and blood! Because others have gone before us, are we ashamed to follow, and not rather ashamed at our not following?" I scarcely knew what I said, and in my excitement I flung away from him, while he gazed at me in silent astonishment. For I did not sound like myself: my face, eyes, color, tone expressed my meaning more clearly than my words.

There was a little garden belonging to our lodging, of which we had the use—as of the whole house—for the master, our landlord, did not live there. The tempest in my breast hurried me out into this garden, where no one might interrupt the fiery struggle in which I was engaged with myself, until it came to the outcome that thou knewest though I did not. But I was mad for health, and dying for life; knowing what evil thing I was, but not knowing what good thing I was so shortly to become.

I fled into the garden, with Alypius following step by step; for I had no secret in which he did not share, and how could he leave me in such distress? We sat down, as far from the house as possible. I was greatly disturbed in spirit, angry at myself with a turbulent indignation because I had not entered thy will and covenant, O my God, while all my bones cried out to me to enter, extolling it to the skies. The way therein is not by ships or chariots or feet—indeed it was not as far as I had come from the house to the place where we were seated. For to go along that road and indeed to reach the goal is nothing else but the will to go. But it must be a strong and single will, not staggering and swaying about this way and that—a changeable, twisting, fluctuating will, wrestling with itself while one part falls as another rises.

20. Finally, in the very fever of my indecision, I made many motions

with my body; like men do when they will to act but cannot, either because they do not have the limbs or because their limbs are bound or weakened by disease, or incapacitated in some other way. Thus if I tore my hair, struck my forehead, or, entwining my fingers, clasped my knee, these I did because I willed it. But I might have willed it and still not have done it, if the nerves had not obeyed my will. Many things then I did, in which the will and power to do were not the same. Yet I did not do that one thing which seemed to me infinitely more desirable, which before long I should have power to will because shortly when I willed, I would will with a single will. For in this, the power of willing is the power of doing; and as yet I could not do it. Thus my body more readily obeyed the slightest wish of the soul in moving its limbs at the order of my mind than my soul obeyed itself to accomplish in the will alone its great resolve.

21. How can there be such a strange anomaly? And why is it? Let thy mercy shine on me, that I may inquire and find an answer, amid the dark labyrinth of human punishment and in the darkest contritions of the sons of Adam. Whence such an anomaly? And why should it be? The mind commands the body, and the body obeys. The mind commands itself and is resisted. The mind commands the hand to be moved and there is such readiness that the command is scarcely distinguished from the obedience in act. Yet the mind is mind, and the hand is body. The mind commands the mind to will, and yet though it be itself it does not obey itself. Whence this strange anomaly and why should it be? I repeat: The will commands itself to will, and could not give the command unless it wills; yet what is commanded is not done. But actually the will does not will entirely; therefore it does not command entirely. For as far as it wills, it commands. And as far as it does not will, the thing commanded is not done. For the will commands that there be an act of will—not another, but itself. But it does not command entirely. Therefore, what is commanded does not happen; for if the will were whole and entire, it would not even command it to be, because it would already be. It is, therefore, no strange anomaly partly to will and partly to be unwilling. This is actually an infirmity of mind, which cannot wholly rise, while pressed down by habit, even though it is supported by the truth. And so there are two wills, because one of them is not whole, and what is present in this one is lacking in the other.

22. Let them perish from thy presence, O God, as vain talkers and deceivers of the soul perish, who, when they observe that there are two wills in the act of deliberation, go on to affirm that there are two kinds of minds in us: one good, the other evil.[8] They are indeed themselves evil when they hold these evil opinions—and they shall become good only when they come to hold the truth and consent to the truth that

---

[8]St. Augustine is attacking the Manicheans, members of a sect founded by a Persian named Manichee in the middle of the third century. Manichee had attempted to create a religion which would include the truths of all previous religions, including Christianity. Manicheism preached a severely ascetic life, and many Christians were influenced by it. But it adopted as its central principle the characteristically Persian idea that good and evil are distinct entities, the result of two gods, one good, one evil, struggling to rule the universe, with man as their battleground. The Church naturally considered Manicheism a dangerous heresy. Augustine, however, in his younger days, had been strongly attracted by the idea as an explanation of the mixture of good and evil in man's make-up.

thy apostle may say to them: "You were formerly in darkness, but now are you in the light in the Lord." But they desired to be light, not "in the Lord," but in themselves. They conceived the nature of the soul to be the same as what God is, and thus have become a thicker darkness than they were; for in their dread arrogance they have gone farther away from thee, from thee "the true Light, that lights every man that comes into the world." Mark what you say and blush for shame; draw near to him and be enlightened, and your faces shall not be ashamed.

While I was deliberating whether I would serve the Lord my God now, as I had long purposed to do, it was I who willed and it was also I who was unwilling. In either case, it was I. I neither willed with my whole will nor was I wholly unwilling. And so I was at war with myself and torn apart by myself. And this strife was against my will; yet it did not show the presence of another mind, but the punishment of my own. Thus it was no more I who did it, but the sin that dwelt in me—the punishment of a sin freely committed by Adam, and I was a son of Adam.

23. For if there are as many opposing natures as there are opposing wills, there will not be two but many more. If any man is trying to decide whether he should go to their conventicle or to the theater, the Manicheans at once cry out, "See, here are two natures—one good, drawing this way, another bad, drawing back that way; for how else can you explain this indecision between conflicting wills?" But I reply that both impulses are bad—that which draws to them and that which draws back to the theater. But they do not believe that the will which draws to them can be anything but good. Suppose, then, that one of us should try to decide, and through the conflict of his two wills should waver whether he should go to the theater or to our church. Would not those also waver about the answer here? For either they must confess, which they are unwilling to do, that the will that leads to our church is as good as that which carries their own adherents and those captivated by their mysteries; or else they must imagine that there are two evil natures and two evil minds in one man, both at war with each other, and then it will not be true what they say, that there is one good and another bad. Else they must be converted to the truth, and no longer deny that when anyone deliberates there is one soul fluctuating between conflicting wills.

24. Let them no longer maintain that when they perceive two wills to be contending with each other in the same man the contest is between two opposing minds, of two opposing substances, from two opposing principles, the one good and the other bad. Thus, O true God, thou dost reprove and confute and convict them. For both wills may be bad: as when a man tries to decide whether he should kill a man by poison or by the sword; whether he should take possession of this field or that one belonging to someone else, when he cannot get both; whether he should squander his money to buy pleasure or hold onto his money through the motive of covetousness; whether he should go to the circus or to the theater, if both are open on the same day; or, whether he should take a third course, open at the same time, and rob another man's house; or, a fourth option, whether he should commit adultery, if he has the opportunity—all these things concurring in the

same space of time and all being equally longed for, although impossible to do at one time. For the mind is pulled four ways by four antagonistic wills—or even more, in view of the vast range of human desires—but even the Manicheans do not affirm that there are these many different substances. The same principle applies as in the action of good wills. For I ask them, "Is it a good thing to have delight in reading the apostle, or is it a good thing to delight in a sober psalm, or is it a good thing to discourse on the gospel?" To each of these, they will answer, "It is good." But what, then, if all delight us equally and all at the same time? Do not different wills distract the mind when a man is trying to decide what he should choose? Yet they are all good, and are at variance with each other until one is chosen. When this is done the whole united will may go forward on a single track instead of remaining as it was before, divided in many ways. So also, when eternity attracts us from above, and the pleasure of earthly delight pulls us down from below, the soul does not will either the one or the other with all its force, but still it is the same soul that does not will this or that with a united will, and is therefore pulled apart with grievous perplexities, because for truth's sake it prefers this, but for custom's sake it does not lay that aside.

25. Thus I was sick and tormented, reproaching myself more bitterly than ever, rolling and writhing in my chain till it should be utterly broken. By now I was held but slightly, but still was held. And thou, O Lord, didst press upon me in my inmost heart with a severe mercy, redoubling the lashes of fear and shame; lest I should again give way and that same slender remaining tie not be broken off, but recover strength and enchain me yet more securely.

I kept saying to myself, "See, let it be done now; let it be done now." And as I said this I all but came to a firm decision. I all but did it—yet I did not quite. Still I did not fall back to my old condition, but stood aside for a moment and drew breath. And I tried again, and lacked only a very little of reaching the resolve—and then somewhat less, and then all but touched and grasped it. Yet I still did not quite reach or touch or grasp the goal, because I hesitated to die to death and to live to life. And the worse way, to which I was habituated, was stronger in me than the better, which I had not tried. And up to the very moment in which I was to become another man, the nearer the moment approached, the greater horror did it strike in me. But it did not strike me back, nor turn me aside, but held me in suspense.

26. It was, in fact, my old mistresses, trifles of trifles and vanities of vanities, who still enthralled me. They tugged at my fleshly garments and softly whispered: "Are you going to part with us? And from that moment will we never be with you any more? And from that moment will not this and that be forbidden you forever?" What were they suggesting to me in those words "this or that"? What is it they suggested, O my God? Let thy mercy guard the soul of thy servant from the vileness and the shame they did suggest! And now I scarcely heard them, for they were not openly showing themselves and opposing me face to face; but muttering, as it were, behind my back; and furtively plucking at me as I was leaving, trying to make me look back at them. Still they delayed me, so that I hesitated to break loose and shake myself free of

them and leap over to the place to which I was being called—for unruly habit kept saying to me, "Do you think you can live without them?"

27. But now it said this very faintly; for in the direction I had set my face, and yet toward which I still trembled to go, the chaste dignity of continence appeared to me—cheerful but not wanton, modestly alluring me to come and doubt nothing, extending her holy hands, full of a multitude of good examples—to receive and embrace me. There were there so many young men and maidens, a multitude of youth and every age, grave widows and ancient virgins; and continence herself in their midst: not barren, but a fruitful mother of children—her joys—by thee, O Lord, her husband. And she smiled on me with a challenging smile as if to say: "Can you not do what these young men and maidens can? Or can any of them do it of themselves, and not rather in the Lord their God? The Lord their God gave me to them. Why do you stand in your own strength, and so stand not? Cast yourself on him; fear not. He will not flinch and you will not fall. Cast yourself on him without fear, for he will receive and heal you." And I blushed violently, for I still heard the muttering of those "trifles" and hung suspended. Again she seemed to speak: "Stop your ears against those unclean members of yours, that they may be mortified. They tell you of delights, but not according to the law of the Lord thy God." This struggle raging in my heart was nothing but the contest of self against self. And Alypius kept close beside me, and awaited in silence the outcome of my extraordinary agitation.

28. Now when deep reflection had drawn up out of the secret depths of my soul all my misery and had heaped it up before the sight of my heart, there arose a mighty storm, accompanied by a mighty rain of tears. That I might give way fully to my tears and lamentations, I stole away from Alypius, for it seemed to me that solitude was more appropriate for the business of weeping. I went far enough away that I could feel that even his presence was no restraint upon me. This was the way I felt at the time, and he realized it. I suppose I had said something before I started up and he noticed that the sound of my voice was choked with weeping. And so he stayed alone, where we had been sitting together, greatly astonished. I flung myself down under a fig tree—how I know not—and gave free course to my tears. The streams of my eyes gushed out an acceptable sacrifice to thee. And, not indeed in these words, but to this effect, I cried to thee: "And thou, O Lord, how long? How long, O Lord? Wilt thou be angry forever? Oh, remember not against us our former iniquities." For I felt that I was still enthralled by them. I sent up these sorrowful cries: "How long, how long? Tomorrow and tomorrow? Why not now? Why not this very hour make an end to my uncleanness?"

29. I was saying these things and weeping in the most bitter contrition of my heart, when suddenly I heard the voice of a boy or a girl—I know not which—coming from the neighboring house, chanting over and over again, "Pick it up, read it; pick it up, read it." Immediately I ceased weeping and began most earnestly to think whether it was usual for children in some kind of game to sing such a song, but I could not remember ever having heard the like. So, damming the torrent of my tears,

I got to my feet, for I could not but think that this was a divine command to open the Bible and read the first passage I should light upon. For I had heard how Anthony, accidentally coming into church while the gospel was being read, received the admonition as if what was read had been addressed to him: "Go and sell what you have and give it to the poor, and you shall have treasure in heaven; and come and follow me." By such an oracle he was forthwith converted to thee.

So I quickly returned to the bench where Alypius was sitting, for there I had put down the apostle's book when I had left there. I snatched it up, opened it, and in silence read the paragraph on which my eyes first fell: "Not in rioting and drunkenness, not in chambering and wantonness, not in strife and envying, but put on the Lord Jesus Christ, and make no provision for the flesh to fulfill the lusts thereof." I wanted to read no further, nor did I need to. For instantly, as the sentence ended, there was infused in my heart something like the light of full certainty and all the gloom of doubt vanished away.

30. Closing the book, then, and putting my finger or something else for a mark I began—now with a tranquil countenance—to tell it all to Alypius. And he in turn disclosed to me what had been going on in himself, of which I knew nothing. He asked to see what I had read. I showed him, and he looked on even further than I had read. I had not known what followed. But indeed it was this, "Him that is weak in the faith, receive." This he applied to himself, and told me so. By these words of warning he was strengthened, and by exercising his good resolution and purpose—all very much in keeping with his character, in which, in these respects, he was always far different from and better than I—he joined me in full commitment without any restless hesitation.

Then we went in to my mother, and told her what happened, to her great joy. We explained to her how it had occurred—and she leaped for joy triumphant; and she blessed thee, who art "able to do exceedingly abundantly above all that we ask or think." For she saw that thou hadst granted her far more than she had ever asked for in all her pitiful and doleful lamentations. For thou didst so convert me to thee that I sought neither a wife nor any other of this world's hopes, but set my feet on that rule of faith which so many years before thou hadst showed her in her dream about me. And so thou didst turn her grief into gladness more plentiful than she had ventured to desire, and dearer and purer than the desire she used to cherish of having grandchildren of my flesh.

[After concluding the autobiographical portion of the *Confessions* in the ninth book, St. Augustine devotes the last four books to examining the processes by which his experiences have come to have meaning for him. The results are profound analyses of the nature of memory, time, and creation itself. The following selection illustrates the kind of thinking he brings to these subjects.]

Book X

11. What is it, then, that I love when I love my God? Who is he that is beyond the topmost point of my soul? Yet by this very soul will I mount

up to him. I will soar beyond that power of mine by which I am united to the body, and by which the whole structure of it is filled with life. Yet it is not by that vital power that I find my God. For then "the horse and the mule, that have no understanding," also might find him, since they have the same vital power, by which their bodies also live. But there is, besides the power by which I animate my body, another by which I endow my flesh with sense—a power that the Lord hath provided for me; commanding that the eye is not to hear and the ear is not to see, but that I am to see by the eye and to hear by the ear; and giving to each of the other senses its own proper place and function, through the diversity of which I, the single mind, act. I will soar also beyond this power of mine, for the horse and mule have this too, for they also perceive through their bodily senses.

12. I will soar, then, beyond this power of my nature also, still rising by degrees toward him who made me. And I enter the fields and spacious halls of memory, where are stored as treasures the countless images that have been brought into them from all manner of things by the senses. There, in the memory, is likewise stored what we cogitate, either by enlarging or reducing our perceptions, or by altering one way or another those things which the senses have made contact with; and everything else that has been entrusted to it and stored up in it, which oblivion has not yet swallowed up and buried.

When I go into this storehouse, I ask that what I want should be brought forth. Some things appear immediately, but others require to be searched for longer, and then dragged out, as it were, from some hidden recess. Other things hurry forth in crowds, on the other hand, and while something else is sought and inquired for, they leap into view as if to say, "Is it not we, perhaps?" These I brush away with the hand of my heart from the face of my memory, until finally the thing I want makes its appearance out of its secret cell. Some things suggest themselves without effort, and in continuous order, just as they are called for—the things that come first give place to those that follow, and in so doing are treasured up again to be forthcoming when I want them. All of this happens when I repeat a thing from memory.

13. All these things, each one of which came into memory in its own particular way, are stored up separately and under the general categories of understanding. For example, light and all colors and forms of bodies came in through the eyes; sounds of all kinds by the ears; all smells by the passages of the nostrils; all flavors by the gate of the mouth; by the sensation of the whole body, there is brought in what is hard or soft, hot or cold, smooth or rough, heavy or light, whether external or internal to the body. The vast cave of memory, with its numerous and mysterious recesses, receives all these things and stores them up, to be recalled and brought forth when required. Each experience enters by its own door, and is stored up in the memory. And yet the things themselves do not enter it, but only the images of the things perceived are there for thought to remember. And who can tell how these images are formed, even if it is evident which of the senses brought which perception in and stored it up? For even when I am in darkness and silence I can bring out colors in my memory if I wish, and discern between black and white and the other shades as I wish; and at the same

time, sounds do not break in and disturb what is drawn in by my eyes, and which I am considering, because the sounds which are also there are stored up, as it were, apart. And these too I can summon if I please and they are immediately present in memory. And though my tongue is at rest and my throat silent, yet I can sing as I will; and those images of color, which are as truly present as before, do not interpose themselves or interrupt while another treasure which had flowed in through the ears is being thought about. Similarly all the other things that were brought in and heaped up by all the other senses, I can recall at my pleasure. And I distinguish the scent of lilies from that of violets while actually smelling nothing; and I prefer honey to mead, a smooth thing to a rough, even though I am neither tasting nor handling them, but only remembering them.

14. All this I do within myself, in that huge hall of my memory. For in it, heaven, earth, and sea are present to me, and whatever I can cogitate about them—except what I have forgotten. There also I meet myself and recall myself—what, when, or where I did a thing, and how I felt when I did it. There are all the things that I remember, either having experienced them myself or been told about them by others. Out of the same storehouse, with these past impressions, I can construct now this, now that, image of things that I either have experienced or have believed on the basis of experience—and from these I can further construct future actions, events, and hopes; and I can meditate on all these things as if they were present. "I will do this or that"—I say to myself in that vast recess of my mind, with its full store of so many and such great images—"and this or that will follow upon it." "O that this or that could happen!" "God prevent this or that." I speak to myself in this way; and when I speak, the images of what I am speaking about are present out of the same store of memory; and if the images were absent I could say nothing at all about them.

15. Great is this power of memory, exceedingly great, O my God —a large and boundless inner hall! Who has plumbed the depths of it? Yet it is a power of my mind, and it belongs to my nature. But I do not myself grasp all that I am. Thus the mind is far too narrow to contain itself. But where can that part of it be which it does not contain? Is it outside and not in itself? How can it be, then, that the mind cannot grasp itself? A great marvel rises in me; astonishment seizes me. Men go forth to marvel at the heights of mountains and the huge waves of the sea, the broad flow of the rivers, the vastness of the ocean, the orbits of the stars, and yet they neglect to marvel at themselves. Nor do they wonder how it is that, when I spoke of all these things, I was not looking at them with my eyes—and yet I could not have spoken about them had it not been that I was actually seeing within, in my memory, those mountains and waves and rivers and stars which I have seen, and that ocean which I believe in—and with the same vast spaces between them as when I saw them outside me. But when I saw them outside me, I did not take them into me by seeing them; and the things themselves are not inside me, but only their images. And yet I knew through which physical sense each experience had made an impression on me.

16. And yet this is not all that the unlimited capacity of my memory

stores up. In memory, there are also all that one has learned of the liberal sciences, and has not forgotten—removed still further, so to say, into an inner place which is not a place. Of these things it is not the images that are retained, but the things themselves. For what literature and logic are, and what I know about how many different kinds of questions there are—all these are stored in my memory as they are, so that I have not taken in the image and left the thing outside. It is not as though a sound had sounded and passed away like a voice heard by the ear which leaves a trace by which it can be called into memory again, as if it were still sounding in mind while it did so no longer outside. Nor is it the same as an odor which, even after it has passed and vanished into the wind, affects the sense of smell—which then conveys into the memory the *image* of the smell which is what we recall and re-create; or like food which, once in the belly, surely now has no taste and yet does have a kind of taste in the memory; or like anything that is felt by the body through the sense of touch, which still remains as an image in the memory after the external object is removed. For these things themselves are not put into the memory. Only the images of them are gathered with a marvelous quickness and stored, as it were, in the most wonderful filing system, and are thence produced in a marvelous way by the act of remembering.

17. But now when I hear that there are three kinds of questions— "Whether a thing is? What it is? Of what kind it is?"—I do indeed retain the images of the sounds of which these words are composed and I know that those sounds pass through the air with a noise and now no longer exist. But the things themselves which were signified by those sounds I never could reach by any sense of the body nor see them at all except by my mind. And what I have stored in my memory was not their signs, but the things signified.

How they got into me, let them tell who can. For I examine all the gates of my flesh, but I cannot find the door by which any of them entered. For the eyes say, "If they were colored, we reported that." The ears say, "If they gave any sound, we gave notice of that." The nostrils say, "If they smell, they passed in by us." The sense of taste says, "If they have no flavor, don't ask me about them." The sense of touch says, "If it had no bodily mass, I did not touch it, and if I never touched it, I gave no report about it."

Whence and how did these thing enter into my memory? I do not know. For when I first learned them, it was not that I believed them on the credit of another man's mind, but I recognized them in my own; and I saw them as true, took them into my mind and laid them up, so to say, where I could get at them again whenever I willed. There they were, then, even before I learned them, but they were not in my memory. Where were they, then? How does it come about that when they were spoken of, I could acknowledge them and say, "So it is, it is true," unless they were already in the memory, though far back and hidden, as it were, in the more secret caves, so that unless they had been drawn out by the teaching of another person, I should perhaps never have been able to think of them at all?

18. Thus we find that learning those things whose images we do not

take in by our senses, but which we intuit within ourselves without images and as they actually are, is nothing else except the gathering together of those same things which the memory already contains—but in an indiscriminate and confused manner—and putting them together by careful observation as they are at hand in the memory; so that where-as they formerly lay hidden, scattered, or neglected, they now come easily to present themselves to the mind which is now familiar with them. And how many things of this sort my memory has stored up, which have already been discovered and, as I said, laid up for ready reference. These are the things we may be said to have learned and to know. Yet, if I cease to recall them even for short intervals of time, they are again so submerged—and slide back, as it were, into the further reaches of the memory—that they must be drawn out again as if new from the same place (for there is nowhere else for them to have gone) and must be collected so that they can become known. In other words, they must be gathered up from their dispersion. This is where we get the word *cogitate.* For *cogo* [collect] and *cogito* [to go on collecting] have the same relation to each other as *ago* [do] and *agito* [do frequently], and *facio* [make] and *factito* [make frequently]. But the mind has properly laid claim to this word [cogitate] so that not everything that is gathered together anywhere, but only what is collected and gathered together in the mind, is properly said to be "cogitated."

19. The memory also contains the principles and the unnumbered laws of numbers and dimensions. None of these has been impressed on the memory by a physical sense, because they have neither color nor sound, nor taste, nor sense of touch. I have heard the sound of the words by which these things are signified when they are discussed: but the sounds are one thing, the things another. For the sounds are one thing in Greek, another in Latin; but the things themselves are neither Greek nor Latin nor any other language. I have seen the lines of the craftsmen, the finest of which are like a spider's web, but mathe-matical lines are different. They are not the images of such things as the eye of my body has showed me. The man who knows them does so without any cogitation of physical objects whatever, but intuits them within himself. I have perceived with all the senses of my body the num-bers we use in counting; but the numbers by which we count are far different from these. They are not the images of these; they simply are. Let the man who does not see these things mock me for saying them; and I will pity him while he laughs at me.

20. All these things I hold in my memory, and I remember how I learned them. I also remember many things that I have heard quite falsely urged against them, which, even if they are false, yet it is not false that I have remembered them. And I also remember that I have distinguished between the truths and the false objections, and now I see that it is one thing to distinguish these things and another to re-member that I did distinguish them when I have cogitated on them. I remember, then, both that I have often understood these things and also that I am now storing away in my memory what I distinguish and comprehend of them so that later on I may remember just as I under-stand them now. Therefore, I remember that I remembered, so that

if afterward I call to mind that I once was able to remember these things it will be through the power of memory that I recall it.

The Manual

---

30. But now, can that part of the human race to whom God hath promised deliverance and a place in the eternal Kingdom be restored through the merits of their own works? Of course not! For what good works could a lost soul do except as he had been rescued from his lostness? Could he do this by the determination of his free will? Of course not! For it was in the evil use of his free will that man destroyed himself and his will at the same time. For as a man who kills himself is still alive when he kills himself, but having killed himself is then no longer alive and cannot resuscitate himself after he has destroyed his own life—so also sin which arises from the action of the free will turns out to be victor over the will and the free will is destroyed. "By whom a man is overcome, to this one he then is bound as slave." This is clearly the judgment of the apostle Peter. And since it is true, I ask you what kind of liberty can one have who is bound as a slave except the liberty that loves to sin?

He serves freely who freely does the will of his master. Accordingly he who is slave to sin is free to sin. But thereafter he will not be free to do right unless he is delivered from the bondage of sin and begins to be the servant of righteousness. This, then, is true liberty: the joy that comes in doing what is right. At the same time, it is also devoted service in obedience to righteous precept.

But how would a man, bound and sold, get back his liberty to do good, unless he could regain it from Him whose voice saith, "If the Son shall make you free, then you will be free indeed"? But before this process begins in man, could anyone glory in his good works as if they were acts of his free will, when he is not yet free to act rightly? He could do this only if, puffed up in proud vanity, he were merely boasting. This attitude is what the apostle was reproving when he said, "By grace you have been saved by faith."

31. And lest men should arrogate to themselves saving faith as their own work and not understand it as a divine gift, the same apostle who says somewhere else that he had "obtained mercy of the Lord to be trustworthy" makes here an additional comment: "And this is not of yourselves; rather it is a gift of God—not because of works either, lest any man should boast." But then, lest it be supposed that the faith-

---

From *Augustine: Confessions and Enchiridion*, LCC, Vol. VII, ed. Albert C. Outler. Published 1955, The Westminster Press. Used by permission of The Westminster Press and Student Christian Movement Press Limited.

ful are lacking in good works, he added further, "For we are his workmanship, created in Christ Jesus to good works, which God hath prepared beforehand for us to walk in them."

We are then truly free when God ordereth our lives, that is, formeth and createth us not as men—this he hath already done—but also as good men, which he is now doing by his grace, that we may indeed be new creatures in Christ Jesus. Accordingly, the prayer: "Create in me a clean heart, O God." This does not mean, as far as the natural human heart is concerned, that God hath not already created this.

32. Once again, lest anyone glory, if not in his own works, at least in the determination of his free will, as if some merit had originated from him and as if the freedom to do good works had been bestowed on him as a kind of reward, let him hear the same herald of grace, announcing: "For it is God who is at work in you both to will and to do according to his good will." And, in another place: "It is not therefore a matter of man's willing, or of his running, but of God's showing mercy." Still, it is obvious that a man who is old enough to exercise his reason cannot believe, hope, or love unless he wills it, nor could he run for the prize of his high calling in God without a decision of his will. In what sense, therefore, is it "not a matter of human willing or running but of God's showing mercy," unless it be that "the will itself is prepared by the Lord," even as it is written? This saying, therefore, that "it is not a matter of human willing or running but of God's showing mercy," means that the action is from both, that is to say, from the will of man and from the mercy of God. Thus we accept the dictum, "It is not a matter of human willing or running but of God's showing mercy," as if it meant, "The will of man is not sufficient by itself unless there is also the mercy of God." By the same token, the mercy of God is not sufficient by itself unless there is also the will of man. But if we say rightly that "it is not a matter of human willing or running but of God's showing mercy," because the will of man alone is not enough, why, then, is not the contrary rightly said, "It is not a matter of God's showing mercy but of a man's willing," since the mercy of God by itself alone is not enough? Now, actually, no Christian would dare to say, "It is not a matter of God's showing mercy but of man's willing," lest he explicitly contradict the apostle. The conclusion remains, therefore, that this saying: "Not man's willing or running but God's showing mercy," is to be understood to mean that the whole process is credited to God, who both prepareth the will to receive divine aid and aideth the will which has been thus prepared.

For a man's good will comes before many other gifts from God, but not all of them. One of the gifts it does not antedate is—just itself! Thus in the Sacred Eloquence we read both, "His mercy goes before me," and also, "His mercy shall follow me." It predisposes a man before he wills, to prompt his willing. It follows the act of willing, lest one's will be frustrated. Otherwise, why are we admonished to pray for our enemies, who are plainly not now willing to live piously, unless it be that God is even now at work in them and in their wills? Or again, why are we admonished to ask in order to receive, unless it be that He who grants us what we will is he through whom it comes to pass that we will?

We pray for enemies, therefore, that the mercy of God should go before them, as it goes before us; we pray for ourselves that his mercy shall follow us.

96. Nor should we doubt that God doth well, even when he alloweth whatever happens ill to happen. For he alloweth it only through a just judgment—and surely all that is just is good. Therefore, although evil, in so far as it is evil, is not good, still it is a good thing that not only good things exist but evil as well. For if it were not good that evil things exist, they would certainly not be allowed to exist by the Omnipotent Good, for whom it is undoubtedly as easy not to allow to exist what he does not will, as it is for him to do what he does will.

Unless we believe this, the very beginning of our Confession of Faith is imperiled—the sentence in which we profess to believe in God the Father Almighty. For he is called Almighty for no other reason than that he can do whatsoever he willeth and because the efficacy of his omnipotent will is not impeded by the will of any creature.

97. Accordingly, we must now inquire about the meaning of what was said most truly by the apostle concerning God, "Who willeth that all men should be saved." For since not all—not even a majority—*are* saved, it would indeed appear that the fact that what God willeth to happen does not happen is due to an embargo on God's will by the human will.

Now, when we ask for the reason why not all are saved, the customary answer is: "Because they themselves have not willed it." But this cannot be said of infants, who have not yet come to the power of willing or not willing. For, if we could attribute to their wills the infant squirmings they make at baptism, when they resist as hard as they can, we would then have to say that they were saved against their will. But the Lord's language is clearer when, in the Gospel, he reproveth the unrighteous city: "How often," he saith, "would I have gathered your children together, as a hen gathers her chicks, and you would not." This sounds as if God's will had been overcome by human wills and as if the weakest, by not willing, impeded the Most Powerful so that he could not do what he willed. And where is that omnipotence by which "whatsoever he willed in heaven and on earth, he has done," if he willed to gather the children of Jerusalem together, and did not do so? Or, is it not rather the case that, although Jerusalem did not will that her children be gathered together by him, yet, despite her unwillingness, God did indeed gather together those children of hers whom he would? It is not that "in heaven and on earth" he hath willed and done some things, and willed other things and not done them. Instead, "all things whatsoever he willed, he hath done."

98. Furthermore, who would be so impiously foolish as to say that God cannot turn the evil wills of men—as he willeth, when he willeth, and where he willeth—toward the good? But, when he acteth, he acteth through mercy; when he doth not act, it is through justice. For, "he hath mercy on whom he willeth; and whom he willeth, he hardeneth."

Now when the apostle said this, he was commending grace, of which he had just spoken in connection with the twin children in Rebecca's womb: "Before they had yet been born, or had done anything good or bad, in order that the electing purpose of God might continue—not through works but through the divine calling—it was said of them, 'The elder shall serve the younger.'" Accordingly, he refers to another prophetic witness, where it is written, "Jacob I loved, but Esau have I hated." Then, realizing how what he said could disturb those whose understanding could not penetrate to this depth of grace, he adds: "What therefore shall we say to this? Is there unrighteousness in God? God forbid!" Yet it does seem unfair that, without any merit derived from good works or bad, God should love the one and hate the other. Now, if the apostle had wished us to understand that there were future good deeds of the one, and evil deeds of the other—which God, of course, foreknew—he would never have said "not of good works" but rather "of *future* works." Thus he would have solved the difficulty; or, rather, he would have left no difficulty to be solved. As it is, however, when he went on to exclaim, "God forbid!"—that is, "God forbid that there should be unfairness in God"—he proceeds immediately to add (to prove that no unfairness in God is involved here), "For he says to Moses, 'I will have mercy on whom I will have mercy, and I will show pity to whom I will show pity.'" Now, who but a fool would think God unfair either when he imposes penal judgment on the deserving or when he shows mercy to the undeserving? Finally, the apostle concludes and says, "Therefore, it is not a question of him who wills nor of him who runs but of God's showing mercy."

Thus, both the twins were "by nature children of wrath," not because of any works of their own, but because they were both bound in the fetters of damnation originally forged by Adam. But He who said, "I will have mercy on whom I will have mercy," loved Jacob in unmerited mercy, yet hated Esau with merited justice. Since this judgment of wrath was due them both, the former learned from what happened to the other that the fact that he had not, with equal merit, incurred the same penalty gave him no ground to boast of his own distinctive merits—but, instead, that he should glory in the abundance of divine grace, because "it is not a question of him who wills nor of him who runs, but of God's showing mercy." And, indeed, the whole visage of Scripture and, if I may speak so, the lineaments of its countenance, are found to exhibit a mystery, most profound and salutary, to admonish all who carefully look thereupon "that he who glories, should glory in the Lord."

99. Now, after the apostle had commended God's mercy in saying, "So then, there is no question of him who wills nor of him who runs, but of God's showing mercy," next in order he intends to speak also of his judgment—for where his mercy is not shown, it is not unfairness but justice. For with God there is no injustice. Thus, he immediately added, "For the Scripture says to Pharaoh, 'For this very purpose I raised you up, that I may show through you my power, and that my name may be proclaimed in all the earth.'" Then, having said this, he draws a conclusion that looks both ways, that is, toward mercy and toward judgment: "Therefore," he says, "he hath mercy on whom he willeth, and whom he willeth he hardeneth." He showeth mercy out of his great goodness; he hardeneth out of no unfairness at all. In this way,

neither does he who is saved have a basis for glorying in any merit of his own: nor does the man who is damned have a basis for complaining of anything except what he has fully merited. For grace alone separates the redeemed from the lost, all having been mingled together in the one mass of perdition, arising from a common cause which leads back to their common origin. But if any man hears this in such a way as to say: "Why then does he find fault? For who resists his will?"—as if to make it seem that man should not therefore be blamed for being evil *because* God "hath mercy on whom he willeth and whom he willeth he hardeneth"—God forbid that we should be ashamed to give the same reply as we see the apostle giving: "O man, who are you to reply to God? Does the molded object say to the molder, 'Why have you made me like this?' Or is not the potter master of his clay, to make from the same mass one vessel for honorable, another for ignoble, use?"

There are some stupid men who think that in this part of the argument the apostle had no answer to give; and, for lack of a reasonable rejoinder, simply rebuked the audacity of his gainsayer. But what he said—"O man, who are you?"—has actually great weight and in an argument like this recalls man, in a single word, to consider the limits of his capacity and, at the same time, supplies an important explanation.

For if one does not understand these matters, who is he to talk back to God? And if one does understand, he finds no better ground even then for talking back. For if he understands, he sees that the whole human race was condemned in its apostate head by a divine judgment so just that not even if a single member of the race were ever saved from it, no one could rail against God's justice. And he also sees that those who are saved had to be saved on such terms that it would show—by contrast with the greater number of those not saved but simply abandoned to their wholly just damnation—what the whole mass deserved and to what end God's merited judgment would have brought them, had not his undeserved mercy interposed. Thus every mouth of those disposed to glory in their own merits should be stopped, so that "he that glories may glory in the Lord."

100. These are "the great works of the Lord, well-considered in all his acts of will"—and so wisely well-considered that when his angelic and human creation sinned (that is, did not do what he willed, but what it willed) he could still accomplish what he himself had willed and this through the same creaturely will by which the first act contrary to the Creator's will had been done. As the Supreme Good, he made good use of evil deeds, for the damnation of those whom he had justly predestined to punishment and for the salvation of those whom he had mercifully predestined to grace.

For, as far as they were concerned, they did what God did not will that they do, but as far as God's omnipotence is concerned, they were quite unable to achieve their purpose. In their very act of going against his will, his will was thereby accomplished. This is the meaning of the statement, "The works of the Lord are great, well-considered in all his acts of will"—that in a strange and ineffable fashion even that which is done against his will is not done without his will. For it would not be done without his allowing it—and surely his permission is not unwilling but willing—nor would he who is good allow the evil to be done, unless in his omnipotence he could bring good even out of evil.

101. Sometimes, however, a man of good will wills something that God doth not will, even though God's will is much more, and much more certainly, good—for under no circumstances can it ever be evil. For example, it is a good son's will that his father live, whereas it is God's good will that he should die. Or, again, it can happen that a man of evil will can will something that God also willeth with a good will—as, for example, a bad son wills that his father die and this is also God's will. Of course, the former wills what God doth not will, whereas the latter does will what God willeth. Yet the piety of the one, though he wills not what God willeth, is more consonant with God's will than is the impiety of the other, who wills the same thing that God willeth. There is a very great difference between what is fitting for man to will and what is fitting for God—and also between the ends to which a man directs his will—and this difference determines whether an act of will is to be approved or disapproved. Actually, God achieveth some of his purposes —which are, of course, all good—through the evil wills of bad men. For example, it was through the ill will of the Jews that, by the good will of the Father, Christ was slain for us—a deed so good that when the apostle Peter would have nullified it he was called "Satan" by him who had come in order to be slain. How good seemed the purposes of the pious faithful who were unwilling that the apostle Paul should go to Jerusalem, lest there he should suffer the things that the prophet Agabus had predicted! And yet God had willed that he should suffer these things for the sake of the preaching of Christ, and for the training of a martyr for Christ. And this good purpose of his he achieved, not through the good will of the Christians, but through the ill will of the Jews. Yet they were more fully his who did not will what he willed than were those who were willing instruments of his purpose—for while he and the latter did the very same thing, he worked through them with a good will, whereas they did his good will with their ill will.

102. But, however strong the wills either of angels or of men, whether good or evil, whether they will what God willeth or will something else, the will of the Omnipotent is always undefeated. And this will can never be evil, because even when it inflicts evils, it is still just; and obviously what is just is not evil. Therefore, whether through pity "he hath mercy on whom he willeth," or in justice "whom he willeth, he hardeneth," the omnipotent God never doth anything except what he doth will, and doth everything that he willeth.

103. Accordingly, when we hear and read in sacred Scripture that God "willeth that all men should be saved," although we know well enough that not all men are saved, we are not on that account to underrate the fully omnipotent will of God. Rather, we must understand the Scripture, "Who will have all men to be saved," as meaning that no man is saved unless God willeth his salvation: not that there is no man whose salvation he doth not will, but that no one is saved unless He willeth it. Moreover, his will should be sought in prayer, because if he willeth, then what he willeth must necessarily be. And, indeed, it was of prayer to God that the apostle was speaking when he made that statement.

Thus, we are also to understand what is written in the Gospel about Him "who enlighteneth every man." This means that there is no man who is enlightened except by God.

In any case, the word concerning God, "who will have all men to be saved," does not mean that there is no one whose salvation he doth not will—he who was unwilling to work miracles among those who, he said, would have repented if he had wrought them—but by "all men" we are to understand the whole of mankind, in every single group into which it can be divided: kings and subjects; nobility and plebeians; the high and the low; the learned and unlearned; the healthy and the sick; the bright, the dull, and the stupid; the rich, the poor, and the middle class; males, females, infants, children, the adolescent, young adults and middle-aged and very old; of every tongue and fashion, of all the arts, of all professions, with the countless variety of wills and minds and all the other things that differentiate people. For from which of these groups doth not God will that some men from every nation should be saved through his only-begotten Son our Lord? Therefore, he doth save them since the Omnipotent cannot will in vain, whatsoever he willeth.

Now, the apostle had enjoined that prayers should be offered "for all men" and especially "for kings and all those of exalted station," whose worldly pomp and pride could be supposed to be a sufficient cause for them to despise the humility of the Christian faith. Then, continuing his argument, "for this is good and acceptable in the sight of God our Saviour"—that is, to pray even for such as these kings—the apostle, to remove any warrant for despair, added, "Who willeth that all men be saved and come to the knowledge of the truth." Truly, then, God hath judged it good that through the prayers of the lowly he would deign to grant salvation to the exalted—a paradox we have already seen exemplified. Our Lord also useth the same manner of speech in the Gospel, where he saith to the Pharisees, "You tithe mint and rue and every herb." Obviously, the Pharisees did not tithe what belonged to others, nor all the herbs of all the people of other lands. Therefore, just as we should interpret "every herb" to mean "every kind of herb," so also we can interpret "all men" to mean "all kinds of men." We could interpret it in any other fashion, as long as we are not compelled to believe that the Omnipotent hath willed anything to be done which was not done. "He hath done all things in heaven and earth, whatsoever he willed," as Truth sings of him, and surely he hath not willed to do anything that he hath not done. There must be no equivocation on this point.

104. Consequently, God would have willed to preserve even the first man in that state of salvation in which he was created and would have brought him in due season, after the begetting of children, to a better state without the intervention of death—where he not only would have been unable to sin, but would not have had even the will to sin—if he had foreknown that man would have had a steadfast will to continue without sin, as he had been created to do. But since he did foreknow that man would make bad use of his free will—that is, that he would sin—God prearranged his own purpose so that he could do good to

man, even in man's doing evil, and so that the good will of the Omnipotent should be nullified by the bad will of men, but should nonetheless be fulfilled.

105. Thus it was fitting that man should be created, in the first place, so that he could will both good and evil—not without reward, if he willed the good; not without punishment, if he willed the evil. But in the future life he will not have the power to will evil; and yet this will not thereby restrict his free will. Indeed, his will will be much freer, because he will then have no power whatever to serve sin. For we surely ought not to find fault with such a will, nor say it is no will, or that it is not rightly called free, when we so desire happiness that we not only are unwilling to be miserable, but have no power whatsoever to will it.

And, just as in our present state, our soul is unable to will unhappiness for ourselves, so then it will be forever unable to will iniquity. But the ordered course of God's plan was not to be passed by, wherein he willed to show how good the rational creature is that is able not to sin, although one unable to sin is better. So, too, it was an inferior order of immortality—but yet it was immortality—in which man was capable of not dying, even if the higher order which is to be is one in which man will be incapable of dying.

106. Human nature lost the former kind of immortality through the misuse of free will. It is to receive the latter through grace—though it was to have obtained it through merit, if it had not sinned. Not even then, however, could there have been any merit without grace. For although sin had its origin in free will alone, still free will would not have been sufficient to maintain justice, save as divine aid had been afforded man, in the gift of participation in the immutable good. Thus, for example, the power to die when he wills it is in a man's own hands—since there is no one who could not kill himself by not eating (not to mention other means). But the bare will is not sufficient for maintaining life, if the aids of food and other means of preservation are lacking.

Similarly, man in paradise was capable of self-destruction by abandoning justice by an act of will; yet if the life of justice was to be maintained, his will alone would not have sufficed, unless He who made him had given him aid. But, after the Fall, God's mercy was even more abundant, for then the will itself had to be freed from the bondage in which sin and death are the masters. There is no way at all by which it can be freed by itself, but only through God's grace, which is made effectual in the faith of Christ. Thus, as it is written, even the will by which "the will itself is prepared by the Lord" so that we may receive the other gifts of God through which we come to the Gift eternal—this too comes from God.

107. Accordingly, even the life eternal, which is surely the wages of good works, is called a *gift* of God by the apostle. "For the wages of sin," he says, "is death; but the gift of God is eternal life in Christ Jesus our Lord." Now, wages for military service are paid as a just debit, not as a gift. Hence, he said "the wages of sin is death," to show that death was not an unmerited punishment for sin but a just debit. But a gift, unless it be gratuitous, is not grace. We are, therefore, to understand that even man's merited goods are gifts from God, and when life eternal

is given through them, what else do we have but "grace upon grace returned"?

Man was, therefore, made upright, and in such a fashion that he could either continue in that uprightness—though not without divine aid —or become perverted by his own choice. Whichever of these two man had chosen, God's will would be done, either by man or at least *concerning* him. Wherefore, since man chose to do his own will instead of God's, God's will *concerning* him was done; for, from the same mass of perdition that flowed out of that common source, God maketh "one vessel for honorable, another for ignoble use"; the ones for honorable use through his mercy, the ones for ignoble use through his judgment; lest anyone glory in man, or—what is the same thing—in himself.

Comments / on St. Augustine

[Augustine] has everything that Jerome lacks: the most delicate emotional life and spiritual fire; that longing to know essence which soars above all factual science. *E. R. CURTIUS (1948)*

[St. Augustine] has the power . . . of making what is intensely personal pass into the universal, so that the reader seems to be following his own story. To use the language of his system, his own experience evokes in the memory of others an echo which is recognized to be true. Hence his mark on philosophy has been described by a modern writer as that of *interiorizing* it. He is the first explorer of the hinterland of the self. *M. C. D'ARCY (1930)*

Augustine's psychological genius has given an account of the trouble of having a divided self which has never been surpassed. . . . There could be no more perfect description of the divided will, when the higher wishes lack just that last acuteness, that touch of explosive intensity, that dynamogenic quality (to use the slang of the psychologists) that enables them to burst their shell and to make the inruption efficaciously into life and quell the lower tendencies forever. *WILLIAM JAMES (1902)*

[I]n connection with the problem of moral evil, St. Augustine makes a creative contribution unrivaled in Christian thought. He did so by isolating the inner fact of the human will and seeing in it the ultimate source of moral evil. . . . [H]e had an insatiable urge to get at the truth of things. When he followed along this path and became convinced intellectually that the Christian answer was correct, even then he only experienced a paralysis of the will. He wanted to become a Christian, but yet he could not, so deep was his entanglement in his worldly desires and passions. . . .

Then suddenly came the mysterious incident in the garden at Milan. . . .
The miracle happened. St. Augustine was now free to act righteously. . . .
Whatever may be the inadequacies of this theory of moral evil when it
is subjected to rational analysis, it constitutes a powerful answer and one
which is consistent with man's deepest inner experience of the fact that
he possesses a will.   *W. J. OATES (1948)*

The motive that inspires a work like the *Confessions* is open to criticism;
it is a question whether a wholesome mind is anxious to write minutely
about itself.   *E. K. RAND (1928)*

Augustine was perfectly aware that everyone would read the *Confessions,*
and indeed would have been sorry if they did not: but he assumed that
they would be quite sure that they were truthful—so much so that the
whole of the *Confessions* is an outpouring of his soul to God—God is the
immediate audience; and only now and again does the author look aside
(and down) towards his human hearers. This *public spontaneity* is alien
to our sentiment, and must not be judged, as probable or improbable,
according to it.   *C. C. MARTINDALE (1930)*

The emotional progress which Augustine has described in the *Confessions* represented a search for the proper symbols in which he might
express the two most passionate drives of his passionate nature: his
adoration for the immaterial and the absolute, his detestation for the relative and the material. . . . The intensity of his conversion—it was, of
course, the ecstasy of mysticism—served not only as a fitting climax to
Augustine's passionate search for the absolute; it determined, as his
subsequent writings were to show, the boundaries of his *Weltanschauung:*
the ineffable power of God, and the hideous evil of the world, the flesh,
the unsaved man.

Augustine's radical departure from the humanistic tradition is apparent
in his substitution of will for reason in his hierarchy of value. . . . For
him, will, not reason, is the dominant force in the universe, and God
Himself, the sum of all absolutes, is the absolute will. Like man, He is
a creature of will, but His will is *ipso facto* for good while man's is ordinarily for evil. What God wills must be good because He wills it, not because it is rational: sovereignty supplants intelligence. . . . It is this
glorification of will that makes possible the doctrine of original sin.

The Greeks had accepted the notion of fate *(nemesis)* and had erected
a great dramatic literature around it, but for them fate was the inexorable
working out of cause and effect; it proved the fact of a rational moral
order in the universe. Augustine preserved the idea of *nemesis,* along with
the Stoic idea of providence, but he called it predestination and he made
it the suprarational manifestation of God's inscrutable will.
                                                 HERSCHEL BAKER (1947)

[Augustine] possessed a strong, capacious, argumentative mind; he
boldly sounded the dark abyss of grace, predestination, free will, and

original sin; and the rigid system of Christianity which he framed or re-stored, has been entertained with public applause and secret reluctance by the Latin Church. *EDWARD GIBBON (1781)*

The doctrine of sin and grace marks, in its most acute form, the breach between Classicism and Christianity. It had been the considered judg-ment of Aristotle that 'virtue and vice are both alike in our power'. . . . To Augustine, however, there was no such folly among the many follies of philosophy as to suppose that mankind, by reason of any capacity inherent in himself, possessed the ability to discover a good independent of that which was intrinsic to him as a created being, much less to gener-ate within himself the impulse needed for its realization. Thus, for him, the classical ideal of perfectibility through knowledge or enlightenment was wholly illusory; and, for the aberrations of humanity, he saw no remedy through education, whether conceived as intellectual discipline or moral habituation or both, *apart from* a recognition of the creative truth in the light of which alone these processes might properly be understood. *C. N. COCHRANE (1940)*

Boethius
480?—524?

The difficulty in reconciling the idea of a divine power ruling the universe with the notion that man is responsible for his own actions has always troubled thoughtful men. For Christian thinkers the problem has been particularly troublesome, since God's omnipotence and omniscience are basic tenets of Christianity. St. Augustine, who had dealt with the problem in a number of treatises, showed through extensive theological analysis that divine predestination is not necessarily incompatible with human free will. In the few chapters devoted to the subject in the *Manual,* however, he put considerably more emphasis on the power of God than on the moral freedom of man. As a result, even though he had a great deal to do with establishing the position ultimately adopted by Catholic theology on this question—that man has at least enough freedom of the will to make him responsible for his actions—St. Augustine hardly appeared as a champion of free will to the casual reader. The essential features of his complex demonstration of the existence of free will usually reached a general audience in later ages through the medium of Boethius' *Consolation of Philosophy.*

Anicius Manlius Severinus Boethius was born in Rome of a patrician family. He had a distinguished political career in a number of high public offices under Theodoric, a Germanic chieftain from Eastern Europe who had become king of Italy. Eventually, however, Boethius was accused of treason, imprisoned, and executed by Theodoric. The political circumstances surrounding Boethius' downfall are obscure; but it seems likely that he was innocent and that Theodoric, who belonged to a Christain sect condemned as heretical by the Western Church, was motivated against him at least partly because of his Catholic faith.

Boethius combined a busy life in politics with an active dedication to the advancement of learning. He set for himself the enormous task of translating all the works of Plato and Aristotle into Latin, and though he never completed the project, he did make considerable headway. Whatever knowledge of Aristotle was current in Western Europe before the twelfth century was due mainly to Boethius. He also composed influential works, based on Greek sources, dealing with arithmetic, geometry, and music, as well as a number of important philosophical and theological treatises.

Boethius wrote the *Consolation of Philosophy* while in prison awaiting execution. He gave it the form of a dialogue between himself and Philosophy, allegorized as a gracious lady who undertakes to answer for him the question of why a good man should suffer unjustly in a world supposedly ruled by a just God. Her explanation stretches over five books; ranges through adaptations of Aristotelian, Platonic, and Augustinian thought on such subjects as fortune, fate, chance, providence, free will, and predestination; and provides so much consolation that the book was one of the most widely read in Europe throughout the Middle Ages and was repeatedly translated into the vernacular languages. Among the English translators were two of the most effective monarchs in English history, famed as rulers rather than as philosophers: King Alfred the Great, who considered it essential that his people have the book available in their own language; and Queen Elizabeth I, who undertook her translation to help recover from her consternation when the king of France renounced Protestantism.

Consolation of Philosophy

Book V

Here she [Philosophy] made an end and was for turning the course of her speaking to the handling and explaining of other subjects. Then said I: "Your encouragement is right and most worthy in truth of your name and weight. But I am learning by experience what you just now said of Providence; that the question is bound up in others. I would ask you whether you think that Chance exists at all, and what you think it is?"

Then she answered: "I am eager to fulfil my promised debt, and to shew you the path by which you may seek your home. But these things, though all-expedient for knowledge, are none the less rather apart from our path, and we must be careful lest you become wearied by our turnings aside, and so be not strong enough to complete the straight journey."

"Have no fear at all thereof," said I. "It will be restful to know these

From *Tractates Consolation,* translated by H. E. Stewart and E. K. Rand (Cambridge, Mass.: Harvard University Press). Reprinted by permission of the publishers and The Loeb Classical Library. The poetry insertions are from *Consolation of Philosophy,* 1902 translation by W. V. Cooper (New York: Carlton House, n.d.).

things in which I have so great a pleasure; and when every view of your reasoning has stood firm with unshaken credit, so let there be no doubt of what shall follow."

"I will do your pleasure," she made answer, and thus she began to speak:

"If chance is defined as an outcome of random influence, produced by no sequence of causes, I am sure that there is no such thing as chance, and I consider that it is but an empty word, beyond shewing the meaning of the matter which we have in hand. For what place can be left for anything happening at random, so long as God controls everything in order? It is a true saying that nothing can come out of nothing. None of the old philosophers has denied that, though they did not apply it to the effective principle,[1] but to the matter operated upon—that is to say, to nature; and this was the foundation upon which they built all their reasoning. If anything arises from no causes, it will appear to have risen out of nothing. But if this is impossible, then chance also cannot be anything of that sort, which is stated in the definition which we mentioned."

"Then is there nothing which can be justly called chance, nor anything 'by chance'?" I asked. "Or is there anything which common people know not, but which those words do suit?"

"My philosopher, Aristotle, defined it in his *Physics* shortly and well-nigh truly."

"How?" I asked.

"Whenever anything is done with one intention, but something else, other than was intended, results from certain causes, that is called chance: as, for instance, if a man digs the ground for the sake of cultivating it, and finds a heap of buried gold. Such a thing is believed to have happened by chance, but it does not come from nothing, for it has its own causes, whose unforeseen and unexpected coincidence seem to have brought about a chance. For if the cultivator did not dig the ground, if the owner had not buried his money, the gold would not have been found. These are the causes of the chance piece of good fortune, which comes about from the causes which meet it, and move along with it, not from the intention of the actor. For neither the burier nor the tiller intended that the gold should be found; but, as I said, it was a coincidence, and it happened that the one dug up what the other buried. We may therefore define chance as an unexpected result from the coincidence of certain causes in matters where there was another purpose. The order of the universe, advancing with its inevitable sequences, brings about this coincidence of causes. This order itself emanates from its source, which is Providence, and disposes all things in their proper time and place.

I

"In the Achaemenian rocks, where Parthians with their darts
In their dissembled flight do wound their enemies,

---

[1] The *effective principle* is a technical philosophical term, also known as the *efficient cause*, which signifies the immediate agent in the production of an effect. The effective principle of a brick wall is a bricklayer.

Tigris from the same head doth with Euphrates rise,[2]
And forthwith they themselves divide in several parts;
But if they join again, and them one channel bound,
Bringing together all that both their waves do bear;
The ships and trees, whose roots they from the bank do tear,
Will meet, and they their floods will mingle and confound,
Yet run this wandering course in places which are low,
And in these sliding streams a settled law remains.
So fortune, though it seems to run with careless reins,
Yet hath it certain rule, and doth in order flow."

"I have listened to you," I said, "and agree that it is as you say. But in this close sequence of causes, is there any freedom for our judgment, or does this chain of fate bind the very feelings of our minds too?"

"There is free will," she answered. "Nor could there be any reasoning nature without freedom of judgment. For any being that can use its reason by nature, has a power of judgment by which it can without further aid decide each point, and so distinguish between objects to be desired and objects to be shunned. Each therefore seeks what it deems desirable, and flies from what it considers should be shunned. Wherefore all who have reason have also freedom of desiring and refusing in themselves. But I do not lay down that this is equal in all beings. Heavenly and divine beings have with them a judgment of great insight, an imperturbable will, and a power which can effect their desires. But human spirits must be more free when they keep themselves safe in the contemplation of the mind of God; but less free when they sink into bodies, and less still when they are bound by their earthly members. The last stage is mere slavery, when the spirit is given over to vices and has fallen away from the possession of its reason. For when the mind turns its eyes from the light of truth on high to lower darkness, soon they are dimmed by the clouds of ignorance, and become turbid through ruinous passions; by yielding to these passions and consenting to them, men increase the slavery which they have brought upon themselves, and their true liberty is lost in captivity. But God, looking upon all out of the infinite, perceives the views of Providence, and disposes each as its destiny has already fated for it according to its merits: 'He looketh over all and heareth all.'

II

"Sweet Homer sings the praise
Of Phoebus[3] clear and bright,
And yet his strongest rays
Cannot with feeble light
Cast through the secret ways
Of earth and seas his sight,

---

[2]Achaemenia is an ancient name for Persia; the Parthians were one of the peoples included in the Persian Empire; the Tigris and the Euphrates are great rivers, both of which have their source in what was in ancient times the Persian Empire.
[3]The sun.

Though 'all lies open to his eyes.'
But He who did this world devise—

The earth's vast depths unseen
From his sight are not free,
No clouds can stand between,
He at one time doth see
What are, and what have been,
And what shall after be.
Whom, since he only vieweth all,
You rightly the true Sun may call."

Then said I, "Again am I plunged in yet more doubt and difficulty."

"What are they," she asked, "though I have already my idea of what your trouble consists?"

"There seems to me," I said, "to be such incompatibility between the existence of God's universal foreknowledge and that of any freedom of judgment. For if God foresees all things and cannot in anything be mistaken, that, which His Providence sees will happen, must result. Wherefore if it knows beforehand not only men's deeds but even their designs and wishes, there will be no freedom of judgment. For there can neither be any deed done, nor wish formed, except such as the infallible Providence of God has foreseen. For if matters could ever so be turned that they resulted otherwise than was foreseen of Providence, this foreknowledge would cease to be sure. But, rather than knowledge, it is opinion which is uncertain; and that, I deem, is not applicable to God. And, further, I cannot approve of an argument by which some men think that they can cut this knot; for they say that a result does not come to pass for the reason that Providence has foreseen it, but the opposite rather, namely, that because it is about to come to pass, therefore it cannot be hidden from God's Providence. In that way it seems to me that the argument must resolve itself into an argument on the other side. For in that case it is not necessary that that should happen which is foreseen, but that that which is about to happen should be foreseen; as though, indeed, our doubt was whether God's foreknowledge is the certain cause of future events, or the certainty of future events is the cause of Providence. But let our aim be to prove that, whatever be the shape which this series of causes takes, the fulfilment of God's foreknowledge is necessary, even if this knowledge may not seem to induce the necessity for the occurrence of future events. For instance, if a man sits down, it must be that the opinion, which conjectures that he is sitting, is true; but conversely, if the opinion concerning the man is true because he is sitting, he must be sitting down. There is therefore necessity in both cases: the man must be sitting, and the opinion must be true. But he does not sit because the opinion is true, but rather the opinion is true because his sitting down has preceded it. Thus, though the cause of the truth of the opinion proceeds from the other fact, yet there is a common necessity on both parts. In like manner we must reason of Providence and future events. For even though they are foreseen because they are about to happen, yet they do not happen because they are foreseen. None the less it is necessary that either what is about to happen should be foreseen of God, or that what has been foreseen should happen; and this alone is enough to destroy all free will.

"Yet how absurd it is that we should say that the result of temporal affairs is the cause of eternal foreknowledge! And to think that God foresees future events because they are about to happen, is nothing else than to hold events of past time to be the cause of that highest Providence. Besides, just as, when I know a present fact, that fact must be so; so also when I know of something that will happen, that must come to pass. Thus it follows that the fulfilment of a foreknown event must be inevitable.

"Lastly, if any one believes that any matter is otherwise than the fact is, he not only has not knowledge, but his opinion is false also, and that is very far from the truth of knowledge. Wherefore, if any future event is such that its fulfilment is not sure or necessary, how can it possibly be known beforehand that it will occur? For just as absolute knowledge has no taint of falsity, so also that which is conceived by knowledge cannot be otherwise than as it is conceived. That is the reason why knowledge cannot lie, because each matter must be just as knowledge knows that it is. What then? How can God know beforehand these uncertain future events? For if He thinks inevitable the fulfilment of such things as may possibly not result, He is wrong; and that we may not believe, nor even utter, rightly. But if He perceives that they will result as they are in such a manner that He only knows that they may or may not occur, equally, how is this foreknowledge, this which knows nothing for sure, nothing absolutely? How is such a foreknowledge different from the absurd prophecy which Horace puts in the mouth of Tiresias:[4] 'Whatever I shall say, will either come to pass, or it will not'? How, too, would God's Providence be better than man's opinion, if, as men do, He only sees to be uncertain such things as have an uncertain result? But if there can be no uncertainty with God, the most sure source of all things, then the fulfilment of all that He has surely foreknown, is certain. Thus we are led to see that there is no freedom for the intentions or actions of men; for the mind of God, foreseeing all things without error or deception, binds all together and controls their results. And when we have once allowed this, it is plain how complete is the fall of all human actions in consequence. In vain are rewards or punishments set before good or bad, for there is no free or voluntary action of the mind to deserve them; and what we just now determined was most fair, will prove to be most unfair of all, namely to punish the dishonest or reward the honest, since their own will does not put them in the way of honesty or dishonesty, but the unfailing necessity of development constrains them. Wherefore neither virtues nor vices are anything, but there is rather an indiscriminate confusion of all deserts. And nothing could be more vicious than this; since the whole order of all comes from Providence, and nothing is left to human intention, it follows

---

[4]Horace (65—8 B.C.) was a famous Roman lyric poet. Tiresias was a legendary Greek prophet supposed to have lived in Homeric times.

that our crimes, as well as our good deeds, must all be held due to the author of all good. Hence it is unreasonable to hope for or pray against aught. For what could any man hope for or pray against, if an undeviating chain links together all that we can desire? Thus will the only understanding between God and man, the right of prayer, be taken away. We suppose that at the price of our deservedly humbling ourselves before Him we may win a right to the inestimable reward of His divine grace: this is the only manner in which men can seem to deal with God, so to speak, and by virtue of prayer to join ourselves to that inaccessible light, before it is granted to us; but if we allow the inevitability of the future, and believe that we have no power, what means shall we have to join ourselves to the Lord of all, or how can we cling to Him? Wherefore, as you sang but a little while ago, the human race must be cut off from its source and ever fall away.

III

"What cause of discord breaks the bands of love?
What God between two truths such wars doth move?
That things which severally well settled be
Yet joined in one will never friendly prove?
Or in true things can we no discord see,
Because all certainties do still agree?
But our dull soul, covered with members blind,
Knows not the secret laws which things do bind,
By the drowned light of her oppressed fire.
Why then, the hidden notes of things to find,
Doth she with such a love of truth desire?
If she knows that which she doth so require,
Why wisheth she known things to know again?
If she knows not, why strives she with blind pain?
Who after things unknown will strive to go?
Or will such ignorant pursuit maintain?
How shall she find them out? Or having so,
How shall she then their forms and natures know?
Because this soul the highest mind did view,
Must we needs say that it all nature knew?
Now she, though clouds of flesh do her debar,
Forgets not all that was her ancient due,
But in her mind some general motions are,
Though not the skill of things particular.
He that seeks truth in neither course doth fall;
Not knowing all, nor ignorant of all,
He marketh general things which he retains,
And matters seen on high doth back recall,
And things forgotten to his mind regains,
And joins them to that part which there remains."

Then said she, "This is the old plaint concerning Providence which was so strongly urged by Cicero when treating of Divination, and you yourself have often and at length questioned the same subject. But so far, none of you have explained it with enough diligence or certainty. The cause of this obscurity is that the working of human reason cannot approach the directness of divine foreknowledge. If this could be understood at all, there would be no doubt left. And this especially will I try to make plain, if I can first explain your difficulties.

"Tell me why you think abortive the reasoning of those who solve the question thus; they argue that foreknowledge cannot be held to be a cause for the necessity of future results, and therefore free will is not in any way shackled by foreknowledge. Whence do you draw your proof of the necessity of future results if not from the fact that such things as are known beforehand cannot but come to pass? If, then (as you yourself admitted just now), foreknowledge brings no necessity to bear upon future events, how is it that the voluntary results of such events are bound to find a fixed end? Now for the sake of the argument, that you may turn your attention to what follows, let us state that there is no foreknowledge at all. Then are the events which are decided by free will, bound by any necessity, so far as this goes? Of course not. Secondly, let us state that foreknowledge exists, but brings no necessity to bear upon events; then, I think, the same free will will be left, intact and absolute. 'But,' you will say, 'though foreknowledge is no necessity for a result in the future, yet it is a sign that it will necessarily come to pass.' Thus, therefore, even if there had been no foreknowledge, it would be plain that future results were under necessity; for every sign can only shew what it is that it points out; it does not bring it to pass. Wherefore we must first prove that nothing happens but of necessity, in order that it may be plain that foreknowledge is a sign of this necessity. Otherwise, if there is no necessity, then foreknowledge will not be a sign of that which does not exist. Now it is allowed that proof rests upon firm reasoning, not upon signs or external arguments; it must be deduced from suitable and binding causes. How can it possibly be that things, which are foreseen as about to happen, should not occur? That would be as though we were to believe that events would not occur which Providence foreknows as about to occur, and as though we did not rather think this, that though they occur, yet they have had no necessity in their own natures which brought them about. We can see many actions developing before our eyes; just as chariot drivers see the development of their actions as they control and guide their chariots, and many other things likewise. Does any necessity compel any of those things to occur as they do? Of course not. All art, craft, and intention would be in vain, if everything took place by compulsion. Therefore, if things have no necessity for coming to pass when they do, they cannot have any necessity to be about to come to pass before they do. Wherefore there are things whose results are entirely free from necessity. For I think not that there is any man who will say this, that things, which are done in the present, were not about to be done in the past, before they are done. Thus these foreknown events have their free results. Just as foreknowledge of present things brings no necessity to bear upon them as they come to pass, so also foreknowledge of future things brings no necessity to bear upon things which are to come.

"But you will say that there is no doubt of this too, whether there can be any foreknowledge of things which have not results bounden by necessity. For they do seem to lack harmony: and you think that if they are foreseen, the necessity follows; if there is no necessity, then they cannot be foreseen; nothing can be perceived certainly by knowledge, unless it be certain. But if things have uncertainty of result, but are foreseen as though certain, this is plainly the obscurity of opinion, and not the truth of knowledge. For you believe that to think aught other than it is, is the opposite of true knowledge. The cause of this error is that every man believes that all the subjects, that he knows, are known by their own force or nature alone, which are known; but it is quite the opposite. For every subject, that is known, is comprehended not according to its own force, but rather according to the nature of those who know it. Let me make this plain to you by a brief example: the roundness of a body may be known in one way by sight, in another way by touch. Sight can take in the whole body at once from a distance by judging its radii, while touch clings, as it were, to the outside of the sphere, and from close at hand perceives through the material parts the roundness of the body as it passes over the actual circumference. A man himself is differently comprehended by the senses, by imagination, by reason, and by intelligence. For the senses distinguish the form as set in the matter operated upon by the form; imagination distinguishes the appearance alone without the matter. Reason goes even further than imagination; by a general and universal contemplation it investigates the actual kind which is represented in individual specimens. Higher still is the view of the intelligence, which reaches above the sphere of the universal, and with the unsullied eye of the mind gazes upon that very form of the kind in its absolute simplicity. Herein the chief point for our consideration is this: the higher power of understanding includes the lower, but the lower never rises to the higher. For the senses are capable of understanding naught but the matter; imagination cannot look upon universal or natural kinds; reason cannot comprehend the absolute form; whereas the intelligence seems to look down from above and comprehend the form, and distinguishes all that lie below, but in such a way that it grasps the very form which could not be known to any other than itself. For it perceives and knows the general kind, as does reason; the appearance, as does the imagination; and the matter, as do the senses, but with one grasp of the mind it looks upon all with a clear conception of the whole. And reason too, as it views general kinds, does not make use of the imagination nor the senses, but yet does perceive the objects both of the imagination and of the senses. It is reason which thus defines a general kind according to its conception: Man, for instance, is an animal, biped and reasoning. This is a general notion of a natural kind, but no man denies that the subject can be approached by the imagination and by the senses, just because reason investigates it by a reasonable conception and not by the imagination or senses. Likewise, though imagination takes its beginning of seeing and forming appearances from the senses, yet without their aid it surveys each subject by an imaginative faculty of distinguishing, not by the distinguishing faculty of the senses.

"Do you see then, how in knowledge of all things, the subject uses its own standard of capability, and not those of the objects known? And this is but reasonable, for every judgment formed is an act of the person who judges, and therefore each man must of necessity perform his own action from his own capability and not the capability of any other.

IV

"Cloudy old prophets of the Porch[5] once taught
That sense and shape presented to the thought
   From outward objects their impression take,
As when upon a paper smooth and plain
On which as yet no marks of ink have lain
   We with a nimble pen do letters make.
But if our minds to nothing can apply
Their proper motions, but do patient lie
   Subject to forms which do from bodies flow,
As a glass[6] renders empty shapes of things,
Who then can show from whence that motion springs
   By force of which the mind all things doth know?
Or by what skill are several things espied?
And being known what power doth them divide,
   And thus divided doth again unite,
And with a various journey oft aspires
To highest things, and oft again retires
   To basest, nothing being out of sight,
And when she back unto herself doth move,
Doth all the falsehoods by the truth reprove?
   This vigour needs must be an active cause,
And with more powerful forces must be deckt,
Than that which from those forms, that do reflect
   From outward matter, all her virtue draws.
And yet in living bodies passion's might
Doth go before, whose office is to incite,
   And the first motions in the mind to make.
As when the light unto our eyes appears,
Or some loud voice is sounded in our ears,
   Then doth the strength of the dull mind awake
Those phantasies which she retains within;
She stirreth up such notions to begin,
   Whose objects with their natures best agree,
And thus applying them to outward things,
She joins the external shapes which thence she brings
   With forms which in herself included be.

"With regard to feeling the effects of bodies, natures which are brought

---

[5] I.e., Stoic philosophers.
[6] A mirror.

into contact from without may affect the organs of the senses, and the body's passive affection may precede the active energy of the spirit, and call forth to itself the activity of the mind; if then, when the effects of bodies are felt, the mind is not marked in any way by its passive reception thereof, but declares that reception subject to the body of its own force, how much less do those subjects, which are free from all affections of bodies, follow external objects in their perceptions, and how much more do they make clear the way for the action of their mind? By this argument many different manners of understanding have fallen to widely different natures of things. For the senses are incapable of any knowledge but their own, and they alone fall to those living beings which are incapable of motion, as are sea shell-fish, and other low forms of life which live by clinging to rocks; while imagination is granted to animals with the power of motion, who seem to be affected by some desire to seek or avoid certain things. But reason belongs to the human race alone, just as the true intelligence is God's alone. Wherefore that manner of knowledge is better than others, for it can comprehend of its own nature not only the subject peculiar to itself, but also the subjects of the other kinds of knowledge. Suppose that the senses and imagination thus oppose reasoning, saying, 'The universal natural kinds, which reason believes that it can perceive, are nothing; for what is comprehensible to the senses and the imagination cannot be universal: therefore either the judgment of reason is true, and that which can be perceived by the senses is nothing; or, since reason knows well that there are many subjects comprehensible to the senses and imagination, the conception of reason is vain, for it holds to be universal what is an individual matter comprehensible to the senses.' To this reason might answer, that 'it sees from a general point of view what is comprehensible to the senses and the imagination, but they cannot aspire to a knowledge of universals, since their manner of knowledge cannot go further than material or bodily appearances; and in the matter of knowledge it is better to trust to the stronger and more nearly perfect judgment.' If such a trial of argument occurred, should not we, who have within us the force of reasoning as well as the powers of the senses and imagination, approve of the cause of reason rather than that of the others? It is in like manner that human reason thinks that the divine intelligence cannot perceive the things of the future except as it conceives them itself. For you argue thus: 'If there are events which do not appear to have sure or necessary results, their results cannot be known for certain beforehand: therefore there can be no foreknowledge of these events; for if we believe that there is any foreknowledge thereof, there can exist nothing but such as is brought forth of necessity.' If therefore we, who have our share in possession of reason, could go further and possess the judgment of the mind of God, we should then think it most just that human reason should yield itself to the mind of God, just as we have determined that the senses and imagination ought to yield to reason.

"Let us therefore raise ourselves, if so be that we can, to that height of the loftiest intelligence. For there reason will see what it cannot of itself perceive, and that is to know how even such things as have uncertain results are perceived definitely and for certain by foreknowledge; and such foreknowledge will not be mere opinion, but rather the single and direct form of the highest knowledge unlimited by any finite bounds.

V

"What several figures things that live upon the earth do keep!
Some have their bodies stretched in length by which the dust
    they sweep
And do continual furrows make while on their breasts they creep.
Some lightly soaring up on high with wings the wind do smite
And through the longest airy space pass with an easy flight.
Some by their paces to imprint the ground with steps delight,
Which through the pleasant fields do pass or to the woods do go,
Whose several forms though to our eyes they do a difference show,
Yet by their looks cast down on earth their senses heavy grow.
Men only with more stately shape to higher objects rise,
Who with erected bodies stand and do the earth despise.
These figures warn (if baser thoughts blind not thine earthly eyes)
That thou who with an upright face dost look upon the sky,
Shouldst also raise thy mind aloft, lest while thou bearest high
Thine earthly head, thy soul opprest beneath thy body lie.

"Since then all that is known is apprehended, as we just now shewed, not according to its own nature but according to the nature of the knower, let us examine, so far as we lawfully may, the character of the divine nature, so that we may be able to learn what its knowledge is.

"The common opinion, according to all men living, is that God is eternal. Let us therefore consider what is eternity. For eternity will, I think, make clear to us at the same time the divine nature and knowledge.

"Eternity is the simultaneous and complete possession of infinite life. This will appear more clearly if we compare it with temporal things. All that lives under the conditions of time moves through the present from the past to the future; there is nothing set in time which can at one moment grasp the whole space of its lifetime. It cannot yet comprehend to-morrow; yesterday it has already lost. And in this life of to-day your life is no more than a changing, passing moment. And as Aristotle said of the universe, so it is of all that is subject to time; though it never began to be, nor will ever cease, and its life is co-extensive with the infinity of time, yet it is not such as can be held to be eternal. For though it apprehends and grasps a space of infinite lifetime, it does not embrace the whole simultaneously; it has not yet experienced the future. What we should rightly call eternal is that which grasps and possesses wholly and simultaneously the fulness of unending life, which lacks naught of the future, and has lost naught of the fleeting past; and such an existence must be ever present in itself to control and aid itself, and also must keep present with itself the infinity of changing time. Therefore, people who hear that Plato thought that this universe had no beginning of time and will have no end, are not right in thinking that in this way the created world is co-eternal with its creator. For to pass through unending life, the attribute which Plato ascribes to the universe is one thing; but it is another thing to grasp simultaneously the whole of unending life in the present; this is plainly a peculiar property of the mind of God.

"And further, God should not be regarded as older than His creations by any period of time, but rather by the peculiar property of His own single nature. For the infinite changing of temporal things tries to imitate the ever simultaneously present immutability of His life: it cannot succeed in imitating or equalling this, but sinks from immutability into change, and falls from the single directness of the present into an infinite space of future and past. And since this temporal state cannot possess its life completely and simultaneously, but it does in the same manner exist for ever without ceasing, it therefore seems to try in some degree to rival that which it cannot fulfil or represent, for it binds itself to some sort of present time out of this small and fleeting moment; but inasmuch as this temporal present bears a certain appearance of that abiding present, it somehow makes those, to whom it comes, seem to be in truth what they imitate. But since this imitation could not be abiding, the unending march of time has swept it away, and thus we find that it has bound together, as it passes, a chain of life, which it could not by abiding embrace in its fulness. And thus if we would apply proper epithets to those subjects, we can say, following Plato, that God is eternal, but the universe is continual.

"Since then all judgment apprehends the subject of its thought according to its own nature, and God has a condition of ever-present eternity, His knowledge, which passes over every change of time, embracing infinite lengths of past and future, views in its own direct comprehension everything as though it were taking place in the present. If you would weigh the foreknowledge by which God distinguishes all things, you will more rightly hold it to be a knowledge of a never-failing constancy in the present, than a foreknowledge of the future. Whence Providence is more rightly to be understood as a looking forth than a looking forward, because it is set far from low matters and looks forth upon all things as from a lofty mountain-top above all. Why then do you demand that all things occur by necessity, if divine light rests upon them, while men do not render necessary such things as they can see? Because you can see things of the present, does your sight therefore put upon them any necessity? Surely not. If one may not unworthily compare this present time with the divine, just as you can see things in this your temporal present, so God sees all things in His eternal present. Wherefore this divine foreknowledge does not change the nature or individual qualities of things: it sees things present in its understanding just as they will result some time in the future. It makes no confusion in its distinctions, and with one view of its mind it discerns all that shall come to pass whether of necessity or not. For instance, when you see at the same time a man walking on the earth and the sun rising in the heavens, you see each sight simultaneously, yet you distinguish between them, and decide that one is moving voluntarily, the other of necessity. In like manner the perception of God looks down upon all things without disturbing at all their nature, though they are present to Him but future under the conditions of time. Wherefore this foreknowledge is not opinion but knowledge resting upon truth, since He knows that a future event is, though He knows too that it will not occur of necessity. If you answer here that what God sees about to happen, cannot but happen, and that what cannot but happen is bound by necessity, you fasten me down to the word necessity. I will grant that we have a matter of most firm truth, but it is one to which scarce any man can approach unless he be a contemplator of the divine. For I shall answer that such a thing will occur of necessity, when it is viewed from the point of divine knowledge; but when it is examined in its own nature, it seems perfectly free and unrestrained. For there are two kinds of necessities; one is simple: for instance, a necessary fact, 'all men are mortal'; the other is conditional; for instance, if you know that a man is walking, he must be walking: for what each man knows cannot be otherwise than it is known to be; but the conditional one is by no means followed by this simple and direct necessity; for there is no necessity to compel a voluntary walker to proceed, though it is necessary that, if he walks, he should be proceeding. In the same way, if Providence sees an event in its present, that thing must be, though it has no necessity of its own nature. And God looks in His present upon those future things which come to pass through free will. Therefore if these things be looked at from the point of view of God's insight, they come to pass of necessity under the condition of divine knowledge; if, on the other hand, they are viewed by themselves, they do not lose the perfect freedom of their nature. Without doubt, then, all things that God foreknows do come to pass, but some of them proceed from free will; and though they result by coming into existence, yet they do not lose their own nature, because before they came to pass they could also not have come to pass.

"'What then,' you may ask, 'is the difference in their not being bound by necessity, since they result under all circumstances as by necessity, on account of the condition of divine knowledge?' This is the difference, as I just now put forward: take the sun rising and a man walking; while these operations are occurring, they cannot but occur: but the one was bound to occur before it did; the other was not so bound. What God has in His present, does exist without doubt; but of such things some follow by necessity, others by their authors' wills. Wherefore I was justified in saying that if these things be regarded from the view of divine knowledge, they are necessary, but if they are viewed by themselves, they are perfectly free from all ties of necessity: just as when you refer all, that is clear to the senses, to the reason, it becomes general truth, but it remains particular if regarded by itself. 'But,' you will say, 'if it is in my power to change a purpose of mine, I will disregard Providence, since I may change what Providence forsees.' To which I answer, 'You can change your purpose, but since the truth of Providence knows in its present that you can do so, and whether you do so, and in what direction you may change it, therefore you cannot escape that divine foreknowledge: just as you cannot avoid the glance of a present eye, though you may by your free will turn yourself to all kinds of different actions.' 'What?' you will say, 'can I by my own action change divine knowledge, so that if I choose now one thing, now another, Providence too will seem to change its knowledge?' No; divine insight precedes all future things, turning them back and recalling them to the present time of its own peculiar knowledge. It does not change, as you may think, between this and that alternation of foreknowledge. It is constant in preceding and embracing by one glance all your changes. And God does not receive this ever present grasp of all things and vision of the present at the occurrence of future events, but from His own peculiar directness. Whence also is that difficulty solved which you laid down a little while ago, that it was not worthy to say that our future events were the cause of God's knowledge. For this power of knowledge, ever in the present and embracing all things in its perception, does itself constrain all things, and owes naught to following events from which it has received naught. Thus, therefore, mortal men have their freedom of judgment intact. And since their wills are freed from all binding necessity, laws do not set rewards or punishments unjustly. God is ever the constant foreknowing overseer, and the ever-present eternity of His sight moves in harmony with the future nature of our actions, as it dispenses rewards to the good, and punishments to the bad. Hopes are not vainly put in God, nor prayers in vain offered: if these are right, they cannot but be answered. Turn therefore from vice: ensue virtue: raise your soul to upright hopes: send up on high your prayers from this earth. If you would be honest, great is the necessity enjoined upon your goodness, since all you do is done before the eyes of an all-seeing Judge."

Comments / on Boethius

. . . [Boethius], the holy soul who, to those who listened well, unmasked the deceitful world.   *DANTE (1317?)*

Like Plato, Boethius had the mind of a poet with which to take his flights, and like Aristotle a rational conscience for ballast.

Were the philosophical treatises of [important medieval philosophers like] Alcuin or Abelard or Thomas Aquinas translated before the nineteenth century? Not for popular sale in any case. But the *Consolatio Philosophiae* was pondered over and passed about for admiration in royal halls as well as in the gloom of a medieval study.
                                                        H. R. PATCH (1935)

If [Boethius] has not quite solved the problem of freedom, we may pertinently ask who has? His solution, at any rate, is in accord with Christian theology in its insistence on the two opposing and logically contradictory principles of human freedom and divine omniscience.

E. K. RAND (1928)

Even when he is speaking only as a philosopher, Boethius thinks as a Christian. *ETIENNE GILSON (1955)*

Although doubtless a professing Christian, [Boethius'] sentiments were those of pagan philosophy. *H. O. TAYLOR (1925)*

St. Thomas Aquinas
1225?–1274

One of the main intellectual forces in the newly flourishing civilization of Western Europe in the twelfth and thirteenth centuries was the translation of the complete works of Aristotle into Latin. They came by a circuitous route. Western philosophers still could not read Greek, but Arabic philosophers, who could, had begun translating Aristotle into their own language as early as the ninth century. Arabic and Christian thought had a meeting ground in Spain, where a Moslem culture had flourished alongside a Christian one since the eighth century. Toward the middle of the twelfth century Christian scholars in Spain began translating the works of Arabic philosophers into Latin, and by the end of the century almost the entire body of Aristotelian thought was available in that language. Until that time, Christian thinkers had been pretty much confined in their knowledge of Greek thought to the adaptations of Platonic philosophy incorporated into the writings of the Fathers of the Church. They now found themselves confronted with a comprehensive, orderly, generally convincing philosophic system that accounted for every phenomenon of human experience on the basis of reason alone. It posed a challenge of the same kind as that met by the early Fathers—to show that the Christian faith was not at odds with, but was a necessary addition to, human reason. Establishing a harmony between faith and reason, between Christian theology and Aristotelian philosophy, became the main concern of theologians during the next few centuries.

St. Thomas Aquinas was the greatest of these harmonizers. He came from a well-to-do family in southern Italy and was educated at the monastery of Monte Cassino and at the University of Naples. When he was about twenty, he joined the Dominican friars, an order noted for its emphasis on scholarship. He had a brilliant career as a teacher and writer and could have reached high ecclesiastical office but refused the chances offered him, choosing to concentrate his energies on scholarship. Within a half century after his death he was canonized as a saint, primarily because of his theological achievements. His influence has been felt by all subsequent Catholic thinkers and was formally recognized by Pope Leo XIII, in 1879, and by Pope Pius XII, in 1950, both of whom declared in papal encyclicals that the writings of St. Thomas should serve as a basis for contemporary theological speculation.

St. Thomas outranks even St. Augustine as the most prolific writer in the history of the Church. The author of massive treatises touching upon almost every conceivable topic relevant to the Christian faith and upon almost every significant preceding discussion of those topics, he strove to synthesize whatever knowledge from whatever source was available into a comprehensive system expounding all the principles of Christian belief. His most ambitious work is the *Summa Theologica (The Summation of Theology),* designed to stand as a complete, reasoned summation of opinion about every detail in the whole of Christian theology. It also stands as a characteristic expression of scholasticism, the intellectual method and viewpoint that dominated medieval thought from the twelfth through the fourteenth centuries. In a strict sense, *scholasticism* is a term designating method only—the procedures for scholarly exposition and argumentation developed in medieval schools and universities and usually followed by medieval scholars. In a broader sense, however, the term is commonly used in reference not only to the method but also to the substance of this kind of medieval thinking. The scholastic program of studies emphasized dialectics, natural philosophy, and metaphysics, but held that all these disciplines were subordinate to, and valuable mainly for their contribution to, the study of theology. The scholastic method was founded on the principle of minute, detailed analysis. In scholastic argumentation, such as the *Summation of Theology* engages in, the writer organizes his thought into a series of topics or questions and divides each question into a series of separate articles, each dealing with a specific issue raised by the question. For each article he lists objections to his position; then expresses his own point of view, citing authorities to support it; and finally replies to each objection in sequence.

In the following selections, the first question has been presented in full to demonstrate the method; in the remaining questions, much of the scholastic apparatus has been omitted to allow St. Thomas' statements of his own position to stand plain. The length at which the first question is handled will provide some idea of the magnitude of St. Thomas' achievement; the *Summation of Theology* contains 631 questions and, under them, some 10,000 replies to specific objections.

The Summation of Theology

QUESTION I / *The Nature and Extent of Sacred Doctrine*

To place our purpose within proper limits, we first endeavour to investigate the nature and extent of this sacred doctrine. Concerning this there are ten points of inquiry:—

From *Summa Theologica*, 2nd ed., Part I, Vols. I, V. Published, 1941, by Burns & Oates Ltd. Reprinted by permission of Burns & Oates Ltd. and Benziger Brothers, Inc.

(1) Whether it is necessary? (2) Whether it is a science? (3) Whether it is one or many? (4) Whether it is speculative or practical? (5) How it is compared with other sciences? (6) Whether it is the same as wisdom? (7) Whether God is its subject-matter? (8) Whether it is a matter of argument? (9) Whether it rightly employs metaphors and similes? (10) Whether the Sacred Scripture of this doctrine may be expounded in different senses?

FIRST ARTICLE / WHETHER, BESIDES PHILOSOPHY, ANY FURTHER DOCTRINE IS REQUIRED?

We proceed thus to the First Article:—

Objection 1. It seems that, besides philosophical science, we have no need of any further knowledge. For man should not seek to know what is above reason: *Seek not the things that are too high for thee* (Ecclus. iii. 22). But whatever is not above reason is fully treated of in philosophical science. Therefore any other knowledge besides philosophical science is superfluous.

Obj. 2. Further, knowledge can be concerned only with being, for nothing can be known, save what is true; and all that is, is true. But everything that is, is treated of in philosophical science—even God Himself; so that there is a part of philosophy called theology, or the divine science, as Aristotle has proved (*Metaph.* vi.). Therefore, besides philosophical science, there is no need of any further knowledge.

On the contrary, It is written (2 Tim. iii. 16): *All Scripture inspired of God is profitable to teach, to reprove, to correct, to instruct in justice.* Now Scripture, inspired of God, is no part of philosophical science, which has been built up by human reason. Therefore it is useful that besides philosophical science there should be other knowledge—*i.e.,* inspired of God.

I answer that, It was necessary for man's salvation that there should be a knowledge revealed by God, besides philosophical science built up by human reason. Firstly, indeed, because man is directed to God, as to an end that surpasses the grasp of his reason; *The eye hath not seen, O God, besides Thee, what things Thou hast prepared for them that wait for Thee* (Isa. lxiv. 4). But the end must first be known by men who are to direct their thoughts and actions to the end. Hence it was necessary for the salvation of man that certain truths which exceed human reason should be made known to him by divine revelation. Even as regards those truths about God which human reason could have discovered, it was necessary that man should be taught by a divine revelation; because the truth about God such as reason could discover, would only be known by a few, and that after a long time, and with the admixture of many errors. Whereas man's whole salvation, which is in God, depends upon the knowledge of this truth. Therefore, in order that the salvation of men might be brought about more fitly and more surely, it was necessary that they should be taught divine truths by divine revelation. It was therefore necessary that, besides philosophical science built up by reason there should be a sacred science learnt through revelation.

Reply Obj. 1. Although those things which are beyond man's knowledge may not be sought for by man through his reason, nevertheless, once they are revealed by God they must be accepted by faith. Hence the sacred text continues, *For many things are shown to thee above the understanding of man* (Ecclus. iii. 25). And in this the sacred science consists.

Reply Obj. 2. Sciences are differentiated according to the various means through which knowledge is obtained. For the astronomer and the physicist both may prove the same conclusion—that the earth, for instance, is round: the astronomer by means of mathematics (*i.e.,* abstracting from matter), but the physicist by means of matter itself. Hence there is no reason why those things which may be learnt from philosophical science, so far as they can be known by natural reason, may not also be taught us by another science so far as they fall within revelation. Hence theology included in sacred doctrine differs in kind from that theology which is part of philosophy.

SECOND ARTICLE / WHETHER SACRED DOCTRINE IS A SCIENCE?

We proceed thus to the Second Article:—

Objection 1. It seems that sacred doctrine is not a science. For every science proceeds from self-evident principles. But sacred doctrine proceeds from articles of faith which are not self-evident, since their truth is not admitted by all: *For all men have not faith* (2 Thess. iii. 2). Therefore sacred doctrine is not a science.

Obj. 2. Further, no science deals with individual facts. But this sacred science treats of individual facts, such as the deeds of Abraham, Isaac, and Jacob, and such like. Therefore sacred doctrine is not a science.

On the contrary, Augustine says (*De Trin.* xiv. 1), *to this science alone belongs that whereby saving faith is begotten, nourished, protected, and strengthened.* But this can be said of no science except sacred doctrine. Therefore sacred doctrine is a science.

I answer that, Sacred doctrine is a science. We must bear in mind that there are two kinds of sciences. There are some which proceed from a principle known by the natural light of the intelligence, such as arithmetic and geometry and the like. There are some which proceed from principles known by the light of a higher science: thus the science of perspective proceeds from principles established by geometry, and music from principles established by arithmetic. So it is that sacred doctrine is a science, because it proceeds from principles established by the light of a higher science, namely, the science of God and the blessed. Hence, just as the musician accepts on authority the principles taught him by the mathematician, so sacred science is established on principles revealed by God.

Reply Obj. 1. The principles of any science are either in themselves self-evident, or reducible to the conclusions of a higher science; and such, as we have said, are the principles of sacred doctrine.

Reply Obj. 2. Individual facts are treated of in sacred doctrine, not because it is concerned with them principally: but they are introduced rather both as examples to be followed in our lives (as in moral sciences), and in order to establish the authority of those men through whom the divine revelation, on which this sacred scripture or doctrine is based, has come down to us.

THIRD ARTICLE / WHETHER SACRED DOCTRINE IS ONE SCIENCE?

We proceed thus to the Third Article:—
Objection 1. It seems that sacred doctrine is not one science; for according to the Philosopher[1] (*Poster.* i.) *that science is one which treats only of one class of subjects.* But the creator and the creature, both of whom are treated of in sacred doctrine, cannot be grouped together under one class of subjects. Therefore sacred doctrine is not one science.
Obj. 2. Further, in sacred doctrine we treat of angels, corporeal creatures, and human morality. But these belong to separate philosophical sciences. Therefore sacred doctrine cannot be one science.
On the contrary, Holy Scripture speaks of it as one science: *Wisdom gave him the knowledge* [*scientiam*] *of holy things* (Wisd. x. 10).
I answer that, sacred doctrine is one science. The unity of a faculty or habit is to be gauged by its object, not indeed, in its material aspect, but as regards the precise formality under which it is an object. For example, man, ass, stone, agree in the one precise formality of being coloured; and colour is the formal object of sight. Therefore, because Sacred Scripture considers things precisely under the formality of being divinely revealed, whatever has been divinely revealed·possesses the one precise formality of the object of this science; and therefore is included under sacred doctrine as under one science.
Reply Obj. 1. Sacred doctrine does not treat of God and creatures equally, but of God primarily; and of creatures only so far as they are referable to God as their beginning or end. Hence the unity of this science is not impaired.
Reply Obj. 2. Nothing prevents inferior faculties or habits from being differentiated by something which falls under a higher faculty or habit as well; because the higher faculty or habit regards the object in its more universal formality, as the object of the *common sense* is whatever affects the senses, including, therefore, whatever is visible or audible. Hence the *common sense,* although one faculty, extends to all the objects of the five senses. Similarly, objects which are the subject-matter of different philosophical sciences can yet be treated of by this one single sacred science under one aspect precisely so far as they can be included in revelation. So that in this way sacred doctrine bears, as it were, the stamp of the divine science, which is one and simple, yet extends to everything.

---

[1]Aristotle's reputation among the scholastics was so great that they honored him by referring to him simply as "the Philosopher," as though no further identification were required.

FOURTH ARTICLE / WHETHER SACRED DOCTRINE
IS A PRACTICAL SCIENCE?

We proceed thus to the Fourth Article:—
Objection 1. It seems that sacred doctrine is a practical science; for
a practical science is that which ends in action according to the Philosopher (*Metaph.* ii.). But sacred doctrine is ordained to action; *Be ye
doers of the word, and not hearers only* (Jas. i. 22). Therefore sacred doctrine is a practical science.

Obj. 2. Further, sacred doctrine is divided into the Old and the New
Law.[2] But law implies a moral science, which is a practical science.
Therefore sacred doctrine is a practical science.

On the contrary, Every practical science is concerned with human
operations; as moral science is concerned with human acts, and architecture with buildings. But sacred doctrine is chiefly concerned with
God, whose handiwork is especially man. Therefore it is not a practical
but a speculative science.

I answer that, Sacred doctrine, being one, extends to things which
belong to different philosophical sciences, because it considers in each
the same formal aspect, namely so far as they can be known through
divine revelation. Hence, although among the philosophical sciences
one is speculative and another practical, nevertheless sacred doctrine
includes both; as God, by one and the same science, knows both Himself
and His works. Still, it is speculative rather than practical, because
it is more concerned with divine things than with human acts; though it
does treat even of these latter, inasmuch as man is ordained by them to
the perfect knowledge of God, in which consists eternal bliss. This is
a sufficient answer to the Objections.

FIFTH ARTICLE / WHETHER SACRED DOCTRINE IS NOBLER
THAN OTHER SCIENCES?

We proceed thus to the Fifth Article:—
Objection 1. It seems that sacred doctrine is not nobler than other
sciences; for the nobility of a science depends on the certitude it establishes. But other sciences, the principles of which cannot be doubted,
seem to be more certain than sacred doctrine; for its principles—namely,
articles of faith—can be doubted. Therefore other sciences seem to
be nobler.

Obj. 2. Further, it is the sign of a lower science to depend upon a
higher; as music depends upon arithmetic. But sacred doctrine does
in a sense depend upon the philosophical sciences; for Jerome observes,
in his Epistle to Magnus, that *the ancient doctors so enriched their books
with the ideas and phrases of the philosophers, that thou knowest not what
more to admire in them, their profane erudition or their scriptural learning.*
Therefore sacred doctrine is inferior to other sciences.

---

[2]The *Old Law* and the *New Law* are designations for the Old Testament and New Testament, respectively.

On the contrary, Other sciences are called the handmaidens of this one: *Wisdom sent her maids to invite to the tower* (Prov. ix. 3).

I answer that, Since this science is partly speculative and partly practical, it transcends all others speculative and practical. Now one speculative science is said to be nobler than another, either by reason of its greater certitude, or by reason of the higher worth of its subject-matter. In both these respects this science surpasses other speculative sciences; in point of greater certitude, because other sciences derive their certitude from the natural light of human reason, which can err; whereas this derives its certitude from the light of the divine knowledge, which cannot be misled: in point of the higher worth of its subject-matter, because this science treats chiefly of those things which by their sublimity transcend human reason; while other sciences consider only those things which are within reason's grasp. Of the practical sciences, that one is nobler which is ordained to a further purpose, as political science is nobler than military science; for the good of the army is directed to the good of the State. But the purpose of this science, in so far as it is practical, is eternal bliss; to which as to an ultimate end the purposes of every practical science are directed. Hence it is clear that from every standpoint it is nobler than other sciences.

Reply Obj. 1. It may well happen that what is in itself the more certain may seem to us the less certain on account of the weakness of our intelligence, "which is dazzled by the clearest objects of nature; as the owl is dazzled by the light of the sun" (*Metaph.* ii., *lect.* i.). Hence the fact that some happen to doubt about articles of faith is not due to the uncertain nature of the truths, but to the weakness of human intelligence; yet the slenderest knowledge that may be obtained of the highest things is more desirable than the most certain knowledge obtained of lesser things, as is said in *de Animalibus* xi.

Reply Obj. 2. This science can in a sense depend upon the philosophical sciences, not as though it stood in need of them, but only in order to make its teaching clearer. For it accepts its principles not from other sciences; but immediately from God, by revelation. Therefore it does not depend upon other sciences as upon the higher, but makes use of them as of the lesser, and as handmaidens: even so the master sciences make use of the sciences that supply their materials, as political of military science. That it thus uses them is not due to its own defect or insufficiency, but to the defect of our intelligence, which is more easily led by what is known through natural reason (from which proceed the other sciences), to that which is above reason, such as are the teachings of this science.

SIXTH ARTICLE / WHETHER THIS DOCTRINE IS THE SAME AS WISDOM?

We proceed thus to the Sixth Article:—

Objection 1. It seems that this doctrine is not the same as wisdom. For no doctrine which borrows its principles is worthy of the name of wisdom; seeing that the wise man directs, and is not directed (*Metaph.* i.). But this doctrine borrows its principles. Therefore this science is not wisdom.

Obj. 2. Further, it is a part of wisdom to prove the principles of other sciences. Hence it is called the chief of sciences, as is clear in *Ethic* vi. But this doctrine does not prove the principles of other sciences. Therefore it is not the same as wisdom.

Obj. 3. Further, this doctrine is acquired by study, whereas wisdom is acquired by God's inspiration; so that it is numbered among the gifts of the Holy Spirit (Isa. xi. 2). Therefore this doctrine is not the same as wisdom.

On the contrary, It is written (Deut. iv. 6): *This is your wisdom and understanding in the sight of nations.*

I answer that, This doctrine is wisdom above all human wisdom; not merely in any one order, but absolutely. For since it is the part of a wise man to arrange and to judge, and since lesser matters should be judged in the light of some higher principle, he is said to be wise in any one order who considers the highest principle in that order: thus in the order of building he who plans the form of the house is called wise and architect, in opposition to the inferior labourers who trim the wood and make ready the stones: *As a wise architect I have laid the foundation* (I Cor. iii. 10). Again, in the order of all human life, the prudent man is called wise, inasmuch as he directs his acts to a fitting end: *Wisdom is prudence to a man* (Prov. x. 23). Therefore he who considers absolutely the highest cause of the whole universe, namely God, is most of all called wise. Hence wisdom is said to be the knowledge of divine things, as Augustine says (*De Trin.* xii. 14). But sacred doctrine essentially treats of God viewed as the highest cause—not only so far as He can be known through creatures just as philosophers knew Him—*That which is known of God is manifest in them* (Rom. i. 19)—but also so far as He is known to Himself alone and revealed to others. Hence sacred doctrine is especially called wisdom.

Reply Obj. 1. Sacred doctrine derives its principles not from any human knowledge, but from the divine knowledge, through which, as through the highest wisdom, all our knowledge is set in order.

Reply Obj. 2. The principles of other sciences either are evident and cannot be proved, or are proved by natural reason through some other science. But the knowledge proper to this science comes through revelation, and not through natural reason. Therefore it has no concern to prove the principles of other sciences, but only to judge of them. Whatsoever is found in other sciences contrary to any truth of this science, must be condemned as false: *Destroying counsels and every height that exalteth itself against the knowledge of God* (2 Cor. x 4, 5).

Reply Obj. 3. Since judgment appertains to wisdom, the twofold manner of judging produces a twofold wisdom. A man may judge in one way by inclination, as whoever has the habit of a virtue judges rightly of what concerns that virtue by his very inclination towards it. Hence it is the virtuous man, as we read, who is the measure and rule of human acts. In another way, by knowledge, just as a man learned in moral science might be able to judge rightly about virtuous acts, though he had not the virtue. The first manner of judging divine things belongs to that wisdom which is set down among the gifts of the Holy Ghost: *The spiritual man judgeth all things* (I Cor. ii. 15). And Dionysius[3] says (*Div. Nom.* ii.): *Hierotheus is taught not by mere learning, but by experience of divine things.* The second manner of judging belongs to this doctrine, which is acquired by study, though its principles are obtained by revelation.

SEVENTH ARTICLE / WHETHER GOD IS THE OBJECT OF THIS SCIENCE?

We proceed thus to the Seventh Article:—

Objection 1. It seems that God is not the object of this science. For in every science the nature of its object is presupposed. But this science cannot presuppose the essence of God, for Damascene[4] says (*De Fid. Orth.* I iv.): *It is impossible to define the essence of God.* Therefore God is not the object of this science.

Obj. 2. Further, whatever conclusions are reached in any science must be comprehended under the object of the science. But in Holy Writ we reach conclusions not only concerning God, but concerning many other things, such as creatures and human morality. Therefore God is not the object of this science.

On the contrary, The object of the science is that of which it principally treats. But in this science the treatment is mainly about God; for it is called theology, as treating of God. Therefore God is the object of this science.

I answer that, God is the object of this science. The relation between a science and its object is the same as that between a habit or faculty and its object. Now properly speaking the object of a faculty or habit is the thing under the aspect of which all things are referred to that faculty or habit, as man and stone are referred to the faculty of sight in that they are coloured. Hence coloured things are the proper objects of sight. But in sacred science all things are treated of under the aspect of God; either because they are God Himself; or because they refer to God as their beginning and end. Hence it follows that God is in very truth the object of this science. This is clear also from the principles of this science, namely, the articles of faith, for faith is about God. The object of the principles and of the whole science must be the same, since the whole science is contained virtually in its principles. Some, however, looking to what is treated of in this science, and not to the aspect under which it is treated, have asserted the object of this science to be something other than God—that is, either things and signs; or the works of salvation; or the whole Christ, as the head and members. Of all these things, in truth, we treat in this science, but so far as they have reference to God.

Reply Obj. 1. Although we cannot know in what consists the essence of God, nevertheless in this science we make use of His effects, either

---

[3] An Athenian of the first century converted to Christianity by St. Paul. During the later Middle Ages he was considered to be the author of a number of philosophical and theological works written around the beginning of the sixth century by an anonymous author who pretended they had been written by Dionysius. The anonymous author is now generally known as Pseudo-Dionysius, and it is to his work that St. Thomas refers.

[4] An eighth-century theologian who lived in the Near East and who wrote what became the standard works of dogmatic theology in Greek Orthodox Christianity. He was canonized by both the Eastern and the Western Churches.

of nature or of grace, in place of a definition, in regard to whatever is treated of in this science concerning God; even as in some philosophical sciences we demonstrate something about a cause from its effect, by taking the effect in place of a definition of the cause.

Reply Obj. 2. Whatever other conclusions are reached in this sacred science are comprehended under God, not as parts or species or accidents, but as in some way related to Him.

EIGHTH ARTICLE / WHETHER SACRED DOCTRINE IS A MATTER OF ARGUMENT?

We proceed thus to the Eighth Article:—

Objection 1. It seems this doctrine is not a matter of argument. For Ambrose[5] says (*De Fide,* I): *Put arguments aside where faith is sought.* But in this doctrine faith especially is sought: *But these things are written that you may believe* (John xx. 31). Therefore sacred doctrine is not a matter of argument.

Obj. 2. Further, if it is a matter of argument, the argument is either from authority or from reason. If it is from authority, it seems unbefitting its dignity, for the proof from authority is the weakest form of proof. But if from reason, this is unbefitting its end, because, according to Gregory[6] (*Homil.* 26), *faith has no merit in those things of which human reason brings its own experience.* Therefore sacred doctrine is not a matter of argument.

On the contrary, The Scripture says that a bishop should *embrace that faithful word which is according to doctrine, that he may be able to exhort in sound doctrine and to convince the gainsayers* (Tit. i. 9).

I answer that, As other sciences do not argue in proof of their principles, but argue from their principles to demonstrate other truths in these sciences: so this doctrine does not argue in proof of its principles, which are the articles of faith, but from them it goes on to prove something else; as the Apostle[7] from the resurrection of Christ argues in proof of the general resurrection (I Cor. xv.). However, it is to be borne in mind, in regard to the philosophical sciences, that the inferior sciences neither prove their principles nor dispute with those who deny them, but leave this to a higher science; whereas the highest of them, viz., metaphysics, can dispute with one who denies its principles, if only the opponent will make some concession; but if he concede nothing, it can have no dispute with him, though it can answer his objections. Hence Sacred Scripture, since it has no science above itself, can dispute with one who denies its principles only if the opponent admits some at least of the truths obtained through divine revelation; thus we can argue with heretics from texts in Holy Writ, and against those who

---

[5]One of the great Fathers of the Western Church (340?—397). He was bishop of Milan at the time of Augustine's conversion.

[6]An outstanding theologian and the greatest pope during the first millennium of Western Christianity (540?—604).

[7]Just as the role played by Aristotle in the development of philosophy was indicated by calling him simply "the Philosopher," the role of St. Paul in the spread of Christianity was indicated by calling him simply "the Apostle."

deny one article of faith we can argue from another. If our opponent believes nothing of divine revelation, there is no longer any means of proving the articles of faith by reasoning, but only of answering his objections—if he has any—against faith. Since faith rests upon infallible truth, and since the contrary of a truth can never be demonstrated, it is clear that the arguments brought against faith cannot be demonstrations, but are difficulties that can be answered.

Reply Obj. 1. Although arguments from human reason cannot avail to prove what must be received on faith, nevertheless this doctrine argues from articles of faith to other truths.

Reply Obj. 2. This doctrine is especially based upon arguments from authority, inasmuch as its principles are obtained by revelation: thus we ought to believe on the authority of those to whom the revelation has been made. Nor does this take away from the dignity of this doctrine, for although the argument from authority based on human reason is the weakest, yet the argument from authority based on divine revelation is the strongest. But sacred doctrine makes use even of human reason, not, indeed, to prove faith (for thereby the merit of faith would come to an end), but to make clear other things that are put forward in this doctrine. Since therefore grace does not destroy nature, but perfects it, natural reason should minister to faith as the natural bent of the will ministers to charity. Hence the Apostle says: *Bringing into captivity every understanding unto the obedience of Christ* (2 Cor. x. 5). Hence sacred doctrine makes use also of the authority of philosophers in those questions in which they were able to know the truth by natural reason, as Paul quotes a saying of Aratus:[8] *As some also of your own poets said; For we are also His offspring* (Acts xvii. 28). Nevertheless, sacred doctrine makes use of these authorities as extrinsic and probable arguments; but properly uses the authority of the canonical Scriptures as an incontrovertible proof, and the authority of the doctors of the Church as one that may properly be used, yet merely as probable. For our faith rests upon the revelation made to the apostles and prophets, who wrote the canonical books, and not on the revelations (if any such there are) made to other doctors. Hence Augustine says (*Epist. ad Hieron.* xix. I.): *Only those books of Scripture which are called canonical have I learnt to hold in such honour as to believe their authors have not erred in any way in writing them. But other authors I so read as not to deem anything in their works to be true, merely on account of their having so thought and written, whatever may have been their holiness and learning.*

NINTH ARTICLE / WHETHER HOLY SCRIPTURE SHOULD USE METAPHORS?

We proceed thus to the Ninth Article:—

Objection 1. It seems that Holy Scripture should not use metaphors. For that which is proper to the lowest science seems not to befit this science, which holds the highest place of all. But to proceed by the aid

---

[8] Greek general and statesman of the third century B.C.

of various similitudes and figures is proper to poetry, the least of all the sciences. Therefore it is not fitting that this science should make use of such similitudes.

Obj. 2. Further, this doctrine seems to be intended to make truth clear. Hence a reward is held out to those who manifest it: *They that explain me shall have life everlasting* (Ecclus. xxiv. 31). But by such similitudes truth is obscured. Therefore to put forward divine truths by likening them to corporeal things does not befit this science.

Obj. 3. Further, the higher creatures are, the nearer they approach to the divine likeness. If therefore any creature be taken to represent God, this representation ought chiefly to be taken from the higher creatures, and not from the lower; yet this is often found in the Scriptures.

On the contrary, It is written (Osee xii. 10): *I have multiplied visions, and I have used similitudes by the ministry of the prophets.* But to put forward anything by means of similitudes is to use metaphors. Therefore this sacred science may use metaphors.

I answer that, It is befitting Holy Writ to put forward divine and spiritual truths by means of comparisons with material things. For God provides for everything according to the capacity of its nature. Now it is natural to man to attain to intellectual truths through sensible objects,[9] because all our knowledge originates from sense. Hence in Holy Writ spiritual truths are fittingly taught under the likeness of material things. This is what Dionysius says (*Cælest. Hierarch.* i.): *We cannot be enlightened by the divine rays except they be hidden within the covering of many sacred veils.* It is also befitting Holy Writ, which is proposed to all without distinction of persons—*To the wise and to the unwise I am a debtor* (Rom. i. 14)—that spiritual truths be expounded by means of figures taken from corporeal things, in order that thereby even the simple who are unable by themselves to grasp intellectual things may be able to understand it.

Reply Obj. 1. Poetry makes use of metaphors to produce a representation, for it is natural to man to be pleased with representations. But sacred doctrine makes use of metaphors as both necessary and useful.

Reply Obj. 2. The ray of divine revelation is not extinguished by the sensible imagery wherewith it is veiled, as Dionysius says (*Cælest. Hierarch.* i.); and its truth so far remains that it does not allow the minds of those to whom the revelation has been made, to rest in the metaphors, but raises them to the knowledge of truths; and through those to whom the revelation has been made others also may receive instruction in these matters. Hence those things that are taught metaphorically in one part of Scripture, in other parts are taught more openly. The very hiding of truth in figures is useful for the exercise of thoughtful minds, and as a defence against the ridicule of the impious, according to the words *Give not that which is holy to dogs* (Matth. vii. 6).

Reply Obj. 3. As Dionysius says, (*loc. cit.*) it is more fitting that divine truths should be expounded under the figure of less noble than of nobler bodies, and this for three reasons. Firstly, because thereby men's minds are the better preserved from error. For then it is clear that these things

---

[9] I.e., objects perceived through the senses.

are not literal descriptions of divine truths, which might have been open
to doubt had they been expressed under the figure of nobler bodies,
especially for those who could think of nothing nobler than bodies.
Secondly, because this is more befitting the knowledge of God that we
have in this life. For what He is not is clearer to us than what He is.
Therefore similitudes drawn from things farthest away from God form
within us a truer estimate that God is above whatsoever we may say or
think of Him. Thirdly, because thereby divine truths are the better
hidden from the unworthy.

TENTH ARTICLE / WHETHER IN HOLY SCRIPTURE A WORD
MAY HAVE SEVERAL SENSES?

We proceed thus to the Tenth Article:—
Objection 1. It seems that in Holy Writ a word cannot have several
senses, historical or literal, allegorical, tropological or moral, and
anagogical. For many different senses in one text produce confusion and
deception and destroy all force of argument. Hence no argument, but
only fallacies, can be deduced from a multiplicity of propositions. But
Holy Writ ought to be able to state the truth without any fallacy. Therefore in it there cannot be several senses to a word.
Obj. 2. Further, Augustine says (*De util. cred.* iii.) that *the Old Testament has a fourfold division as to history, etiology, analogy, and allegory.* Now
these four seem altogether different from the four divisions mentioned
in the first objection. Therefore it does not seem fitting to explain the
same word of Holy Writ according to the four different senses mentioned above.
Obj. 3. Further, besides these senses, there is the parabolical, which
is not one of these four.
On the contrary, Gregory says (*Moral.* xx., I): *Holy Writ by the manner
of its speech transcends every science, because in one and the same sentence,
while it describes a fact, it reveals a mystery.*
I answer that, The author of Holy Writ is God, in whose power it
is to signify His meaning, not by words only (as man also can do), but
also by things themselves. So whereas in every other science things are
signified by words, this science has the property, that the things signified
by the words have themselves also a signification. Therefore that first
signification whereby words signify things belongs to the first sense,
the historical or literal. That signification whereby things signified
by words have themselves also a signification is called the spiritual sense,
which is based on the literal, and presupposes it. Now this spiritual sense
has a threefold division. For as the Apostle says (Heb. x. I) the Old
Law is a figure of the New Law, and Dionysius says (*Cœl. Hier.* i.) *the New
Law itself is a figure of future glory.* Again, in the New Law, whatever
our Head has done is a type of what we ought to do. Therefore, so far
as the things of the Old Law signify the things of the New Law, there is
the allegorical sense; so far as the things done in Christ, or so far as
the things which signify Christ, are types of what we ought to do, there
is the moral sense. But so far as they signify what relates to eternal

glory, there is the anagogical sense. Since the literal sense is that which the author intends, and since the author of Holy Writ is God, Who by one act comprehends all things by His intellect, it is not unfitting, as Augustine says (*Confess.* xii.), if, even according to the literal sense, one word in Holy Writ should have several senses.

Reply Obj. 1. The multiplicity of these senses does not produce equivocation or any other kind of multiplicity, seeing that these senses are not multiplied because one word signifies several things; but because the things signified by the words can be themselves types of other things. Thus in Holy Writ no confusion results, for all the senses are founded on one—the literal—from which alone can any argument be drawn, and not from those intended in allegory, as Augustine says (*Epist.* xlviii.). Nevertheless, nothing of Holy Scripture perishes on account of this, since nothing necessary to faith is contained under the spiritual sense which is not elsewhere put forward by the Scripture in its literal sense.

Reply Obj. 2. These three—history, etiology, analogy—are grouped under the literal sense. For it is called history, as Augustine expounds (*loc. cit.*), whenever anything is simply related; it is called etiology when its cause is assigned, as when Our Lord gave the reason why Moses allowed the putting away of wives—namely, on account of the hardness of men's hearts; it is called analogy whenever the truth of one text of Scripture is shown not to contradict the truth of another. Of these four, allegory alone stands for the three spiritual senses. Thus Hugh of S. Victor[10] (*Sacram.* iv. 4 *Prolog.*) includes the anagogical under the allegorical sense, laying down three senses only—the historical, the allegorical, and the tropological.

Reply Obj. 3. The parabolical sense[11] is contained in the literal, for by words things are signified properly and figuratively. Nor is the figure itself, but that which is figured, the literal sense. When Scripture speaks of God's arm, the literal sense is not that God has such a member, but only what is signified by this member, namely, operative power. Hence it is plain that nothing false can ever underlie the literal sense of Holy Writ.

QUESTION 2 | *The Existence of God*

FIRST ARTICLE | WHETHER THE EXISTENCE OF GOD IS SELF-EVIDENT?

. . . A thing can be self-evident in either of two ways; on the one hand, self-evident in itself, though not to us; on the other, self-evident in itself, and to us. A proposition is self-evident because the predicate is included in the essence of the subject, as 'Man is an animal,' for animal is contained in the essence of man. If, therefore, the essence of the predicate and subject be known to all, the proposition will be self-evident to all; as is clear with regard to the first principles of demonstration, the terms

---

[10]French theologian (1096?—1141).
[11]The meaning based on parables.

of which are common things that no one is ignorant of, such as being and non-being, whole and part, and suchlike. If, however, there are some to whom the essence of the predicate and subject is unknown, the proposition will be self-evident in itself, but not to those who do not know the meaning of the predicate and subject of the proposition. Therefore, it happens, as Boethius says *(Hebdom., the title of which is: 'Whether all that is, is good'),* 'that there are some mental concepts of self-evident only to the learned, as that incorporeal substances are not in space.' Therefore I say that this proposition, 'God exists,' of itself is self-evident, for the predicate is the same as the subject; because God is His own existence as will be hereafter shown (Q. III., A. 4). Now because we do not know the essence of God, the proposition is not self-evident to us; but needs to be demonstrated by things that are more known to us, though less known in their nature—namely, by effects. . . .

SECOND ARTICLE / WHETHER IT CAN BE DEMONSTRATED THAT GOD EXISTS?

. . . Demonstration can be made in two ways: One is through the cause, and is called *a priori,* and this is to argue from what is prior absolutely. The other is through the effect, and is called a demonstration *a posteriori;* this is to argue from what is prior relatively only to us. When an effect is better known to us than its cause, from the effect we proceed to the knowledge of the cause. And from every effect the existence of its proper cause can be demonstrated, so long as its effects are better known to us; because since every effect depends upon its cause, if the effect exists, the cause must pre-exist. Hence the existence of God, in so far as it is not self-evident to us, can be demonstrated from those of His effects which are known to us. . . .

THIRD ARTICLE / WHETHER GOD EXISTS?

. . . The existence of God can be proved in five ways.
The first and more manifest way is the argument from motion. It is certain, and evident to our senses, that in the world some things are in motion. Now whatever is in motion is put in motion by another, for nothing can be in motion except it is in potentiality to that towards which it is in motion; whereas a thing moves inasmuch as it is in act. For motion is nothing else than the reduction of something from potentiality to actuality. But nothing can be reduced from potentiality to actuality, except by something in a state of actuality. Thus that which is actually hot, as fire, makes wood, which is potentially hot, to be actually hot, and thereby moves and changes it. Now it is not possible that the same thing should be at once in actuality and potentiality in the same respect, but only in different respects. For what is actually hot cannot simultaneously be potentially hot; but it is simultaneously potentially cold. It is therefore impossible that in the same respect and in the same way a thing should be both mover and moved, *i.e.,* that it should move itself. There-

fore, whatever is in motion must be put in motion by another. If that by which it is put in motion be itself put in motion, then this also must needs be put in motion by another, and that by another again. But this cannot go on to infinity, because then there would be no first mover, and, consequently, no other mover; seeing that subsequent movers move only inasmuch as they are put in motion by the first mover; as the staff moves only because it is put in motion by the hand. Therefore it is necessary to arrive at a first mover, put in motion by no other; and this everyone understands to be God.

The second way is from the nature of the efficient cause. In the world of sense we find there is an order of efficient causes. There is no case known (neither is it, indeed, possible) in which a thing is found to be the efficient cause of itself; for so it would be prior to itself, which is impossible. Now in efficient causes it is not possible to go on to infinity, because in all efficient causes following in order, the first is the cause of the intermediate cause, and the intermediate is the cause of the ultimate cause, whether the intermediate cause be several, or one only. Now to take away the cause is to take away the effect. Therefore, if there be no first cause among efficient causes, there will be no ultimate, nor any intermediate cause. But if in efficient causes it is possible to go on to infinity, there will be no first efficient cause, neither will there be an ultimate effect, nor any intermediate efficient causes; all of which is plainly false. Therefore it is necessary to admit a first efficient cause, to which everyone gives the name of God.

The third way is taken from possibility and necessity, and runs thus. We find in nature things that are possible to be and not to be, since they are found to be generated, and to corrupt, and consequently, they are possible to be and not to be. But it is impossible for these always to exist, for that which is possible not to be at some time is not. Therefore, if everything is possible not to be, then at one time there could have been nothing in existence. Now if this were true, even now there would be nothing in existence, because that which does not exist only begins to exist by something already existing. Therefore, if at one time nothing was in existence, it would have been impossible for anything to have begun to exist; and thus even now nothing would be in existence— which is absurd. Therefore, not all beings are merely possible, but there must exist something the existence of which is necessary. But every necessary thing either has its necessity caused by another, or not. Now it is impossible to go on to infinity in necessary things which have their necessity caused by another, as has been already proved in regard to efficient causes. Therefore we cannot but postulate the existence of some being having of itself its own necessity, and not receiving it from another, but rather causing in others their necessity. This all men speak of as God.

The fourth way is taken from the gradation to be found in things. Among beings there are some more and some less good, true, noble, and the like. But 'more' and 'less' are predicated of different things, according as they resemble in their different ways something which is the maximum, as a thing is said to be hotter according as it more nearly resembles that which is hottest; so that there is something which is truest, something best, something noblest, and, consequently, something which is uttermost being; for those things that are greatest in truth are greatest in being, as it is written in *Metaph.* ii. Now the maximum in any genus is the cause of all in that genus; as fire, which is the maximum of heat, is the cause of all hot things. Therefore there must also be something which is to all beings the cause of their being, goodness, and every other perfection; and this we call God.

The fifth way is taken from the governance of the world. We see that things which lack intelligence, such as natural bodies, act for an end and this is evident from their acting always, or nearly always, in the same way, so as to obtain the best result. Hence it is plain that not fortuitously, but designedly, do they achieve their end. Now whatever lacks intelligence cannot move towards an end, unless it be directed by some being endowed with knowledge and intelligence; as the arrow is shot to its mark by the archer. Therefore some intelligent being exists by whom all natural things are directed to their end; and this being we call God. . . .

QUESTION 15 / *Of Ideas*

FIRST ARTICLE / WHETHER THERE ARE IDEAS?

. . . It is necessary to suppose ideas in the divine mind. For the Greek word *Idea* is in Latin *Forma*. Hence by ideas are understood the forms of things, existing apart from the things themselves. Now the form of anything existing apart from the thing itself can be for one of two ends; either to be the type of that of which it is called the form, or to be the principle of the knowledge of that thing, inasmuch, as the forms of things knowable are said to be in him who knows them. In either case we must suppose ideas, as is clear for the following reason:

In all things not generated by chance, the form must be the end of any generation whatsoever. But an agent does not act on account of the form, except in so far as the likeness of the form is in the agent, as may happen in two ways. For in some agents the form of the thing to be made pre-exists according to its natural being, as in those that act by their nature; as a man generates a man, or fire generates fire. Whereas in other agents the form of the thing to be made pre-exists according to intelligible being, as in those that act by the intellect; and thus the likeness of a house pre-exists in the mind of the builder. And this may be called the idea of the house, since the builder intends to build his house like to the form conceived in his mind. As then the world was not made by chance, but by God acting by His intellect . . . there must exist in the divine mind a form to the likeness of which the world was made. And in this the notion of an idea consists. . . .

SECOND ARTICLE / WHETHER IDEAS ARE MANY?

. . . It must necessarily be held that ideas are many. In proof of which it is to be considered that in every effect the ultimate end is the proper intention of the principal agent, as the order of an army is the proper intention of the general. Now the highest good existing in things is the good of the order of the universe, as the Philosopher clearly teaches in *Metaph.* xii. Therefore the order of the universe is properly intended by God, and is not the accidental result of a succession of agents, as has been supposed by those who have taught that God created only the first creature, and that this creature created the second creature, and so on, until this great multitude of beings was produced. According to this opinion God would have the idea of the first created thing alone; whereas, if the order itself of the universe was created by Him immediately, and intended by Him, He must have the idea of the order of the universe. Now there cannot be an idea of any whole, unless particular ideas are had of those parts of which the whole is made; just as a builder cannot conceive the idea of a house unless he has the idea of each of its parts. So, then, it must needs be that in the divine mind there are the proper ideas of all things. Hence Augustine says (*Octog. Tri. Quæst.; qu.* xlvi.), *that each thing was created by God according to the idea proper to it,* from which it follows that in the divine mind ideas are many. Now it can easily be seen how this is not repugnant to the simplicity of God, if we consider that the idea of a work is in the mind of the operator as that which is understood, and not as the image whereby he understands, which is a form that makes the intellect in act. For the form of the house in the mind of the builder, is something understood by him, to the likeness of which he forms the house in matter. Now, it is not repugnant to the simplicity of the divine mind that it understand many things; though it would be repugnant to its simplicity were His understanding to be formed by a plurality of images. Hence many ideas exist in the divine mind, as things understood by it; as can be proved thus. Inasmuch as He knows His own essence perfectly, He knows it according to every mode in which it can be known. Now it can be known not only as it is in itself, but as it can be participated in by creatures according to some degree of likeness. But every creature has its own proper species, according to which it participates in some degree in likeness to the divine essence. So far, therefore, as God knows His essence as capable of such imitation by any creature, He knows it as the particular type and idea of that creature: and in like manner as regards other creatures. So it is clear that God understands many particular types of many things, and these are many ideas. . . .

THIRD ARTICLE / WHETHER THERE ARE IDEAS OF ALL THINGS THAT GOD KNOWS?

. . . As ideas, according to Plato, are principles of the knowledge of things and of their generation, an idea has this twofold office, as it exists in the mind of God. So far as the idea is the principle of the making of things, it may be called an *exemplar,* and belongs to practical knowledge. But so far as it is a principle of knowledge, it is properly called a *type,* and may belong to speculative knowledge also. As an exemplar, therefore, it has respect to everything made by God in any period of time; whereas as a principle of knowledge it has respect to all things known by God, even though they never come to be in time; and to all things that He knows according to their proper type, in so far as they are known by Him in a speculative manner. . . .

QUESTION 103 / *Of the Government of Things in General*

FIRST ARTICLE / WHETHER THE WORLD IS GOVERNED BY ANYONE?

. . . Certain ancient philosophers denied the government of the world, saying that all things happened by chance. But such an opinion can be refuted as impossible in two ways. First, by observation of things themselves: for we observe that in nature things happen always or nearly always for the best; which would not be the case unless some sort of providence directed nature towards good as an end; which is to govern. Wherefore the unfailing order we observe in things is a sign of their being governed; for instance, if we enter a well-ordered house we gather therefrom the intention of him that put it in order, as Tullius[12] says (*De Nat. Deorum* ii.), quoting Aristotle. Secondly, this is clear from a consideration of Divine goodness, which . . . was the cause of the production of things in existence. For as *it belongs to the best to produce the best,* it is not fitting that the supreme goodness of God should produce things without giving them their perfection. Now a thing's ultimate perfection consists in the attainment of its end. Therefore it belongs to the Divine goodness, as it brought things into existence, so to lead them to their end: and this is to govern. . . .

SECOND ARTICLE / WHETHER THE END OF THE GOVERNMENT
OF THE WORLD IS SOMETHING OUTSIDE THE WORLD?

. . . As the end of a thing corresponds to its beginning, it is not possible to be ignorant of the end of things if we know their beginning. Therefore, since the beginning of all things is something outside the universe, namely, God, it is clear . . . that we must conclude that the end of all things is some extrinsic good. This can be proved by reason. For it is clear that good has the nature of an end; wherefore, a particular end of anything consists in some particular good; while the universal end of all things is the Universal Good; Which is good of Itself by virtue of Its Essence, Which is the very essence of goodness; whereas a particular good is good by participation. Now it is manifest that in the whole created universe there is not a good which is not such by participation. Wherefore that good which is the end of the whole universe must be a good outside the universe. . . .

THIRD ARTICLE / WHETHER THE WORLD IS GOVERNED BY ONE?

. . . We must of necessity say that the world is governed by one. For since the end of the government of the world is that which is essentially

---

[12]Cicero.

good, which is the greatest good; the government of the world must be the best kind of government. Now the best government is government by one. The reason of this is that government is nothing but the directing of the things governed to the end; which consists in some good. But unity belongs to the idea of goodness, as Boëthius proves (*De Consol.* iii. II) from this, that, as all things desire good, so do they desire unity; without which they would cease to exist. For a thing so far exists as it is one. Whence we observe that things resist division, as far as they can; and the dissolution of a thing arises from some defect therein. Therefore the intention of a ruler over a multitude is unity, or peace. Now the proper cause of unity is one. For it is clear that several cannot be the cause of unity or concord, except so far as they are united. Furthermore, what is one in itself is a more apt and a better cause of unity than several things united. Therefore a multitude is better governed by one than by several. From this it follows that the government of the world, being the best form of government, must be by one. This is expressed by the Philosopher (*Metaph.* xii., Did. xi. 10): *Things refuse to be ill governed; and multiplicity of authorities is a bad thing, therefore there should be one ruler. . . .*

FOURTH ARTICLE / WHETHER THE EFFECT OF GOVERNMENT IS ONE OR MANY?

. . . The effect of any action may be judged from its end; because it is by action that the attainment of the end is effected. Now the end of the government of the world is the essential good, to the participation and similarity of which all things tend. Consequently the effect of the government of the world may be taken in three ways. First, on the part of the end itself; and in this way there is but one effect, that is, assimilation to the supreme good. Secondly, the effect of the government of the world may be considered on the part of those things by means of which the creature is made like to God. Thus there are, in general, two effects of the government. For the creature is assimilated to God in two things; first, with regard to this, that God is good; and so the creature becomes like Him by being good: and secondly, with regard to this, that God is the cause of goodness in others; and so the creature becomes like God by moving others to be good. Wherefore there are two effects of government, the preservation of things in their goodness, and the moving of things to good. Thirdly, we may consider in the individual the effects of the government of the world; and in this way they are without number. . . .

FIFTH ARTICLE / WHETHER ALL THINGS ARE SUBJECT TO THE DIVINE GOVERNMENT?

. . . For the same reason is God the ruler of things as He is their cause, because the same gives existence as gives perfection; and this belongs to government. Now God is the cause not indeed only of some particular kind of being, but of the whole universal being. . . . Wherefore, as there can be nothing which is not created by God, so there can be nothing which is not subject to His government. This can also be proved from the nature of the end of government. For a man's government extends over all those things which come under the end of his government. Now the end of the Divine government is the Divine goodness; as we have shown (A. 2). Wherefore, as there can be nothing that is not ordered to the Divine goodness as its end, . . . so it is impossible for anything to escape from the Divine government.

Foolish therefore was the opinion of those who said that the corruptible lower world, or individual things, or that even human affairs, were not subject to the Divine government. These are represented as saying, *God hath abandoned the earth* (Ezech. ix. 9). . . .

SIXTH ARTICLE / WHETHER ALL THINGS ARE IMMEDIATELY GOVERNED BY GOD?

. . . In government there are two things to be considered; the design of government, which is providence itself; and the execution of the design. As to the design of government, God governs all things immediately; whereas in its execution, He governs some things by means of others.

The reason of this is that as God is the very essence of goodness, so everything must be attributed to God in its highest degree of goodness. Now the highest degree of goodness in any practical order, design, or knowledge (and such is the design of government) consists in knowing the individuals acted upon; as the best physician is not the one who can only give his attention to general principles, but who can consider the least details; and so on in other things. Therefore we must say that God has the design of the government of all things, even of the very least.

But since things which are governed should be brought to perfection by government, this government will be so much the better in the degree the things governed are brought to perfection. Now it is a greater perfection for a thing to be good in itself and also the cause of goodness in others, than only to be good in itself. Therefore God so governs things that He makes some of them to be causes of others in government; as a master, who not only imparts knowledge to his pupils, but gives also the faculty of teaching others. . . .

SEVENTH ARTICLE / WHETHER ANYTHING CAN HAPPEN OUTSIDE THE ORDER OF THE DIVINE GOVERNMENT?

. . . It is possible for an effect to result outside the order of some particular cause; but not outside the order of the universal cause. The reason of this is that no effect results outside the order of a particular cause, except through some other impeding cause; which other cause must itself be reduced to the first universal cause; as indigestion may occur outside the order of the nutritive power by some such impediment as the coarseness of the food, which again is to be ascribed to some other cause, and so on till we come to the first universal cause. Therefore as God is the first universal cause, not of one genus only, but of all being in general, it is impossible for anything to occur outside the order of the Divine government; but from the very fact that from one point of view something seems to evade the order of Divine providence considered in regard to one particular cause, it must necessarily come back to that order as regards some other cause. . . .

EIGHTH ARTICLE / WHETHER ANYTHING CAN RESIST THE ORDER OF THE DIVINE GOVERNMENT?

. . . We may consider the order of Divine providence in two ways; in general, inasmuch as it proceeds from the governing cause of all; and in particular, inasmuch as it proceeds from some particular cause which executes the order of the Divine government.

Considered in the first way, nothing can resist the order of the Divine government. This can be proved in two ways: firstly from the fact that the order of the Divine government is wholly directed to good, and everything by its own operation and effort tends to good only; *for no one acts intending evil,* as Dionysius says (*Div. Nom.* iv.): secondly from the fact that, as we have said above (A. 1, *ad* 3; A. 5, *ad* 2), every inclination of anything, whether natural or voluntary, is nothing but a kind of impression from the first mover; as the inclination of the arrow towards a fixed point is nothing but an impulse received from the archer. Wherefore every agent, whether natural or free, attains to its divinely appointed end, as though of its own accord. For this reason God is said *to order all things sweetly.* . . .

Comments / on St. Thomas

Despite their radical opposition, the Theologism and the Rationalism of the thirteenth century had at least one common feature; their one-sidedness. Theologism would maintain that every part of Revelation should be understood, while Rationalism would uphold the view that no part of Revelation can be understood. The historical significance of St. Thomas Aquinas rests with the fact that he was the first medieval thinker to go to the root of the difficulty. . . . Ever since the beginning of the thirteenth century, there had been a growing tendency among the Christian theologians themselves, to draw a dividing line between the order of what we believe and the order of what we know. . . . St. Thomas Aquinas was wonderfully equipped to solve a problem of this kind, because it was a problem of order. Now anyone who is at all familiar with his work knows full well that he simply could not help putting everything in its proper place. Each thing in its own place, a place for each thing.

ETIENNE GILSON (1938)

To diversify wisdom in this way—to distinguish between learning divine things by experiencing them and learning them by the human understanding of revelation, to recognize therefore the meaning and the method of reason in all its naturalness—is, in its largest terms, the problem facing the thirteenth century. Hitherto Christian thinkers had sought wisdom and understanding in a truly breathless way: in the ecstatic vision of God. But confronted by Greek reason, they began to discover another understanding and another wisdom; and alongside the contemplative and mystic there began to emerge within Christian thought the theologian and the philosopher, even as alongside the monastery there emerged the university.

A. C. PEGIS (1945)

[St. Thomas] found the means to solve all the riddles of the world by this process of rationalizing the irrational allegorically and of elevating what had been so rationalized by means of mystical symbolism. Thomas can never be refuted by his own method. As the rational conceptions are uplifted to the realm of faith, his opponent has not time to assail them. So Thomism appeals against criticism to belief, and against unbelief to criticism; it overthrows erroneous opinions with the aid of philosophy, but escapes from philosophic criticism behind the mysticism of ecclesiastical dogma. Thomas moves within this circle with a nimbleness and agility unheard of before.

KARL VOSSLER (1925)

Thomas Aquinas . . . [and certain other scholastics] are systematic minds; their philosophy is an intellectual monument, and the sense of proportion which it reveals is the same as that of the Gothic cathedral to which it has so often been compared. It is just because everything is so fittingly combined in the scholastic philosophy, and because it does satisfy the mind's most exacting demands for coherence, in which its very life consists, that it has charmed through the ages so many successive generations of thinkers.

MAURICE DE WULF (1922)

Thomas' teaching, although it culminates in purely theological doctrines, claims to have a foundation in natural reason independent of, and separable from, revealed doctrine. . . . [Nevertheless, in the *Summation of Theology*] the ultimate authority is revelation. Although Thomas assumes the impossibility of any real conflict between the teachings of right reason and revelation, this assumption cannot be made by anyone who does not accept his views either of natural reason or of revelation. If any actual conflict does exist, Thomas must of necessity have distorted one teaching or the other, or both. . . . To repeat, in Thomas' own system theology, or, more correctly, revealed theology, takes precedence over the teachings of natural reason. And, although Thomas affirms the independence and separability from revealed theology of the teachings of natural reason, those who dissent from his theology have the understandable suspicion that such "harmony" as Thomas finds between the teachings of reason and of revelation is primarily due to a corruption of the former.

H. V. JAFFA (1952)

Aquinas is not regarded by modern Thomists as a man who has answered all questions, once and for all. He is considered a model of what the open-minded student may achieve in rethinking the problems of reality, knowledge, and human life, with the aid of what is best in contemporary science and learning. . . . Every problem in his *Summa of Theology* is presented as an open question. . . .

V. J. BOURKE (1960)

Early Italian Poets

The Idea of Romantic Love

In classical times women, as women, were not very important in the affairs of men. As queens, as wives, as mothers, as daughters, they were given the respect due those positions in society. Their sexual attractions were acknowledged as one of the pleasures of life. But the notion of romantic love as we understand it—the idealization of woman as man's inspiration and the source of his greatest happiness—simply did not exist. Or if it did, virtually no record of it has survived in the writings that have come down to us from Greek and Roman antiquity. The noblest kind of emotional and spiritual gratification was to be experienced only between man and man.

The Christian era introduced no change. If anything, Christianity—with its tendency toward asceticism, its emphasis on divine rather than human love, and its consciousness of original sin, for which a woman could so easily be blamed—pushed women even lower in men's scale of values. At least, again, none of the writings extant from the first millennium of Christianity indicate otherwise. The noblest kind of emotional and spiritual gratification was to be experienced only between man and God.

But in the twelfth century, for reasons that we do not yet fully understand and as a result of influences about which we are still uncertain —perhaps merely as part of the quickening felt by every aspect of civilization in western Europe at that time—signs of a change in man's attitude toward woman started to appear, most noticeably in imaginative literature. Early in the century in the Provençal region of southern France, lyric poetry glorifying the love of woman began to be written; by the end of the century this theme dominated both lyric and narrative poetry throughout western Europe. Woman was both idealized and idolized as man's inspiration to greater achievement and, as Chantecleer put it in Chaucer's *Canterbury Tales,* "man's joy and all his bliss." How much this attitude was reflected in the actualities of contemporary society is open to question; the likelihood is, not very much. But once an idea has been accepted in principle, it tends eventually to become accepted in practice. The notion of romantic love, needless to say, has become firmly embedded in the patterns of Western culture.

But one essential modification was made in this conception which completed the idea of romantic love as we know it today. The twelfth-century poets, while recognizing to some extent the spiritual satisfactions to be gained from love of woman, put considerably more emphasis on its physical qualities. What was necessary was a shift in emphasis from the physical to the spiritual. This shift can best be seen in the works of a number of thirteenth-century Italian poets culminating with Dante. After that time, for most of Western society the noblest kind of emotional and spiritual gratification was to be experienced only between man and woman.

Giacomo da Lentino (?—1250?) was the Imperial Notary at the court of Frederick II, King of Sicily and Emperor of the Holy Roman Empire. Frederick, a poet himself, encouraged and sponsored poets at his court writing in the Provençal tradition. Giacomo, who was the outstanding member of the group and who probably is to be credited with inventing the sonnet as a poetic form, shows in his work how far the unmodified Provencal tradition could go toward a spiritual conception of love.

Guido Guinizelli (1240?—1276), a Bolognese lawyer, was named by Dante as his own poetic father. He was the originator of the *dolce stil nuovo,* the "sweet new style" which changed the tone of romantic poetry by stressing as love's primary attribute the spiritual elevation it produced.

Guido Cavalcanti (1250?—1300) belonged to one of the great families of Florence, studied deeply in scholastic philosophy, and was a close friend of Dante's. His attempts to establish a philosophic basis for the romantic conception of love guided Dante in the same direction.

Dino Frescobaldi (?—1320?), a Florentine of noble birth and a friend of Dante's, was famed as a poet in his own day. In his work appear the typical qualities of the fully developed *dolce stil nuovo.*

Giacomo da Lentino

Sonnet

Of His Lady in Heaven

I have it in my heart to serve God so
   That into Paradise I shall repair,—
   The holy place through the which everywhere
I have heard say that joy and solace flow.
Without my lady I were loth to go,—
   She who has the bright face and the bright hair;
   Because if she were absent, I being there,
My pleasure would be less than nought, I know.

From *Early Italian Poets,* edited by Dante Gabriel Rossetti (London: Simpkin, Marshall, Hamilton, Kent & Co., originally published 1861).

Look you, I say not this to such intent
As that I there would deal in any sin:
I only would behold her gracious mien,
And beautiful soft eyes, and lovely face,
That so it should be my complete content
To see my lady joyful in her place.

Guido Guinizelli

Canzone

Of the Gentle Heart

Within the gentle heart Love shelters him,
  As birds within the green shade of the grove.
Before the gentle heart, in Nature's scheme,
  Love was not, nor the gentle heart ere Love.
    For with the sun, at once,
So sprang the light immediately; nor was
    Its birth before the sun's.
And Love hath his effect in gentleness
    Of very self; even as
Within the middle fire the heat's excess.

The fire of Love comes to the gentle heart
  Like as its virtue to a precious stone;
To which no star its influence can impart
  Till it is made a pure thing by the sun:
    For when the sun hath smit
From out its essence that which there was vile,
    The star endoweth it.
And so the heart created by God's breath
    Pure, true, and clean from guile,
A woman, like a star, enamoureth.

In gentle heart Love for like reason is
  For which the lamp's high flame is fann'd and bow'd:
Clear, piercing bright, it shines for its own bliss;
  Nor would it burn there else, it is so proud.
    For evil natures meet
With Love as it were water met with fire,
    As cold abhorring heat.
Through gentle heart Love doth a track divine,—
    Like knowing like; the same
As diamond runs through iron in the mine.

From *Early Italian Poets,* edited by Dante Gabriel Rossetti (London: Simpkin, Marshall, Hamilton, Kent & Co., originally published 1861).

The sun strikes full upon the mud all day:
  It remains vile, nor the sun's worth is less.
"By race I am gentle," the proud man doth say:
  He is the mud, the sun is gentleness.
    Let no man predicate
That aught the name of gentleness should have,
    Even in a king's estate,
Except the heart there be a gentle man's.
    The star-beam lights the wave,—
Heaven holds the star and the star's radiance.

God, in the understanding of high Heaven,
  Burns more than in our sight the living sun:
There to behold His Face unveil'd is given;
  And Heaven, whose will is homage paid to One,
    Fulfils the things which live
In God, from the beginning excellent.
    So should my lady give
That truth which in her eyes is glorified,
    On which her heart is bent,
To me whose service waiteth at her side.

My lady, God shall ask, "What dared'st thou?
  (When my soul stands with all her acts review'd;)
"Thou passed'st Heaven, into My sight, as now,
  To make Me of vain love similitude.
    To me doth praise belong,
And to the Queen of all the realm of grace
    Who endeth fraud and wrong."
Then may I plead: "As though from Thee he came,
    Love wore an angel's face:
Lord, if I loved her, count it not my shame."

Guido Cavalcanti

Sonnets

He Compares All Things with His Lady, and Finds Them Wanting

Beauty in woman; the high will's decree;
  Fair knighthood arm'd for manly exercise;
  The pleasant song of birds; love's soft replies;
The strength of rapid ships upon the sea;

From *Early Italian Poets,* edited by Dante Gabriel Rossetti (London: Simpkin, Marshall, Hamilton, Kent & Co., originally published 1861).

The serene air when light begins to be;
   The white snow, without wind that falls and lies;
   Fields of all flower; the place where waters rise;
Silver and gold; azure in jewellery:—
Weigh'd against these, the sweet and quiet worth
   Which my dear lady cherishes at heart
     Might seem a little matter to be shown;
   Being truly, over these, as much apart
As the whole heaven is greater than this earth.
   All good to kindred natures cleaveth soon.

In Praise of Guido Orlandi's[1] Lady

A lady in whom love is manifest—
   That love which perfect honour doth adorn—
Hath ta'en the living heart out of thy breast,
   Which in her keeping to new life is born:
For there by such sweet power it is possest
   As even is felt of Indian unicorn:[2]
And all its virtue now, with fierce unrest,
   Unto thy soul makes difficult return.
For this thy lady is virtue's minister
   In suchwise that no fault there is to show,
     Save that God made her mortal on this ground,
     And even herein His wisdom shall be found:
   For only thus our intellect could know
That heavenly beauty which resembles her.

Dino Frescobaldi

Sonnet

Of the Star of His Love

That star the highest seen in heaven's expanse
   Not yet forsakes me with its lovely light:
   It gave me her who from her heaven's pure height
Gives all the grace mine intellect demands.

---

[1]A member of the circle of Florentine poets which included Dante and Guido Cavalcanti.

[2]A mythical beast supposedly indigenous to India, mentioned as early as the fifth century B.C. by the Greek historian Ctesias. It was usually described as having the head and body of a horse, the hind legs of an antelope, the tail of a lion, sometimes the beard of a goat, and, as its chief feature, a long, sharp horn set in the middle of its forehead. According to medieval legend, it was exceedingly fierce and could not be caught by any hunter in an ordinary way. It could be trapped only by the following strategem: if a virgin girl were sent off into the woods where the unicorn lurked, it would leap into her lap when it saw her, embrace her, and thus get caught.

From *Early Italian Poets,* edited by Dante Gabriel Rossetti (London: Simpkin, Marshall, Hamilton, Kent & Co., originally published 1861).

Thence a new arrow of strength is in my hands
  Which bears good will whereso it may alight;
    So barb'd, that no man's body or soul its flight
Has wounded yet, nor shall wound any man's.
Glad am I therefore that her grace should fall
  Not otherwise than thus; whose rich increase
    Is such a power as evil cannot dim.
My sins within an instant perish'd all
  When I inhaled the light of so much peace.
    And this Love knows; for I have told it him.

Comments / on the Early Italian Poets

[For Guinizelli] the demonstration, almost the essence, of love is pure contemplation of the beauty of the beloved. Feminine beauty, as Guinizelli thinks of it, is the outer gleam of an interior beauty of soul. This beauty reveals itself not only in harmony of lineaments, but also in chaste and decorous actions. . . . And this beauty is also, if not essentially at least in tendency, a moral beauty, which purifies and transfigures . . . a passion closely connected with the sexual instinct. . . . The adored lady, then, without ceasing to be considered as a real woman, becomes a symbol of the celestial intelligences, *i.e.,* the angels; allegiance to the lady becomes a species of religious cult. Guinizelli reconciles amatory desire and service with the theological doctrine that love is a desire for something eternally and infinitely better than ourselves.

BERNARD STAMBLER (1957)

But the beauty which moved the interest of the *stilnovisti* [poets writing in the "sweet new style"] was not primarily sensual in its character. It required an effort of the intellect to perceive its nature. For these poets love was an intellectual longing, a desire which had almost nothing in common with the yearnings of the unlettered for sensual gratification.

Through [Guinizelli] love had vastly broadened its scope. Without quite relinquishing its foothold on earth, it now reached far into the skies, and the poet of love was able to employ his intellect, his learning, and his imagination for the first time to some purpose.

By assimilating the desire for beauty of woman to the longing of the soul for the absolute, the *stilnovisti* put the entire relation of true love on a new footing. The lady became an ideal. . . . In exalting the beloved lady to the point where she might be loved with intellectual love, it was necessary to divest her of her womanhood. The poet's love now acquired the necessary nobility; but the lady vanished.

MAURICE VALENCY (1958)

Dante Alighieri

1265–1321

Dante Alighieri, like the other early Italian poets, was a well-born man for whom literary endeavor was an avocation rather than a career. He took an active part in civic life and, as a result of the savage Florentine politics of that time, was banished from his native city in 1302 and condemned to death if he should ever return. He spent the rest of his life as an exile in the service of various cities in northern Italy and in the creation of great literature—important treatises on philosophy, government, and language, and the *Divine Comedy.*

La Vita Nuova *(The New Life)* is a product of Dante's youth, composed some ten years before he went into exile. In it he collected a number of poems he had written celebrating his love for a certain Beatrice and connected them with a prose commentary explaining how each came to be written. Much of what we know about Beatrice is derived from the *New Life* itself, so that for centuries the question has been debated whether she was a real woman who had lived and been loved by Dante or was simply a creation of his imagination, a fictional symbol for his idea of love. Current opinion pretty much agrees that she was both. She is identified with Beatrice Portinari, daughter of an eminent Florentine family. She was married at twenty-one and died a few years later in 1290. Dante was strongly attracted to her, but he too had married and was raising a family. He sublimated his emotion by idealizing her into a symbol of spiritual love and described the course of that love in *New Life.* The book stands as a record of Dante's progress in understanding both what love is and what love poetry should be. The early poems are written in the Provencal style and represent the attitude toward love inherent in that tradition. The poem beginning with the line "Ladies that have intelligence in love" is referred to in the *Divine Comedy* as representative of the "sweet new style" and in the *New Life* marks the shift to the attitude toward love inherent in that style. In spirit the work as a whole is akin to, and valuable for the same reason as, St. Augustine's *Confessions,* a book Dante had read closely. Like St. Augustine, Dante examines his own emotional experiences to show how his conception of the true meaning of love developed within him. The difference between the two is instructive: St. Augustine experienced divine love directly, Dante through the medium of love for a woman.

The *New Life* leads directly to the *Divine Comedy.* Dante's masterpiece has as one of its main themes the celebration of his love for Beatrice, and it is surely the finest testament of the spiritual elevation resulting from love of a woman ever written. The genesis of that conception of love is to be seen in the *New Life.*

The New Life

In that part of the book of my memory before the which is little that can be read, there is a rubric, saying, *Incipit Vita Nova.*[1] Under such rubric I find written many things; and among them the words which I purpose to copy into this little book; if not all of them, at the least their substance.

Nine times already since my birth had the heaven of light returned to the selfsame point almost, as concerns its own revolution, when first the glorious Lady of my mind was made manifest to mine eyes; even she who was called Beatrice by many who knew not wherefore.[2] She had already been in this life for so long as that, within her time, the starry heaven had moved towards the Eastern quarter one of the twelve parts of a degree; so that she appeared to me at the beginning of her ninth year almost, and I saw her almost at the end of my ninth year. Her dress, on that day, was of a most noble colour, a subdued and goodly crimson, girdled and adorned in such sort as best suited with her very tender age. At that moment, I say most truly that the spirit of life, which hath its dwelling in the secretest chamber of the heart, began to tremble so violently that the least pulses of my body shook therewith; and in trembling it said these words: *Ecce deus fortior me, qui veniens dominabitur mihi.*[3] At that moment the animate spirit, which dwelleth in the lofty chamber whither all the senses carry their perceptions, was filled with wonder, and speaking more especially unto the spirits of the eyes, said these words: *Apparuit jam beatitudo vestra.*[4] At that moment the natural spirit, which dwelleth there where our nourishment is administered, began to weep, and in weeping said these words: *Heu miser! quia frequenter impeditus ero deinceps.*[5]

From *Early Italian Poets,* edited by Dante Gabriel Rossetti (London: Simpkin, Marshall, Hamilton, Kent & Co., originally published 1861).

[1]"Here begins the new life."

[2]The name Beatrice in Italian means "she who confers blessing." It is derived from the same Latin root as the English words *beatify* or *beatitude.*

[3]"Here is a deity stronger than I, who, coming, shall rule over me."

[4]"Your beatitude has now been shown to you."

[5]"Alas! how often shall I be disturbed from this time forth!"

I say that, from that time forward, Love quite governed my soul; which was immediately espoused to him, and with so safe and undisputed a lordship (by virtue of strong imagination) that I had nothing left for it but to do all his bidding continually. He oftentimes commanded me to seek if I might see this youngest of the Angels: wherefore I in my boyhood often went in search of her, and found her so noble and praiseworthy that certainly of her might have been said those words of the poet Homer, "She seemed not to be the daughter of a mortal man, but of God." And albeit her image, that was with me always, was an exultation of Love to subdue me, it was yet of so perfect a quality that it never allowed me to be overruled by Love without the faithful counsel of reason, whensoever such counsel was useful to be heard. But seeing that were I to dwell overmuch on the passions and doings of such early youth, my words might be counted something fabulous, I will therefore put them aside; and passing many things that may be conceived by the pattern of these, I will come to such as are writ in my memory with a better distinctness.

After the lapse of so many days that nine years exactly were completed since the above-written appearance of this most gracious being, on the last of those days it happened that the same wonderful lady appeared to me dressed all in pure white, between two gentle ladies elder than she. And passing through a street, she turned her eyes thither where I stood sorely abashed: and by her unspeakable courtesy, which is now guerdoned in the Great Cycle, she saluted me with so virtuous a bearing that I seemed then and there to behold the very limits of blessedness. The hour of her most sweet salutation was certainly the ninth[6] of the day; and because it was the first time that any words from her reached mine ears, I came into such sweetness that I parted thence as one intoxicated. And betaking me to the loneliness of mine own room, I fell to thinking of this most courteous lady, thinking of whom I was overtaken by a pleasant slumber, wherein a marvellous vision was presented to me: for there appeared to be in my room a mist of the colour of fire, within the which I discerned the figure of a lord of terrible aspect to such as should gaze upon him, but who seemed therewithal to rejoice inwardly that it was a marvel to see. Speaking he said many things, among the which I could understand but few; and of these, this: *Ego dominus tuus.*[7] In his arms it seemed to me that a person was sleeping, covered only with a blood-coloured cloth; upon whom looking very attentively, I knew that it was the lady of the salutation who had deigned the day before to salute me. And he who held her held also in his hand a thing that was burning in flames; and he said to me, *Vide cor tuum.*[8] But when he had remained with me a little while, I thought that he set himself to awaken her that slept; after the which he made her to eat that thing which flamed in his hand; and she ate as one fearing. Then, having

---

[6]Dante's insistence on the number nine throughout this work (even the *nuova* in its title could be translated as "ninth" rather than as "new") is due to the mystic symbolism which numbers had in medieval thought. Nine was a holy number because it represented three times itself, three being a holy number because it symbolized the Christian Trinity.

[7]"I am your master."

[8]"Behold your heart."

waited again a space, all his joy was turned into most bitter weeping; and as he wept he gathered the lady into his arms, and it seemed to me that he went with her up towards heaven: whereby such a great anguish came upon me that my light slumber could not endure through it, but was suddenly broken. And immediately having considered, I knew that the hour wherein this vision had been made manifest to me was the fourth hour (which is to say, the first of the nine last hours) of the night.

Then, musing on what I had seen, I proposed to relate the same to many poets who were famous in that day: and for that I had myself in some sort the art of discoursing with rhyme, I resolved on making a sonnet, in the which, having saluted all such as are subject unto Love, and entreated them to expound my vision, I should write unto them those things which I had seen in my sleep. And the sonnet I made was this:—

> To every heart which the sweet pain doth move,
>   And unto which these words may now be brought
>   For true interpretation and kind thought,
> Be greeting in our Lord's name, which is Love.
> Of those long hours wherein the stars, above,
>   Wake and keep watch, the third was almost nought
>   When Love was shown me with such terrors fraught
> As may not carelessly be spoken of.
>
> He seem'd like one who is full of joy, and had
>   My heart within his hand, and on his arm
>   My lady, with a mantle round her, slept;
> Whom (having waken'd her) anon he made
>   To eat that heart; she ate, as fearing harm.
>   Then he went out; and as he went, he wept.

This sonnet is divided into two parts. In the first part I give greeting, and ask an answer; in the second, I signify what thing has to be answered to. The second part commences here: "Of those long hours."[9]

To this sonnet I received many answers, conveying many different opinions; of the which one was sent by him whom I now call the first among my friends,[10] and it began thus, "Unto my thinking thou beheld'st all worth." And indeed, it was when he learned that I was he who had sent those rhymes to him, that our friendship commenced. But the true meaning of that vision was not then perceived by any one, though it be now evident to the least skilful.

From that night forth, the natural functions of my body began to be vexed and impeded, for I was given up wholly to thinking of this most gracious creature: whereby in short space I became so weak and so reduced that it was irksome to many of my friends to look upon me; while others, being moved by spite, went about to discover what it

---

[9]Dante subjects most of the poems in the *New Life* to this sort of typically scholastic "division." All subsequent divisions have been omitted.
[10]Guido Cavalcanti.

was my wish should be concealed. Wherefore I, (perceiving the drift of their unkindly questions,) by Love's will, who directed me according to the counsels of reason, told them how it was Love himself who had thus dealt with me: and I said so, because the thing was so plainly to be discerned in my countenance that there was no longer any means of concealing it. But when they went on to ask, "And by whose help hath Love done this?" I looked in their faces smiling, and spake no word in return.

Now it fell on a day, that this most gracious creature was sitting where words were to be heard of the Queen of Glory;[11] and I was in a place whence mine eyes could behold their beatitude: and betwixt her and me, in a direct line, there sat another lady of pleasant favour; who looked round at me many times, marvelling at my continued gaze which seemed to have *her* for its object. And many perceived that she thus looked; so that departing thence, I heard it whispered after me, "Look you to what a pass *such a lady* hath brought him"; and in saying this they named her who had been midway between the most gentle Beatrice and mine eyes. Therefore I was reassured, and knew that for that day my secret had not become manifest. Then immediately it came into my mind that I might make use of this lady as a screen to the truth: and so well did I play my part that the most of those who had hitherto watched and wondered at me, now imagined they had found me out. By her means I kept my secret concealed till some years were gone over; and for my better security, I even made divers rhymes in her honour; whereof I shall here write only as much as concerneth the most gentle Beatrice, which is but a very little. Moreover, about the same time while this lady was a screen for so much love on my part, I took the resolution to set down the name of this most gracious creature accompanied with many other women's names, and especially with hers whom I spake of. And to this end I put together the names of sixty the most beautiful ladies in that city where God had placed mine own lady; and these names I introduced in an epistle in the form of a *sirvent,*[12] which it is not my intention to transcribe here. Neither should I have said anything of this matter, did I not wish to take note of a certain strange thing, to wit: that having written the list, I found my lady's name would not stand otherwise than ninth in order among the names of these ladies.

Now it so chanced with her by whose means I had thus long time concealed my desire, that it behoved her to leave the city I speak of, and to journey afar: wherefore I, being sorely perplexed at the loss of so excellent a defence, had more trouble than even I could before have supposed. And thinking that if I spoke not somewhat mournfully of her departure, my former counterfeiting would be the more quickly perceived, I determined that I would make a grievous sonnet thereof;[13] the which I will write here, because it hath certain words in it whereof

---

[11]I.e., in a church.

[12]A lyric form developed by the Provençal poets. Its substance was usually prosaic, the exposition of some kind of information. Hence the name of the form: it was called a *sirvent* because it "served" a specific, usually utilitarian, purpose.

[13]The whole business of elaborate pretenses and devices for secrecy are part of the Provençal tradition of love and are characteristic of Provençal love poetry.

my lady was the immediate cause as will be plain to him that understands. And the sonnet was this:—

> All ye that pass along Love's trodden way,
> Pause ye awhile and say
>   If there be any grief like unto mine:
> I pray you that you hearken a short space
> Patiently, if my case
>   Be not a piteous marvel and a sign.
> Love (never, certes, for my worthless part,
> But of his own great heart,)
>   Vouchsafed to me a life so calm and sweet
> That oft I heard folk question as I went
> What such great gladness meant:—
>   They spoke of it behind me in the street.
>
> But now that fearless bearing is all gone
>   Which with Love's hoarded wealth was given me;
>   Till I am grown to be
> So poor that I have dread to think thereon.
>
> And thus it is that I, being like as one
>   Who is ashamed and hides his poverty,
>   Without seem full of glee,
> And let my heart within travail and moan.

[Dante has a vision in which a certain youth (whom he later realizes
was the God of Love) appears to him and tells him that it is time to lay
aside pretenses and to make Beatrice known, though circumspectly, that
it is she whom he loves.]

After this vision I have recorded, and having written those words
which Love had dictated to me, I began to be harassed with many and
divers thoughts, by each of which I was sorely tempted; and in especial,
there were four among them that left me no rest. The first was this:
"Certainly the lordship of Love is good; seeing that it diverts the mind
from all mean things." The second was this: "Certainly the lordship
of Love is evil; seeing that the more homage his servants pay to him,
the more grievous and painful are the torments wherewith he torments
them." The third was this: "The name of Love is so sweet in the hearing
that it would not seem possible for its effects to be other than sweet;
seeing that the name must needs be like unto the thing named: as it
is written: *Nomina sunt consequentia rerum.*"[14] And the fourth was this:
"The lady whom Love hath chosen out to govern thee is not as other
ladies, whose hearts are easily moved."
And by each one of these thoughts I was so sorely assailed that I
was like unto him who doubteth which path to take, and wishing to
go, goeth not. And if I bethought myself to seek out some point at the

---

[14]"Names are the results of things."

which all these paths might be found to meet, I discerned but one way, and that irked me; to wit, to call upon Pity, and to commend myself unto her. And it was then that, feeling a desire to write somewhat thereof in rhyme, I wrote this sonnet:—

All my thoughts always speak to me of Love,
    Yet have between themselves such difference
    That while one bids me bow with mind and sense,
A second saith, "Go to: look thou above;"
The third one, hoping, yields me joy enough;
    And with the last come tears, I scarce know whence:
    All of them craving pity in sore suspense,
Trembling with fears that the heart knoweth of.
And thus, being all unsure which path to take,
    Wishing to speak I know not what to say,
    And lose myself in amorous wanderings:
Until, (my peace with all of them to make,)
    Unto mine enemy I needs must pray,
    My Lady Pity, for the help she brings.

After this battling with many thoughts, it chanced on a day that my most gracious lady was with a gathering of ladies in a certain place; to the which I was conducted by a friend of mine; he thinking to do me a great pleasure by showing me the beauty of so many women. Then I, hardly knowing whereunto he conducted me, but trusting in him (who yet was leading his friend to the last verge of life), made question: "To what end are we come among these ladies?" and he answered: "To the end that they may be worthily served." And they were assembled around a gentlewoman who was given in marriage on that day; the custom of the city being that these should bear her company when she sat down for the first time at table in the house of her husband. Therefore I, as was my friend's pleasure, resolved to stay with him and do honour to those ladies.

But as soon as I had thus resolved, I began to feel a faintness and a throbbing at my left side, which soon took possession of my whole body. Whereupon I remember that I covertly leaned my back unto a painting that ran round the walls of that house; and being fearful lest my trembling should be discerned of them, I lifted mine eyes to look on those ladies, and then first perceived among them the excellent Beatrice. And when I perceived her, all my senses were overpowered by the great lordship that Love obtained, finding himself so near unto that most gracious being, until nothing but the spirits of sight remained to me; and even these remained driven out of their own instruments because Love entered in that honoured place of theirs, that so he might the better behold her. And although I was other than at first, I grieved for the spirits so expelled, which kept up a sore lament, saying: "If he had not in this wise thrust us forth, we also should behold the marvel of this lady." By this, many of her friends, having discerned my confusion, began to wonder; and together with herself, kept whispering of me and mocking me. Whereupon my friend, who knew not what to conceive, took me by the hands, and drawing me forth from among them, required to know what ailed me. Then, having first held me at quiet for a space until my perceptions were come back to me, I made answer to my friend: "Of a surety I have now set my feet on that point of life, beyond the which he must not pass who would return."[15]

Afterwards, leaving him, I went back to the room where I had wept before; and again weeping and ashamed, said: "If this lady but knew of my condition, I do not think that she would thus mock at me; nay, I am sure that she must needs feel some pity." And in my weeping I bethought me to write certain words, in the which, speaking to her, I should signify the occasion of my disfigurement, telling her also how I knew that she had no knowledge thereof: which, if it were known, I was certain must move others to pity. And then, because I hoped that peradventure it might come into her hearing, I wrote this sonnet.

> Even as the others mock, thou mockest me;
>   Not dreaming, noble lady, whence it is
>   That I am taken with strange semblances,
> Seeing thy face which is so fair to see:
> For else, compassion would not suffer thee
>   To grieve my heart with such harsh scoffs as these.
>   Lo! Love, when thou art present, sits at ease,
> And bears his mastership so mightily,
> That all my troubled senses he thrusts out,
>   Sorely tormenting some, and slaying some,
>   Till none but he is left and has free range
>   To gaze on thee. This makes my face to change
> Into another's; while I stand all dumb,
> And hear my senses clamour in their rout.

A while after this strange disfigurement, I became possessed with a strong conception which left me but very seldom, and then to return quickly. And it was this: "Seeing that thou comest into such scorn by the companionship of this lady, wherefore seekest thou to behold her? If she should ask thee this thing, what answer couldst thou make unto her? yea, even though thou wert master of all thy faculties, and in no way hindered from answering." Unto the which, another very humble thought said in reply: "If I were master of all my faculties, and in no way hindered from answering, I would tell her that no sooner do I image to myself her marvellous beauty than I am possessed with the desire to behold her, the which is of so great strength that it kills and destroys in my memory all those things which might oppose it; and it is therefore that the great anguish I have endured thereby is yet not enough to restrain me from seeking to behold her." And then, because of these thoughts, I resolved to write somewhat, wherein, having pleaded mine excuse, I should tell her of what I felt in her presence. Whereupon I wrote this sonnet:—

---

[15]One of the most perplexing things about the *New Life* is that nowhere in it does Dante mention the fact of Beatrice's marriage. It is possible that this passage is his way of alluding to it and that she herself was the bride.

The thoughts are broken in my memory,
   Thou lovely Joy, whene'er I see thy face;
   When thou art near me, Love fills up the space,
Often repeating, "If death irk thee, fly."
My face shows my heart's colour, verily,
   Which, fainting, seeks for any leaning-place;
   Till, in the drunken terror of disgrace,
The very stones seem to be shrieking, "Die!"
It were a grievous sin, if one should not
   Strive then to comfort my bewilder'd mind
    (Though merely with a simple pitying)
For the great anguish which thy scorn hath wrought
   In the dead sight o' the eyes grown nearly blind,
    Which look for death as for a blessed thing.

Thereafter, this sonnet bred in me desire to write down in verse four other things touching my condition, the which things it seemed to me that I had not yet made manifest. The first among these was the grief that possessed me very often, remembering the strangeness which Love wrought in me; the second was, how Love many times assailed me so suddenly and with such strength that I had no other life remaining except a thought which spake of my lady; the third was, how when Love did battle with me in this wise, I would rise up all colourless, if so I might see my lady, conceiving that the sight of her would defend me against the assault of Love, and altogether forgetting that which her presence brought unto me; and the fourth was, how when I saw her, the sight not only defended me not, but took away the little life that remained to me. And I said these four things in a sonnet, which is this:—

At whiles (yea oftentimes) I muse over
   The quality of anguish that is mine
   Through Love: then pity makes my voice to pine
Saying, "Is any else thus, anywhere?"
Love smiteth me, whose strength is ill to bear;
   So that of all my life is left no sign
   Except one thought; and that, because 'tis thine,
Leaves not the body but abideth there.
And then if I, whom other aid forsook,
   Would aid myself, and innocent of art
    Would fain have sight of thee as a last hope,
No sooner do I lift mine eyes to look
   Than the blood seems as shaken from my heart,
    And all my pulses beat at once and stop.

After I had written these three last sonnets, wherein I spake unto my lady, telling her almost the whole of my condition, it seemed to me that I should be silent, having said enough concerning myself. But albeit I spake not to her again, yet it behoved me afterward to write of another matter, more noble than the foregoing. And for that the occasion of what I then wrote may be found pleasant in the hearing, I will relate it as briefly as I may.

Through the sore change in mine aspect, the secret of my heart was now understood of many. Which thing being thus, there came a day when certain ladies to whom it was well known (they having been with me at divers times in my trouble) were met together for the pleasure of gentle company. And as I was going that way by chance, (but I think rather by the will of fortune,) I heard one of them call unto me, and she that called was a lady of very sweet speech. And when I had come close up with them, and perceived that they had not among them mine excellent lady, I was reassured; and saluted them, asking of their pleasure. The ladies were many; divers of whom were laughing one to another, while divers gazed at me as though I should speak anon. But when I still spake not, one of them, who before had been talking with another, addressed me by my name, saying, "To what end lovest thou this lady, seeing that thou canst not support her presence? Now tell us this thing, that we may know it: for certainly the end of such a love must be worthy of knowledge." And when she had spoken these words, not she only, but all they that were with her, began to observe me, waiting for my reply. Whereupon I said thus unto them:—"Ladies, the end and aim of my Love was but the salutation of that lady of whom I conceive that ye are speaking; wherein alone I found that beatitude which is the goal of desire. And now that it hath pleased her to deny me this, Love, my Master, of his great goodness, hath placed all my beatitude there where my hope will not fail me." Then those ladies began to talk closely together; and as I have seen snow fall among the rain, so was their talk mingled with sighs. But after a little, that lady who had been the first to address me, addressed me again in these words: "We pray thee that thou wilt tell us wherein abideth this thy beatitude." And answering, I said but thus much: "In those words that do praise my lady." To the which she rejoined: "If thy speech were true, those words that thou didst write concerning thy condition would have been written with another intent."

Then I, being almost put to shame because of her answer, went out from among them; and as I walked, I said within myself: "Seeing that there is so much beatitude in those words which do praise my lady, wherefore hath my speech of her been different?" And then I resolved that thenceforward I would choose for the theme of my writings only the praise of this most gracious being. But when I had thought exceedingly, it seemed to me that I had taken to myself a theme which was much too lofty, so that I dared not begin; and I remained during several days in the desire of speaking, and the fear of beginning. After which it happened, as I passed one day along a path which lay beside a stream of very clear water, that there came upon me a great desire to say somewhat in rhyme: but when I began thinking how I should say it, methought that to speak of her were unseemly, unless I spoke to other ladies in the second person; which is to say, not to *any* other ladies, but only to such as are so called because they are gentle, let alone for mere womanhood. Whereupon I declare that my tongue spake as though by its own impulse, and said, "Ladies that have intelligence in love."

These words I laid up in my mind with great gladness, conceiving to take them as my commencement. Wherefore, having returned to the city I spake of, and considered thereof during certain days, I began a poem with this beginning, constructed in the mode which will be seen below in its division. The poem begins here:—[16]

> Ladies that have intelligence in love,
> > Of mine own lady I would speak with you;
> > Not that I hope to count her praises through,
> > > But telling what I may, to ease my mind.
> And I declare that when I speak thereof
> Love sheds such perfect sweetness over me
> That if my courage fail'd not, certainly
> > To him my listeners must be all resign'd.
> > Wherefore I will not speak in such large kind
> That mine own speech should foil me, which were base;
> But only will discourse of her high grace
> > In these poor words, the best that I can find,
> With you alone, dear dames and damozels:
> 'Twere ill to speak thereof with any else.
>
> An Angel, of his blessed knowledge, saith
> > To God: "Lord, in the world that Thou hast made,
> > A miracle in action is display'd
> > > By reason of a soul whose splendors fare
> Even hither: and since Heaven requireth
> > Nought saving her, for her it prayeth Thee,
> > Thy Saints crying aloud continually."
> > > Yet Pity still defends our earthly share
> > > In that sweet soul; God answering thus the prayer:
> "My well-belovèd, suffer that in peace
> Your hope remain, while so My pleasure is,
> > There where one dwells who dread the loss of her;
> And who in Hell unto the doom'd shall say,
> I have look'd on that for which God's chosen pray."
>
> My lady is desired in the high Heaven:
> > *Wherefore,* it now behoveth me to tell,
> > Saying: Let any maid that would be well
> > > Esteem'd keep with her: for as she goes by,
> Into foul hearts a deathly chill is driven
> By Love, that makes ill thought to perish there;
> While any who endures to gaze on her
> > Must either be made noble, or else die.
> > When one deserving to be raised so high
> Is found, 'tis then her power attains its proof,
> Making his heart strong for his soul's behoof

---

[16]This is the poem mentioned in the *Divine Comedy* under circumstances indicating that Dante meant it to be taken as an exemplar of the "sweet new style."

With the full strength of meek humility.
Also this virtue owns she, by God's will:
Who speaks with her can never come to ill.

Love saith concerning her: "How chanceth it
   That flesh, which is of dust, should be thus pure?"
   Then, gazing always, he makes oath: "Forsure,
     This is a creature of God till now unknown."
She hath that paleness of the pearl that's fit
In a fair woman, so much and not more;
She is as high as Nature's skill can soar;
   Beauty is tried by her comparison.
   Whatever her sweet eyes are turn'd upon,
Spirits of love do issue thence in flame,
Which through their eyes who then may look on them
     Pierce to the heart's deep chamber every one.
And in her smile Love's image you may see;
Whence none can gaze upon her steadfastly.

Dear Song, I know thou wilt hold gentle speech
   With many ladies, when I send thee forth:
   Wherefore, (being mindful that thou hadst thy birth
     From Love, and art a modest, simple child,)
Whomso thou meetest, say thou this to each:
"Give me good speed! To her I wend along
In whose much strength my weakness is made strong."
   And if, i' the end, thou wouldst not be beguiled
   Of all thy labour, seek not the defiled
And common sort; but rather choose to be
Where man and woman dwell in courtesy.
   So to the road thou shalt be reconciled,
And find the lady, and with the lady, Love.
Commend thou me to each, as doth behove.

When this song was a little gone abroad, a certain one of my friends, hearing the same, was pleased to question me, that I should tell him what thing love is; it may be, conceiving from the words thus heard a hope of me beyond my desert. Wherefore I, thinking that after such discourse it were well to say somewhat of the nature of Love, and also in accordance with my friend's desire, proposed to myself to write certain words in the which I should treat of this argument. And the sonnet that I then made is this:—

Love and the gentle heart are one same thing,
   Even as the wise man in his ditty saith.[17]
   Each, of itself, would be such life in death
As rational soul bereft of reasoning.
'Tis Nature makes them when she loves: a king

---

[17] Guido Guinizelli, in "Of the Gentle Heart."

Love is, whose palace where he sojourneth
Is call'd the Heart; there draws he quiet breath
At first, with brief or longer slumbering.
Then beauty seen in virtuous womankind
   Will make the eyes desire, and through the heart
   Send the desiring of the eyes again;
Where often it abides so long enshrined
   That Love at length out of this sleep will start.
   And women feel the same for worthy men.

Having treated of love in the foregoing, it appeared to me that I should also say something in praise of my lady, wherein it might be set forth how love manifested itself when produced by her; and how not only she could awaken it where it slept, but where it was not she could marvellously create it. To the which end I wrote another sonnet; and it is this:—

My lady carries love within her eyes;
   All that she looks on is made pleasanter;
   Upon her path men turn to gaze at her;
He whom she greeteth feels his heart to rise,
And droops his troubled visage, full of sighs,
   And of his evil heart is then aware:
   Hate loves, and pride becomes a worshipper.
O women, help to praise her in somewise.
Humbleness, and the hope that hopeth well,
   By speech of hers into the mind are brought,
   And who beholds is blessed oftenwhiles.
   The look she hath when she a little smiles
   Cannot be said, nor holden in the thought;
'Tis such a new and gracious miracle.

[Beatrice's father dies, and during the course of mourning, Dante is suddenly overwhelmed by the thought that Beatrice too is mortal. He dreams that she dies and describes all the details of mourning and of his emotional anguish over the fact of her death—which he does not do when he comes to mention her actual death later in the book.]

But returning to the matter of my discourse. This excellent lady, of whom I spake in what hath gone before, came at last into such favour with all men, that when she passed anywhere folk ran to behold her; which thing was a deep joy to me: and when she drew near unto any, so much truth and simpleness entered into his heart, that he dared neither to lift his eyes nor to return her salutation: and unto this, many who have felt it can bear witness. She went along crowned and clothed with humility, showing no whit of pride in all that she heard and saw: and when she had gone by, it was said of many, "This is not a woman, but one of the beautiful angels of Heaven," and there were some that said: "This is surely a miracle; blessed be the Lord, who hath power to work thus marvellously." I say, of very sooth, that she showed herself so gentle and so full of all perfection, that she bred in those who looked upon her a soothing quiet beyond any speech; neither could any look upon her without sighing immediately. These things, and things yet more wonderful, were brought to pass through her miraculous virtue. Wherefore I, considering thereof and wishing to resume the endless tale of her praises, resolved to write somewhat wherein I might dwell on her surpassing influence; to the end that not only they who had beheld her, but others also, might know as much concerning her as words could give to the understanding. And it was then that I wrote this sonnet:—

> My lady looks so gentle and so pure
>> When yielding salutation by the way,
>> That the tongue trembles and has nought to say,
> And the eyes, which fain would see, may not endure.
> And still, amid the praise she hears secure,
>> She walks with humbleness for her array;
>> Seeming a creature sent from Heaven to stay
> On earth, and show a miracle made sure.
> She is so pleasant in the eyes of men
> That through the sight the inmost heart doth gain
>> A sweetness which needs proof to know it by:
> And from between her lips there seems to move
> A soothing spirit that is full of love,
>> Saying for ever to the soul, "O sigh!"

This sonnet is so easy to understand, from what is afore narrated, that it needs no division: and therefore, leaving it, I say also that this excellent lady came into such favour with all men, that not only she herself was honoured and commended; but through her companionship, honour and commendation came unto others. Wherefore I, perceiving this and wishing that it should be made manifest to those that beheld it not, wrote the sonnet here following; wherein is signified the power which her virtue had upon other ladies:—

> For certain he hath seen all perfectness
>> Who among other ladies hath seen mine:
>> They that go with her humbly should combine
> To thank their God for such peculiar grace.
> So perfect is the beauty of her face
>> That it begets in no wise and any sign
>> Of envy, but draws round her a clear line
> Of love, and blessed faith, and gentleness.
> Merely the sight of her makes all things bow:
>> Not she herself alone is holier
>>> Than all; but hers, through her, are raised above.
> From all her acts such lovely graces flow
>> That truly one may never think of her
>>> Without a passion of exceeding love.

Thereafter on a day, I began to consider that which I had said of my lady: to wit, in these two sonnets aforegone: and becoming aware that I had not spoken of her immediate effect on me at that especial time, it seemed to me that I had spoken defectively. Whereupon I resolved to write somewhat of the manner wherein I was then subject to her influence, and of what her influence then was. And conceiving that I should not be able to say these things in the small compass of a sonnet, I began therefore a poem with this beginning:—

> Love hath so long possess'd me for his own
>   And made his lordship so familiar
> That he, who at first irk'd me, is now grown
>   Unto my heart as its best secrets are.
>   And thus, when he in such sore wise doth mar
> My life that all its strength seems gone from it,
> Mine inmost being then feels throughly quit
>   Of anguish, and all evil keeps afar.
> Love also gathers to such power in me
>   That my sighs speak, each one a grievous thing,
>   Always soliciting
> My lady's salutation piteously.
>   Whenever she beholds me, it is so,
>   Who is more sweet than any words can show.

Quomodo sedet sola civitas plena populo! facta est quasi vidua domina gentium![18]

I was still occupied with this poem, (having composed thereof only the above-written stanza,) when the Lord God of justice called my most gracious lady unto Himself, that she might be glorious under the banner of that blessed Queen Mary, whose name had always a deep reverence in the words of holy Beatrice. And because haply it might be found good that I should say somewhat concerning her departure, I will herein declare what are the reasons which make that I shall not do so.

And the reasons are three. The first is, that such matter belongeth not of right to the present argument, if one consider the opening of this little book. The second is, that even though the present argument required it, my pen doth not suffice to write in a fit manner of this thing. And the third is, that were it both possible and of absolute necessity, it would still be unseemly for me to speak thereof, seeing that thereby it must behove me to speak also mine own praises: a thing that in whosoever doeth it is worthy of blame. For the which reasons, I will leave this matter to be treated of by some other than myself.

Nevertheless, as the number nine, which number hath often had mention in what hath gone before, (and not, as it might appear, without reason,) seems also to have borne a part in the manner of her death: it is

---

[18]"How doth the city sit solitary, that was full of people! how is she become as a widow, she that was great among the nations!" (Book of Lamentations 1:1.)

therefore right that I should say somewhat thereof. And for this cause, having first said what was the part it bore herein, I will afterwards point out a reason which made that this number was so closely allied unto my lady.

I say, then, that according to the division of time in Italy, her most noble spirit departed from among us in the first hour of the ninth day of the month; and according to the division of time in Syria, in the ninth month of the year: seeing that Tismim, which with us is October, is there the first month. Also she was taken from among us in that year of our reckoning (to wit, of the years of our Lord) in which the perfect number was nine times multiplied within that century wherein she was born into the world: which is to say, the thirteenth century of Christians.[19]

And touching the reason why this number was so closely allied unto her, it may peradventure be this. According to Ptolemy,[20] (and also to the Christian verity,) the revolving heavens are nine; and according to the common opinion among astrologers, these nine heavens together have influence over the earth. Wherefore it would appear that this number was thus allied unto her for the purpose of signifying that, at her birth, all these nine heavens were at perfect unity with each other as to their influence. This is one reason that may be brought: but more narrowly considering, and according to the infallible truth, this number was her own self: that is to say, by similitude. As thus. The number three is the root of the number nine; seeing that without the interposition of any other number, being multiplied merely by itself, it produceth nine, as we manifestly perceive that three times three are nine. Thus, three being of itself the efficient of nine, and the Great Efficient of Miracles being of Himself Three Persons (to wit: the Father, the Son, and the Holy Spirit), which, being Three, are also One:—this lady was accompanied by the number nine to the end that men might clearly perceive her to be a nine, that is, a miracle, whose only root is the Holy Trinity. It may be that a more subtile person would find for this thing a reason of greater subtilty: but such is the reason that I find, and that liketh me best.

After this most gracious creature had gone out from among us, the whole city came to be as it were widowed and despoiled of all dignity. Then I, left mourning in this desolate city, wrote unto the principal persons thereof, in an epistle, concerning its condition; taking for my commencement those words of Jeremias: *Quomodo sedet sola civitas! etc.* And I make mention of this, that none may marvel wherefore I set down these words before, in beginning to treat of her death. Also if any should blame me, in that I do not transcribe that epistle whereof I have spoken, I will make it mine excuse that I began this little book with the intent that it should be written altogether in the vulgar tongue; wherefore, seeing that the epistle I speak of is in Latin, it belongeth not to mine undertaking: more especially as I know that my chief

---

[19]I.e., Beatrice died on June 9, 1290.

[20]An astronomer, mathematician, and geographer of the second century A.D. whose theories about the structure of the universe were generally accepted until the seventeenth century.

friend, for whom I write this book, wished also that the whole of it should be in the vulgar tongue.

When mine eyes had wept for some while, until they were so weary with weeping that I could no longer through them give ease to my sorrow, I bethought me that a few mournful words might stand me instead of tears. And therefore I proposed to make a poem, that weeping I might speak therein of her for whom so much sorrow had destroyed my spirit; and I then began "The eyes that weep."

> The eyes that weep for pity of the heart
>   Have wept so long that their grief languisheth
>   And they have no more tears to weep withal:
> And now, if I would ease me of a part
>   Of what, little by little, leads to death,
>   It must be done by speech, or not at all.
>   And because often, thinking, I recall
> How it was pleasant, ere she went afar,
>   To talk of her with you, kind damozels,
>   I talk with no one else,
> But only with such hearts as women's are.
>   And I will say,—still sobbing as speech fails,—
> That she hath gone to Heaven suddenly,
> And hath left Love below, to mourn with me.
>
> Beatrice is gone up into high Heaven,
>   The kingdom where the angels are at peace;
>   And lives with them; and to her friends is dead.
> Not by the frost of winter was she driven
>   Away, like others; nor by summer-heats;
>   But through a perfect gentleness, instead.
>   For from the lamp of her meek lowlihead
> Such an exceeding glory went up hence
>   That it woke wonder in the Eternal Sire,
>   Until a sweet desire
> Enter'd Him for that lovely excellence,
>   So that He bade her to Himself aspire;
> Counting this weary and most evil place
> Unworthy of a thing so full of grace.
>
> Wonderfully out of the beautiful form
>   Sear'd her clear spirit, waxing glad the while;
>   And is in its first home, there where it is.
> Who speaks thereof, and feels not the tears warm
>   Upon his face, must have become so vile
>   As to be dead to all sweet sympathies.
>   Out upon him! an abject wretch like this
> May not imagine anything of her,—
>   He needs no bitter tears for his relief.
>   But sighing comes, and grief,
> And the desire to find no comforter,

(Save only Death, who makes all sorrow brief,)
To him who for a while turns in his thought
How she hath been among us, and is not.

With sighs my bosom always laboureth
  In thinking, as I do continually,
    Of her for whom my heart now breaks apace;
And very often when I think of death,
  Such a great inward longing comes to me
    That it will change the colour of my face;
    And, if the idea settles in its place,
All my limbs shake as with an ague-fit;
  Till, starting up in wild bewilderment,
  I do become so shent
That I go forth, lest folk misdoubt of it.
  Afterward, calling with a sore lament
On Beatrice, I ask, "Canst thou be dead?"
And calling on her, I am comforted.

Grief with its tears, and anguish with its sighs,
  Come to me now whene'er I am alone;
    So that I think the sight of me gives pain.
And what my life hath been, that living dies,
  Since for my lady the New Birth's begun,
    I have not any language to explain.
    And so, dear ladies, though my heart were fain,
I scarce could tell indeed how I am thus.
  All joy is with my bitter life at war;
  Yea, I am fallen so far
That all men seem to say, "Go out from us,"
  Eyeing my cold white lips, how dead they are.
But she, though I be bow'd unto the dust,
Watches me; and will guerdon me, I trust.

Weep, piteous Song of mine, upon thy way,
  To the dames going and the damozels,
  For whom, and for none else,
Thy sisters have made music many a day.
Thou, that art very sad and not as they,
  Go dwell thou with them as a mourner dwells.

[Dante describes some of the sorrows over Beatrice's loss which oppressed him during the first year after her death.]

Then, having sat for some space sorely in thought because of the time that was now past, I was so filled with dolorous imaginings that it became outwardly manifest in mine altered countenance. Whereupon, feeling this and being in dread lest any should have seen me, I lifted mine eyes to look; and then perceived a young and very beautiful lady, who was gazing upon me from a window with a gaze full of pity, so that the very sum of pity appeared gathered together in her. And seeing that unhappy persons, when they beget compassion in others, are then most moved unto weeping, as though they also felt pity for themselves, it came to pass that mine eyes began to be inclined unto tears. Wherefore, becoming fearful lest I should make manifest mine abject condition, I rose up, and went where I could not be seen of that lady; saying afterwards within myself: "Certainly with her also must abide most noble Love." And with that, I resolved upon writing a sonnet, wherein, speaking unto her, I should say all that I have just said. And as this sonnet is very evident, I will not divide it.

> Mine eyes beheld the blessed pity spring
>   Into thy countenance immediately,
>   A while agone, when thou beheld'st in me
> The sickness only hidden grief can bring;
> And then I knew thou wast considering
>   How abject and forlorn my life must be;
>   And I became afraid that thou shouldst see
> My weeping, and account it a base thing.
> Therefore I went out from thee; feeling how
>   The tears were straightway loosen'd at my heart
>   Beneath thine eyes' compassionate control.
>   And afterwards I said within my soul:
> "Lo! with this lady dwells the counterpart
> Of the same Love who holds me weeping now."

It happened after this, that whensoever I was seen of this lady, she became pale and of a piteous countenance, as though it had been with love; whereby she remembered me many times of my own most noble lady, who was wont to be of a like paleness. And I know that often, when I could not weep nor in any way give ease unto mine anguish, I went to look upon this lady, who seemed to bring the tears into my eyes by the mere sight of her. Of the which thing I bethought me to speak unto her in rhyme, and then made this sonnet: which begins, "Love's pallor," and which is plain without being divided, by its exposition aforesaid.

> Love's pallor and the semblance of deep ruth
>   Were never yet shown forth so perfectly
>   In any lady's face, chancing to see
> Grief's miserable countenance uncouth,
> As in thine, lady, they have sprung to soothe,
>   When in mine anguish thou hast look'd on me;
>   Until sometimes it seems as if, through thee,
> My heart might almost wander from its truth.
> Yet so it is, I cannot hold mine eyes
>   From gazing very often upon thine
>   In the sore hope to shed those tears they keep;
> And at such time, thou mak'st the pent tears rise
>   Even to the brim, till the eyes waste and pine;
>   Yet cannot they, while thou art present, weep.

At length, by the constant sight of this lady, mine eyes began to be gladdened overmuch with her company; through which thing many times I had much unrest, and rebuked myself as a base person: also, many times I cursed the unsteadfastness of mine eyes, and said to them inwardly: "Was not your grievous condition of weeping wont one while to make others weep? And will ye now forget this thing because a lady looketh upon you? who so looketh merely in compassion of the grief ye then showed for your own blessed lady. But whatso ye can, that do ye, accursed eyes! many a time will I make you remember it! for never, till death dry you up, should ye make an end of your weeping." And when I had spoken thus unto mine eyes, I was taken again with extreme and grievous sighing. And to the end that this inward strife which I had undergone might not be hidden from all saving the miserable wretch who endured it, I proposed to write a sonnet, and to comprehend in it this horrible condition. And I wrote this which begins, "The very bitter weeping."

"The very bitter weeping that ye made
  So long a time together, eyes of mine,
  Was wont to make the tears of pity shine
In other eyes full oft, as I have said.
But now this thing were scarce rememberèd
  If I, on my part, foully would combine
  With you, and not recall each ancient sign
Of grief, and her for whom your tears were shed.
It is your fickleness that doth betray
  My mind to fears, and makes me tremble thus
    What while a lady greets me with her eyes.
Except by death, we must not any way
  Forget our lady who is gone from us."
    So far doth my heart utter, and then sighs.

The sight of this lady brought me into so unwonted a condition that I often thought of her as of one too dear unto me; and I began to consider her thus: "This lady is young, beautiful, gentle, and wise: perchance it was Love himself who set her in my path, that so my life might find peace." And there were times when I thought yet more fondly, until my heart consented unto its reasoning. But when it had so consented, my thought would often turn round upon me, as moved by reason, and cause me to say within myself: "What hope is this which would console me after so base a fashion, and which hath taken the place of all other imagining?" Also there was another voice within me, that said: "And wilt thou, having suffered so much tribulation through Love, not escape while yet thou mayst from so much bitterness? Thou must surely know that this thought carries with it the desire of Love, and drew its life from the gentle eyes of that lady who vouchsafed thee so much pity." Wherefore I, having striven sorely and very often with myself, bethought me to say somewhat thereof in rhyme. And seeing that in the battle of doubts, the victory most often remained with such as inclined towards the lady of whom I speak, it seemed to me that I should address this sonnet unto her: in the first line whereof, I call that thought which spake of her a gentle thought, only because it spoke of one who was gentle; being of itself most vile.

> A gentle thought there is will often start,
>   Within my secret self, to speech of thee;
>   Also of Love it speaks so tenderly
> That much in me consents and takes its part.
> "And what is this," the soul saith to the heart,
>   "That cometh thus to comfort thee and me,
>   And thence where it would dwell, thus potently
> Can drive all other thoughts by its strange art?"
> And the heart answers: "Be no more at strife
>   'Twixt doubt and doubt: this is Love's messenger
>   And speaketh but his words, from him received;
> And all the strength it owns and all the life
>   It draweth from the gentle eyes of her
>   Who, looking on our grief, hath often grieved."

But against this adversary of reason, there rose up in me on a certain day, about the ninth hour, a strong visible phantasy, wherein I seemed to behold the most gracious Beatrice, habited in that crimson raiment which she had worn when I had first beheld her; also she appeared to me of the same tender age as then. Whereupon I fell into a deep thought of her: and my memory ran back, according to the order of time, unto all those matters in the which she had borne a part; and my heart began painfully to repent of the desire by which it had so basely let itself be possessed during so many days, contrary to the constancy of reason.

And then, this evil desire being quite gone from me, all my thoughts turned again unto their excellent Beatrice. And I say most truly that from that hour I thought constantly of her with the whole humbled and ashamed heart; the which became often manifest in sighs, that had among them the name of that most gracious creature, and how she departed from us. Also it would come to pass very often, through the bitter anguish of some one thought, that I forgot both it, and myself, and where I was. By this increase of sighs, my weeping, which before had been somewhat lessened, increased in like manner; so that mine eyes seemed to long only for tears and to cherish them, and came at last to be circled about with red as though they had suffered martyrdom; neither were they able to look again upon the beauty of any face that might again bring them to shame and evil: from which things it will appear that they were fitly guerdoned for their unsteadfastness. Wherefore I, (wishing that mine abandonment of all such evil desires and vain temptations should be certified and made manifest, beyond all doubts which might have been suggested by the rhymes aforewritten,) proposed to write a sonnet, wherein I should express this purport. And I then wrote, "Woe's me!"

> Woe's me! by dint of all these sighs that come
>   Forth of my heart, its endless grief to prove,

Mine eyes are conquer'd, so that even to move
Their lids for greeting is grown troublesome.
They wept so long that now they are grief's home
 And count their tears all laughter far above:
 They wept, till they are circled now by Love
With a red circle in sign of martyrdom.
These musings, and the sighs they bring from me,
 Are grown at last so constant and so sore
  That Love swoons in my spirit with faint breath;
Hearing in those sad sounds continually
 The most sweet name that my dead lady bore,
  With many grievous words touching her death.

About this time, it happened that a great number of persons undertook a pilgrimage, to the end that they might behold that blessed portraiture bequeathed unto us by our Lord Jesus Christ as the image of His beautiful countenance,[21] (upon which countenance my dear lady now looketh continually.) And certain among these pilgrims, who seemed very thoughtful, passed by a path which is wellnigh in the midst of the city where my most gracious lady was born, and abode, and at last died.

Then I, beholding them, said within myself: "These pilgrims seem to be come from very far; and I think they cannot have heard speak of this lady, or know anything concerning her. Their thoughts are not of her, but of other things; it may be, of their friends who are far distant, and whom we, in our turn, know not." And I went on to say: "I know that if they were of a country near unto us, they would in some wise seem disturbed, passing through this city which is so full of grief." And I said also: "If I could speak with them a space, I am certain that I should make them weep before they went forth of this city; for those things that they would hear from me must needs beget weeping in any."

And when the last of them had gone by me, I bethought me to write a sonnet, showing forth mine inward speech; and that it might seem the more pitiful, I made as though I had spoken it indeed unto them. And I wrote this sonnet, which beginneth: "Ye pilgrim-folk." I made use of the word *pilgrim* for its general signification; for "pilgrim" may be understood in two senses, one general, and one special. General, so far as any man may be called a pilgrim who leaveth the place of his birth; whereas, more narrowly speaking, he only is a pilgrim who goeth towards or frowards the House of St. James. For there are three separate denominations proper unto those who undertake journeys to the glory of God. They are called Palmers who go beyond the seas eastward, whence often they bring palm-branches. And Pilgrims, as I have said, are they who journey unto the holy House of Gallicia; seeing that no other apostle was buried so far from his birth-place as was the blessed Saint James. And there is a third sort who are called Romers; in that they go whither these whom I have called pilgrims went: which is to say, unto Rome.

---

[21]Veronica's veil. According to legend, a woman of Jerusalem named Veronica wiped the face of Christ on the way to the Crucifixion with a cloth which miraculously retained the imprint of Christ's countenance.

Ye pilgrim-folk, advancing pensively
  As if in thought of distant things, I pray,
  Is your own land indeed so far away
As by your aspect it would seem to be,—
That nothing of our grief comes over ye
  Though passing through the mournful town midway;
  Like unto men that understand to-day
Nothing at all of her great misery?
Yet if ye will but stay, whom I accost,
  And listen to my words a little space,
    At going ye shall mourn with a loud voice.
It is her Beatrice that she hath lost;
  Of whom the least word spoken holds such grace
    That men weep hearing it, and have no choice.

A while after these things, two gentle ladies sent unto me, praying that I would bestow upon them certain of these my rhymes. And I, (taking into account their worthiness and consideration,) resolved that I would write also a new thing, and send it them together with those others, to the end that their wishes might be more honourably fulfilled. Therefore I made a sonnet, which narrates my condition, and which I caused to be conveyed to them, accompanied with the one preceding, and with that other which begins, "Stay now with me and listen to my sighs." And the new sonnet is, "Beyond the sphere."

Beyond the sphere which spreads to widest space
  Now soars the sigh that my heart sends above:
  A new perception born of grieving Love
Guideth it upward the untrodden ways.
When it hath reach'd unto the end, and stays,
  It sees a lady round whom splendours move
  In homage; till, by the great light thereof
Abash'd, the pilgrim spirit stands at gaze.
It sees her such, that when it tells me this
  Which it hath seen, I understand it not,
    It hath a speech so subtle and so fine.
And yet I know its voice within my thought
  Often remembereth me of Beatrice:
    So that I understand it, ladies mine.

After writing this sonnet, it was given unto me to behold a very wonderful vision;[22] wherein I saw things which determined me that I would say nothing further of this most blessed one, until such time as I could discourse more worthily concerning her. And to this end I labour all I can; as she well knoweth. Wherefore if it be His pleasure through whom is the life of all things, that my life continue with me a few years, it is my hope that I shall yet write concerning her what hath not before been written of any woman. After the which, may it seem good unto Him

---

[22]Presumably the idea for the *Divine Comedy*.

who is the Master of Grace, that my spirit should go hence to behold
the glory of its lady: to wit, of that blessed Beatrice who now gazeth
continually on His countenance *qui est per omnia sæcula benedictus.
Laus Deo.*[23]

Comments / on *The New Life*

The *Vita Nuova*, taken as a whole, is the poetic embodiment of a spiritual
development, actually and historically lived out, through who can say how
many single experiences. He who composed the *Vita Nuova* must already
have had the *Divine Comedy* more or less clearly in mind; as he gazed
back on his youth, he must have recognized or dimly felt in all its experiences an inner destiny, a divine guidance, that drew him on to something greater. To work out this appointed destiny from the motley material
of a series of events and experiences which extend from the ninth to the
twenty-second [*sic*] year of the poet's life, is if not the only, at least the
chief, purpose of the *Vita Nuova.*

In the *Vita Nuova* the courtly homage to women changes, unnoted and
as if of its own volition, to saintly worship, and the latter in turn to metaphysical speculation. The poet gradually passes from knightly homage
to mystical adoration and philosophic contemplation.

KARL VOSSLER (1925)

From the *Vita Nuova* we get the impression of a rather moony and sentimental young man, engaged in making more or less serious love to various young women, staring them out of countenance in church, circulating
sonnets among a small circle of friends, attending parties, and weeping
a great deal over a passionate attachment which subjected him to a certain amount of ridicule among his acquaintances. He displays himself
in these attitudes with a sort of humorous compassion . . . but also with
an overpowering conviction that in his vision of what Beatrice was he
had got hold of something of enormous importance—some experience
which held the clue to *all* experience, if only he could get it across to us.

D. L. SAYERS (1957)

[T]he *Vita Nuova*, besides being a sequence of beautiful poems connected
by a curious vision-literature prose, is, I believe, a very sound psychological treatise on something related to what is now called "sublimation."
There is also a practical sense of realities behind it, which is antiro-

---

[23]"Who is blessed throughout all ages. Praise God."

mantic: not to expect more from *life* than it can give or from *human* beings than they can give; to look to *death* for what life cannot give.

T. S. ELIOT (1929)

We are too often kept from feeling great things greatly for want of power to assimilate them to the little things which we feel keenly and sincerely. Dante had, in this respect, the art of a Platonic lover: he could enlarge the object of his passion, and keep the warmth and ardor of it undiminished. . . . Of this Platonic expansion of emotion, till it suffuses all that deserves to kindle it, we have a wonderful version in Dante's *Vita Nuova.* . . . The learned will dispute forever on the exact basis and meaning of these confessions of Dante. The learned are perhaps not those best fitted to solve the problem. It is a matter for literary tact and sympathetic imagination. It must be left to the delicate intelligence of the reader, if he has it; and if he has not, Dante does not wish to open his heart to him. His enigmatical manner is his protection against the intrusion of uncongenial minds.

GEORGE SANTAYANA (1910)

It was inevitable that between two such divergent conceptions of love as troubadour [Provencal] love of woman and Christian love of God conflict should arise: inevitable because in his "philosophy" the troubadour found no place for Christian love as such. Neither did the Christian love make any room at all for troubadour love. . . . [Dante] found a way to go beyond the conflict of love of woman with love of God, bringing to the thesis and the antithesis of the one and the other that synthesis which managed to reject neither the one nor the other but to keep both in a single suspension—in a single theory of love. The *Vita Nuova* is that theory.

C. S. SINGLETON (1949)

Letter to Can Grande

Probably no other work in the literature of the world, except for the Bible, has been the subject of as much commentary as Dante's *Divine Comedy.* The poem demands commentary, as Dante himself was the first to realize, and consequently, he was the first to write one. In a letter dedicating the third section of the work, the *Paradiso,* to Can Grande della Scala, Lord of Verona and one of Dante's principal benefactors in exile, Dante presented his own views of how his creation should be read. Much of his exposition consists of minute analysis in the scholastic manner, likely to be more of a hindrance than a help to the modern reader. However, the passages in which he described the method and purpose of his conception of allegory—which is based on the medieval notion voiced in

St. Thomas Aquinas' *Summation of Theology* that every phenomenon within human experience has some sort of spiritual significance—are fundamental to an understanding of the *Divine Comedy.*

---

6. If any one, therefore, is desirous of offering any sort of introduction to part of a work, it behoves him to furnish some notion of the whole of which it is a part. Wherefore I, too, being desirous of offering something by way of introduction to the above-mentioned part of the whole *Comedy,* thought it incumbent on me in the first place to say something concerning the work as a whole, in order that access to the part might be the easier and the more perfect. There are six points, then, as to which inquiry must be made at the beginning of every didactic work; namely, the subject, the author, the form, the aim, the title of the book, and the branch of philosophy to which it belongs. Now of these six points there are three in respect of which the part which I have had in mind to address to you differs from the whole work; namely, the subject, the form, and the title; whereas in respect of the others there is no difference, as is obvious to any one who considers the matter. Consequently, in an examination of the whole, these three points must be made the subject of a separate inquiry; which being done, the way will be sufficiently clear for the introduction to the part. Later we will examine the other three points, not only with reference to the whole work, but also with reference to the particular part which is offered to you.

7. For the elucidation, therefore, of what we have to say, it must be understood that the meaning of this work is not of one kind only; rather the work may be described as 'polysemous', that is, having several meanings; for the first meaning is that which is conveyed by the letter, and the next is that which is conveyed by what the letter signifies; the former of which is called literal, while the latter is called allegorical, or mystical. And for the better illustration of this method of exposition we may apply it to the following verses: 'When Israel went out of Egypt, the house of Jacob from a people of strange language; Judah was his sanctuary, and Israel his dominion'. For if we consider the letter alone, the thing signified to us is the going out of the children of Israel from Egypt in the time of Moses; if the allegory, our redemption through Christ is signified; if the moral sense, the conversion of the soul from the sorrow and misery of sin to a state of grace is signified; if the anagogical, the passing of the sanctified soul from the bondage of the corruption of this world to the liberty of everlasting glory is signified. And although these mystical meanings are called by various names, they may one and all in a general sense be termed allegorical, inasmuch as they are different *(diversi)* from the literal or historical; for the word 'allegory' is so called from the Greek *alleon,* which in Latin is *alienum* (strange) or *diversum* (different).

From *The Letters of Dante,* edited by Paget Toynbee. Reprinted by permission of the Clarendon Press, Oxford.

8. This being understood, it is clear that the subject, with regard to which the alternative meanings are brought into play, must be twofold. And therefore the subject of this work must be considered in the first place from the point of view of the literal meaning, and next from that of the allegorical interpretation. The subject, then, of the whole work, taken in the literal sense only, is the state of souls after death, pure and simple. For on and about that the argument of the whole work turns. If, however, the work be regarded from the allegorical point of view, the subject is man according as by his merits or demerits in the exercise of his free will he is deserving of reward or punishment by justice.

9. And the form is twofold—the form of the treatise, and the form of the treatment. The form of the treatise is threefold, according to the threefold division. The first division is that whereby the whole work is divided into three cantiche; the second, whereby each cantica is divided into cantos; and the third, whereby each canto is divided into rhymed lines. The form or manner of treatment is poetic, fictive, descriptive, digressive, and figurative; and further, it is definitive, analytical, probative, refutative, and exemplificative.

10. The title of the book is 'Here begins the *Comedy* of Dante Alighieri, a Florentine by birth, not by disposition'. For the understanding of which it must be noted that 'comedy' is so called from *comos,* a village, and *oda,* a song; whence comedy is as it were a 'rustic song'. Now comedy is a certain kind of poetical narration which differs from all others. It differs, then, from tragedy in its subject-matter, in that tragedy at the beginning is admirable and placid, but at the end or issue is foul and horrible. And tragedy is so called from *tragos,* a goat, and *oda;* as it were a 'goat-song', that is to say foul like a goat, as appears from the tragedies of Seneca.[1] Whereas comedy begins with sundry adverse conditions, but ends happily, as appears from the comedies of Terence.[2] And for this reason it is the custom of some writers in their salutation to say by way of greeting: 'a tragic beginning and a comic ending to you!' Tragedy and comedy differ likewise in their style of language; for that of tragedy is high-flown and sublime, while that of comedy is unstudied and lowly. And this is implied by Horace[3] in the *Art of Poetry,* where he grants that the comedian may on occasion use the language of tragedy, and vice versa:

> Yet sometimes comedy her voice will raise,
> And angry Chremes[4] scold with swelling phrase;
> And prosy periods oft our ears assail
> When Telephus and Peleus[5] tell their tragic tale.

---

[1]Roman playwright (4? B.C.—65 A.D.).

[2]Roman playwright (190?—159? B.C.). Dante's etymologies for the origins of the words *comedy* and *tragedy* have been discredited by modern scholarship, but his explanation of them as literary forms reflects the usual medieval conception of their meaning.

[3]Roman poet (65—8 B.C.).

[4]A reference to a play no longer extant.

[5]Telephus and Peleus are both figures from Greek mythology who appear in the works of the fifth-century B.C. tragic playwrights.

And from this it is clear that the present work is to be described as a comedy. For if we consider the subject-matter, at the beginning it is horrible and foul, as being *Hell;* but at the close it is happy, desirable, and pleasing, as being *Paradise.* As regards the style of language, the style is unstudied and lowly, as being in the vulgar tongue, in which even women-folk hold their talk. And hence it is evident why the work is called a comedy. And there are other kinds of poetical narration, such as the pastoral poem, the elegy, the satire, and the votive song, as may also be gathered from Horace in the *Art of Poetry;* but of these we need say nothing at present.

11. It can now be shown in what manner the subject of the part offered to you is to be determined. For if the subject of the whole work taken in the literal sense is the state of souls after death, pure and simple, without limitation; it is evident that in this part the same state is the subject, but with a limitation, namely the state of blessed souls after death. And if the subject of the whole work from the allegorical point of view is man according as by his merits or demerits in the exercise of his free will he is deserving of reward or punishment by justice, it is evident that in this part this subject has a limitation, and that it is man according as by his merits he is deserving of reward by justice.

12. In like manner the form of the part is determined by that of the whole work. For if the form of the treatise as a whole is threefold, in this part it is twofold only, the division being that of the cantica and of the cantos. The first division (into cantiche) cannot be applicable to the form of the part, since the cantica is itself a part under the first division.

13. The title of the book also is clear. For the title of the whole book is 'Here begins the *Comedy*', &c., as above; but the title of the part is 'Here begins the third cantica of the *Comedy* of Dante, which is called *Paradise*'.

14. These three points, in which the part differs from the whole, having been examined, we may now turn our attention to the other three, in respect of which there is no difference between the part and the whole. The author, then, of the whole and of the part is the person mentioned above, who is seen to be such throughout.

15. The aim of the whole and of the part might be manifold; as, for instance, immediate and remote. But leaving aside any minute examination of this question, it may be stated briefly that the aim of the whole and of the part is to remove those living in this life from a state of misery, and to bring them to a state of happiness.

16. The branch of philosophy to which the work is subject, in the whole as in the part, is that of morals or ethics; inasmuch as the whole as well as the part was conceived, not for speculation, but with a practical object. For if in certain parts or passages the treatment is after the manner of speculative philosophy, that is not for the sake of speculation, but for a practical purpose; since, as the Philosopher says in the second book of the *Metaphysics:* 'practical men occasionally speculate on things in their particular and temporal relations'.

Comments / on *Letter to Can Grande*

. . . letter to Can Grande, that precious document for the understanding of the *Paradiso,* of the poet's mind, and of the amazingly intricate rhetorical doctrine through which [Dante] made his way to the crystal clarity of his poetry.   *E. K. RAND (1928)*

. . . letter to Can Grande, where [Dante's] thought may be heard creaking scholastically, as he describes the nature of his poem. . . .

                                                                      H. O. TAYLOR (1925)

The Letter [to Can Grande] is speaking of the way in which a poem is to be understood. And in choosing its example of allegory from Holy Scripture, the Letter is clearly looking to the kind of allegory which is the allegory of theologians; and is thus pointing to a poem in which the first and literal sense is to be taken as the first and literal sense of Scripture is taken, namely as an historical sense . . . if we take the allegory of the *Divine Comedy* to be the allegory of theologians, we shall expect to find in the poem a first literal meaning presented as a meaning which is not fictive but true, because the words which give that meaning point to events which are seen as historically true. And we shall see these events themselves reflecting a second meaning because their author, who is God, can use events as men use words. *But,* we shall not demand at every moment that the event signified by the words be in its turn as a word, because this is not the case in Holy Scripture. . . . And [in paraphrase of one of Dante's fourteenth-century commentators] if you say: "I do not believe that Dante ever went to the other world," then I say that with those who deny what a poem asks to be granted, there is no further disputing.

                                                                  C. S. SINGLETON (1954)

On World Government

The relationship between religion and government has always been a troublesome problem for all societies, raising all sorts of difficult questions about just how much influence one should have on the operations of the other. During the later Middle Ages the division of powers between Church and State constituted the most controversial political issue in Western Europe. Kingship was a secular office, but coronations were religious ceremonies; kings ruled their domains, but they ruled by divine right, and the pope was the chief representative of God on earth. Did the pope's authority transcend the king's in matters concerning his own kingdom? If so, to what extent? Only in ecclesiastical affairs? What about matters in which ecclesiastical interests came into conflict with secular interests? Or even in purely secular affairs where a moral, and therefore spiritual, issue was involved? Although these questions and the countless ramifications emanating from them were continually being argued in every kingdom, the arguments tended to be colored by local circumstances. The general principles at stake can be seen most clearly in the conflicts between the popes and the Holy Roman Emperors.

The Holy Roman Empire represented the Church's dream of a world wholly Christian united under a single supreme secular ruler just as it was already united, in theory at least, under a single supreme spiritual ruler. It was to be a revival of the Roman Empire as it had existed under the Caesars, but under Christian auspices. Charlemagne was crowned as the first Holy Roman Emperor in the year 800, and for a time the dream was close to a reality, since Charlemagne did in fact rule over most of that part of the Christian world which acknowledged the spiritual authority of the pope. Although in later periods the emperor usually managed to rule only those domains that were his by right of family inheritance or military conquest, the concept of a Holy Roman Empire and the title of *emperor* survived into the nineteenth century. For much of that time the popes and emperors were at odds about the proper limits of each other's authority.

The popes, claiming supreme authority over all the affairs of Christendom because all human affairs affected human salvation and were therefore the ultimate responsibility of the papacy, argued that the emperor's main function was to provide the secular power to enforce the pope's authority. The broad answer to this argument, based on one of the fundamental principles underlying the theory of the separation of Church and State, was that spiritual authority should confine itself solely to spiritual affairs; otherwise, it would tend to diminish its spiritual force. Dante believed fervently in this principle, just as he believed in the idea of a Holy Roman Empire as the means by which a single, stable, orderly government might be achieved for the whole of Christendom. One of the main themes in the *Divine Comedy* is Dante's political conviction that the fragmentation of secular authority and the meddling of the Church in secular affairs were responsible for many of the ills in contemporary society. He put the same convictions into comprehensive, detailed, systematic form in his political treatise, *De Monarchia (On World Government)*. It stands as a classic statement of position for one side of the controversy between Church and State.

Book I

(1) It would seem that all men on whom the Higher Nature has stamped the love of truth must make it their chief concern, like as they have been enriched by the toil of those who have gone before,

---

From *The Latin Works of Dante*, translated by Philip Wicksteed. Published, 1904, by J. M. Dent & Sons Ltd. Reprinted by permission of the publishers.

so themselves in like manner to toil in advance for those that shall be hereafter, that posterity may have of them whereby to be enriched.

For he who, himself imbued with public teachings, yet cares not to contribute aught to the public good, may be well assured that he has fallen far from duty; for he is not "a tree by the streams of waters, bearing his fruit in due season," but rather a devouring whirlpool, ever sucking in, and never pouring back what it has swallowed. Wherefore, often pondering these things with myself, lest I should one day be convicted of the charge of the buried talent, I long not only to burgeon, but also to bear fruit for the public advantage, and to set forth truths unattempted by others. For what fruit would he bear who should demonstrate once more some theorem of Euclid; who should strive to expound anew felicity, which Aristotle has already expounded; who should undertake again the apology of old age, which Cicero has pleaded? Naught at all, but rather would such wearisome superfluity provoke disgust.

And inasmuch as amongst other unexplored and important truths the knowledge of the temporal monarchy is most important and least explored, and (for that it stands in no direct relation to gain) has been attempted by none; therefore am I minded to extract it from its recesses, on the one hand that I may keep vigil for the good of the world, and on the other that I may be the first to win for my glory the palm of so great a prize. A hard task in truth do I attempt, and beyond my strength, trusting not so much in my proper power as in the light of that giver who giveth to all liberally and upbraideth not.

(2) First, therefore, we have to consider what the temporal monarchy means; in type to wit, and after intention. The temporal monarchy, then, which is called empire is "a unique princedom extending over all persons in time," or, "in and over those things which are measured by time." And there rise three main inquiries concerning the same: for in the first place we may inquire and examine whether it is needful for the well-being of the world; in the second, whether the Roman people rightfully assumed to itself the function of monarchy; and in the third, whether the authority of the monarchy depends immediately upon God, or upon some other minister or vicar of God. . . .

(3) So now we must consider what is the goal of human civilisation as a whole, which, when we see, more than half our work will be done, according to the Philosopher *Ad Nicomachum.* . . . [T]here is one end for which nature produces . . . the individual man, another for which the domestic group, another for which the district, another for which the city-state, and another for which the kingdom; and lastly, there is an ultimate goal for which the eternal God, by his art, which is nature, brings into being the human race in its universality. And it is this last for which we are now seeking as the first principle to direct our inquiry. . . .

. . . [W]hat this function is will be obvious if the specific potentiality of mankind generally be made clear. I say, then, that no capacity which is shared by many beings, differing in species, is the specific capacity of any one of them. For since that which is specific constitutes a species, it would follow that one essence would be specifically assigned to several species, which is impossible. The specific capacity, then, which differentiates man is not merely *being,* taken without qualification, for this he shares with the elements; neither *compound being,* for this we find in the minerals; nor *animated being,* for this is in plants; nor *appre-hension,* for this is shared by the brutes; but *apprehension by means of the potential intellect,* which mode of being is not competent to any other save man, either above him or below. . . . It is plain, then, that the specific potentiality of humanity as such is a potentiality or capacity of intellect. . . .

Moveover, the intellectual faculty of which I am speaking deals not only with universal forms or species, but also, by a kind of extension, with particular ones. Whence it is commonly said that the speculative intellect by extension becomes the practical intellect, the end of which is *doing* and *making.* And I draw this distinction because there are things to be *done* which are regulated by political wisdom, and things to be *made,* which are regulated by art. But they are all alike handmaids of speculation, as the supreme function for which the Prime Excellence brought the human race into being. And now we have already reached a point at which that saying of the *Politics* begins to be luminous: "The intellectually vigorous have natural sway over others."

(4) . . . And since it is with the whole as it is with the part, and it is the fact that in sedentary quietness the individual man is perfected in knowledge and in wisdom, it is evident that in the quiet or tranquillity of peace the human race is most freely and favourably disposed towards the work proper to it (which is almost divine, even as it is said "Thou hast made him a little lower than the angels"). Whence it is manifest that universal peace is the best of all those things which are ordained for our blessedness. And that is why there rang out to the shepherds from on high, not riches, not pleasures, not honours, not length of life, not health, not strength, not beauty, but peace. For the celestial soldiery proclaims, "Glory to God in the highest; and, on earth, peace to men of good will." Hence, also, "Peace be with you" was the salutation of him who was the salvation of man. For it was meet that the supreme saviour should utter the supreme salutation. . . .

(5) And now, to resume what we said at the outset, three main questions are raised and discussed about the temporal monarchy, more commonly called the empire; concerning which, as already declared, we purpose to make inquiry, in the order indicated above, under the first principle now laid down. Let us therefore first discuss whether a temporal monarchy is needful for the well-being of the world.

Now against its being needful there is no force either of argument or of authority, whereas most powerful and most patent arguments establish that it is. Of which let the first be drawn from the authority of the Philosopher in his *Politics.* For there his venerable authority asserts that when more things than one are ordained for a single purpose, needs must one of them guide or rule, and the others be guided or ruled. And to this not only the glorious name of the author, but inductive argument also forces assent. . . .

Now it is admitted that the whole human race is ordained for a single end, as was set forth before. Therefore there must be one guiding or ruling power. And this is what we mean by monarch or emperor. Thus it appears that for the well-being of the world there must be a monarchy or empire.

(8) And everything is well and best disposed which is disposed

after the intention of the prime agent, which is God. And this is self-evident to all who deny not that the divine excellence attains the height of perfection. It is of the intention of God that every created thing should present the divine likeness in so far as its proper nature is capable of receiving it. Wherefore it is said, "Let us make man after our image and likeness." And although "after our image" may not be said of things lower than man, yet "after our likeness" may be said of all things soever, since the whole universe is nought else than a certain footprint of the divine excellence. Therefore the human race is well and best disposed when, to the measure of its power, it is likened to God. . . .

But the human race is then most one when it is all united in one, which can not be save when it is subject in its totality to one prince, as is self-evident. Therefore, it is when subject to one prince that the human race is most likened to God, and consequently most conforms to the divine intention. . . .

(10) Wheresoever contention may arise there must needs be judgment, else there were an imperfection without its proper perfector; which is impossible, since God and nature fails not in things necessary. Now between any two princes, one of whom is in no way subject to the other, contention may arise, either through their own fault or that of their subjects, as is self-evident. Wherefore there must needs be judgment between such. And since the one may not take cognisance of what concerns the other, the one not being subject to the other (for a peer has no rule over his peer), there must needs be a third of wider jurisdiction who, within the compass of his right, has princedom over both. . . . Therefore monarchy is necessary for the world. And this reasoning was perceived by the Philosopher when he said, "Things love not to be ill-disposed; but a multiplicity of princedoms is ill; therefore, one prince."

(11) Moreover, the world is best disposed when justice is most potent therein; whence Virgil, in praise of that age which was visibly rising in his own day, sang in his *Bucolics:*—

"Iam redit et Virgo, redeunt Saturnia regna."[1]

By "Virgin" he meant Justice, who was also called Astraea. By "Saturnian kingdoms" he meant the best ages, which were also called the golden.

Justice is most potent under a monarch only; therefore for the best disposition of the world it is needful that there should be a monarchy or empire. . . .

. . . [W]e must note that greed is the chief opponent of justice, as Aristotle indicates in the fifth *Ad Nicomachum.* If greed be absolutely removed, nothing is left to oppose justice; whence it is the opinion of the Philosopher that such things as can be determined by law should in no case be left to the judge. And this for fear of greed, which readily turns the minds of men aside. Now where there is nought that can be desired, there it is impossible for greed to be; for when their objects are de-

---

[1] "At last the Virgin and the Saturnian kingdoms are returning."

stroyed the passions cannot persist. But the monarch has nought that he can desire, for his jurisdiction is bounded by the ocean alone, which is not the case with other princes, since their principalities are bounded by others; as for instance the King of the Castile's by the King of Aragon's. Whence it follows that the monarch may be the purest subject of justice amongst mortals.

Moreover, just as greed, though it be never so little, clouds to some extent the disposition of justice, so does charity or right love sharpen and brighten it. In whomsoever therefore right love has the greatest power of inhering, in him justice may take the most commanding place. The monarch is such; therefore when he exists justice is most powerful, or at any rate may be so. Now, that right love has the action I have said may be shown thus. Greed, scorning the intrinsic significance of man, seeks other things; but charity, scorning all other things, seeks God and man, and consequently the good of man. And since, amongst the other blessings of man, living in peace is the chief (as was said above), and justice is the chiefest and mightiest accomplisher of this, therefore charity will chiefly give vigour to justice; and the stronger she is, the more.

And that right love should inhere in the monarch most of all men is shown thus. Everything lovable is the more loved the closer it is to the lover. But men are closer to the monarch than to other princes; therefore they are most loved by him, or at least they ought to be. The first proposition is manifest if the nature of patients and agents be considered. The second proposition is demonstrated thus. Men only come into contact with other princes partwise, but with the monarch in their totality. And again, men come into contact with other princes through the monarch, and not conversely; and thus, charge of all men primarily and immediately inheres in the monarch, and in other princes only through the monarch, inasmuch as their charge is derived from that supreme charge. . . .

(12) And the human race when most free is best disposed. This will be clear if the principle of freedom be understood. Wherefore be it known that the first principle of our freedom is freedom of choice, which many have on their lips but few in their understanding. . . .

. . . I say that judgment is the link between apprehension and appetite. For first a thing is apprehended, then when apprehended it is judged to be good or bad, and finally he who has so judged it pursues or shuns it. If, then, the judgment altogether sets the appetite in motion, and is in no measure anticipated by it, it is free. But if the judgment is moved by the appetite, which to some extent anticipates it, it cannot be free, for it does not move of itself, but is drawn captive by another. And hence it is that brutes cannot have free judgment because their judgments are always anticipated by appetite. And hence too it may be seen that the intellectual substances whose wills are immutable, and separated souls departing from this life in grace, do not lose their freedom of choice because of the immutability of their wills, but retain it in its most perfect and potent form.

When we see this we may further understand that this freedom (or this principle of all our freedom) is the greatest gift conferred by God on human nature; for through it we have our felicity here as men, through it we have our felicity elsewhere as deities. . . . It is only when a monarch is reigning that the human race exists for its own sake, and not for the sake of something else. For it is only then that perverted forms of government are made straight, to wit democracies, oligarchies, and tyrannies, which force the human race into slavery (as is obvious to whosoever runs through them all), and that government is conducted by kings, aristocrats (whom they call *optimates*), and zealots for the people's liberty. . . . And such right governments purpose freedom, to wit that men should exist for their own sakes. For the citizens are not there for the sake of the consuls, nor the nation for the sake of the king, but conversely the consuls for the sake of the citizens, the king for the sake of the nation. For just as the body politic is not established for the benefit of the laws, but the laws for the benefit of the body politic, so too they who live under the law are not ordained for the benefit of the legislator, but rather he for theirs, as saith the Philosopher again in what has been left by him on the present matter. Hence it is clear that, albeit the consul or king be masters of the rest as regards the way, yet as regards the end they are their servants; and the monarch most of all, for he must assuredly be regarded as the servant of all. Hence it may begin to appear at this point how the monarch is conditioned in laying down the laws by the end set before him.

Therefore the human race is best disposed when under a monarchy. Whence it follows that for the well-being of the world the existence of a monarchy is necessary.

(14) . . . [D]oubtless, we should note that when we say the human race can be ruled by one supreme prince we are not to be so understood, as that every petty decision of each municipality (since even the bye-laws sometimes leave us in the lurch and themselves need direction, as is clear from the Philosopher in the fifth *Ad Nicomachum,* in his commendation of *epyekia*) could issue from him immediately. For nations, kingdoms, and cities have their special conditions which ought to be regulated by different laws. For a law is a rule to direct life. And naturally the Scythians who live outside the seventh clima, and experience great inequality of days and nights, and are oppressed by an almost intolerable chill of frost, must needs be regulated in a different way from the Garamantes who live under the equinoctial circle and always have the light of day equal in length to the darkness of night, and because of the excessive heat of the air cannot endure to be covered with a superfluity of garments. But it must be thus understood, that the human race in those things which are common, and are inherent in all, should be ruled by him, and guided by his common rule to peace. And this rule or law, the particular princes ought to receive from him, as the practical intellect receives the major proposition from the speculative intellect, and adds under it the particular proposition which is properly its own, and so proceeds to the particular practical conclusion. And not only is this possible to one; but it must of necessity flow from one, that all confusion concerning universal principles may be removed. And thus Moses writes in the Law that he himself did; for joining to himself the chiefs of the tribes of the sons of Israel, he relegated to them the in-

ferior judgments, reserving to himself alone the higher and more general; which more general judgments the chieftains made use of throughout their tribes according as they were applicable to each of them. . . .

(15) . . . All concord depends on unity in wills. The human race when best disposed is a concord. For as a single man when best disposed both as to mind and body is a concord, and so also a house, a city, and a kingdom, so likewise is the whole human race. Therefore the human race when best disposed depends upon a unity in wills. But this unity cannot be unless there is one will dominating and ruling all the rest to oneness; inasmuch as the wills of mortals, because of the seductive delights of youth, have need of a directive principle, as the Philosopher teaches in the last *Ad Nicomachum.* Nor can that one will exist unless there be a single prince of all, whose will may be the mistress and ruler of all others. . . .

(16) All the reasons set forth above are confirmed by a memorable experience; namely, of that state of mortal things which the Son of God, when about to become man for man's salvation, either awaited, or, when he would, produced. For if we go through all the states and periods of man, even from the fall of our first parents, which was the point at which we turned aside on our wanderings, we shall find that the world was never quiet on every side except under divus Augustus, the monarch, when there was a perfect monarchy. And that in truth the human race was then blessed in the tranquillity of universal peace is witnessed by all the historians, witnessed by illustrious poets. To this the scribe of the gentleness of Christ has likewise deigned to bear witness; and finally Paul has called that most happy state the "fulness of time." Verily the time and all temporal things were full, for no ministry to our felicity was then vacant of its minister.

But what the state of the world has been since that seamless garment first suffered rending by the nail of covetousness we may read—would that we might not also see! O race of men in what storms and losses, in what shipwrecks must thou needs be tossed, so long as, transformed into a beast of many heads, thou strivest after many things! Thou art sick in either intellect, sick in affection. Thou dost not minister to the higher intellect by reasonings that cannot be gainsaid, nor to the lower by the aspect of experience, nor even to thy affection by the sweetness of divine persuasion, when there sounds to thee through the trumpet of the Holy Spirit, "Behold how good and how pleasant it is for brethren to dwell together in unity."

[In Book II, Dante argues that the original Roman Empire rightfully exercised dominion over the world.]

Book III

(1) . . . In the beginning of this work it was proposed to inquire into three questions in such fashion as their subject-matter would allow.[2]

---

[2] See opening paragraph of Chapter 2 in Book I.

And in the foregoing books I believe the task has been sufficiently accomplished with respect to the first two of them. . . .

The present question, then, concerning which we are to make inquiry, lies between two great lights, to wit the Roman pontiff and the Roman prince; and we are to ask whether the authority of the Roman monarch, who is monarch of the world by right, as proved in the second book, is immediately dependent upon God; or rather on some vicar or minister of God, by whom I understand the successor of Peter, who in very truth bears the keys of the kingdom of heaven.

(4) Now those for whom the whole disputation that follows will be conducted assert that the authority of the empire depends upon the authority of the church, as the inferior artisan is dependent on the architect; and thereto they are moved by sundry adverse arguments which they draw from sacred scripture, and from certain things done alike by the supreme pontiff and by the emperor himself; though they strive also to gain some support from reason.

For they say firstly, following the scripture of Genesis, that God made two great luminaries, a greater luminary and a lesser luminary, that the one might rule over the day and the other the night. And these they have been accustomed to understand as spoken allegorically of those two regimens, to wit the spiritual and the temporal. Thence they argue that like as the moon, which is the lesser luminary, has no light save as she receives it from the sun, so neither has the temporal regimen any authority save as it receives it from the spiritual regimen. . . .

. . . But it may be shown in two ways that this interpretation of the passage can by no means be defended. First, since such regimens are certain accidents of man himself, God would seem to have followed a perverse order in producing the accidents before their proper subject, and to say this of God is absurd. For those two luminaries were produced on the fourth day, and man on the sixth day, as may be seen in the text.

Moreover, since those regimens exist to direct men to certain ends (as will be shown below), if man had remained in the state of innocence in which he was made by God he would have had no need of such directive regimens. Such regimens, then, are remedial against the infirmity of sin. Now since on the fourth day not only was man not sinful but man was not at all, to produce remedies would have been superfluous, which is counter to the divine excellence. For a physician were foolish to prepare a plaster to apply to the future abscess of one as yet not born. It must not be said, then, that on the fourth day God made these two regimens; and consequently Moses cannot have meant what they make out that he did.

But even if we allow this false statement we may disarm it by the method of distinction. And this is a gentler way of proceeding with an adversary, for it does not show that he is uttering an absolute falsehood, as the method by destruction does. I say, then, that although the moon has no abundant light save as she receives it from the sun, it does not therefore follow that the moon herself is derived from the sun. Wherefore be it known that the existence of the moon is one thing, her virtue another, and her operation yet a third. As to her existence the moon is in no way dependent on the sun, neither is she with respect to her virtue, and not absolutely with respect to her operation; for her motion is derived from her proper mover, and her influence from her proper rays. For she has a certain light from herself as is manifest in her eclipse. But with respect to her better and more virtuous operation she does receive something from the sun, to wit, abundance of light by the receipt of which she operates with more virtue. . . .

(5) They also draw an argument from the text of Moses, saying that from the loins of Jacob flowed the type of these two regimens, to wit, Levi and Judah, the one of whom was the father of the priesthood, and the other of the temporal regimen. Then they argue from them thus: "As Levi was related to Judah so is the church related to the empire. Levi preceded Judah in birth, as is evident in the text, therefore the church precedes the empire in authority."

This is easily indeed refuted; for the assertion that Levi and Judah, the sons of Jacob, represent those regimens I might refute as before by denying it; but let it be granted; yet when they infer in their argument that as Levi was first in birth so the church is first in authority, I say, as before, that the predicate of the conclusion is one and the major term is another; for authority is one thing and nativity another, both in subject and sense. Therefore there is an error in form. And it runs like this: "A preceded B in C; D is in the same relation to E that A is in to B; therefore D preceded E in F," whereas F and C are different.

And if, by way of rejoinder, they should say that F follows from C, that is to say authority from seniority, and that the consequent may be substituted in an inference for the antecedent (as animal for man), I reply that it is false; for there are many seniors by birth who not only do not precede those younger than themselves in authority but are preceded by them; as is evident when bishops are younger in years than their arch-presbyters. And thus the objection is seen to err in alleging as a cause what is not a cause.

(8) They also allege from the text of the same that word of Christ to Peter, "And whatsoever thou hast bound on earth shall be bound in heaven also, and whatsoever thou hast loosed on earth shall be loosed in heaven also." And they gather from this text of Matthew, and likewise from the text of John, that the same was said to all the apostles. Whence they argue that, by concession of God, the successor of Peter can both bind and loose everything; and hence they infer that he can loose the laws and decrees of the empire, and bind laws and decrees for the temporal regimen; from which what they assert would really follow.

We must proceed against this by distinction, applied to the major of the syllogism they employ. For their syllogism runs: "Peter had power to loose and bind all things. Peter's successor has whatsoever Peter had. Therefore Peter's successor has power to loose and bind all things." Whence they infer that he has power to loose and bind the authority and decrees of the empire.

I grant the minor, but the major only with a distinction. And therefore I say that this sign of universality "all," which is implied in "whatsoever," never distributes beyond the scope of the term distributed.

For if I say "every animal runs," the distribution of "every" covers all that is included under the genus "animal." But if I say "every man runs," then the universal qualification only distributes over what is covered by this term "man." And when I say "every grammarian" the distribution is still further contracted.

Wherefore we must always consider what it is which the universal qualification has to distribute, and when we do so we shall easily see how far the distribution extends, on considering the nature and scope of the distributed term. Wherefore when it is said "Whatsoever thou hast bound," if this "whatsoever" were to be taken absolutely their contention would be true, and he would not only be able to do what they assert, but to loose a wife from her husband and bind her to another while the first still lived, which he by no means can. He would also be able to absolve me while I am not penitent, which even God himself could not do.

Since this, then, is so, it is manifest that the distribution in question is not to be taken absolutely, but relatively to something. And to what it is relative is sufficiently evident when we consider what it was that was being granted to him, in connection with which that distributive qualification was added. For Christ says to Peter, "I will give thee the keys of the kingdom of heaven," that is, "I will make thee doorkeeper of the kingdom of heaven." Then he adds, "And whatsoever," that is "everything which," that is "everything which has reference to that office" thou shalt have power to loose and bind. And thus the sign of universality which is implied in "whatsoever" is restricted in its distribution by the office of the keys of the kingdom of heaven. And taken thus the proposition under discussion is true; but absolutely it clearly is not so. And therefore I say that although Peter's successor can loose and bind within the requirements of the office committed to Peter, yet it does not follow from that that he can loose or bind the decrees of the empire, or the laws (as was their contention), unless it could be further proved that this concerns the office of the keys; and the contrary of this will be shown below.

(10) It is further urged by some that the Emperor Constantine, when cleansed of his leprosy at the intercession of Sylvester, who was then supreme pontiff, granted the seat of empire, to wit Rome, to the church, together with many other dignities of the empire.[3] Whence they argue that no one can assume those dignities thenceforth except he receive them from the church, whose they say they are. And from this it would certainly follow that the one authority is dependent on the other, as they would have it. . . .

. . . I say that it has no force, because Constantine had no power to alienate the imperial dignity, nor had the church power to receive it. . . .

. . . [I]t were counter to human right should the empire destroy itself.

---

[3]Constantine (280?–337) became emperor in 306 and was converted to Christianity in 313, in which year he proclaimed Christianity the official religion of the Roman Empire. Dante refers to the so-called "Donation of Constantine," a document which is now known to have been forged probably during the eighth century but which was accepted throughout the later Middle Ages as genuine and used as one of the main arguments in asserting papal authority over the emperors. The authenticity of the Donation was first questioned in the fifteenth century, but it was not until the end of the eighteenth that its spurious character was generally acknowledged.

Therefore the empire may not destroy itself. Since, then, to rend the empire were to destroy it (inasmuch as the empire consists in the unity of universal monarchy), it is manifest that he who wields the authority of the empire may not rend the empire. And that it is counter to human right to destroy the empire is manifest from what has gone before.

Moreover, every jurisdiction is prior to its judge, for the judge is appointed to the jurisdiction, and not conversely. But the empire is a jurisdiction embracing every temporal jurisdiction in its scope; therefore it is prior to its judge, who is the emperor, because the emperor is appointed to it, and not conversely. Whence it is clear that the emperor, as emperor, cannot change it since it is the source of his being what he is. Now I say thus: Either he was emperor when he is said to have made the grant to the church, or he was not. And if not, it is obvious that he had no power of making grants with respect to the empire. If he was, then, since such a grant was to the prejudice of his jurisdiction, he, as emperor, had no power to make it.

Further, if one emperor had power to tear never so little a piece from the jurisdiction of the empire, so on the same showing had another also. And since the temporal jurisdiction is finite, and any finite thing can be used up by finite subtractions, it would follow that the prime jurisdiction might be reduced to nothing, which is contrary to reason.

And again, . . . in order for a grant to be legitimate there must be the due disposition not only of him who grants but of him to whom the grant is made. For it seems that the acts of the agents inhere in a suitably disposed patient. But the church was entirely undisposed for receiving temporal things, in virtue of express prohibitive command, as we learn from Matthew, thus: "Possess not gold nor silver, nor money in your girdles, nor purse for your journey," and the rest. For, although we find in Luke a relaxation of the precept with respect to certain things, yet nowhere have I been able to find that permission was given to the church, after that prohibition, to possess gold and silver. Wherefore if the church had no power to receive, then even if Constantine, as far as he was concerned, had power to give, still the action was impossible because the patient had not the due disposition. . . .

(11) They further say that pope Hadrian summoned Charles the Great to his aid and the church's, because of the wrongs wrought by the Lombards in the time of Desiderius, their king; and that Charles received from him the dignity of the empire, notwithstanding that Michael was the ruling emperor at Constantinople.[4] Wherefore they say that all who have been emperors of the Romans after him are themselves advocates of the church, and by the church must be called to office. And from this, too, that dependence which they wish to prove would follow.

---

[4]Dante is referring to events which occurred at the end of the eighth century. Constantinople had been a capital for Roman emperors since the time of Constantine, who had named the city after himself and made it his imperial city. Late in the fourth century the Roman Empire had been divided into two portions, the western emperor ruling from Rome and the eastern emperor from Constantinople. Dante's point is that at the time that Charlemagne was crowned Holy Roman Emperor in 800, there was actually already a Roman emperor, Michael, ruling at Constantinople.

And to invalidate this, I say that their contention amounts to nothing; for the usurpation of a right does not create a right. Else in the same way it might be shown that the authority of the church depends upon the emperor, since the emperor Otho restored pope Leo, and deposed Benedict and carried him off into exile in Saxony.[5]

(12) But their argument from reason is this. . . . [A]ll men are of one kind; therefore they must be reduced to the unit, as measure of them all. And, since the supreme pontiff and the emperor are men, if that conclusion is true they must be reduced to the unit man; and since the pope must not be reduced to any other, it remains that the emperor, together with all others, must be reduced to him, as the measure and norm. . . .

. . . [T]hey fall into a fallacy *secundum accidens.*[6]

To demonstrate which, be it known that it is one thing to be a man and another thing to be pope. And in like manner it is one thing to be a man and another to be emperor; just as it is one thing to be a man and another to be a father and master; for a man is such in virtue of a substantial form from which he acquires his species and genus, and by which he is brought under the predicament of substance. But a father is such in virtue of an accidental form, or relation, from which indeed he acquires a species and genus, in a sense, but is brought under the class *ad aliquid,* or relativity. Otherwise, since no accidental form exists in itself, apart from the foundation of the substance that underlies it, everything would be reduced to the predicament of substance; and this is false. . . .

Wherefore I maintain that the standard to which they must be reduced as men is one, and that to which they must be reduced as pope and emperor another. For as men they have to be referred to the best man, whoever that may be; who is the standard and idea of all others, so to speak; that is, to him who is most supremely one in his own kind, as may be gathered from the last *Ad Nicomachum.* . . .

(13) Having set forth and refuted the errors on which they chiefly rely who say that the authority of the Roman prince depends on the Roman pontiff, we must return to the demonstration of the truth as to this third matter which was laid down for discussion from the beginning. And this truth will be sufficiently unfolded if I show, under the principle of inquiry which we have laid down, that the said authority depends immediately upon the summit of all being, which is God. And this will be shown if we either disprove the church's authority over it (since no other is even alleged), or prove by direct demonstration that it depends immediately on God.

Now that the authority of the church is not the cause of the imperial authority is thus proved. If, while one thing does not exist or is not exercising its virtue, another thing has its full virtue, the first thing is

---

[5]Dante is referring to events which occurred in the third quarter of the tenth century, when the emperors still had a good deal of authority in the selection of popes. Emperor Otto I had made Leo VIII pope in 963; but a synod of Churchmen had deposed him the next year in favor of Pope John XII. After the death of John XII that same year, a synod had elected Benedict V as pope, but Otto managed to have Benedict deposed and Leo restored.

[6]To argue on the basis of the accidental, i.e., nonessential, attributes of something.

not the cause of that virtue. But when the church did not exist, or was not exercising its virtue, the empire had its full virtue. . . .

The major proposition of this demonstration is explained by the terms; the second, Christ and the church confirm, Christ by his birth and death as set forth above, the church when Paul in the Acts of the Apostles says to Festus, "I stand at the judgment seat of Caesar where I must be judged"; and also when the angel of God says to Paul a little after, "Fear not, Paul. It behoves thee to stand before Caesar." And below Paul says again to the Jews in Italy, "Now when the Jews opposed I was compelled to appeal to Caesar, not as having aught of which to accuse my nation, but that I might snatch my soul from death.". . .

And if Constantine had not possessed authority over the patronage of the church, what he deputed to her from the empire he could not have deputed of right, and thus the church would be wrongfully enjoying that grant, since God will have offerings without spot, according to that of Leviticus, "every offering which ye shall bring to the Lord shall be without leaven.". . .

(15) Again, that which is against the nature of anything is not in the number of its virtues, since the virtues of each thing follow its nature, for the attainment of its end. But virtue to authorise rule over our mortality is contrary to the nature of the church. Therefore it is not of the number of her virtues.

To prove the minor be it known that the nature of the church is the form of the church. For though nature is predicated of material and of form, yet it is more properly predicated of form as is shown in the *De Naturali Auditu.* But the form of the church is no other than the life of Christ, embraced both in his words and in his deeds. For his life was the idea and exemplar of the church militant, especially of pastors, and most of all of the supreme pastor, whose it is to feed the lambs and sheep. Whence he himself in John, when bequeathing the form of his life, says, "I have given you an example that as I have done to you should ye also do." And specifically to Peter when he had committed to him the office of pastor, as we learn from the same source, he said, "Peter, follow thou me." But Christ in the presence of Pilate renounced any such regimen as that in question. "My kingdom," said he, "is not of this world. If my kingdom were of this world, my servants would fight that I should not be given over to the Jews. But now my kingdom is not hence."

. . . Whence we gather that the power of authorising this kingdom is counter to the nature of the church. . . .

(16) . . . [I]t has been shown . . . that the authority of the empire is not caused by the authority of the supreme pontiff, yet it has not been altogether proved that it depends immediately on God, save by consequential inference; for the consequential inference is that if it does not depend on the vicar of God it depends on God. And, therefore, for the perfect establishment of the proposition, we must prove by direct demonstration that the emperor or monarch of the world is in immediate relation to the Prince of the universe, who is God.

Now to understand this be it known that man alone of beings holds a mid-place between corruptible and incorruptible; wherefore he is rightly likened by the philosophers to the horizon which is between two hemispheres. For man, if considered after either essential part, to wit soul and body, is corruptible if considered only after the one, to wit the body, but if after the other, to wit the soul, he is incorruptible. Wherefore the Philosopher says well of the soul (in that it is incorruptible), in the second *De Anima,* "And it alone is capable of being separated from the corruptible as perpetual."

If man, then, is a kind of mean between corruptible and incorruptible things, since every mean savours of the nature of the extremes, it is necessary that man should savour of either nature. And since every nature is ordained to a certain end it follows that there must be a twofold end of man, so that like as he alone amongst all beings partakes of corruptibility and incorruptibility, so he alone amongst all beings should be ordained for two final goals, of which the one should be his goal as a corruptible being, and the other as an incorruptible.

That unutterable providence, then, has set two ends before man to be contemplated by him: the blessedness, to wit, of this life, which consists in the exercise of his proper power and is figured by the terrestrial paradise, and the blessedness of eternal life, which consists in the fruition of the divine aspect, to which his proper power may not ascend unless assisted by the divine light. And this blessedness is given to be understood by the celestial paradise.

Now to these two as to diverse ends it behoves him to come by diverse means. For to the first we attain by the teachings of philosophy, following them by acting in accordance with the moral and intellectual virtues. To the second by spiritual teachings, which transcend human reason, as we follow them by acting according to the theological virtues: faith, hope, to wit, and charity. Now albeit these ends and means are made plain to us, the one by human reason (which the philosophers have wholly brought to our knowledge), the other by the Holy Spirit (which hath revealed the truth that is beyond our nature, but yet needful to us, by means of the prophets and sacred writers and by Jesus Christ the Son of God co-eternal with the said Spirit, and by his disciples), yet would human greed cast them behind were not men, like horses going astray in their brutishness, held in the way by bit and rein.

Wherefore man had need of a twofold directive power according to his twofold end, to wit, the supreme pontiff, to lead the human race, in accordance with things revealed, to eternal life; and the emperor, to direct the human race to temporal felicity in accordance with the teachings of philosophy. And since none, or few (and they with extremest difficulty) could reach this port, were not the waves of seductive greed assuaged and the human race left free to rest in the tranquillity of peace, this is that mark on which he who has charge of the world and is called the Roman prince should chiefly fix his mind, to wit, that on this threshing floor of mortality life should be lived in freedom and in peace. And since the disposition of this world follows the disposition that inheres in the circulation of the heavens, in order to accomplish this end, namely, that the charters which conduce to liberty and peace should be applied by the ruler in question with due reference to time and place, it is needful that they should be dispensed by him who looks upon the whole disposition of the heavens presently. And that is he only who so preordained that disposition that by it he in his providence might weave all things together, each in its due order.

But if this be so, God alone chooses, he alone confirms, since he hath no superior. Whence we may further gather that neither they who now are, nor such others of any kind as have ever been called the electors,[7] should so be called; but rather should they be reckoned the heralds of divine providence. Whence it comes to pass that they to whom is granted the honour of making the proclamation are subject from time to time to dissent; because either all or some of them are clouded by the mists of greed, and discern not the face of the divine dispensation.

Thus, then, it is plain that the authority of the temporal monarch descends upon him without any mean from the Fountain of universal authority. Which Fountain, one in the citadel of Its simplicity, flows into manifold channels out of the abundance of Its excellence.

And now already methinks I have sufficiently reached the mark I set before myself. For the truth of that question has been searched out in which was asked whether the office of monarch were necessary to the well-being of the world, and of that in which was asked whether the Roman people acquired empire for itself by right, and also of that last question in which was asked whether the monarch's authority depended from God, or immediately from some other. The truth concerning which last question is not to be received in such narrow sense as that the Roman prince is subordinate in naught to the Roman pontiff; inasmuch as mortal felicity is in a certain sense ordained with reference to immortal felicity. Let Caesar, therefore, observe that reverence to Peter which a first-born son should observe to a father, so that illuminated by the light of paternal grace he may with greater power irradiate the world, over which he is set by him alone who is ruler of all things spiritual and temporal.

Comments / on *World Government*

Some ten years after Dante's death Pope John XXII ordered that the *Monarchia* be burned.   *E. H. WILKINS (1954)*

How is one to persuade the theologians that, for the very reason that makes them abandon philosophy to Aristotle, they should abandon the Empire to the Emperor? Such is the problem whose solution Dante's *Monarchy* offered to the world. . . . Dante's doctrine touching the rela-

---

[7]As early as the eleventh century the election of the Holy Roman Emperor had been claimed as a right by certain powerful German princes. They and their descendants were given the hereditary title of "Electors."

tions between the Priesthood and the Empire has been interpreted in almost every conceivable way. Some conceive it as teaching the total isolation of the two powers: each is competent in its own sphere and owes absolutely nothing to the other. Others maintain that, whatever he may seem to say, Dante recognizes the subordination of the Emperor to the Pope. Others maintain, on the contrary, that Dante subordinates the Pope to the Emperor. Finally, some, disturbed at all these contradictions, come to the conclusion that the historians would agree more wholeheartedly if *Dante* had not contradicted himself.   *ETIENNE GILSON (1939)*

Pope Gregory VIII coined a simile of "two lights in the firmament of the Church militant," the Pope as the sun and the Emperor as the moon. The simile was a two-edged sword that pricked the Emperors when they came in conflict with the Pope. "And as moonlight is to the sunlight," says Bryce, "so was the Empire to the Papacy. The rays of the one were borrowed, feeble, and often interrupted; the other shone with an unquenchable brilliance all her own." Dante felt the force of this simile in defending the Empire, but could only counter with his unpersuasive comparison of Pope and Emperor with two suns. . . .   *C. W. JONES (1950)*

The political theory of Dante is a sublime and largely original one. It suffers only from its extreme ideality, which makes it inapplicable. . . . Nor does it seem that at bottom Dante's political philosophy, any more than that of the Hebrew prophets, missed the great causes and the great aims of human progress. Behind mythical and narrow conceptions of history, he had a true sense for the moral principles that really condition our well-being. A better science need subtract nothing from the insight he had into the difference between political good and evil. What in his day seemed a dream—that mankind should be one great commonwealth —is now obvious to the idealist, the socialist, the merchant.
        GEORGE SANTAYANA (1910)

We thus see that Dante in supporting his conviction of the necessity of a world-rule falls back upon the fiction of divine inspiration, so often resorted to in elections whether by reliance upon chance, as in antiquity, or on spiritual visitation, as among Christians.
        DINO BIGONGIARI (1949)

No wonder that the ideal empire which Dante, by speculation, by faith, and by hope, shaped . . . in the *De Monarchia,* resembles remarkably the papacy of his day. The emperor derives his rights from the same original source as the pope, and in like manner. They both wield universal power. Though separate, they are parallel not only in their functions, but in their substances as well. . . . The very last words of the *De Monarchia* show most clearly that a distinct worldly political principle cannot be derived from the premises of the transcendental, theological, and ecclesiastical view of life taken by the Middle Ages. Dante flatters himself, to be sure, that he has completely proved the utter independence of the *imperium* from the *sacerdotium;* but he ends his investigation with a paragraph which once more leaves everything that seemed juridically determined to the good pleasure of the parties concerned; as though conscience was appealed to against the verdict of the law. . . . Surprise has been expressed that Dante did not perceive the vicious circle of this argument. But as a medieval thinker, he could not recognize it as such. For neither the secular nor the ecclesiastical power was regarded in the Middle Ages as absolute or sovereign, in the modern sense of the word. Above all authorities and rulers of mankind stood the divine, or if you will the natural, law; they were all limited, relative, and subject to the living God. . . .   *KARL VOSSLER (1925)*

Francesco Petrarch
1304–1374

In just about the same way that scholasticism typifies the modes of thought characteristic of the later Middle Ages, humanism typifies the characteristic intellectual attitudes of the Renaissance. Today, broadly speaking, humanism implies a wide range of activities that enrich the human spirit by helping men develop a full awareness both of the distinctively human ideals and values that have been created by and have shaped human experience and of the distinctively human intellectual capabilities and resources men possess as human beings. Originally, though, the term had a much more narrow meaning. It was first used early in the nineteenth century to express an emphasis in education on the Greek and Latin classics as opposed to more practical and scientific subjects. In that sense it could be, and soon was, applied by historians investigating the Renaissance to describe the activities of the *humanists,* a term used as early as the fifteenth century to designate men engaged in *studia humanitatis,* the study of the humanities. This term, too, had a much more narrow meaning in the fifteenth century, referring to a program of education and scholarship in rhetoric, grammar, history, poetry, and moral philosophy based on the reading and interpretation of the classical Latin, and to some extent Greek, authors. A program of this sort was, in the long run, bound to produce a different kind of outlook and set of values than resulted from the scholastic disciplines of dialectic, natural philosophy, metaphysics, and theology. It led almost inevitably to increased respect for human worth and dignity and increased emphasis on the purely secular value of man's achievements in this world. These attitudes, combined with a scholarly interest in classical antiquity, distinguish Renaissance humanism from medieval scholasticism and thus mark a new stage in the development of Western civilization.

But civilization develops as a continuum, and the lines dividing new stages from old are always blurred. Francesco Petrarch, generally regarded as the founder of humanism, was nevertheless very much a medieval man. Although born into a Florentine family, he was raised near the French city of Avignon, where the papacy was located during much of the fourteenth century and where his father, a notary, derived much of his business from ecclesiastical affairs. Petrarch first looked to a career as a lawyer but never finished his course of typically scholastic legal education, preferring to devote himself to humanistic studies. In his mid-twenties he entered the service of an ecclesiastical patron, occupying an ill-defined position in the household of Cardinal Giovanni Colonna as a sort of intellectual handyman—secretary, tutor, legal advisor, poet, scholar, table companion, or whatever the occasion demanded. He lived on patronage of this kind or on outright subsidies, ecclesiastical and secular, throughout his career. To the extent that his life was bound up with the Church and its theological convictions, Petrarch is characteristically medieval. To the extent that his life demonstrated, as the lives of earlier humanists did not, the value of secular learning and experience in cultivating the human personality for the fuller enjoyment of earthly existence, he can well be viewed as the founder of humanism.

Petrarch's literary and scholarly works are of considerable volume, and a large part of them are concerned, in one way or another, with himself. Probably his greatest achievement, the one from which all his others derive, was the deliberate construction of his own personality. He was acutely and persistently conscious of his hopes, fears, triumphs, failures, likes, and dislikes; and he made everybody else conscious of them too, establishing his own conception of himself as a model for the European intellectual community of what a humanist should be. The chief medium through which he accomplished this was his letters, which fill some thirteen hundred large pages in the modern Latin edition. Written to people all over Europe, and later revised and edited by him for formal publication, they were mainly literary essays describing his own humanistic preoccupations. They were received in the same spirit in which they were written, and interested audiences would often collect to hear them read aloud. Petrarch liked the epistolary style so much that when in his late forties he composed an autobiographical sketch, he put it into the form of a "Letter to Posterity." He also wrote a whole series of essays on classical authors in the guise of letters to them.

His most ambitious work, *Africa,* was a *magnum opus* modeled on classical epic, which he never finished. However, he publicized it so widely while it was in progress that he managed to have himself crowned poet laureate, in a magnificent public ceremony at Rome in 1341, in official recognition of him as the outstanding poet and scholar of his time. Among his other works are a number of treatises on various humanistic subjects, and a substantial body of lyric poetry that ranks him with the world's great poets and is the chief source of his fame today. His lyrics were written to celebrate his love for a certain Laura—with whom his relationship was much like that of Dante with Beatrice—and were influenced to some extent by the "sweet new style." In their treatment of idealized love and of the lover's conflicting spiritual and sensual emotions, these poems became the model for serious love poetry throughout Europe for several centuries. In *Secretum meum (My Secret),* written when he was nearly forty years old, Petrarch attempted to appraise the meaning of love within the context of all his experience—much like St. Augustine, whom he acknowledges as a guide, and like Dante, whom he does not. No other work of Petrarch's so clearly illustrates the tension created within him by the clash between the conventional values of his society and the values he set for himself—a tension that we, some six centuries later, can see as a clash between the values of thē Middle Ages and of the Renaissance.

Letter to Posterity

Greeting.—It is possible that some word of me may have come to you, though even this is doubtful, since an insignificant and obscure name will scarcely penetrate far in either time or space. If, however, you should have heard of me, you may desire to know what manner of man I was, or what was the outcome of my labours, especially those of which some description or, at any rate, the bare titles may have reached you. . . .

I have taken pride in others, never in myself, and however insignificant I may have been, I have always been still less important in my own judgment. My anger has very often injured myself, but never others. I have always been most desirous of honourable friendships, and have faithfully cherished them. I make this boast without fear, since I am confident that I speak truly. While I am very prone to take offence, I am equally quick to forget injuries, and have a memory tenacious of benefits. In my familiar associations with kings and princes, and in my friendship with noble personages, my good fortune has been such as to excite envy. But it is the cruel fate of those who are growing old that they can commonly only weep for friends who have passed away. The greatest kings of this age have loved and courted me. They may know why; I certainly do not. With some of them I was on such terms that they seemed in a certain sense my guests rather than I theirs; their lofty position in no way embarrassing me, but, on the contrary, bringing with it many advantages. I fled, however, from many of those to whom I was greatly attached; and such was my innate longing for liberty, that I studiously avoided those whose very name seemed incompatible with the freedom that I loved.

I possessed a well-balanced rather than a keen intellect, one prone to all kinds of good and wholesome study, but especially inclined to moral philosophy and the art of poetry. The latter, indeed, I neglected as time went on, and took delight in sacred literature. Finding in that a hidden sweetness which I had once esteemed but lightly, I came to regard the works of the poets as only amenities. Among the many subjects which interested me, I dwelt especially upon antiquity, for our own age has always repelled me, so that, had it not been for the love of those dear to me, I should have preferred to have been born in any other period than our own. In order to forget my own time, I have constantly striven to place myself in spirit in other ages, and consequently I delighted in history; not that the conflicting statements did not offend me, but when in doubt I accepted what appeared to me most probable, or yielded to the authority of the writer. . . .

On my return,[1] since I experienced a deep-seated and innate repugnance to town life, especially in that disgusting city of Avignon which I heartily abhorred, I sought some means of escape. I fortunately discovered, about fifteen miles from Avignon, a delightful valley, narrow and secluded, called Vaucluse, where the Sorgue, the prince of streams, takes its rise. Captivated by the charms of the place, I transferred thither myself and my books. Were I to describe what I did there during many years, it would prove a long story. Indeed, almost every bit of writing which I have put forth was either accomplished or begun, or at least conceived, there, and my undertakings have been so numerous that they still continue to vex and weary me. My mind, like my body, is characterised by a certain versatility and readiness, rather than by strength, so that many tasks that were easy of conception have been given up by reason of the difficulty of their execution. The character of my surroundings suggested the composition of a sylvan or bucolic song. I also dedicated a work in two books upon *The Life of Solitude,* to Philip, now exalted to the Cardinal-bishopric of Sabina. Although always a great man, he was, at the time of which I speak, only the humble Bishop of Cavaillon. He is the only one of my old friends who is still left to me, and he has always loved and treated me not as a bishop (as Ambrose did Augustine), but as a brother.

While I was wandering in those mountains upon a Friday in Holy Week, the strong desire seized me to write an epic in an heroic strain, taking as my theme Scipio Africanus the Great,[2] who had, strange to say, been dear to me from my childhood. But although I began the execution of this project with enthusiasm, I straightway abandoned it, owing to a variety of distractions. The poem was, however, christened *Africa,* from the name of its hero, and, whether from his fortunes or mine, it did not fail to arouse the interest of many before they had seen it.

While leading a leisurely existence in this region, I received, remarkable as it may seem, upon one and the same day,[3] letters both from the Senate at Rome and the Chancellor of the University of Paris, pressing me to appear in Rome and Paris, respectively, to receive the poet's crown of laurel. In my youthful elation I convinced myself that I was quite worthy of this honour; the recognition came from eminent judges, and I accepted their verdict rather than that of my own better judgment. I hesitated for a time which I should give ear to, and sent a letter to Cardinal Giovanni Colonna,[4] . . . asking his opinion. He was

---

[1] From Rome to Avignon in 1337.
[2] Roman general and statesman (237?–183 B.C.), renowned for conquering the forces of Carthage led by Rome's great enemy Hannibal.
[3] September 1, 1340.
[4] Petrarch's first ecclesiastical patron. He was a scion of a family that was an important, often dominant, force in Roman politics from the twelfth through sixteenth centuries.

so near that, although I wrote late in the day, I received his reply before the third hour on the morrow. I followed his advice, and recognised the claims of Rome as superior to all others. My acceptance of his counsel is shown by my twofold letter to him on that occasion, which I shall keep. I set off accordingly; but although, after the fashion of youth, I was a most indulgent judge of my own work, I still blushed to accept in my own case the verdict even of such men as those who summoned me, despite the fact that they would certainly not have honoured me in this way, had they not believed me worthy.

So I decided, first to visit Naples, and that celebrated king and philosopher, Robert, who was not more distinguished as a ruler than as a man of culture. He was, indeed, the only monarch of our age who was the friend at once of learning and of virtue, and I trusted that he might correct such things as he found to criticise in my work. The way in which he received and welcomed me is a source of astonishment to me now, and, I doubt not, to the reader also, if he happens to know anything of the matter. Having learned the reason of my coming, the King seemed mightily pleased. He was gratified, doubtless, by my youthful faith in him, and felt, perhaps, that he shared in a way the glory of my coronation, since I had chosen him from all others as the only suitable critic. After talking over a great many things, I showed him my *Africa,* which so delighted him that he asked that it might be dedicated to him in consideration of a handsome reward. This was a request that I could not well refuse, nor, indeed, would I have wished to refuse it, had it been in my power. He then fixed a day upon which we could consider the object of my visit. This occupied us from noon until evening, and the time proving too short, on account of the many matters which arose for discussion, we passed the two following days in the same manner. Having thus tested my poor attainments for three days, the King at last pronounced me worthy of the laurel. He offered to bestow that honour upon me at Naples, and urged me to consent to receive it there, but my veneration for Rome prevailed over the insistence of even so great a monarch as Robert. At length, seeing that I was inflexible in my purpose, he sent me on my way accompanied by royal messengers and letters to the Roman Senate, in which he gave enthusiastic expression to his flattering opinion of me. This royal estimate was, indeed, quite in accord with that of many others, and especially with my own, but to-day I cannot approve either his or my own verdict. In his case, affection and the natural partiality to youth were stronger than his devotion to truth.

On arriving at Rome, I continued, in spite of my unworthiness, to rely upon the judgment of so eminent a critic, and, to the great delight of the Romans who were present, I who had been hitherto a simple student received the laurel crown.[5] This occasion is described elsewhere in my letters, both in prose and verse. The laurel, however, in no way increased my wisdom, although it did arouse some jealousy—but this is too long a story to be told here. . . .

---

[5]On Easter Sunday, April 8, 1341.

Letter to Homer

I have long desired to address thee in writing, and would have done so without hesitation if I had had a ready command of thy tongue. But alas! Fortune was unkind to me in my study of Greek. Thou, on the other hand, seemest to have forgotten the Latin which it was formerly customary for our authors to bring to thy assistance, but which their descendants have failed to place at thy disposal.[1] And so, excluded from the one and the other means of communication, I kept my peace.

One man has once again restored thee to our age as a Latin.[2] Thy Penelope did not longer nor more anxiously await her Ulysses than I thee. My hopes, indeed, had been deserting me one by one. Excepting the opening lines of several books of thy poem, wherein I beheld thee as one sees, from a distance, the doubtful and rapid look of a wished-for friend, or perhaps, catches a glimpse of his streaming hair—with this exception, then, no portion of thy works had come into my hands in Latin translation. Nothing, in fine, warranted the hope that I might some day behold thee nigh at hand. For that little book which commonly passes as thine, though it is clearly taken from thee and is inscribed with thy name, is nevertheless not thine.[3] Who the author of it may be is not certain. That other person (to whom I have already referred) will restore thee to us in thy entirety, if he lives. Indeed, he has already begun his task, in order that we may derive pleasure not merely from the excellent contents of thy divine poem, but also from the charms of conversing with thee. The Greek flavor has recently been enjoyed by me from a Latin flagon.

This experience brought forcibly home to me the fact that a vigorous and keen intellect can [do] all things. Cicero was, in many instances, merely an expounder of thy thoughts; Vergil was even more frequently a borrower; both, however, were the princes of the Latin speech. And though Annaeus Seneca assert that Cicero loses all his eloquence when dabbling in verse and that Vergil's felicity of expression deserts him when venturing into the realms of prose, still I maintain that it is but right that each of them be compared with himself and not with the other. From such comparison it would clearly result that each should be considered as having fallen below his own highest level. Judged by themselves, I insist that I have read verses of Cicero that are not mere doggerel, and prose letters of Vergil that are not disagreeable.

I am now experiencing the same emotions in thy case, for thy great

---

Reprinted from *Petrarch's Letters to Classical Authors* edited by M. E. Cosenza by permission of The University of Chicago Press. Copyright 1910 by The University of Chicago.

[1]Petrarch is referring to some Latin translations of Homer that had circulated in Europe during the earlier Middle Ages. He knew of them by reputation but had never been able to find one himself.

[2]A reference to Leonzio Pilato, whom Petrarch had sponsored to render a complete translation of Homer into Latin. It turned out that Leonzio was neither very knowledgeable in ancient Greek nor skilled in contemporary literary Latin; however, he did complete the translation three years later, in 1363.

[3]Petrarch refers here to a brief, crude, poetic Latin abridgment of Homer's works which had been made during Roman times and was in the fourteenth century still the main version of Homer's works known in western Europe.

work, too, is a poetical masterpiece. In obedience to the maxim laid down by St. Jerome (a Latin author of exceptional skill in languages), I wrote once upon a time that if thou wert to be translated literally, not merely into Latin prose, but even into Greek prose, from being most eloquent of poets thou wouldst be made of none effect. Now, on the contrary, thou dost still retain thy hidden power to please, though turned into prose, and what is more, into Latin prose. This fact compels admiration. Whatever, therefore, may be said of me, let no one marvel that I have addressed Vergil in verse, but thee in the more tractable and yielding prose. Him I addressed of my own free will; in thy case, I am answering a letter received.[4] Furthermore, with Vergil I employed the idiom which we possessed in common; with thee I have adopted, not thy ancient language, but a certain new speech in which the letter I received was couched, a speech which I use daily, but which is not, I suppose, the one to which thou art accustomed.

But after all, why should I dignify my talk with both of you by giving it the name conversation? Our very best must appear to you mere prattle and chattering. Ye are unapproachable; ye are more than mortal, and your heads pierce the clouds. Yet it is with me as with a babe: I love to babble with those who feed me, even though they are skilled masters of speech. But enough on the subject of style. I now come to the contents of thy letter. . . .

. . . Thou grievest that thou hast been mangled and dismembered by thy imitators. It had needs be so, Homer. No man's intellect was sufficiently vigorous to grasp thee whole. Thou dost wax indignant, moreover, that they should shower abuse upon thee though clothed in thy spoils. Alas! it is only what thou must expect; no one can be particularly ungrateful except him who has previously been the recipient of a great boon. Thy next charge is that, whereas thy name was held in great honor by the early jurists and physicians, to their successors it has become a subject of mockery and contempt. Thou dost not observe how different the later generations are from the preceding. If they were of a like stamp, they would love and cherish the same things. Let thy indignation cease, and thy sorrow as well. On the contrary, take comfort in hoping for the best. To be in disfavor with the wicked and the ignorant is the first sign of virtue and intelligence. The radiance of thy genius is so brilliant that our weak sight cannot endure it. It is with thee as with the sun, for which it is not reckoned a disgrace but praise most high, that it conquers the vision of the weak and puts to flight the birds of night. Among the ancients, and indeed also among men of today —if any there are in whom there still lives even a small spark of our early nature—thou must be esteemed not merely a holy philosopher (as thou thyself sayest) but greater and superior to any philosopher, as I have said above. Thou dost cover a most beautiful philosophy with a very charming and transparent veil. . . .

I come now to myself, so that, being the least in intellect and in years, I may also form the last topic of my letter. In thy adversity thou dost beg me to come to thy aid. Oh, cruel and inexorable fate! In succoring

---

[4]Apparently Petrarch had received a letter purporting to be from the spirit of Homer, presumably sent by one of his literary friends carrying on the game Petrarch had started with his letters to dead authors.

so great a man as thou I could forever boast of a better claim to glory than any I have yet attained or hope to attain. I call Christ to witness —a God to thee unknown—that there is absolutely nothing which I can offer for thy relief except affectionate, tender pity and loyal advice. What assistance, indeed, can be received from one who can do nothing for himself? Hast thou not heard that even thy followers were reviled out of hatred for thy name, and that they were judged insane by an assembly of insane? If this could happen in thine own age and in Athens, most cultured of cities, what dost thou suppose will be the case today with other poets in cities entirely devoted to the pursuit of pleasure? I am one of those at whom the vulgar and the ignorant aim their shafts. I am astonished and wonder why it is so. If only I had given cause for some justifiable hatred! But it matters not how just the cause may or may not have been; the reality of their hatred is undeniable. And is it on my bosom, then, that thou wouldst seek refuge? Oh, insensate turn of fortune's wheel! No palace could be sufficiently spacious and resplendent for thee, Homer, if great intellects were to strive for such material honors as fortune can bestow. But not so: genius spurns the turrets and castles of the ignorant, and delights in the lonely and lowly hut. For my part, although I do not consider myself worthy of so great a guest, I have already harbored thee at my home both in Greek[5] and (as far as it was possible) in Latin. I trust to have thee entire before long, provided thy Thessalian will complete what he has begun.[6] Know, however, that thou art to be received in an even more sacred inclosure: I have made preparations to welcome thee with the greatest eagerness and devotion to the innermost recesses of my heart. In a word, my love for thee is greater and warmer than the rays of the sun, and my esteem such that no one could cherish a greater. . . .

Written in the world above, in that city lying between the famous rivers Po, Ticino, Adda, and others, whence some say Milan derives its name, on the ninth of October in the thirteen hundred and sixtieth year of this last era.

The Ascent of Mount Ventoux [1]

To-day I made the ascent of the highest mountain in this region, which is not improperly called Ventosum.[2] My only motive was the wish

---

[5]Petrarch had made some attempt to learn Greek soon after being crowned poet laureate. But he never made any great progress in it. In one of his letters he describes his joy at having been able to obtain a Greek text of Homer and his sorrow at not being able to understand a word of it.

[6]Petrarch is referring to the translation undertaken by Leonzio shortly before the letter to Homer was written. From *Petrarch*, 2nd ed., by J. H. Robinson and H. W. Rolfe, copyright, 1914, by Putnam's & Coward-McCann. Reprinted by permission of Putnam's & Coward-McCann.

[1]Petrarch wrote this letter from the neighborhood of Avignon in 1336, when he was about thirty-two years old, to a close friend who was an Augustinian monk and a professor of theology and philosophy at the University of Paris.

[2]I.e., windy.

to see what so great an elevation had to offer. I have had the expedition in mind for many years; for, as you know, I have lived in this region from infancy, having been cast here by that fate which determines the affairs of men. Consequently the mountain, which is visible from a great distance, was ever before my eyes, and I conceived the plan of some time doing what I have at last accomplished to-day. The idea took hold upon me with especial force when, in re-reading Livy's[3] *History of Rome,* yesterday, I happened upon the place where Philip of Macedon,[4] the same who waged war against the Romans, ascended Mount Hæmus in Thessaly, from whose summit he was able, it is said, to see two seas, the Adriatic and the Euxine. Whether this be true or false I have not been able to determine, for the mountain is too far away, and writers disagree. Pomponius Mela,[5] the cosmographer—not to mention others who have spoken of this occurrence—admits its truth without hesitation; Titus Livius, on the other hand, considers it false. I, assuredly, should not have left the question long in doubt, had that mountain been as easy to explore as this one. Let us leave this matter [to] one side, however, and return to my mountain here,—it seems to me that a young man in private life may well be excused for attempting what an aged king could undertake without arousing criticism.

When I came to look about for a companion I found, strangely enough, that hardly one among my friends seemed suitable, so rarely do we meet with just the right combination of personal tastes and characteristics, even among those who are dearest to us. This one was too apathetic, that one over-anxious; this one too slow, that one too hasty; one was too sad, another over-cheerful; one more simple, another more sagacious, than I desired. I feared this one's taciturnity and that one's loquacity. The heavy deliberation of some repelled me as much as the lean incapacity of others. I rejected those who were likely to irritate me by a cold want of interest, as well as those who might weary me by their excessive enthusiasm. Such defects, however grave, could be borne with at home, for charity suffereth all things, and friendship accepts any burden; but it is quite otherwise on a journey, where every weakness becomes much more serious. So, as I was bent upon pleasure and anxious that my enjoyment should be unalloyed, I looked about me with unusual care, balanced against one another the various characteristics of my friends, and without committing any breach of friendship I silently condemned every trait which might prove disagreeable on the way. And—would you believe it?—I finally turned homeward for aid, and proposed the ascent to my only brother, who is younger than I, and with whom you are well acquainted. He was delighted and gratified beyond measure by the thought of holding the place of a friend as well as of a brother.

At the time fixed we left the house, and by evening reached Malaucène, which lies at the foot of the mountain, to the north. Having rested there a day, we finally made the ascent this morning, with no

---

[3]Titus Livius, Roman historian (59 B.C.—17 A.D.).
[4]Father of Alexander the Great and conqueror of all Greece; reigned 359—336 B.C.
[5]Roman geographer of the first century A.D.

companions except two servants; and a most difficult task it was. The mountain is a very steep and almost inaccessible mass of stony soil. But, as the poet[6] has well said, "Remorseless toil conquers all." It was a long day, the air fine. We enjoyed the advantages of vigour of mind and strength and agility of body, and everything else essential to those engaged in such an undertaking, and so had no other difficulties to face than those of the region itself. We found an old shepherd in one of the mountain dales, who tried, at great length, to dissuade us from the ascent, saying that some fifty years before he had, in the same ardour of youth, reached the summit, but had gotten for his pains nothing except fatigue and regret, and clothes and body torn by the rocks and briars. No one, so far as he or his companions knew, had ever tried the ascent before or after him. But his counsels increased rather than diminished our desire to proceed, since youth is suspicious of warnings. So the old man, finding that his efforts were in vain, went a little way with us, and pointed out a rough path among the rocks, uttering many admonitions, which he continued to send after us even after we had left him behind. Surrendering to him all such garments or other possessions as might prove burdensome to us, we made ready for the ascent, and started off at a good pace. But, as usually happens, fatigue quickly followed upon our excessive exertion, and we soon came to a halt at the top of a certain cliff. Upon starting on again we went more slowly, and I especially advanced along the rocky way with a more deliberate step. While my brother chose a direct path straight up the ridge, I weakly took an easier one which really descended. When I was called back, and the right road was shown me, I replied that I hoped to find a better way round on the other side, and that I did not mind going farther if the path were only less steep. This was just an excuse for my laziness; and when the others had already reached a considerable height I was still wandering in the valleys. I had failed to find an easier path, and had only increased the distance and difficulty of the ascent. At last I became disgusted with the intricate way I had chosen, and resolved to ascend without more ado. When I reached my brother, who, while waiting for me, had had ample opportunity for rest, I was tired and irritated. We walked along together for a time, but hardly had we passed the first spur when I forgot about the circuitous route which I had just tried, and took a lower one again. Once more I followed an easy, roundabout path through winding valleys, only to find myself soon in my old difficulty. I was simply trying to avoid the exertion of the ascent; but no human ingenuity can alter the nature of things, or cause anything to reach a height by going down. Suffice it to say that, much to my vexation and my brother's amusement, I made this same mistake three times or more during a few hours.

After being frequently misled in this way, I finally sat down in a valley and transferred my winged thoughts from things corporeal to the immaterial, addressing myself as follows:—"What thou hast repeatedly

---

[6]Virgil, who was *the* poet in much the same way that Aristotle was *the* Philosopher and St. Paul was *the* Apostle.

experienced to-day in the ascent of this mountain, happens to thee, as to many, in the journey toward the blessed life. But this is not so readily perceived by men, since the motions of the body are obvious and external while those of the soul are invisible and hidden. Yes, the life which we call blessed is to be sought for on a high eminence, and strait is the way that leads to it. Many, also, are the hills that lie between, and we must ascend, by a glorious stairway, from strength to strength. At the top is at once the end of our struggles and the goal for which we are bound. All wish to reach this goal, but, as Ovid[7] says, 'To wish is little; we must long with the utmost eagerness to gain our end.' Thou certainly dost ardently desire, as well as simply wish, unless thou deceivest thyself in this matter, as in so many others. What, then, doth hold thee back? Nothing, assuredly, except that thou wouldst take a path which seems, at first thought, more easy, leading through low and worldly pleasures. But nevertheless in the end, after long wanderings, thou must perforce either climb the steeper path, under the burden of tasks foolishly deferred, to its blessed culmination, or lie down in the valley of thy sins, and (I shudder to think of it!), if the shadow of death overtake thee, spend an eternal night amid constant torments." These thoughts stimulated both body and mind in a wonderful degree for facing the difficulties which yet remained. Oh, that I might traverse in spirit that other road for which I long day and night, even as to-day I overcame material obstacles by my bodily exertions! And I know not why it should not be far easier, since the swift immortal soul can reach its goal in the twinkling of an eye, without passing through space, while my progress to-day was necessarily slow, dependent as I was upon a failing body weighed down by heavy members.

One peak of the mountain, the highest of all, the country people call "Sonny," why, I do not know, unless by antiphrasis, as I have sometimes suspected in other instances; for the peak in question would seem to be the father of all the surrounding ones. On its top is a little level place, and here we could at last rest our tired bodies.

Now, my father, since you have followed the thoughts that spurred me on in my ascent, listen to the rest of the story, and devote one hour, I pray you, to reviewing the experiences of my entire day. At first, owing to the unaccustomed quality of the air and the effect of the great sweep of view spread out before me, I stood like one dazed. I beheld the clouds under our feet, and what I had read of Athos and Olympus seemed less incredible as I myself witnessed the same things from a mountain of less fame. I turned my eyes toward Italy, whither my heart most inclined. The Alps, rugged and snow-capped, seemed to rise close by, although they were really at a great distance; the very same Alps through which that fierce enemy of the Roman name once made his way, bursting the rocks, if we may believe the report, by the application of vinegar.[8] I sighed, I must confess, for the skies of Italy, which I beheld rather with my mind than with my eyes. An inexpressible longing

---

[7]Roman poet (43 B.C. – 17? A.D.).
[8]Hannibal of Carthage. Livy tells the story in his *History of Rome,* assigning the event to the year 218 B.C.

came over me to see once more my friend[9] and my country. At the same time I reproached myself for this double weakness, springing, as it did, from a soul not yet steeled to manly resistance. And yet there were excuses for both of these cravings, and a number of distinguished writers might be summoned to support me.

Then a new idea took possession of me, and I shifted my thoughts to a consideration of time rather than place. "To-day it is ten years since, having completed thy youthful studies, thou didst leave Bologna. Eternal God! In the name of immutable wisdom, think what alterations in thy character this intervening period has beheld! I pass over a thousand instances. I am not yet in a safe harbour where I can calmly recall past storms. The time may come when I can review in due order all the experiences of the past, saying with St. Augustine, 'I desire to recall my foul actions and the carnal corruption of my soul, not because I love them, but that I may the more love thee, O my God.' Much that is doubtful and evil still clings to me, but what I once loved, that I love no longer. And yet what am I saying? I still love it, but with shame, but with heaviness of heart. Now, at last, I have confessed the truth. So it is. I love, but love what I would not love, what I would that I might hate. Though loath to do so, though constrained, though sad and sorrowing, still I do love, and I feel in my miserable self the truth of the well known words, 'I will hate if I can; if not, I will love against my will.' Three years have not yet passed since that perverse and wicked passion which had a firm grasp upon me and held undisputed sway in my heart began to discover a rebellious opponent, who was unwilling longer to yield obedience. These two adversaries have joined in close combat for the supremacy, and for a long time now a harassing and doubtful war has been waged in the field of my thoughts."[10]

Thus I turned over the last ten years in my mind, and then, fixing my anxious gaze on the future, I asked myself, "If, perchance, thou shouldst prolong this uncertain life of thine for yet two lustres,[11] and shouldst make an advance toward virtue proportionate to the distance to which thou hast departed from thine original infatuation during the past two years, since the new longing first encountered the old, couldst thou, on reaching thy fortieth year, face death, if not with complete assurance, at least with hopefulness, calmly dismissing from thy thoughts the residuum of life as it faded into old age?"

These and similar reflections occurred to me, my father. I rejoiced in my progress, mourned my weaknesses, and commiserated the universal instability of human conduct. I had well-nigh forgotten where I was and our object in coming; but at last I dismissed my anxieties, which were better suited to other surroundings, and resolved to look about me and see what we had come to see. The sinking sun and the

---

[9]Petrarch is referring to Giacomo Colonna, younger brother of Cardinal Giovanni Colonna. Giacomo had been instrumental in helping Petrarch secure Cardinal Giovanni's patronage. Although he was bishop of a diocese in southern France, Giacomo had at this time been in Rome for several years.

[10]Petrarch is referring to his passion for Laura and the conflict between it and his desire for spiritual perfection.

[11]A *lustre* is a period of five years.

lengthening shadows of the mountain were already warning us that the time was near at hand when we must go. As if suddenly wakened from sleep, I turned about and gazed toward the west. I was unable to discern the summits of the Pyrenees, which form the barrier between France and Spain; not because of any intervening obstacle that I know of but owing simply to the insufficiency of our mortal vision. But I could see with the utmost clearness, off to the right, the mountains of the region about Lyons, and to the left the bay of Marseilles and the waters that lash the shores of Aigues Mortes, altho' all these places were so distant that it would require a journey of several days to reach them. Under our very eyes flowed the Rhone.

While I was thus dividing my thoughts, now turning my attention to some terrestrial object that lay before me, now raising my soul, as I had done my body, to higher planes, it occurred to me to look into my copy of St. Augustine's *Confessions,* a gift that I owe to your love, and that I always have about me, in memory of both the author and the giver. I opened the compact little volume, small indeed in size, but of infinite charm, with the intention of reading whatever came to hand, for I could happen upon nothing that would be otherwise than edifying and devout. Now it chanced that the tenth book presented itself. My brother, waiting to hear something of St. Augustine's from my lips, stood attentively by. I call him, and God too, to witness that where I first fixed my eyes it was written: "And men go about to wonder at the heights of the mountains, and the mighty waves of the sea, and the wide sweep of rivers, and the circuit of the ocean, and the revolution of the stars, but themselves they consider not." I was abashed, and, asking my brother (who was anxious to hear more), not to annoy me, I closed the book, angry with myself that I should still be admiring earthly things who might long ago have learned from even the pagan philosophers that nothing is wonderful but the soul, which, when great itself, finds nothing great outside itself. Then, in truth, I was satisfied that I had seen enough of the mountain; I turned my inward eye upon myself, and from that time not a syllable fell from my lips until we reached the bottom again. Those words had given me occupation enough, for I could not believe that it was by a mere accident that I happened upon them. What I had there read I believed to be addressed to me and to no other, remembering that St. Augustine had once suspected the same thing in his own case, when, on opening the book of the Apostle, as he himself tells us, the first words that he saw there were, "Not in rioting and drunkenness, not in chambering and wantonness, not in strife and envying. But put ye on the Lord Jesus Christ, and make not provision for the flesh, to fulfil the lusts thereof."

The same thing happened earlier to St. Anthony,[12] when he was listening to the Gospel where it is written, "If thou wilt be perfect, go and sell that thou hast, and give to the poor, and thou shalt have treasure in heaven: and come and follow me." Believing this scripture to have been read for his especial benefit, as his biographer Athanasius[13] says,

---

[12] The first Christian monk (*c.* 250–350).
[13] One of the great Fathers of the Eastern Church (293?–373).

he guided himself by its aid to the Kingdom of Heaven. And as Anthony on hearing these words waited for nothing more, and as Augustine upon reading the Apostle's admonition sought no farther, so I concluded my reading in the few words which I have given. I thought in silence of the lack of good counsel in us mortals, who neglect what is noblest in ourselves, scatter our energies in all directions, and waste ourselves in a vain show, because we look about us for what is to be found only within. I wondered at the natural nobility of our soul, save when it debases itself of its own free will, and deserts its original estate, turning what God has given it for its honour into dishonour. How many times, think you, did I turn back that day, to glance at the summit of the mountain, which seemed scarcely a cubit high compared with the range of human contemplation,—when it is not immersed in the foul mire of earth? With every downward step I asked myself this: If we are ready to endure so much sweat and labour in order that we may bring our bodies a little nearer heaven, how can a soul struggling toward God, up the steeps of human pride and human destiny, fear any cross or prison or sting of fortune? How few, I thought, but are diverted from their path by the fear of difficulties or the love of ease! How happy the lot of those few, if any such there be! It is of them, assuredly, that the poet was thinking, when he wrote:

> Happy the man who is skilled to understand
> Nature's hid causes; who beneath his feet
> All terrors casts, and death's relentless doom,
> And the loud roar of greedy Acheron.[14]

How earnestly should we strive, not to stand on mountain-tops, but to trample beneath us those appetites which spring from earthly impulses.

With no consciousness of the difficulties of the way, amidst these preoccupations which I have so frankly revealed, we came, long after dark, but with the full moon lending us its friendly light, to the little inn which we had left that morning before dawn. The time during which the servants have been occupied in preparing our supper, I have spent in a secluded part of the house, hurriedly jotting down these experiences on the spur of the moment, lest, in case my task were postponed, my mood should change on leaving the place, and so my interest in writing flag.

You will see, my dearest father, that I wish nothing to be concealed from you, for I am careful to describe to you not only my life in general but even my individual reflections. And I beseech you, in turn, to pray that these vague and wandering thoughts of mine may some time become firmly fixed, and, after having been vainly tossed about from one interest to another, may direct themselves at last toward the single, true, certain, and everlasting good.

---

[14]Acheron is in Greek mythology one of the rivers in Hades, the abode of the dead, which the shades of the dead must cross upon entering Hades. The verse passage is from Virgil's *Georgics*.

My Secret

Proem

Bemused, as is my frequent case, in reflections on how I had come into this life and how I should leave it, I was suddenly aware of a woman clothed in light and beauty. She said to me: "Fear not. In pity for your errors, I have descended from afar to bring you timely aid. Enough, and more than enough, have you gazed with clouded eyes at the ground. If hitherto they have found pleasure in mortal things, what may you not hope if you raise them to look at eternal matters?" "Who are you?" I asked, trembling. "I am Truth." Looking at her glorious face, I knew she could be none other.

As I was gazing on her with ineffable delight I perceived a venerable, majestic person by her side. I did not need to ask his name; his religious aspect, his modest air, his grave eyes, his sober bearing, his African dress, his Roman style, identified that most glorious Father, Augustine. His loving regard, sweeter than that of any human, removed all doubt. Truth turned to him and interrupted his profound meditation with the words: "O Augustine, dearest to me of all men, you know this man to be your devotee, and you know how he has suffered, all unaware, a long, dangerous illness. You must look to the life of this wasting man. None better than you could do this work of pity, since he has always worshiped your name, and since his miseries are similar to those you suffered when you were locked in the prison of the flesh." Said he: "I shall obey you, who have ever been my guide." And she: "I shall remain by your side during your colloquy."

Then we sat down, all three. And with Truth sitting in silent judgment by our side, the Saint and I engaged in a conversation that lasted three days. That our familiar talk might not be lost I have written it down in the measure of a little book, not that I wish to number it among my published works and attain glory thereby, but that I may read it over whenever I wish and taste again the sweetness of my experience. So, my little book, you will flee all the concourse of men and you will be happy to remain alone with me, and you will never belie your name. For you are my *Secret Book,* and that will be your name. And when I am busy with more serious matters you will recall to me in secret what you have recorded in secret.

To avoid the repetitions of "said he" and "said I" I shall represent our words in the form of a dialogue. I learned this style from my Cicero, and he in his turn had learned it from Plato. But let us not digress. Augustine then addressed me as follows.

From *Petrarch and His World* by Morris Bishop (Bloomington: Indiana University Press, 1963). Reprinted by permission of the publishers and Curtis Brown Ltd.

Book I

AUGUSTINUS: What are you doing, poor little man? What are you dreaming? What do you look forward to? Have you then forgotten all your miseries? Don't you remember that you are mortal?

FRANCISCUS: Certainly I remember it. In fact, that thought never comes to me without bringing a twinge of terror.

AUG.: I wish you did remember it, as you say. You would save me a lot of trouble. The best way to despise properly the temptations of this life is to remember one's own misery and meditate assiduously on death. The thought of death should penetrate to the very marrow of your bones.

FR.: It does indeed. But the thought of death doesn't seem to banish my distress of mind.

AUG.: Anyone who seriously longs to cast off his distresses cannot be disappointed of his desire.

FR.: What's this? Everybody wants to get rid of his woes, and very few have been able to. Most people are unhappy against their will.

AUG.: I thought you were more intelligent. If you had properly absorbed the true and helpful words of the philosophers you have read, if in fact you had studied for yourself and not for others, if you had drawn from the reading of so many books a rule for your own life instead of seeking vaingloriously the windy applause of the vulgar, you wouldn't say such stupid things.

FR.: You make me blush like a schoolboy. But still I don't know what for.

AUG.: For many things; but first of all for your idea that a man can be unhappy against his will.

FR.: Ah, I'll stop blushing! Everybody knows that poverty, pain, ignominy, diseases, death, come against our will and without our agency. Hence it's easy to recognize our distresses and easy to hate them, but it's not easy to get rid of them. The first two points are in our power, the third is in the power of fortune.

AUG.: Your impudence makes me angrier than your mistakes. Idiot, have you forgotten the words of the philosophers and saints, that no one can be made miserable by such miseries? If virtue alone renders man happy, the contrary of virtue must render him unhappy.

FR.: That's Stoic doctrine, more theoretical than practical.

AUG.: Are we agreed on this, that a man becomes unhappy only through vice?

FR.: Well, I've noticed that many, including me, are chiefly tormented by our inability to shake off the yoke of vices, although we have struggled all our lives to that end with all our powers. So one may admit that many are very miserable against their will, while grieving and hoping for deliverance.

AUG.: I'll tell you the method of deliverance. The first step is to meditate on death and human infelicity; the second is to struggle with intense desire to rise.

FR.: It hasn't worked with me.

AUG.: In men's minds there is a perverse and pestilent longing to deceive oneself. You men should fear the frauds you perpetrate on yourselves. Everyone esteems himself at more than his worth and loves himself more than is his due. The deceived is never separate from the deceiver.

FR.: You've said that before. But as far as I can remember I have never deceived myself. I can only wish I hadn't been deceived by others.

AUG.: Right now you are deceiving yourself, in boasting that you have never deceived yourself. Do you think that anyone can sin perforce? Sin is a voluntary action; if the will is lacking, the act ceases to be sinful.

FR.: I'll have to grant that. I feel it in myself and I conjecture it in others. I suspect that I am being punished, that since I didn't stand upright when I could, now that I want to rise from my abjection I no longer can.

AUG.: Instead of "I no longer can," you should say: "I no longer wish to."

FR.: I'll never confess that. Heaven knows—no man does—how I have suffered and how I have longed to rise.

AUG.: Conscience may well have made you weep, but it has not made you change your intentions. Certainly you could have reformed, if you had really wished to. Look at my own story, in my Confessions.

FR.: I know all about that. Every time I read your Confessions I am moved by two contrary feelings, hope and fear. Sometimes it seems to me, in tears, that I am reading not another's story but the record of my own pilgrimage.

AUG.: You must learn from it to desire your amelioration passionately. Consult your own conscience. It is the best interpreter of virtue; it is the infallible, truthful judge of your thoughts and acts. It will tell you that you have never properly aspired to salvation.

FR.: My conscience tells me that is true. But how can this great desire work?

AUG.: In opening a way through difficulties. The desire for virtue is a large part of virtue. And this desire can arise only through the extinction of other desires. One must dare to say: "I have nothing further in common with the body; I am revolted by all the visible world; I aspire to greater felicities."

FR.: How can one attain this state?

AUG.: First, as I have already recommended, by the constant remembrance of your mortality.

FR.: So I don't meditate on death?

AUG.: Very rarely, in fact, and so limply that your meditation does not penetrate to the depths of your calamities.

FR.: I thought the opposite.

AUG.: I am not talking about what you thought, but about what you ought to think. You ought to think constantly about the fragility of your state and bear constantly before your eyes the image of your mortality. Few think profoundly that they must necessarily die. You must ever aspire to that life wherein you will cease to be mortal. So you must look continually on the picture of a dying man, on the chilling limbs, the burning, sweating breast, the gasping breath, the receding, filming, tear-filled eyes, the livid face, the sunken cheeks, the yellowed teeth, the sharp nose, the foam at the lips, the thick, dry tongue, the strangle in the throat, the revolting smell, and above all the horror of a face without intelligence.

FR.: I see that I must tell myself the whole truth.

AUG.: Think also of the final judgment, when you must give an account of all your deeds and words, when you can put no trust in wit and eloquence, riches and power, bodily beauty or worldly fame. You must think of heaven and hell not as possible but as necessary and inevitable. Then you may be sure that you have not meditated in vain.

FR.: You terrify me. And yet such meditations are familiar to me, especially at night, when the spirit, released from its daytime cares, collects itself within itself. Then I compose myself in the attitude of a dying man, and I picture vividly to myself the hour of death and all its horrible accompaniments, so that sometimes I seem to look into hell; and I am so shattered by this vision that I rise up all trembling, and I frighten anyone who is present by crying: "Alas, what is happening to me? And what will happen? Mercy, O dear Jesus, aid me!" I fall in a sort of fit; and when I tell my friends of it I move them to tears. Such being my case, what holds me back? What obstacle lies in my way, so that my nightmare meditations bring me only terror, but I remain what I was before, like those who have never known such experiences? I am worse off than they, for they enjoy their pleasures, whereas for me every pleasure is blended with bitterness.

AUG.: You should rather be happy because you are aware of your state. There is hope for you. You must reflect forever on the imminence of death, thanking God for his warnings. As for these midnight phantasms, they are not divinely sent, but are the products of a tortured spirit. Your salutary purpose for reform is weakened by the excessive mobility of your mind. Hence your inward discord, the anxiety of a mind that tortures itself and cannot bring itself to wash away its own stains. While it recognizes its own tortuous ways it does not desert them; while it fears the imminent danger it does not conjure it away.

FR.: Alas, wretched man that I am!

AUG.: Good! You are shaken out of your torpor. Now let us repose a little in silence, and leave the rest to tomorrow.

FR.: That is what I need: repose and silence.

Book II

AUG.: Did you sleep well?

FR.: Well enough.

AUG.: Let's return to our subject. Many evils assail you, but you don't realize how many and how mighty are your enemies. Let's take the capital sins in their order. First, the most grievous sin of pride. How petty are the superiorities you look on with complacency! You are proud of your intellect, of your reading of many books; you glory in your own high talk and in the shape of your mortal body. And yet you recognize how often that fine intellect fails you, and in how many ways you can't equal the competence of the simplest of men. I'm putting it mildly; there are mean, common animals whose powers you could never imitate by any application. And you would glory in your intelligence! All your reading, what good has it done you? Of all the books you have read, how much has clung in your spirit and taken root there, to produce fruit in its time? Examine yourself, and you will find that all you know, in comparison with what you don't know, is only a tiny trickle compared with the ocean. And what is the use of knowing many things if, when you have learned the dimensions of heaven and earth, the measure of the seas, the courses of the stars, the virtues of plants and stones, the secrets of nature, you still don't know yourself? What difference does it make that others applaud your words, if these are not approved by your own inward judgment? What can be more puerile, nay, insane, than, in your heedlessness and sloth, to spend your time in the study of words, to find your pleasure in talk, not even to perceive your own shame with your bleary eyes? You are like those birds that, according to the story, so delight in their own sweet song that they die of it. How often have I heard you complain that neither tongue nor pen could express the ideas that were clear enough in your thought! What then is this rhetoric, so limited and frail that it can't embrace its own subjects or possess what it has embraced! So much for pride of mind! And as for your pride of body, what pleases you therein? Perhaps its vigor and health? Nothing could be more idiotic. A weakness arising from the slightest of causes, the attacks of illness, the bite of a worm, a poisonous exhalation, may make an end of body. Or perhaps you think you're handsome, and you look admiringly on your features and complexion? Have you forgotten the fable of Narcissus?[1] And the revolting ugliness beneath the skin? And the approach of age's decay?

FR.: Hold on a minute! You say I boast of my intelligence. Well, the only intelligence I claim is that I have never trusted it. Why should I be proud of reading many books, from which I have derived little learning but much distress of mind? You accuse me of seeking glory in fine language when, as you admit, my chief torment is that it can't suffice to express my ideas. And when you talked seriously about my beautiful body you almost made me laugh. So I have put my hope in this wretched mortal frame, which daily warns me of its frailty? Heaven forbid! I admit that when I was a boy I took pleasure in showing off my fine face and licking down my hair, but such vanity disappeared with my youth.

AUG.: There is much I could say in reply, but I prefer to let your conscience shame you. You try to hide your pride, but you reveal it in your depreciation of others. That revelation of self-esteem is more unpleasant than undue exaltation of oneself. I would much rather see you exalt others, even though preserving your own primacy, than watch you

---

[1]In Greek mythology, Narcissus was a beautiful youth who rejected the love of the nymph Echo and was punished by Aphrodite, the goddess of love, who made him fall in love with his own image in a fountain. His fruitless attempts to approach this beautiful object led to his despair and death. He was changed into the flower that bears his name.

trample them down and then haughtily display a shield of humility, made of the scorn of others.

FR.: As you like. I have no very high opinion either of myself or of others. I don't like to say outright what I have learned to think of most men.

AUG.: Well, let's pass on to the other points. Of envy I absolve you. But what about greed for temporal goods?

FR.: Come, come! I never heard anything more absurd. There's nothing I'm freer from than avarice.

AUG.: Not so free as you think. And not so free either from ambition. What are these incessant cares and worries of yours? You may say that you want to be in a position to help your friends. But that would be just a noble excuse.

FR.: I'm not inhuman enough to be unmoved by concern for my friends, especially those who are endeared to me by their virtue and merit. Some I admire, some I venerate, some I love, some I pity. On the other hand I'm not so high-minded as to ruin myself for my friends. I have to think of my own future, provide a competence for old age, and hence combine some material concern with my cultivation of the Muses.

AUG.: A useless labor, and a senseless one. You can get along with very little. You were never so well off as when you were wandering alone and carefree in the hills. Then you thought yourself the richest and happiest of mortals; but now you have abandoned that frugal country peace. You began to despise the berries of your bushes, the rough clothing, and life among peasants, and you have come to learn cupidity amid the city's tumults. You are still hesitant, perhaps because you are caught in the snares of sin, or perhaps because God wills that where you passed your youth under the discipline of others you should, though your own master, drag out a sad old age.

FR.: Well, if I try to provide against poverty in that sad old age, what is wrong with that?

AUG.: The wrong is that you are forever concerned with the ephemeral, and you forget the eternal. Nothing is more senseless than to suffer poverty forever, out of fear of suffering it for a day.

FR.: True; but my desires are modest and limited. I don't want abundance; but I don't want to live in need.

AUG.: Only the gods don't live in need. Don't you know that man is the most needy of all the animals? Cease to hope for the impossible; content yourself with man's lot, and learn to have both too much and too little, to surpass and to be surpassed. You can't shake off the yoke of fortune that rests on the necks of kings. You can be freed from it only when, conquering human passions, you submit yourself totally to the rule of virtue. Then you will be free, needing nothing, subject to no man, finally a king, powerful and absolutely happy.

FR.: I wish that I could wish for nothing. But I am dragged on by perverse habit. I feel forever something unsatisfied in my heart.

AUG.: Let us speak of ambition. Examine your heart and you will find that it has no little place there.

FR.: You think it was nothing that I have fled the cities whenever I could, disdaining assemblies and public ceremonies, seeking the woods and country peace, forswearing vain honors? And I hear myself accused of ambition!

AUG.: You mortals renounce many things not because you despise them but because you despair of attaining them. You haven't proved to me that you haven't desired honors, but only that you hate the trouble of seeking them. Don't hope to hide behind a finger, as the saying goes. This flight from the cities, this longing for the woods of which you are so proud, doesn't excuse you; it's just a shift of blame. All kinds of roads lead to the same goal; and believe me, though you have left the trodden highway, you are trying to reach on a byway those ambitious ends you claim to despise. Your insistence on free time, your solitude, your incuriosity about normal human occupations, your studies, whose purpose is glory, all prove your ambition. But let's get on. I won't mention gluttony; you're free of that. And wrath is no serious fault of yours. But there are more dangerous passions for you.

FR.: Good God, what more dangerous can remain?

AUG.: How great are the flames of lust?

FR.: Sometimes they are so great that I grieve that I wasn't born insensible. I would rather be a motionless stone than feel the upheavals of my body. Sometimes I think I have risen above them; and then I fall again, with bitterness of spirit, into the old miseries.

AUG.: I am not surprised, for I was a witness of your struggles, and I saw you rise and fall; and now, in pity for your prostrate state, I have proposed to bring you aid.

FR.: I thank you. But what human power remains to help me?

AUG.: None; only divine power. A man cannot be chaste without God's gift. You must beg for this gift, humbly and often with tears. He does not deny what is properly asked.

FR.: I have done that so often that I almost fear to bore him.

AUG.: Not humbly enough, not soberly enough. You have always reserved a little place for future desires; you have always set the term of your prayers too far ahead. I speak out of experience; the same thing happened to me. I used to pray: "Lord, grant me to live chaste; but not right away; pretty soon." But a man who prays for tomorrow loses today.

FR.: I shall then pray assiduously, without weariness, shame, or despair.

AUG.: Good. And keep in mind the words of Plato, that nothing hinders knowledge of the divine more than the carnal appetites and the flame of lust. But since we are to return to this subject, I shall deal now with other grievous wounds of your spirit. You are afflicted by a calamitous ailment, which the moderns call *accidia* and the ancients *aegritudo,* or depression, or acute melancholy.

FR.: The very name makes me shudder.

AUG.: I am not surprised, since you have suffered from it long and grievously.

FR.: I admit it. The assaults of the other passions are brief and they contain their modicum of pleasure, but this plague holds me so close that sometimes it tortures me day and night, robbing me of light and life, plunging me into hell. But strangely enough I feed so upon tears and pain with a kind of atrocious black satisfaction that I am unwilling to be torn from them.

AUG.: What is the cause of your depression? Illness, misfortune?

FR.: All kinds of causes. Specific reasons; and in general my abhorrence and contempt for the human condition.

AUG.: What especially afflicts you?

FR.: Everything I see, hear, and feel.

AUG.: Gad! There is nothing you like?

FR.: Nothing—or not very much.

AUG.: All this is what I have called accidia. You loathe all your own concerns.

FR.: Other people's too.

AUG.: Even your advantages, which others envy?

FR.: Only the most wretched of creatures could envy a wretched man.

AUG.: You think that fortune has been unkind to you?

FR.: Very unkind, very evil, very arrogant, very cruel.

AUG.: Well, everybody can't be first.

FR.: I don't want to be first. No one has had more modest ambitions than I, but no one has gained them with more difficulty. I call Truth to witness that I have never desired to stand first. I abhor an existence filled with care and trouble; I much prefer a middle state, Horace's golden mean, *aurea mediocritas*. But even that I haven't been able to attain. Forever doubtful of the future, with my mind in suspense, I have gained no pleasure from fortune's favors. As you know, I have always been dependent on others, and that's the unhappiest of states.

AUG.: You would have it that you alone of all men might live free from care? Very few indeed have been able to live for themselves alone, and the happiest are those who have lived for others. There must be other reasons for your melancholy.

FR.: Don't you know that cruel stroke of fate, which in a single day struck me down, and all my hopes, and my property, and my family and home?[2]

AUG.: I see your eyes flash. Let's go on, for this is no time to deal with that matter.

FR.: Then there's my life in this most horrible of cities.[3] Sometimes it seems to me that I have descended into hell. How can I do here anything really good, think honest thoughts, write proper poetry?

AUG.: Plenty of others, and great men too, have suffered in the same way. You came of your own free will to this city and to this state of mind, and by your own free will you can escape. You can train your ears to listen to the city's din with pleasure, as to a waterfall. By such devices you can banish your melancholy.

FR.: I must yield to you, although I am not entirely convinced. At least, my condition no longer seems so wretched as it did. Let us now postpone further talk till tomorrow.

---

[2]Petrarch is probably referring to the death of his father, which seems to have resulted in a squabble over his inheritance with his stepmother.

[3]Petrarch follows this statement with a long description (omitted in this abridgment) of the repulsive features of life in Avignon.

Book III

AUG.: I haven't yet touched your deepest and most persistent troubles. You are fastened by two mighty chains. You are like a miser in prison shackled by golden fetters; you would like to get free, but you don't want to lose them. But there's a law in this prison: if you don't throw off the chains you can't go free. And you love them; you even boast of them.

FR.: What are these chains you're talking about?

AUG.: Love and glory.

FR.: Gods above, what's this I hear? So you call love and glory chains, and if I permit it you'll take them from me? You want to rob me of the loveliest things in life, and condemn to darkness the fairest part of my being?

AUG.: I'm going to try to, though I doubt if I succeed. Tell me, don't you think love is the utmost madness?

FR.: The fact is, love depends on its object. It can be called either the ugliest passion of the spirit or its noblest activity. If I adore a wicked, contemptible woman, that is madness; but if a rare exemplar of virtue attracts me and I devote myself to loving and venerating her, what of that?

AUG.: There's no difference. In both cases you bid farewell to reason and to awareness of truth.

FR.: You're wasting your time. I've never loved anything foul, anything that was not very beautiful.

AUG.: Even beautiful things can be loved foully.

FR.: Do you know who it is you're talking about?

AUG.: I have thoroughly considered my subject. We are going to talk about a mortal woman, whom you have been admiring and celebrating during a large part of your life. I am amazed at your long insanity.

FR.: Don't be offensive. Do you realize that you are referring to a woman whose mind, ignoring earthly cares, burns with celestial desires? In whose aspect, as truth is truth, shines heavenly beauty? Whose behavior is an example of perfect virtue? Whose voice, whose eyes, are more than mortal, whose very walk seems no human action? Think of that, please, and you will realize what sort of language you must use.

AUG.: Poor fool! So for sixteen years you have fed your flame with false cajolements! How you have suffered! But in the end, when those eyes close in death, you will be ashamed that you tied your immortal soul to a mortal body and you will blush to recall what you have so exalted.

FR.: God forbid! I shall not live to see her death.

AUG.: How do you know? She is getting older; that splendid body, worn out with illness and with frequent childbirths, has already lost much of its old vigor. It is folly to submit your soul to any such mortal thing.

FR.: I have not done so. I have never loved her body so much as her soul. My delight was in her character, transcending mortality, resembling that of the angels. So if—the mere utterance makes me shudder—if she should die first, I would appease my grief by saying, with Laelius,[4] wisest of the Romans: "I loved her virtue, which has not been spent."

AUG.: Well, pour all the praise you like on your little woman. I won't contradict you. She's a queen, a saint, if you like, or as Virgil said, a goddess, a sister of Phoebus,[5] a nymph. But her great virtue won't help to excuse your errors.

FR.: I call Truth here by our side to witness that in my love there has never been anything base, lewd, or in any way culpable, except perhaps in its excess. Nothing more wholly beautiful than my love can be conceived.

AUG.: I'm sorry to hear such nonsense from one who ought to think more clearly.

FR.: Whatever I am is due to her. I should never have gained my present reputation, however one may judge it, if she hadn't tended with her noble sympathy that tiny little seed of virtue that nature sowed in my breast. She recalled my youthful spirit from all turpitude, pulled me back, as they say, with a hook, and forced me to look upward. How could I fail to be transformed by her character? Never has any slanderer, however scurrilous, attacked her good name or dared to find anything reprehensible in her actions, words, or even gestures. Even those who leave nothing unsoiled spared her, in admiration and reverence. It is not strange that her good fame inspired in me the desire for fame, and eased my labors to that end. From my young manhood I longed for nothing else than to please her, who alone had pleased me. You know how, to gain that end, I spurned the temptations of a myriad pleasures and subjected myself prematurely to laborious cares. And you order me to forget her or to love her more temperately!

AUG.: You make me sick at my stomach.

FR.: Why, pray?

AUG.: Because to think falsely is a sign of ignorance; but to proclaim the false impudently is a sign both of ignorance and of vainglory.

FR.: How can you prove that I have either thought or said anything false?

AUG.: By everything you have said! First of all when you say that she has made you what you are. The fact is that she has prevented you from developing. What a man you might have been, if she hadn't captured you with her beauty! It is kind nature that made you what you were; she prevented you from becoming what you might have been, or rather you threw it away for her, for she is innocent. Her beauty seemed to you so sweet and attractive that you destroyed your native possibilities in your longings and wailings. And you boast that she preserved you from all turpitudes! Perhaps she did save you from many, but she forced you into greater calamities. For one who drives us to our downfall while keeping us out of various filthy courses, or who inflicts a mortal wound while healing some minor scratches, can hardly be called our liberator, but rather our murderer. So she whom you call your guide

---

[4]Roman statesman of the second century B.C. who helped introduce Greek culture into Rome and who figures as a speaker in a number of Cicero's philosophical dialogues.

[5]In Greco-Roman mythology, Phoebus Apollo was god of the sun and the patron of music and poetry. His twin sister, Diana, was goddess of the moon and symbolized chastity in woman.

has saved you from foul actions only to lay you out on a splendid bier. And as for her teaching you to look upward, to disdain the mass of men, what else is that than making you slave to her alone, forgetful and scornful of all else on earth? There is nothing worse for a man among men. When you recall that she involved you in innumerable labors you are certainly telling the truth. But you got a good deal out of them! And as for your boast that she made you seek for fame, well, that is the worst burden on your soul. In short, this woman you exalt so highly is ruining you.

FR.: What do you mean?

AUG.: She has distracted your mind from the love of the Creator and has turned it to the love of the creature. You have loved the Creator only as the artificer who made that beautiful body.

FR.: I protest to Truth here present and to my conscience that I never loved her body more than her soul! As she has grown older and her bodily beauty has dwindled I have been the more constant. Although the flower of youth visibly fades with the passage of time, the beauty of her spirit kept increasing, and this has kept me faithful.

AUG.: Are you trying to fool me? If that spirit had inhabited a squalid body, would you have loved it as much?

FR.: I don't dare to assert that, for the spirit is invisible. But if the spirit should make itself manifest, no doubt I would love a beautiful spirit even in an ugly habitation.

AUG.: You are playing on words. For if you can love only what is evident to the eyes, you love the body. However, I won't deny that her spirit and her character have added fuel to your flames, just as her very name greatly increased your passion. You loved body and soul together, and both of them immoderately. And you have fallen into great disasters because of this love.

FR.: That I will never admit, even if you put me to torture.

AUG.: Do you remember your boyhood, your love of God, your meditations on death, your religious feeling, your love of virtue?

FR.: I remember very well, and I grieve that as I have grown older my merits have decreased.

AUG.: When did you lose these good habits?

FR.: I came to a parting of the ways, and I took the downward path. And I have never been able to find the right way again.

AUG.: How old were you when this happened?

FR.: It was in the midst of youth's fevers. If you wait a moment, I can recollect the exact year.

AUG.: And when did this woman's beauty first appear to you?

FR.: Oh, that I'll never forget!

AUG.: How do those two times match?

FR.: Well, in fact her appearance in my life and my steps astray happened at about the same time.

AUG.: That's what I was after. And this glorious woman, this guide to heaven, why didn't she hold you by the hand and show you the right road?

FR.: She did all she could. Unmoved by my prayers and blandishments, in spite of her youth and mine and in spite of certain circumstances that might have moved a heart of stone, she kept her feminine purity and remained firm, impregnable. Isn't that something? She showed me my duty; and when I went my headstrong way she preferred to abandon me rather than to follow me.

AUG.: Ah, then you did sometimes have base desires! You denied that before. Well, that's the familiar madness of lovers, always saying: "Will I, nill I, nill I, will I." You don't know what you want or what you don't want.

FR.: You've tricked me. If perhaps I had such desires at the time, youthful ardor caused them. Now I know better. But she never wavered in her womanly virtue. If at the time I protested against it, now I am glad of it, and I thank her.

AUG.: It's hard to trust someone who has fallen once. That flame of yours may be less intense, it hasn't been extinguished. And in ascribing so much merit to your beloved, in absolving her, you are condemning yourself. Love has made you wretched; that's what I began by saying. Earthly love leads to the forgetfulness of God; it has brought you to the miserable state you have described. In your folly, you were not even content with gazing on her living face, the source of your woes, and you obtained from an illustrious artist a painted image and carried it around with you, to have something to cry over forever. You sought out everything that would provoke and irritate your emotion. And—the final proof of an unhinged mind—you were as much allured by her beautiful name as by her body, and with incredible folly you cultivated every punning significance of it! You loved the laurel, whether of emperors or poets, because it chimed with her name. You could hardly write a poem without dragging in the laurel. And since you couldn't hope for the imperial wreath, you longed for the laurel crown of poetry as immoderately as you had loved the lady. You will be shocked some day when you reflect how much effort you spent in obtaining it, though I grant that you were often borne on the wings of inspiration. Don't speak; I know what is in your mind. I know that you were a poet before you fell in love. But the difficulties and dangers in the way of success would have delayed your effort, if the memory of that sweetest of names hadn't spurred you on over land and sea to Rome and Naples, where finally you gained what you had lusted for so ardently. Anyone who doesn't take this as an indication of notable madness must be mad himself.

FR.: What do you want me to do? Despair?

AUG.: First we'll look for remedies. Cicero says that many think of driving out an old love with a new one, as a nail drives out a nail. That's good advice. A mind dispersed on many objects has the more difficulty in concentrating on one. But the danger is that if you cast off this passion, which I admit is one of the nobler sort, you may get entangled in many, and become, instead of a lover, a libertine. I won't disapprove of your passing from one subjection to another, for perhaps in such excursions you may find your liberty, or a lighter servitude; but I would much reprobate your bowing your neck to a series of sordid involvements.

FR.: May the patient interrupt the doctor for a moment? Let me tell you this—I can never love anyone else. My eyes are so used to gazing upon her, my mind is so used to admiring her, that all that is not she seems dark and ugly. So if you command me to love another in order to free myself from love, you are asking the impossible. It's all over; I am done for.

AUG.: Then you must find some external remedy. Can you persuade yourself to run away?

FR.: Painful though it would be, I could do so.

AUG.: If you can, you're saved. How can you be secure in this place, where remain so many vestiges of your old wounds, where you are oppressed by the present and the past?

FR.: I have often attempted flight, in search of freedom. To obtain it I have wandered far and wide, east and north, even to the edge of Ocean.[6] But wherever I went I bore my hurt within me.

AUG.: As Socrates said, you were always traveling with yourself. You must lay down that old burden of care, and prepare your heart; then at least you will be really fleeing.

FR.: I don't see how that will cure me.

AUG.: I didn't speak of curing or of getting well; I said: "Prepare your heart." You must teach your heart to cast off its burdens; you must go away without hope of return, without a backward glance. But you must beware of a relapse, in revisiting familiar scenes. You yourself have often thought you were cured, and you would have been cured if you had remained away. But walking the well-known streets, recalling old vanities at the mere sight of certain spots, you were struck dumb, you sighed, you stood stock-still and barely refrained from tears. Wounded once more, you fled, murmuring: "I feel that here are still hidden some traps of the old enemy; here remain some relics of death." Is a man ever cured? A look at a comely body arouses lust; a glance from lovely eyes may awaken sleeping love. You must not only quit this pestilential city, you must flee with all diligence whatever recalls your mind to its past occupations.

FR.: I have already been meditating flight, but I am uncertain where to go.

AUG.: Many ways, many harbors are open to you. I know that you love above all Italy and your sweet native soil, and rightfully enough. I therefore advise Italy, for the manners of its people, for its skies and surrounding seas and shores and Apennine hills. Go surely and quickly, and do not turn back. Forget the past, look to what is to come. Too long have you been an exile from your fatherland and from yourself. It is now time to return, for "evening is falling and night is friend of the de- spoiler." But avoid solitude, until you feel that no after-affects of your illness remain. When you said that your rustications were of no benefit to you, you were stating the obvious. What remedies could you expect to find in a remote, solitary country place? I admit that when you fled there alone and kept sighing and looking back at the city, I often laughed

---

[6]Popular geography during classical and medieval times considered the world to consist of the land mass of Europe, Asia, and Africa, which was completely surrounded by Ocean in which there were a few mythical or actual islands but no significant bodies of earth. This theory held whether the world was conceived of as spherical or flat.

at you from on high, and I said to myself: "Love has surrounded that poor fellow with a Lethean[7] cloud, and to flee from his disease he is running toward death!"

FR.: Ovid advised forlorn lovers to avoid solitude. I have known that passage from boyhood.

AUG.: What is the use of knowing so much, if you couldn't make the application to your own necessities? I have been the more surprised at your error in seeking solitude, in that you knew the wise verses of the ancients against it, and you have added a few yourself. You have often complained that solitude has done you no good.

FR.: Have you any other remedies to suggest?

AUG.: To set forth everything one knows is rather to show off than to really help a friend. But Cicero says that three things distract the mind from love: satiety, shame, and reflection. Well, satiety in your case is impossible. As for shame—tell me, and excuse me, have you looked in your mirror lately?

FR.: What do you mean? Yes, I suppose so, as usual.

AUG.: Haven't you noticed that your face is changing, day by day?

FR.: Now that you mention it, yes. Men seem to get old faster now than they used to. Of course I have been white-haired since my youth, like Domitian, Numa Pompilius, and Virgil.[8]

AUG.: If you had been bald you would have dragged in Julius Caesar. At any rate, shame should banish passion. You are too old to play the passionate lover. Most men don't reach your present age.[9] Renounce the follies of youth; extinguish the ardors of adolescence. Don't be forever thinking of what you have been; look around you to realize what you are now.

FR.: Do you know what brings me a little comfort? She is getting old along with me.

AUG: Perhaps you think it's more decent for you to love her when you're both old than to fall in love with a girl? As a matter of fact love is all the uglier as there is less basis for love. You should therefore be ashamed that your mind never changes, while the body is continually changing. That is a subject for reflection, which, as I said, is Cicero's third cure of love. Meditate on your manhood, on the nobility of the human spirit, on the fragility and filth of the body, on the brevity of life, on the flight of time, on the certainty of death. Think how revolting it is to be the world's laughingstock, how improper your behavior is for your clerical profession. Recall all your sufferings for her sake, all your lamentations and tears. Think, at the same time, of her ungrateful and supercilious bearing, how, if she was occasionally kind, it was more briefly than the blowing of a summer breeze. Think how you have added to her fame, and how much she has subtracted from your own life, and how you have protected her own fair name, while she has always been perfectly unconcerned about your state. Think how she has distracted

---

[7]In Roman mythology, Lethe was a river in Hades. Souls about to be reincarnated drank its water, which made them forget their previous existence.

[8]Domitian (51–96 A.D.) was a Roman emperor. Numa Pompilius was a legendary king of Rome supposed to have reigned early in the seventh century B.C.

[9]Petrarch was thirty-eight.

you from the love of God, how she has interfered with the completion of the works you have in hand. And finally think of what she actually is! Few consider with a realizing sense the filthiness of the feminine body. Repel every recollection of your past preoccupations and all thought of the past. And besiege heaven with your prayers; tire the ears of the heavenly king. Let no night or day pass without tears and supplications. But we've talked enough about this. Now I come to your final fault, which I must undertake to cure. You are unduly desirous of worldly glory and of immortality for your name.

FR.: I must confess it. I cannot restrain this appetite.

AUG.: But it is to be feared that the longing for vain immortality may block the road to true immortality. Worldly fame is nothing but the diffuse gabble of many tongues. It is a gust of air, the breath of many men. You despise the vulgar mob; but you delight in the silly little words of the very men whose actions you condemn. Worse, you find the summit of your felicity therein! What is the purpose of your perpetual labors, your night vigils, the fervency of your studies? You may answer: "To learn something useful for my life;" but you already know all that is needful for life and death. It would be better for you to apply what you know to your conduct. And I notice that you have tried in most of your works to tickle the public taste, to please the very people you particularly dislike, plucking posies, in your poems, histories, and speeches, to enrapture your hearers. And not content with their ephemeral applause, you have lusted for fame among posterity. Thus you started a big history of Romans, from Romulus to Titus;[10] and without finishing that, you dispatched a poetic craft to Africa.[11] And so, writing of others, you forget yourself. And death may strike you down before you finish either task.

FR.: I have been afraid of that. I once fell seriously ill, and I thought I was going to die. And what tortured me most was the thought that I was leaving my *Africa* half finished. As I didn't want anyone else to edit it, I had determined to burn it with my own hands. That is a bitter memory.

AUG.: You confirm me in my judgment. But suppose you had plenty of time, leisure, tranquillity, without dull periods or physical weakness, that you were spared all those interruptions that have interfered with your writing, that every condition was favorable. What great thing do you think you would accomplish?

FR.: No doubt some brilliant, rare, excellent book.

AUG.: The more excellent it might be, the more it would detract from the care of your soul. And how vain and transitory is earthly fame!

FR.: Oh, I know all that old stuff of the philosophers about the vanity of human wishes and so forth. But I don't expect to become a god and embrace eternity. Human fame is enough for me. That's what I long for. Being mortal, I desire only mortal rewards.

AUG.: What a calamity, if you are telling the truth! If you don't want

---

[10]Romulus was the legendary founder of Rome in the eighth century B.C. Titus (40?–81 A.D.) was a Roman emperor.

[11]Augustine is referring to *Africa*, the epic poem Petrarch was working on.

immortal rewards, if you don't look to eternity, you are condemned to earth. Your fate is sealed; there is no hope for you.

FR.: All I meant was this: I treat mortal things as mortal, and I don't affront the nature of things by vast, unreasonable desires. I don't abandon eternal concerns; I just defer them.

AUG.: Take care! Death may strike at any moment. Time is short; it is dangerous to make any postponement.

FR.: Still, there is some reason in my stand. That glory which it is permissible to hope for must be sought while we are here below. The greater glory will be enjoyed in heaven by those who will be admitted there; they won't even think of earthly glory. So this is the order: the care for mortal things must come first in mortal minds; eternal concerns will succeed in their turn to the transitory.

AUG.: What a foolish little man you are! You think that all the joys of earth and heaven will shower upon you at your summons! What is earth in comparison with heaven? I hate to hear you sneer at the "old stuff" of the philosophers. Is the geometrical proof that our earth is tiny, just a long island of land, old stuff? Is it old stuff that of the world's five so-called zones the middle one is uninhabitable by men because of the sun's heat, the extreme one to north and south burdened by intolerable cold and perpetual ice, so that only the two temperate zones are habitable? It is doubtful whether the antipodes are inhabited; I don't think so myself. That leaves only the north temperate zone, which, according to some, is divided into two parts, one reserved for our uses, the other cut off by the northern Ocean, which forbids our access to it. In this tiny world glory is of small account.

FR.: Do you then order me to give up my studies and live ingloriously?

AUG.: I will never advise you to live without glory, but I admonish you not to prefer the quest of glory to that of virtue. I will lay down this rule: take no heed for glory; the less you long for it the more of it you will gain. A man would be mad who would bustle about under the midday sun to show others his shadow, and no less mad is he who, in the ardors of life, tries to promote his own fame. Go to your goal, and your shadow will follow you. You wear yourself out writing books; you're making a great mistake, for you forget your own advantage in trying to bring advantage to others, and thus in the vain hope of glory you waste unwitting this brief span of life.

FR.: What shall I do then? Shall I leave my books unfinished? Wouldn't it be more sensible to hurry them to a conclusion, if God grants it, and then, being freed of these tasks, to give myself wholly to higher things? I can't calmly leave half done works that have cost me so much.

AUG.: I know where the shoe pinches. You would rather abandon yourself than your little books. Lay down the burden of your histories; the deeds of the Romans have been sufficiently celebrated by themselves and by others. Abandon Africa and leave it to its inhabitants. You won't increase either Scipio's glory or your own. He can't be any further exalted; you are just creeping along behind him. So surrender all these works, and at last give yourself back to yourself! And, to return to the point from which we started, begin to think deeply about death, which little by little and all unconscious you are approaching.

You are part of the great procession; exulting in the prime of your life, you are treading on the heels of others; but others are treading on yours. Remember Cicero: "All the life of a philosopher is meditation on death." You can find the right path by listening to your own spirit, which tells you: "This is the way home." I pray God that he may accompany you and bring your wandering steps to safety.

FR.: Oh, may your prayer be granted, and by God's favor may I come safe out of the maze, free of my own self-deceptions and delusions! And may the storms of my spirit subside, and the world be silent, and fortune molest me no more!

Comments / on Petrarch

In [Petrarch] for the first time individuality and its rights stood forth strong and free with a claim to the highest significance. . . . Even his unmeasured thirst for fame and his petty vanities belonged as essential parts thereto. Everything that he read or learned, everything that he did or experienced, he related to his own person; the whole external world served him simply as material for his personal education. . . . He searched in the books of Cicero and Augustine for experiences comparable to his own; he sought men in books. Petrarch did much for classical learning; he gave the strongest impulse to the destruction of scholasticism; but the greatest, most arduous, and most serviceable of his achievements was himself.   *GEORG VOIGT (1859)*

Since [Petrarch] was such a keen observer of actual life and so lovingly devoted to the investigation of the human heart, all the records of the past became a living reality to him, and he felt himself sharing in the drama related as if he had an active part in the cast. It was not just a whim that he, the untiring letter-writer, started to 'correspond' with characters of ancient times, as if they could answer him. When he read their works, he almost forgot that they were long since dead. By such intensive reading with a clear comprehension of chronological relations and the inner logic of historical evolution, he developed a conception of history that strikes us very often as thoroughly modern.

HANS NACHOD (1948)

By the time of the humanistic movement . . . the growth of a sense of history was beginning to introduce a further great change [in European thought]. Petrarch's *Letters to the Ancient Dead* revealed an awareness of their author's position in time. . . . Combined with the perception of the ineluctable passage of time there was a sentimental nostalgia for the civilization to which he looked back . . . the development of a sense of historical distance was one of the most distinguishing marks of the cultural movement in Renaissance Italy. . . .   *M. P. GILMORE (1952)*

The decision [to climb Mount Ventoux] was far more original than it would appear today. There is no clear record that anyone ever climbed a mountain for pleasure or mere curiosity from the time of King Philip of Macedon to that of Petrarch. . . . Petrarch remains the first recorded Alpinist, the first to climb a mountain because it is there.
MORRIS BISHOP (1963)

A good deal has been written about Petrarch's famous ascent of Mount Ventoux. Körting assuredly exaggerates its significance when he declares it "an epoch-making deed" which would by itself substantiate Petrarch's title to be called the first modern man. The reader will observe that, however modern may have been the spirit in which the excursion was undertaken, the relapse into medieval sentiment was speedy and complete.
J. H. ROBINSON (1914)

By this narrative of the ascent of Mount Ventoux Petrarch revealed himself in the whole complexity of his personality and in the diversity of his thoughts, feelings, and interests. He was the man of a new age who set out to discover the beauty of the world and relive an experience forgotten for long centuries. He was the humanist who wanted not merely to devote himself to an antiquarian study of the arts and letters, the history and philosophy of Roman days, but who desired to revive the past in the present and for the future by re-enacting what the ancients had done. He was the Italian patriot whose inner eye beheld the unity and splendor of his native country. He was the lover of Laura who was still torn in his human feelings but was beginning to conquer himself. Yet at the end he found himself bound by the traditions of medieval Christianity in which he had been brought up and which he always revered in the person and work of his great guide, St. Augustine. Thus at the culminating point of his new experience Petrarch closed his eyes to the external world and turned to the spiritual problems of his soul.
T. E. MOMMSEN (1946)

For Petrarch, who ignores and dislikes scholastic theology but always emphasizes his religious convictions, Augustine was one of the favorite authors who ever exercised a decisive influence upon his spiritual development. . . . Thus it was the Augustine of the *Confessions,* the man who eloquently expresses his feelings and experiences, not the dogmatic theologian who impressed Petrarch and later humanists and helped them to reconcile their religious convictions with their literary tastes and personal opinions.   *P. O. KRISTELLER (1955)*

It would be a grave misapprehension to suppose that the [*Secret*] does not reflect a very real contradiction in the soul of the writer. No careful reader can fail to see in it the bitterness of a spirit at odds with itself. Indeed, its whole significance lies in the sturdy and heartfelt defence of the intrinsic virtue of the more noble temporal ambitions, especially those of a man of letters, against the deadening suggestions of monasticism.   *J. H. ROBINSON (1914)*

It is significant that in the *Secret* the dialogues between Augustine and Petrarch always end in Augustine's carrying his point. . . . Petrarch is traditionally called one of the first modern men, yet emotionally he lies closer to Augustine than to Galileo; even his subjectivism is strikingly Augustinian; and he was convinced, as many notables of the Renaissance were, that man, a guest in a strange house on this earth, has as his primary obligation the knowledge of God. . . .

HERSCHEL BAKER (1947)

"I am like a man standing between two worlds: I look both forward and backward," [Petrarch] wrote. The context makes clear that he pictured himself standing between an ancient world of light and a present one of ominous darkness. But his statement contains another meaning. He stood between two worlds, the medieval and the modern, the past and the present. He was the hinge of the door, says Whitfield. He was necessarily medieval, a part of his time, a product of his education. However, he was consciously a rebel against his time. He looked for his sanction in the great classic past of Rome; he tried to restore that past as a present lesson to the world.   *MORRIS BISHOP (1963)*

Pico della Mirandola
1463–1494

One striking feature of Renaissance humanism, which offers a sharp contrast to medieval scholasticism, is the emphasis it placed on the idea of human dignity. This idea, one of the perennial topics in the history of Western thought, has challenged men's minds in all ages to determine man's significance in the scheme of things. The opening chapters of Genesis take up the challenge, as did Homer, who was the first of a long line of ancient Greek writers—poets, playwrights, philosophers—who in one way or another were concerned with affirming the dignity of man. The development of classical civilization was based on respect for, and insistence on the necessity of, individual human achievement. No matter what forces ruled the world of man, his intellect, properly used, gave him the means to assert his dignity as a human being. Human dignity was viewed as an internal absolute, dependent on no external power.

Christian thinking, however, introduced an ambivalence into this conception of the dignity of man by denying its independence and judging man in relationship both with God and with the rest of the universe. On the one hand, Christianity stressed the importance of man by emphasizing his central position in the universe, his superiority over all other earthly beings, his creation in the image of God, his possession of an immortal soul, and the special favor shown him by the incarnation and passion of Christ. But on the other hand, Christian theology, by emphasizing the majesty of God in all His attributes and questioning the existence of human free will, tended to minimize man's importance. In other words, man appeared great in contrast with any of the material phenomena of the universe but small in contrast with God. Christian thought from its very beginnings was mindful of both contrasts but until the end of the scholastic era tended to stress the second. Nevertheless, Renaissance humanism, although Christian in belief and conscious of the majesty of God, followed the example of classical thought in emphasizing man's freedom to work out his own destiny and in prizing secular achievement in this world as an assertion of the dignity of man.

Giovanni Pico, Count of Mirandola, voiced the most eloquent expression of the characteristic attitude of Renaissance humanism toward the idea of human dignity in his *Oration on the Dignity of Man.* The youngest son of the ruler of Mirandola, a small principality in northern Italy, Pico was an energetic intellectual. By the time he was in his early twenties, he had traveled through much of France and Italy studying at various universities, establishing friendships with the outstanding humanists of the time, acquiring a thorough knowledge of the Greek and Latin classics and humanistic and scholastic thought, and becoming familiar with Hebrew and Arabic philosophy in their original languages. His intellectual ideal was to show the unity of truth by demonstrating the harmony among all philosophies, synthesizing whatever ideas seemed valid to him from various systems into a single system compatible with Christianity. As a start, when he was twenty-three years old, he published a set of nine hundred theses, philosophical and theological propositions representing the conclusions he had reached from his studies. He intended to defend his theses in an elaborate ceremony of public disputation at Rome, but it was never held because the Church condemned a number of his propositions as heretical. For the next few years Pico was embroiled in controversy with the ecclesiastical authorities. In another few years he died of a fever, leaving only some brief or fragmentary treatises in place of the ambitious philosophical works he had planned.

The two most important philosophical ideas in Pico's theses are his underlying conception of the unity of truth, on which the work as a whole is based, and his affirmation of the dignity of man. The *Oration,* intended as an introductory statement to inaugurate the public disputation and not published until after his death, presents his arguments in defense of these ideas. They were to become standard arguments in humanist thought.

Oration on the Dignity of Man

1. I have read in the records of the Arabians, reverend Fathers, that Abdala the Saracen,[1] when questioned as to what on this stage of the world, as it were, could be seen most worthy of wonder, replied: "There is nothing to be seen more wonderful than man." In agreement with this opinion is the saying of Hermes Trismegistus:[2] "A great miracle, Asclepius,[3] is man." But when I weighed the reason for these

Reprinted from *Renaissance Philosophy of Man* edited by Ernest Cassirer, P. O. Kristeller, and J. H. Randall by permission of The University of Chicago Press. © 1948 by The University of Chicago.

[1]Probably Abd Allah, the cousin of Mohammed, who lived in the late sixth and early seventh centuries A.D.
[2]The name given to the otherwise unknown author of certain Neoplatonic writings dating from the third century A.D.
[3]A speaker in one of Hermes' dialogues, after whom the dialogue is named.

maxims, the many grounds for the excellence of human nature reported by many men failed to satisfy me—that man is the intermediary between creatures, the intimate of the gods, the king of the lower beings, by the acuteness of his senses, by the discernment of his reason, and by the light of his intelligence the interpreter of nature, the interval between fixed eternity and fleeting time, and (as the Persians say) the bond, nay, rather, the marriage song of the world, on David's testimony but little lower than the angels. Admittedly great though these reasons be, they are not the principal grounds, that is, those which may rightfully claim for themselves the privilege of the highest admiration. For why should we not admire more the angels themselves and the blessed choirs of heaven? At last it seems to me I have come to understand why man is the most fortunate of creatures and consequently worthy of all admiration and what precisely is that rank which is his lot in the universal chain of Being[4]—a rank to be envied not only by brutes but even by the stars and by minds beyond this world. It is a matter past faith and a wondrous one. Why should it not be? For it is on this very account that man is rightly called and judged a great miracle and a wonderful creature indeed.

2. But hear, Fathers, exactly what this rank is and, as friendly auditors, conformably to your kindness, do me this favor. God the Father, the supreme Architect, had already built this cosmic home we behold, the most sacred temple of His godhead, by the laws of His mysterious wisdom. The region above the heavens He had adorned with Intelligences, the heavenly spheres He had quickened with eternal souls, and the excrementary and filthy parts of the lower world He had filled with a multitude of animals of every kind. But, when the work was finished, the Craftsman kept wishing that there were someone to ponder the plan of so great a work, to love its beauty, and to wonder at its vastness. Therefore, when everything was done (as Moses and Timaeus[5] bear witness), He finally took thought concerning the creation of man. But there was not among His archetypes that from which He could fashion a new offspring, nor was there in His treasure-houses anything which He might bestow on His new son as an inheritance, nor was there in the seats of all the world a place where the latter might sit to contemplate the universe. All was now complete; all things had been assigned to the highest, the middle, and the lowest orders. But in its final creation it was not the part of the Father's power to fail as though exhausted. It was not the part of His wisdom to waver in a needful matter through poverty of counsel. It was not the part of His kindly love that he who was to praise God's divine generosity in regard to others should be compelled to condemn it in regard to himself.

3. At last the best of artisans ordained that that creature to whom He had been able to give nothing proper to himself should have joint possession of whatever had been peculiar to each of the different kinds of being. He therefore took man as a creature of indeterminate

---

[4]The idea of the Great Chain of Being has influenced Western thought from Plato's time to the present day. The idea conceives of all entities in the universe as existing in hierarchical relationships, from God down to the amoeba.

[5]Pico is referring to a speaker in one of Plato's dialogues, after whom the dialogue is named.

nature and, assigning him a place in the middle of the world, addressed him thus: "Neither a fixed abode nor a form that is thine alone nor any function peculiar to thyself have we given thee, Adam, to the end that according to thy longing and according to thy judgment thou mayest have and possess what abode, what form, and what functions thou thyself shalt desire. The nature of all other beings is limited and constrained within the bounds of laws prescribed by Us. Thou, constrained by no limits, in accordance with thine own free will, in whose hand We have placed thee, shalt ordain for thyself the limits of thy nature. We have set thee at the world's center that thou mayest from thence more easily observe whatever is in the world. We have made thee neither of heaven nor of earth, neither mortal nor immortal, so that with freedom of choice and with honor, as though the maker and molder of thyself, thou mayest fashion thyself in whatever shape thou shalt prefer. Thou shalt have the power to degenerate into the lower forms of life, which are brutish. Thou shalt have the power, out of thy soul's judgment, to be reborn into the higher forms, which are divine."

4. O supreme generosity of God the Father, O highest and most marvelous felicity of man! To him it is granted to have whatever he chooses, to be whatever he wills. Beasts as soon as they are born (so says Lucilius[6]) bring with them from their mother's womb all they will ever possess. Spiritual beings, either from the beginning or soon thereafter, become what they are to be for ever and ever. On man when he came into life the Father conferred the seeds of all kinds and the germs of every way of life. Whatever seeds each man cultivates will grow to maturity and bear in him their own fruit. If they be vegetative, he will be like a plant. If sensitive, he will become brutish. If rational, he will grow into a heavenly being. If intellectual, he will be an angel and the son of God. And if, happy in the lot of no created thing, he withdraws into the center of his own unity, his spirit, made one with God, in the solitary darkness of God, who is set above all things, shall surpass them all. Who would not admire this our chameleon? Or who could more greatly admire aught else whatever? It is man who Asclepius of Athens, arguing from his mutability of character and from his self-transforming nature, on just grounds says was symbolized by Proteus[7] in the mysteries. Hence those metamorphoses renowned among the Hebrews and the Pythagoreans.

5. For the occult theology of the Hebrews sometimes transforms the holy Enoch into an angel of divinity whom they call "Mal'akh Adonay Shebaoth," and sometimes transforms others into other divinities. The Pythagoreans degrade impious men into brutes and, if one is to believe Empedocles,[8] even into plants. Mohammed,[9] in imitation, often had this saying on his tongue: "They who have deviated from divine law become beasts," and surely he spoke justly. For it is not the bark that makes the plant but its senseless and insentient nature; neither is it the hide that

---

[6]Roman satirical poet of the second century B.C.

[7]In Greek mythology, Proteus is "the old man of the sea" who knows all things and has tne power of assuming different shapes.

[8]Greek philosopher of the fifth century B.C.

[9]Arabian prophet and founder of the Mohammedan religion (570?—632 A.D.).

makes the beast of burden but its irrational, sensitive soul; neither is it the orbed form that makes the heavens but their undeviating order; nor is it the sundering from body but his spiritual intelligence that makes the angel. For if you see one abandoned to his appetites crawling on the ground, it is a plant and not a man you see; if you see one blinded by the vain illusions of imagery, as it were of Calypso,[10] and, softened by their gnawing allurement, delivered over to his senses, it is a beast and not a man you see. If you see a philosopher determining all things by means of right reason, him you shall reverence: he is a heavenly being and not of this earth. If you see a pure contemplator, one unaware of the body and confined to the inner reaches of the mind, he is neither an earthly nor a heavenly being; he is a more reverend divinity vested with human flesh.

6. Are there any who would not admire man, who is, in the sacred writings of Moses and the Christians, not without reason described sometimes by the name of "all flesh," sometimes by that of "every creature," inasmuch as he himself molds, fashions, and changes himself into the form of all flesh and into the character of every creature? For this reason the Persian Euanthes, in describing the Chaldaean theology, writes that man has no semblance that is inborn and his very own but many that are external and foreign to him; whence this saying of the Chaldaeans: "Hanorish tharah sharinas," that is, "Man is a being of varied, manifold, and inconstant nature." But why do we emphasize this? To the end that after we have been born to this condition—that we can become what we will—we should understand that we ought to have especial care to this, that it should never be said against us that, although born to a privileged position, we failed to recognize it and became like unto wild animals and senseless beasts of burden, but that rather the saying of Asaph the prophet should apply: "Ye are all angels and sons of the Most High," and that we may not, by abusing the most indulgent generosity of the Father, make for ourselves that freedom of choice He has given into something harmful instead of salutary. Let a certain holy ambition invade our souls, so that, not content with the mediocre, we shall pant after the highest and (since we may if we wish) toil with all our strength to obtain it.

7. Let us disdain earthly things, despise heavenly things, and, finally, esteeming less whatever is of the world, hasten to that court which is beyond the world and nearest to the Godhead. There, as the sacred mysteries relate, Seraphim, Cherubim, and Thrones[11] hold the first places; let us, incapable of yielding to them, and intolerant of a lower place, emulate their dignity and their glory. If we have willed it, we shall be second to them in nothing.

11. If this is what we must practice in our aspiration to the angelic way of life, I ask: "Who will touch the ladder of the Lord either with

---

[10]Pico seems to have Calypso confused with Circe. Both were immortal women inhabiting solitary islands who, according to Homer, kept Odysseus with them for a time. But it was Circe who gave men enchanted banquets to turn them into beasts. Calypso simply offered Odysseus a pleasant place to live, promising to make him immortal if he stayed with her.

[11]Medieval Christian thought conceived of a precise hierarchy of angels in nine different orders. Seraphim, Cherubim, and Thrones are the highest three orders. The specific hierarchy seems to have been originated by Pseudo-Dionysius.

fouled foot or with unclean hands?" As the sacred mysteries have it, it is impious for the impure to touch the pure. But what are these feet? What these hands? Surely the foot of the soul is that most contemptible part by which the soul rests on matter as on the soil of the earth, I mean the nourishing and feeding power, the tinder of lust, and the teacher of pleasurable weakness. Why should we not call the hands of the soul its irascible power, which struggles on its behalf as the champion of desire and as plunderer seizes in the dust and sun what desire will devour slumbering in the shade? These hands, these feet, that is, all the sentient part whereon resides the attraction of the body which, as they say, by wrenching the neck holds the soul in check, lest we be hurled down from the ladder as impious and unclean, let us bathe in moral philosophy as if in a living river. Yet this will not be enough if we wish to be companions of the angels going up and down on Jacob's ladder, unless we have first been well fitted and instructed to be promoted duly from step to step, to stray nowhere from the stairway, and to engage in the alternate comings and goings. Once we have achieved this by the art of discourse or reasoning, then, inspired by the Cherubic spirit,[12] using philosophy through the steps of the ladder, that is, of nature, and penetrating all things from center to center, we shall sometimes descend, with titanic force rending the unity like Osiris into many parts, and we shall sometimes ascend, with the force of Phoebus collecting the parts like the limbs of Osiris into a unity,[13] until, resting at last in the bosom of the Father who is above the ladder, we shall be made perfect with the felicity of theology.

12. Let us also inquire of the just Job, who entered into a life-covenant with God before he himself was brought forth into life, what the most high God requires above all in those tens of hundreds of thousands who attend him. He will answer that it is peace, in accord with what we read in him: "He maketh peace in his high places." And since the middle order expounds to the lower orders the counsel of the highest order, let Empedocles the philosopher expound to us the words of Job the theologian. He indicates to us a twofold nature present in our souls, by one side of which we are raised on high to the heavenly regions, and by the other side plunged downward into the lower, through strife and friendship or through war and peace, as he witnesses in the verses in which he makes complaint that he is being driven into the sea, himself goaded by strife and discord into the semblance of a madman and a fugitive from the gods.

13. Surely, Fathers, there is in us a discord many times as great; we have at hand wars grievous and more than civil, wars of the spirit which, if we dislike them, if we aspire to that peace which may so raise us to the sublime that we shall be established among the exalted of the Lord, only philosophy will entirely allay and subdue in us. In the first

---

[12]Elsewhere, Pico says that the Cherubim "glow with the splendor of intelligence." He uses them to symbolize the contemplative spirit in man.

[13]Pico mingles elements from both Greek and Egyptian mythology in this passage. In Greek mythology the Titans were giants of enormous strength whom Zeus had to overcome before he could become ruler of the gods. Osiris was the chief Egyptian god, who, according to legend, was murdered by his jealous brother, who cut up and scattered his corpse in fourteen parts. These were found and pieced together by Osiris' wife, Isis. Phoebus Apollo is the Greco-Roman god of the sun, who also symbolizes intellectual inspiration.

place, if our man but ask a truce of his enemies, moral philosophy will check the unbridled inroads of the many-sided beast and the leonine passions of wrath and violence. If we then take wiser counsel with ourselves and learn to desire the security of everlasting peace, it will be at hand and will generously fulfil our prayers. After both beasts are felled like a sacrificed sow, it will confirm an inviolable compact of holiest peace between flesh and spirit. Dialectic will appease the tumults of reason made confused and anxious by inconsistencies of statement and sophisms of syllogisms. Natural philosophy will allay the strife and differences of opinion which vex, distract, and wound the spirit from all sides. But she will so assuage them as to compel us to remember that, according to Heraclitus, nature was begotten from war, that it was on this account repeatedly called "strife" by Homer, and that it is not, therefore, in the power of natural philosophy to give us in nature a true quiet and unshaken peace but that this is the function and privilege of her mistress, that is, of holiest theology. She will show us the way and as comrade lead us to her who, seeing us hastening from afar, will exclaim "Come to me, ye who have labored. Come and I will restore you. Come to me, and I will give you peace, which the world and nature cannot give you."

14. When we have been so soothingly called, so kindly urged, we shall fly up with winged feet, like earthly Mercuries,[14] to the embraces of our blessed mother and enjoy that wished-for peace, most holy peace, indivisible bond, of one accord in the friendship through which all rational souls not only shall come into harmony in the one mind which is above all minds but shall in some ineffable way become altogether one. This is that friendship which the Pythagoreans say is the end of all philosophy. This is that peace which God creates in his heavens, which the angels descending to earth proclaimed to men of good will, that through it men might ascend to heaven and become angels. Let us wish this peace for our friends, for our century. Let us wish it for every home into which we go; let us wish it for our own soul, that through it she shall herself be made the house of God, and to the end that as soon as she has cast out her uncleanness through moral philosophy and dialectic, adorned herself with manifold philosophy as with the splendor of a courtier, and crowned the pediments of her doors with the garlands of theology, the King of Glory may descend and, coming with his Father, make his stay with her. If she show herself worthy of so great a guest, she shall, by the boundless mercy which is his, in golden raiment like a wedding gown, and surrounded by a varied throng of sciences, receive her beautiful guest not merely as a guest but as a spouse from whom she will never be parted. She will desire rather to be parted from her own people and, forgetting her father's house and herself, will desire to die in herself in order to live in her spouse, in whose sight surely the death of his saints is precious—death, I say, if we must call death that fulness of life, the consideration of which wise men have asserted to be the aim of philosophy.

---

[14]In Greco-Roman mythology, Mercury was a god distinguished for his speed who often served as the messenger of Zeus or Jupiter.

15. Let us also cite Moses himself, but little removed from the spring-ing abundance of the holy and unspeakable wisdom by whose nectar the angels are made drunk. Let us hearken to the venerable judge in these words proclaiming laws to us who are dwellers in the desert loneliness of this body: "Let those who, as yet unclean, still need moral philosophy, live with the people outside the tabernacle under the sky, meanwhile purifying themselves like the priests of Thessaly. Let those who have already ordered their conduct be received into the sanctuary but not quite yet touch the holy vessels; let them first like zealous Levites in the service of dialectic minister to the holy things of philos-ophy. Then when they have been admitted even to these, let them now behold the many-colored robe of the higher palace of the Lord, that is to say, the stars; let them now behold the heavenly candlestick divided into seven lights; let them now behold the fur tent, that is, the elements, in the priesthood of philosophy, so that when they are in the end, through the favor of theological sublimity, granted entrance into the inner part of the temple, they may rejoice in the glory of the Godhead with no veil before his image." This of a surety Moses commands us and, in commanding, summons, urges, and encourages us by means of philosophy to prepare ourselves a way, while we can, to the heavenly glory to come.

16. But indeed not only the Mosaic and Christian mysteries but also the theology of the ancients show us the benefits and value of the liberal arts, the discussion of which I am about to undertake. For what else did the degrees of the initiates observed in the mysteries of the Greeks mean? For they arrived at a perception of the mysteries when they had first been purified through those expiatory sciences, as it were, moral philosophy and dialectic. What else can that perception possibly be than an interpretation of occult nature by means of philosophy? Then at length to those who were so disposed came that *epopteia*,[15] that is to say, the observation of things divine by the light of theology. Who would not long to be initiated into such sacred rites? Who would not desire, by neglecting all human concerns, by despising the goods of fortune, and by disregarding those of the body, to become the guest of the gods while yet living on earth, and, made drunk by the nectar of eternity, to be endowed with the gifts of immortality though still a mortal being? Who would not wish to be so inflamed with those Socratic frenzies sung by Plato in the *Phaedrus,* that, by the oarage of feet and wings escaping speedily from hence, that is, from a world set on evil, he might be borne on the fastest of courses to the heavenly Jerusalem? Let us be driven, Fathers, let us be driven by the frenzies of Socrates, that they may so throw us into ecstasy as to put our mind and ourselves in God. Let us be driven by them, if we have first done what is in our power. For if through moral philosophy the forces of our passions have by a fitting agreement become so intent on harmony that they can sing together in undisturbed concord, and if through dialectic our reason has moved progressively in a rhythmical measure, then we shall be stirred by the frenzy of the Muses and drink the heavenly har-

---

[15]Initiation in the Eleusinian mysteries, one of the most important ancient Greek religious festivals.

mony with our inmost hearing. Thereupon Bacchus,[16] the leader of the Muses, by showing in his mysteries, that is, in the visible signs of nature, the invisible things of God to us who study philosophy, will intoxicate us with the fulness of God's house, in which, if we prove faithful, like Moses, hallowed theology shall come and inspire us with a doubled frenzy. For, exalted to her lofty height, we shall measure therefrom all things that are and shall be and have been in indivisible eternity; and, admiring their original beauty, like the seers of Phoebus, we shall become her own winged lovers. And at last, roused by ineffable love as by a sting, like burning Seraphim rapt from ourselves, full of divine power we shall no longer be ourselves but shall become He Himself Who made us.

17. If anyone investigates the holy names of Apollo, their meanings and hidden mysteries, these amply show that that god is no less a philosopher than a seer; but, since Ammonius[17] has sufficiently examined this subject there is no reason why I should now treat it otherwise. But, Fathers, three Delphic precepts may suggest themselves to your minds, which are very necessary to those who are to go into the most sacred and revered temple, not of the false but of the true Apollo, who lights every soul as it enters this world. You will see that they give us no other advice than that we should with all our strength embrace this threefold philosophy which is the concern of our present debate. For the saying *meden agan,* that is, "Nothing too much," prescribes a standard and rule for all the virtues through the doctrine of the Mean, with which moral philosophy duly deals. Then the saying *gnothi seauton,* that is, "Know thyself," urges and encourages us to the investigation of all nature, of which the nature of man is both the connecting link and, so to speak, the "mixed bowl." For he who knows himself in himself knows all things, as Zoroaster[18] first wrote, and then Plato in his *Alcibiades.* When we are finally lighted in this knowledge by natural philosophy, and nearest to God are uttering the theological greeting, *ei,* that is, "Thou art," we shall likewise in bliss be addressing the true Apollo on intimate terms.

Comments / on Pico

[W]e shall show how differences of birth had lost their significance in Italy. Much of this was doubtless owing to the fact that men and mankind were

---

[16]In Greco-Roman mythology, the Muses were nine sister goddesses presiding over literature and the arts. Bacchus was the god of luxuriant fertility, and hence the god of wine; he also presided over the effects of wine, conviviality, and the urge for music and poetry.

[17]Christian philosopher who lived in Alexandria, Egypt, during the third century.

[18]Founder of the religion of the ancient Persian peoples (628?–551? B.C.).

here first thoroughly and profoundly understood. This one single result of the Renaissance is enough to fill us with thankfulness. The logical notion of humanity was old enough—but here the notion became a fact. The loftiest conceptions on this subject were uttered by Pico della Mirandola in his speech on the dignity of man, which may justly be called one of the noblest of that great age.   *JACOB BURCKHARDT (1860)*

And yet to read a page of one of Pico's forgotten books is like a glance into one of those sepulchers, upon which the wanderer in classical lands has sometimes stumbled, with the old disused ornaments and furniture of a world wholly unlike ours and still fresh in them. That whole conception of nature is so different from our own. For Pico, the world is a limited place, bounded by actual crystal walls, and a material firmament; it is like a painted toy. . . . How different from this childish dream is our own conception of nature, with its unlimited space, its innumerable suns, and the earth but a mote in the beam; how different the strange new awe and superstition with which it fills our minds! . . . [Pico] wins one on, in spite of oneself, to turn again to the pages of his forgotten books, although we know already that the actual solution proposed in them will satisfy us as little as perhaps it satisfied him.

WALTER PATER (1873)

The early Italian Humanists were primarily concerned not with philosophical speculation but rather with the development of a culture and educational ideal that was based on the study and imitation of classical antiquity. Yet when they were driven to justify that ideal and the significance of their classical studies, they claimed that these studies contribute to the formation of a desirable human being and are hence of particular concern for man as man. . . . When Pico, and Ficino before him, worked out a philosophical theory of the dignity of man in the universe, they were merely giving a more systematic and speculative development to a vague idea that had dominated the thought and aspirations of their Humanist predecessors for several generations.   *P. O. KRISTELLER (1948)*

Niccolò Machiavelli

1469—1527

An almost inevitable consequence of Renaissance humanism was the tendency to look at the circumstances of human life objectively, to see them as determined by the realities of men's relationships with each other rather than as part of a world in which every object and institution had some meaning in terms of God's design for the universe. In political theory, this difference between medieval and Renaissance thinking is particularly striking. The fundamental assumption underlying medieval political thought, typified in a work like Dante's *On World Government,* was that earthly kings held their authority by divine sanction. Political theorists were concerned with the ethical functions and theological implications of kingship, often considering the subject of how a ruler might best be educated to inculcate in him those moral, judicial, and intellectual qualities that would make him a fit representative of God on earth. The theoretical conceptions of kingship, however, were often far removed from reality. Most medieval rulers were more concerned with what was expedient rather than with what was right. Although they acknowledged the moral and religious ideas of kingship in principle, since these served as one source of their authority, in practice most successful rulers had mastered the actual exercise of power. In the Renaissance, political thought began to suit theory to practice, to formulate the principles of political authority on the basis of the actualities of political power.

Niccolò Machiavelli was largely responsible for this change. Often regarded as the founder of modern political science, he was the first man in western Europe to attempt, in *The Prince,* to present a realistic appraisal of how to obtain, use, and retain political power. His main interest in life was practical politics. Born of an established Florentine family and provided with a sound humanistic education, he entered government service in the Republic of Florence as a young man. For almost fifteen years he held the post of what might today be called Secretary for Foreign Affairs, distinguishing himself as an effective statesman with a firm grasp of the realities of contemporary politics. In 1512, when the government of Florence was restored to the Medici, who had been deposed as rulers in 1494, Machiavelli was deprived of office, imprisoned for a time, and then exiled for a year from the city to his country estate. There he devoted himself to humanistic studies and writing, hoping through his books on government to convince the Medici that he would be of value in their service. But although he later performed a number of minor political duties for Florence, he never again held a post of any real importance.

Machiavelli's writings include some comedies modeled on the classical Roman pattern, a treatise on the art of war, a history of Florence commissioned by the government in 1520, and, as his major work, the *Discourses on Livy,* an extensive exposition of his political theories in the form of a commentary on the first-century Roman historian. He planned the *Discourses* in ten books but finished only three, beginning it when he first went into exile and working on it intermittently thereafter. Apparently his work on the *Discourses* gave him the idea of composing a brief treatise on practical politics that might influence the Medici in his favor. The result was *The Prince,* written in 1513 and at once widely circulated in manuscript, even though it was not published until five years after Machiavelli's death. In one sense, then, *The Prince* can be considered a chapter out of the *Discourses,* and in theory, anyhow, no complete understanding of Machiavelli's political thought is possible without reading both works. In practice, however, Machiavelli's ideas have generally been judged by, and his reputation based on, *The Prince* alone.

For centuries critics have argued whether Machiavelli intended *The Prince* to have universal application or designed it as a specific remedy for the particular problems of contemporary Italian politics. There is no question that the situation in Italy did inspire the writing of the book. By the early sixteenth century, both France and Spain had developed strong centralized monarchies, which claimed certain historic territorial rights in Italy. In Italy itself, power was fragmented among five major forces —based in Florence, Milan, Naples, Venice, and Rome, which the papacy used as the base of its strength—and among a great number of smaller principalities, some allied with or controlled by one of the main five and some trying to maintain an independent political existence. These entities were continually beset by internal power struggles, with regimes regularly being overturned; they were continually at odds with one another, with alliances regularly being shifted; and France and Spain were continually capitalizing on these internal dissensions to extend their possessions and authority in Italy. It is this kind of world that stands in the background of Machiavelli's *Prince.*

The Prince

To The Magnificent Lorenzo di Piero de' Medici

Those who strive to obtain the good graces of a prince are accustomed to come before him with such things as they hold most precious, or in which they see him take most delight: whence one often sees horses, arms, cloth of gold, precious stones, and similar ornaments presented to princes, worthy of their greatness.

Desiring therefore to present myself to Your Magnificence with some testimony of my devotion towards you, I have not found among my possessions anything which I hold more dear than, or value so much as, the knowledge of the actions of great men, acquired by long experience in contemporary affairs, and a continual study of antiquity; which, having reflected upon it with great and prolonged diligence, I now send, digested into a little volume, to your Magnificence.

And although I may consider this work unworthy of your countenance, nevertheless I trust much to your benignity that it may be acceptable, seeing that it is not possible for me to make a better gift than to offer you the opportunity of understanding in the shortest time all that I have learnt in so many years, and with so many troubles and dangers; —which work I have not embellished with swelling or magnificent words, nor stuffed with rounded periods, nor with any extrinsic allurements or adornments whatever, with which so many are accustomed to load and embellish their works; for I have wished either that no honour should be given it, or else that the truth of the matter and the weightiness of the theme shall make it acceptable.

Nor do I hold with those who regard it as presumption if a man of low and humble condition dare to discuss and settle the concerns of princes; because, just as those who draw landscapes place themselves below in the plain to contemplate the nature of the mountains and of lofty places, and in order to contemplate the plains place themselves high upon the mountains, even so to understand the nature of the people it needs to be a prince, and to understand that of princes it needs to be of the people.

Take then, your Magnificence, this little gift in the spirit in which I send it; wherein, if it be diligently read and considered by you, you will learn my extreme desire that you should attain that greatness which fortune and your other attributes promise. And if your Magnificence from the summit of your greatness will sometimes turn your eyes to these lower regions, you will see how unmeritedly I suffer a great and continued malignity of fortune.

From *The Prince* by Niccolo Machiavelli. Translated by W. K. Marriott. Everyman's Library Edition. Reprinted by permission of E. P. Dutton & Co., Inc. and J. M. Dent & Sons Ltd.

Chapter 3

Concerning Mixed Principalities

But the difficulties occur in a new principality. And firstly, if it be not entirely new, but is, as it were, a member of a state which, taken collectively, may be called composite, the changes arise chiefly from an inherent difficulty which there is in all new principalities; for men change their rulers willingly, hoping to better themselves, and this hope induces them to take up arms against him who rules: wherein they are deceived, because they afterwards find by experience they have gone from bad to worse. This follows also on another natural and common necessity, which always causes a new prince to burthen those who have submitted to him with his soldiery and with infinite other hardships which he must put upon his new acquisition.

In this way you have enemies in all those whom you have injured in seizing that principality, and you are not able to keep those friends who put you there because of your not being able to satisfy them in the way they expected, and you cannot take strong measures against them, feeling bound to them. For, although one may be very strong in armed forces, yet in entering a province one has always need of the goodwill of the natives.

For these reasons Louis the Twelfth, King of France,[1] quickly occupied Milan, and as quickly lost it; and to turn him out the first time it only needed Lodovico's[2] own forces; because those who had opened the gates to him, finding themselves deceived in their hopes of future benefit, would not endure the ill-treatment of the new prince. It is very true that, after acquiring rebellious provinces a second time, they are not so lightly lost afterwards, because the prince, with little reluctance, takes the opportunity of the rebellion to punish the delinquents, to clear out the suspects, and to strengthen himself in the weakest places. Thus to cause France to lose Milan the first time it was enough for the Duke Lodovico to raise insurrections on the borders; but to cause him to lose it a second time it was necessary to bring the whole world against him, and that his armies should be defeated and driven out of Italy; which followed from the causes above mentioned.

Nevertheless Milan was taken from France both the first and the second time. The general reasons for the first have been discussed; it remains to name those for the second, and to see what resources he had, and what any one in his situation would have had for maintaining himself more securely in his acquisition than did the King of France.

Now I say that those dominions which, when acquired, are added to an ancient state by him who acquires them, are either of the same country and language, or they are not. When they are, it is easier to hold them, especially when they have not been accustomed to self-government; and to hold them securely it is enough to have destroyed the family

---

[1]Reigned 1498—1515.

[2]Ludovico Sforza, Duke of Milan from 1494 to 1500. The events described by Machiavelli in this paragraph began in 1499 and continued for the next few years.

of the prince who was ruling them; because the two peoples, preserving in other things the old conditions, and not being unlike in customs, will live quietly together, as one has seen in Brittany, Burgundy, Gascony, and Normandy, which have been bound to France for so long a time: and, although there may be some difference in language, nevertheless the customs are alike, and the people will easily be able to get on amongst themselves. He who has annexed them, if he wishes to hold them, has only to bear in mind two considerations: the one, that the family of their former lord is extinguished; the other, that neither their laws nor their taxes are altered, so that in a very short time they will become entirely one body with the old principality.

But when states are acquired in a country differing in language, customs, or laws, there are difficulties, and good fortune and great energy are needed to hold them, and one of the greatest and most real helps would be that he who has acquired them should go and reside there. This would make his position more secure and durable, as it has made that of the Turk in Greece,[3] who, notwithstanding all the other measures taken by him for holding that state, if he had not settled there, would not have been able to keep it. Because, if one is on the spot, disorders are seen as they spring up, and one can quickly remedy them; but if one is not at hand, they are heard of only when they are great, and then one can no longer remedy them. Besides this, the country is not pillaged by your officials; the subjects are satisfied by prompt recourse to the prince; thus, wishing to be good, they have more cause to love him, and wishing to be otherwise, to fear him. He who would attack that state from the outside must have the utmost caution; as long as the prince resides there it can only be wrested from him with the greatest difficulty.

The other and better course is to send colonies to one or two places, which may be as keys to that state, for it is necessary either to do this or else to keep there a great number of cavalry and infantry. A prince does not spend much on colonies, for with little or no expense he can send them out and keep them there, and he offends a minority only of the citizens from whom he takes lands and houses to give them to the new inhabitants; and those whom he offends, remaining poor and scattered, are never able to injure him; whilst the rest being uninjured are easily kept quiet, and at the same time are anxious not to err for fear it should happen to them as it has to those who have been despoiled. In conclusion, I say that these colonies are not costly, they are more faithful, they injure less, and the injured, as has been said, being poor and scattered, cannot hurt. Upon this one has to remark that men ought either to be well treated or crushed, because they can avenge themselves of lighter injuries, of more serious ones they cannot; therefore the injury that is to be done to a man ought to be of such a kind that one does not stand in fear of revenge.

But in maintaining armed men there in place of colonies one spends much more, having to consume on the garrison all the income from the state, so that the acquisition turns into a loss, and many more are ex-

---

[3]The Turks had conquered Greece in the fourteenth century and were to rule over it until the twentieth.

asperated, because the whole state is injured; through the shifting of the garrison up and down all become acquainted with hardship, and all become hostile, and they are enemies who, whilst beaten on their own ground, are yet able to do hurt. For every reason, therefore, such guards are as useless as a colony is useful.

Again, the prince who holds a country differing in the above respects ought to make himself the head and defender of his less powerful neighbours, and to weaken the more powerful amongst them, taking care that no foreigner as powerful as himself shall, by any accident, get a footing there; for it will always happen that such a one will be introduced by those who are discontented, either through excess of ambition or through fear, as one has seen already. The Romans were brought into Greece by the Ætolians; and in every other country where they obtained a footing they were brought in by the inhabitants. And the usual course of affairs is that, as soon as a powerful foreigner enters a country, all the subject states are drawn to him, moved by the hatred which they feel against the ruling power. So that in respect to these subject states he has not to take any trouble to gain them over to himself, for the whole of them quickly rally to the state which he has acquired there. He has only to take care that they do not get hold of too much power and too much authority, and then with his own forces, and with their goodwill, he can easily keep down the more powerful of them, so as to remain entirely master in the country. And he who does not properly manage this business will soon lose what he has acquired, and whilst he does hold it he will have endless difficulties and troubles.

The Romans, in the countries which they annexed, observed closely these measures; they sent colonies and maintained friendly relations with the minor powers, without increasing their strength; they kept down the greater, and did not allow any strong foreign powers to gain authority. Greece appears to me sufficient for an example. The Achaians and Ætolians were kept friendly by them, the kingdom of Macedonia was humbled, Antiochus[4] was driven out; yet the merits of the Achaians and Ætolians never secured for them permission to increase their power, nor did the persuasions of Philip[5] ever induce the Romans to be his friends without first humbling him, nor did the influence of Antiochus make them agree that he should retain any lordship over the country. Because the Romans did in these instances what all prudent princes ought to do, who have to regard not only present troubles, but also future ones, for which they must prepare with every energy, because, when foreseen, it is easy to remedy them; but if you wait until they approach, the medicine is no longer in time because the malady has become incurable; for it happens in this, as the physicians say it happens in hectic fever, that in the beginning of the malady it is easy to cure but difficult to detect, but in the course of time, not having been either detected nor treated in the beginning, it becomes easy to detect but difficult to cure. Thus it happens in affairs of state, for when the evils

---

[4]Antiochus III (242–187 B.C.), King of Syria who had extended his domain through much of Asia Minor and then attempted to conquer Greece until repulsed by the Romans.

[5]Philip V (237–179 B.C.), King of Macedonia and ostensible ruler of Greece until forced by the Romans to renounce his sovereignty over Greece.

that arise have been foreseen (which it is only given to a wise man to see), they can be quickly redressed, but when, through not having been foreseen, they have been permitted to grow in a way that every one can see them, there is no longer a remedy. Therefore. the Romans, foreseeing troubles, dealt with them at once, and, even to avoid a war, would not let them come to a head, for they knew that war is not to be avoided, but is only put off to the advantage of others; moreover they wished to fight with Philip and Antiochus in Greece so as not to have to do it in Italy; they could have avoided both, but this they did not wish; nor did that ever please them which is for ever in the mouths of the wise ones of our time:—Let us enjoy the benefits of the time —but rather the benefits of their own valour and prudence, for time drives everything before it, and is able to bring with it good as well as evil, and evil as well as good.

But let us turn to France and inquire whether she has done any of the things mentioned. I will speak of Louis (and not of Charles[6]) as the one whose conduct is the better to be observed, he having held possession of Italy for the longest period; and you will see that he has done the opposite to those things which ought to be done to retain a state composed of divers elements.

King Louis was brought into Italy by the ambition of the Venetians, who desired to obtain half the state of Lombardy by his intervention. I will not blame the course taken by the king, because, wishing to get a foot-hold in Italy, and having no friends there—seeing rather that every door was shut to him owing to the conduct of Charles—he was forced to accept those friendships which he could get, and he would have succeeded very quickly in his design if in other matters he had not made some mistakes. The king, however, having acquired Lombardy, regained at once the authority which Charles had lost: Genoa yielded; the Florentines became his friends; the Marquis of Mantua, the Duke of Ferrara, the Bentivogli, my lady of Forli, the Lords of Faenza, of Pesaro, of Rimini, of Camerino, of Piombino, the Lucchese, the Pisanians, the Sienese—everybody made advances to him to become his friend. Then could the Venetians realise the rashness of the course taken by them, which, in order that they might secure two towns in Lombardy, had made the king master of two-thirds of Italy.

Let any one now consider with what little difficulty the king could have maintained his position in Italy had he observed the rules above laid down, and kept all his friends secure and protected; for although they were numerous they were both weak and timid, some afraid of the Church, some of the Venetians, and thus they would always have been forced to stand in with him, and by their means he could easily have made himself secure against those who remained powerful. But he was no sooner in Milan than he did the contrary by assisting Pope Alexander[7] to occupy the Romagna. It never occurred to him that by this action he was weakening himself, depriving himself of friends and of those

[6]Charles VIII (1470–1498), who had preceded his cousin Louis XII as king of France.

[7]Roderigo Borgia (1431–1503), who became Pope Alexander VI in 1492. He used the resources of the papacy to extend both the temporal power of the Church in Italy and the fortunes and possessions of his own family, notably by helping his son Cesare establish dominion in central Italy.

who had thrown themselves into his lap, whilst he aggrandised the Church by adding much temporal power to the spiritual, thus giving it great authority. And having committed this prime error, he was obliged to follow it up, so much so that, to put an end to the ambition of Alexander, and to prevent his becoming the master of Tuscany, he was himself forced to come into Italy.

And as if it were not enough to have aggrandised the Church, and deprived himself of friends, he, wishing to have the kingdom of Naples, divides it with the King of Spain, and where he was the prime arbiter of Italy he takes an associate so that the ambitious of that country and the malcontents of his own should have where to shelter; and where-as he could have left in the kingdom his own pensioner as king, he drove him out, to put one there who was able to drive him, Louis, out in turn.

The wish to acquire is in truth very natural and common, and men al-ways do so when they can, and for this they will be praised not blamed; but when they cannot do so, yet wish to do so by any means, then there is folly and blame. Therefore, if France could have attacked Naples with her own forces she ought to have done so; if she could not, then she ought not to have divided it. And if the partition which she made with the Venetians in Lombardy was justified by the excuse that by it she got a foot-hold in Italy, this other partition merited blame, for it had not the excuse of that necessity.

Therefore Louis made these five errors: he destroyed the minor powers, he increased the strength of one of the greater powers in Italy, he brought in a foreign power, he did not settle in the country, he did not send colonies. Which errors, if he had lived, were not enough to injure him had he not made a sixth by taking away their dominions from the Venetians; because, had he not aggrandised the Church, nor brought Spain into Italy, it would have been very reasonable and neces-sary to humble them; but having first taken these steps, he ought never to have consented to their ruin, for they, being powerful, would always have kept off others from designs on Lombardy, to which the Venetians would never have consented except to become masters themselves there; also because the others would not wish to take Lombardy from France in order to give it to the Venetians, and to run counter to both they would not have had the courage.

And if any one should say: King Louis yielded the Romagna to Alex-ander and the kingdom to Spain to avoid war, I answer for the reasons given above that a blunder ought never to be perpetrated to avoid war, because it is not to be avoided, but is only deferred to your dis-advantage. And if another should allege the pledge which the king had given to the Pope that he would assist him in the enterprise in exchange for the dissolution of his marriage and for the cap to Rouen,[8] to that I reply what I shall write later on concerning the faith of princes, and how it ought to be kept.

Thus King Louis lost Lombardy by not having followed any of the

---

[8]Georges d'Amboise (1460-1510), Archbishop of Rouen and adviser and minister to Louis XII; made a cardinal (given the "cap") by Pope Alexander.

conditions observed by those who have taken possession of countries and wished to retain them. Nor is there any miracle in this, but much that is reasonable and quite natural. And on these matters I spoke at Nantes with Rouen, when Valentino, as Cesare Borgia, the son of Pope Alexander, was usually called, occupied the Romagna, and on Cardinal Rouen observing to me that the Italians did not understand war, I replied to him that the French did not understand statecraft, meaning that otherwise they would not have allowed the Church to reach such greatness. And in fact it has been seen that the greatness of the Church and of Spain in Italy has been caused by France, and her ruin may be attributed to them. From this a general rule is drawn which never or rarely fails: that he who is the cause of another becoming powerful is ruined; because that predominancy has been brought about either by astuteness or else by force, and both are distrusted by him who has been raised to power.

Chapter 6

Concerning New Principalities Which Are Acquired by One's Own Arms and Ability

Let no one be surprised if, in speaking of entirely new principalities as I shall do, I adduce the highest examples both of prince and of state; because men, walking almost always in paths beaten by others, and following by imitation their deeds, are yet unable to keep entirely to the ways of others or attain to the power of those they imitate. A wise man ought always to follow the paths beaten by great men, and to imitate those who have been supreme, so that if his ability does not equal theirs, at least it will savour of it. Let him act like the clever archers who, designing to hit the mark which yet appears too far distant, and knowing the limits to which the strength of their bow attains, take aim much higher than the mark, not to reach by their strength or arrow to so great a height, but to be able with the aid of so high an aim to hit the mark they wish to reach.

I say, therefore, that in entirely new principalities, where there is a new prince, more or less difficulty is found in keeping them, accordingly as there is more or less ability in him who has acquired the state. Now, as the fact of becoming a prince from a private station presupposes either ability or fortune, it is clear that one or other of these two things will mitigate in some degree many difficulties. Nevertheless, he who has relied least on fortune is established the strongest. Further, it facilitates matters when the prince, having no other state, is compelled to reside there in person.

But to come to those who, by their own ability and not through fortune, have risen to be princes, I say that Moses, Cyrus, Romulus, Theseus,[9] and such like are the most excellent examples. And although

---

[9] Cyrus (600?–529 B.C.), founder of the Persian Empire. Romulus, legendary founder of Rome in the eighth century B.C. Theseus, legendary king of Athens who was supposed to have unified the scattered Greek communities into a single state.

one may not discuss Moses, he having been a mere executor of the will of God, yet he ought to be admired, if only for that favour which made him worthy to speak with God. But in considering Cyrus and others who have acquired or founded kingdoms, all will be found admirable; and if their particular deeds and conduct shall be considered, they will not be found inferior to those of Moses, although he had so great a preceptor. And in examining their actions and lives one cannot see that they owed anything to fortune beyond opportunity, which brought them the material to mould into the form which seemed best to them. Without that opportunity their powers of mind would have been extinguished, and without those powers the opportunity would have come in vain.

It was necessary, therefore, to Moses that he should find the people of Israel in Egypt enslaved and oppressed by the Egyptians, in order that they should be disposed to follow him so as to be delivered out of bondage. It was necessary that Romulus should not remain in Alba, and that he should be abandoned at his birth, in order that he should become King of Rome and founder of the fatherland. It was necessary that Cyrus should find the Persians discontented with the government of the Medes, and the Medes soft and effeminate through their long peace. Theseus could not have shown his ability had he not found the Athenians dispersed. These opportunities, therefore, made those men fortunate, and their high ability enabled them to recognise the opportunity whereby their country was ennobled and made famous.

Those who by valorous ways become princes, like these men, acquire a principality with difficulty, but they keep it with ease. The difficulties they have in acquiring it arise in part from the new rules and methods which they are forced to introduce to establish their government and its security. And it ought to be remembered that there is nothing more difficult to take in hand, more perilous to conduct, or more uncertain in its success, than to take the lead in the introduction of a new order of things. Because the innovator has for enemies all those who have done well under the old conditions, and lukewarm defenders in those who may do well under the new. This coolness arises partly from fear of the opponents, who have the laws on their side, and partly from the incredulity of men, who do not readily believe in new things until they have had a long experience of them. Thus it happens that whenever those who are hostile have the opportunity to attack they do it like partisans, whilst the others defend lukewarmly, in such wise that the prince is endangered along with them.

It is necessary, therefore, if we desire to discuss this matter thoroughly, to inquire whether these innovators can rely on themselves or have to depend on others: that is to say, whether, to consummate their enterprise, have they to use prayers or can they use force? In the first instance they always succeed badly, and never compass anything; but when they can rely on themselves and use force, then they are rarely endangered. Hence it is that all armed prophets have conquered, and the unarmed ones have been destroyed. Besides the reasons mentioned, the nature of the people is variable, and whilst it is easy to persuade them, it is difficult to fix them in that persuasion. And thus it is necessary to take such measures that, when they believe no longer, it may be possible to make them believe by force.

If Moses, Cyrus, Theseus, and Romulus had been unarmed they could not have enforced their constitutions for long—as happened in our time to Fra Girolamo Savonarola,[10] who was ruined with his new order of things immediately the multitude believed in him no longer, and he had no means of keeping steadfast those who believed or of making the unbelievers to believe. Therefore such as these have great difficulties in consummating their enterprise, for all their dangers are in the ascent, yet with ability they will overcome them; but when these are overcome, and those who envied them their success are exterminated, they will begin to be respected, and they will continue afterwards powerful, secure, honoured, and happy.

To these great examples I wish to add a lesser one; still it bears some resemblance to them, and I wish it to suffice me for all of a like kind: it is Hiero the Syracusan.[11] This man rose from a private station to be Prince of Syracuse, nor did he, either, owe anything to fortune but opportunity; for the Syracusans, being oppressed, chose him for their captain, afterwards he was rewarded by being made their prince. He was of so great ability, even as a private citizen, that one who writes of him says he wanted nothing but a kingdom to be a king. This man abolished the old soldiery, organised the new, gave up old alliances, made new ones; and as he had his own soldiers and allies, on such foundations he was able to build any edifice: thus, whilst he had endured much trouble in acquiring, he had but little in keeping.

Chapter 7

Concerning New Principalities Which Are Acquired Either by the Arms of Others or by Good Fortune

Those who solely by good fortune become princes from being private citizens have little trouble in rising, but much in keeping atop; they have not any difficulties on the way up, because they fly, but they have many when they reach the summit. Such are those to whom some state is given either for money or by the favour of him who bestows it; as happened to many in Greece, in the cities of Ionia and of the Hellespont, where princes were made by Darius,[12] in order that they might hold the cities both for his security and his glory; as also were those emperors who, by the corruption of the soldiers, from being citizens came to empire. Such stand simply upon the goodwill and the fortune of him who has elevated them—two most inconstant and unstable things. Neither

---

[10]Dominican friar and religious reformer (1452–1498), who was chiefly responsible for driving the Medici out of Florence in 1494. He established a severely puritanical, theocratic government there; but his fanatic beliefs got him into difficulties with the papacy, and in 1497 he was excommunicated as a heretic. The next year the aristocratic party regained control of Florence, and Savonarola was tried and executed for sedition and heresy.

[11]Ruler of the Greek colony of Syracuse, in Sicily, from 478 to 466 B.C. By the end of his reign he had extended his power over the entire island.

[12]Persian emperor (558?–486 B.C.), who ruled over much of Asia, all of Asia Minor, and parts of Greece.

have they the knowledge requisite for the position; because, unless they are men of great worth and ability, it is not reasonable to expect that they should know how to command, having always lived in a private condition; besides, they cannot hold it because they have not forces which they can keep friendly and faithful.

States that rise unexpectedly, then, like all other things in nature which are born and grow rapidly, cannot have their foundations and correspondencies fixed in such a way that the first storm will not over-throw them; unless, as is said, those who unexpectedly become princes are men of so much ability that they know they have to be prepared at once to hold that which fortune has thrown into their laps, and that those foundations, which others have laid *before* they became princes, they must lay *afterwards*.

Concerning these two methods of rising to be a prince by ability or fortune, I wish to adduce two examples within our own recollection, and these are Francesco Sforza[13] and Cesare Borgia. Francesco, by proper means and with great ability, from being a private person rose to be Duke of Milan, and that which he had acquired with a thousand anxieties he kept with little trouble. On the other hand, Cesare Borgia, called by the people Duke Valentino, acquired his State during the ascendency of his father, and on its decline he lost it, notwithstanding that he had taken every measure and done all that ought to be done by a wise and able man to fix firmly his roots in the states which the arms and fortunes of others had bestowed on him.

Because, as is stated above, he who has not first laid his foundations may be able with great ability to lay them afterwards, but they will be laid with trouble to the architect and danger to the building. If, there-fore, all the steps taken by the duke be considered, it will be seen that he laid solid foundations for his future power, and I do not consider it superfluous to discuss them, because I do not know what better precepts to give a new prince than the example of his actions; and if his disposi-tions were of no avail, that was not his fault, but the extraordinary and extreme malignity of fortune.

Alexander the Sixth, in wishing to aggrandise the duke, his son, had many immediate and prospective difficulties. Firstly, he did not see his way to make him master of any state that was not a state of the Church; and if he was willing to rob the Church he knew that the Duke of Milan and the Venetians would not consent, because Faenza and Rimini were already under the protection of the Venetians. Be-sides this, he saw the arms of Italy, especially those by which he might have been assisted, in hands that would fear the aggrandisement of the Pope, namely, the Orsini and the Colonnesi[14] and their following. It behoved him, therefore, to upset this state of affairs and embroil the powers, so as to make himself securely master of part of their states. This was easy for him to do, because he found the Venetians, moved by other reasons, inclined to bring back the French into Italy;

---

[13]A famous soldier and leader of mercenary troops (1401–1466) who established himself as Duke of Milan in 1450 and controlled much of northern Italy by the time of his death.
[14]Two great baronial families that had for centuries been the most important forces in Roman politics.

he would not only not oppose this, but he would render it more easy by dissolving the former marriage of King Louis. Therefore the king came into Italy with the assistance of the Venetians and the consent of Alexander. He was no sooner in Milan than the Pope had soldiers from him for the attempt on the Romagna, which yielded to him on the reputation of the king. The duke, therefore, having acquired the Romagna and beaten the Colonnesi, while wishing to hold that and to advance further, was hindered by two things: the one, his forces did not appear loyal to him, the other, the goodwill of France: that is to say, he feared that the forces of the Orsini, which he was using, would not stand to him, that not only might they hinder him from winning more, but might themselves seize what he had won, and that the king might also do the same. Of the Orsini he had a warning when, after taking Faenza and attacking Bologna, he saw them go very unwillingly to that attack. And as to the king, he learned his mind when he himself, after taking the Duchy of Urbino, attacked Tuscany, and the king made him desist from that undertaking; hence the duke decided to depend no more upon the arms and the luck of others.

For the first thing he weakened the Orsini and Colonnesi parties in Rome, by gaining to himself all their adherents who were gentlemen, making them his gentlemen, giving them good pay, and, according to their rank, honouring them with office and command in such a way that in a few months all attachment to the factions was destroyed and turned entirely to the duke. After this he awaited an opportunity to crush the Orsini, having scattered the adherents of the Colonna house. This came to him soon and he used it well; for the Orsini, perceiving at length that the aggrandisement of the duke and the Church was ruin to them, called a meeting at Magione in Perugia. From this sprung the rebellion at Urbino and the tumults in the Romagna, with endless dangers to the duke, all of which he overcame with the help of the French. Having restored his authority, not to leave it at risk by trusting either to the French or other outside forces, he had recourse to his wiles, and he knew so well how to conceal his mind that, by the mediation of Signor Pagolo[15]—whom the duke did not fail to secure with all kinds of attentions, giving him money, apparel, and horses—the Orsini were reconciled, so that their simplicity brought them into his power at Sinigalia.[16] Having exterminated the leaders, and turned their partisans into his friends, the duke had laid sufficiently good foundations to his power, having all the Romagna and the Duchy of Urbino; and the people now beginning to appreciate their prosperity, he gained them all over to himself. And as this point is worthy of notice, and to be imitated by others, I am not willing to leave it out.

When the duke occupied the Romagna he found it under the rule of weak masters, who rather plundered their subjects than ruled them, and gave them more cause for disunion than for union, so that the country was full of robbery, quarrels, and every kind of violence; and so,

---

[15]An Orsini.
[16]Borgia had arranged what was to be a friendly meeting with the leaders of the Orsini for the purpose of forming an alliance with them. When they met him at Sinigaglia (now, Senigallia), he had them murdered.

wishing to bring back peace and obedience to authority, he considered it necessary to give it a good governor. Thereupon he promoted Messer Ramiro d'Orco, a swift and cruel man, to whom he gave the fullest power. This man in a short time restored peace and unity with the greatest success. Afterwards the duke considered that it was not advisable to confer such excessive authority, for he had no doubt but that he would become odious, so he set up a court of judgment in the country, under a most excellant president, wherein all cities had their advocates. And because he knew that the past severity had caused some hatred against himself, so, to clear himself in the minds of the people, and gain them entirely to himself, he desired to show that, if any cruelty had been practised, it had not originated with him, but in the natural sternness of the minister. Under this pretence he took Ramiro, and one morning caused him to be executed and left on the piazza at Cesena with the block and a bloody knife at his side. The barbarity of this spectacle caused the people to be at once satisfied and dismayed.

But let us return whence we started. I say that the duke, finding himself now sufficiently powerful and partly secured from immediate dangers by having armed himself in his own way, and having in a great measure crushed those forces in his vicinity that could injure him if he wished to proceed with his conquest, had next to consider France, for he knew that the king, who too late was aware of his mistake, would not support him. And from this time he began to seek new alliances and to temporise with France in the expedition which she was making towards the kingdom of Naples against the Spaniards who were besieging Gaeta. It was his intention to secure himself against them, and this he would have quickly accomplished had Alexander lived.

Such was his line of action as to present affairs. But as to the future he had to fear, in the first place, that a new successor to the Church might not be friendly to him and might seek to take from him that which Alexander had given him, so he decided to act in four ways. Firstly, by exterminating the families of those lords whom he had despoiled, so as to take away that pretext from the Pope. Secondly, by winning to himself all the gentlemen of Rome, so as to be able to curb the Pope with their aid, as has been observed. Thirdly, by converting the college more to himself. Fourthly, by acquiring so much power before the Pope should die that he could by his own measures resist the first shock. Of these four things, at the death of Alexander, he had accomplished three. For he had killed as many of the dispossessed lords as he could lay hands on, and few had escaped; he had won over the Roman gentlemen, and he had the most numerous party in the college. And as to any fresh acquisition, he intended to become master of Tuscany, for he already possessed Perugia and Piombino, and Pisa was under his protection. And as he had no longer to study France (for the French were already driven out of the kingdom of Naples by the Spaniards, and in this way both were compelled to buy his goodwill), he pounced down upon Pisa. After this, Lucca and Siena yielded at once, partly through hatred and partly through fear of the Florentines; and the Florentines would have had no remedy had he continued to prosper, as he was prospering the year that Alexander died, for he had acquired so much power and reputation that he would have stood by himself, and no longer have depended on the luck and the forces of others, but solely on his own power and ability.

But Alexander died five years after he had first drawn the sword. He left the duke with the state of Romagna alone consolidated, with the rest in the air, between two most powerful hostile armies, and sick unto death. Yet there were in the duke such boldness and ability, and he knew so well how men are to be won or lost, and so firm were the foundations which in so short a time he had laid, that if he had not had those armies on his back, or if he had been in good health, he would have overcome all difficulties. And it is seen that his foundations were good, for the Romagna awaited him for more than a month. In Rome, although but half alive, he remained secure; and whilst the Baglioni, the Vitelli, and the Orsini might come to Rome, they could not effect anything against him. If he could not have made Pope him whom he wished, at least the one whom he did not wish would not have been elected. But if he had been in sound health at the death of Alexander, everything would have been easy to him. On the day that Julius the Second was elected, he told me that he had thought of everything that might occur at the death of his father, and had provided a remedy for all, except that he had never anticipated that, when the death did happen, he himself would be on the point to die.

When all the actions of the duke are recalled, I do not know how to blame him, but rather it appears to me, as I have said, that I ought to offer him for imitation to all those who, by the fortune or the arms of others, are raised to government. Because he, having a lofty spirit and far-reaching aims, could not have regulated his conduct otherwise, and only the shortness of the life of Alexander and his own sickness frustrated his designs. Therefore, he who considers it necessary to secure himself in his new principality, to win friends, to overcome either by force or fraud, to make himself beloved and feared by the people, to be followed and revered by the soldiers, to exterminate those who had power or reason to hurt him, to change the old order of things for new, to be severe and gracious, magnanimous and liberal, to destroy a disloyal soldiery and to create new, to maintain friendship with kings and princes in such a way that they must help him with zeal and offend with caution, cannot find a more lively example than the actions of this man.

Only can he be blamed for the election of Julius the Second, in whom he made a bad choice, because, as is said, not being able to elect a Pope to his own mind, he could have hindered any other from being elected Pope; and he ought never to have consented to the election of any cardinal whom he had injured or who had cause to fear him if they became pontiffs. For men injure either from fear or hatred. Those whom he had injured, amongst others, were San Pietro ad Vincula,[17] Colonna, San Giorgio, and Ascanio. The rest, in becoming Pope, had to fear him, Rouen and the Spaniards excepted; the latter from their relation-

---

[17]Giuliano della Rovere (1443–1513), who succeeded Pope Alexander as Pope Julius II.

ship and obligations, the former from his influence, the kingdom of France having relations with him. Therefore, above everything, the duke ought to have created a Spaniard Pope and, failing him, he ought to have consented to Rouen and not San Pietro ad Vincula. He who believes that new benefits will cause great personages to forget old injuries is deceived. Therefore, the duke erred in his choice, and it was the cause of his ultimate ruin.

Chapter 9

Concerning a Civil Principality

But coming to the other point—where a leading citizen becomes the prince of his country, not by wickedness or any intolerable violence, but by the favour of his fellow citizens—this may be called a civil principality: nor is genius or fortune altogether necessary to attain to it, but rather a happy shrewdness. I say then that such a principality is obtained either by the favour of the people or by the favour of the nobles. Because in all cities these two distinct parties are found, and from this it arises that the people do not wish to be ruled nor oppressed by the nobles, and the nobles wish to rule and oppress the people; and from these two opposite desires there arises in cities one of three results, either a principality, self-government, or anarchy.

A principality is created either by the people or by the nobles, accordingly as one or other of them has the opportunity; for the nobles, seeing they cannot withstand the people, begin to cry up the reputation of one of themselves, and they make him a prince, so that under his shadow they can give vent to their ambitions. The people, finding they cannot resist the nobles, also cry up the reputation of one of themselves, and make him a prince so as to be defended by his authority. He who obtains sovereignty by the assistance of the nobles maintains himself with more difficulty than he who comes to it by the aid of the people, because the former finds himself with many around him who consider themselves his equal, and because of this he can neither rule nor manage them to his liking. But he who reaches sovereignty by popular favour finds himself alone, and has none around him, or few, who are not prepared to obey him.

Besides this, one cannot by fair dealing, and without injury to others, satisfy the nobles, but you can satisfy the people, for their object is more righteous than that of the nobles, the latter wishing to oppress, whilst the former only desire not to be oppressed. It is to be added also that a prince can never secure himself against a hostile people, because of their being too many, whilst from the nobles he can secure himself, as they are few in number. The worst that a prince may expect from a hostile people is to be abandoned by them; but from hostile nobles he has not only to fear abandonment, but also that they will rise against him; for they, being in these affairs more far-seeing and astute, always come forward in time to save themselves, and to obtain favours from him whom they expect to prevail. Further, the prince is compelled to live always with the same people, but he can do well without the same nobles, being able to make and unmake them daily, and to give or take away authority when it pleases him.

Therefore, to make this point clearer, I say that the nobles ought to be looked at mainly in two ways: that is to say, they either shape their course in such a way as binds them entirely to your fortune, or they do not. Those who so bind themselves, and are not rapacions, ought to be honoured and loved; those who do not bind themselves may be dealt with in two ways; they may fail to do this through pusillanimity and a natural want of courage, in which case you ought to make use of them, especially of those who are of good counsel; and thus, whilst in prosperity you honour yourself, in adversity you have not to fear them. But when for their own ambitious ends they shun binding themselves, it is a token that they are giving more thought to themselves than to you, and a prince ought to guard against such, and to fear them as if they were open enemies, because in adversity they always help to ruin him.

Therefore, one who becomes a prince through the favour of the people ought to keep them friendly, and this he can easily do seeing they only ask not to be oppressed by him. But one who, in opposition to the people, becomes a prince by the favour of the nobles, ought, above everything, to seek to win the people over to himself, and this he may easily do if he takes them under his protection. Because men, when they receive good from him of whom they were expecting evil, are bound more closely to their benefactor; thus the people quickly become more devoted to him than if he had been raised to the principality by their favours; and the prince can win their affections in many ways, but as these vary according to the circumstances one cannot give fixed rules, so I omit them; but, I repeat, it is necessary for a prince to have the people friendly, otherwise he has no security in adversity.

Nabis,[18] Prince of the Spartans, sustained the attack of all Greece, and of a victorious Roman army, and against them he defended his country and his government; and for the overcoming of this peril it was only necessary for him to make himself secure against a few, but this would not have been sufficient if the people had been hostile. And do not let any one impugn this statement with the trite proverb that, "He who builds on the people, builds on the mud," for this is true when a private citizen makes a foundation there, and persuades himself that the people will free him when he is oppressed by his enemies or by the magistrates; wherein he would find himself very often deceived, as happened to the Gracchi[19] in Rome and to Messer Giorgio Scali[20] in Florence. But granted a prince who has established himself as above, who can command, and is a man of courage, undismayed in adversity, who does not fail in other qualifications, and who, by his resolution and energy, keeps the whole people encouraged—such a one will never

---

[18]Ruled Sparta from 207 to 192 B.C.
[19]Two Roman statesmen, brothers, who late in the second century B.C. attempted to support the rights of the Roman people against the aristocracy. Both were killed in riots.
[20]A leader of the Florentine populace who was abandoned by his followers and killed in 1381.

find himself deceived in them, and it will be shown that he has laid his foundations well.

These principalities are liable to danger when they are passing from the civil to the absolute order of government, for such princes either rule personally or through magistrates. In the latter case their government is weaker and more insecure, because it rests entirely on the goodwill of those citizens who are raised to the magistracy, and who, especially in troubled times, can destroy the government with great ease, either by intrigue or open defiance; and the prince has not the chance amid tumults to exercise absolute authority, because the citizens and subjects, accustomed to receive orders from magistrates, are not of a mind to obey him amid these confusions, and there will always be in doubtful times a scarcity of men whom he can trust. For such a prince cannot rely upon what he observes in quiet times, when citizens have need of the state, because then every one agrees with him; they all promise, and when death is far distant they all wish to die for him; but in troubled times, when the state has need of its citizens, then he finds but few. And so much the more is this experiment dangerous, inasmuch as it can only be tried once. Therefore a wise prince ought to adopt such a course that his citizens will always in every sort and kind of circumstance have need of the state and of him, and then he will always find them faithful.

Chapter 14

That Which Concerns a Prince on the Subject of the Art of War

A prince ought to have no other aim or thought, nor select anything else for his study, than war and its rules and discipline; for this is the sole art that belongs to him who rules, and it is of such force that it not only upholds those who are born princes, but it often enables men to rise from a private station to that rank. And, on the contrary, it is seen that when princes have thought more of ease than of arms they have lost their states. And the first cause of your losing it is to neglect this art; and what enables you to acquire a state is to be master of the art. Francesco Sforza, through being martial, from a private person became Duke of Milan; and the sons, through avoiding the hardships and troubles of arms, from dukes became private persons. For among other evils which being unarmed brings you, it causes you to be despised, and this is one of those ignominies against which a prince ought to guard himself, as is shown later on. Because there is nothing proportionate between the armed and the unarmed; and it is not reasonable that he who is armed should yield obedience willingly to him who is unarmed, or that the unarmed man should be secure among armed servants. Because, there being in the one disdain and in the other suspicion, it is not possible for them to work well together. And therefore a prince who does not understand the art of war, over and above the other misfortunes already mentioned, cannot be respected by his soldiers, nor can he rely on them. He ought never, therefore, to have out of his thoughts this subject of war, and in peace he should addict himself more to its exercise than in war; this he can do in two ways, the one by action, the other by study.

As regards action, he ought above all things to keep his men well organised and drilled, to follow incessantly the chase, by which he accustoms his body to hardships, and learns something of the nature of localities, and gets to find out how the mountains rise, how the valleys open out, how the plains lie, and to understand the nature of rivers and marshes, and in all this to take the greatest care. Which knowledge is useful in two ways. Firstly, he learns to know his country, and is better able to undertake its defence; afterwards, by means of the knowledge and observation of that locality, he understands with ease any other which it may be necessary for him to study hereafter; because the hills, valleys, and plains, and rivers and marshes that are, for instance, in Tuscany, have a certain resemblance to those of other countries, so that with a knowledge of the aspect of one country one can easily arrive at a knowledge of others. And the prince that lacks this skill lacks the essential which it is desirable that a captain should possess, for it teaches him to surprise his enemy, to select quarters, to lead armies, to array the battle, to besiege towns to advantage.

Philopoemen,[21] Prince of the Acheans, among other praises which writers have bestowed on him, is commended because in time of peace he never had anything in his mind but the rules of war; and when he was in the country with friends, he often stopped and reasoned with them: "If the enemy should be upon that hill, and we should find ourselves here with our army, with whom would be the advantage? How should one best advance to meet him, keeping the ranks? If we should wish to retreat, how ought we to set about it? If they should retreat, how ought we to pursue?" And he would set forth to them, as he went, all the chances that could befall an army; he would listen to their opinion and state his, confirming it with reasons, so that by these continual discussions there could never arise, in time of war, any unexpected circumstances that he could not deal with.

But to exercise the intellect the prince should read histories, and study there the actions of illustrious men, to see how they have borne themselves in war, to examine the causes of their victories and defeat, so as to avoid the latter and imitate the former; and above all do as an illustrious man did, who took as an exemplar one who had been praised and famous before him, and whose achievements and deeds he always kept in his mind, as it is said Alexander the Great imitated Achilles, Cæsar Alexander, Scipio[22] Cyrus. And whoever reads the life of Cyrus, written by Xenophon, will recognise afterwards in the life of Scipio how that imitation was his glory, and how in chastity, affability, humanity, and liberality Scipio conformed to those things which have been written of Cyrus by Xenophon. A wise prince ought to observe some

---

[21]Greek general and statesman (253?–183 B.C.).
[22]Roman general (237?–183 B.C.), who defeated the great Carthaginian general Hannibal and broke the power of Carthage.

such rules, and never in peaceful times stand idle, but increase his resources with industry in such a way that they may be available to him in adversity, so that if fortune changes it may find him prepared to resist her blows.

Chapter 15

Concerning Things for Which Men, and Especially Princes, Are Praised or Blamed

It remains now to see what ought to be the rules of conduct for a prince towards subject and friends. And as I know that many have written on this point, I expect I shall be considered presumptuous in mentioning it again, especially as in discussing it I shall depart from the methods of other people. But, it being my intention to write a thing which shall be useful to him who apprehends it, it appears to me more appropriate to follow up the real truth of a matter than the imagination of it; for many have pictured republics and principalities which in fact have never been known or seen, because how one lives is so far distant from how one ought to live, that he who neglects what is done for what ought to be done, sooner effects his ruin than his preservation; for a man who wishes to act entirely up to his professions of virtue soon meets with what destroys him among so much that is evil.

Hence it is necessary for a prince wishing to hold his own to know how to do wrong, and to make use of it or not according to necessity. Therefore, putting on one side imaginary things concerning a prince, and discussing those which are real, I say that all men when they are spoken of, and chiefly princes for being more highly placed, are remarkable for some of those qualities which bring them either blame or praise; and thus it is that one is reputed liberal, another miserly, using a Tuscan term (because an avaricious person in our language is still he who desires to possess by robbery, whilst we call one miserly who deprives himself too much of the use of his own); one is reputed generous, one rapacious; one cruel, one compassionate; one faithless, another faithful; one effeminate and cowardly, another bold and brave; one affable, another haughty; one lascivious, another chaste; one sincere, another cunning; one hard, another easy; one grave, another frivolous; one religious, another unbelieving, and the like. And I know that every one will confess that it would be most praiseworthy in a prince to exhibit all the above qualities that are considered good; but because they can neither be entirely possessed nor observed, for human conditions do not permit it, it is necessary for him to be sufficiently prudent that he may know how to avoid the reproach of those vices which would lose him his state; and also to keep himself, if it be possible, from those which would not lose him it; but this not being possible, he may with less hesitation abandon himself to them. And again, he need not make himself uneasy at incurring a reproach for those vices without which the state can only be saved with difficulty, for if everything is considered carefully, it will be found that something which looks like virtue, if followed, would be his ruin; whilst something else, which looks like vice, yet followed brings him security and prosperity.

Chapter 16

Concerning Liberality and Meanness

Commencing then with the first of the above-named characteristics, I say that it would be well to be reputed liberal. Nevertheless, liberality exercised in a way that does not bring you the reputation for it, injures you; for if one exercises it honestly and as it should be exercised, it may not become known, and you will not avoid the reproach of its opposite. Therefore, any one wishing to maintain among men the name of liberal is obliged to avoid no attribute of magnificence; so that a prince thus inclined will consume in such acts all his property, and will be compelled in the end, if he wish to maintain the name of liberal, to unduly weigh down his people, and tax them, and do everything he can to get money. This will soon make him odious to his subjects, and becoming poor he will be little valued by any one; thus, with his liberality, having offended many and rewarded few, he is affected by the very first trouble and imperilled by whatever may be the first danger; recognising this himself, and wishing to draw back from it, he runs at once into the reproach of being miserly.

Therefore, a prince, not being able to exercise this virtue of liberality in such a way that it is recognised, except to his cost, if he is wise he ought not to fear the reputation of being mean, for in time he will come to be more considered than if liberal, seeing that with his economy his revenues are enough, that he can defend himself against all attacks, and is able to engage in enterprises without burdening his people; thus it comes to pass that he exercises liberality towards all from whom he does not take, who are numberless, and meanness towards those to whom he does not give, who are few.

We have not seen great things done in our time except by those who have been considered mean; the rest have failed. Pope Julius the Second was assisted in reaching the papacy by a reputation for liberality, yet he did not strive afterwards to keep it up, when he made war on the King of France; and he made many wars without imposing any extraordinary tax on his subjects, for he supplied his additional expenses out of his long thriftiness. The present King of Spain[23] would not have undertaken or conquered in so many enterprises if he had been reputed liberal. A prince, therefore, provided that he has not to rob his subjects, that he can defend himself, that he does not become poor and abject, that he is not forced to become rapacious, ought to hold of little account a reputation for being mean, for it is one of those vices which will enable him to govern.

And if any one should say: Cæsar obtained empire by liberality, and many others have reached the highest positions by having been liberal,

---

[23]Ferdinand V, reigned 1474–1516, who unified Spain and extended his power into much of Italy.

and by being considered so, I answer: Either you are a prince in fact, or in a way to become one. In the first case this liberality is dangerous, in the second it is very necessary to be considered liberal; and Cæsar was one of those who wished to become pre-eminent in Rome; but if he had survived after becoming so, and had not moderated his expenses, he would have destroyed his government. And if any one should reply: Many have been princes, and have done great things with armies, who have been considered very liberal, I reply: Either a prince spends that which is his own or his subjects' or else that of others. In the first case he ought to be sparing, in the second he ought not to neglect any opportunity for liberality. And to the prince who goes forth with his army, supporting it by pillage, sack, and extortion, handling that which belongs to others, this liberality is necessary, otherwise he would not be followed by soldiers. And of that which is neither yours nor your subjects' you can be a ready giver, as were Cyrus, Cæsar, and Alexander; because it does not take away your reputation if you squander that of others, but adds to it; it is only squandering your own that injures you.

And there is nothing wastes so rapidly as liberality, for even whilst you exercise it you lose the power to do so, and so become either poor or despised, or else, in avoiding poverty, rapacious and hated. And a prince should guard himself, above all things, against being despised and hated; and liberality lead you to both. Therefore it is wiser to have a reputation for meanness which brings reproach without hatred, than to be compelled through seeking a reputation for liberality to incur a name for rapacity which begets reproach with hatred.

Chapter 17

Concerning Cruelty and Clemency, and Whether It Is Better to Be Loved Than Feared

Coming now to the other qualities mentioned above, I say that every prince ought to desire to be considered clement and not cruel. Nevertheless he ought to take care not to misuse this clemency. Cesare Borgia was considered cruel; notwithstanding, his cruelty reconciled the Romagna, unified it, and restored it to peace and loyalty. And if this be rightly considered, he will be seen to have been much more merciful than the Florentine people, who, to avoid a reputation for cruelty, permitted Pistoia to be destroyed. Therefore a prince, so long as he keeps his subjects united and loyal, ought not to mind the reproach of cruelty; because with a few examples he will be more merciful than those who, through too much mercy, allow disorders to arise, from which follow murder or robbery; for these are wont to injure the whole people, whilst those executions which originate with a prince offend the individual only.

And of all princes, it is impossible for the new prince to avoid the imputation of cruelty, owing to new states being full of dangers. Hence Virgil, through the mouth of Dido, excuses the inhumanity of her reign owing to its being new, saying:—

"Res dura, et regni novitas me talia cogunt
Moliri, et late fines custode tueri."[24]

Nevertheless he ought to be slow to believe and to act, nor should he himself show fear, but proceed in a temperate manner with prudence and humanity, so that too much confidence may not make him incautious and too much distrust render him intolerable.

Upon this a question arises: whether it be better to be loved than feared or feared than loved? It may be answered that one should wish to be both, but, because it is difficult to unite them in one person, it is much safer to be feared than loved, when, of the two, either must be dispensed with. Because this is to be asserted in general of men, that they are ungrateful, fickle, false, cowards, covetous, and as long as you succeed they are yours entirely; they will offer you their blood, property, life, and children, as is said above, when the need is far distant; but when it approaches they turn against you. And that prince who, relying entirely on their promises, has neglected other precautions, is ruined; because friendships that are obtained by payments, and not by greatness or nobility of mind, may indeed be earned, but they are not secured, and in time of need cannot be relied upon; and men have less scruple in offending one who is beloved than one who is feared, for love is preserved by the link of obligation which, owing to the baseness of men, is broken at every opportunity for their advantage; but fear preserves you by a dread of punishment which never fails.

Nevertheless a prince ought to inspire fear in such a way that, if he does not win love, he avoids hatred; because he can endure very well being feared whilst he is not hated, which will always be as long as he abstains from the property of his citizens and subjects and from their women. But when it is necessary for him to proceed against the life of some one, he must do it on proper justification and for manifest cause, but above all things he must keep his hand off the property of others, because men more quickly forget the death of their father than the loss of their patrimony. Besides, pretexts for taking away the property are never wanting; for he who has once begun to live by robbery will always find pretexts for seizing what belongs to others; but reasons for taking life, on the contrary, are more difficult to find and sooner lapse. But when a prince is with his army, and has under control a multitude of soldiers, then it is quite necessary for him to disregard the reputation of cruelty, for without it he would never hold his army united or disposed to its duties.

Among the wonderful deeds of Hannibal this one is enumerated: that having led an enormous army, composed of many various races of men, to fight in foreign lands, no dissensions arose either among them or against the prince, whether in his bad or in his good fortune. This arose from nothing else than his inhuman cruelty, which, with his boundless valour, made him revered and terrible in the sight of his soldiers, but without that cruelty, his other virtues were not sufficient

---

[24]". . . my cruel fate
And doubts attending an unsettled state
Force me to guard my coast from foreign foes."

to produce this effect. And short-sighted writers admire his deeds from one point of view and from another condemn the principal cause of them. That it is true his other virtues would not have been sufficient for him may be proved by the case of Scipio, that most excellent man, not only of his own times but within the memory of man, against whom, nevertheless, his army rebelled in Spain; this arose from nothing but his too great forbearance, which gave his soldiers more licence than is consistent with military discipline. For this he was upbraided in the Senate by Fabius Maximus, and called the corruptor of the Roman soldiery. The Locrians were laid waste by a legate of Scipio, yet they were not avenged by him, nor was the insolence of the legate punished, owing entirely to his easy nature. Insomuch that some one in the Senate, wishing to excuse him, said there were many men who knew much better how not to err than to correct the errors of others. This disposition, if he had been continued in the command, would have destroyed in time the fame and glory of Scipio; but, he being under the control of the Senate, this injurious characteristic not only concealed itself, but contributed to his glory.

Returning to the question of being feared or loved, I come to the conclusion that, men loving according to their own will and fearing according to that of the prince, a wise prince should establish himself on that which is in his own control and not in that of others; he must endeavour only to avoid hatred, as is noted.

Chapter 18

Concerning the Way in Which Princes Should Keep Faith

Every one admits how praiseworthy it is in a prince to keep faith, and to live with integrity and not with craft. Nevertheless our experience has been that those princes who have done great things have held good faith of little account, and have known how to circumvent the intellect of men by craft, and in the end have overcome those who have relied on their word. You must know there are two ways of contesting, the one by the law, the other by force; the first method is proper to men, the second to beasts; but because the first is frequently not sufficient, it is necessary to have recourse to the second. Therefore it is necessary for a prince to understand how to avail himself of the beast and the man. This has been figuratively taught to princes by ancient writers, who describe how Achilles and many other princes of old were given to the Centaur Chiron[25] to nurse, who brought them up in his discipline; which means solely that, as they had for a teacher one who was half beast and half man, so it is necessary for a prince to know how to make use of both natures, and that one without the other is not durable. A prince, therefore, being compelled knowingly to adopt the beast, ought to choose the fox and the lion; because the lion cannot defend himself against snares and the fox cannot defend himself against

---

[25]In Greek mythology, the centaurs were a fabulous race of beings. Each was shaped like a horse with the body of a man in place of the horse's neck and head. Chiron was a centaur famous for his wisdom and for having educated a number of the most notable heroes in Greek mythology.

wolves. Therefore, it is necessary to be a fox to discover the snares and a lion to terrify the wolves. Those who rely simply on the lion do not understand what they are about. Therefore a wise lord cannot, nor ought he to, keep faith when such observance may be turned against him, and when the reasons that caused him to pledge it exist no longer. If men were entirely good this precept would not hold, but because they are bad, and will not keep faith with you, you too are not bound to observe it with them. Nor will there ever be wanting to a prince legitimate reasons to excuse this non-observance. Of this endless modern examples could be given, showing how many treaties and engagements have been made void and of no effect through the faithlessness of princes; and he who has known best how to employ the fox has succeeded best.

But it is necessary to know well how to disguise this characteristic, and to be a great pretender and dissembler; and men are so simple, and so subject to present necessities, that he who seeks to deceive will always find some one who will allow himself to be deceived. One recent example I cannot pass over in silence. Alexander the Sixth did nothing else but deceive men, nor ever thought of doing otherwise, and he always found victims; for there never was a man who had greater power in asserting, or who with greater oaths would affirm a thing, yet would observe it less; nevertheless his deceits always succeeded according to his wishes, because he well understood this side of mankind.

Therefore it is unnecessary for a prince to have all the good qualities I have enumerated, but it is very necessary to appear to have them. And I shall dare to say this also, that to have them and always to observe them is injurious, and that to appear to have them is useful; to appear merciful, faithful, humane, religious, upright, and to be so, but with a mind so framed that should you require not to be so, you may be able and know how to change to the opposite.

And you have to understand this, that a prince, especially a new one, cannot observe all those things for which men are esteemed, being often forced, in order to maintain the state, to act contrary to fidelity, friendship, humanity, and religion. Therefore it is necessary for him to have a mind ready to turn itself accordingly as the winds and variations of fortune force it, yet, as I have said above, not to diverge from the good if he can avoid doing so, but, if compelled, then to know how to set about it.

For this reason a prince ought to take care that he never lets anything slip from his lips that is not replete with the above-named five qualities, that he may appear to him who sees and hears him altogether merciful, faithful, humane, upright, and religious. There is nothing more necessary to appear to have than this last quality, inasmuch as men judge generally more by the eye than by the hand, because it belongs to everybody to see you, to few to come in touch with you. Every one sees what you appear to be, few really know what you are, and those few dare not oppose themselves to the opinion of the many, who have the majesty of the state to defend them; and in the actions of all men, and especially of princes, which it is not prudent to challenge, one judges by the result.

For that reason, let a prince have the credit of conquering and holding his state, the means will always be considered honest and he will be praised by everybody; because the vulgar are always taken by what a thing seems to be and by what comes of it; and in the world there are only the vulgar, for the few find a place there only when the many have no ground to rest on.

One prince of the present time, whom it is not well to name, never preaches anything else but peace and good faith, and to both he is most hostile, and either, if he had kept it, would have deprived him of reputation and kingdom many a time.

Chapter 20

Are Fortresses, and Many Things to Which Princes Often Resort, Advantageous or Hurtful?

Some princes, so as to hold securely the state, have disarmed their subjects; others have kept their subject towns distracted by factions; others have fostered enmities against themselves; others have laid themselves out to gain over those whom they distrusted in the beginning of their governments; some have built fortresses; some have overthrown and destroyed them. And although one cannot give a final judgment on all of these things unless one possesses the particulars of those states in which a decision has to be made, nevertheless I will speak as comprehensively as the matter of itself will admit.

There never was a new prince who has disarmed his subjects; rather when he has found them disarmed he has always armed them, because, by arming them, those arms become yours, those men who were distrusted become faithful, and those who were faithful are kept so, and your subjects become your adherents. And whereas all subjects cannot be armed, yet when those whom you do arm are benefited, the others can be handled more freely, and this difference in their treatment, which they quite understand, makes the former your dependents, and the latter, considering it to be necessary that those who have the most danger and service should have the most reward, excuse you. But when you disarm them, you at once offend them by showing that you distrust them, either for cowardice or for want of loyalty, and either of these opinions breeds hatred against you. And because you cannot remain unarmed, it follows that you turn to mercenaries . . . ; even if they should be good they would not be sufficient to defend you against powerful enemies and distrusted subjects. Therefore, as I have said, a new prince in a new principality has always distributed arms. Histories are full of examples. But when a prince acquires a new state, which he adds as a province to his old one, then it is necessary to disarm the men of that state, except those who have been his adherents in acquiring it; and these again, with time and opportunity, should be rendered soft and effeminate; and matters should be managed in such a way that all the armed men in the state shall be your own soldiers who in your old state were living near you.

Our forefathers, and those who were reckoned wise, were accustomed to say that it was necessary to hold Pistoia by factions and Pisa by fortresses; and with this idea they fostered quarrels in some of their tributary towns so as to keep possession of them the more easily. This may have been well enough in those times when Italy was in a way balanced, but I do not believe that it can be accepted as a precept for to-day, because I do not believe that factions can ever be of use; rather it is certain that when the enemy comes upon you in divided cities you are quickly lost, because the weakest party will always assist the outside forces and the other will not be able to resist. The Venetians, moved, as I believe, by the above reasons, fostered the Guelph and Ghibelline[26] factions in their tributary cities; and although they never allowed them to come to bloodshed, yet they nursed these disputes amongst them, so that the citizens, distracted by their differences, should not unite against them. Which, as we saw, did not afterwards turn out as expected, because, after the rout at Vaila, one party at once took courage and seized the state. Such methods argue, therefore, weakness in the prince, because these factions will never be permitted in a vigorous principality; such methods for enabling one the more easily to manage subjects are only useful in times of peace, but if war comes this policy proves fallacious.

Without doubt princes become great when they overcome the difficulties and obstacles by which they are confronted, and therefore fortune, especially when she desires to make a new prince great, who has a greater necessity to earn renown than an hereditary one, causes enemies to arise and form designs against him, in order that he may have the opportunity of overcoming them, and by them to mount higher, as by a ladder which his enemies have raised. For this reason many consider that a wise prince, when he has the opportunity, ought with craft to foster some animosity against himself, so that, having crushed it, his renown may rise higher.

Princes, especially new ones, have found more fidelity and assistance in those men who in the beginning of their rule were distrusted than among those who in the beginning were trusted. Pandolfo Petrucci,[27] Prince of Siena, ruled his state more by those who had been distrusted than by others. But on this question one cannot speak generally, for it varies so much with the individual; I will only say this, that those men who at the commencement of a princedom have been hostile, if they are of a description to need assistance to support themselves, can always be gained over with the greatest ease, and they will be tightly held to serve the prince with fidelity, inasmuch as they know it to be very necessary for them to cancel by deeds the bad impression which he had formed of them; and thus the prince always extracts more profit from them than from those who, serving him in too much security, may neglect his affairs. And since the matter demands it, I must not fail to warn a prince, who by means of secret favours has acquired a new state, that he must well consider the reasons which induced those to favour him who did

---

[26]The Guelphs and Ghibellines represented a fundamental cleavage in Italian politics. Roughly speaking, the Guelphs supported the papacy in its political conflicts with the Holy Roman Emperors, while the Ghibellines supported the emperors against the papacy. Local politics often obscured the fundamental issues, but the division into Guelphs and Ghibellines was general throughout Italy.

[27]Ruled Siena from 1497 until his death in 1512.

so; and if it be not a natural affection towards him, but only discontent with their government, then he will only keep them friendly with great trouble and difficulty, for it will be impossible to satisfy them. And weighing well the reasons for this in those examples which can be taken from ancient and modern affairs, we shall find that it is easier for the prince to make friends of those men who were contented under the former government, and are therefore his enemies, than of those who, being discontented with it, were favourable to him and encouraged him to seize it.

It has been a custom with princes, in order to hold their states more securely, to build fortresses that may serve as a bridle and bit to those who might design to work against them, and as a place of refuge from a first attack. I praise this system because it has been made use of formerly. Notwithstanding that, Messer Nicolo Vitelli in our times has been seen to demolish two fortresses in Citta di Castello so that he might keep that state; Guido Ubaldo, Duke of Urbino, on returning to his dominion, whence he had been driven by Cesare Borgia, rased to the foundations all the fortresses in that province, and considered that without them it would be more difficult to lose it; the Bentivogli returning to Bologna came to a similar decision. Fortresses, therefore, are useful or not according to circumstances; if they do you good in one way they injure you in another. And this question can be reasoned thus: the prince who has more to fear from the people than from foreigners ought to build fortresses, but he who has more to fear from foreigners than from the people ought to leave them alone. The castle of Milan, built by Francesco Sforza, has made, and will make, more trouble for the house of Sforza than any other disorder in the state. For this reason the best possible fortress is—not to be hated by the people, because, although you may hold the fortresses, yet they will not save you if the people hate you, for there will never be wanting foreigners to assist a people who have taken arms against you. It has not been seen in our times that such fortresses have been of use to any prince, unless to the Countess of Forli, when the Count Girolamo, her consort, was killed; for by that means she was able to withstand the popular attack and wait for assistance from Milan, and thus recover her state; and the posture of affairs was such at that time that the foreigners could not assist the people. But fortresses were of little value to her afterwards when Cesare Borgia attacked her, and when the people, her enemy, were allied with foreigners. Therefore, it would have been safer for her, both then and before, not to have been hated by the people than to have had the fortresses. All these things considered then, I shall praise him who builds fortresses as well as him who does not, and I shall blame whoever, trusting in them, cares little about being hated by the people.

Chapter 23

How Flatterers Should Be Avoided

I do not wish to leave out an important branch of this subject, for it is a danger from which princes are with difficulty preserved, unless they are very careful and discriminating. It is that of flatterers, of whom courts are full, because men are so self-complacent in their own affairs, and in a way so deceived in them, that they are preserved with difficulty from this pest, and if they wish to defend themselves they run the danger of falling into contempt. Because there is no other way of guarding oneself from flatterers except letting men understand that to tell you the truth does not offend you; but when every one may tell you the truth, respect for you abates.

Therefore a wise prince ought to hold a third course by choosing the wise men in his state, and giving to them only the liberty of speaking the truth to him, and then only of those things of which he inquires, and of none others; but he ought to question them upon everything, and listen to their opinions, and afterwards form his own conclusions. With these councillors, separately and collectively, he ought to carry himself in such a way that each of them should know that, the more freely he shall speak, the more he shall be preferred; outside of these, he should listen to no one, pursue the thing resolved on, and be steadfast in his resolutions. He who does otherwise is either overthrown by flatterers, or is so often changed by varying opinions that he falls into contempt.

I wish on this subject to adduce a modern example. Fra Luca, the man of affairs to Maximilian, the present Emperor, speaking of his majesty, said: He consulted with no one, yet never got his own way in anything. This arose because of his following a practice the opposite to the above; for the emperor is a secretive man—he does not communicate his designs to any one, nor does he receive opinions on them. But as in carrying them into effect they become revealed and known, they are at once obstructed by those men whom he has around him, and he, being pliant, is diverted from them. Hence it follows that those things he does one day he undoes the next, and no one ever understands what he wishes or intends to do, and no one can rely on his resolutions.

A prince, therefore, ought always to take counsel, but only when he wishes and not when others wish; he ought rather to discourage every one from offering advice unless he asks it; but, however, he ought to be a constant inquirer, and afterwards a patient listener concerning the things of which he inquired; also, on learning that any one, on any consideration, has not told him the truth, he should let his anger be felt.

And if there are some who think that a prince who conveys an impression of his wisdom is not so through his own ability, but through the good advisers that he has around him, beyond doubt they are deceived, because this is an axiom which never fails: that a prince who is not wise himself will never take good advice, unless by chance he has yielded his affairs entirely to one person who happens to be a very prudent man. In this case indeed he may be well governed, but it would not be for long, because such a governor would in a short time take away his state from him.

But if a prince who is not experienced should take counsel from more than one he will never get united counsels, nor will he know how to unite them. Each of the counsellors will think of his own interests, and the prince will not know how to control them or to see through them. And they are not to be found otherwise, because men will always prove untrue to you unless they are kept honest by constraint. Therefore it must be inferred that good counsels, whencesoever they come, are born of the wisdom of the prince, and not the wisdom of the prince from good counsels.

Chapter 24

Why the Princes of Italy Have Lost Their States

The previous suggestions, carefully observed, will enable a new prince to appear well established, and render him at once more secure and fixed in the state then if he had been long seated there. For the actions of a new prince are more narrowly observed than those of an hereditary one, and when they are seen to be able they gain more men and bind far tighter than ancient blood; because men are attracted more by the present than by the past, and when they find the present good they enjoy it and seek no further; they will also make the utmost defence for a prince if he fails them not in other things. Thus it will be a double glory to him to have established a new principality, and adorned and strengthened it with good laws, good arms, good allies, and with a good example; so will it be a double disgrace to him who, born a prince, shall lose his state by want of wisdom.

And if those seigniors are considered who have lost their states in Italy in our times, such as the King of Naples, the Duke of Milan, and others, there will be found in them, firstly, one common defect in regard to arms from the causes which have been discussed at length; in the next place, some one of them will be seen, either to have had the people hostile, or if he has had the people friendly, he has not known how to secure the nobles. In the absence of these defects states that have power enough to keep an army in the field cannot be lost.

Philip of Macedon,[28] not the father of Alexander the Great, but he who was conquered by Titus Quintius, had not much territory compared to the greatness of the Romans and of Greece who attacked him, yet being a warlike man who knew how to attract the people and secure the nobles, he sustained the war against his enemies for many years, and if in the end he lost the dominion of some cities, nevertheless he retained the kingdom.

Therefore, do not let our princes accuse fortune for the loss of their principalities after so many years' possession, but rather their own sloth, because in quiet times they never thought there could be a change (it is a common defect in man not to make any provision in the calm against the tempest), and when afterwards the bad times came they thought of flight and not of defending themselves, and they hoped that the people, disgusted with the insolence of the conquerors, would recall them. This course, when others fail, may be good, but it is very bad to have neglected all other expedients for that, since you would never wish to fall because you trusted to be able to find some one later on to restore you. This again either does not happen, or, if it does, it will not be for your security, because that deliverance is of no avail which does

---

[28]Philip V (cf. fn. 5).

not depend upon yourself; those only are reliable, certain, and durable that depend on yourself and your valour.

Chapter 25

What Fortune Can Effect in Human Affairs, and How to Withstand Her

It is not unknown to me how many men have had, and still have, the opinion that the affairs of the world are in such wise governed by fortune and by God that men with their wisdom cannot direct them and that no one can even help them; and because of this they would have us believe that it is not necessary to labour much in affairs, but to let chance govern them. This opinion has been more credited in our times because of the great changes in affairs which have been seen, and may still be seen, every day, beyond all human conjecture. Sometimes pondering over this, I am in some degree inclined to their opinion. Nevertheless, not to extinguish our free will, I hold it to be true that fortune is the arbiter of one half of our actions, but that she still leaves us to direct the other half, or perhaps a little less.

I compare her to one of those raging rivers, which when in flood overflows the plains, sweeping away trees and buildings, bearing away the soil from place to place; everything flies before it, all yield to its violence, without being able in any way to withstand it; and yet, though its nature be such, it does not follow therefore that men, when the weather becomes fair, shall not make provision, both with defences and barriers, in such a manner that, rising again, the waters may pass away by canal, and their force be neither so unrestrained nor so dangerous. So it happens with fortune, who shows her power where valour has not prepared to resist her, and thither she turns her forces where she knows that barriers and defences have not been raised to constrain her.

And if you will consider Italy, which is the seat of these changes, and which has given to them their impulse, you will see it to be an open country without barriers and without any defence. For if it had been defended by proper valour, as are Germany, Spain, and France, either this invasion would not have made the great changes it has made or it would not have come at all. And this I consider enough to say concerning resistance to fortune in general.

But confining myself more to the particular, I say that a prince may be seen happy to-day and ruined to-morrow without having shown any change of disposition or character. This, I believe, arises firstly from causes that have already been discussed at length, namely, that the prince who relies entirely upon fortune is lost when it changes. I believe also that he will be successful who directs his actions according to the spirit of the times, and that he whose actions do not accord with the times will not be successful. Because men are seen, in affairs that lead to the end which every man has before him, namely, glory and riches, to get there by various methods; one with caution, another with haste; one by force, another by skill; one by patience, another by its opposite; and each one succeeds in reaching the goal by a different method. One can also see of two cautious men the one attain his end, the other fail; and similarly, two men by different observances are equally successful, the one being cautious, the other impetuous; all this arises from nothing else than whether or not they conform in their methods to the spirit of the times. This follows from what I have said, that two men working differently bring about the same effect, and of two working similarly, one attains his object and the other does not.

Changes in estate also issue from this, for if, to one who governs himself with caution and patience, times and affairs converge in such a way that his administration is successful, his fortune is made; but if times and affairs change, he is ruined if he does not change his course of action. But a man is not often found sufficiently circumspect to know how to accommodate himself to the change, both because he cannot deviate from what nature inclines him to, and also because, having always prospered by acting in one way, he cannot be persuaded that it is well to leave it; and, therefore, the cautious man, when it is time to turn adventurous, does not know how to do it, hence he is ruined; but had he changed his conduct with the times fortune would not have changed.

Pope Julius the Second went to work impetuously in all his affairs, and found the times and circumstances conform so well to that line of action that he always met with success. Consider his first enterprise against Bologna, Messer Giovanni Bentivogli being still alive. The Venetians were not agreeable to it, nor was the King of Spain, and he had the enterprise still under discussion with the King of France; nevertheless he personally entered upon the expedition with his accustomed boldness and energy, a move which made Spain and the Venetians stand irresolute and passive, the latter from fear, the former from desire to recover all the kingdom of Naples; on the other hand, he drew after him the King of France, because that king, having observed the movement, and desiring to make the Pope his friend so as to humble the Venetians, found it impossible to refuse him soldiers without manifestly offending him. Therefore Julius with his impetuous action accomplished what no other pontiff with simple human wisdom could have done; for if he had waited in Rome until he could get away, with his plans arranged and everything fixed, as any other pontiff would have done, he would never have succeeded. Because the King of France would have made a thousand excuses, and the others would have raised a thousand fears.

I will leave his other actions alone, as they were all alike, and they all succeeded, for the shortness of his life did not let him experience the contrary; but if circumstances had arisen which required him to go cautiously, his ruin would have followed, because he would never have deviated from those ways to which nature inclined him.

I conclude therefore that, fortune being changeful and mankind steadfast in their ways, so long as the two are in agreement men are successful, but unsuccessful when they fall out. For my part I consider that it is better to be adventurous than cautious, because fortune is a woman, and if you wish to keep her under it is necessary to beat and ill-use her; and it is seen that she allows herself to be mastered by the adventurous rather than by those who go to work more coldly. She is, therefore, always, woman-like, a lover of young men, because they are less cautious, more violent, and with more audacity command her.

Chapter 26

An Exhortation to Liberate Italy from the Barbarians

Having carefully considered the subject of the above discourses, and wondering within myself whether the present times were propitious to a new prince, and whether there were the elements that would give an opportunity to a wise and virtuous one to introduce a new order of things which would do honour to him and good to the people of this country, it appears to me that so many things concur to favour a new prince that I never knew a time more fit than the present.

And if, as I said, it was necessary that the people of Israel should be captive so as to make manifest the ability of Moses; that the Persians should be oppressed by the Medes so as to discover the greatness of the soul of Cyrus; and that the Athenians should be dispersed to illustrate the capabilities of Theseus: then at the present time, in order to discover the virtue of an Italian spirit, it was necessary that Italy should be reduced to the extremity she is now in, that she should be more enslaved than the Hebrews, more oppressed than the Persians, more scattered than the Athenians; without head, without order, beaten, despoiled, torn, overrun; and to have endured every kind of desolation.

Although lately some spark may have been shown by one, which made us think he was ordained by God for our redemption, nevertheless it was afterwards seen, in the height of his career, that fortune rejected him;[29] so that Italy, left as without life, waits for him who shall yet heal her wounds and put an end to the ravaging and plundering of Lombardy, to the swindling and taxing of the Kingdom and of Tuscany, and cleanse those sores that for long have festered. It is seen how she entreats God to send some one who shall deliver her from these wrongs and barbarous insolencies. It is seen also that she is ready and willing to follow a banner if only some one will raise it.

Nor is there to be seen at present one in whom she can place more hope than in your illustrious house, with its valour and fortune, favoured by God and by the Church of which it is now the chief, and which could be made the head of this redemption. This will not be difficult if you will recall to yourself the actions and lives of the men I have named. And although they were great and wonderful men, yet they were men, and each one of them had no more opportunity than the present offers, for their enterprises were neither more just nor easier than this, nor was God more their friend than He is yours.

With us there is great justice, because that war is just which is necessary, and arms are hallowed when there is no other hope but in them. Here there is the greatest willingness, and where the willingness is great the difficulties cannot be great if you will only follow those men to whom I have directed your attention. Further than this, how extraor-

---

[29]Probably a reference to Cesare Borgia.

dinarily the ways of God have been manifested beyond example; the sea is divided, a cloud has led the way, the rock has poured forth water, it has rained manna, everything has contributed to your greatness; you ought to do the rest. God is not willing to do everything, and thus take away our free will and that share of glory which belongs to us.

And it is not to be wondered at if none of the above-named Italians have been able to accomplish all that is expected from your illustrious house; and if in so many revolutions in Italy, and in so many campaigns, it has always appeared as if military virtue were exhausted, this has happened because the old order of things was not good, and none of us have known how to find a new one. And nothing honours a man more than to establish new laws and new ordinances when he himself has newly risen. Such things when they are well founded and dignified will make him revered and admired, and in Italy there are not wanting opportunities to bring such into use in every form.

Here there is great valour in the limbs whilst it fails in the head. Look attentively at the duels and the hand-to-hand combats, how superior the Italians are in strength, dexterity, and subtlety. But when it comes to armies they do not bear comparison, and this springs entirely from the insufficiency of the leaders, since those who are capable are not obedient, and each one seems to himself to know, there having never been any one so distinguished above the rest, either by valour or fortune, that others would yield to him. Hence it is that for so long a time, and during so much fighting in the past twenty years, whenever there has been an army wholly Italian, it has always given a poor account of itself; the first witness to this is Il Taro, afterwards Alexandria, Capua, Genoa, Vaila, Bologna, Mestri.

If, therefore, your illustrious house wishes to follow those remarkable men who have redeemed their country, it is necessary before all things, as a true foundation for every enterprise, to be provided with your own forces, because there can be no more faithful, truer, or better soldiers. And although singly they are good, altogether they will be much better when they find themselves commanded by their prince, honoured by him, and maintained at his expense. Therefore it is necessary to be prepared with such arms, so that you can be defended against foreigners by Italian valour.

And although Swiss and Spanish infantry may be considered very formidable, nevertheless there is a defect in both, by reason of which a third order would not only be able to oppose them, but might be relied upon to overthrow them. For the Spaniards cannot resist cavalry, and the Switzers are afraid of infantry whenever they encounter them in close combat. Owing to this, as has been and may again be seen, the Spaniards are unable to resist French cavalry, and the Switzers are overthrown by Spanish infantry. And although a complete proof of this latter cannot be shown, nevertheless there was some evidence of it at the battle of Ravenna, when the Spanish infantry were confronted by German battalions, who follow the same tactics as the Swiss; when the Spaniards, by agility of body and with the aid of their shields, got in under the pikes of the Germans and stood out of danger, able to attack, while the Germans stood helpless, and, if the cavalry had not dashed up, all would have been over with them. It is possible, therefore, knowing the defects of both these infantries, to invent a new one, which will resist cavalry and not be afraid of infantry; this need not create a new order of arms, but a variation upon the old. And these are the kind of improvements which confer reputation and power upon a new prince.

This opportunity, therefore, ought not to be allowed to pass for letting Italy at last see her liberator appear. Nor can one express the love with which he would be received in all those provinces which have suffered so much from these foreign scourings, with what thirst for revenge, with what stubborn faith, with what devotion, with what tears. What door would be closed to him? Who would refuse obedience to him? What envy would hinder him? What Italian would refuse him homage? To all of us this barbarous dominion stinks. Let, therefore, your illustrious house take up this charge with that courage and hope with which all just enterprises are undertaken, so that under its standard our native country may be ennobled, and under its auspices may be verified that saying of Petrarch:—

> Virtù contro al Furore
> Prenderà l'arme, e fia il combatter corto:
>   Che l'antico valore
> Negli italici cuor non è ancor morto.[30]

Discourses on Livy

Book I / Chapter 3

Of the Events That Caused the Creation of Tribunes[1] in Rome; Which Made the Republic More Perfect

All those who have written upon civil institutions demonstrate (and history is full of examples to support them) that whoever desires to found a state and give it laws, must start with assuming that all men are bad and ever ready to display their vicious nature, whenever they may find occasion for it. If their evil disposition remains concealed for

---

[30] "Valour against fell wrath
Will take up arms; and be the combat quickly sped!
  For, sure, the ancient worth
That in Italians stirs the heart, is not yet dead."

From *The Prince and the Discourses* by Niccolò Machiavelli, translated by C. E. Detmold (New York: Random House, Inc., 1940).

[1] Magistrates whose specific function was to protect the individual plebeian (common) citizen from the arbitrary action of the patrician (aristocratic) magistrates.

a time, it must be attributed to some unknown reason; and we must assume that it lacked occasion to show itself; but time, which has been said to be the father of all truth, does not fail to bring it to light. After the expulsion of the Tarquins[2] the greatest harmony seemed to prevail between the Senate and the people. The nobles seemed to have laid aside all their haughtiness and assumed popular manners, which made them supportable even to the lowest of the citizens. The nobility played this role so long as the Tarquins lived, without their motive being divined; for they feared the Tarquins, and also lest the ill-treated people might side with them. Their party therefore assumed all possible gentleness in their manners towards the people. But so soon as the death of the Tarquins had relieved them of their apprehensions, they began to vent upon the people all the venom they had so long retained within their breasts, and lost no opportunity to outrage them in every possible way; which is one of the proofs of the argument we have advanced, that men act right only upon compulsion; but from the moment that they have the option and liberty to commit wrong with impunity, then they never fail to carry confusion and disorder everywhere. It is this that has caused it to be said that poverty and hunger make men industrious, and that the law makes men good; and if fortunate circumstances cause good to be done without constraint, the law may be dispensed with. But when such happy influence is lacking, then the law immediately becomes necessary. Thus the nobles, after the death of the Tarquins, being no longer under the influence that had restrained them, determined to establish a new order of things, which had the same effect as the misrule of the Tarquins during their existence; and therefore, after many troubles, tumults, and dangers occasioned by the excesses which both the nobles and the people committed, they came, for the security of the people, to the creation of the Tribunes, who were endowed with so many prerogatives, and surrounded with so much respect, that they formed a powerful barrier between the Senate and the people, which curbed the insolence of the former.

Chapter 4

The Disunion of the Senate and the People Renders the Republic of Rome Powerful and Free

I shall not pass over in silence the disturbances that occurred in Rome from the time of the death of the Tarquins to that of the creation of the Tribunes; and shall afterwards refute the opinion of those who claim that the Roman republic has always been a theatre of turbulence and disorder, and that if its extreme good fortune and the military discipline had not supplied the defects of her constitution, she would have deserved the lowest rank amongst the republics.

It cannot be denied that the Roman Empire was the result of good

---

[2]The last of the semilegendary kings who were supposed to have ruled Rome from the eighth into the sixth century B.C.

fortune and military discipline; but it seems to me that it ought to be perceived that where good discipline prevails there also will good order prevail, and good fortune rarely fails to follow in their train. Let us, however, go into details upon this point. I maintain that those who blame the quarrels of the Senate and the people of Rome condemn that which was the very origin of liberty, and that they were probably more impressed by the cries and noise which these disturbances occasioned in the public places, than by the good effect which they produced; and that they do not consider that in every republic there are two parties, that of the nobles and that of the people; and all the laws that are favorable to liberty result from the opposition of these parties to each other, as may easily be seen from the events that occurred in Rome. From the time of the Tarquins to that of the Gracchi, that is to say, within the space of over three hundred years, the differences between these parties caused but very few exiles, and cost still less blood; they cannot therefore be regarded as having been very injurious and fatal to a republic, which during the course of so many years saw on this account only eight or ten of its citizens sent into exile, and but a very small number put to death, and even but a few condemned to pecuniary fines. Nor can we regard a republic as disorderly where so many virtues were seen to shine. For good examples are the result of good education, and good education is due to good laws; and good laws in their turn spring from those very agitations which have been so inconsiderately condemned by many. For whoever will carefully examine the result of these agitations will find that they have neither caused exiles nor any violence prejudicial to the general good, and will be convinced even that they have given rise to laws that were to the advantage of public liberty. And if it be said that these are strange means,—to hear constantly the cries of the people furious against the Senate, and of a Senate declaiming against the people, to see the populace rush tumultuously through the streets, close their houses, and even leave the city of Rome, —I reply, that all these things can alarm only those who read of them, and that every free state ought to afford the people the opportunity of giving vent, so to say, to their ambition; and above all those republics which on important occasions have to avail themselves of this very people. Now such were the means employed at Rome; when the people wanted to obtain a law, they resorted to some of the extremes of which we have just spoken, or they refused to enroll themselves to serve in the wars, so that the Senate was obliged to satisfy them in some measure. The demands of a free people are rarely pernicious to their liberty; they are generally inspired by oppressions, experienced or apprehended; and if their fears are ill founded, resort is had to public assemblies where the mere eloquence of a single good and respectable man will make them sensible of their error. "The people," says Cicero, "although ignorant, yet are capable of appreciating the truth, and yield to it readily when it is presented to them by a man whom they esteem worthy of their confidence."

One should show then more reserve in blaming the Roman government, and consider that so many good effects, which originated in that republic, cannot but result from very good causes. If the troubles of

Rome occasioned the creation of Tribunes, then they cannot be praised too highly, for besides giving to the people a share in the public administration, these Tribunes were established as the most assured guardians of Roman liberty. . . .

Chapter 9

To Found a New Republic, or to Reform Entirely the Old Institutions of an Existing One, Must Be the Work of One Man Only

It may perhaps appear to some that I have gone too far into the details of Roman history before having made any mention of the founders of that republic, or of her institutions, her religion, and her military establishment. Not wishing, therefore, to keep any longer in suspense the desires of those who wish to understand these matters, I say that many will perhaps consider it an evil example that the founder of a civil society, as Romulus was, should first have killed his brother, and then have consented to the death of Titus Tatius, who had been elected to share the royal authority with him; from which it might be concluded that the citizens, according to the example of their prince, might, from ambition and the desire to rule, destroy those who attempt to oppose their authority. This opinion would be correct, if we do not take into consideration the object which Romulus had in view in committing that homicide. But we must assume, as a general rule, that it never or rarely happens that a republic or monarchy is well constituted, or its old institutions entirely reformed, unless it is done by only one individual; it is even necessary that he whose mind has conceived such a constitution should be alone in carrying it into effect. A sagacious legislator of a republic, therefore, whose object is to promote the public good, and not his private interests, and who prefers his country to his own successors, should concentrate all authority in himself; and a wise mind will never censure any one for having employed any extraordinary means for the purpose of establishing a kingdom or constituting a republic. It is well that, when the act accuses him, the result should excuse him; and when the result is good, as in the case of Romulus, it will always absolve him from blame. For he is to be reprehended who commits violence for the purpose of destroying, and not he who employs it for beneficent purposes. The lawgiver should, however, be sufficiently wise and virtuous not to leave this authority which he has assumed either to his heirs or to any one else; for mankind, being more prone to evil than to good, his successor might employ for evil purposes the power which he had used only for good ends. Besides, although one man alone should organize a government, yet it will not endure long if the administration of it remains on the shoulders of a single individual; it is well, then, to confide this to the charge of many, for thus it will be sustained by the many. Therefore, as the organization of anything cannot be made by many, because the divergence of their opinions hinders them from agreeing as to what is best, yet, when once they do understand it, they will not readily agree to abandon it. That Romulus deserves to be excused for the death of his brother and that of his associate, and that what he had done was for the general good, and not for the gratification of his own ambition, is proved by the fact that he immediately instituted a Senate with which to consult, and according to the opinions of which he might form his resolutions. And on carefully considering the authority which Romulus reserved for himself, we see that all he kept was the command of the army in case of war, and the power of convoking the Senate. This was seen when Rome became free, after the expulsion of the Tarquins, when there was no other innovation made upon the existing order of things than the substitution of two Consuls, appointed annually, in place of an hereditary king; which proves clearly that all the original institutions of that city were more in conformity with the requirements of a free and civil society than with an absolute and tyrannical government.

The above views might be corroborated by any number of examples, such as those of Moses, Lycurgus, Solon,[3] and other founders of monarchies and republics, who were enabled to establish laws suitable for the general good only by keeping for themselves an exclusive authority; but all these are so well known that I will not further refer to them. I will adduce only one instance, not so celebrated, but which merits the consideration of those who aim to become good legislators: it is this. Agis,[4] king of Sparta, desired to bring back the Spartans to the strict observance of the laws of Lycurgus, being convinced that, by deviating from them, their city had lost much of her ancient virtue, and consequently her power and dominion; but the Spartan Ephores[5] had him promptly killed, as one who attempted to make himself a tyrant. His successor, Cleomenes, had conceived the same desire, from studying the records and writings of Agis, which he had found, and which explained his aims and intentions. Cleomenes was convinced that he would be unable to render this service to his country unless he possessed sole authority; for he judged that, owing to the ambitious nature of men, he could not promote the interests of the many against the will of the few; and therefore he availed of a convenient opportunity to have all the Ephores slain, as well as all such others as might oppose his project, after which he restored the laws of Lycurgus entirely. This course was calculated to resuscitate the greatness of Sparta, and to give Cleomenes a reputation equal to that of Lycurgus, had it not been for the power of the Macedonians and the weakness of the other Greek republics. For being soon after attacked by the Macedonians, and Sparta by herself being inferior in strength, and there being no one whom he could call to his aid, he was defeated; and thus his project, so just and laudable, was never put into execution. Considering, then, all these things, I conclude that, to found a republic, one must be alone; and that Romulus

---

[3]Lycurgus was the semilegendary king of Sparta who was supposed to have trained that city's constitution and code of laws during the ninth century B.C. Solon was an Athenian statesman famous for the just system of laws and social reforms he devised at the beginning of the sixth century B.C.

[4]Reigned 244–241? B.C.

[5]A board of five magistrates, elected annually, who had supreme authority in the government of Sparta.

deserves to be absolved from, and not blamed for, the death of Remus and of Tatius.

Chapter 12

The Importance of Giving Religion a Prominent Influence in a State, and How Italy Was Ruined Because She Failed in This Respect Through the Conduct of the Church of Rome

Princes and republics who wish to maintain themselves free from corruption must above all things preserve the purity of all religious observances, and treat them with proper reverence; for there is no greater indication of the ruin of a country than to see religion contemned. And this is easily understood, when we know upon what the religion of a country is founded; for the essence of every religion is based upon some one main principle. The religion of the Gentiles had for its foundation the responses of the oracles, and the tenets of the augurs and aruspices; upon these alone depended all their ceremonies, rites, and sacrifices. For they readily believed that the Deity which could predict their future good or ill was also able to bestow it upon them. Thence arose their temples, their sacrifices, their supplications, and all the other ceremonies; for the oracle of Delphos, the temple of Jupiter Ammon, and other celebrated oracles, kept the world in admiration and devoutness. But when these afterwards began to speak only in accordance with the wishes of the princes, and their falsity was discovered by the people, then men became incredulous, and disposed to disturb all good institutions. It is therefore the duty of princes and heads of republics to uphold the foundations of the religion of their countries, for then it is easy to keep their people religious, and consequently well conducted and united. And therefore everything that tends to favor religion (even though it were believed to be false) should be received and availed of to strengthen it; and this should be done the more, the wiser the rulers are, and the better they understand the natural course of things. Such was, in fact, the practice observed by sagacious men; which has given rise to the belief in the miracles that are celebrated in religions, however false they may be. For the sagacious rulers have given these miracles increased importance, no matter whence or how they originated; and their authority afterwards gave them credence with the people. Rome had many such miracles; and one of the most remarkable was that which occurred when the Roman soldiers sacked the city of Veii; some of them entered the temple of Juno, and, placing themselves in front of her statue, said to her, "Will you come to Rome?" Some imagined that they observed the statue make a sign of assent, and others pretended to have heard her reply, "Yes." Now these men, being very religious, as reported by Titus Livius,[6] and having entered the temple quietly, they were filled with devotion and reverence, and might really have believed that they had heard a reply

---

[6]Livy (59 B.C. – 17 A.D.), the Roman historian whose works Machiavelli is using as the basis for his *Discourses*.

to their question, such as perhaps they could have presupposed. But this opinion and belief was favored and magnified by Camillus[7] and the other Roman chiefs.

And certainly, if the Christian religion had from the beginning been maintained according to the principles of its founder, the Christian states and republics would have been much more united and happy than what they are. Nor can there be a greater proof of its decadence than to witness the fact that the nearer people are to the Church of Rome, which is the head of our religion, the less religious are they. And whoever examines the principles upon which that religion is founded, and sees how widely different from those principles its present practice and application are, will judge that her ruin or chastisement is near at hand. But as there are some of the opinion that the well-being of Italian affairs depends upon the Church of Rome, I will present such arguments against that opinion as occur to me; two of which are most important, and cannot according to my judgment be controverted. The first is, that the evil example of the court of Rome has destroyed all piety and religion in Italy, which brings in its train infinite improprieties and disorders; for as we may presuppose all good where religion prevails, so where it is wanting we have the right to suppose the very opposite. We Italians then owe to the Church of Rome and to her priests our having become irreligious and bad; but we owe her a still greater debt, and one that will be the cause of our ruin, namely, that the Church has kept and still keeps our country divided. And certainly a country can never be united and happy, except when it obeys wholly one government, whether a republic or a monarchy, as is the case in France and in Spain; and the sole cause why Italy is not in the same condition, and is not governed by either one republic or one sovereign, is the Church; for having acquired and holding a temporal dominion, yet she has never had sufficient power or courage to enable her to seize the rest of the country and make herself sole sovereign of all Italy. And on the other hand she has not been so feeble that the fear of losing her temporal power prevented her from calling in the aid of a foreign power to defend her against such others as had become too powerful in Italy; as was seen in former days by many sad experiences, when through the intervention of Charlemagne she drove out the Lombards, who were masters of nearly all Italy;[8] and when in our times she crushed the power of the Venetians by the aid of France, and afterwards with the assistance of the Swiss drove out in turn the French. The Church, then, not having been powerful enough to be able to master all Italy, nor having permitted any other power to do so, has been the cause why Italy has never been able to unite under one head, but has always remained under a number of princes and lords, which occasioned her so many dissensions and so much weakness that she became a prey not only to the powerful barbarians, but of whoever chose to assail her. This we other Italians owe to the Church of Rome, and to none other. And any one, to be promptly convinced by experiment of the truth of all this, should have the power to transport the court of Rome to reside, with all the power

[7]Roman soldier and statesman of the fourth century B.C.

it has in Italy, in the midst of the Swiss, who of all peoples nowadays live most according to their ancient customs so far as religion and their military system are concerned; and he would see in a very little while that the evil habits of that court would create more confusion in that country than anything else that could ever happen there.

Chapter 34

The Authority of the Dictatorship[9] Has Always Proved Beneficial to Rome, and Never Injurious; It Is the Authority Which Men Usurp, and Not That Which Is Given Them by the Free Suffrages of Their Fellow-Citizens, That Is Dangerous to Civil Liberty

Some writers have blamed those Romans who first introduced the practice of creating Dictators, as being calculated in time to lead to despotism in Rome; alleging that the first tyrant of that city governed her under the title of Dictator, and saying that, if it had not been for this office, Cæsar never could under any other public title have imposed his despotism upon the Romans. Evidently the subject could not have been thoroughly considered by those who advance this opinion, so generally adopted without good reasons; for it was neither the name nor the rank of the Dictator that subjected Rome to servitude, but it was the authority which citizens usurped to perpetuate themselves in the government. And if the title of Dictator had not existed in Rome, some other would have been taken; for power can easily take a name, but a name cannot give power. And it is seen that the dictatorship, whenever created according to public law and not usurped by individual authority, always proved beneficial to Rome; it is the magistracies and powers that are created by illegitimate means which harm a republic, and not those that are appointed in the regular way, as was the case in Rome, where in the long course of time no Dictator ever failed to prove beneficial to the republic. The reason of this is perfectly evident: first, before a citizen can be in a position to usurp extraordinary powers, many things must concur, which in a republic as yet uncorrupted never can happen; for he must be exceedingly rich, and must have many adherents and partisans, which cannot be where the laws are observed; and even if he had them, he would never be supported by the free suffrages of the people, for such men are generally looked upon as dangerous. Besides this, Dictators were appointed only for a limited term, and not in perpetuity, and their power to act was confined to the particular occasion for which they were created. This power consisted in being able to decide alone upon the measures to be adopted for averting the pressing danger, to do whatever he deemed proper without consultation, and to inflict punishment upon any one without appeal. But the Dictator

---

[9] A dictator was a magistrate appointed to rule the Republic during a period of special, originally only military, emergency. His appointment could not exceed six months.

could do nothing to alter the form of the government, such as to diminish the powers of the Senate or the people, or to abrogate existing institutions and create new ones. So that, taking together the short period for which he held the office, and the limited powers which he possessed, and the fact that the Roman people were as yet uncorrupted, it is evident that it was impossible for him to exceed his powers and to harm the republic; which on the contrary, as all experience shows, was always benefited by him.

And truly, of all the institutions of Rome, this one deserves to be counted amongst those to which she was most indebted for her greatness and dominion. For without some such an institution Rome would with difficulty have escaped the many extraordinary dangers that befell her; for the customary proceedings of republics are slow, no magistrate or council being permitted to act independently, but being in almost all instances obliged to act in concert one with the other, so that often much time is required to harmonize their several opinions; and tardy measures are most dangerous when the occasion requires prompt action. And therefore all republics should have some institution similar to the dictatorship. The republic of Venice, which is pre-eminent amongst modern ones, had reserved to a small number of citizens the power of deciding all urgent matters without referring their decisions to a larger council. And when a republic lacks some such system, a strict observance of the established laws will expose her to ruin; or, to save her from such danger, the laws will have to be disregarded. Now in a well-ordered republic it should never be necessary to resort to extra-constitutional measures; for although they may for the time be beneficial, yet the precedent is pernicious, for if the practice is once established of disregarding the laws for good objects, they will in a little while be disregarded under that pretext for evil purposes. Thus no republic will ever be perfect if she has not by law provided for everything, having a remedy for every emergency, and fixed rules for applying it. And therefore I will say, in conclusion, that those republics which in time of danger cannot resort to a dictatorship, or some similar authority, will generally be ruined when grave occasions occur. It is well to note with reference to this institution how wisely the Romans had provided the mode of electing the Dictator. For as his creation reflected in some measure discredit upon the Consuls, who as chiefs of the republic had to submit to his authority the same as the other citizens, and apprehending that this might possibly excite indignation amongst the citizens, it was decided that the nomination of the Dictator should be made by the Consuls themselves; so that when an emergency occurred in which Rome needed this quasi regal power, the Consuls, having the right of creating it themselves, might thus be less sensitive than if it were imposed upon them by others. For the wounds and every other evil that men inflict upon themselves spontaneously, and of their own choice, are in the long run less painful than those inflicted by others. In later times, however, the Romans, instead of appointing a Dictator, used to confer that extraordinary power upon the Consuls in these words: "Let the Consuls see that the republic suffers no detriment." But to return now to our subject, I conclude that the neighboring tribes of Rome, in attempting to oppress her, caused her not only to adopt new means for defending herself, but also to prepare with greater force, abler counsels, and greater authority to attack them.

Book II

Introduction

Men ever praise the olden time, and find fault with the present, though often without reason. They are such partisans of the past that they extol not only the times which they know only by the accounts left of them by historians, but, having grown old, they also laud all they remember to have seen in their youth. Their opinion is generally erroneous in that respect, and I think the reasons which cause this illusion are various. The first I believe to be the fact that we never know the whole truth about the past, and very frequently writers conceal such events as would reflect disgrace upon their century, whilst they magnify and amplify those that lend lustre to it. The majority of authors obey the fortune of conquerors to that degree that, by way of rendering their victories more glorious, they exaggerate not only the valiant deeds of the victor, but also of the vanquished; so that future generations of the countries of both will have cause to wonder at those men and times, and are obliged to praise and admire them to the utmost. Another reason is that men's hatreds generally spring from fear or envy. Now, these two powerful reasons of hatred do not exist for us with regard to the past, which can no longer inspire either apprehension or envy. But it is very different with the affairs of the present, in which we ourselves are either actors or spectators, and of which we have a complete knowledge, nothing being concealed from us; and knowing the good together with many other things that are displeasing to us, we are forced to conclude that the present is inferior to the past, though in reality it may be much more worthy of glory and fame. I do not speak of matters pertaining to the arts, which shine by their intrinsic merits, which time can neither add to nor diminish; but I speak of such things as pertain to the actions and manners of men, of which we do not possess such manifest evidence.

I repeat, then, that this practice of praising and decrying is very general, though it cannot be said that it is always erroneous; for sometimes our judgment is of necessity correct, human affairs being in a state of perpetual movement, always either ascending or declining. We see, for instance, a city or country with a government well organized by some man of superior ability; for a time it progresses and attains a great prosperity through the talents of its lawgiver. Now, if any one living at such a period should praise the past more than the time in which he lives, he would certainly be deceiving himself; and this error will be found due to the reasons above indicated. But should he live in that city or country at the period after it shall have passed the zenith of its glory and in the time of its decline, then he would not be wrong in praising the past. Reflecting now upon the course of human affairs, I think that, as a whole, the world remains very much in the same condition, and the good in it always balances the evil; but the good and the evil change from one country to another, as we learn from the history of those ancient kingdoms that differed from each other in manners, whilst the world at large remained the same. The only difference being, that all the virtues that first found a place in Assyria were thence transferred to Media, and afterwards passed to Persia, and from there they came into Italy and to Rome. And if after the fall of the Roman Empire none other sprung up that endured for any length of time, and where the aggregate virtues of the world were kept together, we nevertheless see them scattered amongst many nations, as, for instance, in the kingdom of France, the Turkish empire, or that of the Sultan of Egypt, and nowadays the people of Germany, and before them those famous Saracens, who achieved such great things and conquered so great a part of the world, after having destroyed the Roman Empire of the East. The different peoples of these several countries, then, after the fall of the Roman Empire, have possessed and possess still in great part that virtue which is so much lamented and so sincerely praised. And those who live in those countries and praise the past more than the present may deceive themselves; but whoever is born in Italy and Greece, and has not become either an Ultramontane in Italy or a Turk in Greece, has good reason to find fault with his own and to praise the olden times; for in their past there are many things worthy of the highest admiration, whilst the present has nothing that compensates for all the extreme misery, infamy, and degradation of a period where there is neither observance of religion, law, or military discipline, and which is stained by every species of the lowest brutality; and these vices are the more detestable as they exist amongst those who sit in the tribunals as judges, and hold all power in their hands, and claim to be adored.

But to return to our argument, I say that, if men's judgment is at fault upon the point whether the present age be better than the past, of which latter, owing to its antiquity, they cannot have such perfect knowledge as of their own period, the judgment of old men of what they have seen in their youth and in their old age should not be false, inasmuch as they have equally seen both the one and the other. This would be true, if men at the different periods of their lives had the same judgment and the same appetites. But as these vary (though the times do not), things cannot appear the same to men who have other tastes, other delights, and other considerations in age from what they had in youth. For as men when they age lose their strength and energy, whilst their prudence and judgment improve, so the same things that in youth appeared to them supportable and good, will of necessity, when they have grown old, seem to them insupportable and evil; and when they should blame their own judgment they find fault with the times. Moreover, as human desires are insatiable, (because their nature is to have and to do everything whilst fortune limits their possessions and capacity of enjoyment,) this gives rise to a constant discontent in the human mind and a weariness of the things they possess; and it is this which makes them decry the present, praise the past, and desire the future, and all this without any reasonable motive. I know not, then, whether

I deserve to be classed with those who deceive themselves, if in these Discourses I shall laud too much the times of ancient Rome and censure those of our own day. And truly, if the virtues that ruled then and the vices that prevail now were not as clear as the sun, I should be more reticent in my expressions, lest I should fall into the very error for which I reproach others. But the matter being so manifest that everybody sees it, I shall boldly and openly say what I think of the former times and of the present, so as to excite in the minds of the young men who may read my writings the desire to avoid the evils of the latter, and to prepare themselves to imitate the virtues of the former, whenever fortune presents them the occasion. For it is the duty of an honest man to teach others that good which the malignity of the times and of fortune has prevented his doing himself; so that amongst the many capable ones whom he has instructed, some one perhaps, more favored by Heaven, may perform it.

Having in the preceding Book treated of the conduct of the Romans in matters relating to their internal affairs, I shall in this Book speak of what the Roman people did in relation to the aggrandizement of their empire.

Chapter 2

What Nations the Romans Had to Contend Against, and with What Obstinacy They Defended Their Liberty

Nothing required so much effort on the part of the Romans to subdue the nations around them, as well as those of more distant countries, as the love of liberty which these people cherished in those days; and which they defended with so much obstinacy, that nothing but the exceeding valor of the Romans could ever have subjugated them. For we know from many instances to what danger they exposed themselves to preserve or recover their liberty, and what vengeance they practised upon those who had deprived them of it. The lessons of history teach us also, on the other hand, the injuries people suffer from servitude. And whilst in our own times there is only one country in which we can say that free communities exist, in those ancient times all countries contained numerous cities that enjoyed entire liberty. In the times of which we are now speaking[10] there were in Italy from the mountains that divide the present Tuscany from Lombardy, down to the extreme point, a number of independent nations, such as the Tuscans, the Romans, the Samnites, and many others, that inhabited the rest of Italy. Nor is there ever any mention of there having been other kings besides those that reigned in Rome, and Porsenna, king of the Tuscans, whose line became extinct in a manner not mentioned in history. But we do see that, at the time when the Romans went to besiege Veii, Tuscany was free, and so prized her liberty and hated the very name of king, that when the Veienti had created a king in their city for its defence,

---

[10]Sixth century B.C.

and applied to the Tuscans for help against the Romans, it was resolved, after repeated deliberations, not to grant such assistance to the Veienti so long as they lived under that king; for the Tuscans deemed it not well to engage in the defence of those who had voluntarily subjected themselves to the rule of one man. And it is easy to understand whence that affection for liberty arose in the people, for they had seen that cities never increased in dominion or wealth unless they were free. And certainly it is wonderful to think of the greatness which Athens attained within the space of a hundred years after having freed herself from the tyranny of Pisistratus;[11] and still more wonderful is it to reflect upon the greatness which Rome achieved after she was rid of her kings. The cause of this is manifest, for it is not individual prosperity, but the general good, that makes cities great; and certainly the general good is regarded nowhere but in republics, because whatever they do is for the common benefit, and should it happen to prove an injury to one or more individuals, those for whose benefit the thing is done are so numerous that they can always carry the measure against the few that are injured by it. But the very reverse happens where there is a prince whose private interests are generally in opposition to those of the city, whilst the measures taken for the benefit of the city are seldom deemed personally advantageous by the prince. This state of things soon leads to a tyranny, the least evil of which is to check the advance of the city in its career of prosperity, so that it grows neither in power nor wealth, but on the contrary rather retrogrades. And if fate should have it that the tyrant is enterprising, and by his courage and valor extends his dominions, it will never be for the benefit of the city, but only for his own; for he will never bestow honors and office upon the good and brave citizens over whom he tyrannizes, so that he may not have occasion to suspect and fear them. Nor will he make the states which he conquers subject or tributary to the city of which he is the despot, because it would not be to his advantage to make that city powerful, but it will always be for his interest to keep the state disunited, so that each place and country shall recognize him only as master; thus he alone, and not his country, profits by his conquests. Those who desire to have this opinion confirmed by many other arguments, need but read Xenophon's treatise "On Tyranny."

It is no wonder, then, that the ancients hated tyranny and loved freedom, and that the very name of Liberty should have been held in such esteem by them; as was shown by the Syracusans when Hieronymus, the nephew of Hiero, was killed.[12] When his death became known to his army, which was near Syracuse, it caused at first some disturbances, and they were about committing violence upon his murderers; but when they learnt that the cry of Liberty had been raised in Syracuse, they were delighted, and instantly returned to order. Their fury against the tyrannicides was quelled, and they thought only of how a free government might be established in Syracuse. Nor can we wonder that the people indulge in extraordinary revenge against those who have robbed

---

[11]Ruled Athens 560?–527 B.C

[12]These events occurred in the fourth decade of the fifth century B.C.

them of their liberty; of which we could cite many instances, but will quote only one that occurred in Corcyra, a city of Greece, during the Peloponnesian war.[13] Greece was at that time divided into two parties, one of which adhered to the Athenians, and the other to the Spartans, and a similar division of parties existed in most of the Greek cities. It happened that in Corcyra the nobles, being the stronger party, seized upon the liberties of the people; but with the assistance of the Athenians the popular party recovered its power, and, having seized the nobles, they tied their hands behind their backs, and threw them into a prison large enough to hold them all. They thence took eight or ten at a time, under pretence of sending them into exile in different directions; but instead of that they killed them with many cruelties. When the remainder became aware of this, they resolved if possible to escape such an ignominious death; and having armed themselves as well as they could, they resisted those who attempted to enter the prison; but when the people heard this disturbance, they pulled down the roof and upper portion of the prison, and suffocated the nobles within under its ruins. Many such notable and horrible cases occurred in that country, which shows that the people will avenge their lost liberty with more energy than when it is merely threatened.

Reflecting now as to whence it came that in ancient times the people were more devoted to liberty than in the present, I believe that it resulted from this, that men were stronger in those days, which I believe to be attributable to the difference of education, founded upon the difference of their religion and ours. For, as our religion teaches us the truth and the true way of life, it causes us to attach less value to the honors and possessions of this world; whilst the Pagans, esteeming those things as the highest good, were more energetic and ferocious in their actions. We may observe this also in most of their institutions, beginning with the magnificence of their sacrifices as compared with the humility of ours, which are gentle solemnities rather than magnificent ones, and have nothing of energy or ferocity in them, whilst in theirs there was no lack of pomp and show, to which was superadded the ferocious and bloody nature of the sacrifice by the slaughter of many animals, and the familiarity with this terrible sight assimilated the nature of men to their sacrificial ceremonies. Besides this, the Pagan religion deified only men who had achieved great glory, such as commanders of armies and chiefs of republics, whilst ours glorifies more the humble and contemplative men than the men of action. Our religion, moreover, places the supreme happiness in humility, lowliness, and a contempt for worldly objects, whilst the other, on the contrary, places the supreme good in grandeur of soul, strength of body, and all such other qualities as render men formidable; and if our religion claims of us fortitude of soul, it is more to enable us to suffer than to achieve great deeds.

These principles seem to me to have made men feeble, and caused them to become an easy prey to evil-minded men, who can control them more securely, seeing that the great body of men, for the sake of gaining Paradise, are more disposed to endure injuries than to avenge

---

[13]These events occurred in the seventh decade of the fifth century B.C.

them. And although it would seem that the world has become effeminate and Heaven disarmed, yet this arises unquestionably from the
baseness of men, who have interpreted our religion according to the
promptings of indolence rather than those of virtue. For if we were
to reflect that our religion permits us to exalt and defend our country,
we should see that according to it we ought also to love and honor our
country, and prepare ourselves so as to be capable of defending her.
It is this education, then, and this false interpretation of our religion,
that is the cause of there not being so many republics nowadays as there
were anciently; and that there is no longer the same love of liberty
amongst the people now as there was then. I believe, however, that
another reason for this will be found in the fact that the Roman Empire,
by force of arms, destroyed all the republics and free cities; and although that empire was afterwards itself dissolved, yet these cities
could not reunite themselves nor reorganize their civil institutions,
except in a very few instances.

Be that, however, as it may, the Romans found everywhere a league
of republics, well armed for the most obstinate defence of their liberties,
showing that it required the rare ability and extreme valor of the Romans
to subjugate them. And to give but one example of this, we will confine
ourselves to the case of the Samnites, which really seems marvelous.
This people Titus Livius himself admits to have been so powerful
and valiant in arms that, until the time of the Consul Papirius Cursor,
grandson of the first Papirius, a period of forty years,[14] they were able
to resist the Romans, notwithstanding their many defeats, the destruction of their cities, and much slaughter. That country, which was then
so thickly inhabited and contained so many cities, is now almost a desert;
and yet it was originally so powerful and well governed that it would
have been unconquerable by any other than Roman valor. It is easy to
discover the cause of this different state of things, for it all comes from
this, that formerly that people enjoyed freedom, and now they live in
servitude; for, as I have already said above, only those cities and countries
that are free can achieve greatness. Population is greater there because
marriages are more free and offer more advantages to the citizen; for
people will gladly have children when they know that they can support
them, and that they will not be deprived of their patrimony, and where
they know that their children not only are born free and not slaves, but,
if they possess talents and virtue, can arrive at the highest dignities of
the state. In free countries we also see wealth increase more rapidly,
both that which results from the culture of the soil and that which is
produced by industry and art; for everybody gladly multiplies those
things, and seeks to acquire those goods the possession of which he can
tranquilly enjoy. Thence men vie with each other to increase both private and public wealth, which consequently increase in an extraordinary
manner. But the contrary of all this takes place in countries that are
subject to another; and the more rigorous the subjection of the people,
the more will they be deprived of all the good to which they had previously been accustomed. And the hardest of all servitudes is to be sub-

---

[14]First third of the third century B.C.

ject to a republic, and this for these reasons: first, because it is more enduring, and there is no hope of escaping from it; and secondly, because republics aim to enervate and weaken all other states so as to increase their own power. This is not the case with a prince who holds another country in subjection, unless indeed he should be a barbarous devastator of countries and a destroyer of all human civilization, such as the princes of the Orient. But if he be possessed of only ordinary humanity, he will treat all cities that are subject to him equally well, and will leave them in the enjoyment of their arts and industries, and measurably all their ancient institutions. So that if they cannot grow the same as if they were free, they will at least not be ruined whilst in bondage; and by this is understood that bondage into which cities fall that become subject to a stranger, for of that to one of their own citizens we have already spoken above.

Considering now all that has been said, we need not wonder at the power which the Samnites possessed, so long as they were free, nor at the feeble condition to which they afterwards became reduced when they were subjugated. Titus Livius testifies to this in several instances, and mainly in speaking of the war with Hannibal, where he states that the Samnites, pressed by a legion of Romans which was at Nola, sent messengers to Hannibal to implore his assistance. These said in their address that for a hundred years they had combated the Romans with their own soldiers and generals, and had many times sustained the contest against two consular armies and two Consuls at once; but that now they had been reduced so low that they were hardly able to defend themselves against the one small Roman legion that was stationed at Nola.

Comments / on Machiavelli

I am at my farm; and, since my last misfortunes, have not been in Florence twenty days. I rise with the sun, and go into a wood of mine that is being cut, where I remain two hours inspecting the work of the previous day and conversing with the woodcutters, who have always some trouble on hand among themselves or with their neighbors. . . . Next I take the road, enter the inn door, talk with the passers-by, inquire the news of the neighborhood, listen to a variety of matters, and make note of the different tastes and humors of men. This brings me to dinnertime, when I join my family and eat the poor produce of my farm. After dinner I go back to the inn, where I generally find the host and a butcher, a miller, and a pair of bakers. With these companions I play the fool all day at cards or backgammon: a thousand squabbles, a thousand insults and abusive dialogues take place, while we haggle over a farthing, and shout loud enough to be heard from San Casciano. But when evening falls I go home and enter my study. On the threshold I put off my country clothing, filthy with mud and mire, and array myself in royal courtly garments; thus worthily attired, I make my entrance into the ancient courts of the men of old, where they receive me with love, and where I feed upon that food which only is my own and for which I was born. . . . For four hours' space I feel no annoyance, forget all care; poverty cannot frighten, nor death appal me. I am carried away to their society. And since Dante says "that there is no science unless we retain what we have learned," I have set down what I have gained from their discourse, and composed a treatise, *De Principatibus,* in which I enter as deeply as I can into the science of the subject. . . . To a prince, and especially to a new prince, it ought to prove welcome. Therefore I am dedicating it to The Magnificence Guliano.[15] . . . I have talked with Filippo Casavecchia about this little work of mine, whether I ought to present it or not; and if so, whether I ought to send or take it myself to him. . . . I am prompted to present it by the necessity which pursues me, seeing that I am consuming myself in idleness, and I cannot continue long in this way without becoming contemptible through poverty. I wish these Signori Medici would begin to make some use of me, if it were only to set me to the work of rolling a stone. If I did not win them over to me afterwards, I should only complain of myself. As for my book, if they read it, they would perceive that the fifteen years I have spent in studying statecraft have not been wasted in sleep or play; and everybody ought to be glad to make use of a man who has so filled himself with experience at the expense of others.

NICCOLÒ MACHIAVELLI (1513)

What means a prince whose sole motive is lust of mastery should use to establish and maintain his dominion, the most ingenious Machiavelli has set forth at large; but with what design one can hardly be sure. . . . He perhaps wished to show how cautious a free multitude should be of entrusting its welfare absolutely to one man, who . . . must be in daily fear of plots, and so is forced to look chiefly after his own interest, and, as for the multitude, rather to plot against it than consult its good. And I am the more led to this opinion concerning that most farseeing man, because it is known that he was favorable to liberty, for the maintenance of which he has besides given the most wholesome advice.

BARUCH SPINOZA (1670)

If Machiavelli had had a prince for a disciple, the first thing he would have recommended him to do would have been to write a book against Machiavellism. *VOLTAIRE (1755)*

It is indeed scarcely possible for any person, not well acquainted with the history and literature of Italy, to read without horror and amazement the celebrated treatise which has brought so much obloquy on the name of Machiavelli. Such a display of wickedness, naked yet not ashamed, such cool, judicious, scientific atrocity, seemed rather to belong to a fiend than to the most depraved of men. Principles which the most hardened ruffian would scarcely hint to his most trusted accomplice, or avow, without the disguise of some palliating sophism, even to his own mind, are professed without the slightest circumlocution, and assumed as the fundamental axioms of all political science. . . . After this, it may seem ridiculous to say that we are acquainted with few writings which exhibit so much elevation of sentiment, so pure and warm a zeal for the public good, or so just a view of the duties and rights of citizens, as those of Machiavelli. Yet so it is. And even from *The Prince* itself we could select many passages in support of this remark. . . . It is, therefore, in the state of the moral feeling among the Italians of those times that we must seek for the real explanation of what seems most mysterious in the life and writings of this remarkable man.   *T. B. MACAULAY (1827)*

The authentic interpreter of Machiavelli . . . is the whole course of later history. . . . [Machiavelli] is the earliest conscious and articulate exponent of certain living forces in the present world. Religion, progressive enlightenment, the perpetual vigilance of public opinion, have not reduced his empire, or disproved the justice of his conception of mankind. He obtains a new lease of authority from causes that are still prevailing and from doctrines that are apparent in politics, philosophy and science.
LORD ACTON (1891)

The very realism of *The Prince* defeats its own purpose. The redeemer of the chosen people is the outcome of their defeat: his one goal is success, his one virtue efficiency, his only principle expediency. His morality is the martial law of the soul, in which the normal rights of humanity are suspended. But as politics are a perpetual emergency, either latent or actual, expediency becomes his normal law. He is emancipated from common prejudices; he exists in a moral void; his conduct is to be judged by the mind alone; he is a scientific creation; that is his strength; and it is also his weakness.   *RALPH ROEDER (1933)*

In one sense, at least, it is unfortunate that the study of politics should so generally be called political science. It can never be a science in the same sense that physics is a science, based on experimentation and measurement. In every political decision there must always remain a calculated risk. . . . The best [the political scientist] can do is to study the motivation of princes in concrete situations without any preconceived ideas. Machiavelli held that, of such preconceived ideas which prevent arriving at the truth, the most serious is the idea that princes follow, or should follow, the same moral code that governs the conduct of private individuals. Machiavelli therefore completely divorced the study of politics from the study of ethics. They have nothing in common. But here we quickly run into one of several psychological contradictions into which Machiavelli's rigorous realism leads him. He recommends to the prince that he use hypocrisy, whenever expedient, to gain power. This cannot be effective in the long run, since the prince's important relations are with other princes. . . . When all princes practice deceit it soon fails to get results for any of them.   *CHRISTIAN GAUSS (1952)*

The Prince is neither a moral nor an immoral book: it is simply a technical book. In a technical book we do not seek for rules of ethical conduct, of good and evil. It is enough if we are told what is useful or useless.

The whole argument of Machiavelli is clear and coherent. His logic is impeccable. If we accept his premises we cannot avoid his conclusions. With Machiavelli we stand at the gateway of the modern world. The desired end is attained; the state has won its full autonomy. Yet this result had to be bought dearly. The state is entirely independent; but at the same time it is completely isolated. The sharp knife of Machiavelli's thought has cut off all the threads by which in former generations the state was fastened to the organic whole of human existence. The political world has lost its connections not only with religion or metaphysics but also with all the other forms of man's ethical and cultural life. It stands alone—in an empty space.   *ERNST CASSIRER (1946)*

The famous last chapter of *The Prince* is an appeal to the national senti- ment of the Italians, and an apostrophe to the savior who will deliver Italy from the barbarians. It voices the hope that such a liberator will be welcomed everywhere in Italy and hailed as the father of his country. Whether or not this chapter was written separately from the rest of the book, it hardly accords with the realism Machiavelli had shown through- out the earlier chapters. In many ways these earlier chapters may be in- terpreted as a refutation, chapter by chapter and page by page, of the ethi- cal and idealistic treatises on the virtues of the prince, characteristic of humanistic literature. It almost looks as if Machiavelli, when he came to the end, made a desperate appeal to the existence of a patriotic senti- ment which his whole observation of the Italian scene must have proved simply was not there. He had bewailed its absence; he had studied its effect in Roman history; he had invoked the dictator in Italy precisely be- cause the sense of community was wanting. Yet he seemed in this last chapter to feel that an Italian national sentiment could be created over- night by the provision of forceful leadership. The great analyst of the methods of political realism yielded here to a romantic view of national- ism, the other great force that was to dominate the modern political scene. *Realpolitik* could use nationalism, and indeed became far more powerful when based on nationalism; but it could not create nationalism. Louis XI [of France] and Ferdinand of Aragon could accomplish what they did, not only because of what they were in themselves, but also because of a certain sense of community in their realms. Caesar Borgia was no Rom- ulus. The forceful union of the people under a prince who was feared —a dictator—was a substitute for the sense of community and genuine patriotism that might have flourished in other historic conditions. Had Machiavelli been consistent to the end, he would have realized that, where nationalism did not exist, the most skillful efforts of *Realpolitik* to evoke it were, at least in the short run, doomed to failure.
                                        M. P. GILMORE (1952)

The primordial, ultimate character of this world [Italy at the beginning of the sixteenth century]—devoid of great moral and political motifs, uninfluenced by the masses, having its being solely in the isolated virtue of scattered individuals. who left their own imprint on material that was flabby and incoherent—finds its true expression in *The Prince*. . . . The people, who bring the first book of the *Discorsi* to life and condition its thought, so much so that Machiavelli justly regards the struggle between patricians and plebs as the source of Rome's greatness, are absent from *The Prince.* They do not even appear in the distance as a social and political entity. We have the Prince's subjects, isolated beings, fragments, as it were, of a vast whole which no longer exists, opposed to the sovereign, but as man to man. Hence the necessity for the Prince to humor them, not to dishonor them or violate their property, to keep their friendship. But where is there any reference to the strength that derives from collective action? When the author seems at first sight to be returning to the theme of the organizing capacity of the masses (Chaps. 9, 20) we find ourselves confronted not with the people but with a confused rabble, not with a party, rich in native energy, abounding in enterprises of its own, seeking to fulfill clearly-defined political aspirations and therefore capable of facing the disputes and the free clashes of opinion on which the fortunes of the Republic depend, but with a mob that "does not wish to be oppressed" and judges "a thing by its results." Compare Chapter IX of *The Prince* with the passage in Chapter IV of the first book of the *Discorsi* in which Machiavelli speaks of the struggle between patricians and plebs in Rome, or with Chapter VI. These last-named chapters breathe a living force, ever-present and self-conscious, a force that creates its forms of life and overcomes individual passions by welding them into the compact unity of a common passion, a force that can also err "through excessive love" of its liberty—but in a Republic that is not corrupt its very error is a source of great good "and enables it (the Republic) to lead a free life." In Chapter IX of *The Prince,* on the other hand, we have an amorphous, scattered and truly anonymous mob, in which nothing has any significance except the feelings of the individual persons, who are incapable of perceiving the collective mind that transcends their own, or of aspiring to the grandeur of political resolution, even if the latter be expressed in the communal strife of the parties.

FEDERICO CHABOD (1925)

Baldassare Castiglione
1478—1529

A distinctive characteristic of Renaissance civilization, according to the famous theory expressed by the nineteenth-century Swiss historian Jacob Burckhardt, was the way human life and institutions were treated as though they were works of art—things that men could design and create for their own pleasure. The humanist attitude that men should cultivate their minds to widen the range of pleasures that human existence could offer eventually led to the explicit assertion of an idea which medieval civilization had acknowledged only tacitly—that the conditions of human existence could be shaped by men to provide the fullest satisfaction from life. The expression of this idea brought with it a change in the ideas of the function of human society and the function of man as a social being.

Medieval thought in general had regarded the structure of human society as constituting part of the overall pattern of the universe created by God's design and as functioning to impose order on the relationships among men. In turn, men functioned in specific roles in the social order —the king as ruler, the knight as warrior, the peasant as provider—so that human society might operate as efficiently and harmoniously as the rest of the universe. Medieval men saw themselves as members of a corporate society, their individual existence subordinated to the whole of which they were a part. Seldom in medieval thought was there any indication that the purpose of society might be the achievement not only of efficiency in the conduct of human affairs but of pleasure as well. It was not until the Renaissance that serious attention was given to the idea that human society, by the very fact of its existence, provided the opportunity of cultivating, almost as an end in itself, the art of living graciously. Implicit in this idea is the assumption that the creation of a gracious mode of life is a worth-while human achievement meriting the best efforts of intelligent men. Such an assumption was impossible in the medieval scheme of thought. But it was possible in the kind of thinking that asserted the dignity of man and regarded the phenomena of human existence objectively. The point of view that allowed Machiavelli to conceive of politics as an independent activity that should operate according to purely political considerations likewise allowed the conception of society as an independent activity operating in accord with purely social considerations. In much the same way that Machiavelli—with almost complete disregard for the economic, moral, and religious implications of kingship—could envision an ideal ruler for the realities of one kind of contemporary politics, it was possible to envision an ideal social being for the realities of one kind of contemporary social order.

Baldassare Castiglione gave expression to this ideal in *The Book of the Courtier,* a work that has had a lasting influence on Western culture through his conception of the traits necessary in the make-up of a gentleman. Castiglione himself might well have been the model for his book. Of aristocratic birth, he spent his life in the service of various Italian princes as a soldier, statesman, and ambassador, cultivating at the same time an interest in humanistic studies and a reputation as a man of letters. His contemporaries were full of praise for him as a man, as a diplomat, and as a writer; upon his death, Charles V, King of Spain and Emperor of the Holy Roman Empire, at whose court Castiglione spent his last few years serving as envoy from the pope, is reported to have said to his courtiers: "I tell you that one of the finest gentlemen in the world is dead."

Castiglione began writing *The Courtier* in 1508, in tribute to the memory of the recently deceased Duke Guidobaldo of Urbino, whom he had served for a number of years. The book was finished some ten years later and was widely circulated in manuscript. It was published in 1528 in order that, as Castiglione explained in an introductory letter to the printed text, the many who read it might have an authentic version available. The book takes the form of conversations among the courtiers of Urbino on four successive evenings one spring when Duke Guidobaldo was still alive. The topics each evening concern the idea of the courtier: the qualities requisite to the perfect courtier; how these qualities are to be cultivated and demonstrated in practice; the qualities requisite to the court lady; the relationship to be observed by the courtier toward his prince and toward the court lady. *The Book of the Courtier* furnishes an idealized picture of an ideal society; but it is a humanist ideal, one that has its roots in reality—and Castiglione's picture has ever since been a model for emulation by real courts and real courtiers and by their modern counterparts.

The Book of the Courtier

Book I

To Messer Alfonso Ariosto[1]

Within myself I have long doubted, dearest messer Alfonso, which of two things were the harder for me: to deny you what you have often begged of me so urgently, or to do it. For while it seemed to me very hard to deny anything (and especially a thing in the highest degree laudable) to one whom I love most dearly and by whom I feel myself to be most dearly loved, yet to set about an enterprise that I was not sure of being able to finish, seemed to me ill befitting a man who esteems just censure as it ought to be esteemed. At last, after much thought, I am resolved to try in this matter how much aid my assiduity may gain from that affection and intense desire to please, which in other things are so wont to stimulate the industry of man.

You ask me then to write what is to my thinking the form of Courtiership most befitting a gentleman who lives at the court of princes, by which he may have the ability and knowledge perfectly to serve them in every reasonable thing, winning from them favour, and praise from other men; in short, what manner of man he ought to be who may deserve to be called a perfect Courtier without flaw. Wherefore, considering your request, I say that had it not seemed to me more blameworthy to be reputed somewhat unamiable by you than too conceited by everyone else, I should have avoided this task, for fear of being held over bold by all who know how hard a thing it is, from among such a variety of customs as are in use at the courts of Christendom, to choose the perfect form and as it were the flower of Courtiership. For custom often makes the same thing pleasing and displeasing to us; whence it sometimes follows that customs, habits, ceremonies and fashions that once were prized, become vulgar, and contrariwise the vulgar become prized. Thus it is clearly seen that use rather than reason has power to introduce new things among us, and to do away with the old; and he will often err who seeks to determine which are perfect. Therefore being conscious of this and many other difficulties in the subject set before me to write of, I am constrained to offer some apology, and to testify that this errour (if errour it may indeed be called) is common to us both, to the end that if I be blamed for it, the blame may be shared by you also; for your offence in setting me a task beyond my powers should not be deemed less than mine in having accepted it.

So now let us make a beginning of our subject, and if possible let

From *The Book of the Courtier by Count Baldesar Castiglione*, translated by Leonard Eckstein Opdycke (New York: Charles Scribner's Sons, 1903).

[1]A friend of Castiglione's (1475–1525) who was himself a kind of "perfect courtier." Castiglione appears to have written *The Courtier* at his suggestion.

us form such a Courtier that any prince worthy to be served by him, although of but small estate, might still be called a very great lord.

In these books we shall follow no fixed order or rule of distinct precepts, such as are usually employed in teaching anything whatever; but after the fashion of many ancient writers, we shall revive a pleasant memory and rehearse certain discussions that were held between men singularly competent in such matters; and although I had no part in them personally, being in England at the time they took place,[2] yet having received them soon after my return, from one who faithfully reported them to me, I will try to recall them as accurately as my memory will permit, so that you may know what was thought and believed on this subject by men who are worthy of highest praise, and to whose judgment implicit faith may be given in all things. Nor will it be amiss to tell the cause of these discussions, so that we may reach in orderly manner the end to which our discourse tends.

On the slopes of the Apennines towards the Adriatic sea, almost in the centre of Italy, there lies (as everyone knows) the little city of Urbino. Although amid mountains, and less pleasing ones than perhaps some others that we see in many places, it has yet enjoyed such favour of heaven that the country round about is very fertile and rich in crops; so that besides the wholesomeness of the air, there is great abundance of everything needful for human life. But among the greatest blessings that can be attributed to it, this I believe to be the chief, that for a long time it has ever been ruled by the best of lords; although in the calamities of the universal wars of Italy, it was for a season deprived of them.[3] But without seeking further, we can give good proof of this by the glorious memory of Duke Federico,[4] who in his day was the light of Italy; nor is there lack of credible and abundant witnesses, who are still living, to his prudence, humanity, justice, liberality, unconquered courage, —and to his military discipline, which is conspicuously attested by his numerous victories, his capture of impregnable places, the sudden swiftness of his expeditions, the frequency with which he put to flight large and formidable armies by means of a very small force, and by his loss of no single battle whatever; so that we may not unreasonably compare him to many famous men of old.

Among his other praiseworthy deeds, he built on the rugged site of Urbino a palace regarded by many as the most beautiful to be found in all Italy; and he so well furnished it with everything suitable that it seemed not a palace but a city in the form of a palace; and not merely with what is ordinarily used,—such as silver vases, hangings of richest cloth-of-gold and silk, and other similar things,—but for ornament he added countless antique statues in marble and bronze, pictures most choice, and musical instruments of every sort, nor would he admit anything there that was not very rare and excellent. Then at very great cost he collected a goodly number of most excellent and rare books

---

[2]This is simply a graceful fiction which serves as an excuse for Castiglione himself not appearing as a speaker in the dialogues. Castiglione is known to have been at the court of Urbino at the time when the dialogues are supposed to have taken place.

[3]Cesare Borgia had seized control of Urbino in 1502 and ruled it until the following year.

[4]Ruled Urbino 1444—1482.

in Greek, Latin and Hebrew, all of which he adorned with gold and with silver, esteeming this to be the chiefest excellence of his great palace.

Following then the course of nature, and already sixty-five years old, he died gloriously, as he had lived; and he left as his successor a motherless little boy of ten years, his only son Guidobaldo. Heir to the State, he seemed to be heir also to all his father's virtues, and soon his noble nature gave such promise as seemed not permissible to hope for from mortal man; so that men esteemed none among the notable deeds of Duke Federico to be greater than to have begotten such a son. But envious of so much virtue, fortune thwarted this glorious beginning with all her power; so that before Duke Guido reached the age of twenty years, he fell ill of the gout, which grew upon him with grievous pain, and in a short space of time so crippled all his members that he could neither stand upon his feet nor move; and thus one of the fairest and most promising forms in the world was distorted and spoiled in tender youth.

And not content even with this, fortune was so contrary to him in all his purposes, that he could seldom carry into effect anything that he desired; and although he was very wise of counsel and unconquered in spirit, it seemed that what he undertook, both in war and in everything else whether small or great, always ended ill for him. And proof of this is found in his many and diverse calamities, which he ever bore with such strength of mind, that his spirit was never vanquished by fortune; nay, scorning her assaults with unbroken courage, he lived in illness as if in health and in adversity as if fortunate, with perfect dignity and universal esteem; so that although he was thus infirm of body, he fought with most honourable rank in the service of their Serene Highnesses the Kings of Naples, Alfonso and Ferdinand the Younger; later with Pope Alexander VI, and with the Venetian and Florentine signories.

Upon the accession of Julius II to the pontificate,[5] he was made Captain of the Church; at which time, following his accustomed habit, above all else he took care to fill his household with very noble and valiant gentlemen, with whom he lived most familiarly, delighting in their intercourse: wherein the pleasure he gave to others was not less than that he received from others, he being well versed in both the learned languages, and uniting affability and pleasantness to a knowledge of things without number. And besides this, the greatness of his spirit so set him on, that although he could not practise in person the exercises of chivalry, as he once had done, yet he took the utmost pleasure in witnessing them in others; and by his words, now correcting now praising every man according to desert, he clearly showed his judgment in those matters; wherefore, in jousts and tournaments, in riding, in the handling of every sort of weapon, as well as in pastimes, games, music,—in short, in all the exercises proper to noble cavaliers,—everyone strove so to show himself, as to merit being deemed worthy of such noble fellowship.

Thus all the hours of the day were assigned to honourable and pleasant exercises as well for the body as for the mind; but since my lord Duke

[5] In 1503.

was always wont by reason of his infirmity to retire to sleep very early after supper, everyone usually betook himself at that hour to the presence of my lady Duchess Elisabetta Gonzaga; where also was ever to be found my lady Emilia Pia, who was endowed with such lively wit and judgment that, as you know, it seemed as if she were the Mistress of us all, and as if everyone gained wisdom and worth from her. Here then, gentle discussions and innocent pleasantries were heard, and on the face of everyone a jocund gaiety was seen depicted, so that the house could truly be called the very abode of mirth: nor ever elsewhere, I think, was so relished, as once was here, how great sweetness may flow from dear and cherished companionship; for not to speak of the honour it was to each of us to serve such a lord as he of whom I have just spoken, there was born in the hearts of all a supreme contentment every time we came into the presence of my lady Duchess; and it seemed as if this were a chain that held us all linked in love, so that never was concord of will or cordial love between brothers greater than that which here was between us all.

The same was it among the ladies, with whom there was intercourse most free and honourable; for everyone was permitted to talk, sit, jest and laugh with whom he pleased; but such was the reverence paid to the wish of my lady Duchess, that this same liberty was a very great check; nor was there anyone who did not esteem it the utmost pleasure he could have in the world, to please her, and the utmost pain to displease her. And thus, most decorous manners were here joined with greatest liberty, and games and laughter in her presence were seasoned not only with witty jests, but with gracious and sober dignity; for that modesty and loftiness which governed all the acts, words and gestures of my lady Duchess, bantering and laughing, were such that she would have been known for a lady of noblest rank by anyone who saw her even but once. And impressing herself thus upon those about her, she seemed to attune us all to her own quality and tone; accordingly every man strove to follow this pattern, taking as it were a rule of beautiful behaviour from the presence of so great and virtuous a lady; whose highest qualities I do not now purpose to recount, they not being my theme and being well known to all the world, and far more because I could not express them with either tongue or pen; and those that perhaps might have been somewhat hid, fortune, as if wondering at such rare virtue, chose to reveal through many adversities and stings of calamity, so as to give proof that in the tender breast of woman, in company with singular beauty, there may abide prudence and strength of soul, and all those virtues that even among stern men are very rare.

But leaving this aside, I say that the custom of all the gentlemen of the house was to betake themselves straightway after supper to my lady Duchess; where, among the other pleasant pastimes and music and dancing that continually were practised, sometimes neat questions were proposed, sometimes ingenious games were devised at the choice of one or another, in which under various disguises the company disclosed their thoughts figuratively to whom they liked best. Sometimes other discussions arose about different matters, or biting retorts passed lightly back and forth. Often "devices" *(imprese),* as we now call them, were displayed; in discussing which there was wonderful diversion, the house being (as I have said) full of very noble talents; among whom (as you know) the most famous were my lord Ottaviano Fregoso, his brother messer Federico, the Magnifico Giuliano de' Medici, messer Pietro Bembo, messer Cesare Gonzaga, Count Ludovico da Canossa, my lord Gaspar Pallavicino, my lord Ludovico Pio, my lord Morello da Ortona, Pietro da Napoli, messer Roberto da Bari, and countless other very noble cavaliers. Moreover there were many, who, although usually they did not dwell there constantly, yet spent most of the time there: like messer Bernardo Bibbiena, the Unico Aretino, Giancristoforo Romano, Pietro Monte, Terpandro, messer Niccolò Frisio; so that there always flocked thither poets, musicians and all sorts of agreeable men, and in every walk the most excellent that were to be found in Italy.

Now Pope Julius II, having by his presence and the aid of the French brought Bologna under subjection to the apostolic see in the year 1506, and being on his way back to Rome, passed through Urbino; where he was received with all possible honour and with as magnificent and splendid state as could have been prepared in any other noble city of Italy: so that besides the pope, all the lord cardinals and other courtiers were most highly gratified. And some there were, attracted by the charm of this society, who tarried at Urbino many days after the departure of the pope and his court; during which time not only were the ordinary pastimes and diversions continued in the usual manner, but every man strove to contribute something new, and especially in the games, to which almost every evening was devoted. And the order of them was such that immediately after reaching the presence of my lady Duchess, everyone sat down in a circle as he pleased or as chance decided; and in sitting they were arranged alternately, a man and a woman, as long as there were women, for nearly always the number of men was by far the greater; then they were governed as seemed best to my lady Duchess, who for the most part left this charge to my lady Emilia.

So, the day after the pope's departure, the company being assembled at the wonted hour and place, after much pleasant talk, my lady Duchess desired my lady Emilia to begin the games; and she, after having for a time refused the task, spoke thus:

"My Lady, since it pleases you that I shall be the one to begin the games this evening, not being able in reason to fail to obey you, I will propose a game in which I think I ought to have little blame and less labour; and this shall be for everyone to propose after his liking a game that has never been given; and then we will choose the one that seems best worthy to be played in this company."

[After some members of the group have proposed various games for the evening, it is Federico Fregoso's turn to offer a suggestion.]

"My Lady, I would it were permitted me, as it sometimes is, to assent to another's proposal; since for my part I would readily approve any of the games proposed by these gentlemen, for I really think that all of them would be amusing. But not to break our rule, I say that anyone who wished to praise our court,—laying aside the merit of our lady Duchess, which with her divine virtue would suffice to lift from earth to heaven the meanest souls that are in the world,—might well say without suspicion of flattery, that in all Italy it would perhaps be hard to find so many cavaliers so singularly admirable and so excellent in divers other matters besides the chief concerns of chivalry, as are now to be found here: wherefore if anywhere there be men who deserve to be called good Courtiers and who are able to judge of what pertains to the perfection of Courtiership, it is reasonable to believe that they are here. So, to repress the many fools who by impudence and folly think to win the name of good Courtier, I would that this evening's game might be, that we select some one of the company and give him the task of portraying a perfect Courtier, explaining all the conditions and special qualities requisite in one who deserves this title; and as to those things that shall not appear sound, let everyone be allowed to contradict, as in the schools of the philosophers it is allowed to contradict anyone who proposes a thesis."

Messer Federico was continuing his discourse still further, when my lady Emilia interrupted him and said:

"This, if it pleases my lady Duchess, shall for the present be our game."

My lady Duchess answered:

"It does please me."

Then nearly all those present began to say, both to my lady Duchess and among themselves, that this was the finest game that could possibly be; and without waiting for each other's answer, they entreated my lady Emilia to decide who should begin. She turned to my lady Duchess and said:

"Command, my Lady, him who it best pleases you should have this task; for I do not wish, by selecting one rather than another, to seem to decide whom I think more competent in this matter than the rest, and so do wrong to anyone."

My lady Duchess replied:

"Nay, make this choice yourself, and take heed lest by not obeying you give an example to the others, so that they too prove disobedient in their turn."

At this my lady Emilia laughed and said to Count Ludovico da Canossa:

"Then not to lose more time, you, Count, shall be the one to take this enterprise after the manner that messer Federico has described; not indeed because we account you so good a Courtier that you know what befits one, but because, if you say everything wrong as we hope you will, the game will be more lively, for everyone will then have something to answer you; while if someone else had this task who knew more than you, it would be impossible to contradict him in anything, because he would tell the truth, and so the game would be tedious."

The Count answered quickly:

"Whoever told the truth, my Lady, would run no risk of lacking contradiction, so long as you were present;" and after some laughter at this retort, he continued: "But truly I would fain escape this burden, it seeming to me too heavy, and I being conscious that what you said in jest is very true; that is, that I do not know what befits a good Courtier: and I do not seek to prove this with further argument, because, as I do not practice the rules of Courtiership, one may judge that I do not know them; and I think my blame may be the less, for sure it is worse not to wish to do well than not to know how. Yet, since it so happens that you are pleased to have me bear this burden, I neither can nor will refuse it, in order not to contravene our rule and your judgment, which I rate far higher than my own."

Then messer Cesare Gonzaga said:

"As the early evening is now spent and many other kinds of entertainment are ready, perhaps it will be well to put off this discussion until to-morrow and give the Count time to think of what he has to say; for it is difficult indeed to speak unprepared on such a subject."

The Count replied:

"I do not wish to be like the fellow who, when stripped to his shirt, vaulted less well than he had done in his doublet; hence it seems to me good fortune that the hour is late, for I shall be obliged by the shortness of the time to say but little, and my not having taken thought will excuse me, so that I shall be allowed to say without blame whatever first comes to my lips.

"Therefore, not to carry this burden of duty longer on my shoulders, I say that in everything it is so hard to know the true perfection as to be well nigh impossible; and this because of the variety of opinions. Thus there are many that will like a man who speaks much, and will call him pleasing; some will prefer modesty; some others, an active and restless man; still others, one who shows calmness and deliberation in everything; and so every man praises or decries according to his mind, always clothing vice with the name of its kindred virtue, or virtue with the name of its kindred vice; for example. calling an impudent man frank, a modest man dull, an ignorant man good, a knave discreet; and so in all things else. Yet I believe that there exists in everything its own perfection, although concealed; and that this can be determined through rational discussion by any having knowledge of the thing in hand. And since, as I have said, the truth often lies concealed, and I do not profess to have this knowledge, I can only praise the kind of Courtier that I most esteem, and approve him who seems to me nearest right, according to my poor judgment; the which you will follow if you find it good, or you will hold to your own if it differs from mine. Nor shall I at all insist that mine is better than yours; not only because you may think one thing and I another, but I myself may sometimes think one thing, and sometimes another.

"I wish, then, that this Courtier of ours should be nobly born and of gentle race; because it is far less unseemly for one of ignoble birth to fail in worthy deeds, than for one of noble birth, who, if he strays from the path of his predecessors, stains his family name, and not only fails to achieve but loses what has been achieved already; for noble birth is like a bright lamp that manifests and makes visible good and evil deeds, and kindles and stimulates to virtue both by fear of shame and by hope of praise. And since his splendour of nobility does not illumine the deeds of the humbly born, they lack that stimulus and fear of shame, nor do they feel any obligation to advance beyond what their predecessors have done; while to the nobly born it seems a reproach not to reach at least the goal set them by their ancestors. And thus it nearly always happens that both in the profession of arms and in other worthy pursuits the most famous men have been of noble birth, because nature has implanted in everything that hidden seed which gives a certain force and quality of its own essence to all things that are derived from it, and makes them like itself: as we see not only in the breeds of horses and of other animals, but also in trees, the shoots of which nearly always resemble the trunk; and if they sometimes degenerate, it arises from poor cultivation. And so it is with men, who if rightly trained are nearly always like those from whom they spring, and often better; but if there be no one to give them proper care, they become like savages and never reach perfection.

"It is true that, by favour of the stars or of nature, some men are endowed at birth with such graces that they seem not to have been born, but rather as if some god had formed them with his very hands and adorned them with every excellence of mind and body. So too there are many men so foolish and rude that one cannot but think that nature brought them into the world out of contempt or mockery. Just as these can usually accomplish little even with constant diligence and good training, so with slight pains those others reach the highest summit of excellence. And to give you an instance; you see my lord Don Ippolito d'Este, Cardinal of Ferrara, who has enjoyed such fortune from his birth, that his person, his aspect, his words and all his movements are so disposed and imbued with this grace, that—although he is young—he exhibits among the most aged prelates such weight of character that he seems fitter to teach than to be taught; likewise in conversation with men and women of every rank, in games, in pleasantry and in banter, he has a certain sweetness and manners so gracious, that whoso speaks with him or even sees him, must needs remain attached to him forever.

"But to return to our subject: I say that there is a middle state between perfect grace on the one hand and senseless folly on the other; and those who are not thus perfectly endowed by nature, with study and toil can in great part polish and amend their natural defects. Besides his noble birth, then, I would have the Courtier favoured in this regard also, and endowed by nature not only with talent and beauty of person and feature, but with a certain grace and (as we say) air that shall make him at first sight pleasing and agreeable to all who see him; and I would have this an ornament that should dispose and unite all his actions, and in his outward aspect give promise of whatever is worthy the society and favour of every great lord."

Here, without waiting longer, my lord Gaspar Pallavicino said:

"In order that our game may have the form prescribed, and that we may not seem to slight the privilege given us to contradict, I say that this nobility of birth does not appear to me so essential in the Courtier; and if I thought I were saying what was new to any of us, I should cite instances of many men born of the noblest blood who have been full of vices; and on the other hand, of many men among the humbly born who by their virtue have made their posterity illustrious. And if what you just said be true, namely that there is in everything this occult influence of the original seed, then we should all be in the same case, because we had the same origin, nor would any man be more noble than another. But as to our differences and grades of eminence and obscurity, I believe there are many other causes: among which I rate fortune to be chief; for we see her holding sway in all mundane affairs, often amusing herself by lifting to heaven whom she pleases (although wholly without merit), and burying in the depths those most worthy to be exalted.

"I quite agree with what you say as to the good fortune of those endowed from birth with advantages of mind and body: but this is seen as well among the humbly born as among the nobly born, since nature has no such subtle distinctions as these; and often, as I said, the highest gifts of nature are found among the most obscure. Therefore, since this nobility of birth is won neither by talent nor by strength nor by craft, and is rather the merit of our predecessors than our own, it seems to me too extravagant to maintain that if our Courtier's parents be humbly born, all his good qualities are spoiled, and that all those other qualifications that you mentioned do not avail to raise him to the summit of perfection; I mean talent, beauty of feature, comeliness of person, and that grace which makes him always charming to everyone at first sight."

Then Count Ludovico replied:

"I do not deny that the same virtues may rule the low-born and the noble: but (not to repeat what we have said already or the many other arguments that could be adduced in praise of noble birth, which is honoured always and by everyone, it being reasonable that good should beget good), since we have to form a Courtier without flaw and endowed with every praiseworthy quality, it seems to me necessary to make him nobly born, as well for many other reasons as for universal opinion, which is at once disposed in favour of noble birth. For if there be two Courtiers who have as yet given no impression of themselves by good or evil acts, as soon as the one is known to have been born a gentleman and the other not, he who is low-born will be far less esteemed by everyone than he who is high-born, and will need much effort and time to make upon men's minds that good impression which the other will have achieved in a moment and merely by being a gentleman. And how important these impressions are, everyone can easily understand: for in our own case we have seen men present themselves in this house, who, being silly and awkward in the extreme, yet had throughout Italy the reputation of very great Courtiers; and although they were detected and recognized at last, still they imposed upon us for many days, and maintained in our minds that opinion of them which they first found impressed there, although they conducted themselves after the slightness of their worth. We have seen others, held at first in small esteem, then admirably successful at the last.

"And of these mistakes there are various causes: and among others, the regard of princes, who in their wish to perform miracles sometimes undertake to bestow favour on a man who seems to them to merit disfavour. And often too they are themselves deceived; but since they always have a host of imitators, their favour begets very great fame, which chiefly guides our judgments: and if we find anything that seems contrary to common opinion, we suspect that it is we ourselves who are wrong, and always seek for something hidden: because it seems that these universal opinions must after all be founded on fact and spring from rational causes; and because our minds are very prone to love and hate, as is seen in battleshows and games and every other sort of contest, wherein the spectators without apparent cause become partisans of one side, with eager wish that it may win and the other lose. In our opinion of men's character also, good or evil fame sways our minds to one of these two passions from the start; and thus it happens that we usually judge with love or hate. You see then how important this first impression is, and how he ought to strive to make a good one at the outset, who thinks to hold the rank and name of good Courtier.

"But to come to some details, I am of opinion that the principal and true profession of the Courtier ought to be that of arms; which I would have him follow actively above all else, and be known among others as bold and strong, and loyal to whomsoever he serves. And he will win a reputation for these good qualities by exercising them at all times and in all places, since one may never fail in this without severest censure. And just as among women, their fair fame once sullied never recovers its first lustre, so the reputation of a gentleman who bears arms, if once it be in the least tarnished with cowardice or other disgrace, remains forever infamous before the world and full of ignominy. Therefore the more our Courtier excels in this art, the more he will be worthy of praise; and yet I do not deem essential in him that perfect knowledge of things and those other qualities that befit a commander; since this would be too wide a sea, let us be content, as we have said, with perfect loyalty and unconquered courage, and that he be always seen to possess them. For the courageous are often recognized even more in small things than in great; and frequently in perils of importance and where there are many spectators, some men are to be found, who, although their hearts be dead within them, yet, moved by shame or by the presence of others, press forward almost with their eyes shut, and do their duty God knows how. While on occasions of little moment, when they think they can avoid putting themselves in danger without being detected, they are glad to keep safe. But those who, even when they do not expect to be observed or seen or recognized by anyone, show their ardour and neglect nothing, however paltry, that may be laid to their charge,—they have that strength of mind which we seek in our Courtier.

"Not that we would have him look so fierce, or go about blustering, or say that he has taken his cuirass to wife, or threaten with those grim scowls that we have often seen in Berto;[6] because to such men as this, one might justly say that which a brave lady jestingly said in gentle company to one whom I will not name at present; who, being invited by her out of compliment to dance, refused not only that, but to listen to the music, and many other entertainments proposed to him,—saying always that such silly trifles were not his business; so that at last the lady said, 'What is your business, then?' He replied with a sour look, 'To fight.' Then the lady at once said, 'Now that you are in no war and out

[6]Probably one of the many buffoons about the papal court in the time of Julius II.

of fighting trim, I should think it were a good thing to have yourself well oiled, and to stow yourself with all your battle harness in a closet until you be needed, lest you grow more rusty than you are;' and so, amid much laughter from the bystanders, she left the discomfited fellow to his silly presumption.

"Therefore let the man we are seeking, be very bold, stern, and always among the first, where the enemy are to be seen; and in every other place, gentle, modest, reserved, above all things avoiding ostentation and that impudent self-praise by which men ever excite hatred and disgust in all who hear them."

Then my lord Gaspar replied:

"As for me, I have known few men excellent in anything whatever, who do not praise themselves; and it seems to me that this may well be permitted them; for when anyone who feels himself to be of worth, sees that he is not known to the ignorant by his works, he is offended that his worth should lie buried, and needs must in some way hold it up to view, in order that he may not be cheated of the fame that is the true reward of worthy effort. Thus among the ancient authors, whoever carries weight seldom fails to praise himself. They indeed are insufferable who do this without desert, but such we do not presume our Courtier to be."

The Count then said:

"If you heard what I said, it was impudent and indiscriminate self-praise that I censured: and as you say, we surely ought not to form a bad opinion of a brave man who praises himself modestly, nay we ought rather to regard such praise as better evidence than if it came from the mouth of others. I say, however, that he, who in praising himself runs into no errour and incurs no annoyance or envy at the hands of those that hear him, is a very discreet man indeed and merits praise from others in addition to that which he bestows upon himself; because it is a very difficult matter."

Then my lord Gaspar said:

"You must teach us that."

The Count replied:

"Among the ancient authors there is no lack of those who have taught it; but to my thinking, the whole art consists in saying things in such a way that they shall not seem to be said to that end, but let fall so naturally that it was impossible not to say them, and while seeming always to avoid self-praise, yet to achieve it; but not after the manner of those boasters, who open their mouths and let the words come forth haphazard. Like one of our friends a few days ago, who, being quite run through the thigh with a spear at Pisa, said he thought it was a fly that had stung him; and another man said he kept no mirrour in his room because, when angry, he became so terrible to look at, that the sight of himself would have frightened him too much."

Everyone laughed at this, but messer Cesare Gonzaga added:

"Why do you laugh? Do you not know that Alexander the Great, on hearing the opinion of a philosopher to be that there was an infinite number of worlds, began to weep, and being asked why he wept, replied, 'Because I have not yet conquered one of them;' as if he would fain have vanquished all? Does not this seem to you a greater boast than that about the fly-sting?"

Then the Count said:

"Yes, and Alexander was a greater man than he who made the other speech. But extraordinary men are surely to be pardoned when they assume much; for he who has great things to do must needs have daring to do them, and confidence in himself, and must not be abject or mean in spirit, yet very modest in speech, showing less confidence in himself than he has, lest his self-confidence lead to rashness."

The Count now paused a little, and messer Bernardo Bibbiena said, laughing:

"I remember what you said earlier, that this Courtier of ours must be endowed by nature with beauty of countenance and person, and with a grace that shall make him so agreeable. Grace and beauty of countenance I think I certainly possess, and this is the reason why so many ladies are ardently in love with me, as you know; but I am rather doubtful as to the beauty of my person, especially as regards these legs of mine, which seem to me decidedly less well proportioned than I should wish: as to my bust and other members however, I am quite content. Pray, now, describe a little more in particular the sort of body that the Courtier is to have, so that I may dismiss this doubt and set my mind at rest."

After some laughter at this, the Count continued:

"Of a certainty that grace of countenance can be truly said to be yours, nor need I cite further example than this to show what manner of thing it is, for we unquestionably perceive your aspect to be most agreeable and pleasing to everyone, albeit the lineaments of it are not very delicate. Still it is of a manly cast and at the same time full of grace; and this characteristic is to be found in many different types of countenance. And of such sort I would have our Courtier's aspect; not so soft and effeminate as is sought by many, who not only curl their hair and pluck their brows, but gloss their faces with all those arts employed by the most wanton and unchaste women in the world; and in their walk, posture and every act, they seem so limp and languid that their limbs are like to fall apart; and they pronounce their words so mournfully that they appear about to expire upon the spot: and the more they find themselves with men of rank, the more they affect such tricks. Since nature has not made them women, as they seem to wish to appear and be, they should be treated not as good women but as public harlots, and driven not merely from the courts of great lords but from the society of honest men.

"Then coming to the bodily frame, I say it is enough if this be neither extremely short nor tall, for both of these conditions excite a certain contemptuous surprise, and men of either sort are gazed upon in much the same way that we gaze on monsters. Yet if we must offend in one of the two extremes, it is preferable to fall a little short of the just measure of height than to exceed it, for besides often being dull of intellect, men thus huge of body are also unfit for every exercise of agility, which thing I should much wish in the Courtier. And so I would have him well built and shapely of limb, and would have him show strength and lightness and suppleness, and know all bodily exercises that befit a man of war: whereof I think the first should be to handle every sort of weapon well on foot and on horse, to understand the advantages of each, and especially to be familiar with those weapons that are ordinarily used among gentlemen; for besides the use of them in war, where such subtlety in contrivance is perhaps not needful, there frequently arise differences between one gentleman and another, which afterwards result in duels often fought with such weapons as happen at the moment to be within reach: thus knowledge of this kind is a very safe thing. Nor am I one of those who say that skill is forgotten in the hour of need; for he whose skill forsakes him at such a time, indeed gives token that he has already lost heart and head through fear.

"Moreover I deem it very important to know how to wrestle, for it is a great help in the use of all kinds of weapons on foot. Then, both for his own sake and for that of his friends, he must understand the quarrels and differences that may arise, and must be quick to seize an advantage, always showing courage and prudence in all things. Nor should he be too ready to fight except when honour demands it; for besides the great danger that the uncertainty of fate entails, he who rushes into such affairs recklessly and without urgent cause, merits the severest censure even though he be successful. But when he finds himself so far engaged that he cannot withdraw without reproach, he ought to be most deliberate, both in the preliminaries to the duel and in the duel itself, and always show readiness and daring. Nor must he act like some, who fritter the affair away in disputes and controversies, and who, having the choice of weapons, select those that neither cut nor pierce, and arm themselves as if they were expecting a cannonade; and thinking it enough not to be defeated, stand ever on the defensive and retreat,—showing therein their utter cowardice. And thus they make themselves a laughing-stock for boys, like those two men of Ancona who fought at Perugia not long since, and made everyone laugh who saw them."

"And who were they?" asked my lord Gaspar Pallavicino.

"Two cousins," replied messer Cesare.

Then the Count said:

"In their fighting they were as like as two brothers;" and soon continued: "Even in time of peace weapons are often used in various exercises, and gentlemen appear in public shows before the people and ladies and great lords. For this reason I would have our Courtier a perfect horseman in every kind of seat; and besides understanding horses and what pertains to riding, I would have him use all possible care and diligence to lift himself a little beyond the rest in everything, so that he may be ever recognized as eminent above all others. And as we read of Alcibiades that he surpassed all the nations with whom he lived, each in their particular province, so I would have this Courtier of ours excel all others, and each in that which is most their profession. And as it is the especial pride of the Italians to ride well with the rein, to govern wild horses with consummate skill, and to play at tilting and jousting,—in these things let him be among the best of the Italians. In tourneys and in the arts of defence and attack, let him shine among the best in France. In stick-throwing, bull-fighting, and in casting spears and darts, let him excel among the Spaniards. But above everything he should temper all his movements with a certain good judgment and grace, if he wishes to merit that universal favour which is so greatly prized.

"There are also many other exercises, which although not immediately dependent upon arms, yet are closely connected therewith, and greatly foster manly sturdiness; and one of the chief among these seems to me to be the chase, because it bears a certain likeness to war: and truly it is an amusement for great lords and befitting a man at court, and furthermore it is seen to have been much cultivated among the ancients. It is fitting also to know how to swim, to leap, to run, to throw stones, for besides the use that may be made of this in war, a man often has occasion to show what he can do in such matters; whence good esteem is to be won, especially with the multitude, who must be taken into account withal. Another admirable exercise, and one very befitting a man at court, is the game of tennis, in which are well shown the disposition of the body, the quickness and suppleness of every member, and all those qualities that are seen in nearly every other exercise. Nor less highly do I esteem vaulting on horse, which although it be fatiguing and difficult, makes a man very light and dexterous more than any other thing; and besides its utility, if this lightness is accompanied by grace, it is to my thinking a finer show than any of the others.

"Our Courtier having once become more than fairly expert in these exercises, I think he should leave the others on one side: such as turning summersaults, rope-walking, and the like, which savour of the mountebank and little befit a gentleman.

"But since one cannot devote himself to such fatiguing exercises continually, and since repetition becomes very tiresome and abates the admiration felt for what is rare, we must always diversify our life with various occupations. For this reason I would have our Courtier sometimes descend to quieter and more tranquil exercises, and in order to escape envy and to entertain himself agreeably with everyone, let him do whatever others do, yet never departing from praiseworthy deeds, and governing himself with that good judgment which will keep him from all folly; but let him laugh, jest, banter, frolic and dance, yet in such fashion that he shall always appear genial and discreet, and that everything he may do or say shall be stamped with grace."

Then messer Cesare Gonzaga said:

"We certainly ought on no account to hinder the course of this discussion; but if I were to keep silence, I should be neglectful both of the right I have to speak and of my desire to know one thing: and let me be pardoned if I ask a question instead of contradicting; for this I think may be permitted me, after the precedent of messer Bernardo here, who in his over desire to be held comely, broke the rules of our game by asking a question instead of contradicting."

Then my lady Duchess said:

"You see how one errour begets many. Therefore he who transgresses and sets a bad example, like messer Bernardo, deserves to be punished not only for his own transgression but also for the others'."

Then messer Cesare replied:

"In that case, my Lady, I shall be exempt from penalty, since messer Bernardo is to be punished for his own fault as well as mine."

"Nay," said my lady Duchess, "you both ought to have double punishment: he for his own transgression and for leading you to transgress; you for your own transgression and for imitating him."

"My Lady," replied messer Cesare, "as yet I have not transgressed; so, to leave all this punishment to messer Bernardo alone, I will keep silence."

And indeed he remained silent; when my lady Emilia laughed and said:

"Say whatever you like, for under leave of my lady Duchess I pardon him that has transgressed and him that shall transgress, in so small a degree."

"I consent," continued my lady Duchess. "But take care lest perchance you fall into the mistake of thinking to gain more by being merciful than by being just; for to pardon him too easily that has transgressed is to wrong him that transgresses not. Yet I would not have my severity reproach your indulgence, and thus be the cause of our not hearing this question of messer Cesare."

And so, being given the signal by my lady Duchess and by my lady Emilia, he at once said:

"If I remember rightly, Sir Count, I think you have repeated several times this evening that the Courtier must accompany his actions, gestures, habits, in short his every movement, with grace; and this you seem to regard as an universal seasoning, without which all other properties and good qualities are of little worth. And indeed I think that in this everyone would allow himself to be persuaded easily, since from the very force of the word, it may be said that he who has grace finds grace. But since you said that this is oftentimes the gift of nature and of heaven and, even when not thus perfect, can with care and pains be made much greater,—those men who are born so fortunate and so rich in this treasure as are some we see, seem to me in this to have little need of other master; because that benign favour of heaven almost in despite of themselves leads them higher than they will, and makes them not only pleasing but admirable to all the world. Therefore I do not discuss this, it not being in our power to acquire it of ourselves. But they who have received from nature only so much, that they are capable of becoming graceful by pains, industry and care,—I long to know by what art, by what training, by what method, they can acquire this grace, as well in bodily exercises (in which you esteem it to be so necessary) as also in everything else that they may do or say. Therefore, since by much praise of this quality you have aroused in all of us, I think, an ardent thirst to pursue it, you are further bound, by the charge that my lady Emilia laid upon you, to satisfy that thirst by teaching us how to attain it."

"I am not bound," said the Count, "to teach you how to become graceful, or anything else; but only to show you what manner of man a perfect Courtier ought to be. Nor would I in any case undertake the task of teaching you this perfection; especially having said a little while ago that the Courtier must know how to wrestle, vault, and do many other things, which I am sure you all know quite as well as if I, who have never learned them, were to teach you. For just as a good soldier knows how to tell the smith what fashion, shape and quality his armour ought to have, but cannot show how it is to be made or forged or tempered; so I perhaps may be able to tell you what manner of man a perfect Courtier ought to be, but cannot teach you what you must do to become one.

"Yet to comply with your request as far as is within my power,—although it is almost a proverb that grace is not to be learned,—I say that whoever would acquire grace in bodily exercises (assuming first that he be by nature not incapable), ought to begin early and learn the rudiments from the best masters. And how important this seemed to King Philip of Macedon, may be seen from the fact that he chose Aristotle, the famous philosopher and perhaps the greatest that has ever been in the world, to teach his son Alexander the first elements of letters. And of the men whom we know at the present day, consider how well and how gracefully my lord Galeazzo Sanseverino, Grand Equerry of France, performs all bodily exercises; and this because in addition to the natural aptitude of person that he possesses, he has taken the utmost pains to study with good masters, and always to have about him men who excel and to select from each the best of what they know: for just as in wrestling, vaulting and in the use of many sorts of weapons, he has taken for his guide our friend messer Pietro Monte, who (as you know) is the true and only master of every form of trained strength and agility, —so in riding, jousting and all else, he has ever had before his eyes the most proficient men that were known in those matters.

"Therefore he who wishes to be a good pupil, besides performing his tasks well, must put forth every effort to resemble his master, and, if it were possible, to transform himself into his master. And when he feels that he has made some progress, it will be very profitable to observe different men of the same calling, and governing himself with that good judgment which must ever be his guide, to go about selecting now this thing from one and that thing from another. And as the bee in the green meadows is ever wont to rob the flowers among the grass, so our Courtier must steal this grace from all who seem to possess it, taking from each that part which shall most be worthy praise; and not act like a friend of ours whom you all know, who thought he greatly resembled King Ferdinand the Younger of Aragon, and made it his care to imitate the latter in nothing but a certain trick of continually raising the head and twisting one side of the mouth, which the king had contracted from some infirmity. And there are many such, who think they gain a point if only they be like a great man in some thing; and frequently they devote themselves to that which is his only fault.

"But having before now often considered whence this grace springs, laying aside those men who have it by nature, I find one universal rule concerning it, which seems to me worth more in this matter than any other in all things human that are done or said: and that is to avoid affectation to the uttermost and as it were a very sharp and dangerous rock; and, to use possibly a new word, to practise in everything a certain nonchalance that shall conceal design and show that what is done and said is done without effort and almost without thought. From this I believe grace is in large measure derived, because everyone knows the difficulty of those things that are rare and well done, and therefore facility in them excites the highest admiration; while on the other hand, to strive and as the saying is to drag by the hair, is extremely ungraceful, and makes us esteem everything slightly, however great it be.

"Accordingly we may affirm that to be true art which does not appear to be art; nor to anything must we give greater care than to conceal art, for if it is discovered, it quite destroys our credit and brings us into small esteem. And I remember having once read that there were several very excellent orators of antiquity, who among their other devices strove to make everyone believe that they had no knowledge of letters; and hiding their knowledge they pretended that their orations were composed very simply and as if springing rather from nature and truth than from study and art; the which, if it had been detected, would have made men wary of being duped by it.

"Thus you see how the exhibition of art and study so intense destroys the grace in everything. Which of you is there who does not laugh when our friend messer Pierpaolo dances in his peculiar way, with those capers of his,—legs stiff to the toe and head motionless, as if he were a stick, and with such intentness that he actually seems to be counting the steps? What eye so blind as not to see in this the ungracefulness of affectation,—and in many men and women who are here present, the grace of that nonchalant ease (for in the case of bodily movements many call it thus), showing by word or laugh or gesture that they have no care and are thinking more of everything else than of that, to make the onlooker think they can hardly go amiss?"

Messer Bernardo Bibbiena here said, without waiting:

"Now at last our friend messer Roberto has found someone to praise the manner of his dancing, as all the rest of you seem to value it lightly; because if this merit consists in nonchalance, and in appearing to take no heed and to be thinking more of everything else than of what you are doing, messer Roberto in dancing has no peer on earth; for to show plainly that he is not thinking about it, he often lets the cloak drop from his shoulders and the slippers from his feet, and still goes on dancing without picking up either the one or the other."

Then the Count replied:

"Since you insist on my talking, I will speak further of our faults. Do you not perceive that what you call nonchalance in messer Roberto, is really affectation? For it is clearly seen that he is striving with all his might to seem to be taking no thought, and this is taking too much thought; and since it passes the true limits of moderation, his nonchalance is affected and unbecoming; and it is a thing that works precisely the reverse of the effect intended, that is the concealment of art. Thus in nonchalance (which is praiseworthy in itself), I do not think that it is less a vice of affectation to let the clothes fall from one's back, than in care of dress (which also is praiseworthy in itself) to hold the head stiff for fear of disarranging one's locks, or to carry a mirrour in the peak of one's cap and a comb in one's sleeve, and to have a valet follow one about the streets with sponge and brush: for such care in dress and such nonchalance both touch upon excess, which is always offensive and contrary to that pure and charming simplicity which is so pleasing to the human mind.

"You see how ungraceful a rider is who strives to sit bolt upright in the saddle after the manner we are wont to call Venetian,—as compared with another who seems not to be thinking about it, and sits his horse as free and steady as if he were afoot. How much more pleasing and how much more praised is a gentleman who carries arms, if he be modest, speak little and boast little, than another who is forever sounding his own praises, and with blasphemy and bluster seems to be hurling defiance at the world! This too is naught but affectation of wishing to appear bold. And so it is with every exercise, nay with everything that can be done or said in the world."

Then my lord Magnifico said:

"This is true also with music, wherein it is a very great fault to place two perfect consonances one after the other, so that our very sense of hearing abhors it and often enjoys a second or seventh, which in itself is a harsh and intolerable discord. And the reason is that repetition of perfect consonances begets satiety and exhibits a too affected harmony; which is avoided by introducing imperfect consonances, and thus a kind of contrast is given, whereby our ears are held more in suspense, and more eagerly await and enjoy the perfect consonances, and sometimes delight in that discord of the second or seventh, as in something unpremeditated."

"You see then," replied the Count, "the harmful effect of affectation in this as in other things. It is said also to have been proverbial among some very excellent painters of antiquity, that over diligence is harmful, and Protogenes is said to have been censured by Apelles because he did not know when to take his hand from the tablet."[7]

Then messer Cesare said:

"Methinks our friend fra Serafino has this same fault, of not knowing when to take his hands from the table, at least until all the food has been taken from it too."

The Count laughed, and continued:

"Apelles meant that in his painting Protogenes did not know when he had finished, which was the same thing as reproving him for being affected in his work. Thus this excellence, which is the opposite of affectation and which for the present we call nonchalance, besides being the true fountain from which grace springs, carries with it another ornament, which, in accompanying any human action whatever and however trifling it be, not only at once reveals the knowledge of him who performs it, but often leads us to rate his knowledge as much greater than in fact it is; because it impresses upon the minds of the bystanders the idea that he who does well so easily, knows much more than he does, and that if he were to use care and effort in what he did, he could do it far better.

---

[7]Two famous Greek painters of the late fourth century B.C. Historians record that although the two were friendly and admired each other's work, Apelles maintained that he excelled Protogenes in knowing when to cease elaborating his paintings.

"And to multiply like examples, here is a man who handles weapons, either about to throw a dart or holding a sword in his hand or other weapon; if he nimbly and without thinking puts himself in an attitude of readiness, with such ease that his body and all his members seem to fall into that posture naturally and quite without effort,—although he do no more, he will prove himself to everyone to be perfect in that exercise. Likewise in dancing, a single step, a single movement of the person that is graceful and not forced, soon shows the knowledge of the dancer. A musician who in singing utters a single note ending with sweet tone in a little group of four notes with such ease as to seem spontaneous, shows by that single touch that he can do much more than he is doing. Often too in painting, a single line not laboured, a single brush-stroke easily drawn, so that it seems as if the hand moves unbidden to its aim according to the painter's wish, without being guided by care or any skill, clearly reveals the excellence of the craftsman, which every man appreciates according to his capacity for judging. And the same is true of nearly everything else.

"Our Courtier then will be esteemed excellent and will attain grace in everything, particularly in speaking, if he avoids affectation; into which fault many fall, and often more than others, some of us Lombards, who, if they have been a year away from home, on their return at once begin to speak Roman, sometimes Spanish or French, and God knows how. And all this comes from over zeal to appear widely informed; in such fashion do men devote care and assiduity to acquiring a very odious fault. And truly it would be no light task for me, if I were to try in these discussions of ours to use those antique Tuscan words that are quite rejected by the usage of the Tuscans of to-day; and besides I think everyone would laugh at me."

[The conversation takes up at some length the details of language, diction, manner of speaking, and so forth appropriate to the Courtier. From there, the subject changes to the kind of learning suitable for a Courtier.]

"I would have him more than passably accomplished in letters, at least in those studies that are called the humanities, and conversant not only with the Latin language but with the Greek, for the sake of the many different things that have been admirably written therein. Let him be well versed in the poets, and not less in the orators and historians, and also proficient in writing verse and prose, especially in this vulgar tongue of ours; for besides the enjoyment he will find in it, he will by this means never lack agreeable entertainment with ladies, who are usually fond of such things. And if other occupations or want of study prevent his reaching such perfection as to render his writings worthy of great praise, let him be careful to suppress them so that others may not laugh at him, and let him show them only to a friend whom he can trust: because they will at least be of this service to him, that the exercise will enable him to judge the work of others. For it very rarely happens that a man who is not accustomed to write, however learned he may be, can ever quite appreciate the toil and industry of writers, or taste the sweetness and excellence of style, and those latent niceties that are often found in the ancients.

"Moreover these studies will also make him fluent, and as Aristippus[8] said to the tyrant, confident and assured in speaking with everyone. Hence I would have our Courtier keep one precept fixed in mind; which is that in this and everything else he should be always on his guard, and diffident rather than forward, and that he should keep from falsely persuading himself that he knows that which he does not know. For by nature we all are fonder of praise than we ought to be, and our ears love the melody of words that praise us more than any other sweet song or sound; and thus, like sirens' voices, they are often the cause of shipwreck to him who does not close his ears to such deceptive harmony. Among the ancient sages this danger was recognized, and books were written showing in what way the true friend may be distinguished from the flatterer. But what does this avail, if there be many, nay a host, of those who clearly perceive that they are flattered, yet love him who flatters them, and hold him in hatred who tells them the truth? And often when they find him who praises them too sparing in his words, they even help him and say such things of themselves, that the flatterer is put to shame, most impudent though he be.

"Let us leave these blind ones to their errour, and have our Courtier of such good judgment that he will not take black for white, or have more self-confidence than he clearly knows to be well founded; and especially in those peculiarities which (if you remember) messer Cesare in his game said we had often used as an instrument to bring men's folly to light.[9] On the contrary, even if he well knows the praises bestowed upon him to be true, let him not err by accepting them too openly or confirming them without some protest; but rather let him as it were disclaim them modestly, always showing and really esteeming arms as his chief profession, and all other good accomplishments as an ornament thereto. And particularly among soldiers let him not act like those who insist on seeming soldiers in learning, and learned men among soldiers. In this way, for the reasons we have alleged, he will avoid affectation, and even the middling things that he does, shall seem very great."

Messer Pietro Bembo here replied:

"Count, I do not see why you insist that this Courtier, being lettered and endowed with so many other admirable accomplishments, should hold everything as an ornament of arms, and not arms and the rest as an ornament of letters; which without other accompaniment are as superior in dignity to arms as the mind is to the body, for the practice of them properly pertains to the mind, as that of arms does to the body."

Then the Count replied:

"Nay, the practice of arms pertains to both mind and body. But I would not have you judge in such a cause, messer Pietro, for you would be too much suspected of bias by one of the two sides: and as the controversy has already been long waged by very wise men, there is no

---

[8]Greek philosopher (435?–356? B.C.) who lived for a time at the court of Dionysius of Syracuse, a ruler whom Plato also served.

[9]At the beginning of the evening, Cesare Gonzaga had suggested that they discuss each person present in turn, describing the ways in which each was most likely to make a fool of himself.

need to renew it; but I regard it as settled in favour of arms, and would have our Courtier so regard it too, since I may form him as I wish. And if you are of contrary mind, wait till you hear of a contest wherein he who defends the cause of arms is allowed to use arms, just as those who defend letters make use of letters in their defence; for if everyone avails himself of his proper weapons, you shall see that men of letters will be worsted."

"Ah," said messer Pietro, "a while ago you blamed the French for prizing letters little, and told what glorious lustre is shed on man by letters and how they make him immortal; and now it seems you have changed your mind. Do you not remember that

> Before the famous tomb of brave Achilles
> Thus spake the mighty Alexander, sighing:
> 'O happy youth, who found so clear a trumpet,
> And lofty bard to make thy deeds undying!'[10]

And if Alexander envied Achilles not for his deeds, but for the fortune that had granted him the happiness of having his exploits celebrated by Homer, we may conclude that Alexander esteemed Homer's poems above Achilles's arms. For what other judge do you wait then, or for what other sentence upon the dignity of arms and letters, than that pronounced by one of the greatest commanders that have ever been?"

Then the Count replied:

"I blame the French for thinking that letters are a hindrance to the profession of arms, and I hold that learning is more proper to no one than to a warrior; and in our Courtier I would have these two accomplishments joined and each aided by the other, as is most proper: nor do I think I have changed my mind in this. But as I said, I do not wish to discuss which of the two is more worthy of praise. It is enough that men of letters almost never select for praise any but great men and glorious deeds, which in themselves merit praise for the mere essential quality from which they spring; besides this they are very noble material for writers: which is a great ornament, and in part the cause of perpetuating writings, which perhaps would not be so much read and appreciated if they lacked their noble theme, but vain and of little moment.

"And if Alexander was envious that Achilles should be praised by Homer, it does not therefore follow that he esteemed letters above arms; wherein if he had felt himself as far behind Achilles as he deemed all those who wrote of him were behind Homer, I am sure he would far rather have desired fine acts on his part than fine speeches on the part of others. Hence I believe that saying of his to have been a tacit eulogy of himself, and that he was expressing a desire for what he thought he did not possess (that is, the supreme excellence of a writer), and not for what he believed he already had attained (that is, prowess in arms, wherein he did not deem Achilles at all his superior). Thus he called Achilles happy, as if hinting that although his own fame had

---

[10]The first quatrain of a sonnet by Petrarch.

hitherto not been so celebrated in the world as Achilles's, which was made bright and illustrious by that poem so divine,—it was not because his valour and merits were less or deserving of less praise, but because fortune bestowed upon Achilles that miracle of nature as a glorious trumpet for his achievements. Perhaps also he wished to incite some noble genius to write about him, by showing that this must be as pleasing to him as were his love and veneration for the sacred monuments of letters: whereof we have spoken long enough for the present."

"Nay, too long," replied my lord Ludovico Pio; "for I believe that in the whole world it would be impossible to find a receptacle large enough to hold all the things you would have in our Courtier."

Then the Count said:

"Wait a little, for there are many more that he must have."

"In that case," replied Pietro da Napoli, "Grasso de' Medici would have a great advantage over messer Pietro Bembo."[11]

Here everyone laughed, and the Count began anew and said:

"My lords, you must know that I am not content with the Courtier unless he be also a musician and unless, besides understanding and being able to read notes, he can play upon divers instruments. For if we consider rightly, there is to be found no rest from toil or medicine for the troubled spirit more becoming and praiseworthy in time of leisure, than this; and especially in courts, where besides the relief from tedium that music affords us all, many things are done to please the ladies, whose tender and gentle spirit is easily penetrated by harmony and filled with sweetness. Thus it is no marvel that in both ancient and modern times they have always been inclined to favour musicians, and have found refreshing spiritual food in music."

Then my lord Gaspar said:

"I admit that music as well as many other vanities may be proper to women and perhaps to some that have the semblance of men, but not to those who really are men; for these ought not to enervate their mind with delights and thus induce therein a fear of death."

"Say not so," replied the Count; "for I shall enter upon a vast sea in praise of music. And I shall call to mind how it was always celebrated and held sacred among the ancients, and how very sage philosophers were of opinion that the world is composed of music, that the heavens make harmony in their moving, and that the soul, being ordered in like fashion, awakes and as it were revives its powers through music.

"Thus it is written that Alexander was sometimes excited by it so passionately, that he was forced almost against his will to leave the banquet table and rush to arms; and when the musician changed the temper of the tune, he grew calm again, laid aside his arms, and returned to the banquet table. Moreover I will tell you that grave Socrates learned to play the cithern at a very advanced age. And I remember having once heard that Plato and Aristotle would have the man of culture a musician also; and they show by a host of arguments that the power of music over

---

[11]Bembo was slender; *Grasso* means "fat man." The reference here is probably to a corpulent soldier nicknamed Grasso, who was in the service of the Medici.

us is very great, and (for many reasons which would be too long to tell now) that it must needs be taught from childhood, not so much for the mere melody that we hear, but for the power it has to induce in us a fresh and good habit of mind and an habitual tendency to virtue, which renders the soul more capable of happiness, just as bodily exercise renders the body more robust; and that music is not only no hindrance in the pursuits of peace and war, but is very helpful therein.

"Again, Lycurgus approved of music in his harsh laws. And we read that in their battles the very warlike Lacedemonians and Cretans used the cithern and other dulcet instruments; that many very excellent commanders of antiquity, like Epaminondas,[12] practised music; and that those who were ignorant of it, like Themistocles,[13] were far less esteemed. Have you not read that music was among the first accomplishments which the worthy old Chiron taught Achilles in tender youth, whom he reared from the age of nurse and cradle? and that the sage preceptor insisted that the hands which were to shed so much Trojan blood, should be often busied with the cithern? Where is the soldier who would be ashamed to imitate Achilles,—to say nothing of many other famous commanders whom I could cite?

"Therefore seek not to deprive our Courtier of music, which not only soothes men's minds, but often tames wild beasts; and he who enjoys it not, may be sure that his spirit is ill attuned. See what power it has, to make (as once it did) a fish submit to be ridden by a man upon the boisterous sea. We find it used in holy temples to render praise and thanks to God; and we must believe that it is pleasing to Him and that He has given it to us as most sweet alleviation for our fatigues and troubles. Wherefore rough toilers of the field under a burning sun often cheat their weariness with crude and rustic song. With music the rude peasant lass, who is up before the day to spin or weave, wards off her drowsiness and makes her toil a pleasure; music is very cheering pastime for poor sailors after rain, wind and tempest: a solace to tired pilgrims on their long and weary journeys, and often to sorrowing captives in their chains and fetters. Thus, as stronger proof that melody even if rude is very great relief from every human toil and care, nature seems to have taught it to the nurse as chief remedy for the continual wailing of frail children, who by the sound of her voice are brought restful and placid sleep, forgetful of the tears so proper to them and given us in that age by nature as a presage of our after life."

As the Count now remained silent for a little, the Magnifico Giuliano said:

"I do not at all agree with my lord Gaspar. Nay I think, for the reasons you give and for many others, that music is not only an ornament but a necessity to the Courtier. Yet I would have you declare in what way this and the other accomplishments that you prescribe for him, are to be practised, and at what time and in what manner. For many things that are praiseworthy in themselves often become very inappropriate when

---

[12]Greek statesman and general (418?−362 B.C.).
[13]Greek statesman and general (527?−460? B.C.).

practised out of season, and on the other hand, some that seem of little moment are highly esteemed when made use of opportunely."

Then the Count said:

"Before we enter upon that subject, I wish to discuss another matter, which I deem of great importance and therefore think our Courtier ought by no means to omit: and this is to know how to draw and to have acquaintance with the very art of painting.

"And do not marvel that I desire this art, which to-day may seem to savour of the artisan and little to befit a gentleman; for I remember having read that the ancients, especially throughout Greece, had their boys of gentle birth study painting in school as an honourable and necessary thing, and it was admitted to the first rank of liberal arts, while by public edict they forbade that it be taught to slaves. Among the Romans too, it was held in highest honour, and the very noble family of the Fabii took their name from it; for the first Fabius was given the name *Pictor,* because,—being indeed a most excellent painter, and so devoted to painting that when he painted the walls of the temple of Health,—he inscribed his own name thereon;[14] for although he was born of a family thus renowned and honoured with so many consular titles, triumphs and other dignities, and although he was a man of letters and learned in the law, and numbered among the orators,—yet he thought to add splendour and ornament to his fame by leaving a memorial that he had been a painter. Nor is there lack of many other men of illustrious family, celebrated in this art; which besides being very noble and worthy in itself, is of great utility, and especially in war for drawing places, sites, rivers, bridges, rocks, fortresses, and the like; since however well we may keep them in memory (which is very difficult), we cannot show them to others.

"And truly he who does not esteem this art, seems to me very unreasonable; for this universal fabric that we see,—with the vast heaven so richly adorned with shining stars, and in the midst the earth girdled by the seas, varied with mountains, valleys and rivers, and bedecked with so many divers trees, beautiful flowers and grasses,—may be said to be a great and noble picture, composed by the hand of nature and of God; and whoever is able to imitate it, seems to me deserving of great praise: nor can it be imitated without knowledge of many things, as he knows well who tries. Hence the ancients greatly prized both the art and the artist, which thus attained the summit of highest excellence; very sure proof of which may be found in the antique marble and bronze statues that yet are seen. And although painting is different from sculpture, both the one and the other spring from the same source, which is good design. Therefore, as the statues are divine, so we may believe the pictures were also; the more indeed because they are susceptible of greater skill."

[The remainder of the first evening's conversation continues on the subject of painting and sculpture as suitable accomplishments for the Courtier.]

---

[14]This event occurred in 300 B.C. Actually, the Fabii had been an important family since early in the fifth century B.C.

Comments / on Castiglione

Three books only the king [Charles V] read with great delight and had them translated into his native tongue; one for the ordering of society: *The Courtier,* by Count Baldassare de Castiglione; one for its relevance to affairs of State: *The Prince* and the *Discourses* of Machiavelli; and the third on the conduct of war, Polybios' history and all his works.

JACOPO SANSOVINO (1570?)

For to princes and great men, [*The Courtier*] is a rule, to rule themselves that rule others. . . . To men grown in years, [*The Courtier*] is a pathway to the beholding and musing of the mind, and to whatsoever else is meet for that age; to young gentlemen, an encouraging to garnish their minds with moral virtues, and their bodies with comely exercises, and both the one and the other with honest qualities to attain unto their noble end. To ladies and gentlewomen, a mirror to deck and trim themselves with virtuous conditions, comely behaviors, and honest entertainment toward all men. And to them all in general, a store house of most necessary implements for the conversation, use, and training up of man's life with courtly demeanors.   *SIR THOMAS HOBY (1561)*

[T]he Courtier, as described to us by Castiglione . . . was the ideal man of society, and was regarded by the civilization of that age as its choicest flower; and the court existed for him rather than he for the court. Indeed, such a man would have been out of place at any court, since he himself possessed all the gifts and the bearing of an accomplished ruler, and because his calm supremacy in all things, both outward and spiritual, implied too independent a nature. The inner impulse which inspired him was directed, though our author does not acknowledge the fact, not to the service of the prince, but to his own perfection.

JACOB BURCKHARDT (1860)

Castiglione's treatise may therefore be called an essay on the character of the true gentleman as he appeared in Italy. Eliminating all qualities that are special to any art or calling, he defines those essential characteristics which were requisite for social excellence in the sixteenth century. It is curious to observe how unchangeable are the laws of real politeness and refinement. Castiglione's courtier is, with one or two points of immaterial difference, a modern gentleman, such as all men of education at the present day would wish to be.   *J. A. SYMONDS (1875)*

The book, which [Castiglione] had begun . . . as a memorial to Duke Guidobaldo and the Court of Urbino, had grown into a profession of faith, embodying the social and moral code of his calling; and he had his reasons for writing . . . the theory of the leisure classes. . . . Castiglione sat down to claim for his profession, as the preserve of an aristocracy, the chastening discipline of the aristocratic view of life, for which the aim of life was the manner of living it. If such moral elegance was ornamental, it was not useless. In the vast confusion and futility of life, which no man could comprehend or control, one could answer for nothing and no one but oneself; and to perfect oneself was perhaps the only service which anyone could render to his kind.   *RALPH ROEDER (1933)*

Thomas More
1478–1535

One of the most enticing ideas in Western thought—the dream of an ideal commonwealth—reappears in the Renaissance as a sign of the connection between humanism and the classical Greek tradition. Among the Greeks, the idea had flourished for centuries both before and after Plato had provided its most eloquent expression in the *Republic*. But in Roman times the dream faded, probably because the practical and patriotic Romans felt that the Roman form of government *was* ideal. Medieval Christianity, for almost precisely opposite reasons, was likewise uninfluenced by the dream: Christian theology viewed man, because of his inherent imperfection, as incapable of creating an ideal society in this world; such a society was to be found, and indeed could only exist, in the next world. Medieval thinkers, to be sure, did speculate about the nature of ideal social and political organization, but, like Dante in *On World Government* they emphasized theoretical description of how existing political, social, and religious institutions ideally ought to function within the existing framework of Christian society. Roman philosophers had done much the same thing in terms of the existing framework of Roman society. But serious visions of a wholly new ideal order of society do not show up either in Roman or in medieval Christian thinking. It remained for the Renaissance humanists—with their renewed emphasis on the dignity of human achievement and on the potentialities of human reason, together with their susceptibility to the influence of classical Greek thought—to inspire once again an interest in the dream of an ideal commonwealth.

Another factor that probably contributed to this interest during the Renaissance was the great expansion of knowledge about the world beyond Europe and the Mediterranean. An increasing number of encounters with different civilizations stimulated an increased curiosity about exotic peoples, places, and customs—and about the stories told by travelers who had seen them. To the man who wanted to describe an imaginary society, the vogue for travel narrative offered an almost ready-made medium of expression. The medium itself was by no means new: medieval literature contains a certain amount of travel writing, much of which consists of highly imaginary accounts purporting to describe the wonders of fantastic places. But the emphasis is on the marvelous aspects of these places, sometimes so much so that they assume the features of an earthly paradise. In very few of these accounts is there anything resembling a comprehensive description of a strange society, and in none of them is there any attempt at a reasoned exposition of a system of social and political institutions that would make for an ideal commonwealth.

Medieval travel literature lacked seriousness, while medieval political theory lacked humor; but a vision of an ideal commonwealth requires both—humor to mark the author's awareness that, men being what they are, his vision is likely to remain imaginary, and seriousness to show his purpose that, even though his vision is imaginary, at least some of its components may strike the mind with enough force to move men toward converting them from theory to practice. There is no real likelihood, Socrates wryly admits in the *Republic,* that philosophers will ever become kings, but Plato nonetheless invested some of his most profound thought in the creation of the *Republic.*

The reappearance of this attitude in the Renaissance was first marked by Sir Thomas More's *Utopia,* a work second only to the *Republic* in its influence on the conception of an ideal commonwealth and even more influential in the sense that it provided what has become the generic name for such a conception. More came from a well-to-do London family, received a thorough humanistic education, and was trained as a lawyer. Before he was thirty years old he had already attained a brilliant reputation, both politically as a member of Parliament and intellectually as one of the outstanding humanists in England. (In 1509, the famous Dutch humanist Erasmus wrote his *Praise of Folly* at More's house and dedicated it to his English host.) In 1515, More entered the service of the government of King Henry VIII and eventually became Lord Chancellor, the most important royal office in England. When Henry's long standing dispute with the papacy over obtaining a divorce resulted in the King's outright denial of papal authority in 1532, More, an intensely pious Roman Catholic noted for his intolerance of heresy and his persecution of heretics, resigned his post as Lord Chancellor. Two years later, Henry, who had finally disavowed the papacy and established the Church of England with himself as Head, demanded that More subscribe to an oath acknowledging him as Supreme Head of the Church. More refused, was imprisoned on a trumped-up charge of treason, was tried and convicted on perjured evidence, and was beheaded the following year.

More began writing the *Utopia,* in Latin, while he was on a diplomatic mission to Flanders in 1515. (Historians like to point out that the three classic expressions of Renaissance social and political thought—*The Prince, The Courtier,* and *Utopia*—were all written within a few years of each other, none influenced by either of the others.) He wrote the second part first, a description of the imaginary state of Utopia, a name he coined from two Greek words that in combination mean "nowhere." On his return to England the next year he composed an introductory first part to achieve a double purpose: to serve as social satire through its criticism of contemporary European institutions to be contrasted with the state of affairs in Utopia; and to explain his knowledge of Utopia by acquainting his readers with a man supposed to have been there, the imaginary traveler Raphael Hythloday, whose surname More coined from Greek words that in combination mean "distributor of nonsense." The completed book was published abroad that same year and quickly attained wide circulation among well-educated people throughout Europe. It was first translated into English some sixteen years after More's death.

Critics have always had difficulty squaring the facts of More's life—his political and religious conservatism—with the visionary society he describes in Utopia. The answer to the questions at issue probably depends on how seriously he meant the work to be taken. Clearly, he was not composing an inflammatory tract calling for immediate social revolution: revolutionaries neither compose their work in esoteric languages, thereby restricting their ideas to a limited and usually by no means activist public, nor do they give humorous names to their own conceptions. But it is equally clear, from the trenchant social commentary in the first part and from the marked influence of Plato's *Republic* in the second, that More did have a serious purpose in mind. The ambiguity posed by the relationship between More and his Utopia is probably best illustrated by two facts of recent history: More was canonized as a saint by the Roman Catholic Church in 1935, and within the same decade his *Utopia* was adopted as an official school textbook by the government of Soviet Russia.

Utopia

Book I

The most victorious and triumphant King of England, Henry the Eighth of that name, in all royal virtues a prince most peerless, had recently some differences with Charles, the most serene Prince of Castile, and sent me into Flanders to negotiate and compose matters between them. I was colleague and companion to that incomparable man, Cuthbert Tunstall, whom the king lately made Master of the Rolls to the great satisfaction of all. I will say nothing of this man, not because I fear the testimony of a friend will be questioned, but because his learning and virtues are greater than I can describe. And also they are so well-known that they do not need my commendation, unless I would, according to the proverb, "Show the sun with a lantern."

From *Utopia* by Thomas More translated and edited by H. V. S. Ogden. Copyright, 1949, by Appleton-Century-Crofts, Inc. Reprinted by permission of Appleton-Century-Crofts, Division of Meredith Publishing Company.

The men appointed by the prince to treat with us, all excellent men, met us at Bruges according to agreement. The chief man among them and their leader was the Margrave of Bruges, a distinguished man. But the wisest and best spoken was George Temse, the Provost of Cassel, a man eloquent both by nature and training, very learned in the law, and most skillful in affairs through his capacity and long practice. After we had met several times and could not come to an agreement, they went to Brussels for some days to learn their prince's pleasure.

Meanwhile I went to Antwerp, since our business permitted it. Of those who visited me while I was there, Peter Giles was more congenial to me than any of the others. He was a native of Antwerp, a man much respected there and worthy of the highest regard. I do not know of a more cultivated or a better bred young man anywhere. He is, indeed, the best and most learned of men, and besides, very courteous to all. To his intimates he is so loving, so trustworthy, and so deeply affectionate that it would be very hard to find another friend like him anywhere. No man is more modest or more candid. No man unites more simplicity with prudence. His conversation is so pleasant, and so witty without vulgarity, that the fervent desire I felt to see my native country and my wife and children (from whom I had been away more than four months) was much eased by his company.

One day after I had heard mass at Nôtre Dame, the most beautiful and most frequented church in Antwerp, I was about to return to my lodgings when I happened to see him talking with a stranger, a man well advanced in years. The stranger had a sunburned face, a long beard, and a cloak hanging carelessly from his shoulders. From his appearance and clothing I took him to be a seaman. When Peter saw me, he approached and greeted me. As I was returning his salutation, he took me aside, and pointing to the stranger, said, "Do you see that man? I was just thinking of bringing him to you."

"He would have been very welcome on your account," I answered.

"And on his own, too," he said, "if you knew him, for there is no man alive who can tell you so much about unknown peoples and countries. And I know that you are most eager for such information."

"Then," said I, "I did not guess badly, for at first sight I took him for a seaman."

"No," he replied, "you are mistaken, for he has sailed not as the sailor Palinurus, but as Ulysses, or rather as Plato. This Raphael, surnamed Hythloday (for so he is called), though not ignorant of the Latin tongue, is eminently learned in the Greek. He has applied himself more particularly to Greek because he has given himself wholly to philosophy, in which he knew that the Romans have left us nothing that is valuable except what is to be found in Seneca and Cicero. He was so desirous of seeing the world that he divided his patrimony among his brothers (he is Portuguese by birth), and threw in his lot with Americus Vespucius. He took part in the last three of Vespucius's four voyages, accounts of which are now published. But he did not return home with him on the last voyage. After much effort, he won permission from Americus to be one of the twenty-four who were left in a fort at the farthest place at which they touched in their last voyage. Being left thus was highly gratifying to a man who gave more thought to his travels than to his burial place, and who often used to say that one who has no grave is covered by the sky and that the road to heaven is equally short from all places.

"Yet this disposition of mind would have cost him dear if God had not been very gracious to him. After the departure of Vespucius he traveled over many countries with five companions from the fort. At last by singular good fortune he got to Ceylon and from thence to Calcutta, where he very happily found some Portuguese ships. And so, beyond anyone's expectation, he came back to his own country."

When Peter had told me this, I thanked him for his kindness in wishing to make me acquainted with a man whose conversation he knew would be so acceptable to me, and I turned toward Raphael. Upon that Raphael and I greeted one another. And after the ordinary civilities of strangers upon their first meeting, we all went to my house. There in the garden we sat down on a grassy bank and conversed.

He told us that when Vespucius had sailed away, he and his companions that had stayed behind in the fort often met the people of the country, and by fair and gentle speech gradually won their favor. Before long they came to dwell with them quite safely and even familiarly. He also told us that they were esteemed by the prince (I have forgotten his name and his country), who furnished them plentifully with all things necessary, and who also gave them the means of traveling, both boats when they went by water and wagons when they traveled over land. He sent with them a faithful guide who was to introduce and recommend them to such other princes as they had a mind to see. After many days' journey, they came to towns and cities, and to commonwealths that were both well peopled and happily governed.

Under the equator and as far on both sides of it as the sun moves, there lie vast deserts parched with the perpetual heat of the sun. The whole region is desolate and gloomy, savage and uncultivated, inhabited by wild beasts and serpents, and by a few men as wild and dangerous as the beasts themselves. As they went on, conditions gradually grew milder. The heat was less burning, the earth greener, and even the beasts less fierce. At last they found nations, cities, and towns that had mutual commerce among themselves and with their neighbors, and that traded by sea and land with remote countries. From then on, he said, they were able to visit many lands on all sides, for they were welcome on board any ship about to make a voyage.

The first vessels that they saw were flat-bottomed, with sails made of close-woven reeds and wicker, or in some places of leather. Farther on they found ships made with round keels and canvas sails, in all ways like our ships. The seamen were skillful both in sailing and in navigation. They were most grateful to him, Raphael said, for showing them the use of the compass, of which they had been ignorant. For that reason they had sailed with great caution and only in summer. Now they have such confidence in the compass that they no longer fear winter, and are carefree rather than safe. This discovery, which they thought so much to their advantage, may become the cause of much mischief to them through their imprudence.

It would take too long to set forth all that Raphael told us he had observed, and it would be a digression from our present purpose. Perhaps in another place we shall tell more about the things that are worth knowing, especially about the wise and prudent institutions that he observed among the civilized nations. We asked him many questions about such things and he answered us very willingly. We made no inquiries, however, about monsters, which are common enough. Scyllas, ravenous harpies, and cannibals are easy to find anywhere, but it is not so easy to find states that are well and wisely governed.

While he told us of many things which are amiss among those new-found nations, he also reckoned up not a few things from which patterns might be taken for correcting the errors of our own cities and kingdoms. These I shall treat in another place, as I have said. Now I intend to relate only what he told us about the manners and laws of the Utopians, first setting forth the occasion that led us to speak of that commonwealth. Raphael had been talking very wisely about the numerous errors and also the wise institutions found both among those nations and us, speaking as intimately about the customs and government of each place he had visited as though he had lived there all his life. Peter was struck with admiration.

"I wonder, Master Raphael," he said, "why you do not enter some king's service, for I know of no prince who would not be eager to have you. Your learning and your knowledge of places and men would entertain him pleasantly, while your advice and your examples would be invaluable. Thus you would serve your own interest and be useful to all your friends."

"I am not greatly concerned about my friends," he said, "for I have already done my duty toward them. While I was still young and healthy, I distributed among my relations and friends the possessions which other men do not part with till they are old and sick (and then only grudgingly and because they can no longer keep them). I think my friends should rest content with this and not expect that for their sake I should enslave myself to any king whatsoever."

"Well-said," Peter replied, "but I do not mean that you should be a slave to any king, only that you should be of service to him."

"The difference is a mere matter of words," Raphael replied.

"As you will," said Peter, "but I do not see any other way in which you can be so useful either to your friends or to the public, to say nothing of making yourself happier."

"Happier?" exclaimed Raphael. "Would a way of life so abhorrent to my nature make my life happier? Now I live as I will, and I believe very few courtiers can say that. As a matter of fact, there are so many men courting the favor of the great that it will be no great loss if they have to do without me or others like me."

Then I said, "It is clear, Master Raphael, that you desire neither wealth nor power, and indeed I value and admire such a man much more than I do any of the great men in the world. Yet I think, if you would give your time and effort to public affairs, you would do a thing worthy of a generous and philosophical nature like yours, even though you might not enjoy it. You could best perform such a service by belonging to the council of some great prince, whom you would urge on to whatever is noble and just. I know you would do this, if you were in such a post. And your efforts would be effective, because a people's welfare or misery flows wholly from their prince, as from a never-failing spring. Your learning is so full, even when not combined with experience, and your experience so great, even without learning, that you would be an exceptional councillor to any king whatsoever."

"You are doubly mistaken, my dear More," said he, "both in your opinion of me and in your estimate of the situation itself. I do not have that capacity which you fancy to be in me, and if I had it, the public would not be any better off through the sacrifice of my leisure; for most princes apply themselves to warlike pursuits (in which I have no skill or interest) rather than to the useful arts of peace. They are generally more set on acquiring new kingdoms rightly or wrongly, than on governing well those that they already have. Moreover the councillors of kings are so wise that they need no advice from others (or at least so it seems to themselves). At the same time they accept and even applaud the most absurd statements of men whose favor they seek for the sake of standing well with the prince. It is natural that each man should flatter himself by thinking his own opinions best. The old crow loves his young and the ape his cubs. Now in a court made up of those who envy all others and admire only themselves, if a man should propose something that he had read in history or observed in his travels, the other councillors would fear that their whole reputation for wisdom was in danger, and that they would be regarded as plain fools unless they could show his suggestion was weak and defective. If all else failed, they would take refuge in the retort that such and such things pleased our ancestors and would that we could match their wisdom! With this they would settle down as though they had said the last word on the subject and as though there were a terrible danger in finding a man wiser than our ancestors in anything. We readily follow whatever they did, as though it were necessarily best. But if something better is proposed, we seize the excuse of reverence for past times and cling to it doggedly. I have met with these proud, absurd, and morose judgments in many places, and once even in England."

[Hythloday attacks the practices of contemporary governments, especially their resistance to any sort of social reform.]

"And this is all I could achieve in a prince's court. For either I would think different thoughts from the rest, and that would be as if I had no thoughts, or else I would agree with them and thus . . . be an accessory to their madness. I do not understand what you mean by saying that a man should guide policy indirectly and should strive to make the best of things, so that what is bad will at least be made as good as possible. In councils there is no place for silent and unwilling acquiescence. A man must openly approve of the worst plans and consent to the most pernicious resolutions. One would pass for a spy or even a traitor, if he approved of such plans only grudgingly. A man has no chance to do good when his colleagues are more likely to corrupt the best of men than be corrected themselves. He will either be corrupted himself by his colleagues, or, if he remains sound and innocent, he will be blamed for the folly and knavery of others. He is far from being able to mend matters by guiding policy indirectly!

"That is why Plato in an excellent simile showed that wise men will not meddle in affairs of state. They see the people swarm into the streets and get drenched with rain, and they cannot persuade them to go out of the rain and back to their houses. They know that if they should go out to them, they would accomplish nothing, and be drenched themselves. So they stay indoors. Although they cannot remedy the folly of others, they can at least be wise themselves.

"But, Master More, to speak plainly what is in my mind, as long as there is private property and while money is the standard of all things, I do not think that a nation can be governed either justly or happily: not justly, because the best things will fall to the worst men; nor happily, because all things will be divided among a few. Even these few are not really well off, while the rest are utterly miserable.

"So I reflect on the wise and sacred institutions of the Utopians, who are so well governed with so few laws. Among them virtue has its due reward, yet everything is shared equally and every man lives in plenty. I contrast them with other nations that are still making laws and yet can never order their affairs satisfactorily. Although each man calls the property he has obtained his own, the many laws passed every day do not enable him to obtain or keep it or to distinguish satisfactorily what he calls his own from another's. This is clear from the many lawsuits unceasingly arising and never ending. When I consider these things, I grow more favorable to Plato's opinion and do not wonder that he refused to make laws for any people who will not share all their goods equally. Wisest of men, he easily perceived that the one and only way to make a people happy is to establish equality of property. I doubt whether this equality can be achieved where property belongs to individual men. For when every man gets as much as he can for himself by one device or another, the few divide the whole wealth among themselves and leave want to the rest. The result generally is that there will be two sorts of people, and their fortunes ought to be interchanged: one sort are useless, but ravenous and wicked, while the other sort are unassuming, modest men who serve the public more than themselves by their daily work.

"By this I am persuaded that unless private property is entirely done away with, there can be no fair distribution of goods, nor can the world be happily governed. As long as private property remains, the largest and far the best part of mankind will be oppressed with an inescapable load of cares and anxieties. This load, I admit, may be lightened somewhat, but cannot be entirely removed. Laws might be made that no one should own more than a certain amount of land nor possess more than a certain sum of money. Or laws might be passed to prevent the prince from growing too powerful and the populace from becoming too strong. It might be made unlawful for public offices to be solicited, or sold, or made burdensome for the officeholder by great expense. Otherwise officeholders are tempted to reimburse themselves by dishonesty and force, and it becomes necessary to find rich men for those offices which ought rather to be held by wise men. Such laws, I say, may have as much effect as good nursing has on men who are dangerously sick. Social evils may be allayed and mitigated, but so long as private property remains, there is no hope at all that they may be healed and society restored to good health. While you try to cure one part, you aggravate the disease in other parts. In redressing one evil another is committed, since you cannot give something to one man without taking the same thing from another."

"On the contrary," I replied, "it seems to me that men cannot live well where all things are in common. How can there be plenty where every man stops working? The hope of gain will not drive him; he will rely on others and become lazy. If men are stirred by want, and yet no one can legally protect what he has earned, what can follow but continual bloodshed and turmoil, especially when the respect for and the authority of magistrates are lost? I cannot conceive of authority among men that are equal to one another in all things."

"I do not wonder," said Raphael, "that it appears so to you, since you have no idea, or only a false idea of such a state. But if you had been with me in Utopia and had seen their customs and institutions as I did at first hand for the five years that I spent among them, you would frankly confess that you had never seen a people ordered so well as they were. Indeed I would never willingly have left, if it had not been to make known that new world to others."

"You will not easily persuade me," Peter Giles said, "that people in that new land are better governed than in our known world. Our abilities are not inferior to theirs, and our government, I believe, is older. Long experience has helped us to find out many conveniences of life, and by good luck we have discovered other things which man's abilities could never have invented."

"As for the age of their commonwealth," Raphael replied, "you might judge more correctly if you had read their histories. If these may be trusted, they had cities even before there were inhabitants here. What chance has hit on or ingenuity has discovered, these things might have been found there as well as here. As a matter of fact I believe that we surpass them in natural abilities, but we are left far behind them in diligence and in zeal to learn. According to their chronicles they had heard nothing about the men from beyond the equator (as they call us) before our landing there, except that once about twelve hundred years ago a ship which a storm had carried toward Utopia was wrecked on their island. Some Romans and Egyptians from the ship were cast up on the island and never departed. Now note how the Utopians profited from this chance event by their diligence. They learned all the useful arts of Roman civilization either directly from their ship-wrecked guests or indirectly from hints given in answer to inquiries. What benefits from the mere fact that some Europeans landed there! If a similar accident has hitherto brought any men here from their land, it has been completely forgotten, as doubtless it will be forgotten in time to come that I was ever in their country. From one such accident they made themselves masters of all our useful inventions, but I believe it will be a long time before we accept any of their institutions which are better than ours. This willingness to learn, I think, is the real reason for their being better governed and for their living more happily than we do, though we are not behind them in ingenuity or riches."

"Then I earnestly beg you, Master Raphael," I said, "to describe that island to us. Do not try to be brief, but explain in order everything relating to their soil, rivers, towns, people, manners, institutions, laws, and, in fact, everything you think we would like to know. And you may take it for granted that we want to know whatever we do not know yet."

"There is nothing," he said, "that I would be happier to do, for these things are fresh in my mind. But it will take some time."

"Let us first go to dinner," I said, "and afterward we shall have time enough."

"Let us do so," he said. So we went in and had dinner. Then we came back and sat down on the same bench. I ordered my servants to take care that no one should interrupt us. Peter Giles and I besought Raphael to be as good as his word. When he saw that we were eager to hear him, he sat silent and thoughtful a moment, and then began as follows. . . .

Book II

Their Country and Agriculture

The island of Utopia is two hundred miles in breadth in the middle part where it is widest, and it is nowhere much narrower than this except toward the two ends. These ends, drawn around in a five hundred-mile curve, make the island crescent-shaped. Between the horns of the crescent, which are some eleven miles apart, the sea comes in and spreads into a great bay. Being well secured from the wind, the bay does not rage with great waves, but is quiet like a lake. This makes nearly the whole inner coast a harbor, greatly facilitating mutual trade. But the entrance into the bay, what with shallows on one side and rocks on the other, is very dangerous. Near the middle there is one rock that rises above the water, and so is not dangerous. On the top of it a tower has been built, in which a garrison is kept. The other rocks lie under water and are very treacherous. The channels are known only to the Utopians, so if any stranger should chance to enter the bay without one of their pilots, he would run a great danger of shipwreck. Even they themselves could not enter safely if some marks on the coast did not direct their way. If these were shifted even a little, any fleet coming against them, no matter how great it was, would certainly be lost.

On the other side of the island there are likewise many harbors, and the coast is so fortified by nature and art that a small number of men could hold off the attack of a great force. They say (and the appearance of the place bears this out) that their land was once not an island. But Utopus, who conquered the country and gave it his name (it was previously called Abraxa), brought its rude and uncivilized inhabitants to such a high level of culture and humanity that now they excel all other people in that part of the world. When he had subdued them, he cut a channel fifteen miles long where their land joined the continent and thus brought the sea entirely around their land. He not only forced the natives to work at it, but his soldiers too, so that the natives would not think they were treated like slaves. By putting so many men to work, he finished the project quickly, and the neighbors, who at first had laughed at his folly, were struck with admiration and terror at his success.

There are fifty-four cities on the island, all large and well built, and with the same language, customs, institutions, and laws. All of them are built on the same plan, as far as the location permits. The nearest are at least twenty-four miles apart, and those that are farthest are not so far but that a man can go on foot from one city to the next in a day.

Once a year each city sends three of its wisest elders to Amaurot[1] to consult about their common concerns. Amaurot is the chief city of the island and lies near its center, so that it is the most convenient place for the elders to meet. Every city has enough ground assigned to it so that it has at least ten miles of farm land in every direction. Where the cities are farther apart, they have more ground. No city desires to enlarge its bounds, for the inhabitants consider themselves husbandmen rather than landlords. They have built houses all over the countryside, well designed and furnished with farm equipment. These houses are inhabited by citizens who come to the country by turns to dwell in them. No country household has fewer than forty men and women in it, besides two bondmen. A master and mistress, serious and mature persons, are in charge of each household. A magistrate is placed over every thirty households. Every year twenty from each household move back to the city, after completing a two-year turn in the country. In their place twenty others are sent out from town, to learn farm work from those that have already been in the country for a year and are somewhat skilled in it. In turn they must teach those who come the following year. If they were all equally ignorant of farm work and new to it, they might damage the crops through ignorance. This custom of shifting the farm workers is established in order that no one will have to do this hard work against his will for more than two years, but many of them ask to stay longer because they take a natural delight in farm life.

The farm workers till the soil, care for the cattle, hew wood, and take it to the city by land or water, as is most convenient. They breed an enormous number of chickens by a marvelous method. Men hatch the eggs, not hens, by keeping them in a warm place at an even temperature. The chicks, as soon as they come out of the shell, recognize and follow men instead of their mothers.

They raise very few horses, but these are full of mettle and are kept only for exercising the youth in the art of horsemanship. For the work of plowing and hauling they employ only oxen. They think horses are stronger than oxen, but they find that oxen can hold out longer and are less subject to disease, and so can be kept with less cost and effort. Moreover, when they are too old for work, they can be used for meat.

They raise grain only for bread. They drink wine, apple or pear cider,

---

[1] From the Greek word *amauros*, meaning "dim" or "uncertain."

or water, sometimes clear, but often mixed with honey or liquorish, of which they have an abundance. Although they know just how much grain each city and its district will consume, they sow more grain and breed more cattle than they need for their own use, and share the surplus with their neighbors. When they need goods on the farms which they do not make there, they get them from the town magistrates without giving anything in exchange. This is not inconvenient, since most of them go to town once a month, especially on holidays. When harvest time comes, the country magistrates notify the towns how many hands will be needed. The harvesters come at the right time, and commonly get in the whole harvest in one fair day.

Their Cities and Especially Amaurot

If you know one of their cities, you know them all, so like are they to one another, except where the location makes some difference. So I shall describe one of them, and no matter which. But what one rather than Amaurot, whose eminence the other cities acknowledge in sending their elders to the annual meeting there, and which I know best because I lived there five years?

Amaurot lies on a gently sloping hill, and is almost square in shape. From a little below the top of the hill it runs down two miles to the river Anyder,[2] and it follows along the river bank for a somewhat greater distance. The Anyder rises about eighty miles above Amaurot in a small spring, but other streams flow into it, two of them being of some size, so that, as it runs past Amaurot, it has grown to the width of half a mile. It grows larger and larger, until at last sixty miles farther along it is lost in the ocean. In this stretch of river between the city and the sea, and also for some miles above the city, the water ebbs and flows every six hours with a strong current. When the tide comes in, it fills the whole Anyder with salt water for about thirty miles, and forces back the fresh water. Above this for several miles the water is brackish, but a little higher up, as it runs past the city, it is quite fresh. When the tide ebbs, the water is fresh all the way to the sea. Over the river there is a bridge, not built on wooden piles, but on many stately arches of stone. It is placed at the part of the city farthest from the sea, so that ships can sail along the entire side of the city without being stopped. They have also another stream, not large to be sure, but very gentle and pleasing. It rises out of the hill, and after flowing through the town in a steep descent, joins the Anyder. The inhabitants have fortified the fountainhead of this river, which rises a little outside the town, so that if they should be attacked, the enemy would not be able to cut off or divert the stream or poison it. Water from it is carried in pipes into the lower section of town. Where the water of the small river cannot be conveyed, they collect rain water in cisterns.

The town is surrounded by a high thick wall with many towers and forts. Also running around the city on three sides, there is a dry ditch, broad and deep and thick-set with a thorn hedge. The river is on the

---

[2]From the Greek *an-hudor*, meaning "without water."

fourth side. The streets are conveniently laid out both for vehicles and for protection from the wind. Their buildings are by no means unsightly, with unbroken rows of houses facing each other and running along the streets through the whole town. The streets are twenty feet wide. Through the whole length of the city there are large gardens behind the houses and enclosed by them.

Every house has a door to the street and another to the garden. The doors, which are made with two leaves, open easily and swing shut of their own accord, freely letting anyone in (for there is no private property). Every ten years they change houses by lot. They think much of their gardens. They raise vines, fruits, herbs, and flowers, all so tastefully arrayed and so well kept that I have never seen any gardens more fruitful or more beautiful than theirs. Their interest in gardening is kept up both by the pleasure they find in it and also by the rivalry between the inhabitants of the different streets, who vie with each other in this matter. Indeed you will find nothing else in this whole city more useful to the citizens or more pleasant. It seems that the founder of the city arranged for nothing more carefully than the gardens.

They say that the whole city was planned by King Utopus himself, but that he left to posterity matters of ornamentation and improvement which could not be perfected in one man's lifetime. Their records go back 1760 years to the conquest of the island and are preserved with the greatest care. From these it appears that at first their houses were small, like cottages and peasant huts, built out of any sort of timber with mud walls and thatched roofs. Now their houses are three stories high; their fronts are faced with stone, cement, or brick, with rubble thrown in between the facings of the walls. The roofs are flat, and are covered with a kind of plaster that is cheap and fireproof and that resists weather better than lead. They use glass very frequently in their windows to keep out the wind. They also use thin linen cloth treated with oil or gum so that it lets in the light and keeps out the wind better.

Their Magistrates

Each year thirty households choose a magistrate, formerly called the syphogrant, but now called the phylarch. Over each ten syphogrants and the households subject to them there is another magistrate, once called the tranibor but now called the chief phylarch.[3] All the syphogrants, two hundred in number, choose the prince by secret vote from the list of four men whom the people of the four sections of the city have nominated. The syphogrants are under oath to choose the man they think fittest. The prince is chosen for life, unless he is suspected of trying to become a dictator. They choose the tranibors annually, but they rarely change them. All their other magistrates hold office for only a year.

The tranibors meet every third day, and more often if necessary, to consult with the prince on affairs of state or on the few disputes between private persons. The tranibors always call in two syphogrants

---

[3]*Phylarch* is a Greek word meaning "chief of a tribe or clan." No satisfactory derivation of *syphogrant* or *tranibor* has yet been proposed.

to the senate, different ones every day. It is a rule that no decision on public business can be made unless the matter has been considered on three different days in the senate. It is a capital offense to consult together on public affairs outside the senate or the people's assembly.

These provisions have been made so that the prince and the tranibors may not conspire together to change the government and enslave the people. Matters of great importance are first brought to the assembly of the syphogrants. When they have discussed the matter with their households and have themselves consulted together, the syphogrants report their decision to the senate. Sometimes an issue is referred to the council of the whole island. One practice observed in their senate is never to debate a matter on the same day on which it was first introduced. Instead, they defer the question to the next meeting, so that a man will not let his tongue run away with him and then strive to defend his foolish first-thoughts instead of considering the public good. They know that through a perverse and preposterous pride a man may prefer to sacrifice the common good to his own hasty opinions for fear of being thought heedless and shortsighted. To prevent this, they take care to deliberate wisely rather than speedily.

Their Economy and Occupations

All the Utopians, men and women alike, work at agriculture, and no one is inexperienced in it. They are trained in it from childhood, partly by school instruction and partly by practice. School children are often taken into the nearby fields as though for play, where they not only see men and women working, but get exercise by working themselves.

Besides sharing in the farm work, every person has some particular trade of his own, such as the manufacture of wool or linen, masonry, metal work, or carpentry. There is no other craft which is practiced by any considerable number of them. People wear the same sort of clothes throughout the island, except for the distinctions which mark the difference between the married and the unmarried. The fashion of clothing never changes. Their clothing looks well, does not hinder their movements, and is suitable both for summer and winter. Every household makes its own clothing, but each man and woman also learns one of the other trades I have mentioned. The women, being the weaker, practice the lighter crafts, such as working with wool or linen. The heavier crafts are left to the men. Generally the same trade passes down from father to son, often by natural inclination. But if anyone's interest lies elsewhere, he is adopted into a family practicing the trade he prefers. When anyone makes such a change, both his father and the magistrates see to it that he is transferred to a responsible and upright householder. After a man has learned one trade, if he desires to acquire another, it is managed in the same manner. When he has learned both, he follows whichever he likes better, unless the public has special need for the other.

The chief and almost the only business of the syphogrants is to see that no one sits around in idleness, and that everyone works hard at his trade. But no one has to wear himself out with endless toil from morning till night, as if he were a beast of burden. Such a life, though it is the common life of workmen in all other countries, is no better than a slave's. The Utopians work six hours out of the twenty-four. They work three hours before dinner. After dinner they rest two hours, and then go to work for another three hours. Then they have supper and at eight o'clock, counting from noon, they go to bed and sleep eight hours.

The other hours of the day, those that are not used for work, sleep, and meals, are left to their individual choice, on the understanding that they shall not waste them idly and wantonly. They use their free time busily on any pursuit that pleases them. Many of them fill these intervals with reading. They have the custom of giving public lectures daily before daybreak, which none are obliged to attend except such as are selected for the pursuit of learning. Yet a great many from all ranks, both men and women, go to hear lectures of one sort or another, according to their interests. If anyone whose mind does not delight in intellectual pursuits prefers to spend his free time at his trade, as many do, this is not forbidden, but commended as beneficial to the commonwealth. After supper they spend an hour in some recreation, in summer gardening, in winter diverting themselves in their dining halls with music or talk. They know nothing about gambling with dice or other such foolish and ruinous games. They play two games not unlike our chess. One is a battle of numbers, in which one number plunders another. The other is a game in which the vices battle against the virtues. In this game the co-operation of the vices against the virtues and their opposition to each other is shown up very cleverly, as well as the special oppositions between particular virtues and vices, and the methods by which the vices openly assault or secretly undermine the virtues, and how the virtues break the strength of the vices and by what means finally one side or the other wins the victory.

To understand their way of life fully we must look at one point more carefully. They allot only six hours to labor, and you might think that a scarcity of essential goods would result. Actually their working hours are sufficient to provide not only an abundance, but even a superabundance of all the necessities and conveniences of life. You will easily understand this if you consider how large a part of the population in other countries is idle. In the first place, the women (and they are half the whole population) usually do not work, or if they do, their husbands lie snoring. Secondly, there is the multitude of priests and socalled religious men, as numerous as they are idle. Add to these all the rich men, especially great landlords, who are commonly called well-born and noble. Add their henchmen, the whole flock of swaggering bullies. Reckon in with these the strong and lusty beggars, who go about feigning some disease to excuse their laziness. You will find that the actual number of workers who supply the needs of mankind is much smaller than you would think. And now consider how few of these workers are employed in really necessary work. Because we measure values by money, we have to carry on many superfluous trades to support luxury and wantoness. If the multitude of our workers produced only what men need for good living, there would be such an abundance of goods that prices would go down and workmen could not subsist. You can easily imagine how little time would be enough to produce the goods that man's needs and convenience demand (and his pleasure too if it were true and natural pleasure), if only the workers in useless trades were placed in worthwhile occupations and all the idlers who languish in sloth but eat twice as much as laborers were put to work on useful tasks.

The truth of this supposition is very apparent in Utopia. Out of all the men and women whose age or health permit them to work, scarcely five hundred are exempted in each city and its surrounding area. Among these are the syphogrants, who are excused from labor by law. Yet they do not excuse themselves from it, because they incite others to work more easily by setting them an example. The Utopians grant the same exemption to some who apply themselves exclusively to learning, but only at the recommendation of the priests and in accordance with a secret vote of the syphogrants. If one of these persons disappoints their hopes, he is made a workman again. On the other hand it sometimes happens that a worker devotes his free time so zealously to learning and progresses so far through his diligence, that he is excused from his trade and is transferred to the class of the learned men. From this class are chosen ambassadors, priests, tranibors, and the prince himself (of old called the Barzanes, but later the Ademus).[4] Since the rest of the entire population is neither idle nor engaged in useless occupations, it is easy to understand how they produce so much in so short a work day.

Besides all this, it should be noted that they accomplish more with less work than people do elsewhere. Among other people the building and repair of houses requires the continuous labor of many workmen. Often a thriftless heir lets the house which his father built fall into disrepair, and his successor must repair at great cost what he might have kept up at small charge. It also happens oftentimes that a house built at a vast expense is scorned and neglected by an heir of supposedly finer taste, and when in a short time it falls into ruin, he builds another somewhere else at no less expense. But among the Utopians things are so ordered that they seldom choose a new location for building a house. They are quick to make present repairs and careful to preserve their buildings for a very long time with a minimum of labor. In the interims craftsmen in the building trades have hardly anything to do, unless they hew timber and square stones for future building.

Consider how little labor their clothing requires. For work they wear loose-fitting leather clothes, which last as long as seven years. When they go out, they put on a cloak which covers up their rougher clothing. Throughout the entire island their cloaks are the same color, the natural color of wool. They need less cloth than is used elsewhere and what they do need is much less costly. They use linen cloth most, because it takes less work to make. They like linen cloth to be white and woolen cloth to be clean, but they are indifferent to fineness of texture. Each person is generally satisfied with one cloak every two years, whereas in other countries four or five woolen coats of different colors and

---

[4] *Ademus* is from the Greek *a-demos,* meaning "without a people." No satisfactory derivation of *Barzanes* has yet been proposed.

the same number of silk cloaks will scarcely suffice for one man, and for more fastidious men even ten are not enough. Among the Utopians there is no reason why a person should want more clothes. If he had them, he would not be any better protected against the cold, nor would he seem at all better dressed.

When they have accumulated a great abundance of everything as a result of their moderate consumption and of their all working, great numbers of them go out to work on the roads, if any need repairing. Often when there is no need for public work, the magistrates proclaim a shorter workday, since they never employ the citizens on needless labor. For the chief aim of their institutions and government, above all else, is to give all citizens as much time as public needs permit for freeing and developing their minds. In this they suppose the felicity of man's life to consist.

Their Social and Business Relations

Now I must explain the social arrangements of these people, their dealings with each other, and how they distribute their goods among themselves.

Each community consists of households for the most part made up of kinsfolk. When the women grow up and are married, they move to their husbands' homes. The sons and grandsons remain in the household and obey their oldest common parent, unless his mind has begun to fail with age. In that case the next oldest takes his place. In order that their cities may not have too many or too few inhabitants, they allow no city to have over six thousand households (exclusive of the surrounding country district) and no household to have fewer than ten or more than sixteen adults. The number of children is not restricted, but the number is easily controlled by transferring the children of a household that has too many to one that does not have enough. Likewise if any city has too many people, that city makes good any shortage in the other cities.

If there is too great an increase throughout the entire island, they take a certain number of citizens from the different cities and plant a colony on the adjoining mainland, where the inhabitants still have more land than they can well cultivate. If the natives wish to live with the Utopians, they are taken in. Since they join the colony willingly, they quickly adopt the same institutions and customs. This is advantageous for both peoples. For by their policies and practices the Utopians make the land yield an abundance for all, which before seemed too small and barren for the natives alone. If the natives will not conform to their laws, they drive them out of the area they claim for themselves, waging war if they meet resistance. Indeed they account it a very just cause of war if a people possess land that they leave idle and uncultivated and refuse the use and occupancy of it to others who according to the law of nature ought to be supported from it.

If the population of any of their cities happens to decline so much that it cannot be made good from other parts of the island without reducing the size of the other cities too much, then the population is built up with citizens from the colonies. This has happened only twice in all their history, both times the result of a devastating plague. They prefer their colonies to die off rather than allow any of their island cities to grow too small.

To return to their manner of living together: as I said, the eldest of every household governs it. Wives are subject to their husbands, children to their parents, and the younger to their elders. Every city is divided into four equal parts, and in the middle of each quarter is a market place for all kinds of goods. The products of each household are brought here and stored in warehouses, where each kind of goods is kept in its proper place. Here the head of each household looks for what he needs, and takes what he wants without payment or obligation. Why should anything be refused him? There is enough of everything, and no fear that anyone will claim more than he needs. Why should anyone be suspected of asking for more than is necessary, when there is never any shortage? Men and animals alike are greedy and rapacious from fear of want. Only human pride glories in surpassing others in conspicuous consumption. For this kind of vice there is no room whatsoever in the Utopian way of life.

Adjoining the warehouses there are food markets where all sorts of vegetables, fruit, and bread are brought. Fish, meat, and poultry are also brought there from places outside the city near running water, where bondmen do the slaughtering and cleaning. The citizens are not allowed to do the slaughtering. The Utopians think that slaughtering destroys the sense of compassion, the most distinctively human feeling of our nature. They do not allow anything dirty or filthy to be brought into the city, to keep the air from becoming tainted with the stench and as a result infectious.

Every street has its great public halls, equally distant from each other and each known by its own name. The syphogrants live in these. Fifteen of the thirty households of a syphogrant live on one side of the hall, fifteen on the other. Here the thirty households are assigned to eat their meals. The stewards of each hall go to the market place at a certain time to secure food.

In distributing food, the Utopians' first concern is for the sick, who are cared for in public hospitals. Every city has four hospitals, generally built outside the walls and so roomy that they might pass for little towns. No matter how great the number of sick people, they need not be crowded closely or uncomfortably. And if the sick have some contagious disease, they can be isolated. These hospitals are well arranged and well supplied with everything needed to cure the patients, who are nursed with watchful and tender care. They are constantly attended by most skillful physicians. Consequently no one objects to being sent to the hospital, everyone preferring to be sick there than at home.

[Hythloday then describes the following features of Utopian civilization: their manner of dining; their attitude toward and modes of travel; their foreign trade; their coinage and their manner of handling money; their philosophical beliefs and intellectual pursuits; their use of slaves;

their care for the sick and their practice of euthanasia for the incurably and painfully ill; their marriage customs.]

Their Punishments, Their Legal Procedure, and Other Matters

Their law lays down no other fixed penalties, but the senate fixes the punishment according to the wickedness of the crime. Husbands punish their wives, and parents their children, unless the offense is so great that a public punishment seems to be for the common good. Generally the most serious crimes are punished by bondage, for they think this no less terrible to criminals than death. And it is more beneficial to the commonwealth, for a bondman's labor is worth more to the state than his death. Moreover the sight of bondage longer deters other men from similar crimes. If bondmen rebel and refuse to work, they are put to death like wild beasts which neither captivity nor chains can restrain. Those who bear their bondage patiently are not left hopeless. After they have been tamed by long hardship, if they show by their repentance that their wrongdoing troubles them more than their punishment, their bondage is modified or remitted, sometimes by the prince's prerogative and sometimes by popular vote.

A man who attempts to seduce a woman risks the same punishment as if he had actually done it. They think that an attempted crime is as bad as one committed, and that a man's failure should not mitigate his punishment when he did all he could to succeed.

They take pleasure in fools. While they think it contemptible to mistreat them, they do not forbid men to enjoy their foolishness, and even regard this as beneficial to the fools. No fools are entrusted to the care of serious and stern men who do not laugh at their ridiculous behavior and jests, for fear that a man who finds no enjoyment in a fool's only gift will not treat him kindly.

To jeer at a person for being deformed or crippled is not considered a reproach to him. But the mocker, who stupidly upbraids the cripple for something he cannot help, is held in contempt.

They consider it a sign of sluggish disposition to neglect one's natural beauty, but they think it is detestable to use rouge. They have learned by experience that no physical beauty recommends a wife to her husband as much as uprightness and obedience. Though some men are won by beauty, none are held except by virtue and compliance.

They deter men from crime by penalties and incite them to virtue by public honors. They set up statues of distinguished men who have deserved well of their country in the market places, to preserve the memory of their good deeds and to spur on the citizens to emulate the glory of their ancestors.

Any man who campaigns too zealously for a magistracy is sure to fail. They live together harmoniously and the magistrates are never proud or cruel. Instead they are called fathers, and deservedly. Because the magistrates do not exact honor from the people against their will, the people honor them willingly, as they should. Not even the prince has the distinction of robe or diadem; he is known only by a sheaf of grain carried before him. In the same way the priest is known by a wax candle.

They have few laws, and such are their institutions that they need few. They strongly censure other nations, which cannot get along without an infinite number of laws and interpretations. They think it highly unjust to bind men by laws that are too numerous to be read and too obscure to be readily understood. As for lawyers, a kind of men who handle matters craftily and interpret laws subtly, they have none at all. They maintain that it is better for each man to plead his own case, and to entrust to the judge what he would elsewhere tell his lawyer. Thus there is less delay, and the truth is brought out more readily. A man speaks without the help of a lawyer's wily instruction, and the judge examines each point carefully, and protects the simpler sort against the falsehoods of crafty men. It is hard to find such equitable procedure among other nations, with their multitude of intricate laws.

But in Utopia everyone is skillful in the law. For the laws are very few, as I have said, and the plainest interpretation is the fairest. All laws, according to their view, are promulgated for the single purpose of teaching each man his duty. Subtle interpretations teach very few, for there are few who can understand them; the simpler and more obvious sense of the laws is clear to all. If laws are not clear, they are useless for the masses of people who need their guidance most. There might as well be no laws at all as to have laws which only men of great ability and long training can interpret. Most men lack the brains for this task and cannot spare the time from their work.

Their Foreign Relations

In times past the Utopians have helped some of their neighbors gain freedom from tyrants. These people admire the virtues of the Utopians so much that of their own accord they have asked the Utopians to send men to be their rulers. Some of these rulers serve for a year, others for five. When their term is finished, they come back bringing with them praise and esteem, and others are sent in their place. These nations seem to have found an excellent plan for their happiness and safety. As the welfare or evil of a state depends on the moral character of its magistrates, what men could they choose more wisely than these, who cannot be tempted by money? For money is useless to them when they go home. And because they are not natives, they are not swayed by rivalries and strife. When these two evils, avarice and partiality, afflict judges, they are the destruction of all justice, which is the chief bond of society. The Utopians call those people that seek magistrates from them neighbors, and those whom they have aided still more, friends.

Whereas other nations are continually making alliances, breaking them, and then renewing them, the Utopians make no alliances with any nation. If nature, they say, will not make man friendly with man, will an alliance do so? Will a man who scorns nature respect mere words? They have been confirmed in this view all the more, because among neighboring nations the alliances and pacts of princes are usually so carelessly observed.

In Europe, especially where the Christian religion prevails, treaty agreements are sacred and inviolable. This is partly owing to the justice and goodness of princes, and partly to the reverence and fear they feel toward the popes, who themselves observe their agreements very religiously. The popes order all other chiefs of state to abide by their promises, even bringing pressure upon evaders by pontifical censure. And the popes rightly point out that it would be most ignominious if men who are specifically called "the faithful" were faithless to their treaties.

But in this new world, which is as far from us in distance as our customs are different from theirs, no confidence is put in alliances, even though they are contracted with the most sacred ceremonies. The greater the formalities, the sooner the treaty may be dissolved by twisting the words, which are often purposely ambiguous. A treaty can never be bound with chains so strong, but that a government can somehow evade it and thereby break both the treaty and its faith. If statesmen found such craftiness and fraud in the contracts of business men, they would scornfully brand them as sacrilegious and worthy of the gallows. These very statesmen, however, take pride in giving just such counsel to princes. Thus justice seems to be a low and humble virtue, one which dwells far beneath the high dignity of kings. Or there may be two kinds of justice, one the people's justice, mean, lowly, bound by fetters on every side so that it cannot jump the fences, the other the justice of princes, which is more majestic and so much freer than the other that it may take whatever it wants.

This practice of keeping treaties so badly is the reason why the Utopians make no alliances. They might indeed change their minds if they lived here. However, they think it a bad custom to make treaties at all, even if they are well observed. To do so makes it seem as if men who are separated by only a hill or a river were bound by no tie of nature, but were born natural enemies and therefore rightly attacked each other unless restrained by treaties. Moreover they see that these alliances do not cement friendship; the two countries still have licence to prey upon each other, unless sufficient caution is used in making the treaty to see that there is no loophole in the wording. The Utopians' view is that no man should be esteemed an enemy if he has done no injury, that the fellowship of nature among men serves instead of a treaty, and that men are bound more adequately by good will than by pacts, more strongly by their hearts than by their words.

Their Warfare

They hate and detest war as a thing manifestly brutal, and yet practiced by man more constantly than by any kind of beast. Contrary to almost all other peoples they consider nothing so inglorious as the glory won in war. Nevertheless both the men and the women of Utopia regularly practice military exercises on certain days, so that they will be prepared when the need arises. They go to war cautiously and reluctantly, only to protect their own territory or that of their friends if an enemy has invaded it, or to free some wretched people from tyrannous oppression and servitude. They help their friends not only in defense, but also to avenge injuries. They do this only if they are consulted in the whole affair, if the facts are proved, and if the stolen plunder is not returned. Then they think they should wage war against the aggressor. They decide on this policy when booty is taken from their friends by force or when the merchants of one country are oppressed in another country by unjust laws or by twisting good laws. This they think is a greater evil than direct attack.

This was the sole cause of the war which the Utopians waged against the Alaopolitans for the sake of the Nephelogetes[5] some time before our arrival, when a wrong seemed to have been done under pretext of right to Nephelogete merchants resident among the Alaopolitans. Whether or not an injustice was done, it was avenged by a terrible war, the strength of each side being augmented by the resources and the hatred of their neighbors. Some prosperous nations were ruined and others were greatly shaken. In the end after a series of misfortunes, the Alaopolitans, who had been a very thriving people compared to the Nephelogetes, were conquered and reduced to bondage by the Nephelogetes. Vigorously as the Utopians stood by their friends in the matter of reparations, they sought none for themselves.

If the Utopians themselves are cheated in this way, they carry their anger only to the point of cutting off trade with that country, provided no bodily injury is done. Not that they care less for their own citizens than for their neighbors, but they think it worse for their neighbors' property to be seized than their own. Their neighbors' merchants suffer a great injury because they lose their own property, but the Utopians think little of their loss, for only common goods have been lost. Besides whatever is exported must be in superfluous abundance at home, or it would not be shipped out. So they think it cruel to avenge a relatively unimportant loss by killing many men, whose death would only affect the lives and livelihood of others. But if any Utopian citizens are unjustly hurt or killed, whether by private or public policy, they send envoys demanding that the guilty persons be handed over to them. If that is refused, they declare war. If the guilty men are given up, their punishment is death or bondage.

The Utopians are troubled and ashamed when they gain a bloody victory, like merchants who have paid too high a price for what they have bought. If they overwhelm the enemy by skill and cunning, they exult and celebrate a public triumph, and erect a memorial for a victory efficiently won. When they win a victory by the strength of understanding (as only men can), they pride themselves on acting bravely and manfully. Bears, lions, boars, wolves, dogs, and other wild beasts fight with their bodies, and many of them surpass us in strength and ferocity as much as we surpass them in understanding and reason.

The Utopians have this one aim in war, to accomplish what they would gladly have achieved without war if just terms had been granted in time. Or if that cannot be done, they aim to exact so severe a revenge from those that have injured them that they will be afraid to do it again.

---

[5] Both names are coined from Greek words. *Nephelogetes* means "men from cloudland"; *Aleopolitanes* means "men from the dark city."

Their policies are directed to these ends, which they strive toward in such a way as to avoid danger rather than to attain glory and fame.

As soon as war is declared, they at once arrange to have many small notices, which are marked with their official seal, set up by stealth in the most conspicuous places in the enemy's country. In these proclamations they promise great rewards to any one who will kill the enemy's king, and smaller rewards (but still very great) for killing those whom they regard as most responsible after the king for plotting aggression against them. They double the reward for anyone who brings in the proscribed man alive. Also they offer like rewards, as well as exemption from punishment, to any of the proscribed men who turn against their countrymen. As a result the proscribed men soon suspect everyone, distrust each other, and become distracted by their danger. It has often turned out that many of them, and even princes, have been betrayed by those whom they most trusted. The Utopians realize that rewards will spur men on to any sort of crime, and consequently they promise incredible gifts. Mindful of the danger which the assassins run, they see to it that the compensation is proportionate to the risk, and promise an immense amount of gold and also rich estates safely placed in neighboring countries. They keep these promises most faithfully. Though this manner of waging war by bidding for and buying enemies may seem like the cruel villainy of an ignoble mind, it is considered by the Utopians as a wise and praiseworthy policy, since it enables them to wage great wars without any battle at all. They even think themselves humane and merciful, because by the death of a few bad men they spare the lives of many innocent men who would otherwise die in battle, some fighting on their own side, some on the enemy's. Indeed they pity the mass of enemy soldiers no less than their own, for they know that they do not fight willingly, but are driven to it by the madness of their rulers.

If this method does not succeed, they sow the seeds of discord among the enemy by inciting the king's brother or some member of the nobility to plot for the crown. If these internal factions languish, then they arouse the neighboring people against the enemy and induce them to revive some old claims, such as kings never lack.

When they promise their resources to help in a war, they furnish money abundantly, but citizens very sparingly. They hold their own men most dear and of such account that they will not willingly exchange one of the citizens for an enemy's king. Since they keep their gold and silver for this single purpose, they spend it without reluctance, the more so as they will live no less well if they spend it all. Besides the wealth which they have at home, they have also boundless treasure abroad, many neighboring nations being in their debt, as I have said. So they hire mercenary soldiers from all sides, especially from the Zapoletes.[6]

These people live five hundred miles from Utopia toward the east. They are a rude, fierce, wild people, who delight in the forests and mountains among which they are brought up. They are sturdy, well able to endure heat, cold, and hard work. They are unacquainted with luxuries

---

[6]A name coined from Greek words to mean "ready-seller."

or with agriculture, and are indifferent about housing and clothing. Their only productive occupation is taking care of cattle. For the most part they live by hunting and theft. It is as if they were born for war, and they watch carefully for any chance to engage in it. When they find such a chance they eagerly embrace it, great numbers of them going out and offering themselves at a low price to any one seeking soldiers. They know only one art for earning a living, the art of taking away life. They fight for their employers fiercely and with incorruptible fidelity. But they will not bind themselves to serve for any set time. They stipulate that they may fight next day for the enemy, if higher pay is offered, and come back on the day after that for still higher pay. There is seldom a war in which a considerable number of them are not fighting on both sides. So it commonly happens that men who are related to one another by blood and have served together in intimacy in the same campaigns are enlisted on opposite sides. Forgetful of their relationship and their friendship, they kill one another for no other reason than that they have been hired for a paltry wage by different kings. They think so much of money that they will change sides readily for an increase of only a penny a day. Thus they grow greedier and greedier for money, but money is of no use to them, for what they acquire with their blood, they soon waste profligately on contemptible pleasures.

This nation serves the Utopians against all people whatsoever, for they give higher pay than any others. Just as the Utopians seek out the best possible men to use at home, by the same principle they seek the worst men to misuse in war. When need requires, they induce the Zapoletes with promises of rich rewards to face hazards from which most of them never return. The Utopians pay the rewards in good faith to those who escape death, to incite them to similar deeds of daring later. And the Utopians have no concern over how many are killed, thinking they would deserve the thanks of the human race if they could purge the world of the whole of that disgusting and vicious people.

In addition to these, they use the soldiers of the people for whom they are fighting, and the troops of other friends as auxiliaries. Finally they add some of their own citizens, including some man of approved valor to command the entire army. They add two substitutes, who serve as privates while the commander is safe. But if he is captured or killed, one of the two succeeds him, and then in case of a mishap to him, the other. In this way they provide that in the varying fortunes of war the whole army may not be endangered by an accident befalling their leader. For their own soldiers they take men from each city who volunteer freely. No one is forced into service away from home against his will. They think that a man who is naturally timid will act weakly, and even dishearten his companions. But if their own country is invaded, they use even these faint-hearted men, provided they are sound in body. They place them on shipboard among better men, or here and there on fortifications where there is no chance of flight. Shame, the immediate presence of the foe, and the hopelessness of flight overcome their fear, and they often show themselves brave from sheer necessity.

Just as no one is forced to go into a foreign war unwillingly, so women are allowed to follow their husbands to war if they wish and are encouraged and praised for doing so. They place each woman beside her husband in the front line of battle. They also station each man's children, kinsmen, and connections around him in order that those whom nature most incites to help one another may be nearest at hand to give mutual aid. It is considered a matter of great reproach for one spouse to survive the other, or for a son to survive his parent. Therefore when battle is joined, they fight it out in a long and bloody struggle to the last man, if the enemy stands fast.

If possible they use only their mercenaries and so avoid sending their own citizens to battle. When this is impossible and they must take part in the fighting themselves, they join battle with a boldness as great as their prudence in avoiding it. They do not begin with a fierce impulsive charge, but gradually as the fighting goes on they increase in valor, becoming so stubborn that they die rather than yield ground. They are free from the cares which often weaken noble spirits. Their own security at home and their confidence in their children's welfare make them stout-hearted and too proud to be conquered. Moreover their skill in warfare increases their valor, and the sound ideas instilled into them in childhood by instruction and the wise institutions of their commonwealth add to their courage. They do not hold life so cheap that they waste it, nor do they hold it so dear that they avidly and shamefully grasp it when duty bids them give it up.

When the battle rages hottest, the bravest young men, who have joined themselves together by oaths, take upon themselves to destroy the leader of the enemy's forces. They assault him openly, they ambush him, they attack him hand to hand. Fresh men replace those who are worn out in the continuous struggle. In the end they rarely fail to kill or capture him, unless he takes to flight.

When they win a battle, they are more ready to take prisoners than to make a great slaughter. They never pursue fugitives without keeping part of their army in good order arrayed under their standards. If the rest of their army has been overcome and they have only gained the victory with their reserve troops, they think it better to let the enemy slip away with forces intact rather than pursue them with their own ranks in disorder. For they remember what happened more than once to themselves. After the enemy's main army had been overcome, the Utopians, scattered and apprehensive of no danger, were pursuing the retreating foe in the glow of victory. Among this conquered army some few men had been placed in reserve and were watching for their opportunity. Suddenly they attacked and changed the course of the whole battle. The conquered seized the victory from the seeming victors and in turn became the conquerors.

They are equally shrewd in laying ambushes and in avoiding them. Sometimes they seem to be preparing to flee, when their real intention is the opposite. Again, when they are planning flight, you would never guess it. If they think they are too few in number or are in a poor position, they either move camp silently in the night, or slip off by some other stratagem. Or they fall back in the daytime so gradually and in such good order, that it is as dangerous to attack them in their retreat as in their advance.

They fortify their camps very carefully with a wide and very deep trench. They throw the earth inward, where it is used for a wall. They do not use bondmen for this work. The entire army takes part except for those who serve in front of the rampart as an armed guard against sudden attack. With so many hands at work they complete great fortifications around a large area in an incredibly short time.

The armor they use is strong for resisting blows, but does not interfere with their bodily movements. In fact, they can even swim in it. Part of their training in warfare is learning to swim in armor. For fighting at a distance they use arrows, which both infantry and cavalry shoot with speed and sureness. For close fighting their weapons are not swords but sharp and heavy axes used with a forward lunge or a downstroke. They devise ingenious engines of war and then keep them well hidden, for fear that if these were known before they were needed and if the enemy discovered them, they would be useless except as a butt for the enemy's jokes. In designing them, the first consideration is that they may be easily carried and manipulated.

When the Utopians agree to a truce, they observe it so religiously that they will not violate it even though provoked. They do not lay waste the enemy's country nor burn his grain. In their marches they take care that neither the men nor the horses trample down the grain, for they may need it themselves. They attack no man who is disarmed unless he is a spy. When cities are surrendered, they take them under their protection. If they carry a place by storm, they do not plunder it, but kill those who opposed the surrender and reduce the rest of the garrison to bondage, leaving the inhabitants unharmed. If the Utopians find any of the inhabitants who recommended surrender, they share with them part of the property of those who have been condemned, and then divide the rest among the auxiliary troops. None of the Utopians themselves want any of the spoils.

When a war is ended, they charge the cost to the conquered, not to the friends for whom they undertook it. They take the indemnity either in the form of money, which they set aside for future use in war, or in the form of land, which produces a constant revenue of considerable amount. At the present time they draw this sort of revenue from many peoples, amounting with gradual increases from various sources to more than 700,000 ducats a year. They send some of their own citizens abroad as tax collectors to receive these revenues, with orders to live sumptuously and to conduct themselves like great personages. Even then much remains, which they are to bring home to their own treasury or which, as often happens, they lend to the people who already have it in hand, until it is needed at home. They seldom call it all in. They assign part of the lands as rewards to those whom they have urged to risk great dangers, such as I have mentioned.

If any prince has taken up arms and is preparing to invade their realm, they at once attack him in strength outside their own territory. For they do not willingly wage war on their own soil, and no necessity could force them to admit foreign auxiliaries to their island to aid them.

The Religion of the Utopians

There are different kinds of religion throughout the island, as well as in each city. Some worship the sun as a god, others the moon, and still others some one of the planets. Others worship some man pre-eminent in virtue or glory, not only as a god, but as the supreme god. But by far the greatest number of the Utopians, and among these the wisest, worship none of these. They think there is one unknown, eternal, infinite, and unknowable deity, transcending human comprehension and pervading the whole universe not physically but in virtue and power. Him they call Father of all. They acknowledge that from Him alone comes the beginning, increase, progress, change, and end of all things. They do not offer divine honors to any other god.

Though they hold different beliefs on other matters of religion, all the Utopians agree with their wiser sort in this, that there is only one supreme power, the Maker and Ruler of the universe, whom they all call in their native language Mithra. But they differ as to who he is; some think he is one god, others another. But whatever god each person regards as the chief god, they all agree in thinking that God is the very Being to whose power and majesty the supremacy over all things is attributed by universal consent.

By degrees all the Utopians are coming to forsake their various superstitions and to agree upon this one religion that seems to excel the others in reason. No doubt the other religions would have vanished long ago, had it not happened that whenever one of the Utopians who was planning to change his religion met with misfortune, the rest regarded it not as an accident but as something sent by a divinity as a punishment for the desertion of his worship.

We told them of the name, doctrine, manner of life, and miracles of Christ, and of the wonderful constancy of the many martyrs, who willingly sacrificed their blood to bring so many nations far and wide to Christianity. You will hardly believe with what favorably disposed minds they received this account, either because God secretly incited them or because this religion is most like the belief already very strong among them. I thought that they were also somewhat influenced by learning that Christ instituted community of goods and that this custom was still in practice among the most sincere of the Christians. Whatever the reason, many came over to our religion and were baptized. Two of our number had died and none of us four survivors, I regret to say, were priests, so though they received instruction in other matters they did not receive those sacraments which in our religion only priests can administer. But they understand them and long for them ardently. In fact, they argue vigorously with one another as to whether a man chosen from among them without the Pope's authorization would have the true character of a priest. Though they seemed determined to choose such a one, they had not chosen him at the time of my leaving.

Those among them that have not yet accepted the Christian religion do not restrain others from it nor abuse the converts to it. While I was there, only one man among the Christians was punished. This newly baptized convert, in spite of all our advice, was preaching in public on the Christian worship more zealously than wisely. He grew so heated that he not only put our worship before all others, but also condemned all other rites as profane and loudly denounced their celebrants as wicked and impious men fit for hell fire. After he had been preaching these things for a long time, they seized him. They convicted him not on a charge of disparaging their religion, but of arousing public disorder among the people, and sentenced him to exile. For they count it among their oldest institutions that no man shall be made to suffer for his religion.

In the early days King Utopus learned that before his coming the inhabitants had quarreled violently over religion. He found that it was easy to conquer them all, because the different sects in fighting for their country fought by themselves instead of together. Therefore after his victory he decreed that each man might follow whatever religion he wished and might try to persuade others to join it amicably and temperately and without bitterness toward others. If persuasion failed, a person was forbidden to use force or to indulge in wrangling. If anyone argued for his religion contentiously, he was to be punished by exile or bondage.

Utopus made this law partly for the sake of peace, which he saw was in danger of being completely destroyed by constant strife and implacable hatred, and partly for the sake of religion. He did not venture to make dogmatic decisions in regard to religion, perhaps from some idea that God likes and inspires a variety and multiplicity of worship. He deemed it foolish and insolent for anyone to try to make all men accept his own beliefs by force and by threats. If one religion is true and the others false, and if men use reason and moderation, he clearly foresaw that the truth would prevail by its own strength. But if men fight and riot, as evil and headstrong men will do, then the best and holiest religion in the world will be crowded out by the emptiest superstitions, like wheat choked by thorns and briars. So he imposed no one religion on his people, and left each man free to believe what he would, with one exception. He made a solemn and severe law against any who sink so far below the dignity of human nature as to think that the soul dies with the body, or that the universe is carried along by chance without an over-ruling providence.

The Utopians believe that after this life there are punishments for wickedness and rewards for virtue. They consider one who thinks otherwise as hardly a man, since he has degraded the human soul to the low level of a beast's body. Such a man they do not count fit for human society, for if he dares, he will scorn all its laws and customs. Who can doubt that a man who fears nothing but the law and apprehends nothing after death would secretly flout his country's laws or break them by force to satisfy his greed? Therefore no preferment is awarded to one with such views, and no magistracy or any public responsibility is entrusted to him. Instead, he is generally looked down upon as a man of worthless and sordid nature. Yet they do not punish such a man further, for they are persuaded that no one can make himself believe anything at will. Nor do they force him by threats to conceal his thoughts, and so open the door to deceit and lying, which they detest as the next thing to fraud. But they take care that he does not argue for his opinions, especially before the common people. They permit and even encourage him to discuss these matters with their priests and other serious men, in full confidence that finally his mad opinions will yield to reason.

There are others, in fact a considerable number, who go to the opposite extreme, and believe that the souls of animals are immortal, though not comparable with the human soul in excellence nor capable of as great happiness. These men are not thought to be bad or altogether lacking in reason, and their opinion is not discouraged.

Almost all the Utopians believe so firmly that man's happiness after death is endless, that they lament sickness but not death. They only mourn a man's death if they see that he parts with life reluctantly. This they take as a very bad sign, as if his soul dreaded death because of hopelessness or from some secret and guilty foreboding of impending punishment. The coming of a man who does not run gladly at the call, but is dragged off like a shirker, cannot be pleasing to God. They feel horror at such a death, and after carrying out the body in sorrow and with silent prayers to God mercifully to pardon the man's weakness, they bury the body in the earth. When a man dies cheerfully and full of good hope, they do not grieve, but follow the body singing, earnestly commending the man's soul to God. Then they cremate him reverently rather than sadly, and in the place where the funeral pyre was made, they set up a tombstone with the dead man's honors engraved upon it. When they return from the funeral, they relate his life and good deeds, and no part of his life is more frequently nor more gladly rehearsed than his cheerful death.

They think that remembering his good qualities is a powerful incitement to virtue among the living and the most pleasing honor to the dead. For they believe that the dead are present among us and hear the talk about themselves, though they are invisible through the dullness of human sight. They think that the dead, in keeping with their happy condition, can go where they want, and in affectionate loyalty visit those they loved and esteemed during their lives. They also believe that in good men these affections, like other good things, are increased rather than decreased after death, and that the dead come among the living observing their words and deeds. Consequently they enter into their undertakings all the more confidently because of their trust in such protectors. And they are deterred from secret wrongdoing by the belief that their forefathers are present.

They laugh at auguries and other superstitious forms of divination that are common among other nations. But they revere miracles which cannot flow from the powers of nature, looking on them as the works and witnesses of God. They say that such miracles have frequently occurred among them. Sometimes they have won safety and success amid great dangers and uncertainties through public prayers offered with assured confidence.

They hold that the careful observation of nature and the reflection on it and the reverence that arises from this is a kind of worship very pleasing to God.

Not a few among them are led by their religion to neglect learning, to pursue no sort of study, nor even to allow themselves any leisure, but are always busy about good works. They believe that their future happiness after death is increased by good works toward others. Some of them visit the sick, others mend roads, clean ditches, repair bridges, dig turf, gravel, and stones, fell and cut up trees, and bring wood, grain, and other things into the cities by wagon. They work for private citizens as well as the public, and do even more work than bondmen. They undertake willingly and cheerfully any work that is rough, hard, or dirty, or such as frightens away most people because it is heavy, loathsome, and discouraging. By this means they secure leisure for others while they themselves are continually at work. They take no pay, and they do not reprove others for their way of living. They do not boast of their own lives. The more they serve others, the more they are held in honor among all people.

These persons are of two kinds. The first are celibates, and abstain entirely from meat as well as from women, some of them from every sort of flesh whatsoever. They utterly reject the pleasures of this life as harmful; they eagerly and earnestly strive for the joys of the life to come, hoping soon to attain it by watches and severe toil. The other kind are no less eager to work, but they marry. They do not scorn the solace of marriage, and they feel that they owe toil to nature (to make nature productive) and children to their native land. They avoid no pleasure so long as it does not interfere with their labor. They enjoy meat because they think that by it they are made stronger for labor. The Utopians consider these the wiser men, but the other kind the holier ones. If any man claimed that he preferred celibacy to marriage and a hard life to an easy one on the grounds of reason, they would laugh at him. But since the ascetics claim to be moved to their way of life by religion, the Utopians look up to them and revere them. They are very careful to state anything concerning religion precisely, so they call these ascetic men *buthrescas* in their language, a term which may be translated as "men in religious orders."

Their priests are men of great holiness, and are therefore few in number. In fact not over thirteen are permitted in each city, one for each temple. If there is a war, seven of them go out with the army and others fill their places temporarily. When the war is over, each priest returns to his former place. Until the substitute priests succeed priests who die, they live as companions to the chief priest. For one priest is in authority over the others. The priests are chosen by secret popular vote, as are the other magistrates, in order to avoid strife. After election they are consecrated by the college of priests. They are in charge of all sacred affairs, they supervise worship, and they act as overseers of the people's conduct. It is a great disgrace for anyone to be summoned to them and taken to task for living a dishonorable life. The priests' duty is only to counsel and advise. The prince and the other magistrates correct and punish offenders, though the priests excommunicate those that are very bad. No form of punishment is more dreaded than this. It burdens the wrongdoer with infamy and torments him with religious fear. Not even his body is safe for long, for unless he speedily convinces the priests of his repentance, he will be arrested and punished by the senate for impiety.

The priests are the teachers of the boys and youths. Instruction in good manners and virtue is considered as important as instruction in learning. The priests make the greatest effort to inculcate sound beliefs and concepts into the malleable minds of the boys, in order to preserve the commonwealth. When such ideas have been deeply impressed, they stay with a man throughout his life and make him most valuable in preserving the well-being of the state, which only declines from the vices which arise from bad moral attitudes.

Women are not excluded from the priesthood, but are chosen less often, and only if they are elderly widows. The wives of the priests are the chief women in the whole country, except for the women priests.

No greater honor is paid to any magistrate among the Utopians than to the priests. Even if one of them does something criminal, he is not subject to any state trial. Instead the judgment is left to God and to his own conscience. They do not think it right to lay hands on any priest, no matter how bad he is, since a priest is specially dedicated to God as if he were a sacred offering. This custom they observe all the more easily because the priests are few in number and selected with such care. It rarely happens that a man chosen as a singularly good man and raised to such an honor wholly because of his character falls into corruption and vice. If such a thing should happen, for human nature is changeable, no great harm to the state is to be feared from their immunity, because priests are few in number and without any power except that arising from the respect paid them. They prefer to have few priests, lest the dignity of that order which they esteem so highly grow cheap if shared among many, and because they think it hard to find men equal to that dignity to which the ordinary virtues do not suffice to raise them.

Their priests are venerated as much among foreign nations as they are among themselves, as is very clear from the following custom. When their soldiers engage in battle, the priests of the Utopians kneel down not far away, wearing their sacred vestments. With hands uplifted to heaven, they pray first of all for peace, then for victory for themselves without much bloodshed on either side. And when the victory turns to their side, the priests run among their own battle lines and restrain the fury of their soldiers. If any of the enemy soldiers see these priests and call to them, that is enough to save their lives. And if they touch the garments of a priest, that will save their property from all injury. Their priests are so greatly reverenced and venerated among all the peoples in that part of the world, that they have preserved the Utopians from the fury of the enemy as often as they have saved the enemy from their own soldiers. Sometimes when the Utopian line of battle has been broken and all hope lost, and the enemy in fierce pursuit thirsting for slaughter and plunder, the priests have stopped the bloodshed, separated the troops, and made a fair peace. There is nowhere any tribe so fierce, cruel, and barbarous as not to hold their persons sacred and inviolable.

The Utopians celebrate the first and last days of each month as holidays. They divide the year into months, which they measure by the course of the moon, just as they measure the year by the circuit of the sun. The first day they call in their language the Cynemern, the last day the Trapemern, which may be translated as the first and the last festival day.

They have magnificent temples, built with great effort and able to hold a great many people. This is a necessity, since they have built so few of them. The temples are somewhat dark inside, not from any error in architecture, but by the advice of the priests, who think that in a strong light the thoughts are scattered, but in a rather dim light the thoughts are collected and devotion heightened.

Though there are many different religions among them, yet all these, no matter how different, agree in the main point, the worship of the one Divine Nature, as though they were all going toward one destination by different routes. So nothing is seen or heard in the temples which does not suit all their religions. Any rite that is peculiar to some one sect is celebrated in a private home, but the public worship is performed in such a way as not to interfere with the private rites. There are no images of God in their temples, so that everyone may conceive of God in any form he wishes. They do not call upon God by different names, but use only the name Mithra. However they may conceive of him, all alike agree in calling the one Divine Majesty by this name. They offer no prayers that will offend any sect.

They meet in their temples on the evening of the holiday which closes the month, and while still feasting they thank God for their good fortune during that month or year which is ending. On the next day, which is the first festival day of the new month, they meet in the morning in their temples to pray for the prosperous and happy outcome of their affairs in the ensuing month or year. On each last holiday, before going to the temple, wives fall on their knees before their husbands, children before their parents. They confess every misdeed or failure, and ask forgiveness for their offenses. Thus any cloud of domestic discord is removed, and they may engage in their devotions with a serene and untroubled mind. They hold it wrong to worship with a troubled conscience. If they are aware of hatred or anger in their hearts toward anyone, they do not presume to take part in the service until they have been reconciled and their feelings purified, for fear of some great and immediate punishment. In the temples the men and women are separated, the men going to the right, the women to the left. The men of each household seat themselves in front of the master of their household and the women in front of the mistress. In this way their behavior in public may be seen by those who manage and direct them at home. They take great care that younger and older may be seated here and there promiscuously. If the boys sat together, they might waste in childish foolery the time in which they ought to develope a religious dread of God, which is the greatest and almost the only incitement to virtue.

They do not offer animal sacrifices. They think that a kind god, who gives these creatures life, will not be pleased by their slaughter. They burn incense and scatter perfumes and offer wax candles, not with the thought that this profits the Divine Nature in any way, for not even prayers do that. But they think that this is a harmless sort of worship, and that men are somehow elevated by odors, lights, and ritual, and take part in divine worship with a more fervent spirit.

In the temple the people wear white, and the priest wears a vari-colored robe that is marvelous in workmanship and appearance, but is not made of costly material. It is not interwoven with thread of gold nor set with precious stones, but is so skillfully inwrought with various kinds of feathers that the value of the workmanship could not be exceeded by the costliest materials. Moreover they say that certain mysteries are symbolized in the pattern of the feathers on the priestly vestments, the meaning of which is carefully handed down among the priests to remind them of God's benefits to men and their duties both to God and to one another.

As soon as the priest comes from the vestry in his robes, the people all prostrate themselves reverently on the ground with so deep a silence that the very sight strikes a certain dread, as though a divinity were actually present. After they have remained in this posture for some time, they rise at a sign from the priest. Then they sing hymns, accompanied by musical instruments different from those seen in our part of the world. Many of theirs are sweeter than ours, but some are much inferior. Without doubt they excel us in one thing: all their music, both vocal and instrumental, imitates and expresses the feelings and is well suited in sound to the occasion or subject. Whether the mood of the hymn is cheerful, pleading, troubled, sad, or angry, the music penetrates and inspires the minds of the hearers. Finally the priest and the people offer solemn prayers in a set form, so composed that what they all recite in unison each one applies to himself.

In these prayers each one acknowledges God to be the creator, ruler, and author of all good things, thanking Him for the many benefits received and in particular for the fact that through God's favor they have been born into this commonwealth, which is the happiest, and into this religion, which they hope is the truest. If they are mistaken in this, and if there be any kind of society or religion that is more acceptable to God, they pray that in His goodness He will reveal this to them, for they are ready to follow wherever he leads them. But if their social organization is the best and their religion is the truest, then they pray that He will make them steadfast therein and bring the rest of mankind to the same rules of life and the same concept of God, unless by His inscrutable will He prefers the present diversity of religions.

Then they pray that after an easy death God will receive each of them to Himself. They do not presume to set a time, how soon or how late their passing shall be. But if it may be wished for, without offense to His divine majesty, they pray to go to God soon, even though by the hardest death, rather than be kept away from Him longer by the most prosperous course of life! When this prayer has been finished, they bow again to the ground and after a little they rise again and go home to dinner. The rest of the day they spend in games and martial exercises.

Now I have described to you as truthfully as I could the structure of this commonwealth, which I think the best, and indeed the only one which can rightfully be called by that name. In other places where they speak of the common good, every man is looking out for his own good. But in Utopia where there is no private property and where they zealously pursue the public business, there the name commonwealth is doubly deserved. Elsewhere, even though the state is prosperous, most men know that they may die of hunger if they do not look out for themselves, and so they are forced to take care of themselves rather than other people. In Utopia where everything belongs to everybody, they know that if the public warehouses and granaries are full, no one will lack anything for his personal use.

Among them there is no mal-distribution of goods, nor is anyone poor and indigent. When no one owns anything, all are rich. What greater riches can there be than to live cheerfully and serenely, free from all anxieties, without worries about making a living and unvexed by the complaints of one's wife about money? No one has to worry about his son's being poor, or about his daughter's dowry. Each man's livelihood and happiness are secure, and the same is true of all his relations, his wife, sons, grandsons, great-grandsons, and the whole line of descendants that highborn men assume will follow them. Why should he look forward to less, since those who can no longer work are cared for as well as those who do?

How could anyone dare to compare the justice of the Utopians with that of other nations? If there is any trace of justice or equity among other nations, may I perish among them! What justice is there in this, that a nobleman, a goldsmith, a moneylender, or some other man who does nothing at all for a living or does something that is of no use to the public, lives a sumptuous and elegant life? In the meantime a servant, a driver, a blacksmith, or a farmer works as hard as a beast at labor so necessary that the commonwealth could not last a year without it. Yet they earn so poor a living and lead such miserable lives that their condition seems worse than that of draft animals. Beasts do not work so incessantly and do not live much worse—in fact they live better—and they have no worries about the future. But working men are burdened with barren and fruitless toil, and live in fear of want in their old age. Their daily wage is insufficient to support them for the present, so they can have no surplus to lay up for the future.

Is not a government unjust and ungrateful that squanders rich rewards on noblemen (as they are called), goldsmiths, and others that do not work but live only by flattery or by catering to useless pleasures? And is it just for a government to ignore the welfare of farmers, charcoal burners, servants, drivers, and blacksmiths, without whom the commonwealth could not exist at all? After their best years have been consumed by labor and they are worn out by age and sickness, they are still penniless, and the thankless state, unmindful of their many great services, rewards them with nothing but a miserable death. Furthermore the rich constantly try to whittle away something from the pitiful wages of the poor by private fraud and even by public laws. To pay so little to men who deserve the best from the state is in itself unjust, yet it is made "just" legally by passing a law.

So when I weigh in my mind all the other states which flourish today, so help me God, I can discover nothing but a conspiracy of the rich, who pursue their own aggrandizement under the name and title of the Commonwealth. They devise ways and means to keep safely what they have unjustly acquired, and to buy up the toil and labor of the poor as cheaply as possible and oppress them. When these schemes of the rich become established by the government, which is meant to protect the poor as well as the rich, then they are law. With insatiable greed these wicked men divide among themselves the goods which would have been enough for all.

And yet they are far short of the happiness of the Utopians, who have abolished the use of money, and with it greed. What evils they avoid! What a multitude of crimes they prevent! Everyone knows that frauds, thefts, quarrels, contentions, uprisings, murders, betrayals, and poisonings (evils which are commonly punished rather than checked by the severities of the law) would wither away if money were eradicated! Fear, anxiety, worry, care, toil, and sleepless nights would disappear at the same time as money! Even poverty, which seems to need money more than anything else for its relief, would vanish if money were gone.

To see this more clearly, consider this one example. Take some poor and unfruitful year in which hunger has carried off many thousands of men. If the barns of the rich were searched at the end of the year, I maintain that enough grain would be found to feed everyone, and to save those who died from the famine and from the plague caused by the famine. How easily the bare needs of life might be provided, if money, which is meant to procure us the necessities of life, did not itself deter us! Certainly rich men know this. They also know that it would be more practicable to provide the necessities of life for everyone than to supply superfluities for a few, and much better to eradicate our innumerable evils than to be burdened with great concentrations of wealth.

If that one monster pride, the first and foremost of all evils, did not forbid it, the whole world would doubtless have adopted the laws of the Utopians long before this, drawn on by a rational perception of what each man's true interest is or else by the authority of Christ our Saviour, who in His great wisdom knows what is best and in His loving kindness bids us do it. Pride measures her prosperity not by her own goods but by others' wants. Pride would not deign to be a goddess, if there were no inferiors she could rule and triumph over. Her happiness shines brightly only in comparison to others' misery, and their poverty binds them and hurts them the more as her wealth is displayed. Pride is the infernal serpent that steals into the hearts of men, thwarting and holding them back from choosing the better way of life.

Pride is far too deeply rooted in men's hearts to be easily torn out. I am glad, therefore, that the Utopians have achieved their social organization, which I wish all mankind would imitate. Their institutions give their commonwealth a moral and social foundation for living happy lives, and as far as man can predict, these institutions will last forever. Because they have rooted out ambition and strife along with other vices, they are in no danger of civil wars, which have ruined many states that seemed secure. And as long as they maintain sound institutions and domestic harmony, they can never be overcome by the envious rulers near by, who have often attempted their ruin in vain.

*　　　*　　　*

Thus Raphael finished speaking. I admit that not a few things in the manners and laws of the Utopians seemed very absurd to me: their way of waging war, their religious customs, as well as other matters, but especially the keystone of their entire system, namely, their communal living without the use of money. This one thing takes away all the nobility, magnificence, splendor, and majesty which public opinion commonly regards as the true ornaments of a nation. But I saw that Raphael was tired with talking, and I was not sure that he could bear contradiction in these matters. I remembered that he had spoken ill of certain men who feared they would not be thought wise unless they could find something to criticize in other men's opinions.

So with praise for the Utopian institutions and for his account of them, I took him by the hand and led him in to supper, adding that we would find some other time for considering these things more thoroughly and for talking with him in greater detail about them. I hope that such an opportunity may come some time. Meanwhile I cannot agree with everything that he said, though he was singularly well informed and also highly experienced in worldly affairs. Yet I must confess that there are many things in the Utopian Commonwealth that I wish rather than expect to see followed among our citizens.

Comments / on More

I say therefore in these days in which men by their own default misconstrue and take harm of the very scripture of God, until men better amend, if any man would now translate *Utopia* into English, or some works either that I myself have written ere this, albeit there be none harm therein—folk yet being (as they be) given to take harm of that that is good, I would, not only my darling's [Erasmus] books but mine own also, help burn them both with mine own hands, rather than folk should (though through their own fault) take any harm of them, seeing that I see them likely in these days so to do.   *THOMAS MORE (1533)*

As a Humanist and a politician, More was in the front rank of his contemporaries, as a Socialist he was far ahead of them. His political, religious, and Humanist writings are to-day only read by a small number of historians. Had he not written *Utopia* his name would scarcely be better known to-day than that of the friend who shared his fate, Bishop Fisher of Rochester. His socialism made him immortal. . . . [A] thinker who takes his stand on the material conditions [of society] may be a whole epoch in advance of his time, if he perceives a newly evolving mode of production and its social consequences not only sooner than most of his contemporaries, but straining far into the future, also glimpses the more rational mode of production into which it will develop.

Thomas More is one of the few who have been capable of this bold intellectual leap; at a time when the capitalist mode of production was in its infancy, he mastered its essential features so thoroughly that the alternative mode of production which he elaborated and contrasted with it as a remedy for its evils, contained several of the most important ingredients of Modern Socialism. The drift of his speculations, of course, escaped his contemporaries, and can only be properly appreciated by us to-day. Despite the immense economic and technical transformations of the last three hundred years, we find in *Utopia* a number of tendencies which are still operative in the Socialist Movement of our time.

KARL KAUTSKY (1890)

[F]ew books have been more misunderstood than *Utopia*. It has given the English language a word "Utopian" to signify something visionary and unpractical. Yet the remarkable thing about *Utopia* is the extent to which it adumbrates social and political reforms which have either been actually carried into practice, or which have come to be regarded as very practical politics. Utopia is depicted as a sternly righteous and puritanical State, where few of us would feel quite happy; yet we go on using the word "Utopia" to signify an easy-going paradise, whose only fault is that it is too happy and ideal to be realized. . . .

It is noteworthy that the two most potent books on the State written in the Sixteenth Century were written within so few years of each other. Parts of *Utopia* read like a commentary on parts of *The Prince*. . . . There is a reason for the coincidence; before *The Prince* was written, ideas used in *The Prince* had been gaining ground. They were the "progressive" ideas, and we may regard *Utopia* as a "reaction" against them. Over and over again, in Book I of *Utopia,* Raphael Hythloday imagines himself as counselling a prince, telling him what he ought to do, against those who are telling him what he *can* do; and always Raphael admits that these ideas of justice which he has brought from Utopia are opposed to all that the most up-to-date statesmen of Europe are thinking and doing.

And so, from the point of view of the new age of Machiavellian statesmanship and commercial exploitation *Utopia* is old-fashioned.

R. W. CHAMBERS (1935)

[Utopia] is a non-Christian state founded on reason and nature, unperfected by faith and grace. . . . It is none the less of supreme importance to observe that the Commonwealth of Utopia is founded not only on reason but also on religion.   *RICHARD O'SULLIVAN (1936)*

There were quite a number of movements in the later Middle Ages which proclaimed community of possessions as their principle. But all these movements were religious in character. They preached the principle of community as "the law of God." More divested the principle of this religious integument, he proclaimed it on the grounds of reason. The

Utopian order is to him the best because it is the most rational and the most conducive to man's well-being on earth.

VYACHESLAV VOLGIN (1953)

In sixteenth-century English culture . . . the religious atmosphere of the Renaissance not only asserts itself, but presses forward ever more triumphantly. Thomas More in his *Utopia* attempts to oppose to the system of dogmatic theology an entirely new form of religion. He outlines here the ideal of religion without dogma as the purest and best worship of the divine being. *ERNST CASSIRER (1932)*

All seem to be agreed that [*Utopia*] is a great book, but hardly any two agree as to its real significance: we approach it through a cloud of contradictory eulogies. In such a state of affairs a good, though not a certain, clue is the opinion of those who lived nearer the author's time than we. Our starting-point is that Erasmus speaks of it as if it were primarily a comic book; Tyndale despises it as "poetry"; for Harpsfield it is a "jolly invention", "pleasantly" set forth; More himself in later life classes it and the *Praise of Folly* together as books fitter to be burned than translated in an age prone to misconstruction. . . . It all sounds as if we had to do with a book whose real place is not in the history of political thought so much as in that of fiction and satire. It is, of course, possible that More's sixteenth-century readers, and More himself, were mistaken. But it is at least equally possible that the mistake lies with those modern readers who take the book *au grand sérieux*. There is a cause specially predisposing them to error in such a matter. They live in a revolutionary age, an age which modern weapons and the modern revolutionary technique have made it only too easy to produce in the real world states recognizably like those we invent on paper: writing Utopias is now a serious matter. In More's time . . . there was no real hope or fear that the paper states could be "drawn into practice": the man engaged in blowing such bubbles did not need to talk as if he were on his oath. . . .

The *Utopia* has its serious, even its tragic, elements. It is, as its [first] translator Robinson says, "fruteful and profitable." But it is not a consistently serious philosophical treatise, and all attempts to treat it as such break down sooner or later. The interpretation which breaks down soonest is the "liberal" interpretation. There is nothing in the book on which the later More, the heretic-hunter, need have turned his back. There is no freedom of speech in Utopia. There is nothing liberal in Utopia. From it, as from all other imaginary states, liberty is more successfully banished than the real world, even at its worst, allows. The very charm of these paper citizens is that they cannot in any way resist their author: every man is a dictator in his own book. It is not love of liberty that makes men write Utopias. *C. S. LEWIS (1954)*

The revered name of Thomas More has been invoked in support of the radical socialist states of the Soviet world empire, as well as in support of the anti-Communist position of the Papacy. Both interpretations purport to be founded on a critical reading of *Utopia*.

One literary reason why *Utopia* has lent itself to such divergence of

opinion is its basic genre: the dialogue. . . . Hythloday and the *persona*
More who may or may not represent the views of Thomas More the writer
. . . present two fundamental sides to the question. Hythloday's platform
is common ownership of property, and he refuses to concede the feasi-
bility of gradual reform of monarchical society. The *persona* More is
often forthrightly opposed to the doctrine of common ownership, and
argues instead for a policy of compromise and slow change within the
limitations of practical politics. Their dialogue concludes in apparent
lack of reconciliation of these opposing points of view. Accordingly,
the critic can choose his hero. . . . Between the cry of voices from both
sides, [there is] the middle position of regarding *Utopia* as the impartial
presentation of two points of view, as a dialogue of the mind with itself.
. . . Hythloday and *persona* More represent the two polarities of More's
own mind. . . .   *D. M. BEVINGTON (1961)*

The description of Utopia by itself may be considered one or more of a
great many different things: 1. A fantastic escape from unpleasant reality.
2. A blueprint for a better society which More thought men might soon
establish. 3. A better society which might exist in some far-off time.
4. A better society which More desired but did not believe possible.
5. A reconstruction of medieval social virtues. 6. A revival of primitive
Christian communism. 7. A speculative portrait of rumored American
societies, like that of the Incas. 8. A strictly rational philosophic construction, minus Christianity, for the purposes of moral instruction.
9. A pleasant fable written by a humanist for the amusement of himself
and his scholarly friends. 10. A fruit of classical studies, following
Plato's *Republic*. 11. An early plan for British imperialism. 12. A Christian
humanist account of a scholar's paradise, where philosophers are kings
and the church is purified. 13. A society constructed as the direct opposite to England for the purpose of disguising social criticism. 14. A
description of a desirable and possible organization of city republics.
　Long as it is, the above list could be longer. Each interpretation has
some truth in it, though all can hardly be equally true. Most commonly
advanced have been the eighth, ninth, tenth, and twelfth.
                                 RUSSELL AMES (1949)

Desiderius Erasmus and Martin Luther
1466?—1536   1483—1546

The Humanist and the Reformer

The sixteenth century saw, among other things, the "great debate" between humanism and the Reformation. This confrontation is highlighted by the dispute between Erasmus and Luther on the perennial question of the freedom of the will. In 1524, Erasmus, vexed by the excessive predestinarianism contained in the emerging Protestant creed and urged on by some of his Catholic friends, wrote his urbane and scholarly tract *On Free Will (De libero arbitrio).* Luther, after some delay caused by his active involvement in political strife, answered in kind but interspersed his long treatise *The Enslaved Will (De servo arbitrio,* 1525) with thunderous rhetoric, the sheer force of which momentarily seemed to reduce his opponent to silence. But in 1526—1527 Erasmus retaliated with two lengthy and carefully argued volumes, *Hyperaspistes (The Defender),* in which he offered a detailed explanation of Christian humanism and its theology and at the same time castigated Luther as the destroyer of civil, religious, and cultural harmony. Careful scrutiny of argument and counterargument suggests that the forensic joust ended in a draw, as did ultimately the exhaustive struggle on the political level between Catholic and Protestant factions.

Erasmus, who was originally well disposed toward Luther's valiant fight to cleanse the Church from a host of flagrant abuses and who throughout his life evinced great respect for the reformer's scholarly achievements, finally had to break with Luther's intransigent denial of free will. He thereby drew the battle line between the evolving Catholic and Protestant positions concerning the doctrine of justification, i.e., man's way to salvation. Luther, who reciprocated Erasmus' respect and had long hoped for a powerful assist in theological matters from the most eminent humanist of the times, was deeply offended by the latter's refusal to endorse the new creed. Luther knew that Erasmus had aimed his thrust at the very heart of Protestant theology. From its inception,

Luther's reform was concerned primarily with the theological foundations of the Church, although by sheer accident of history and fate, political, economic, and sociological problems tended to overshadow Luther's true concerns. His deep disappointment over his former friend's cautious moderation accounts partly for the often ruthless polemic of his rebuttal. The two protagonists of the great debate never met in person. But besides carrying on a sporadic correspondence, they knew each other well through their writings. The trajectories of their careers ran parallel in their youth but then, through stormy years, carried them to fundamentally different modes of life and thought.

Desiderius Erasmus was born out of wedlock in Rotterdam, the son of a priest and a physician's daughter. Throughout his life Erasmus seemed to suffer from the illegitimacy of his birth, and in times of turmoil and violent partisanship, he vainly craved the comfort of intimate family ties. He obtained a thorough education at the famous school of the Brethren of the Common Life at Deventer (1474–1484). The various schools of the Brethren, located in several places throughout northern Europe, propagated a religion of personal piety with an anticlerical bias, a kind of lay spirituality which deeply affected northern humanism. They also equipped their students with solid classical learning. It was here that Erasmus acquired his superb command of Latin.

Erasmus became a monk and in 1492 was ordained a priest at the Augustinian monastery at Steyn. He did not relish the ascetic life; although he wrote an essay deprecating mundane pleasures, it was ostensibly to convince himself of his fitness for monasticism. Poor health and his irrepressible love for humanistic studies gained him a temporary dispensation from the pope which, as it turned out, proved to be permanent.

In 1495 Erasmus enrolled at the University of Paris. Repulsed by the arid debates of the scholastic theologians, he taught himself Greek and classical philology. At the behest of various benefactors, he soon undertook repeated trips to England and a journey to Italy, which widened his intellectual horizon. Study, scholarly research, writing, and good companionship filled much of his peripatetic life thereafter.

From 1505 on to the end of his days Erasmus published a steady stream of writings—both serious and satiric—whose eloquence and broad learning earned him the admiration of friends and enemies alike. In 1516 he published his most important contribution to Renaissance scholarship: The *Novum Instrumentum* (later, *Testamentum*), a critical revision of the Greek text of the New Testament with a new Latin translation and a commentary. Presuming to improve upon Jerome's Latin version, long hallowed as the "Vulgate," this work marked the application of humanistic learning to early Christian literature and the beginning of modern textual criticism of the Bible.

In 1517, the very year Luther nailed his portentous 95 Theses to the door of the castle church at Wittenberg, Erasmus was completely freed—by papal decree and with his ready acquiescence—from his monastic vows. Henceforth, on his various travels he observed with a sympathetic eye the development of Luther's reform movement in Germany. Only around 1520, as the Lutheran revolt passed from criticism of indulgences to rejection of the papacy and councils, did he demur. The Church, although its theology might be shot through with nonsense, still appeared to him as a bulwark of social order and individual morality. Two popes, Adrian VI and his successor, Clement VII, beseeched him to enter the lists against Luther. When he finally acceded to their demands, he did not launch an all-out attack against the Reformation but engaged upon a mannerly and objective discussion of Luther's denial of free will.

In his treatise *On Free Will* Erasmus readily admits that, logically, the beliefs in divine omnipotence and man's moral freedom seem mutually exclusive. But as a humanist, he is repelled by the doctrines of predestination and determinism because they do violence to the notions of human dignity and the value of human life. His deeply felt opposition to predestinarianism is based not upon theological cogency but rather on the humanist's instinctive respect for the autonomy of the individual. Luther, in his fiery retort to Erasmus, shows no such tender compunctions. Their differing views on human dignity cast a glaring light on the basic cleavage between humanism and Reformation in sixteenth-century Europe.

Martin Luther, seventeen years younger than Erasmus, was born in Eisleben, Saxony, to a mining family of peasant stock. His youthful experiences were strikingly similar to Erasmus': his relationships with his family were marred by insecurity and friction; he was sent to a Brethren school at Magdeburg to imbibe the *devotio moderna;* and after a stint as a student of law at the University of Erfurt, he entered the local Augustinian monastery. Although he was remarkably well read, his growing interest in the Bible made him virtually immune to the mere literary and philological interests of many humanists. St. Paul and St. Augustine kept him under their spell, while Erasmus, for instance, found his inspiration primarily in the Platonists or the most scholarly of the early Church Fathers, such as St. Jerome and Origen.

Luther rose fast in the ranks of his order, earned his doctorate, and was made professor at the new University of Wittenberg. He first taught Aristotle, whom he soon came to abhor (at one time he dubbed him a "rancid philosopher") and then Scriptural exegesis. Increasingly fascinated by the doctrines of certain German mystics who stressed the weakness of the human will and the pervasive power of divine grace, he became aware of the ever-widening chasm between his own inner religious experience and the official dogma of the Church. St. Paul's epistles, especially Romans, seemed to confirm his own religious sensibilities, while Erasmus' annotated Greek edition of the New Testament aided him in his exegetical work.

In 1517, after he had been appointed his order's vicar of the districts of Meissen and Thuringia and entrusted with the supervision of eleven monasteries, he made public his discontent with the prevailing doctrine of justification by brashly attacking the practice of indulgences. Indulgences were letters of reprieve, sold by agents of some powerful ecclesiastic dignitary, which promised remission of penalties in purgatory and in some cases even rescindment of sin altogether. The efficacy of these letters of indulgence was directly proportionate to their cost. The practice, prompted largely by economic motives, had its theological basis in the Catholic doctrine of a "Treasury of Goodness" amassed by the Saints, the Virgin Mary, and Christ himself, who had been infinitely better than they needed to be for their own salvation. God's vicar on earth, the pope, was empowered to tap this inexhaustible reservoir of goodness through his emissaries and to transfer some of its bounty to those whose accounts were in arrears. All individual sins had to be accounted for in minute detail. The Church obviously took a corporate view of goodness but an individualistic view of sin. The sale of indulgences was an excrescence, deplored by many a good Catholic, of an already elaborate sacramental system deemed indispensable to man's salvation.

Luther's 95 Theses, while directly assailing the flagrant abuses perpetrated by the hawkers of indulgences, were based on his deep conviction that the Church had too low an opinion of God's majesty and too high an opinion of the role of man's will and human institutions in the economy of salvation. In all of his subsequent writings he never veered from his basic Paulinistic-Augustinian position: personal faith in Christ is the avenue to salvation and not the mechanical performance of institutionalized "works," i.e., sacraments.

In the emerging fight with the papal see, Luther's humanist sympathizers wished Erasmus on their side. But Luther's three fighting challenges to the existing authorities—namely, *Address to the German Nobility, The Babylonian Captivity of the Church,* and *The Liberty of a Christian Man*—brought the incurable rupture with Rome and with it Erasmus' estrangement from the more militant elements in the Reform Movement. In 1520, a papal bull *Exsurge Domine* chastised Luther. But Luther retorted with unflagging zeal in his *Assertions,* which contained, among other things, an impassioned denial of free will. In 1521, Luther was excommunicated, but he continued to stand firmly by his convictions when he was summoned before the Diet of Worms later that same year.

Political events finally forced Luther to go into hiding at the Wartburg (the castle of the Elector of Saxony, Luther's protector), where he accomplished his magisterial German translation of the New Testament. Erasmus, loath to be drawn into debate, moved from his sensitive position of professor at Louvain to the more sheltered atmosphere of a town house in Basle. But in 1524, the great debate could no longer be staved off, and with Erasmus' treatise *On Free Will* the issue was joined. Luther's answer, four times longer than Erasmus' tract, is perhaps as unsystematic as Erasmus' piece, but it is certainly overwhelming in its conviction. For the rest of his days, Luther considered *The Enslaved Will* his masterwork, the capstone of his theology, alongside with his *Little* and his *Great Catechism.*

To Erasmus, freedom of the will is primarily a speculative question which should be approached from a dispassionate, scholarly standpoint. To Luther, it is unmistakably a soteriological question—i.e., one vitally concerned with man's salvation—that allows no erosive temporizing and cautious fence-straddling but calls for whole-hearted personal commitment. Erasmus saw a personal attack in Luther's blunt arguments and denunciations, and his attitude toward Luther from then on was irreconcilably hostile.

In their personal styles of life and writing, Erasmus and Luther were direct opposites. Erasmus was a retiring intellectual who preferred the reflective calm of his study to the bustle of the outside world, but who nevertheless remained sensitive to his position as the acknowledged head of a cosmopolitan community of scholars. Luther was a brooding, yet exuberant leader of men who loved to mingle with common folk, proud of his peasant ancestry and the strong ties that bound him to his native soil. Characteristically, Erasmus used to advantage the polished Latin of Renaissance tract literature while Luther preferred to write in a powerful, ringing German. Thus, although they had shared much common ground in their youth, Erasmus and Luther were finally cast by these and other fundamental differences into the roles of protagonists in the greatest debate of their time.

On Free Will / Erasmus

Preface: Man and Truth

Among the many difficulties encountered in Holy Scripture—and there are many of them—none presents a more perplexed labyrinth than the problem of the freedom of the will. In ancient and more recent times philosophers and theologians have been vexed by it to an astonishing degree, but, as it seems to me, with more exertion than success on their part. Recently, Carlstadt and Eck[1] restored interest in the problem, debating it, however, with moderation. Soon thereafter, Martin Luther took up the whole controversy once more—and in a rather heated fashion—with his formal *Assertion* concerning the freedom of the will. And although more than one has answered his *Assertion,* I, too, encouraged by my friends, am going to try to see whether, by the following brief discussion, the truth might not become more visible.

2) *Objectivity and Scepticism*

Let no one misinterpret our battle. We are not two gladiators incited against each other. I want to argue only against one of Luther's teachings, illuminating, if this be possible, in the subsequent clash of scriptural passages and arguments, the truth, the investigation of which has always been the most reputable activity of scholars. There will be no invective, and for two reasons: it does not behoove Christians so to act; and moreover, the truth, which by excessive quarreling is often lost, is discovered with greater certainty without it. . . .

From *Discourse on Free Will*, translated by Ernst F. Winter. Copyright, 1961, by Frederick Ungar Publishing Co., Inc. Reprinted by permission of the publishers.
[1]Andreas Carlstadt (1480−1541), at one time an ardent follower of Luther's, was challenged by Johann Maier von Eck (1486−1543), a German Catholic theologian and Luther's lifelong foe, to debate the question of free will at the University of Leipzig (June 27, 1519).

3) *Having an Open Mind*

For these reasons then, I must confess that I have not yet formed a definite opinion on any of the numerous traditional views regarding the freedom of the will; all I am willing to assert is that the will enjoys some power of freedom. My reading of Martin Luther's *Assertion* was quite unprejudiced, except that I felt towards him a favor such as a lawyer feels towards a hard pressed defendant. Though Luther's argument is defended with every means at his disposal and presented with great verve, I must honestly confess that he has not yet convinced me. . . . Therefore, I merely want to analyze and not to judge, to inquire and not to dogmatize. I am ready to learn from anyone who advances something more accurate or more reliable, though I would rather persuade mediocre minds not to argue too stubbornly on such matters. It harms Christian concord more than it helps piety.

4) *Difficulties in the Scripture*

Holy Scripture contains secrets into which God does not want us to penetrate too deeply, because if we attempt to do so, increasing darkness envelopes us, so that we might come to recognize in this manner both the unfathomable majesty of divine wisdom and the feebleness of the human mind. . . . Much will have to wait for that time when we shall see no longer in a mirror and in an enigma, but shall contemplate in its glory the unveiled face of the Lord.

5) *Essence of Christian Piety*

In my opinion the implications of the freedom of the will in Holy Scripture are as follows: if we are on the road to piety, we should continue to improve eagerly and forget what lies behind us; if we have become involved in sin, we should make every effort to extricate ourselves, to accept the remedy of penance, and to solicit the mercy of the Lord, without which neither the human will nor its striving is effective; for all evil let us consider ourselves responsible, but let us ascribe all good to Divine Benevolence alone, for to It we owe even what we are; and in all things must we believe that whatever delightful or sad happens to us during life, God has caused it for our salvation, and that no injustice can come from Him who is by nature just, even if something should befall us which we deem undeserved; nobody should despair of forgiveness by a God who is by nature most merciful. In my opinion, it used to be sufficient for Christian piety to cling to these truths.

7) *Unsuitableness of Luther's Teachings*

Let us assume the truth of what Wycliffe[2] has taught and Luther has asserted, namely, that everything we do happens not on account of our

---

[2]John Wycliffe (1330?–1384) was one of the early influential English reformers.

free will, but out of sheer necessity. What could be more useless than
to publish this paradox to the world? Secondly, let us assume that it
is true, as Augustine has written somewhere, that God causes both
good and evil in us, and that he rewards us for his good works wrought
in us and punishes us for the evil deeds done in us. What a loophole
the publication of this opinion would open to godlessness among innumerable people? In particular: mankind is lazy, indolent, malicious,
and, in addition, incorrigibly prone to every impious outrage. How many
weak ones would continue in their perpetual and laborious battle
against their own flesh? What wicked fellow would henceforth try to
better his conduct? Who could love with all his heart a God who fires
a hell with eternal pain, in order to punish there poor mankind for his
own evil deeds, as if God enjoyed human distress? Most people would
react as they are sketched above. People are universally ignorant and
carnal-minded. They tend towards unbelief, wickedness and blasphemy. There is no sense in pouring oil upon the fire.

Thus Paul, the prudent disburser of the divine word, frequently
consults charity and prefers to pursue what serves the neighbor, rather
than what is permissible. Among the mature he speaks with the wisdom
he possesses. But before the weak he displays no other knowledge but
that of Jesus Christ, the crucified. Holy Scripture knows how to adjust
its language to our human condition. In it are passages where God is
angry, grieved, indignant, furious; where he threatens and hates. Again
in other places he has mercy, he regrets, he changes his intentions.
This does not mean that such changes really take place in the nature of
God. These are rather modes of expression, benefitting our weak-
mindedness and dullness. The same prudence should, I believe, adorn
all who have taken up preaching the divine word. Some things can be
noxious, because like wine for the feverish, they are not fitting. Hence
such matters might be treated in discourses among the educated or also
in theological schools, although it is not expedient even there I think
unless done with caution. Definitely, it seems to me, it is not only unsuitable, but truly pernicious to carry on such disputations when everybody can listen.

In short, one should be persuaded to waste neither time nor ingenuity
in such labyrinths; neither to refute nor to endorse Luther's teachings.
Perhaps I deserve the reproach of having been too verbose in this preface. But all of it appears more important than the disputation proper.

Introduction: Objective Criterion for Truth

Since Luther recognizes no authority of any author, however approved,
except that of the canonical books, I gladly accept this diminution of
labor. Both among the Greeks and the Latins exist innumerable thinkers
who deal explicitly or cursorily with the freedom of the will. It would
have been a formidable task to gather all the quotations for and against
free will; to explain every passage as well as to refute it. This irksome
exertion would have been wasted on Luther and his friends, particularly

since they not only hold different opinions, but also contradict themselves extensively.

10) *Miracles and Exemplary Life*

. . .

I do not want to accuse Luther, whom I don't know personally, but whose writings have made a mixed impression on me. I am addressing this to others who are better known to me and who interrupt us by saying, "They were simply men," every time we advance an interpretation by an orthodox elder for the purpose of understanding a controversial passage. When we ask, what are the marks of a true scriptural interpretation, since both sides are represented only by human beings, their answer is "The mark of the Holy Spirit." If you ask why the Holy Spirit should have forsaken the side which is also distinguished by miracles, and be found rather amongst them, they answer as if during all these hundreds of years there had been no Gospel in the world. If one misses among them a conduct of life commensurate with the Spirit, they answer that they are saved by faith and not by works. If one misses miracles, they say these have stopped long ago and are no longer needed, since now the light of Scripture shines so wonderfully. If one contests that Scripture is clear in our case, otherwise so many excellent men would also have been blind, one has moved in a full cycle to the beginning of the argument.

11) *Infallible Church*

Let us assume that he who has the Spirit is sure of the meaning of Scripture. How can I also possess the certainty which the other pretends to have? What can I do when several persons claim different interpretations, but each one swears to have the Spirit? Moreover, since the Spirit does not inspire the same person with everything, some who have the Spirit may be mistaken on a point.

This then I want to reply to those who discard without hesitation the old interpretation of sacred books, and instead submit their own, as if an oracle had proclaimed it. Finally, even though Christ's Spirit might permit His people to be in error in an unimportant question on which man's salvation does not depend, no one could believe that this Spirit has deliberately overlooked error in His Church for 1300 years, and that He did not deem one of all the pious and saintly Church Fathers worthy enough to be inspired, with what, they contend, is the very essence of all evangelical teaching.

13) *Definition of Free Will*

I have completed half of this work. To those whom I have convinced, as I intended, that it were better not to cavil and quibble about such questions, especially not before the common people, I will not have to

present the further proof to which I shall now proceed, hoping that
truth will prevail everywhere, which will perhaps sparkle from a comparison of scriptural passages like fire struck from flint. Nobody can
deny that Sacred Scripture contains many passages stating the obvious
freedom of the human will. On the other hand, there are some passages
which seem to deny the former. Yet, it is certain that Scripture cannot
contradict itself, since all passages are inspired by the same Spirit. Therefore, we shall first examine those passages which confirm our view and
then we shall try to dispose of those that seem to be opposed.[3]

By freedom of the will we understand in this connection the power
of the human will whereby man can apply to or turn away from that
which leads unto eternal salvation.

Old Testament Proofs Supporting the Free Will

17) *Law of Nature, Law of Good Works, Law of Faith*

Therefore we are born under three kinds of laws: the law of nature,
the law of good works, and the law of faith, to use Paul's expression.

The Law of Nature, carved deeply into the minds of all, tells Scythians
as well as Greeks that it is unjust to do to another what one does not
wish to suffer himself. Without the help of Scripture and without the
light of faith, philosophers have gained a knowledge of divine kindness
and greatness by observing the created world. They have left us many
moral precepts which bear an astounding resemblance to the precepts
of the Gospels. We possess many of their sayings, encouraging virtue
and detesting turpitude. Thus it seems probable that they had a will
tending to moral good, but incapable of eternal salvation, unless grace
be added through faith.

The Law of Good Works, on the other hand, issues commands and
sanctions them with punishment. It increases sin and causes death,
not because it is evil, but because it requires good works which, without
grace, we could not possibly perform.

The Law of Faith which, posing even more difficult commandments
than the law of works, makes what would be impossible, not only easy
but also pleasant, as long as we are supported by abundant grace. Thus
faith heals our reason which has suffered through sin, and charity helps
our weakened will to act. . . .

18) *Freedom and Grace According to Pelagius. . .*

Views concerning the capacity of our free will after the Fall of Man
and before the reception of grace differ astonishingly among ancient
and modern thinkers, with one or the other aspect being emphasized.
Whoever wanted to counter despair or a false sense of security, and
thereby spur man to hope and aspiration, has actually overrated the freedom of the will.

---

[3]In these excerpts only a few examples of the Biblical passages in support of free will cited and discussed
by Erasmus will be included.

Pelagius[4] taught that no new grace was needed once grace had liberated and healed the free will of man. Thus the free will by itself was deemed sufficient to achieve eternal salvation. But we owe salvation solely to God without whose grace the will of man could not be effectively free to achieve good. The strength of soul, with which man can pursue the good he knows and avoid all evil, is in itself a gift of the creator who could have made a frog instead of man. . . .

19) *Freedom and Grace According to St. Augustine and the Reformers*

Diametrically opposed is the view that all morally good deeds without grace are detestable in God's sight no less than criminal deeds such as murder and adultery, because they do not originate in faith nor in love of God. This judgment is obviously too severe. The fact remains that there have been philosophers who possessed some knowledge of God, and hence perhaps also some trust and love of God, and did not act solely out of vainglory's sake, but rather out of love of virtue and goodness, which, they taught, was to be loved for no other reason but that it is good. For, whether a man who risks death for his country out of vainglory performs a morally good act in the general concrete or in the morally abstract, I do not know.

St. Augustine and his followers give a greater stress to the role of grace, as Paul also affirms it at every opportunity, because they are all conscious of how it debases true piety if man relies solely on his own strength. Thus Augustine challenges the view that man, subject to sin, can better himself or act to save himself. Only undeserved divine grace can spur man supernaturally to wish that which will lead to eternal life. This is known to some as prevenient grace. Augustine calls it operative grace. For him faith, through which we enter eternity, is also a free gift of God. So is charity an additional gift of the Spirit. Augustine calls it cooperative grace. It assists those who strive until they have reached their goal. Although free will and grace together accomplish the same work, grace is the leading cause and not just a concomitant one. But some are divided even on this opinion and say: if one considers the act according to its nature, then the will of man is the more important cause; if one considers, however, the meritorious aspects of the act, then grace is the more important.

Now, it appears that faith which evinces our desire to do salutary things, and charity which wishes us not to be frustrated in our desire, are not distinct in time, as they are different in their nature. Both can however be intensified in time.

20) *Four Varieties of Grace*

Since grace means a freely given gift, we may enumerate three or four varieties of grace.

---

[4]Pelagius (355?–425?), rejecting St. Augustine's teachings on predestination and grace, argued that grace consists of the "natural" attributes of man: reason, free will, and understanding of the Gospel.

The first kind of grace we possess by nature. Sin has corrupted, but not extinguished it, as we said before, and some call it the natural influence. Even the most obstinate sinner will retain this grace which is common to all mankind. Thus, everyone is free to speak or to keep silent, to sit or to stand up, to help the poor, to read holy books, to listen to sermons. Some now hold that such acts in themselves can in no way lead to eternal life. Others assert that such works, because of God's immense goodness can prepare for the reception of grace, and can move God to be merciful. True, some deny that this can happen without special grace. Therefore, this first kind of grace, common to all, is seldom called grace. Yet, it actually is such. For God as creator, conservor and governor of this world every day achieves greater miracles than the healing of a leper or the exorcism of demons. But we don't call these divine acts of maintaining the world miracles, because they are obvious to us every day.

A second variety is extraordinary grace. God through mercy moves the undeserving sinner to contrition. But God does not yet infuse that ultimate grace which can eliminate his sin and make him once more pleasing to Himself. Thus a sinner aided by this second kind of grace, which we had called operative, is displeased with himself. Yet, though he has not abandoned the inclination to sin, he is capable of giving alms, can pray, practice pious exercises, listen to sermons, request pious people to intercede for him with God, and thus by means of these and other ethically good works, apply in a way for obtaining the ultimate grace.

The goodness of God does not refuse to any mortals this second grace. The mercy of God offers everyone favorable opportunities for repentance. One needs only to attach the rest of one's own will to God's help, which merely invites to, but does not compel to betterment. Furthermore, one finds the opinion, that it is within our power to turn our will towards or away from grace—just as it is our pleasure to open or close our eyes against light. It is incompatible with the infinite love of God for man that a man's striving with all his might for grace should be frustrated. Through that grace, which they call sanctifying, if he inspires to it with all his power, it results that no sinner should be overconfident, none again should despair. No one perishes except through his own fault.

There are then first natural grace, second an exciting or operative grace, which is, to be sure, imperfect, third an efficient grace, which we have called cooperative, and which promotes that which is begun, and fourth a grace which leads to the final goal. The last three are supposedly one and the same grace, even though according to its operation in us, we call it by different names. Thus, the first excites, the second promotes and the third leads to the goal.

21) *Views of Thomists, Carlstadt, and Luther*

There are then those who are quite removed from Pelagius in ascribing more to grace and hardly anything to the free will, though not completely abolishing it. They deny that man could desire anything good without extraordinary grace, that he can initiate, continue and reach the goal without the guiding and continuous help of divine grace. Such an opinion appears quite probable, because it leaves man the possibility of exerting himself and striving, and nevertheless relinquishing to him nothing which he could solely ascribe to his own powers.[5]

But more objectionable is the opinion of those who emphatically affirm that the will in itself can only commit sin and that only grace can cause good; and this grace operates not through or with the will but merely within the will; in such wise that the will is in this case like wax in the hands of the sculptor; that it takes on any form pleasing to the craftsman.[6] These people, I think, have so great a fear of and distrust of meritorious human acts that they go too far.

Yet, worst of all is obviously the opinion of those who maintain that the free will is an empty name and that neither among the angels, nor Adam, nor us, nor before or after receiving grace did it or could it accomplish anything;[7] that rather God causes in us evil as well as good, and that everything happens of mere necessity.

23) *Additional Old Testament Proofs*

Now God has offered already in paradise the choice between life and death. If you obey my laws you shall live; if you disobey, you must die; beware of evil and choose the good. In the same vein he spoke to Cain: "Why are you angry and why are you downcast? If you do well, will you not be accepted; but if you do not well, will not sin crouch at the door? Its desire is for you, but you must master it" (Genesis 4,6-7). Here reward is in prospect for whoever chooses the good, and punishment for whoever prefers evil. Simultaneously this passage shows that bad inclinations can be overcome and that they don't necessitate sinning. With this passage agrees also the Lord's saying to Moses: "I have set before you life and death. Choose the good and follow me."[8] Could it be stated any more plainly? God shows what is good and what is evil. He offers as recompense death or life. He relinquishes to man the freedom of choice. It would be ridiculous to command one to make a choice, if he were incapable of turning in either direction. That's like saying to someone who stands at the crossroads "choose either one," when only one is passable. . . .

New Testament Proofs Supporting the Free Will

25) *God's Judgment*

Now we want to investigate whether also in Paul, the zealous advocate of grace, who storms the works of the Jewish laws, we find something which implies the freedom of the will. Thus we meet above all a passage in the Epistle to the Romans: "Dost thou despise the riches of his good-

---

[5]This seems to be an oversimplification of the Thomistic position.
[6]Here Erasmus outlines Carlstadt's views.
[7]This is Erasmus view of Luther's doctrine.
[8]Possibly a free rendition of Deuteronomy 30:19.

ness and patience and long-suffering? Dost thou not know that the greatness of God is meant to lead thee to repentance?" (Romans 2,4). How could the disdain of a commandment be imputed, if there is no free will? And how could God invite us to do penance, when he has caused impenitence? And how could a condemnation be justified, when the judge himself has compelled the committing of an outrage? But Paul had just finished saying, "and we know that the judgment of God is according to truth against those who do such things" (Romans 2,2). Here he speaks of "doing," and of a judgment according to truth. Where is mere necessity? Where is the will that merely suffers? Mark well whom Paul does blame for evil: "But according to thy hardness and unrepented heart, thou dost treasure up to thyself wrath in the day of wrath, and of the revelation of the just judgment of God who will render to every man according to his works" (Romans 2,5). The reference here is to a just judgment of God and to works which deserve punishment. If God ascribes to us only his own good works which he performs through us, and we thus earn glory, honor and immortality, then his goodness appears plausible. Although even in such a case the Apostle adds, "life eternal indeed he will give to those who by patience in good works seek glory and honor and immortality" (Romans 2,7). But how could it be justified that "wrath and indignation . . . tribulation and anguish" (Romans 12, 8-9) shall be visited upon the transgressor, if he is doing nothing freely, but everything through necessity?

Apparent Proofs Against the Free Will

33) *God's Foreknowledge*

The knotty point how God's foreknowledge is compatible with our free will has often been amplified. But in my opinion Lorenzo Valla[9] has been most successful at it: Foreknowledge does not cause what is to take place. Even we know many things which will be happening. They will not happen because we know them, but vice versa. An eclipse of the sun does not occur because astronomers predict it, but it can be predicted, precisely because it will take place.

34) *God's Predestination*

More difficult becomes the question when we consider God's will or determination, meaning that God wills that which He knows beforehand. Somehow He must wish the foreknown, seeing that He does not prevent it though he could do so. This is what Paul means when he comments: "For who resists his will?" (Romans 9,19). "He has mercy on whom he will, and whom he will he hardens" (Romans 9,18). Assuming a king could do, unopposed, as he pleases, then everything he wishes would be called his "doing."

---

[9]Lorenzo Valla (1405?–1457) was foremost among Italian humanists. He was the author of many scholarly works (one of which was a pioneer in the field of textual criticism) and a treatise on free will.

Thus it might appear that God's will, which is the first cause of all that happens, seems to deprive us of the free will. Paul does not discuss this question, rather he scolds those who want to investigate it, "O man, who art thou to reply to God?" (Romans 9,20). However, he scolds the man who would impiously complain, just as a master might well say to his stubborn servant that he should not inquire after the why of a given order, but rather carry it out. The master's answer would be different if an understanding and willing servant desires modestly to know why the master wants something to be done which appears to be useless.

God had wanted the Pharaoh to perish miserably. He was justified in wishing this, and it was good that the tyrant did perish. The will of God, however, did not force him to persist in his wrong. Thus a master may give an order to a servant whose bad character he knows. Such an order may offer the opportunity for sin and, caught in it, his punishment may serve as a lesson to others. The master knows beforehand that the servant will sin, and thus display his real character; in a certain sense, he wills his destruction and his sin. Nonetheless, this does not excuse the servant, for he sins out of his own malice. He has deserved that his malice be known to all and be punished. But where could you assume the beginning of merit where there is eternal necessity and where there is no free will?

Summary and Conclusion

52) *Some Reformers' Views Justified*

Evidently these people considered it quite apt for the simple obedience of a Christian that man depend completely on the will of God when he places his entire trust and all his hopes in his promises; when he, conscious of his own wretchedness, admires and loves his immense mercy which he gives us plentifully without charge; when he, furthermore, subjects himself completely to his will, no matter whether he wants to save or destroy him; when he accepts no praise whatsoever for his works, and rather ascribes all glory to His grace, thinking that man is nothing else but a living tool of the divine Spirit, which the latter has cleansed and sanctified for himself through his undeserved goodness, and which he guides and governs according to his inscrutable wisdom; furthermore, when there exists nothing anybody could claim as his own accomplishment, and when he hopes for eternal life as reward for steadfast faith in God, not because he had earned it by his own good works, but because the goodness of God was pleased to promise that reward to those who have trust in him; whereby, consequently, man has the duty to beg God assiduously for imparting and augmenting his Spirit in us, to thank him for every success and to adore in all cases God's omnipotence, to admire everywhere his wisdom, and to love everywhere his goodness.

These utterances are also very praiseworthy to me, because they agree with Holy Scripture. They conform to the creed of those who died once and for all to this world, through their baptism have been buried with Christ, and after the mortification of the flesh live henceforth with the Spirit of Jesus, into whose body they have been ingrafted, through faith.[10] This is incontestably a pious and captivating conception, which takes from us every conceit, which transfers all glory and confidence to Christ, which expels from us the fear of men and demons, and which, though making us distrustful of our human potentialities, makes us nonetheless strong and courageous in God. This we applaud freely, up to the point of exaggeration which we want to avoid.

53) *Errors and Injustice in the Reformers*

But the rational soul in me has many doubts when I hear the following: there is no merit in man; all his works, even the pious ones, are sin; our will can do no more than the clay in the potter's hand; everything we do or want to do is reduced to unconditional necessity.

First, why do you read so often that the saints, rich in good work, have acted with justice, have walked upright in the sight of God, never deviating to the right or to the left, if everything is sin, even what the most pious does—in fact such a sin that one for whom Christ has died would nonetheless be condemned to inferno, were it not for God's mercy?

Secondly, why does one so often hear of reward, if there is no merit at all? How would disobedience of those following God's commandments be praised, and disobedience be damned? Why does Holy Scripture so frequently mention judgment, if merit cannot be weighed at all? Or why must we stand before the seat of judgment if nothing has happened according to our will, but everything according to mere necessity? It is disturbing to think of all the many admonitions, commandments, threats, exhortations and complaints, if we can do nothing, but God's unchangeable will causes the willing as well as the carrying out in us. He wants us to pray perseveringly. He wants us to watch, to fight and to struggle for the reward of eternal life. Why does he continuously want to be asked, when he has already decided whether to give us or not to give us, and when he himself, unchangeable, is unable to change his resolutions? Why does he command us to strive laboriously for what he has decided to give freely? God's grace fights and triumphs in us when we are afflicted, ejected, derided, tortured and killed. Such atrocities the martyrs suffered. Nonetheless such a martyr is to have no merit. Indeed, it is called a sin, if he submits his body to tortures, in the hope of heavenly life. But why would an exceedingly merciful God wish to be thus engaged with his martyrs? Cruel would appear a man if he did not give, unless having tortured to despair, that which he had already decided to bestow freely upon his friend.

Perhaps, as soon as one confronts this obscurity in the divine decision, one ought to adore that which we are not supposed to comprehend, so that man says, "he is the Lord, he can do everything he wishes, and since he is by nature good, everything he wills can only be very good." It is still plausible enough to say that God crowns his gifts in us; he permits his benefits to be our advantage; he deigns with undeserved good-

---

[10]Erasmus is referring here to the Mystical Body of Christ (Romans 6:4).

ness to attribute to us what he has caused in us, well deserved, as it were, if we trust in him, and in order to obtain immortality. But I don't know how those can be consistent who exaggerate God's mercy towards the pious in such a way as to permit him to be almost cruel against the others.

A goodness which imputes to us its excellence might possibly be tolerable to a pious soul. But it is difficult to explain how it is compatible with justice (not to speak with mercy), to condemn the others, in whom God did not deign to cause good, to eternal tortures, although on their own they could not possibly effect any good, since they either possessed no free will, or only one good for sinning.

57) Human Nature and Salvation

In my opinion the free will could have been so defined as to avoid overconfidence in our merits and the other disadvantages which Luther shuns, as well as to avoid such as we recited above, and still not lose the advantages which Luther admires. This, it seems to me, is accomplished by those who attribute everything to the pulling by grace which is the first to excite our spirit, and attribute only something to human will in its effort to continue and not withdraw from divine grace. But since all things have three parts, a beginning, a continuation and an end, grace is attributed to the two extremities, and only in continuation does the free will effect something. Two causes meet in this same work, the grace of God and the human will, grace being the principal cause and will a secondary, since it is impotent without the principal cause, while the latter has sufficient strength by itself. Thus, while the fire burns through its natural strength, the principal cause is still God, who acts through the fire. God alone would indeed suffice, and without Him fire could not burn. Due to this combination, man must ascribe his total salvation to divine grace, since it is very little that the free will can effect, and even that comes from divine grace which has at first created free will and then redeemed and healed it. Thus are placated, if they can be placated, those who will not tolerate that man has some good which he does not owe to God. He owes this also to God, but in another way and under another title. Just as an inheritance coming in equal share to the children, is not called a benevolence, because it belongs by common law to all. If beyond this common right a donation is made to this or that child, it is called liberality. But children owe gratitude to their parents also under the title of their inheritance.

I will try to express in parables what we have been saying. Even the healthy eye of a man does not see in the darkness, and when it is blinded, it does not see anything in light either. Thus the will can do nothing, though free, if withdrawing from grace. But the one with good eyes can close his eyes before the light and see nothing. He can also turn his eyes away. They will not see what he could have seen. The one with blind eyes owes his gratitude in the first place to God, and only then to the doctor. Before sinning our eyes were healthy. Sin has ruined them. Whoever sees, what can he pride himself in? He can impute to himself his cautious closing and turning away of the eyes.

Listen to another parable. A father raises his child, which is yet unable to walk, which has fallen and which exerts himself, and shows him an apple, placed in front of him. The boy likes to go and get it, but due to his weak bones would soon have fallen again, if the father had not supported him by his hand and guided his steps. Thus the child comes, led by the father, to the apple which the father places willingly into his hand, like a reward for his walking. The child could not have raised itself without the father's help; would not have seen the apple without the father's showing; would not have stepped forward without the father's helping his weak little steps; would not have reached the apple without the father's placing it into his hand. What can the child claim for himself? Yet, he did do something, but he must not glory in his own strength, since he owes everything to the father.

Let us assume it is the same with God. What does the child do? As the boy is being helped up, he makes an effort and tries to accommodate his weak steps to the father's guidance. The father could have pulled him against his will. A childish whim could have refused the apple. The father could have given the apple without his running, but he would rather give it in this manner, because it is better for the boy. I readily admit that our striving contributes less to the gaining of eternal life, than the boy's running at the hand of his father.

59) *Addressed to Luther*

Those who deny any freedom of the will and affirm absolute necessity, admit that God works in man not only the good works, but also evil ones. It seems to follow that inasmuch as man can never be the author of good works, he can also never be called the author of evil ones. This opinion seems obviously to attribute cruelty and injustice to God, something religious ears abhor vehemently. (He would no longer be God if anything vicious and imperfect were met in him.) Nonetheless those holding such an implausible view have an answer: He is God; He is able to do only the best and most beautiful. If you observe the fittingness of the universe, even what is evil in itself, is good in it and illustrates the glory of God. No creature can adjudge the Creator's intentions. Man must subject himself completely to them. In fact, if it pleases God to damn this or that one, nobody must grumble, but accept what pleases him, and be convinced that he does everything for the best. What would come of it if man were to ask God why he did not make him an angel? . . .

60) *Further Exaggeration and Difficulties*

But let us cease reasoning with those devoid of reason. We began our disputation with man, created in the image and likeness of God, and for whose pleasure He created all things. We note that some are born with healthy bodies and good minds, as though born for virtue, again others with monstrous bodies and horrible sickness, others so stupid that they almost have fallen to the level of brute animals, some even more brutish than the brutes, others so disposed toward disgraceful passions, that it seems a strong fate is impelling them, others insane and possessed by the devils. How will we explain the question of God's justice and mercy in such cases? Shall we say with Paul: "O the depth . . ." (Romans 11,33)? I think this would be better than to judge with impious rashness God's decisions, which man cannot explore. And truly, it is even more difficult to explain how God crowns his favors in some with immortal life, and punishes his misdeeds in others with eternal suffering. In order to defend such a paradox they resort to other paradoxes and to maintain the battle against their adversary. They immensely exaggerate original sin which supposedly has corrupted even the most excellent faculties of human nature, makes man incapable of anything, save only ignoring and hating God, and not even after grace and justification by faith can he effect any work which wouldn't be sin. They make that inclination to sin in us, remaining after the sin of our first parents, an invincible sin in itself, so that not one divine precept exists which even a man justified by faith could possibly keep. All the commandments of God have supposed no other purpose than to amplify the grace of God, which, irrespective of merit, grants salvation. . . .

Luther seems to enjoy such exaggerations. He pushes other people's exaggerations even further, driving out bad knots with worse wedges, as the saying goes. Some had daringly advanced another exaggeration, selling not only their own, but also the merits of all the saints. What kind of works is meant: songs, chanting the psalms, eating of fishes, fasting, dressing simply, titles? Thus Luther drove one nail through with another, when he said the saints had no merits whatsoever, and that the works of even the most pious men were sin and would adduce eternal damnation if faith and divine mercy had not come to the rescue. The other side was making a considerable profit with confession and reparation. Human conscience was thereby exceedingly entangled. Likewise, all kinds of strange things were related concerning purgatory. The opponents [i.e. Luther] correct these mistakes by saying confession is the Devil's invention, and should not be required, and they think no satisfaction is necessary for sin, because Christ has atoned for the sin of all; and think there is no purgatory. One side goes so far as to say that the orders of any prior of a monastery are binding under pain of hell, while they have no scruples in promising eternal life to those who obey them. The opponents answer this exaggeration by saying that all the orders of popes, councils and bishops are heretical and anti-Christian. The one side exalts papal power in an exaggerated way, the other side speaks of the pope such that I do not dare to repeat it. Again, one side says the vows of monks and priests fetter man forever under punishment of hell, the others say such vows are godless and not to be made, and once made, to be broken.

62) *Final Conclusions*

Hence, if it has sufficiently been demonstrated, this matter is as follows: It does not promote piety to investigate this any further than must be, especially before those who are unlearned. We have proven that our opinion is more evident in scriptural testimony than the opinion of the opponents. It is a fact that Holy Scripture is in most instances either obscure and figurative, or seems, at first sight, to contradict itself. Therefore, whether we like it or not, we sometimes had to recede from the literal meaning, and had to adjust its meaning to an interpretation. Finally, it has been plainly shown how many unreasonable, not to say absurd things follow, if we eliminate the freedom of the will. It has been made plain that the opinion, as I have been elucidating it, when accepted, does not eliminate the pious and Christian things Luther argues for—concerning the highest love of God; the rejection of exclusive faith in merits, works and our strength; the complete trust in God according to his promises. Hence, I want the reader to consider whether he thinks it is fair to condemn the opinion offered by the Church Fathers, approved for so many centuries by so many people, and to accept some paradoxes which are at present disturbing the Christian world. If the latter are true, I admit freely to my mental sloth and inability to grasp. I know for certain that I am not resisting the truth, that I love from the bottom of my heart true evangelical liberty, and that I detest everything adverse to the Gospels. Thus I am here not as a judge, as I said at the outset, but as a disputer. Nevertheless, I can truly affirm that I have served religiously in this debate, as was demanded once upon a time of judges trying matters of life and death. Though I am an old man, I'm neither ashamed nor irked to be taught by a younger if he teaches with evangelical gentleness more evident truths.

Here some will say: Erasmus should learn about Christ and disregard human prudence. This nobody understands, unless he has the Spirit of God.

Now, if I do not yet understand what Christ is, certainly we must have gone far astray from our topic and goal, though I should love nothing more than to learn which Spirit so many doctors and Christian people possessed—because it seems probable that the people believed what their bishops have already taught for thirteen centuries—who did not understand this.

I have come to the end. It is for others to judge.

The Enslaved Will / Luther

Introduction

To the Venerable Master Erasmus of Rotterdam, Martin Luther wishes Grace and Peace in Christ.

That I have been so long in answering your Diatribe on the free will,

From *Discourse on Free Will*, translated by Ernst F. Winter. Copyright, 1961, by Frederick Ungar Publishing Co., Inc. Reprinted by permission of the publishers.

venerable Erasmus, has happened against the expectation of all and
against my usual wont, because thus far I have not only gladly embraced
such opportunities for writing, but have also freely searched for them.
. . . I concede to you openly, a thing I have never done before, that you
not only surpass me by far in literary prowess and intellectuality (which
we all grant to you as your due, and the more so, since I am a barbarian
occupied with the barbarous), but that you have in two ways also damp-
ened my spirits and impetuousness, and slackened my strength before
the battle began. First, because artfully you debate this matter with
wonderful and continuous restraint, preventing thereby my becoming
angry with you. Second, because by chance or fortune or fate you say
nothing on so great a subject which has not already been stated before,
and you say even less, and attribute more to free will than the Sophists[1]
hitherto did (I shall speak more of this later), so that it seemed quite
superfluous to answer your invalid arguments.

. . . If I do answer, it is because faithful brethren in Christ press me
to it. . . . And who knows but that God may even condescend to visit
you, dearest Erasmus, through me, His poor weak vessel, and that I
may (which from my heart I desire of the Father of mercies through
Jesus Christ our Lord) come to you in this book in a happy hour and
gain a dearest brother. For although you write wrongly concerning free
will, I owe you no small thanks, because you have confirmed my own
view. Seeing the case for free will argued with such great talents, yet
leaving it worse than it was before, is an evident proof that free will
is a downright lie. It is like the woman of the gospel: the more the physicians treat her case, the worse it gets.[2]

Therefore I shall be even more grateful if you gain greater certainty
through me, just as I have gained in assurance through you. But both
are the gift of the Spirit, and not the work of our own endeavors. So
we should pray to God that He will open my mouth, and your and all
men's hearts: that He may be the teacher in the midst of us, who may in
us speak and hear.

My friend Erasmus, may I ask you to suffer my lack of eloquence,
as I in return will bear with your ignorance in these matters. God does
not give everything to each and we cannot all do everything. As Paul
says, "Now there are varieties of gifts, but the same Spirit" (1 Corinthians 12,4). It remains, therefore, that these gifts render a mutual
service. One with his gift bear the burden of the other's lack. Thus we
shall fulfill the law of Christ.

Refutation of Erasmus' Preface

(ERASMUS 4) *Clarity of Scriptures*

. . . I hope you credit Luther with some acquaintance with and judgment in the sacred writings. If not, beware and I'll wring the admission
from you! This is the distinction which I make (for I too am going to

---

[1]Luther means the scholastics, whose theology he condemns as sophistry.
[2]Cf. Luke 8:43 and Mark 5:26.

act a little the rhetorician and logician): God and the Scriptures are two things, just like God and creation are two things. Nobody doubts that in God many things are hidden of which we know nothing. . . . But that there are in Scriputes some things abstruse and not quite plain, was spread by the godless Sophists, whom you echo, Erasmus. They have never yet produced one article to prove this their madness. Satan has frightened men from reading the sacred writings, and has rendered Holy Scriptures contemptible, so as to ensure his poisonous philosophy to prevail in the church. I admit that many passages in Scriptures are obscure and abstruse. But that is due to our ignorance of certain terms and grammatical particulars, and not to the majesty of the subject. This ignorance does not in any way prevent our knowing all the contents of Scriptures. What things can Scriptures still be concealing, now that the seals are broken, the stone rolled from the door of the sepulchre, and that greatest of all mysteries brought to light: Christ became man; God is Trinity and Unity; Christ suffered for us and will reign forever? Are not these things known and proclaimed even in our streets? Take Christ out of Scriptures and what will you find remaining in them? All the things contained in the Scriptures, therefore, are made manifest (even though some passages containing unknown words are yet obscure). But it is absurd and impious to say that things are obscure, because of a few obscure words, when you know the contents of Scriptures being set in the clearest light. And if the words are obscure in one place, yet they are clear in another. . . .

(ERASMUS 5 & 6) *The Crucial Issue: Knowing Free Will*

. . . You draft for us a list of those things which you consider sufficient for Christian piety. Any Jew or Gentile utterly ignorant of Christ could easily draw up the same, because you do not mention Christ in a single letter. As though you thought that Christian piety is possible without Christ, if God be but worshipped with one's whole heart as being a "naturally most benign God." What shall I say here, Erasmus? You ooze Lucian[3] from every pore; you swill Epicurus by the gallons. If you consider this subject not necessary to Christians, I ask you to withdraw from the debate. We have no common ground. I consider it vital.

If, as you say, it be irreligious, curious, superfluous to know whether God's foreknowledge is contingent; whether our will can contribute anything pertinent to our eternal salvation, or whether it simply endures operative grace; whether everything we do, good or evil, is done out of mere necessity, or whether we are rather enduring, what then, I ask, is religious, serious and useful knowledge? This is weak stuff, Erasmus. *Das ist zu viel!*[4]

It is difficult to attribute this to your ignorance, because you are now old, you have lived among Christians and you have long been studying the sacred writings. You leave me no room for excusing or thinking

---

[3]Lucian was a second-century A.D. Greek prose writer famous for his wit and vigorous satire. He ridiculed not only the Christian religion but also ancient mythology and certain philosophers.

[4]"That's too much!" Luther's lapse into German in the midst of his Latin is a sign of his irritation with Erasmus.

well of you. And yet the Papists pardon and put up with these outrageous statements, because you are writing against Luther. Without
a Luther in the case, they would tear you apart. Here I must speak like
Aristotle when arguing with his master Plato: Plato is my friend, but
truth must be honored above all. Granted you have but little understanding of Scripture and Christian piety, surely even an enemy of
Christians ought to know what Christians do, consider useful and necessary. But you, a theologian and teacher of Christianity, wanting to write
an outline guide for Christianity, forget your own sceptical way. Otherwise you would vacillate as to what is profitable and necessary for Christians. In fact, you defy your own principles and make an unheard of
assertion that here is something nonessential. If it is really unessential,
and not surely known, then neither God, Christ, the gospel, faith nor
anything else even of Judaism, let alone Christianity, is left. In the
name of the immortal God, Erasmus, how wide a window, how big a
field are you opening up for attack against you.

. . . The essence of Christianity which you describe . . . is without
Christ, without the Spirit, and chillier than ice. . . . You plainly assert
that the will is effective in things pertaining to eternal salvation, when
you speak of its striving. And again you assert that it is passive, when
saying that without the mercy of God it is ineffective. But you fail to
define the limits within which we should think of the will as acting and
as being acted upon. Thus you keep us in ignorance as to how far the
mercy of God extends, and how far our own will extends; what man's
will and God's mercy really *do* effect. That prudence of yours carries
you along. You side with neither party and escape safely through Scylla
and Charybdis, in order that coming into open sea, overwhelmed and
confounded by the waves, you can then assert all that you now deny,
and deny all that you now assert! . . .

. . . It is not irreligious, curious or superfluous, but extremely wholesome and necessary for a Christian to know whether or not his will has
anything to do in matters pertaining to salvation. This, let me tell you,
is the very hinge upon which our disputation turns. It is the crucial
issue between you and me. It is our aim to inquire what free will can
do, in what it is passive, and how it is related to the grace of God. If
we know nothing of these things, we shall know nothing whatsoever
of Christianity, and shall be worse off than all the heathens. Whoever
does not understand this, let him confess that he is not a Christian.
But he who derides and ridicules it, should know that he is the greatest
foe of Christians. . . . It is necessary to distinguish most clearly between
the power of God and our own, between God's works and ours, if we
are to live a godly life.

Foreknowledge of God

. . . In this book, therefore, I shall harry you and all the Sophists
until you shall define for me the power of free will. And I hope so to
harry you (Christ helping me) as to make you heartily repent ever having
published your Diatribe. It is then essentially necessary and wholesome for Christians to know that God foreknows nothing contingently,

but that he foresees, purposes and does all things according to His immutable, eternal and infallible will. This thunderbolt throws free will flat and utterly dashes it to pieces. Those who want to assert it must either deny this thunderbolt or pretend not to see it. . . .

(ERASMUS 7) *The Christian's Peace*

. . . You make it clear that this peace and tranquility of the flesh are to you far more important than faith, conscience, salvation, the word of God, the glory of Christ and God himself. Therefore, let me tell you, and I beg you to let it sink deep into your mind, I am concerned with a serious, vital and eternal verity, yes such a fundamental one, that it ought to be maintained and defended at the cost of life itself, and even though the whole world should not only be thrown into turmoil and fighting, but shattered in chaos and reduced to nothing. If you don't grasp this, or if you are not moved by this, then mind your own business, and leave us to whom God has given it to grasp and to be affected by it. . . .

Christian Liberty

. . . The doctrine that confession and satisfaction ought to be free, you either deny, or you do not know that there exists a word of God. I for my part know for sure that there is a word of God which asserts Christian liberty, in order that we may not be ensnared into bondage by human traditions and human laws. . . . The prince of this world does not allow that the laws of the Popes and his bishops be kept in liberty. His intention is to entangle and bind consciences. This the true God will not bear. Therefore, the word of God and the traditions of men oppose each other in irreconcilable discord. . . .

And as to your fear that many depraved persons will abuse this liberty, this must be considered among those turmoils, as part of that temporal leprosy which we must bear, and the evil we must endure. . . . You are ridiculous enough to misquote Paul. But Paul does not speak of teaching or of teaching doctrinal truth, as you confound his words and twist their meaning to please you. On the contrary, he would have the truth spoken everywhere, at all times, and in every way. He is even delighted when Christ is preached out of envy and hatred, and plainly says so. "Provided only that in every way, whether in pretense or in truth, Christ is being proclaimed". . . . Truth and doctrine should always be preached openly and firmly, without compromise or concealment. . . .

. . . If we ask you to determine for us when, to whom, and how truth is to be spoken, could you give an answer? . . . Perhaps you have in mind to teach the truth so that the Pope does not object, Caesar is not enraged, bishops and princes are not upset, and furthermore no uproar and turmoil are caused in the wide world, lest many be offended and grow worse? . . . His Gospel which all need should not be confined to any place or time. It should be preached to all men, at all times and in all places. I have already proved above that what is written in Scriptures is plain to all, and is wholesome, and must be proclaimed abroad. . . .

With the same prudence you advise that wrong decisions made in councils should not be openly acknowledged, lest ground for denying the authority of the fathers be thus afforded. This is indeed just what the Pope wanted you to say! And he hears it with greater pleasure than the Gospel itself. He will be most ungrateful, if he does not honor you in return with a cardinal's cap, together with all the revenues belonging to it. . . . I must tell you again: men's ordinances cannot be observed together with the word of God, because the former bind consciences and the latter looses them. . . . The authority of the Fathers is therefore nothing . . . for Christ is a higher authority.

Spontaneity of Necessitated Acts

You say: Who will endeavor to reform his life? I answer: Nobody! No man can! God has no time for your self-reformers, for they are hypocrites. The elect who fear God will be reformed by the Holy Spirit. The rest will perish unreformed. Note how Augustine does not say that the works of none or of all are crowned, but that the works of some are. "Therefore there will be some who reform their lives."

You say, by our doctrine a floodgate of iniquity is opened. Be it so. Ungodly men are part of that evil leprosy spoken of before. Nevertheless, these are the same doctrines which throw open to the elect, who fear God, a gateway to righteousness, an entrance into heaven, a way unto God. . . . These truths are published for the sake of the elect, that they may be humbled and brought down to nothing and so be saved. The rest resist this humiliation. They condemn the teaching of self-desperation. They wish to have left a little something that they may do themselves. Secretly they continue proud, and enemies of the grace of God.

. . . As to the other paradox you mention, that whatever is done by us, is not done by free will, but of mere necessity, let us briefly consider it, lest we should let such a pernicious remark go unchallenged. I observe: if it be proved that our salvation is not of our own strength or counsel, but depends on the working of God alone (which I hope I shall clearly prove later in the main discussion), does it not evidently follow that when God is not present to work in us, everything we do is evil, and that we of necessity act in a way not availing unto our salvation? For if it is not we ourselves, but God only, who works salvation in us, it follows that nothing we do before His working in us avails unto salvation. By necessity I do not mean compulsion. I meant what they term the necessity of immutability. That is to say, a man void of the Spirit of God does not do evil against his will, under pressure, as though taken by the neck and forced into it, . . . but he does it spontaneously and willingly. And this willingness and desire of doing evil he cannot, by his own strength, eliminate, restrain or change. He goes on still desiring and craving to do evil. And if external pressure compels him to act outwardly to the contrary, yet the will within remains averse and chafes under such constraint. But it would not thus rise in indignation, if it were changed, and made willing to yield to a constraining power. This is what we mean by the necessity of immutability: that the will cannot change itself, nor give itself another bent, but, rather, the more it is resisted, the more it is irritated to crave, as its indignation proves. This would not be the case if it were free or had a free will. . . .

. . . On the other hand, when God works in us, the will is changed under the sweet influence of the Spirit of God. It desires and acts not from compulsion, but responsively of its own desire and inclination. It cannot be altered by any opposition. It cannot be compelled or overcome even by the gates of hell. It still goes on to desire, crave after and love that which is good, just as once it desired, craved after and loved evil. . . . Thus the human will is like a beast of burden. If God rides it, it wills and goes whence God wills; as the Psalm says, "I was as a beast of burden before thee" (Psalm 72,22). If Satan rides, it wills and goes where Satan wills. Nor may it choose to which rider it will run, nor which it will seek. But the riders themselves contend who shall have and hold it.

Grace and Free Will

. . . And now, what if I prove from your own words, in which you assert the freedom of the will, that there is no such thing as free will at all? What, if I should show that you unwittingly deny what you labor with so much sagacity to affirm? If I fail here, I promise to revoke all that I wrote against you in this book; and all that your Diatribe advances against me shall be confirmed!

You make the power of free will small and utterly ineffective apart from the grace of God. Acknowledged? Now then, I ask you: If God's grace is wanting, or if it be taken away from that certain small degree of power, what can it do for itself? You say it is ineffective and can do nothing good. Therefore it will not do what God or His grace wills. And why? Because we have now taken God's grace away from it, and what the grace of God does not do is not good. Hence it follows that free will without the grace of God is not free at all, but is the permanent bondslave and servant of evil, since it cannot turn itself unto good. This being determined, I allow you to enlarge the power of free will as much as you like, make it angelic, divine, if you can. But once you add this doleful postscript, that it is ineffective apart from God's grace, you at once rob it of all its power. What is ineffective power, but plainly no power at all. Therefore, to say that free will exists and has power, though ineffective, is, what the Sophists call a contradiction in terms. It is like saying, free will is something which is not free.

. . . But, if we do not want to drop this term altogether (which would be the safest and most Christian thing to do), we may still use it in good faith denoting free will in respect not of what is above him, but of what is below him. This is to say, man should know in regard to his goods and possessions the right to use them, to do or to leave undone, according to his free will. Although at the same time, that same free will is overruled by the free will of God alone, just as He pleases. However, with regard to God, and in all things pertaining to salvation or damnation, man has no free will, but is a captive, servant and bondslave, either to the will of God, or to the will of Satan. . . .

Refutation of Erasmus' Introduction

(ERASMUS 8) *Denying Church Fathers' Authority*

... At the beginning of our disputation proper you promised to argue according to the canonical books, "since Luther recognizes no extra-canonical authority." Very well! I welcome your promise. . . . You tell us that you are much influenced by so great a number of the most learned men. . . . Biblical scholars, holy martyrs, many renowned for miracles, together with the more recent theologians, many schools, councils, bishops and popes. In a word, on your side, you say, is learning, ability, numbers, greatness, courage, holiness, miracles, while on my side there are only Wycliffe and Lorenzo Valla. . . . But tell me this: was anyone of them made a saint, did anyone of them receive the Spirit or work miracles in the name of the free will, or by the power of the free will, or to confirm the free will? Far from it, you will say, but in the name and by the power of Jesus Christ were all those things done, and for the confirmation of the doctrine of Christ. . . . Wherefore your appeal to the holiness, the Spirit and the miracles of the Fathers is pointless. These do not prove the free will, but the doctrine of Jesus Christ which contradicts free will. . . . Those who assert the free will . . . in blindness and ignorance, pick that which the Fathers, stumbling in the weakness of their flesh have said in favor of free will, and oppose it to that which the same Fathers, in the power of the Spirit, have elsewhere said against free will. . . .

(ERASMUS 9–12) *Invisible Church and Clarity of Scriptures*

... The Creed which we all hold runs thus, "I believe in the holy catholic Church". . . . Show me under the kingdom of the Pope one single bishop discharging his office. Show me a single council at which they dealt with matters of religion, and not with gowns, dignities, revenues and other profanities, which only the mad could consider pertaining to the Holy Spirit! Nevertheless they are called the Church. . . . And yet even under them Christ has preserved His Church, though it is not called the church. How many saints do you imagine the inquisition having burned and killed, such as John Hus?[5] No doubt, many holy men of the same spirit lived in those times.

Why don't you rather marvel at this, Erasmus, that in general there were, from the beginning of time, superior talents, greater learning, a more ardent pursuit among pagans than among Christians and the people of God? As Christ Himself declares, "The children of this world . . . are more prudent than the children of light" (Luke 16,8). . . . Therefore, what shall we do? The Church is hidden, the saints are unknown. What and whom shall we believe? . . . Scriptures, because they are called a way and a path, doubtless because of their perfect certainty. . . . Wherefore, if the doctrine of free will is obscure and ambiguous it is no con-

---

[5]Bohemian religious reformer burned at the stake as a heretic (1369?–1415). He wrote against the abuses of the clergy and the supremacy of the pope in matters of faith, relying on the Scriptures as the sole guide to truth.

cern of Christians and the Scriptures, and should therefore be left alone. . . . But if it does concern Christians and Scriptures, it ought to be clear, open and manifest, just like all the other articles of faith which are quite evident. For all the articles held by Christians should be most evident to themselves and also supported against adversaries by such plain and manifest scriptures as to stop all their mouths, so that they can make no reply. . . . But why need enlarge? Why not conclude the discussion with this your Introduction and give my verdict against you in your own words, according to Christ's saying, "by thy words thou wilt be justified, and by thy words thou wilt be condemned"? (Matthew 12,37). For you say that Scriptures are not clear upon this point. And then suspending all judgment, you discuss throughout your book only the pros and cons on each side! That's why you wish to call it a Diatribe, i.e., discussion, rather than an Apophasis, i.e., denial. . . .

Refutation of Erasmus' Old and New Testament Proofs Supporting the Free Will

(ERASMUS 13) *Refuting Erasmus' Definition of Free Will*

Let us first of all, as is proper, begin with your definition of free will: "Under free will we understand in this connection the ability of the human will whereby man can turn toward or turn away from that which leads unto eternal salvation."

Shrewdly you have stated a bare definition, without explaining any of its parts (as others do). Perhaps you feared more shipwrecks than one. I am therefore forced to investigate the several parts myself. Upon closer examination the thing defined is undoubtedly of a greater extent than the definition. The Sophists call such a definition vicious, i.e., when a definition fails to cover fully the thing defined. For I have shown above that free will belongs to none but God alone. You are perhaps right in assigning to man a will of some sort, but to credit him with free will in the things of God is going too far. For the term free will means in its proper sense for everybody a will that can and does do God-ward whatever it pleases, restrained by no law and no command. . . . Here then at the outset, the definition of the term and the definition of the thing are at odds. The term signifies one thing and what is really meant is another. . . .

(ERASMUS 17–21) *Erasmus' Three Views on Free Will*

Then you invent a fourfold grace, so as to assign a sort of faith and charity even to the philosophers. And with this you also invent a three-fold law, of nature, of works, and of faith, so as to assert boldly that the precepts of the philosophers agree with the precepts of the gospel. . . . Out of one opinion concerning free will you make three. The first opinion, of those who deny that man can will good without special grace, who deny that it can make progress, perfect, etc., seems to you severe, though very probable. And this you approve, because it leaves to man desire and effort, but does not leave anything that he may ascribe to his own power. The second opinion, of those who contend that free will avails for nothing but sinning and that grace alone works good in us, etc., seems to you more severe still. And the third opinion, of those who say that free will is an empty phrase, and God works in us both good and evil, and all that comes to pass is of mere necessity, seems to you most severe. You profess to be writing against those last two.

Do you know what you are saying, friend Erasmus? You are here presenting three opinions, as if belonging to three different sects, simply because you fail to realize that it is the same subject, stated by us, spokesmen of the same party, only in different ways and words. Let me show you your carelessness and sleepy stupidity of your own judgment.

I ask you, how does your previous definition of free will square with this first opinion which you confess to be very probable? For you said that free will is a power of the human will by which a man can turn towards good, whereas here you say approvingly that man without grace cannot will good. The definition affirms what its example denies. Hence there are found in your free will a yes and a no. In one and the same doctrine and article in the same breath you approve and condemn us; approve and condemn yourself. Do you believe that to apply itself to what pertains unto eternal salvation, a power your definition assigns to free will, is not good? If there is so much good in free will that it could apply itself unto good, it would have no need of grace. Therefore, the free will which you define is one, and the free will you defend is another. . . .

. . . But perhaps this is the dream of the Diatribe that between these two, the "ability to will good" and the "inability to will good," there may be a middle ground, i.e., to will is absolute, without respect to good and evil. So that by a logical subtlety we may steer clear of the rocks and say that in the will of man there is a certain willing which indeed cannot will good without grace, but which nevertheless does not forthwith will only evil. It is a sort of mere abstract willing, pure and simple, either upward unto God by grace, or downwards unto evil by sin. But then what becomes of your statement that when it has lost its liberty it is compelled to serve sin? Where then is that desire and effort that you left it? Where is its power to apply itself to that which pertains to eternal salvation? For that power of applying itself unto salvation cannot be a mere willing, unless the salvation itself is said to be nothing. Nor again can that desire and endeavor be a mere willing, because desire must strive and aim for something (such as good), and cannot go forth into nothing, nor be absolutely inactive. In a word, wherever the Diatribe turns, it cannot keep clear of inconsistencies and contradictory assertions, nor avoid making that very free will which it defends, as much a prisoner as it is itself. In attempting to free the will it gets so entangled that it ends up bound together with free will in bonds indissoluble!

(ERASMUS 14–16, 22–23) *Erasmus' Confusion in Scriptural Proofs*

.   .   .

. . . The New Testament proper consists of promises and exhortations, just as the Old Testament proper consists of laws and threats. In the

New Testament the gospel is preached. This is nothing else than the word that offers the Spirit and grace for the remission of sins, obtained for us by Christ crucified. It is entirely free, given through the mere mercy of God the Father, thus favoring us unworthy creatures who deserve damnation rather than anything else. After this follow exhortations. They are intended to animate those who are already justified and have obtained mercy to be diligent in the fruits of the Spirit and of the righteousness given them, to exercise themselves in love and good works, and to bear courageously the cross and all the other tribulations of this world. This is the whole sum of the New Testament. But how little Erasmus understands of this matter is manifest in not knowing how to distinguish between the Old and the New Testaments. For he sees nothing anywhere but laws and precepts by which men may be formed in good manners. But what the rebirth, renewal, regeneration and the whole work of the Spirit are, he does not see. . . .

Comments on Erasmus' Treatment of Passages Denying Free Will

(ERASMUS 33–37) *Foreknowledge and Necessity*

. . . Let the Diatribe invent and go on inventing, let it cavil and cavil again, if God foreknew that Judas would be a traitor, Judas became a traitor of necessity, and it was not in the power of Judas, nor of any creature, to alter it, or change his will from that which God had foreseen. . . . If God be not deceived in that which he foreknows, then that which He foreknows must of necessity come to pass. Otherwise, who could believe His promises, who would fear His threatenings, if what He promised or threatened did not necessarily ensue? How could He promise or threaten, if His foreknowledge deceives Him or can be hindered by our mutability? This supremely clear light of certain truth manifestly stops all mouths, puts an end to all questions, gives forever victory over all evasive subtleties. . . .

. . . Of course, this seems to give the greatest offense to common sense or natural reason, that God, who is proclaimed as being so full of mercy and goodness, should of His own mere will abandon, harden and damn men, as though delighted in the sins and great eternal torments of the miserable. It seems iniquitous, cruel, intolerable to think thus of God. It has given offense to so many and many great men down the ages. And who would not be offended? I myself have been offended at it more than once, even unto the deepest abyss of despair, so far that I wished I had never been made a man. That was before I knew how healthgiving that despair was and how near it was to grace. This is why so much toil and labor has been devoted to excusing the goodness of God, and to accusing the will of man. Here those distinctions have been invented between the ordinary will of God and the absolute will of God, between the necessity of consequence and the necessity of the thing consequent, and many others. But nothing has been achieved by these means beyond imposing upon the unlearned, by vain words and by "the contradictions of so-called knowledge." For after all, a conscious conviction has been left deeply rooted in the hearts of learned and un-learned alike, whenever they have made a serious approach to this matter, so that they are aware that, if the foreknowledge and omnipotence of God are admitted, we must be under necessity. . . .

Luther's Conclusion

. . . I will not accept or tolerate that moderate middle way which Erasmus would, with good intention, I think, recommend to me: to allow a certain little to free will, in order to remove the contradictions of Scripture. . . . The case is not bettered, nor anything gained by this middle way. Because, unless you attribute all and everything to free will, as the Pelagians do, the contradictions in Scripture still remain, merit and reward, the mercy and justice of God are abolished, and all the difficulties which we try to avoid by allowing this certain little ineffective power to free will, remain just as they were before. Therefore, we must go to extremes, deny free will altogether and ascribe everything to God!

Summary on the Enslaved Will

We are now coming to the last part of this book, in which, as I promised, I am bringing forward my own resources against free will. Not that I shall produce them all, for who could do that within the limits of this small book, when the whole Scriptures, in every letter and iota, stand on my side? There is no need, because free will lies vanquished and prostrate already. . . .

Doctrine of Salvation by Faith in Christ Disproves Free Will

. . . Paul now proclaims with full confidence and authority: "But now the righteousness of God has been made manifest independently of the Law, being attested by the Law and the Prophets; the righteousness of God through faith in Jesus Christ upon all who believe. For there is no distinction, as all have sinned and have need of the glory of God. They are justified freely by his grace through the redemption which is in Christ Jesus, whom God has set forth as a propitiation by his blood through faith, etc." (Romans 3,21-25). Here Paul utters very thunder-bolts against free will. First, he says, the righteousness of God without the law is manifested. He distinguishes the righteousness of God from the righteousness of the Law, because the righteousness of faith comes by grace, without the law. This saying, "without the law" can mean nothing else, but that Christian righteousness exists without the works of the law; the works of the law availing and effecting nothing toward its attainment. As Paul says further on: "For we reckon that a man is justified by faith independently of the works of the law" (Romans 3,28). And earlier he has said: "For by the works of the law no human being shall be justified" (Romans 3,20). From all this it is clearly manifest that the endeavor and effect of free will are simply nothing. For if the righteousness of God exists without the law, and without the works of the law, how shall it not much more exist without free will? The supreme concern of free will is to exercise itself in moral righteousness, or the works of that law by which its blindness and impotency derive their assistance. But this word "without" abolishes all morally good works, all moral righteousness and all preparations for grace. Scrape together every power you can think of as belonging to free will and Paul will still stand invincible saying, the righteousness of God exists without it! And though I should grant that free will by its endeavors can advance in some direction, namely, unto good works, or unto the righteousness of the civil or moral law, it does yet not advance towards God's righteousness, nor does God in any respect allow its devoted efforts to be worthy unto gaining His righteousness; for He says that His righteousness stands without the law. . . .

Personal Comfort in the Doctrine of Bondage

. . . As for myself, I frankly confess, that I should not want free will to be given me, even if it could be, nor anything else be left in my own hands to enable me to strive after my salvation. And that, not merely, because in the face of so many dangers, adversities and onslaughts of devils, I could not stand my ground and hold fast my free will—for one devil is stronger than all men, and on these terms no man could be saved—but because, even though there were no dangers, adversities or devils, I should still be forced to labor with no guarantee of success and to beat the air only. If I lived and worked to all eternity, my conscience would never reach comfortable certainty as to how much it must do to satisfy God. Whatever work it had done, there would still remain a scrupling as to whether or not it pleased God, or whether He required something more. The experience of all who seek righteousness by works proves that. I learned it by bitter experience over a period of many years. But now that God has put my salvation out of the control of my own will and put it under the control of His, and has promised to save me, not according to my effort or running, but . . . according to His own grace and mercy, I rest fully assured that He is faithful and will not lie to me, and that moreover He is great and powerful, so that no devils and no adversities can destroy Him or pluck me out of His hand. . . . I am certain that I please God, not by the merit of my works, but by reason of His merciful favor promised to me. So that, if I work too little or badly, He does not impute it to me, but, like a father, pardons me and makes me better. This is the glorying which all the saints have in their God!

Conclusion

I shall here end this book, though prepared, if necessary, to pursue this Discussion still further. . . . And now, my friend Erasmus, I entreat you for Christ's sake to keep your promise. You promised that you would willingly yield to him who taught better than yourself. . . . I confess that you are a great man, adorned with many of God's noblest gifts, with talent, learning and an almost miraculous eloquence, whereas I have and am nothing, except to glory in being a Christian.

Moreover, I give you hearty praise: alone, in contrast to all others, you have discussed the real thing, i.e., the essential point. You have not wearied me with those irrelevant points about the Papacy, purgatory, indulgences and such trifles. . . . For that I heartily thank you. . . .

However, if you cannot treat this issue differently from the way this Diatribe does, I pray you, remain content with your own gift and study, adorn and promote literature and the languages, as hitherto you have done to great advantage and with much credit. I confess that your studies have also helped me. For them I honor and sincerely respect you. But God has not willed yet, nor granted you to be equal to the subject matter of this debate. I entreat you, do not think me arrogant, when I pray that the Lord may speedily make you as much superior to me in these matters, as you are superior to me in all others. It is nothing new for God to instruct a Moses by a Jethro, or to teach a Paul by an Ananias. And as to what you say, "you have greatly missed the mark, if you are ignorant of Christ": I think you see yourself how matters stand. But not all will err, if you or I may err. God is glorified in a wonderful way in His saints! So that we may consider those being saints that are farthest from sanctity. Nor is it an unlikely thing that you, as being a man, should fail to understand aright, and to note with sufficient care, the Scriptures, or the sayings of the Fathers, under whose guidance you imagine you cannot miss the mark.

That you have failed is quite clear from this: "you assert nothing, but have made comparisons." One who is fully acquainted with the matter and understands it, does not write like that. On the contrary, in this book of mine, I have not made comparisons, but have asserted and still do assert. I wish none to become judges, but urge all men to submit!

May the Lord whose cause this is, enlighten you and make you a vessel of honor and glory. Amen.

The Praise of Folly / Erasmus

The Praise of Folly, published in 1511 while Erasmus sojourned in England, is an encomium, i.e., a kind of oration praising its subject which in the orthodox tradition of serious rhetoric is a person, living or dead. Erasmus' book, however, is a eulogy of an allegorical person, namely Folly, put into the mouth of Folly herself. As the painter Holbein saw her, she is a young woman, fresh and piquant, but wrapped in a scholar's gown and wearing a cap adorned with two long peaks shaped to suggest ass's ears and each ending in a bow—the bells of the jester. The figure of a fool or jester lends itself admirably to Erasmus' satire. Taken seriously by nobody, the jester is in a position to make serious and aggressive pronouncements with impunity. And, indeed, while Erasmus' satire cut deeply in more than one way, it immediately captivated literate Europe.

At first, Folly presents herself as a vital force of nature guarding man's happiness against the deadly assaults of a prying and spying intellect. Then, in a spirit of good-natured fun but perhaps also in the name of true piety, she lays bare the pretensions and the hypocrisies of the various learned professions, above all the clergy. It is just such tongue-lashings of ecclesiastic institutions and dignitaries as are found in *The Praise of Folly* that account for Erasmus' reputation as a forerunner of the Lutheran Reformation. Ultimately, Folly launches into a panegyric of the true Christian spirit, man's loftiest "folly," a kind of madness in which man's mind is possessed, as it were, by the divine.

A comprehensive irony informs the whole book, but its vitality stems primarily from the underlying tolerance with which Erasmus pleads, ever so obliquely, for an understanding of human nature, even its dark and irrational side. In this sense, Erasmus proves to be a humanist of the most generous sort, namely, one who loves humanity despite its follies.

Folly speaks:

1. However mortal folk may commonly speak of me (for I am not ignorant how ill the name of Folly sounds, even to the greatest fools), I am she—the only she, I may say—whose divine influence makes gods and men rejoice. One great and sufficient proof of this is that the instant I stepped up to speak to this crowded assembly, all faces at once brightened with a fresh and unwonted cheerfulness, all of you suddenly unbent your brows, and with frolic and affectionate smiles, you applauded; so that as I look upon all present about me, you seem flushed with nectar, like gods in Homer, not without some nepenthe, also; whereas a moment ago you were sitting moody and depressed, as if you had come out of the cave of Trophonius.[1]. . .

2. Nor do I have any use for those wiseacres who preach that it is most foolish and insolent for a person to praise himself. Yet let it be as foolish as they would have it, if only they will grant that it is proper: and what is more suitable than that Folly herself should be the trumpeter

---

From Desiderius Erasmus, *Praise of Folly,* translated by H. H. Hudson. Copyright, 1941, by Princeton University Press. Reprinted by permission of Princeton University Press.

[1]Greek demigod who had a famous oracle in a cavern at Lebadia, Boeotia. The ritual for consulting the oracle was so funereal that its suppliants left the cave morose and dejected.

of her praises? "She is her own flute-player." Who, indeed, could portray me better than can I myself? Unless it could so happen that I am better known to some one else than I am to myself. On the whole, however, I deem that what I am doing is much more decent than what a host of our best people, and scholars even, do continually. With a certain perverse modesty they are wont to convey instructions to some sycophantic speaker or prattling poet whom they have engaged at a fee; and then they hear back from him their praises, that is to say, some pure fiction. The blushing listener, meanwhile, spreads his plumes like a peacock, and bridles, while the brazen adulator searches among the gods to find a parallel for this good-for-nothing, and proposes him as the complete exemplar of all virtues—from which the man himself knows that he is farther away than twice infinity. . . .

3. . . . I do not feign one thing in my face while I hold something else in my heart. I am in all points so like myself that even those who specially arrogate to themselves the part and name of wise men cannot conceal me, though they walk about "like apes in scarlet or asses in lion-skins." Let them carry it as cunningly as you could ask, the protruding ears will somewhere betray the Midas.[2] An ungrateful class of men that, so help me! Although they are wholly of my party, in public they are so ashamed of my name that they toss it up at others as a great reproach! Wherefore, since in fact they are most foolish, and yet are eager to seem wise men and veritable Thaleses, shall we not with entire justice dub them *morosophers,* "foolosophers"?

5. . . . In the first place, what can be dearer or more precious than life? And the beginning and first principle of life is owed to whom else but me? Not the spear of "potent-fathered" Pallas,[3] not the shield of "cloud-compelling" Jove, procreates the children of men or multiplies their race. Even he, the father of gods and king of men, who shakes all heaven by a nod, is obliged to lay aside his three-pronged thunder and that Titanic aspect by which, when he pleases, he scares all the gods, and assume another character in the slavish manner of an actor, if he wishes to do what he never refrains from doing, that is to say, to beget children. Now the Stoics believe that they are next-door neighbors to gods. But give me a triple Stoic, or a quadruple one, or, if you will, a Stoic multiplied by six hundred; if for this purpose he will not put off his beard, the ensign of wisdom (though displayed also by goats), yet he will certainly lay by his gravity, smooth his brow, renounce his rock-bound principles, and for a few minutes toy and talk nonsense. In fine, the wise man must send for me, I repeat, if he ever wishes to become a father. And why not speak to you still more frankly, as is my fashion? I beg to inquire whether the head, whether the face, the breast, the hand, or the ear—all of them accounted honorable members —generates gods and men? I judge not; nay, rather that foolish, even silly, part which cannot be named without laughter, is the propagator

---

[2]In Greek mythology, the son of a goddess and a satyr, whose stupid blunders became proverbial. Apollo caused long ass ears to grow from his head when he disparaged the god's music

[3]The goddess Pallas Athena, who, according to one mytn, sprang full-grown and fully armed from Zeus' forehead.

of the human race. This is at last that sacred spring from which all things derive existence. . . .

Now tell me, what man, by heaven, could wish to stick his head into the halter of marriage if, as your wiseacres have the habit of doing, he first weighed with himself the inconveniences of wedded life? Or what woman would ever admit her husband to her person, if she had heard or thought about the dangerous pains of childbirth and the irksomeness of bringing up a child? But since you owe your existence to the marriage-bed, and marriage is owing to Anoia,[4] a servant of mine, you can see how vastly indebted you are to me! Then, too, would a woman who has gone through all this, wish to make a second venture, if the power and influence of my Lethe[5] did not attend her? And in spite of what Lucretius claims, Venus herself would not deny that without the addition of my presence her strength would be enfeebled and ineffectual. So it is that from this brisk and silly little game of mine come forth the haughty philosophers (to whose places those who are vulgarly called monks have now succeeded), and kings in their scarlet, pious priests, and triply most holy popes; also, finally, that assembly of the gods of the poets, so numerous that Olympus, spacious as it is, can hardly accommodate the crowd.

6. But let it be accounted a little thing that the seed-plot and source of existence are mine, if I do not show that whatever is profitable in any life is also of my giving. For what about it? Can life be called life at all if you take away pleasure? . . . You applaud! I knew that none of you is so wise—or rather so foolish—no, I prefer to say so wise—as to err on that point. Even the famous Stoics do not really scorn pleasure, but they studiously dissemble and attack it in public with a thousand reproaches, only to the end that, with other people scared off, they may enjoy it more liberally. But let them tell me, by Jove, what part of life is not sad, unpleasant, graceless, flat, and burdensome, unless you have pleasure added to it, that is, a seasoning of folly? As proof of this, there is extant that lovely tribute to me by Sophocles, who can never be sufficiently praised, "To know nothing affords the happiest life"; and he would be authority enough, but come, I will open the whole matter, step by step. . . .

9. . . . Good Lord, what divorces, or worse things, would not happen all over the place, were not the domestic association of man and woman propped up and fostered by flattery, by jesting, by pliableness, ignorance, dissimulation—satellites of mine, remember! Mercy me, how few marriages would come off, if the husband prudently inquired what tricks his seemingly coy and modest little lady had played long before the wedding! And still fewer, though entered upon, would last, did not most of the wife's doings escape her husband's knowledge, through his negligence or stupidity. But these blessings are owed to Folly. She brings it about that the wife pleases the husband, the husband pleases the wife, the household is tranquil, the alliance holds. A husband is laughed at, called cuckoo, cuckold, or what not, when he kisses away

---

[4]Greek for "mindlessness" or "madness."
[5]In Greek mythology, a goddess personifying oblivion.

the tears of his whorish wife; but how much happier thus to be deceived than to harass himself by an unresting jealousy and to spoil everything with distressing brawls.

In sum, no society, no union in life, could be either pleasant or lasting without me. A people does not for long tolerate its prince, or a master tolerate his servant, a handmaiden her mistress, a teacher his student, a friend his friend, a wife her husband, a landlord his tenant, a partner his partner, or a boarder his fellow-boarder, except as they mutually or by turns are mistaken, on occasion flatter, on occasion wisely wink, and otherwise soothe themselves with the sweetness of folly.

16. And now I seem to hear the philosophers disagreeing with me. But the true unhappiness, they say, is to be engrossed in folly, to err, to be deceived, not to know. Nay, this is to live as a man. Why they call it "unhappy" I cannot see. It is simply that men are born thus, trained thus, constituted thus; it is the common lot of all. Nothing can be called unhappy if it fulfils its own nature, unless you would conclude that a man ought to be pitied because he cannot fly about with the birds, and cannot run on four feet like the whole family of beasts, and is not armed with horns like a bull. But by the same token one will call the finest horse miserable because he has not learned grammar and does not eat cheese-cakes; one will call the bull unhappy because he is such a sorry wrestler. Hence, just as a horse ignorant of grammar is not miserable, a man who is a fool is not unhappy; the reason being that in each case the attribute is consistent with the nature.

But our logic-choppers have something else to urge. Knowledge of the sciences, they say, is peculiarly the attribute of man; using them as tools, he makes up in his powers for what nature withheld from him. As if this had the least semblance of truth—that nature, which expended so much exact care upon gnats, and upon herbs and flowers, should have fallen asleep over the making of man! So that he has need of sciences—which [Satan], that evil genius of the human race, excogitated for the hurt of man, and which are so far from furthering his happiness that they actually hinder it. To that end they were discovered, according to report, just as that wise king in Plato wittily proves with respect to the invention of letters. Thus the sciences crept in by stealth, along with other banes of human life, and from the very sources whence all evils flow—devils, let us say. Even the name you call them shows this, for "daemons" means "those who know."

The simple folk of the golden age flourished without any armament of sciences, being guided only by nature and instinct. For what need was there of grammar when all spoke the same language, and had no other aim in speaking but that some one else should understand? What use for dialectic, where there was no battle of opinions ranged in contradiction to each other? What room for rhetoric, when no man cared to make trouble for his neighbor? Wherein was the study of law called for, when folk had not learned the evil ways from which, we must admit, our good laws arose. Then, moreover, they had too much piety to search out, with a profane curiosity, the secrets of nature; to investigate the dimensions, motions, and influences of the stars, or the hidden causes of things; deeming it a sacrilege for mortal man to try to know more than is proper to his station. This madness of inquiring what may lie beyond the sky never entered their heads. But as the pristine simplicity of the golden age little by little slipped away, first the arts were discovered—by evil spirits, as I have told; but they were few in number and accepted by few people. Later on, the superstition of the Chaldeans and the frivolous curiosity of the Greeks added hundreds of them—mere vexations of the spirit, seeing that a single system of grammar will amply provide continuous torture through a long lifetime.

And yet among these disciplines the ones that approach nearest to common sense, that is, to folly, are held in highest esteem. Theologians are starved, naturalists find cold comfort, astrologers are mocked, and logicians are slighted. "The doctor alone is worth all the rest put together." Within the profession of medicine, furthermore, so far as any member is eminently unlearned, impudent, or careless, he is valued the more, even in the chambers of belted earls. For medicine, especially as now practised by many, is but a sub-division of the art of flattery, no less truly than is rhetoric. Lawyers have the next place after doctors, and I do not know but that they should have first place; with great unanimity the philosophers—not that I would say such a thing myself—are wont to ridicule the law as an ass. Yet great matters and little matters alike are settled by the arbitrament of these asses. They gather goodly freeholds with broad acres, while the theologian, after poring over chestfuls of the great corpus of divinity, gnaws on bitter beans, at the same time manfully waging war against lice and fleas. As those arts are more successful which have the greatest affinity with folly, so those people are by far the happiest who enjoy the privilege of avoiding all contact with the learned disciplines, and who follow nature as their only guide, since she is in no respect wanting, except as a mortal wishes to transgress the limits set for his status. Nature hates counterfeits; and that which is innocent of art gets along far the more prosperously. . . .

26. Of the same brand also are those who pursue fame by turning out books. All of them are highly indebted to me, but especially those who blacken paper with sheer triviality. For the ones who write learnedly for the verdict of a few scholars . . . seem to me more pitiable than happy, since they continuously torture themselves: they add, they alter, they blot something out, they put it back in, they do their work over, they recast it, they show it to friends, they keep it for nine years; yet they never satisfy themselves. At such a price they buy an empty reward, namely, praise—and that the praise of a handful. They buy it with such an expense of long hours, so much loss of that sweetest of all things, sleep, so much sweat, so many vexations. Add also the loss of health, the wreck of their good looks, weakness of eyes or even blindness, poverty, malice, denial of pleasures, premature old age, and early death— and if there are other things like these, add them. The scholar considers himself compensated for such ills when he wins the approbation of one or two other weak-eyed scholars. But my author is crazy in a far happier way, since without any prolonged thought he quickly puts in writing whatever has come into his head or chanced to his pen, even his dreams; and all this with little waste of paper, knowing that if the trifles he has written are trivial enough the greater numbers of readers—that is, the

fools and ignoramuses—will approve. Of what consequence is it to ignore the two or three scholars, even if they chance to read the work? Or what weight will the censure of a few learned men have, as against the great multitude of those who will shout acclaim? . . .

28. Perhaps it were better to pass over the theologians in silence, . . . that marvellously supercilious and irascible race. For they may attack me with six hundred arguments, in squadrons, and drive me to make a recantation; which if I refuse, they will straightway proclaim me an heretic. By this thunderbolt they are wont to terrify any toward whom they are ill-disposed. No other people are so loth to acknowledge my favors to them; yet the divines are bound to me by no ordinary obligations. They are happy in their self-love, and as if they already inhabited the third heaven they look down from a height on all other mortal men as on creatures that crawl on the ground, and they come near to pitying them. They are protected by a wall of scholastic definitions, arguments, corollaries, implicit and explicit propositions; they have so many hideaways that they could not be caught even by the net of Vulcan;[6] for they slip out on their distinctions, by which also they cut through all knots as easily as with a double-bitted axe from Tenedos; and they abound with newly-invented terms and prodigious vocables. Furthermore, they explain as pleases them the most arcane matters, such as by what method the world was founded and set in order, through what conduits original sin has been passed down along the generations, by what means, in what measure, and how long the perfect Christ was in the Virgin's womb, and how accidents subsist in the Eucharist without their subject.

But those are hackneyed. Here are questions worthy of the great and (as some call them) illuminated theologians, questions to make them prick up their ears—if ever they chance upon them. Whether divine generation took place at a particular time? Whether there are several sonships in Christ? Whether this is a possible proposition: God the Father hates the Son? Whether God could have taken upon Himself the likeness of a Woman? Or of a devil? Of an ass? Of a gourd? Of a piece of flint? Then how would that gourd have preached, performed miracles, or been crucified? Also, what would Peter have consecrated if he had administered the sacrament while Christ's body hung upon the Cross? Also whether at that moment Christ could be said to be a man? And whether after the resurrection it will be forbidden to eat and drink? (Now, while there is time, they are providing against hunger and thirst!) These finespun trifles are numberless, with others even more subtle, having to do with instants of time, notions, relations, accidents, quiddities, entities, which no one can perceive with his eyes unless, like Lynceus,[7] he can see in blackest darkness things that are not there.

We must put in also those hard sayings, contradictions indeed, compared to which the Stoic maxims which were called paradoxes seem the merest simplicity. For instance: it is less of a crime to cut the throats of a thousand men than to set a stitch on a poor man's shoe on the Lord's

---

[6]Roman god of fire and master craftsman, the same as the Greek Hephaestus. In the *Odyssey,* he threw a net over Ares and Aphrodite while they were engaged in an amorous embrace.

[7]In Greek mythology, one of the Argonauts whose sight was so keen that he could see through the bole of a tree.

day; it is better to choose that the universe should perish, body, boots, and breeches (as the saying is), than that one should tell a single lie, however inconsequential. The methods our scholastics pursue only render more subtle these subtlest of subtleties; for you will escape from a labyrinth more quickly than from the tangles of Realists, Nominalists, Thomists, Albertists, Occamists, Scotists[8]—I have not named all, but the chief ones only. But in all these sects there is so much learning and so much difficulty that I should think the apostles themselves must needs have the help of some other spirit if they were to try disputing on these topics with our new generation of theologues.

Paul could exhibit faith; but when he said, "Faith is the substance of things hoped for, the evidence of things not seen," he did not define it doctorally. The same apostle, though he exemplified charity supremely well, divided and defined it with very little logical skill in his first epistle to the Corinthians, Chapter 13. And no doubt the apostles consecrated the Eucharist devoutly enough; but suppose you had questioned them about . . . transubstantiation—how the body is in many places at once, the difference between the body of Christ when in heaven, when on the Cross, when in the sacrament of the Eucharist, about the point when transubstantiation occurs (seeing that the prayer effecting it is a discrete quantity having extension in time)—they would not have answered with the same acuteness, I suggest, with which the sons of Scotus distinguish and define these matters. The apostles knew the mother of Jesus, but who among them has demonstrated philosophically just how she was kept clear from the sin of Adam, as our theologians have done? Peter received the keys, received them from One who did not commit them to an unworthy person, and yet I doubt that he ever understood—for Peter never did attain to subtlety—that a person who did not have knowledge could have the key to knowledge. They went about baptizing everywhere, and yet they never taught what is the formal, the material, the efficient, and the final cause of baptism, nor is mention made by them that it has both a delible character and an indelible one. They worshipped, to be sure, but in spirit, following no other teaching than that of the Gospel, "God is a spirit, and they that worship Him must worship Him in spirit and in truth." It seems never to have been revealed to them that a picture drawn with charcoal on a wall ought to be worshipped with the same worship as Christ himself—at least if it is drawn with two fingers outstretched and the hair unshorn, and has three sets of rays in the nimbus fastened to the back of the head. For who would comprehend these things if he had not consumed all of thirty-six years upon the physics and metaphysics of Aristotle and the Scotists?[9]

In similar wise, the apostles preach grace, and yet they never determined what the difference is between grace freely given and grace that makes one deserving. They urge us to good works, but do not separate work, work working, and work that has been worked. At all times they

---

[8]Various schools of scholastic philosophy.

[9]The followers of John Duns Scotus (1266?–1308), a scholastic philosopher called "the subtle doctor." For a long time, Scotism was a formidable rival of Thomism.

inculcate charity, but do not distinguish charity which is infused from that which is acquired, or explain whether charity is an accident or a substance, created or uncreated. They abhor sin, but may I be shot if they could define scientifically what it is we call sin, unless they had the luck to be instructed by the spirit of the Scotists.

You can never make me believe that Paul, by whose learning you can judge that of the others, would so often have condemned questions, disputes, genealogies, and what he called "strifes of words," if he had really been a master of those subtleties, especially in view of the fact that all the controversies of that time were mere little backwoods debates, quite without art, when put into comparison with the . . . subtleties of Our Masters. And yet these masters are as modest as can be; for if by chance something was written by the apostles carelessly or not quite doctorally, they do not damn it out of hand, but give it a proper interpretation. Thus much honor they pay, partly to the antiquity of the passage and partly to the apostolic authority. And dear me, it would be almost unjust to look for very scholarly things from the apostles, for they heard no word about them from their Master. . . .

29. . . . Furthermore, they draw exact pictures of every part of hell as if they had spent many years in that commonwealth. They also fabricate new heavenly spheres as fancy dictates, adding the biggest of all and the finest—for there must be a suitable place for the souls of the blessed to take their walks in, to entertain at dinner, or even to play a game of ball. Their heads are so stuffed and stretched with these and two thousand other whim-whams of the same sort that I am sure Jupiter's cerebrum was not any more gravid when he yelled for Vulcan's help to bring forth Pallas.[10] Wherefore do not be astonished when you see at a public disputation the head of one of them all bound round with swathes, for otherwise it would certainly fly to pieces. I often get a good laugh myself when these theologians that loom up so vast in their own eyes begin speaking in their slovenly and barbarous idiom and jabber so that no one except a jabberer can understand them, reaching a pitch—"highest acumen" they call it—whereto the vulgar cannot climb. For they affirm that it suits not with the dignity of sacred discourse to be forced to obey the rules of grammarians. O marvellous prerogative of theologians, if to speak incorrectly is reserved to them alone! . . .

30. Coming nearest to these in felicity are the men who generally call themselves "the religious" and "monks"—utterly false names both, since most of them keep as far away as they can from religion and no people are more in evidence in every sort of place. But I do not see how anything could be more dismal than these monks if I did not succor them in many ways. For though people as a whole so detest this race of men that meeting one by accident is supposed to be bad luck, yet they flatter themselves to the queen's taste. For one thing, they reckon it the highest degree of piety to have no contact with literature, and hence they see to it that they do not know how to read. For another, when with asinine voices they bray out in church those psalms they have learned, by rote

---

[10] At Pallas Athena's birth, Jupiter asked for the help of Vulcan (Hephaestus), who then split open Jupiter's skull with an ax.

rather than by heart, they are convinced that they are anointing God's ears with the blandest of oil. Some of them make a good profit from their dirtiness and mendicancy, collecting their food from door to door with importunate bellowing; nay, there is not an inn, public conveyance, or ship where they do not intrude, to the great disadvantage of the other common beggars. Yet according to their account, by their very dirtiness, ignorance, want of manners, and insolence, these delightful fellows are representing to us the lives of the apostles.

What is funnier than to find that they do everything by rule, employing, as it were, the methods of mathematics; and to slip up is a great crime. There must be just so many knots for each shoe and the shoe-string must be of a certain color; the habit must be decked with just so much trimming; the girdle must be of a certain material and the width of so many straws; the cowl of a certain shape and a certain number of bushels in capacity; the hair so many fingers long; and one must sleep just so many hours. Who does not see that all this equality is really very unequal, in view of the great diversity of bodies and temperaments? Yet on the basis of such details they hold other people as mere nut-shells. What is more, the members of one order, amid all their professions of apostolic charity, will turn and condemn the members of some other, making an admirable hubbub over the way their habit is belted or the slightly darker color of it. Among the monks you will see some so rigorously pious that they will wear no outer garment unless it be of Cilician goat's hair, while their inner garment is of Milesian wool; some others, on the contrary, are linen on the outside, but still wool underneath. Members of certain orders start back from the mere touch of a piece of money as if it were aconite. They do not, however, withdraw from the touch of a glass of wine, or of a woman. In short, all orders take remarkable care that nothing in their way of life shall be consistent; nor is it so much their concern to be like Christ as to be unlike each other. Thus a great part of their felicity derives from their various names. Those of one order delight to call themselves Cordeliers, but among them some are Coletes, some Minors, some Minims, some Crutched. Again, there are the Benedictines and the Bernardines; the Bridgetines and the Augustinians; the Williamists and the Jacobines; as if it were not enough to be called Christians.

The greatest number of them work so hard at their ceremonies and at maintaining the minutiae of tradition that they deem one heaven hardly a suitable reward for their labors; never recalling that the time will come when, with all these things held of no account, Christ will demand a reckoning of that which He has prescribed, namely, charity. One friar will then show a paunch which has been padded out with every kind of fish; another will spill out a hundred bushels of hymns. Another will count off so many myriads of fasts, and will lay the blame for his almost bursting belly upon his having always broken his fasts by a single dinner. Another will point to a pile of ceremonies so big that seven ships could scarcely carry it. Another will boast that for sixty years he never touched money, except when his fingers were protected by two pairs of gloves. Another will wear a cowl so dirty and greasy that no sailor would deign to put it on. Another will celebrate the fact that for more than fifty-five years he lived the life of a sponge, always fastened to one spot. Another will show a voice grown hoarse with assiduous chanting; another, a lethargy contracted by living alone; another, a tongue grown dumb under his vow of silence. But Christ, interrupting their boasts, which otherwise would go on endlessly, will say: "Whence comes this new race of Jews? I recognize one commandment which is truly mine, and of that I hear nothing. Of old in the sight of all men and using no device of parable I promised the inheritance of my Father, not to cowls, orisons, or fasts, but to works of charity. Nor do I acknowledge those who acknowledge too well their own good works; let those that wish to seem holier than myself dwell, if they like, in those six hundred heavens of Basilides,[11] or let them command a new heaven to be built for themselves by the very ones whose petty traditions they have preferred above my commandments." When they shall hear these words and shall see common sailors and teamsters preferred above them, with what faces, think you, will they look wistfully on each other! Yet meanwhile, with some assistance from me, they are happy in their good hope.

Yet nobody dares quite to scorn these people, though they are secluded from the life of the state; and least of all dares one scorn the mendicants, because they get hold of everybody's secrets by means of what they call confessions. To be sure, they account it a crime to publish these, except as it may happen, when they are in drink, that they wish to have some fun telling good stories, and will divulge a matter by hints, but suppressing, of course, the names. If anyone affronts these wasps, they will take suitable revenge in public sermons, and point out their enemy by indirect expressions so cunningly that no one will misunderstand unless he understands nothing. Nor will they make an end of barking until you throw a sop into their mouths.

31. Tell me, what comic actor or mountebank would you rather watch than these monks rhetoricizing in their sermons, droll in every aspect, but neatly exemplifying all the lore which rhetoricians have handed down concerning the art of speaking. Good Lord! How they gesticulate, how aptly they modulate the voice, how they intone, throw themselves about, suddenly put on a new face, and confuse all things by their bawling! And this art of speaking is passed on traditionally from monk to brother monk as if it were a great craft and mystery. It is not lawful for me to know it, but I shall proceed with a few conjectures. They commence with an invocation, a trick which they have borrowed from the poets. Next, if they are to speak of charity, say, they begin their exordium with the river Nile in Egypt. Or if they are to expound the mystery of the Cross, they very happily take a start from Baal, the Babylonian snake-god. If they are to discuss fasting, they set out from the twelve signs of the Zodiac; or if they are to speak on faith, they make a few preliminary remarks on squaring the circle.

I have heard of a certain notable fool—there I go again! I meant to say scholar—who was about to explain the mystery of the Holy Trinity

---

[11]Founder of a gnostic sect who flourished in the second century A.D. In his account of the creation, the original Divine Spirit throws off "emanations" that form a series of heavens in descending order. The earth was on the lowest level of this heavenly hierarchy.

before a very distinguished audience. In order that he might at once make a display of his uncommon learning and give special satisfaction to the divines who were listening, he entered upon his matter in a completely new way—that is, from letters, syllables, and words; then from the agreement of noun and verb, of adjective and noun; while everybody was lost in wonder and some were murmuring to themselves that phrase from Horace, "What is all this stink about?" However, he drew out this observation, that in the elements of grammar he could show a symbol of the Holy Trinity, set forth so plainly that no mathematician could diagram it more clearly in the sand. And this superlative divine had so sweated and toiled on this sermon for the previous eight months that today he is as blind as a mole, all the sharpness of his sight having been exhausted, I fancy, to give edge to his wit. But the man does not begrudge his blindness, reckoning it a small price for the purchase of so much glory.

I heard another, a man of eighty years, and such a theologian that you would have thought Scotus reborn in his person. He was to explain the mystery of the name Jesus, and he showed with admirable subtlety that in the letters of the name was hidden everything that could be said about Him. The circumstance that the name is inflected in but three cases gives us a plain symbol of the threefold nature of God. Then the fact that in one case the name Jesus ends with *s,* in the second case it ends with *m,* and in the third with *u* lies an ineffable mystery, to wit, the three letters show that He is the *s*um, the *m*iddle, and the *u*ltimate. There remained a still more abstruse mystery in these letters treated mathematically; he divided the name Jesus into two equal parts in such a way that a fifth of it (the letter *s*) was left in the middle; then he pointed out that this letter among the Hebrews is called *Schin,* or *Sin;* and that "sin" in the Scottish tongue, as he recalled, means *peccatum.*[12] And from this he was able to declare in the sight of all men that it is Jesus who takes away the sin of the world! All his gaping hearers, and especially the theologues, were struck with admiration of this new approach to the subject. . . . [W]hen did the Greek Demosthenes or the Roman Cicero ever cook up a rhetorical insinuation like that? They held that an introduction was faulty if it began too far from the matter itself, which, in fact, is the very way of beginning used by swineherds, who have mere nature for their guide. But these learned preachers consider that their preamble, for so they call it, will be eminently rhetorical only so far as it has no bearing upon the rest of the argument, to the end that the admiring auditor may murmur to himself, "Now what is he getting at?" . . .

33. Our popes, cardinals, and bishops for some time now have earnestly copied the state and practice of princes, and come near to beating them at their own game. Let a bishop but consider what his alb, the white emblem of sincerity, should teach him, namely, a life in every way blameless; and what is signified on his part by the two-horned miter, the two peaks bound by the same knot—I suppose it is a perfect knowledge of the Old and New Testaments; what is meant by covering his

---

[12]Latin for "sin."

hands with gloves, a clean administration of the sacrament and one unsullied by any taint of human concerns; what the crozier symbolizes, most watchful care of the flock put under his charge; what is indicated by the cross that is carried before him, to wit, a victory over all carnal affections. If he would contemplate these and other lessons of the sort, I say, would he not lead a sad and troubled life? But as it is, they do well enough by way of feeding themselves; as for the other, the care of the sheep, they delegate that to Christ himself, or else refer it to their suffragans, as they call them, or other deputies. Nor do they keep in mind the name they bear, or what the word "bishop" means—labor, vigilance, solicitude. Yet in raking in moneys they truly play the bishop, overseeing everything—and overlooking nothing.

In a similar way the cardinals, if they considered the fact that they have succeeded to the places of the apostles, would see that the same works are required of them as were performed by their predecessors; that they are not lords, but stewards, of spiritual things, and that shortly they are to render an exact account of what they hold in trust. Yes, let them too philosophize a bit concerning their vestments, and question themselves in this fashion: "What does the whiteness of this upper garment mean? Is it not a notable and singular purity of heart? What the crimson lower garment? Is it not a burning love of God? What, again, that outer robe flowing down in broad folds and spreading over the mule of his Exalted Reverence, though it would suffice to cover a camel? Is it not charity ample enough to embrace all men in its helpfulness, by way of teaching, exhorting, chastising, admonishing, ending wars, resisting wicked princes, and freely spending blood—not money alone—for the flock of Christ? And wherefore all this money, anyway, for those who hold the places of the needy apostles?" If they would weigh these things, I repeat, they would not be so ambitious for the post, and would willingly give it up, or at least they would lead a toilsome and watchful life of the sort lived by those ancient apostles.

As to these Supreme Pontiffs who take the place of Christ, if they tried to emulate His life, I mean His poverty, labors, teaching, cross, and contempt for safety, if even they thought upon the title of Pope—that is, Father—or the addition "Most Holy," who on earth would be more afflicted? Who would purchase that seat at the price of every resource and effort? Or who defend it, when purchased, by the sword, by poison, or by anything else? Were wisdom to descend upon them, how it would inconvenience them! Wisdom, did I say? Nay, even a grain of salt would do it—a grain of that salt which is spoken of by Christ. It would lose them all that wealth and honor, all those possessions, triumphal progresses, offices, dispensations, tributes, and indulgences; it would lose them so many horses, mules, and retainers; so many pleasures. (See how I have comprehended in a few words many marketsful, a great harvest, a wide ocean, of goods!) In place of these it would bring vigils, fasts, tears, prayers, sermons, studies, sighs, and a thousand troublesome tasks of the sort. Nor should we pass over the circumstance that all those copyists and notaries would be in want, as would all those advocates, promoters, secretaries, muleteers, grooms, bankers, and pimps—I was about to add something more tender, though rougher, I am afraid, on the ears. In short, that great host of men which burdens—I beg your pardon, I mean adorns—the Roman See would beg for their bread. This would be inhuman and downright abominable, and, what is more accursed, those very princes of the church and true lights of the world would themselves be reduced to a staff and a wallet.

As it is now, what labor turns up to be done they hand over to Peter and Paul, who have leisure for it. But the splendor and the pleasure they take care of personally. And so it comes about—by my doing, remember —that scarcely any kind of men live more softly or less oppressed with care; believing that they are amply acceptable to Christ if with a mystical and almost theatrical finery, with ceremonies, and with those titles of Beatitude and Reverence and Holiness, along with blessing and cursing, they perform the office of bishops. To work miracles is primitive and old-fashioned, hardly suited to our times; to instruct the people is irksome; to interpret the Holy Scriptures is pedantry; to pray is otiose; to shed tears is distressing and womanish; to live in poverty is sordid; to be beaten in war is dishonorable and less than worthy of one who will hardly admit kings, however great, to kiss his sacred foot; and finally, to die is unpleasant, to die on the cross a disgrace. . . .

35. . . . Now to the business, under favorable auguries. Ecclesiastes has written in his first chapter: "The number of fools is infinite." When he terms the number infinite, does he not seem to embrace mortals generally, unless for a few—and I do not know that anyone has ever had the luck to see them. But Jeremiah testifies more ingenuously in his tenth chapter, saying, "Every man is made foolish by his own wisdom." He attributes wisdom to God alone, leaving folly as the portion of all men. And again, a little earlier: "Let not man glory in his wisdom." Why do you not wish man to glory in his wisdom, excellent Jeremiah? For the simple reason, he would of course answer, that he has no wisdom. But I return to Ecclesiastes. Thus when he writes, "Vanity of vanities, all is vanity," what else do you think he means but that, just as I have told you, human life is nothing but a sport of folly? And indeed he adds an affirmative vote to the sentiment of Cicero, over whose great name is set down, as I mentioned just now, "Everything is full of fools." Again, when the wise Ecclesiasticus said that "the fool is changed as the moon," but that "the wise man is as fixed as the sun," what did he intend to show except that the whole human race is foolish, and the attribute of wisdom is meet for God alone? For interpreters always read "moon" as human nature, and "sun," the source of all light, as God. In agreement with this we find Christ in the Gospels forbids that anyone should be called good but one, and that is God. If a man who is not wise, then, is a fool, and whoever is good is *ipso facto* wise, in accordance with Stoic writers, it is a necessary conclusion that folly comprehends all men. . . .

37. Yet why am I so needlessly careful in going about to support these matters by all these proofs and witnesses when in the mystical psalms Christ himself, speaking to the Father, says for all men to hear, "Thou knowest my foolishness"? Nor indeed is it without cause that fools are so vastly pleasing to God; the reason being, I suggest, that just as great

princes look suspiciously on men who are too clever, and hate them—as Julius Caesar suspected and hated Brutus and Cassius while he did not fear drunken Antony at all, Nero was suspicious of Seneca, Dionysius[13] of Plato—while on the other hand they take delight in duller and simpler souls; so Christ detests and condemns those wise men who rely on their own prudence. Paul witnesses to this very clearly when he says, "God has chosen the foolish things of the world," and when he says, "It has pleased God to save the world by foolishness," seeing that it could never be redeemed by wisdom. But God points this out clearly enough, when He cries through the mouth of the prophet, "I will destroy the wisdom of the wise, and I will reject the prudence of the prudent." . . .

What do all these things cry out to us if not this, that mortal men, even the pious, are fools? And that Christ, in order to relieve the folly of mankind, though Himself "the wisdom of the Father," was willing in some manner to be made a fool when He took upon Himself the nature of a man and was found in fashion as a man? And likewise He was made "to be sin" that He might heal sinners. Nor did He wish to bring healing by any other means than by "the foolishness of the cross," and by weak and stupid apostles upon whom He carefully enjoined folly, dissuading them from wisdom, while He incited them by the example of children, lilies, mustard-seed, and sparrows—witless things and deficient in sense, living their lives by the guidance of nature with no art or anxious care. Beyond this, He forbade them to be troubled about what they should say before magistrates and He charged that they should not inquire into times and seasons; in a word, they should not trust to their own wisdom but wholly depend upon Him. To the same effect we learn that God, architect of the world, charged upon pain of death that men should not eat of the tree of knowledge, exactly as if knowledge is the bane of happiness. Likewise Paul specifically disavows knowledge as that which puffs up and works harm. . . .

38. But I should not further pursue that which is infinite; let me speak compendiously. The Christian religion on the whole seems to have a kinship with some sort of folly, while it has no alliance whatever with wisdom. If you want proofs of this statement, observe first of all how children, old people, women, and fools find pleasure beyond other folk in holy and religious things, and to that end are ever nearest the altars, led no doubt solely by an impulse of nature. Then you will notice that the original founders of religion, admirably laying hold of pure simplicity, were the bitterest foes of literary learning. Lastly, no fools seem to act more foolishly than do the people whom zeal for Christian piety has got possession of; for they pour out their wealth, they overlook wrongs, allow themselves to be cheated, make no distinction between friends and enemies, shun pleasure, glut themselves with hunger, wakefulness, tears, toils, and reproaches; they disdain life and dearly prefer death; in short, they seem to have grown utterly numb to ordinary sensations, quite as if their souls lived elsewhere and not in their bodies. What is

---

[13]Dionysius the Younger, a volatile tyrant of Syracuse (395?—343 B.C.), took Plato into his service but, fearful of the power Plato held over men's minds, soon dismissed him.

this, forsooth, but to be mad? Whereby we should find it less strange that the apostles appeared to be drunk with new wine, and that Paul, in the eyes of his judge, Festus, looked as if he had gone mad. . . .

39. Wherefore, since there is so great contrariety between the pious and the vulgar, it comes about that each appears to the other to be mad—though in my opinion, to be sure, the word is more correctly applied to the pious than to the others. This will become clearer if I briefly demonstrate, as I promised to do, that their *summum bonum* itself is no other than a kind of insanity. First, let us suppose that Plato was dreaming of something very like it when he wrote that "the madness of lovers is the happiest state of all." Now he who loves intensely no longer lives in himself but in whatever he loves, and the more he can depart from himself and enter into the other, the happier he is. And when a mind yearns toward travelling out of the body, and does not rightly use its own bodily organs, you doubtless, and with accuracy, call the state of it madness. Otherwise, what do they mean by those common phrases, "he is not at home," and "to come to yourself," and "he is himself again"? Furthermore, so far as the love is more perfect the madness is greater and more delightful. Of what sort, then, is that future life with those who dwell on high, toward which pious hearts aspire with such fervor? First the spirit, as conqueror and the more vital, will overmaster and absorb the body, and this it will do the more easily in that now it is in its own realm, so to speak, and also because already, during life, it has cleansed and lightened the body in preparation for this change. Then the spirit itself will be absorbed in marvellous wise by that supreme spirit, more potent than its infinity of parts. Thus the whole man will be outside of himself, nor will he be happy for any other reason than that, so placed outside of himself, he shall have some ineffable portion in that *summum bonum* which draws all things unto itself. And although this happiness arrives at its perfection only when souls, joined to their former bodies, shall be clothed with immortality, yet because the earthly life of pious folk is nothing but a contemplation and kind of shadowing of that other, they sometimes feel a foretaste and a glow of the reward to come. Although this is as but the least little drop in comparison with that flowing fountain of eternal happiness, yet it far surpasses any bodily pleasure, yes, even if all mortal delights were brought together into one. By so much does the spiritual excel over the corporeal, and the invisible over the visible. This surely is what the prophet has promised: "Eye hath not seen, nor ear heard, neither have entered into the heart of man the things which God hath prepared for them that love Him." And this truly is the portion of Folly, that "good part" which "shall not be taken away" by the transformation of life, but will be perfected.

Hence those who are permitted to have a foretaste of this—and it comes to but few—suffer something very like to madness. They say things that are not quite coherent, and this not in the ordinary way of men, but they make a sound without meaning, and suddenly they change the whole aspect of their faces; now cheerful, now downcast, they will weep, then laugh, and then sigh; in brief, they are truly outside themselves. When presently they return to themselves they say that they do not know where they have been, whether in the body or out of it, waking or sleeping; they do not remember what they have heard, seen, spoken, or done; and yet through a cloud, or as in a dream, they know one thing, that they were at their happiest while they were thus out of their wits. So they are sorry to come to themselves again and would prefer, of all good things, nothing but to be mad always with this madness. And this is a tiny little taste of that future happiness.

40. But indeed I have long since forgotten myself and run out of bounds. If anything I have said shall seem too saucy or too glib, stop and think: 'tis Folly, and a woman, that has spoken. But of course you will also remember that Greek proverb, "Even a foolish man will often speak a word in season," unless, perhaps, you assume that this does not extend to women. I see that you are expecting a peroration, but you are just too foolish if you suppose that after I have poured out a hodgepodge of words like this I can recall anything that I have said. There is an old saying, "I hate a pot-companion with a memory." Here is a new one: "I hate a hearer that remembers anything."

And so farewell. . . . Applaud . . . live . . . drink . . . O most distinguished initiates of Folly!

Table Talk / Luther

In 1525, after his marriage to an erstwhile nun, Luther settled down in the old town of Wittenberg in a house that had once been the Augustinian monastery and, as such, Luther's abode for several years while he was a member of the order. The storm and stress of the previous years—the awful struggle in his own soul, his fierce revolt against the abuse of indulgences, his brave stands against many threats, the numerous political upheavals—all gave place to a period of relative calm. Luther and his bride had before them twenty busy, useful years of comparative quiet and domestic bliss, though not of domestic privacy. They kept open house year in and year out and entertained some of their poor relatives, a host of distinguished strangers who came to Wittenberg to see and hear Luther, and above all, many students.

Luther presided over the table, which was always full. A man of many moods—at times deeply absorbed in thought over some ponderous problem of theology or the exasperating taunts of the "papists" and other "ranters," at times jocose and full of mirth—he set the tone for all the lively conversations. Twelve of his most faithful guests (the number of "disciples" is purely accidental) took to jotting down in their notebooks most of Luther's more memorable statements. These notes were soon collected and published under the title *Table Talk*. Spontaneous and off-the-cuff, the theological inconsistencies which they undeniably contain have given ammunition to Luther's enemies. But from a literary standpoint, the mixture of religious meditations, homilies, outbursts of ire, and robust jokes found in these talks give us a vivid portrait of Luther the man and a good measure of the sincerity and strength of his religious commitment.

If God can pardon me for having crucified and martyred Him over more than twenty years with the celebration of Mass, He will certainly give me credit for the good drinks I swill in His honor every so often, with God's consent let people think whatever they please about it.

When I was still a monk, I was so busy reading, writing, preaching and singing in church that I did not get around to praying. Hence if I could not say my prayers on the week days, I would reserve my Sundays for that purpose, forego dinner and pray the whole long day. Oh, how we were plagued by all the popish decrees and rules. The young people nowadays know nothing of that. I remember some novices in a monastery who asked the Pope for some dispensation from the relentless praying. What did the Pope answer? "Get up earlier in the morning and start your prayers at the very crack of dawn."

Erasmus gives you stealthy stiletto stabs in the back; he does nothing in the open under everyone's eyes, oh no. That's why his books are so venomous. In my will, I shall forbid my children to read his *Colloquies,* for therein he utters many blasphemous things under assumed names, quite obviously to attack and deride the Christian Faith. Let him poke fun at me and at others, but I warn him not to make game of God. God will brook no such affronteries. Indeed, I am very much afraid that Erasmus will come to a miserable end. . . .

Among all the books that the opponents of Truth have written against me, I have read only Erasmus' treatise on Free Will from beginning to end and even that one I read with so much disgust that I was often tempted to fling it under the table. All those others who have taken issue with my views gave me enough grist for salty rebuttals on the very first two or three pages of their scribblings. Some I offered up to Pilate, which means, expressed decently, that I used them to wipe my hinder parts, for there was nothing in them but lies so fat and heavy as to upset my bowels.

He who wants to fathom and probe the riddles of God's will and works on the strength of his own reason and without the aid of Holy Writ, thinks he can catch the wind with a spoon or weigh fire on a butcher's scale. God works at times in mysterious ways which our mind cannot grasp: He consigns one to hell and damnation, another He blesses and makes just. It does not behoove us to cross-examine God about the whys and wherefores but we should rather put our trust in Him that He does nothing without good reason. And, indeed, He would be a paltry

From *Dr. Martin Luthers Tischredon oder Colloquia*, edited by Friedrich von Schmidt (Leipzig: Druck und Verlag von Philipp Reclam, 1879). Translated by Robert E. Helbling.

God if He were to give an account of Himself to every darned fool. Let us be content with the Gospel as He chose to reveal it to us in the Bible.

An Englishman, a very learned and God-fearing gentleman, sat down to dinner with Dr. Martin Luther, but did not understand one word of German. Luther said to him: "I will give you my wife as a tutor, she will teach you German in no time at all, for she is so eloquent, nay downright loquacious, that I can hardly keep up with her conversation. Undeniably, women have a great gift of gab, but one should not praise them for that. It befits them much better when they stammer, hem and haw; indeed, that is much more becoming to them."

A young man is like new cider that ferments and bubbles over, wanting out so as to be noticed by all.

At one time when apples and pears were being served after dinner, Dr. Martin Luther remarked: "If Adam had not sinned, we would never need to eat bread, then we could eat nothing but fruit." When someone asked why Christ had eaten after His resurrection, Dr. Martin replied: "Christ did not eat because he needed or wanted to but to prove and demonstrate that he was Christ and truly resurrected."

There are three types of people. First there are the masses who jog along in life, brutishly content, without a conscience, never aware of their vile and corrupt nature, never apprehending the wrath of God about their sinfulness. The second group are those who are fearful of the Law, who do feel the wrath of God but flee from him in panic only to fight and wrestle with themselves in despair as did Saul of old. The third category are those who recognize the opprobrium of their sin and God's towering rage and feel that they were conceived and born in sin and thus would deem themselves lost and damned, had they not hearkened to the Gospel message which says that God forgives our sin through the atonement of Christ; they believe and embrace the Gospel and thus are justified and blessed in the eyes of God. They also prove their faith through all manner of good works as God commanded us to do. The other two groups of men, however, will find their ruin.

Recently, at court, I delivered a very brisk and mettlesome sermon against boozing; but to no avail. Two of my friends tell me that music and the civilized knightly pastimes of yesteryear have fallen into disrepute there and that solemn courtly ceremonials have given way to tippling and carousing. It is true, of course, that our lord, the Prince Elector, is a strong and sturdy figure of a man who can drink anybody under the table without so much as turning a hair. If he were as much bent on sex as on drink, his mistress would come upon bad days. . . .

A lie is like a snowball; the longer you roll it, the bigger it gets.

. . . Then Dr. Heneck asked: "Do you mean to say that the Holy Ghost instills in us certainty about God? If so, then all sects and cults—all of which assert their doctrine to be the only true one—will claim for themselves the gift of the Holy Ghost." Then Dr. Martin rejoined and said: "Mohammed, the Papists, Anabaptists and other zealots cannot be sure of their dogma, for they do not cling to the Gospel but insist on personal righteousness which they make dependent on the performance of such and such works. And though they perform many a ritual, they cannot but doubt and ask themselves: Who knows whether this be agreeable to God? whether I have done enough? since I am unworthy and a poor sinner and my sins are overwhelming! But a true Christian is only certain of one thing which he will not tire of repeating: I do not inquire after my holiness or my unworthiness, but I believe in Jesus Christ, our sole redeemer, "who of God is made unto us wisdom, and righteousness, and sanctification, and redemption." (I Corinthians 1:30)

Comments / on Erasmus, Luther, and the Reformation

In Erasmus, in spite of all his modernity, there breathes a great deal of the spirit of the Middle Ages and of respect for the Church. Erasmus made the *ex cathedra* rulings of the Church his final court of appeal and accepted them in a true spirit of Catholic obedience.

W. E. CAMPBELL (1949)

"You cannot," said Luther, "accept both the Bible and reason; one or the other must go." Luther condemned the Scholastic philosophers for making so many concessions to reason, for trying to prove Christian dogmas rationally, for trying to harmonize Christianity with the philosophy of that "cursed, conceited, wily heathen" Aristotle.

Nevertheless Luther took two steps in the direction of reason: he made the sermon, not ceremony, the center of religious ritual; and in the early days of his rebellion he proclaimed the right of every individual to interpret the Scriptures for himself. He drew up his own canon of authenticity for the books of the Bible: how far did they agree with the teaching of Christ?

WILL DURANT (1957)

So much had they in common that the opponents of Luther were also the opponents of Erasmus, and regarded them as fellow-workers in the same cause. The great humanist, they held, was the inspirer of the great heretic. They even believed him to be the author of some of Luther's writings. "Erasmus," it was said, "laid the egg that Luther hatched." There was a certain amount of truth in the saying. Erasmus by his critical labours paved the way to a truer knowledge of the original sources, particularly the New Testament writings, from which the evangelical reformers drew their inspiration, though his edition of the New Testament is, of course, very imperfect judged by the standard of modern critical scholarship.   *JAMES MACKINNON (1962)*

Luther, too, was fiercely authoritarian—in practice more so than the Roman Church, whose slackness he despised. Having rejected its authority, he had to base his whole creed on the only other available authority, the Bible. This gave him some difficulties, since the Word of God was not always clear or clearly consistent. Luther had a highhanded way with inconvenient texts, for instance calling the Epistle of James a "mere letter of straw" because it stressed the necessity of good works; and in drawing chiefly on St. Paul, to whom he owed his doctrine of justification by faith, he tended to slight the potentially embarrassing ethical teaching of Jesus. Yet he did not permit others to interpret the Bible as freely as he himself had. Justification was by faith—but only the proper faith; the gospel according to Luther was the only true gospel. He flatly repudiated the principle of freedom of conscience implicit in his initial refusal to violate his own conscience, and his initial teaching that every Christian was his own priest.   *HERBERT J. MULLER (1963)*

Luther's role in the history of the Church was in many respects considerable; it can almost be called providential. Blame for the hideous rent suffered by the Seamless Robe of Christ does not lie at his door alone. Many in the Catholic camp share some of the responsibility. Nevertheless it remains true to say that the greatest guilt was Luther's. He was the initiator, the leader, without whose action none of the events we can observe would have happened in quite the way they did. In making the Church so brutally and tragically aware of her problems, however, he also forced her to emerge at last from that muddy slough of complaisance and collusion which was bogging down the best of Christian spirituality. Without Martin Luther and the fear which he inspired, the Holy Church might never have undertaken that genuine reformation, effected within the bounds of her own loyalties and disciplines—a reformation whose need was recognized by so many, but which so few dared attempt. Dialectically, to a large extent, the Church of the Council of Trent sprang from the Church of Wittenberg and the Confession of Augsburg—Martin Luther, you who read St. Paul so assiduously, did you ever take to heart the terrible meaning of the Apostle's remark to the Christians of Corinth? "Parties (i.e., heretics) there must be among you, so that those who are of true metal may be distinguished from the rest." (I Corinthians XI:19)
                                     H. DANIEL-ROPS (1958)

John Calvin
1509–1564

Perhaps even more than Luther, Calvin stressed the Pauline doctrine of predestination and justification by faith, which he couched in the terms of a systematic theology and ethics. Overawed by the power of God and the bounty of His grace and mercy manifest in Christ, Calvin could not see how man could acquire through self-willed works the righteousness which would justify him before his Maker. Yet he did not therefore advocate simple resignation to one's fate but rather dynamic acceptance of the sacred character of one's earthly duties, for "the sight of good works can strengthen faith." With this attitude, Calvin characterized the ideal of the Christian life as a "calling" which extends not only to man's relations with God and Church but to all activities—domestic, public, and professional, as well as religious. The true Christian, in Calvin's terms, must take his religion to be his whole life. To be among the "elect," then, means to look upon mundane tasks as an exalted summons to do work in God's vineyard—not, of course, for one's own enjoyment but rather for the greater glory of God. In this sense, men are but the "stewards" of goods bestowed upon them by divine grace.

Seemingly, there is a central paradox in Calvinism: men have no power to assure their salvation through their own "works," yet they are instructed to work assiduously in a worldly calling. To the pious Calvinist, however, there was no paradox: the active life was simply a form of religious devotion. While working toward material success, he had his mind on spiritual things and was constantly examining the purity of his motives. In this way Calvinism helped develop one of the prominent facets of religious sensibility in Western culture—the Puritan way of life calling for concentration on fruitful work and abstention from distracting pleasures.

Some historians have pointed out that there have been no more willing slaves than the early Puritan merchants and industrialists who amassed goods and riches in an ascetic spirit of self-denial. Frugality and thrift became divine virtues; the successful pursuit of gain, the religious duty of the businessman. According to one theory, the "spirit of capitalism" is intimately linked with the "ethic of Protestantism" and may even have originated in that ethic. Fruitful work in the world is analogous to faith— God-given to some but not to others—and becomes a touchstone of divine election. The certainty of justification which the devout Catholic could derive from his participation in the sacraments performed in the Church could be captured by the Calvinist and Puritan through "sacred" work in the world.

Born at Noyon in the north of France, John Calvin was destined by his father for priesthood. But when he matriculated at the University of Paris, he came under the influence of the Erasmian spirit which was still potent there. In order to divert his son from his fervent interest in humanistic studies, Calvin's father sent him to the University of Orleans to study law. Young Calvin seemed to comply readily enough, but when he returned to Paris, armed with a law degree, he plunged with renewed ardor into humanistic studies. He wrote an erudite commentary on Seneca's tract *On Clemency,* which promised him a brilliant career as a humanist scholar.

Calvin's interest in humanist culture naturally inclined him toward the Reform Movement in Christianity. He was, in all probability, the principal ghost writer of the inaugural address delivered by the newly appointed rector of the University of Paris, Nicholas Cop—an address which began with an Erasmian plea for a purified Christianity and culminated in a Lutheran doctrine of salvation through faith and grace. Suspect to the Inquisition, Calvin went underground and emerged in Basel, Switzerland, the haven for all harassed and persecuted humanists. There, only twenty-six years of age, he completed his *Christianae religionis institutio (The Institutes of the Christian Religion),* a lucid and uncompromising exposition of the predestinarianism and worldly asceticism which were to become the basis of the Puritan creed.

In 1536, on his way back from Italy, Calvin happened to stop off at Geneva, a city of enterprising merchants and artisans. The city had just thrown off an ecclesiastic–ducal rule and in reaction against the Church had proclaimed the Reformed faith and organized an oligarchic city government. The populace, however, proved to be not only freedom-loving but also rambunctious and hard to discipline. As much to assure the free flow of trade on which the city had grown rich as to bring about a much-needed regeneration of morals, the city fathers prevailed upon Calvin to stay and help them weld the new religion and the young government into an effective instrument of law and order.

Except for one short interruption (1538–1540), when a hostile political faction succeeded in driving him into exile, Calvin managed to keep a tight grip on the affairs of state and the private lives of the Genevan citizenry for the rest of his life. He thus achieved a goal that the medieval Catholic Church had seldom reached: he brought into being the ecclesiastic ideal of a theocratic state. He accomplished this mainly without demagoguery or disregard for legal tradition; for as a trained lawyer he showed a punctilious respect for established institutions. In fact, in his theoretical writings and legalistic maneuvers, Calvin often departed from the medieval, ecclesiastic tendency to exalt the Church above the State. On the other hand, he also saw to it—often against considerable opposition—that the civil authority recognized the spiritual jurisdiction of the Church. Unfortunately, he could not resist the medieval practice of punishing spiritual offenders with the secular arm of the law. And since there were multitudinous ecclesiastic rules governing the daily life and the conscience of each citizen, there was no end to stiff fines, massive imprisonments, cruel tortures, and death penalties. Calvin's aim was to mold the life of the community by the divine Word, as found in the Old Testament and supposedly also in the New, through a rigid system of ecclesiastical discipline backed by the State. Thus Calvin's ideal was practically, if not legally or formally, a theocracy.

The Institutes of the Christian Religion

Book III / Chapter 10

How We Must Use the Present Life and Its Helps

(The good things of this life are to be enjoyed as gifts of God, 1—2)

1. DOUBLE DANGER: MISTAKEN STRICTNESS AND MISTAKEN LAXITY
By such elementary instruction, Scripture at the same time duly informs us what is the right use of earthly benefits—a matter not to be neglected in the ordering of our life. For if we are to live, we have also to use those helps necessary for living. And we also cannot avoid those things which seem to serve delight more than necessity. Therefore we must hold to a measure so as to use them with a clear conscience, whether for necessity or for delight. By his word the Lord lays down this measure when he teaches that the present life is for his people as a pilgrimage on which they are hastening toward the Heavenly Kingdom. If we must simply pass through this world, there is no doubt we ought to use its good things in so far as they help rather than hinder our course. Thus Paul rightly persuades us to use this world as if not using it; and to buy goods with the same attitude as one sells them.

But because this topic is a slippery one and slopes on both sides into error, let us try to plant our feet where we may safely stand. There were some otherwise good and holy men who when they saw intemperance and wantonness, when not severely restrained, ever raging with unbridled excess, desired to correct this dangerous evil. This one plan occurred to them: they allowed man to use physical goods in so far as necessity required. A godly counsel indeed, but they were far too severe. For they would fetter consciences more tightly than does the

Word of the Lord—a very dangerous thing. Now, to them necessity means to abstain from all things that they could do without; thus, according to them, it would scarcely be permitted to add any food at all to plain bread and water. And others are even more severe. We are told of Crates the Theban, that he cast all his goods into the sea; for he thought that unless they were destroyed, they would destroy him.[1]

But many today, while they seek an excuse for the intemperance of the flesh in its use of external things, and while they would meanwhile pave the road to licentious indulgence, take for granted what I do not at all concede to them: that this freedom is not to be restrained by any limitation but to be left to every man's conscience to use as far as seems lawful to him. Certainly I admit that consciences neither ought to nor can be bound here to definite and precise legal formulas; but inasmuch as Scripture gives general rules for lawful use, we ought surely to limit our use in accordance with them.

2. THE MAIN PRINCIPLE

Let this be our principle: that the use of God's gifts is not wrongly directed when it is referred to that end to which the Author himself created and destined them for us, since he created them for our good, not for our ruin. Accordingly, no one will hold to a straighter path than he who diligently looks to this end. Now if we ponder to what end God created food, we shall find that he meant not only to provide for necessity but also for delight and good cheer. Thus the purpose of clothing, apart from necessity, was comeliness and decency. In grasses, trees, and fruits, apart from their various uses, there is beauty of appearance and pleasantness of odor. For if this were not true, the prophet would not have reckoned them among the benefits of God, "that wine gladdens the heart of man, that oil makes his face shine" [Ps. 104:15 p.]. Scripture would not have reminded us repeatedly, in commending his kindness, that he gave all such things to men. And the natural qualities themselves of things demonstrate sufficiently to what end and extent we may enjoy them. Has the Lord clothed the flowers with the great beauty that greets our eyes, the sweetness of smell that is wafted upon our nostrils, and yet will it be unlawful for our eyes to be affected by that beauty, or our sense of smell by the sweetness of that odor? What? Did he not so distinguish colors as to make some more lovely than others? What? Did he not endow gold and silver, ivory and marble, with a loveliness that renders them more precious than other metals or stones? Did he not, in short, render many things attractive to us, apart from their necessary use?

(We are not to use these blessings indulgently, or to seek wealth greedily, but to serve dutifully in our calling, 3—6)

3. A LOOK AT THE GIVER OF THE GIFT PREVENTS NARROW-MINDEDNESS AND IMMODERATION

Away, then, with that inhuman philosophy which, while conceding only a necessary use of creatures, not only malignantly deprives us of

---

[1] An episode from *Lives and Opinions of Eminent Philosophers* by Diogenes Laertius.

the lawful fruit of God's beneficence but cannot be practiced unless it robs a man of all his senses and degrades him to a block.

But no less diligently, on the other hand, we must resist the lust of the flesh, which, unless it is kept in order, overflows without measure. And it has, as I have said, its own advocates, who, under the pretext of the freedom conceded, permit everything to it. First, one bridle is put upon it if it be determined that all things were created for us that we might recognize the Author and give thanks for his kindness toward us. Where is your thanksgiving if you so gorge yourself with banqueting or wine that you either become stupid or are rendered useless for the duties of piety and of your calling? Where is your recognition of God if your flesh boiling over with excessive abundance into vile lust infects the mind with its impurity so that you cannot discern anything that is right and honorable? Where is our gratefulness toward God for our clothing if in the sumptuousness of our apparel we both admire ourselves and despise others, if with its elegance and glitter we prepare ourselves for shameless conduct? Where is our recognition of God if our minds be fixed upon the splendor of our apparel? For many so enslave all their senses to delights that the mind lies overwhelmed. Many are so delighted with marble, gold, and pictures that they become marble, they turn, as it were, into metals and are like painted figures. The smell of the kitchen or the sweetness of its odors so stupefies others that they are unable to smell anything spiritual. The same thing is also to be seen in other matters. Therefore, clearly, leave to abuse God's gifts must be somewhat curbed, and Paul's rule is confirmed: that we should "make no provision for the flesh, to gratify its desires" [Rom. 13:14], for if we yield too much to these, they boil up without measure or control.

4. ASPIRATION TO ETERNAL LIFE ALSO DETERMINES ARIGHT OUR OUTWARD CONDUCT OF LIFE

But there is no surer or more direct course than that which we receive from contempt of the present life and meditation upon heavenly immortality. For from this two rules follow: those who use this world should be so affected as if they did not use it; those who marry, as if they did not marry; those who buy, as if they did not buy, just as Paul enjoins. The other rule is that they should know how to bear poverty peaceably and patiently, as well as to bear abundance moderately. He who bids you use this world as if you used it not destroys not only the intemperance of gluttony in food and drink, and excessive indulgence at table, in buildings and clothing, ambition, pride, arrogance, and over-fastidiousness, but also all care and inclination that either diverts or hinders you from thought of the heavenly life and zeal to cultivate the soul. Long ago Cato truly said: "There is great care about dress, but great carelessness about virtue." To use the old proverb: those who are much occupied with the care of the body are for the most part careless about their own souls.

Therefore, even though the freedom of believers in external matters is not to be restricted to a fixed formula, yet it is surely subject to this law: to indulge oneself as little as possible; but, on the contrary, with unflagging effort of mind to insist upon cutting off all show of superfluous wealth, not to mention licentiousness, and diligently to guard against turning helps into hindrances.

5. FRUGALITY, EARTHLY POSSESSIONS HELD IN TRUST

The second rule will be: they who have narrow and slender resources should know how to go without things patiently, lest they be troubled by an immoderate desire for them. If they keep this rule of moderation, they will make considerable progress in the Lord's school. So, too, they who have not progressed, in some degree at least, in this respect have scarcely anything to prove them disciples of Christ. For besides the fact that most other vices accompany the desire for earthly things, he who bears poverty impatiently also when in prosperity commonly betrays the contrary disease. This is my point: he who is ashamed of mean clothing will boast of costly clothing; he who, not content with a slender meal, is troubled by the desire for a more elegant one, will also intemperately abuse those elegances if they fall to his lot. He who will bear reluctantly, and with a troubled mind, his deprivation and humble condition if he be advanced to honors will by no means abstain from arrogance. To this end, then, let all those for whom the pursuit of piety is not a pretense strive to learn, by the Apostle's example, how to be filled and to hunger, to abound and to suffer want.

Besides, Scripture has a third rule with which to regulate the use of earthly things. . . . It decrees that all those things were so given to us by the kindness of God, and so destined for our benefit, that they are, as it were, entrusted to us, and we must one day render account of them. Thus, therefore, we must so arrange it that this saying may continually resound in our ears: "Render account of your stewardship" [Luke 16:2]. At the same time let us remember by whom such reckoning is required: namely, him who has greatly commended abstinence, sobriety, frugality, and moderation, and has also abominated excess, pride, ostentation, and vanity; who approves no other distribution of good things than one joined with love: who has already condemned with his own lips all delights that draw man's spirit away from chastity and purity, or befog his mind.

6. THE LORD'S CALLING A BASIS OF OUR WAY OF LIFE

Finally, this point is to be noted: the Lord bids each one of us in all life's actions to look to his calling. For he knows with what great restlessness human nature flames, with what fickleness it is borne hither and thither, how its ambition longs to embrace various things at once. Therefore, lest through our stupidity and rashness everything be turned topsy-turvy, he has appointed duties for every man in his particular way of life. And that no one may thoughtlessly transgress his limits, he has named these various kinds of living "callings." Therefore each individual has his own kind of living assigned to him by the Lord as a sort of sentry post so that he may not heedlessly wander about throughout life. Now, so necessary is this distinction that all our actions are judged in his sight by it, often indeed far otherwise than in the judgment of human and philosophical reason. No deed is considered more noble, even among philosophers, than to free one's country from tyranny. Yet a private citizen who lays his hand upon a tyrant is openly condemned by the heavenly judge.

But I will not delay to list examples. It is enough if we know that the Lord's calling is in everything the beginning and foundation of well-doing. And if there is anyone who will not direct himself to it, he will never hold to the straight path in his duties. Perhaps, sometimes, he could contrive something laudable in appearance; but whatever it may be in the eyes of men, it will be rejected before God's throne. Besides, there will be no harmony among the several parts of his life. Accordingly, your life will then be best ordered when it is directed to this goal. For no one, impelled by his own rashness, will attempt more than his calling will permit, because he will know that it is not lawful to exceed its bounds. A man of obscure station will lead a private life ungrudgingly so as not to leave the rank in which he has been placed by God. Again, it will be no slight relief from cares, labors, troubles, and other burdens for a man to know that God is his guide in all these things. The magistrate will discharge his functions more willingly; the head of the household will confine himself to his duty; each man will bear and swallow the discomforts, vexations, weariness, and anxieties in his way of life, when he has been persuaded that the burden was laid upon him by God. From this will arise also a singular consolation: that no task will be so sordid and base, provided you obey your calling in it, that it will not shine and be reckoned very precious in God's sight.

Chapter 12

We Must Lift Up Our Minds to God's Judgment Seat that We May Be Firmly Convinced of His Free Justification

(Justification in the light of the majesty and perfection of God, 1 – 3)

1. NO ONE IS RIGHTEOUS BEFORE GOD'S JUDGMENT SEAT

Even though all these things are by shining testimonies shown to be perfectly true, still, how necessary they are will not be clear to us until we set before our eyes what ought to be the basis of this whole discussion. First, therefore, this fact should occur to us: that our discourse is concerned with the justice not of a human court but of a heavenly tribunal, lest we measure by our own small measure the integrity of works needed to satisfy the divine judgment. Yet it is amazing with what great rashness and boldness this is commonly defined. Indeed, one can see how there are none who more confidently, and as people say, boisterously chatter over the righteousness of works than they who are monstrously plagued with manifest diseases, or creak with defects beneath the skin. That happens because they do not think about God's justice, which they would never hold in such derision if they were affected even by the slightest feeling of it. Yet surely it is held of precious little value if it is not recognized as God's justice and so perfect that nothing can be admitted except what is in every part whole and complete and undefiled by any corruption. Such was never found in man and never will be. In the shady cloisters of the schools anyone can easily and readily prattle about the value of works in justifying men. But when we come before the presence of God we must put away such amusements! For there we deal with a serious matter, and do not engage in frivolous word battles. To this question, I insist, we must apply our mind if we would profitably inquire concerning true righteousness: How shall we reply to the Heavenly Judge when he calls us to account? Let us envisage for ourselves that Judge, not as our minds naturally imagine him, but as he is depicted for us in Scripture: by whose brightness the stars are darkened; by whose strength the mountains are melted; by whose wrath the earth is shaken; whose wisdom catches the wise in their craftiness; beside whose purity all things are defiled; whose righteousness not even the angels can bear; who makes not the guilty man innocent; whose vengeance when once kindled penetrates to the depths of hell. Let us behold him, I say, sitting in judgment to examine the deeds of men: Who will stand confident before his throne? "Who . . . can dwell with the devouring fire?" asks the prophet. "Who . . . can dwell with everlasting burnings? He who walks righteously and speaks the truth" [Isa. 33:14–15 p.], etc. But let such a one, whoever he is, come forward. Nay, that response causes no one to come forward. For, on the contrary, a terrible voice resounds: "If thou, O Lord, shouldst mark iniquities, Lord, who shall stand?" [Ps. 130:3]. Indeed, all must soon perish, as it is written in another place: "Shall a man be justified in comparison with God, or shall he be purer than his maker? Behold, they that serve him are not faithful, and in his angels he found wickedness. How much more shall those who dwell in houses of clay, who have an earthly foundation, be consumed before the moth. From morn to eve they shall be cut down" [Job 4:17–20]. Likewise: "Behold, among his saints none is faithful, and the heavens are not pure in his sight. How much more abominable and unprofitable is man, who drinks iniquity like water?" [Job 15:15–16].

Indeed, I admit that in The Book of Job mention is made of a righteousness higher than the observance of the law, and it is worth-while to maintain this distinction. For even if someone satisfied the law, not even then could he stand the test of that righteousness which surpasses all understanding. Therefore, even though Job has a good conscience, he is stricken dumb with astonishment, for he sees that not even the holiness of angels can please God if he should weigh their works in his heavenly scales. Therefore, I now pass over that righteousness which I have mentioned, for it is incomprehensible. I only say that if our life is examined according to the standard of the written law, we are sluggish indeed if we are not tormented with horrid fear at those many maledictions with which God willed to cleanse us—among others this general curse: "Cursed be everyone who does not abide by everything written in this book" [Gal. 3:10; cf. Deut. 27:26]. In short, this whole discussion will be foolish and weak unless every man admit his guilt before the Heavenly Judge, and concerned about his own acquittal, willingly cast himself down and confess his nothingness.

2. RIGHTEOUSNESS BEFORE MEN AND RIGHTEOUSNESS BEFORE GOD

Hither, hither we ought to have raised up our eyes to learn how to tremble rather than vainly to exult. Indeed, it is easy, so long as the comparison stops with men, for anyone to think of himself as having something that his fellows ought not to despise. But when we rise up toward God, that assurance of ours vanishes in a flash and dies. And exactly the same thing happens to our souls with respect to God as happens to our bodies with respect to the visible heavens. For keenness of sight, so long as it confines itself to examining nearby objects, is convinced of its discernment. But directed toward the sun, stricken and numbed by excessive brightness, our vision feels as weak as it did strong in gazing at objects below. Let us, then, not be deceived by empty confidence. Even though we consider ourselves either equal or superior to other men, that is nothing to God, to whose judgment the decision of the matter must be brought. But if our wildness cannot be tamed by these warnings, he will answer us as he spoke to the Pharisees: "Ye are they that justify yourselves before men; but . . . what is exalted among men is an abomination to God" [Luke 16:15]. Go now and haughtily boast of your righteousness among men, while God from heaven abominates it!

But what say God's servants, truly instructed by his Spirit? "Enter not into judgment with thy servant, for no man living is righteous in thy sight" [Ps. 143:2]. Another servant speaks, although in a slightly different sense: "A man cannot be righteous before God. If he wished to contend with him, he could not answer him once in a thousand times" [Job 9:2 – 3]. Here, then, we are clearly told the nature of God's righteousness, which will indeed not be satisfied by any works of man. When it examines our thousand sins, we cannot be cleansed of even one. Surely that chosen instrument of God, Paul, had sincerely conceived such a righteousness when he confessed that he was not aware of anything against himself but that he was not thereby justified.

(Conscience and self-criticism before God deprive us of all claim to good works and lead us to embrace God's mercy, 4 – 8)

4. THE GRAVITY OF GOD'S JUDGMENT PUTS AN END TO ALL SELF-DECEPTION

This is the truth. Awakened consciences, when they have to do with God's judgment, recognize this as the only safe haven in which they can securely breathe. For if the stars, which seem so very bright at night, lose their brilliance in the sight of the sun, what do we think will happen even to the rarest innocence of man when it is compared with God's purity? For it will be a very severe test, which will penetrate to the most hidden thoughts of the heart; and, as Paul says, "he will bring to light the things hidden in darkness, and will uncover the hidden purposes of hearts" [I Cor. 4:5 p.]. This will compel the lurking and lagging conscience to utter all things that have now even been forgotten. Our accuser the devil, mindful of all the transgressions that he has impelled us to perpetrate, will press us. Outward parade of good works, which alone we now esteem, will be of no benefit there; purity of will alone will be demanded of us. And therefore hypocrisy shall fall down confounded, even as it now vaunts itself with drunken boldness. This applies not only to that hypocrisy by which a man, knowing himself guilty before God, strives to show himself off among men but also to that by which every man deceives himself before God, prone as we are to pamper and flatter ourselves. They who do not direct their attention to such a spectacle can, indeed, for the moment pleasantly and peacefully construct a righteousness for themselves, but one that will soon in God's judgment be shaken from them, just as great riches heaped up in a dream vanish upon awakening. But they who seriously, and as in God's sight, will seek after the true rule of righteousness, will certainly find that all human works, if judged according to their own worth, are nothing but filth and defilement. And what is commonly reckoned righteousness is before God sheer iniquity; what is adjudged uprightness, pollution; what is accounted glory, ignominy.

6. WHAT HUMILITY BEFORE GOD IS

But what way do we have to humble ourselves except that, wholly poor and destitute, we yield to God's mercy? For if we think that we have anything left to ourselves, I do not call it humility. And those who have hitherto joined these two things together—namely, that we must think humbly concerning ourselves before God and must reckon our righteousness to be of some value—have taught a pernicious hypocrisy. For if we confess before God contrary to what we feel, we wickedly lie to him. But we cannot feel as we ought without immediately trampling upon whatever seems glorious in us. Therefore, when you hear in the prophet that salvation has been prepared for the humble people, and abasement for the eyes of the proud, first consider that the gateway to salvation does not lie open unless we have laid aside all pride and taken upon ourselves perfect humility; secondly, that this humility is not some seemly behavior whereby you yield a hair of your right to the Lord, as those who do not act haughtily or insult others are called humble in the sight of men, although they rely upon some consciousness of excellence. Rather, this humility is an unfeigned submission of our heart, stricken down in earnest with an awareness of its own misery and want. For so it is everywhere described by the Word of God.

When the Lord speaks thus in Zephaniah, "I will remove from you the proudly exultant . . . and leave in the midst of your people the afflicted and poor, and they shall hope in the Lord," does he not clearly point out who the humble are? [ch. 3:11–12]. They are those who lie afflicted with the knowledge of their own poverty. On the other hand, Scripture calls the proud ones "exultant" because men happy in their prosperity usually leap for joy. But to the humble, whom he plans to save, he leaves nothing but to hope in the Lord. So also in Isaiah: "But to whom will I look, save to him who is lowly and contrite in spirit, and trembles at my words" [Isa. 66:2]? Likewise: "The high and lofty one who inhabits eternity, whose name is Holy, dwelling in the high and holy place, and with a contrite and humble spirit, to quicken the spirit of the humble and . . . the heart of the contrite" [Isa. 57:15].

Whenever you hear the word "contrition," understand a wound of the heart that does not permit a man cast to the ground to be raised up.

If you would, according to God's judgment, be exalted with the humble, your heart ought to be wounded with such contrition. If that does not happen, you will be humbled by God's powerful hand to your shame and disgrace.

7. CHRIST CALLS SINNERS, NOT THE RIGHTEOUS

And our most excellent Master, not content with words, in a parable represents to us, as in a picture, the image of proper humility. For he brings forward a "publican, standing afar off, and not daring to lift his eyes to heaven, who prays with much weeping, 'Lord, be merciful to me a sinner'" [Luke 18:13 p.]. Let us not think these signs of feigned modesty: that he does not dare to look up to heaven or to come nearer, and that, beating his breast, he confesses himself a sinner. But let us know these to be testimonies of an inner feeling. On the other side he puts the Pharisee, who thanks God because he is not a common man, either an extortioner or unjust, or an adulterer, and since he fasts twice in the week and gives tithes of all that he has. In his open confession he acknowledges that the righteousness he has is a gift of God; but because he is confident that he is righteous, unpleasing and hateful, he departs from God's face. The publican is justified by the acknowledgment of his iniquity. Hence, we may see how much favor our abasement has before the Lord, so that the heart cannot be opened to receive his mercy unless it be utterly empty of all opinion of its own worth. When it has been occupied with these things it closes the entry to him. That no one should doubt concerning this, Christ was sent to the earth by the Father with this commission: "To publish good tidings to the poor, to heal the contrite of heart, to preach liberty to the captives, deliverance to the imprisoned, . . . to console the sorrowing . . . , to give them glory instead of ashes, oil . . . instead of mourning, the mantle of praise instead of a spirit of grief" [Isa. 61:1 – 3 p.]. According to this commandment, he invites to share his beneficence only those who labor and are heavy-laden. And in another passage: "I have come not to call the righteous but sinners" [Matt. 9:13].

8. ARROGANCE AND COMPLACENCY BEFORE GOD BLOCK OUR WAY TO CHRIST

Therefore, if we would give ear to Christ's call, away with all arrogance and complacency! Arrogance arises from a foolish persuasion of our own righteousness, when man thinks that he has something meritorious to commend him before God. Complacency can exist even without any belief in works. For many sinners are so drunk with the sweetness of their vices that they think not upon God's judgment but lie dazed, as it were, in a sort of drowsiness, and do not aspire to the mercy offered to them. Such sloth is no less to be shaken off than any confidence in ourselves is to be cast away in order that we may without hindrance hasten to Christ, and empty and hungering, may be filled with his good things. For we will never have enough confidence in him unless we become deeply distrustful of ourselves; we will never lift up our hearts enough in him unless they be previously cast down in us; we will never have consolation enough in him unless we have already experienced desolation in ourselves.

Therefore we are ready to seize and grasp God's grace when we have utterly cast out confidence in ourselves and rely only on the assurance of his goodness—"when," as Augustine says, "forgetting our own merits, we embrace Christ's gifts." For if he sought merits in us, we would not come to his gifts. Bernard is in agreement with this when he neatly compares to faithless servants the proud, who claim even the slightest thing for their own merits because they wrongfully retain the credit for grace that passes through them, as if a wall should say that it gave birth to a sunbeam that it received through a window. Not to halt any longer with this, let us hold it as a brief but general and sure rule that prepared to share the fruit of God's mercy is he who has emptied himself, I do not say of righteousness, which exists not, but of a vain and airy semblance of righteousness. For to the extent that a man rests satisfied with himself, he impedes the beneficence of God.

Chapter 14

The Beginning of Justification and Its Continual Progress

(Scholastic objections to justification by faith, and doctrine of supererogatory merits[2] of the saints examined and refuted, 12–21)

13. ONE WHO SPEAKS OF "SUPEREROGATORY" WORKS MISUNDERSTANDS THE SHARPNESS OF GOD'S DEMAND AND THE GRAVITY OF SIN
If these things are true, surely no works of ours can of themselves render us acceptable and pleasing to God; nor can even the works themselves please him, except to the extent that a man, covered by the righteousness of Christ, pleases God and obtains forgiveness of his sins. For God has not promised the reward of life for particular works but he only declares that the man who does them shall live, leveling that well-known curse against all those who do not persevere in all things. The fiction of partial righteousness is abundantly refuted by these statements, where no other righteousness than the complete observance of the law is allowed in heaven.

Their usual loose talk about "works of supererogation" providing sufficient compensation is no sounder. Why? Do they not always return to the position from which they have already been driven, that he who partly keeps the law is to that extent righteous by works? What no one of sound judgment will concede to them they too shamelessly assume as a fact. The Lord often testifies that he recognizes no righteousness of works except in the perfect observance of his law. What perversity is it for us, when we lack righteousness, in order not to seem deprived of all glory—that is, utterly to have yielded to God—to boast of some

---

[2]Good deeds done by saints of the Roman Catholic Church in excess of the requirements of divine law; also, voluntary good deeds performed by men over and above God's commandments.

little bits of a few works and try through other satisfactions to pay for what is lacking?

Satisfactions have already been effectively demolished, so that they ought not even to come to our minds in a dream. I say that those who talk such nonsense do not realize what an execrable thing sin is in God's sight. Truly, they should have understood that men's whole righteousness, gathered together in one heap, could not make compensation for a single sin. For we see that man was so cast away and abandoned by God for one transgression that he lost at the same time all capacity to recover his salvation. Therefore, the capacity to make satisfaction was taken away. Those who preen themselves on it surely will never satisfy God, to whom nothing is pleasing or acceptable that comes forth from his enemies. Now God's enemies are all those to whom he determines to impute sins. Therefore, our sins must be covered and forgiven before the Lord recognizes any work of ours. From this it follows that forgiveness of sins is free, and those who thrust in any satisfactions wickedly blaspheme it. Let us therefore, after the apostle's example, "forgetting what lies behind and straining forward to what lies before us," run our race, pressing "on toward . . . the prize of the upward call" [Phil. 3:13 — 14 p.].

14. EVEN THE PERFECT FULFILLMENT OF OUR OBLIGATION WOULD BRING US NO GLORY; BUT THIS ALSO IS NOT AT ALL POSSIBLE!

To boast about works of supererogation—how does this square with the injunction laid upon us that, when we have done whatever is commanded us, we call ourselves "unworthy servants," and say that "we have done no more than we ought to have done" [Luke 17:10 p.]? To speak before God is not to pretend or lie but to determine within yourself what you hold for certain. Therefore, the Lord bids us sincerely perceive and consider within ourselves that we perform no unrequired duties for him but render him our due service. And rightly! For we are servants obligated to render so many services that we cannot perform them, even though all our thoughts and all our members were turned to the duties of the law. Consequently, his statement, "When you have done whatever is commanded you," is as much as to say that all the righteous acts of men—and more—belonged to one alone. How dare we, then, since we, every one, are very far away from this goal, boast that we have accumulated something beyond the measure due?

Now there is no reason for any man to object that, though he partly fails in the necessary duties, nothing prevents him from extending his endeavor beyond them. This fact we must accept completely: that there is nothing that can come to mind which contributes to the honoring of God or the love of neighbor that is not comprised within God's law. But if it is a part of the law, let us not boast of voluntary liberality when we are constrained by necessity.

16. NO TRUST IN WORKS AND NO GLORY IN WORKS!

In this respect there are two plagues that we must especially banish from our minds: we must not put any confidence in the righteousness of works, and we must not ascribe to works any glory.

In teaching that all our righteous deeds are foul in God's sight unless these derive a good odor from Christ's innocence, Scripture consistently dissuades us from confidence. Works can only arouse God's vengeance unless they be sustained by his merciful pardon. Thus they leave us nothing but to implore our Judge for mercy with that confession of David's: that no one will be justified before him if he demands a reckoning from his servants. But when Job says: "If I have acted wickedly, woe to me! but if justly, I will not lift up my head" [Job 10:15 p.], although he is concerned with that highest righteousness of God, to which not even the angels answer, he at the same time shows that when it comes to God's judgment, nothing remains to all mortals but to keep silence. For it not only concerns the fact that Job prefers to yield willingly rather than to struggle perilously against God's severity but signifies that he did not experience any other righteousness in himself than what at the first moment would wither before God's face.

When confidence is banished, all glorying also must necessarily depart. For who would accord credit for righteousness to works, trust in which trembles at God's sight? We must therefore come whither Isaiah calls us: "In God all the seed of Israel shall triumph and glory" [Isa. 45:25 p.]; for what he says elsewhere is very true, that we are "the planting of the glory of God" [Isa. 61:3 p.]. The mind will then be duly cleansed when it does not in any respect settle back in the confidence, or exult in the glory, of works. But this error disposes stupid men to be puffed up with false and lying confidence because they always lodge in works the cause of their salvation.

17. IN NO RESPECT CAN WORKS SERVE AS THE CAUSE OF OUR HOLINESS

The philosophers postulate four kinds of causes to be observed in the outworking of things. If we look at these, however, we will find that, as far as the establishment of our salvation is concerned, none of them has anything to do with works. For Scripture everywhere proclaims that the efficient cause of our obtaining eternal life is the mercy of the Heavenly Father and his freely given love toward us. Surely the material cause is Christ, with his obedience, through which he acquired righteousness for us. What shall we say is the formal or instrumental cause but faith? And John includes these three in one sentence when he says: "God so loved the world that he gave his only-begotten Son that everyone who believes in him may not perish but have eternal life" [John 3:16]. As for the final cause, the apostle testifies that it consists both in the proof of divine justice and in the praise of God's goodness, and in the same place he expressly mentions three others. For so he speaks to the Romans: "All have sinned and lack the glory of God; moreover, they are justified freely by his grace" [Rom. 3:23 – 24]. Here you have the head and primal source: that God embraced us with his free mercy. There follows: "Through the redemption which is in Christ Jesus" [Rom. 3:24]. Here you have, as it were, the material cause by which righteousness is brought about for us. In the words "through faith in his blood" [Rom. 3:25 p.], is shown the instrumental cause whereby the righteousness of Christ is applied to us. Lastly, he adds the final cause when, to demonstrate his righteousness, he says, "In order that he himself may be righteous, and the justifier of him who has faith in Christ" [Rom. 3:26]. And to note also, by the way, that this righteousness stands upon reconciliation, he expressly states that Christ was given as reconciliation. Thus also in the first chapter of Ephesians he teaches that we are received into grace by God out of sheer mercy, that this comes about by Christ's intercession and is apprehended by faith, and that all things exist to the end that the glory of divine goodness may fully shine forth. Since we see that every particle of our salvation stands thus outside of us, why is it that we still trust or glory in works? The most avowed enemies of divine grace cannot stir up any controversy with us concerning either the efficient or the final cause, unless they would deny the whole of Scripture. They falsely represent the material and the formal cause, as if our works held half the place along with faith and Christ's righteousness. But Scripture cries out against this also, simply affirming that Christ is for us both righteousness and life, and that this benefit of righteousness is possessed by faith alone.

18. THE SIGHT OF GOOD WORKS, HOWEVER, CAN STRENGTHEN FAITH

Now the saints quite often strengthen themselves and are comforted by remembering their own innocence and uprightness, and they do not even refrain at times from proclaiming it. This is done in two ways: either comparing their good cause with the evil cause of the wicked, they thence derive confidence of victory, not so much by the commendation of their own righteousness as by the just and deserved condemnation of their adversaries. Or, without comparison with others, while they examine themselves before God, the purity of their own conscience brings them some comfort and confidence.

We shall look at the first reason later. Now concerning the second, let us briefly explain how what we said above agrees with it: that under God's judgment we must not put any trust in works, or glory in any esteem of them. The agreement lies in this: that the saints, when it is a question of the founding and establishing of their own salvation, without regard for works turn their eyes solely to God's goodness. Not only do they betake themselves to it before all things as to the beginning of blessedness but they repose in it as in the fulfillment of this. A conscience so founded, erected, and established is established also in the consideration of works, so far, that is, as these are testimonies of God dwelling and ruling in us. Inasmuch, therefore, as this reliance upon works has no place unless you first cast the whole confidence of your mind upon God's mercy, it ought not to seem contrary to that upon which it depends. Therefore, when we rule out reliance upon works, we mean only this: that the Christian mind may not be turned back to the merit of works as to a help toward salvation but should rely wholly on the free promise of righteousness. But we do not forbid him from undergirding and strengthening this faith by signs of the divine benevolence toward him. For if, when all the gifts God has bestowed upon us are called to mind, they are like rays of the divine countenance by which we are illumined to contemplate that supreme light of goodness; much more is this true of the grace of good works, which shows that the Spirit of adoption has been given to us.

19. WORKS AS FRUITS OF THE CALL

When, therefore, the saints by innocence of conscience strengthen their faith and take from it occasion to exult, from the fruits of their calling they merely regard themselves as having been chosen as sons by the Lord. Accordingly, the statement of Solomon: "In the fear of the Lord one has strong confidence" [Prov. 14:26], and the fact that in order to be heard by him the saints sometimes use this calling of God to witness that they have walked before him in uprightness and simplicity are matters that have no place in laying a foundation to strengthen the conscience but are of value only when taken a posteriori. For there is nowhere that fear which is able to establish full assurance. And the saints are conscious of possessing only such an integrity as intermingled with many vestiges of the flesh. But since they take the fruits of regeneration as proof of the indwelling of the Holy Spirit, from this they are greatly strengthened to wait for God's help in all their necessities, seeing that in this very great matter they experience him as Father. And they cannot do even this unless they first apprehend God's goodness, sealed by nothing else than the certainty of the promise. For if they begin to judge it by good works, nothing will be more uncertain or more feeble; for indeed, if works be judged of themselves, by their imperfection they will no less declare God's wrath than by their incomplete purity they testify to his benevolence.

In sum, they so proclaim God's benefits as not to turn away from God's freely given favor, in which, as Paul testifies, there is set "length, breadth, depth, and height" [Eph. 3:18]. It is as if he said: "Wherever the minds of the godly turn, however high they mount up, however far and wide they extend, still they ought not to depart from the love of Christ but should apply themselves wholly to meditating upon it. For in itself it embraces all dimensions." Therefore, he says that it excels and overtops all knowledge, and that when we acknowledge how much Christ loved us we are "filled with all the fullness of God" [Eph. 3:19]. As elsewhere, while Paul boasts that the godly are victors in every contest, he soon adds the reason: "on account of him who loved us" [Rom. 8:37 p.].

20. WORKS ARE GOD'S GIFT AND CANNOT BECOME THE FOUNDATION OF SELF-CONFIDENCE FOR BELIEVERS

We now see that the saints have not a confidence in works that either attributes anything to their merit, since they regard them solely as gifts of God from which they may recognize his goodness and as signs of the calling by which they realize their election, or in any degree diminishes the free righteousness that we attain in Christ, since it depends upon this and does not subsist without it. Augustine expresses this idea in few words but elegantly when he writes: "I do not say to the Lord, 'Despise not the works of my hands' [Ps. 138:8; cf. Ps. 137:8]. 'I have sought the Lord with my hands and am not deceived' [Ps. 77:2; cf. Ps. 76:3]. But I do not commend the works of my hands, for I fear lest, when Thou lookest upon them, thou mayest find more sins than merits. This only I say, this I ask, this I desire: despise not the works of thy hands; see in me thy work, not mine. For if thou seest mine, thou wilt condemn it. If thou seest thine own, thou wilt crown it. For whatever good works are mine are from thee." He gives two reasons why he dared not vaunt his works before God: because if he has anything of good works, he sees in them nothing of his own; and secondly, because these are also overwhelmed by a multitude of sins. From this it comes about that his conscience feels more fear and consternation than assurance. Therefore, he would like God to look upon his good deeds only that, recognizing the grace of his own call in them, he may finish the work he has begun.

21. SENSE IN WHICH GOOD WORKS ARE SOMETIMES SPOKEN OF AS A REASON FOR DIVINE BENEFITS

The fact that Scripture shows that the good works of believers are reasons why the Lord benefits them is to be so understood as to allow what we have set forth before to stand unshaken: that the efficient cause of our salvation consists in God the Father's love; the material cause in God the Son's obedience; the instrumental cause in the Spirit's illumination, that is, faith; the final cause, in the glory of God's great generosity. These do not prevent the Lord from embracing works as inferior causes. But how does this come about? Those whom the Lord has destined by his mercy for the inheritance of eternal life he leads into possession of it, according to his ordinary dispensation, by means of good works. What goes before in the order of dispensation he calls the cause of what comes after. In this way he sometimes derives eternal life from works, not intending it to be ascribed to them; but because he justifies those whom he has chosen in order at last to glorify them, he makes the prior grace, which is a step to that which follows, as it were the cause. But whenever the true cause is to be assigned, he does not enjoin us to take refuge in works but keeps us solely to the contemplation of his mercy. What sort of thing is this teaching of the apostle: "The wages of sin is death; the grace of the Lord, eternal life" [Rom. 6:23]? Why does he not contrast righteousness with sin, as he contrasts life with death? Why does he not make righteousness the cause of life, as he does sin that of death? For thus an antithesis would duly have been set up that is somewhat broken by this variation. But the apostle intended by this comparison to express what was true: namely, that death is owing to men's deserts but life rests solely upon God's mercy.

In short, by these expressions sequence more than cause is denoted. For God, by heaping grace upon grace, from the former grace takes the cause for adding those which follow that he may overlook nothing for the enrichment of his servants. And he so extends his liberality as to have us always look to his freely given election, which is the source and beginning. For, although he loves the gifts which he daily confers upon us, seeing that they proceed from that source, still it is our part to hold to that free acceptance, which alone can support our souls; and so to subordinate to the first cause the gifts of the Holy Spirit he then bestows, that they may nowise detract from it.

Ordinances for the Supervision of Churches (February 3, 1547)

Sermons

1. Everyone in each house is to come on Sundays, unless it be necessary to leave someone behind to take care of children or animals, under penalty of 3 sous.

2. If there be preaching any weekday, arranged with due notice, those that are able to go and have no legitimate excuse are to attend, at least one from each house, under penalty as above.

3. Those who have man or maid servants, are to bring them or have them conveyed when possible, so that they do not live like cattle without instruction.

4. Everyone is to be present at Sermon when the prayer is begun, under penalty as above, unless he absent himself for legitimate reason.

5. Everyone is to pay attention during Sermon, and there is to be no disorder or scandal.

6. No one is to leave or go out from the church until the prayer be made at the end of Sermon, under penalty as above, unless he have legitimate cause. . . .

Penalties

1. Those who fail in their duty of coming are to be admonished by the Guardians,[1] both themselves and their family.

2. If after intimation they continue to default, they are to be fined three groats for each time. Of this one third will be applied to the Guardians, the other two thirds will be applied to the poor of the parish, and put into the funds of the Church for distribution according to need as it becomes known.

3. If anyone come after Sermon has begun, he is to be admonished, and if after this is done he does not amend, for each fault he is to be fined three sous, which will be applied as above.

4. If during Sermon anyone make any disturbance or scandal, he is to be reported to the Consistory[2] to be cautioned, in order that procedure be in proportion to the fault; that is, if by carelessness he is to be well told off, if it happen by intended malice or rebelliousness he is to be reported to their Lordships[3] to be punished appropriately.

From *Calvin: Theological Treatises.* LCC, Vol. XXII, ed. by J. K. S. Reid. The Westminster Press. Published 1954. Used by permission.

[1]Supervisors of parishes elected by "the more responsible and better part of the parishioners."

[2]The ecclesiastic executive branch of the government of Geneva, composed of five pastors and twelve lay elders. The pastors held tenure throughout their ministry, the elders for only a year.

[3]Since these ordinances applied to both the churches within the city and in the country, the term may refer either to the four Syndics, the secular executive officers of the city government, or to the local country lords.

By Whom Fines Are to Be Exacted

1. The local lord, in conjunction with the Ministers and the Guardians, is to oblige the delinquents to pay the fines they have incurred, when they will not pay of their own free will. Legitimate excuses are to be admitted, but this is to be done without any formal procedure.

2. If there be any so rebellious that, despite the above fines, they do not at all amend, they are to be reported to the Consistory with advice to the effect that their Lordships punish them according to the seriousness of their obstinacy.

3. Fathers are to be responsible for their children, and, if there be a penalty, it is to be exacted from them. . . .

Of the Supper

1. No one is to be received at the Supper unless he first have made confession of his faith. That is to say, he must declare before the Minister that he desires to live according to the reformation of the gospel, and that he knows the Creed, the Lord's Prayer and the Commandments of God.

2. Those who wish to receive the Supper are to come at the beginning of the Service; those who come at the end are not to be received.

3. Other impediments are to be within the cognizance of the Consistory, to deal with them, in accordance with what has been ordained.

4. All are to remain until the end, unless there be a legitimate excuse which is recognized as above. . . .

Faults Contravening the Reformation Besides Those Already Mentioned

First, Superstitions

1. Those found to have any paternosters or idols for adoration are to be brought before the Consistory, and, besides the punishment imposed on them there, they are to be brought before their Lordships.

2. Those who have been on pilgrimages or voyages the same.

3. Those who observe the papistical feasts or fastings are to be admonished only, unless they are obstinate in their rebellion.

4. Those who have attended mass, besides admonition, are to be brought before their Lordships.

5. In such cases, their Lordships will have the right of chastising by means of prison or otherwise, or of punishing by extraordinary fines, at their discretion.

In the case of fines, they are to apply some small portion of them to the Guardians, if the delict was notified by them.

Blasphemies

1. Those who have blasphemed, swearing by the body or by the blood of our Lord, or suchlike, ought to do reverence for the first time; for

the second a penalty of five sous; for the third ten sous; and for the last time put in the pillory for an hour.

2. Anyone who abjures or renounces God or his Baptism is for the first time to be put for ten days on bread and water; for the second and third time he is to be punished with some more rigorous corporal punishment, at the discretion of their Lordships.

Contradiction of the Word

1. If there are any who contradict the Word of God, let them be brought before the Consistory to be admonished, or be remanded to their Lordships to receive chastisement according to the needs of the case.

2. If the contradiction or rebellion amount to scandal which demands prompter remedy, the local lord is to take a hand in the matter for the maintenance of the honour of the Ministry and the Magistracy.

Drunkenness

1. There is to be no treating of one another to drinks, under penalty of three sous.

2. The taverns are to be closed during Service, under penalty that the taverner pay three sous and anyone entering them the same.

3. If anyone be found drunk, he is to pay for the first time three sous and be brought before the Consistory; the second time he must pay the sum of five sous; and the third ten sous and be put in prison.

4. There are to be no carousals, under penalty of ten sous.

Songs and Dances

If anyone sing songs that are unworthy, dissolute or outrageous, or spin wildly round in the dance, or the like, he is to be imprisoned for three days, and then sent on to the Consistory.

Usury

No one is to lend at interest or for profit greater than five per cent,[4] on pain of confiscation of the capital sum and of being required to make appropriate amends according to the needs of the case.

Brawling

1. No one is to cause noise or dispute on pain of being punished according to the needs of the case.

2. If there be any who causes sedition or assembling to make or support quarrels, he is to be punished with more rigorous penalties according to what he merits.

---

[4]A few years later this was changed to ten per cent.

Complaints

If there be a complaint or dispute between two people, the Minister, summoning the Guardians, will do his duty to bring them to accord; and if he is unable to prevail, he will remand them to the Consistory.

Games

No one is to play at games that are dissolute, or at games played for gold or silver or at excessive expense, on pain of five sous and loss of the sum staked.

Fornication

1. As to those who are caught in fornication, if it be an unmarried man with an unmarried woman, they are to be imprisoned for six days on bread and water, and pay sixty sous amends.

2. If it be adultery, one or the other being married, they are to be imprisoned for nine days on bread and water, and pay amends at the discretion of their Lordships, as the crime is much more grave.

3. Those who are promised in marriage are not to cohabit as man and wife until the marriage be celebrated in church, otherwise they will be punished as for fornication. . . .

Comments / on Calvin

It is remarkable how much of Roman Catholic tradition and theory survived in Calvin's theology. He owed something to Stoicism, especially to Seneca, and something to his studies of law; but his chief reliance was on St. Augustine, who drew predestinarianism out of St. Paul, who did not know Christ. Calvin sternly ignored Christ's conception of God as a loving and merciful father, and calmly passed by a multitude of Biblical passages that assumed man's freedom to mold his own destiny. Calvin's genius lay not in conceiving new ideas but in developing the thought of his predecessors to ruinously logical conclusions, expressing these with an eloquence equaled only by Augustine, and formulating their practical implications in a system of ecclesiastical legislation.

WILL DURANT (1957)

Here is one of the most significant differences between Calvin and the previous reformers. He rejected their expectation of the speedy coming of the Lord and projected the final cataclysm into an indefinite future. Luther looked wistfully for the end of the age before his own demise and the Anabaptists often set dates. But Calvin renewed the role of St. Augustine who terminated the early Christian expectation of the speedy coming of the Lord and envisaged successive acts in the historical drama in which the Church came well-nigh to be equated with the kingdom of God. Even so Calvin substituted for the great and imminent day of the Lord the dream of the Holy Commonwealth in the terrestrial sphere.

ROLAND H. BAINTON (1952)

Calvin was unique among Protestants in holding that the Church must manage her own affairs with the greatest possible independence of the temporal authority and yet maintain a real relation with that authority: he alone revived in Protestantism the old papal principle that the temporal and spiritual powers were like two swords in one sheath. New also was Calvin's insistence on the Church's public discipline for all members of the community and on the duty of the temporal authorities as Christian men to maintain this discipline even with legal penalties. This principle of discipline is the most characteristic element in Calvin's Geneva: given the belief that God was sovereign, that man before God was nothing, and that to God was due all glory, it followed inevitably that all men must honour God in their doctrine and life—even if they have to be compelled to do so.

BASIL HALL (1956)

In conformity with the Old Testament and in analogy to the ethical valuation of good works, asceticism looked upon the pursuit of wealth as an end in itself as highly reprehensible; but the attainment of it as a fruit of labour in a calling was a sign of God's blessing. And even more important: the religious valuation of restless, continuous, systematic work in a worldly calling, as the highest means to asceticism, and at the same time the surest and most evident proof of rebirth and genuine faith, must have been the most powerful conceivable lever for the expansion of that attitude toward life which we have here called the spirit of capitalism.

MAX WEBER (1905)

"The capitalist spirit" is as old as history, and was not, as has sometimes been said, the offspring of Puritanism. But it found in certain aspects of later Puritanism a tonic which braced its energies and fortified its already vigorous temper.

R. H. TAWNEY (1926)

Calvin had taught that one must find solace solely on the basis of the true faith. Each man was duty-bound to consider himself chosen and to reject all doubt as a temptation of the devil, for a lack of self-confidence was interpreted as a sign of insufficient faith. To attain that self-confidence, unceasing work in a calling was recommended. By his unceasing activity in the service of God, the believer strengthened his self-confidence as the active tool of the divine will. This idea implied a tremendous tension: Calvinism had eliminated all magical means of attaining salvation.

REINHARD BENDIX (1962)

As a child of the medieval peasant world, Luther had introduced a peasant version of the gospel of work, declaring that humble toil or even housework was "a service of God far surpassing the holiness and asceticism of all the monks and nuns"; but he had denounced the thriving business class, which was squeezing the poor. It was John Calvin who signed the pact with this class, sanctifying its interests and values. A spokesman for the busy city world, Calvin sought to escape the shocking contradictions between medieval theory and practice in economic life by investing this life with a high seriousness, dedicating it to the service of God. He made the pursuit of wealth and preservation of property a Christian duty, calling for the same arduous discipline as the warfare against the temptations of the flesh. He exalted the acquisitive virtues of enterprise, diligence, sobriety, frugality, thrift. He invented an ideal type hitherto unknown to religion and culture, a type neither humanistic nor ascetic—the God-fearing businessman.   *HERBERT J. MULLER (1952)*

There were, however, it must be insisted, allowable pleasures for the Puritan. He did not approve of gluttony, which appears in the sermons along with other vices. But he was not greatly worried over it, and in matters of food and drink he favored solid, sound fare and enough of it. He was not notably abstemious if his digestion was good, and contrary to some opinions his digestion often was good. He took the commandment against adultery at least as seriously as he took the others, but within the due bounds of monogamous marriage there is no evidence that he felt about sexual intercourse any of St. Paul's obvious doubts. The empirical evidence that he enjoyed the pleasures of the bed is overwhelming, especially for the American Puritans, for whom large families were an economic asset.   *CRANE BRINTON (1959)*

Bibliography of Critical Comments

This bibliography contains source information for the critical comments that follow the readings. The list is arranged alphabetically by critic, and the page in this volume on which the comments can be found are indicated by **boldface** numbers in parentheses.

Acton, Lord. *The History of Freedom and Other Essays,* eds. J. N. Figgis and R. V. Laurence. London: Macmillan & Co., Ltd., 1907, pp. 212, 231 (**484**).

Adler, Mortimer J. *The Idea of Freedom: A Dialectical Examination of the Conceptions of Freedom,* Vol. I. Garden City, N.Y.: Doubleday & Company, Inc., 1958, p. 332 (**120**).

Ames, Russell. *Citizen Thomas More and His Utopia.* Princeton, N.J.: Princeton University Press, 1949, p. 5 (**553**).

Aristophanes. *The Frogs,* in *The Eleven Comedies,* trans. anon. New York: Liveright Publishing Corp., 1930, vv. 1482-1499 (**93**).

Aristotle. *The Works of Aristotle, Vol. III: Metaphysics,* trans. W. D. Ross, 2nd ed. Oxford: The Clarendon Press, 1928, p. 987b (**92-93**).

Arnold, E. V. *Roman Stoicism.* New York: Humanities Press, Inc., 1958, pp. 85 (**168**), 120 (**196**), 127 (**203**).

Bainton, Roland H. *The Reformation of the Sixteenth Century.* Boston: Beacon Press, 1956, pp. 114-115 (**626-627**).

Baker, Herschel. *The Image of Man.* New York: Harper & Row, Publishers (Harper Torchbooks), 1961, pp. 161-162, 172-173, 175 (**296**); 169 (**263**); 222 (**422**).

Barrow, R. H. *The Romans.* Baltimore, Md.: Penguin Books, Inc., 1949, pp. 150 (**151**), 155-156 (**187**), 160 (**203**).

Bendix, Reinhard. *Max Weber: An Intellectual Portrait.* Garden City, N.Y.: Doubleday & Company, Inc. (Anchor Books), 1962, p. 60 (**627**).

Bevington, D. M. "The Dialogue in *Utopia:* Two Sides to the Question," in *Studies in Philology,* LVIII (July, 1961), 496-498 (**552-553**).

Bigongiari, Dino. "Introduction," *On World Government (De Monarchia),* by Dante Alighieri, trans. H. W. Schneider, 2nd ed. New York: Liberal Arts Press, Inc., 1957, p. xiii (**388**).

Bishop, Morris. *Petrarch and His World.* Bloomington: Indiana University Press, 1963, pp. 103-104 (**421**), 374 (**422**).

Bourke, V. J., ed. *The Pocket Aquinas.* New York: Washington Square Press, Inc., 1960, pp. xix-xx (**337**).

Bowra, C. M. *The Greek Experience.* New York: New American Library, Inc. (Mentor Books), 1959, p. 210 (**166**).

Brinton, Crane. *A History of Western Morals.* New York: Harcourt, Brace & World, Inc., 1959, pp. 77-78 (**59**), 226 (**628**).

Brown, Norman O., trans. *Hesiod.* New York: Liberal Arts Press, Inc., 1953, pp. 44-45 (**9**).

Bultmann, Rudolf. *Primitive Christianity in Its Contemporary Setting.* New York: Meridian Books, 1956, p. 98 (**216**).

Burckhardt, Jacob. *The Civilization of the Renaissance in Italy,* 2nd ed. London: Phaidon Press, Ltd., 1945, pp. 215 (**431-432**), 235 (**513**).

Campbell, W. E. *Erasmus, Tyndale, and More.* Milwaukee, Wis.: The Bruce Publishing Co., 1949, p. 276 (**604**).

Cassirer, Ernst. *The Myth of the State.* Garden City, N.Y.: Doubleday & Company, Inc. (Anchor Books), 1955, pp. 174, 190-191 (**485**).

————. *The Platonic Renaissance in England.* Austin: University of Texas Press, 1953, p. 108 (**552**).

Chabod, Federico. *Machiavelli and the Renaissance,* trans. D. Moore. London: Bowes & Bowes Publishers, Ltd., 1958, pp. 61, 64-65 (**485-486**).

Chambers, R. W. *Thomas More.* Ann Arbor: University of Michigan Press (Ann Arbor Paperbacks), 1958, pp. 125, 132 (**551**).

Cicero. *Letters and Treatises,* trans. E. S. Shuckburgh. New York: P. F. Collier & Son, Inc. (Harvard Classics), 1909, p. 45 (**187**).

Cochrane, C. N. *Christianity and Classical Culture.* New York: Oxford University Press, 1957, pp. 224 (**250-251**), 451-452 (**297**).

Collingwood, R. G. *The Idea of History.* New York: Oxford University Press, 1956, pp. 19 (**41**), 29 (**59**).

Copleston, Frederick. *A History of Philosophy,* Vol. I. Garden City, N.Y.: Doubleday & Company, Inc. (Image Books), 1962, pp. 78-79 (**120**).

Cornford, F. M. *Before and After Socrates.* New York: Cambridge University Press, 1960, pp. 90-91, 100 (**119**).

Curtius, E. R. *European Literature and the Latin Middle Ages.* New York: Pantheon Books, Inc., 1953, p. 73 (**295**).

Daniel-Rops, H. *The Protestant Reformation.* New York: E. P. Dutton & Co., Inc., 1961, pp. 356-357 (**605**).

Danielou, Jean. *Origen.* New York: Sheed & Ward, 1955, p. 184 (**240-241**).

Dante. *The Divine Comedy of Dante Alighieri: Paradiso,* trans. H. R. Huse. New York: Holt, Rinehart & Winston, Inc. (Rinehart Edition 72), X, ll. 125-126 (**312**).

D'Arcy, M. C. "The Philosophy of St. Augustine," in *A Monument to St. Augustine,* eds. M. C. D'Arcy, *et al.* New York: Meridian Books, 1957, p. 156 (**295**).

De Sélincourt, Aubrey. *The World of Herodotus.* Boston: Little, Brown and Company, 1963, p. 23 (**41-42**).

De Wulf, Maurice. *Philosophy and Civilization in the Middle Ages.* New York: Dover Publications, Inc., 1953, p. 109 (**336**).

Durant, Will. *The Life of Greece.* New York: Simon and Schuster, Inc., 1939, pp. 653, 658 (**169**).

Durant, Will. *The Reformation.* New York: Simon and Schuster, Inc., 1957, pp. 370 (**604**), 465 (**626**).

Eliot, T. S. *Selected Essays.* New York: Harcourt, Brace & World, Inc., 1950, p. 235 (**367-368**).

Eller, Meredith F. *The Beginnings of the Christian Religion.* New Haven, Conn.: College & University Press, 1958, p. 203 (**215-216**).

Emerson, Ralph Waldo. *Representative Men.* New York: Sully and Kleinteich, 1876, pp. 56-57 (**93**).

Enslin, Morton S. *Christian Beginnings.* New York: Harper & Row, Publishers (Harper Torchbooks), 1956, pp. 87-88 (**216**).

Epstein, Isidore. *Judaism: A Historical Presentation.* Baltimore, Md.: Penguin Books, Inc., 1959, p. 198 (**216**).

Fowler, Henry H. "The News of the Week in Review," *The New York Times,* September 5, 1965, Sec. IV, p. 1 (**94**).

Gauss, Christian. "Introduction," *The Prince,* by Niccolò Machiavelli. New York: New American Library, Inc. (Mentor Books), 1952, pp. 21-22 (**484**).

Gibbon, Edward. *Decline and Fall of the Roman Empire.* Chicago: Encyclopaedia Britannica, Inc. (Great Books of the Western World), 1952, p. 542 (**296-297**).

Gilmore, M. P. *The World of Humanism.* New York: Harper & Row, Publishers (Harper Torchbooks), 1962, pp. 134-135 (**485**), 236 (**420-421**).

Gilson, Etienne. *Dante the Philosopher.* London: Sheed & Ward, Ltd., 1952, pp. 165, 184-185 (**387-388**).

———. *History of Christian Philosophy in the Middle Ages.* New York: Random House, Inc., 1955, pp. 10, 13 (**228**); 102 (**313**).

———. *Reason and Revelation in the Middle Ages.* New York: Charles Scribner's Sons, 1952, pp. 8, 10-11 (**251**), 69-70 (**335-336**).

Grant, Michael, trans. *Selected Works of Cicero.* Baltimore, Md.: Penguin Books, Inc., 1960, pp. 12, 15 (**187**).

———. *The World of Rome.* New York: New American Library, Inc. (Mentor Books), 1960, pp. 225-226 (**196**).

Gregory Thaumaturgus, St. Cited in *Origen,* by Jean Danielou. New York: Sheed & Ward, 1955, p. 158 (**240**).

Grene, David. *Man in His Pride: Study in the Political Philosophy of Thucydides and Plato.* Chicago: University of Chicago Press, 1950, pp. 26-27 (**59**).

———, trans. *Three Greek Tragedies in Translation.* Chicago: University of Chicago Press, 1942, p. 1 (**22-23**).

Hadas, Moses. *Ancilla to Classical Reading.* New York: Columbia University Press, 1954, pp. 308 (**196**), 309 (**203**).

———. *Essential Works of Stoicism.* New York: Bantam Books, Inc., 1961, p. xii (**168**).

Hadzits, G. D. *Lucretius and His Influence.* New York: Cooper Square Publishers, Inc., 1963, pp. 98-99 (**151**).

Hall, Basil. *John Calvin.* London: publ. for The Historical Association by George Philip & Son, Ltd., 1956, pp. 24-25 (**627**).

Hamilton, Edith. *The Roman Way.* New York: New American Library, Inc. (Mentor Books), 1957, p. 50 (**187**).

Harnack, Adolf. *History of Dogma.* New York: Russell & Russell Publishers, 1958, pp. 178-179 (**228**).

Hoby, Sir Thomas. Introduction to *The Book of the Courtier,* by Baldassare Castiglione, trans. Sir Thomas Hoby (1561). London: J. M. Dent & Sons, Ltd. (Everyman's Library), 1928, pp. 2-3 (**513**).

How, W. W., and J. Wells. *A Commentary on Herodotus,* Vol. I. London: Oxford University Press, 1961, p. 45 (**42**).

Jaeger, Werner. *Paideia: The Ideals of Greek Culture,* Vol. I. Oxford: Basil Blackwell & Mott, Ltd., 1946, pp. 65 (**77**), 155 (**9**).

Jaffa, H. V. *Thomism and Aristotelianism.* Chicago: University of Chicago Press, 1952, pp. 5, 8, 19-20 (**336-337**).

James, William. *The Varieties of Religious Experience.* New York: Modern Library, Inc., n.d. (orig. 1902), pp. 168-170 (**295**).

Jerome, St. Cited in *The Nicene and Post-Nicene Fathers,* Vol. IV, eds. Philip Schaff and Henry Wace. Grand Rapids, Mich.: Wm. B. Eerdmans Publishing Co., 1954, pp. 85-86 (**240**).

Jones, C. W. *Medieval Literature in Translation.* New York: Longmans, Green & Co., Inc., 1950, p. 753 (**388**).

Kautsky, Karl. *Thomas More and His Utopia,* trans. H. J. Stenning. London: A. & C. Black, Ltd., 1927, pp. 159, 161 (**550-551**).

Kitto, H. D. F. *The Greeks.* Baltimore, Md.: Penguin Books, Inc., 1951, pp. 18, 55 (**9**); 179 (**77**).

Klausner, Joseph. *From Jesus to Paul.* London: George Allen & Unwin, Ltd., 1944, p. 182 (**216**).

Knight, W. F. J. *Roman Vergil.* London: Faber & Faber, Ltd., 1944, p. 45 (**152**).

Kristeller, P. O. "Introduction to Pico della Mirandola," in *The Renaissance Philosophy of Man,* eds. E. Cassirer, P. O. Kristeller, and J. H. Randall. Chicago: University of Chicago Press, 1948, p. 221 (**432**).

————. *Renaissance Thought.* New York: Harper & Row, Publishers (Harper Torchbooks), 1961, p. 84 (**421**).

Krutch, Joseph Wood. *The Modern Temper.* New York: Harcourt, Brace & World, Inc., 1956, p. 83 (**23**).

Latham, R. E., trans. *The Nature of the Universe,* by Lucretius. Baltimore, Md.: Penguin Books, Inc., 1951, p. 12 (**151**).

Lea, H. C. *The History of Sacerdotal Celibacy in the Christian Church.* New York: Russell & Russell Publishers, 1957, pp. 26-27 (**262-263**).

Lewis, C. S. *English Literature in the Sixteenth Century.* Oxford: Oxford University Press, 1954, pp. 167-168 (**552**).

Lipsius, Justus. Cited in *Ancilla to Classical Reading,* by Moses Hadas. New York: Columbia University Press (Columbia Paperback), 1961, p. 308 (**196**).

Macaulay, T. B. *Critical and Historical Essays,* Vol. II. London: J. M. Dent & Sons, Ltd. (Everyman's Library), 1907, pp. 2-4 (**483-484**).

Machiavelli, Niccolò. Letter to Francesco Vettori, in *The Renaissance in Italy, Vol. I: The Age of the Despots,* by J. A. Symonds. New York: G. P. Putnam's Sons (Capricorn Books), 1960, pp. 248-250 (**482-483**).

Mackinnon, James. *Luther and the Reformation,* Vol. III. New York: Russell & Russell Publishers, 1962, p. 225 (**604-605**).

Mahaffy, J. P. *Greek Life and Thought.* London: Macmillan & Co., Ltd., 1896, pp. xxxvii, xxxviii (**166**).

Martindale, C. C. "A Sketch of the Life and Character of St. Augustine," in *A Monument to St. Augustine,* eds. M. C. D'Arcy, *et al.* New York: Meridian Books, 1957, p. 84 (**296**).

Mommsen, T. E. "Introduction," *Sonnets and Songs,* by Francesco Petrarch, trans. A. M. Armi. New York: Pantheon Books, Inc., 1946, p. xli (**421**).

More, Thomas. Cited in *Erasmus, Tyndale, and More,* by W. E. Campbell. Milwaukee, Wis.: The Bruce Publishing Co., 1949, p. 86 (**550**).

Muller, Herbert J. *Freedom in the Ancient World.* New York: Harper & Row, Publishers, 1961, pp. 176 (41), 194 (59).

——. *Freedom in the Western World.* New York: Harper & Row, Publishers, 1963, p. 156 (605).

——. *The Uses of the Past.* New York: Oxford University Press (Galaxy Books), 1957, pp. 272-273 (627-628).

Müller, K. O. *A History of the Literature of Ancient Greece,* Vol. I. London: Longmans, Green & Co., Ltd., 1872, p. 359 (41).

Murray, Gilbert. *Five Stages of Greek Religion.* Garden City, N.Y.: Doubleday & Company, Inc., 1955, pp. 62-63 (9), 92 (166).

Nachod, Hans. "Introduction to Petrarch," in *The Renaissance Philosophy of Man,* eds. E. Cassirer, P. O. Kristeller, and J. H. Randall. Chicago: University of Chicago Press, 1948, p. 25 (420).

Nahm, Milton C., trans. *Selections from Early Greek Philosophy,* 4th ed. New York: Appleton-Century-Crofts, 1947, p. 55 (77).

Oates, W. J., ed. *Basic Writings of St. Augustine.* New York: Random House, Inc., 1948, pp. xxxvi-xxxviii (295-296).

O'Sullivan, Richard. "Social Life and Theories of St. Thomas More," in *The Dublin Review,* CXCIX (July, 1936), 49-50 (551).

Patch, H. R. *The Tradition of Boethius.* New York: Oxford University Press, 1935, pp. 6, 47 (312).

Pater, Walter. *The Renaissance.* New York: New American Library, Inc. (Mentor Books), 1959, pp. 41, 45-46 (432).

Pegis, A. C., ed. *Basic Writings of St. Thomas Aquinas,* Vol. I. New York: Random House, Inc., 1945, p. xxxviii (336).

Rand, E. K. *Founders of the Middle Ages.* New York: Dover Publications, Inc., 1957, pp. 38 (250), 85 (241), 130-131 (263), 177 (313), 254 (296), 259 (272).

Robinson, C. A., Jr. *An Anthology of Greek Drama.* New York: Holt, Rinehart & Winston, Inc., 1956, p. ix (23).

——. *The Spring of Civilization: Periclean Athens.* New York: E. P. Dutton & Co., Inc., 1954, p. 342 (93).

Robinson, J. H., and H. W. Rolfe. *Petrarch,* 2nd ed. New York: G. P. Putnam's Sons, 1914, pp. 307 (421), 417 (421-422).

Roeder, Ralph. *The Man of the Renaissance.* New York: Meridian Books, 1958, pp. 295 (484); 315, 320-321 (513-514).

Rose, H. J. *Religion in Greece and Rome.* New York: Harper & Row, Publishers, 1959, p. 267 (203).

Ross, W. D. *Aristotle: A Complete Exposition of His Works and Thought.* New York: Meridian Books, 1959, pp. 186 (119-120), 280 (22).

Russell, Bertrand. *A History of Western Philosophy.* New York: Simon and Schuster, Inc., 1945, pp. 91 (93-94), 182-183 (119).

Sansovino, Jacopo. Cited in *Charles V, Father of Europe,* by Gertrude von Schwarzenfeld. Chicago: Henry Regnery Co., 1957, pp. 39-40 (513).

Santayana, George. *Three Philosophical Poets.* Garden City, N.Y.: Doubleday & Company, Inc. (Anchor Books), 1953, pp. 81, 85 (388); 86-87 (368).

Sayers, D. L. *Further Papers on Dante.* London: Methuen & Co., Ltd., 1957, p. 40 (367).

Schopenhauer, Arthur. *The World as Will and Idea.* New York: Charles

Scribner's Sons, 1883, Vol. I, pp. 113-114 (**166**); Vol. II, p. 354 (**196**).

Sewall, Richard B. "The Tragic Form," in *Essays in Criticism,* IV, iv (October, 1954), 350-351 (**23**).

Singleton, C. S. *Dante Studies, Vol. I: Commedia: Elements of Structures.* Cambridge: Harvard University Press, 1957, pp. 88-90, 94 (**372**).

——. *An Essay on the Vita Nuova.* Cambridge: Harvard University Press, 1958, pp. 63, 74 (**368**).

Spinoza, Baruch. *Tractatus Theologico-Politicus,* trans. R. H. M. Elwes. London: G. Bell & Sons, Ltd. (Bohn's Philosophical Library), 1900, p. 315 (**483**).

Stambler, Bernard. *Dante's Other World.* New York: New York University Press, 1957, p. 48 (**343**).

Symonds, J. A. *The Renaissance in Italy, Vol. I: The Age of the Despots.* New York: G. P. Putnam's Sons (Capricorn Books), 1960, p. 145 (**513**).

Tawney, R. H. *Religion and the Rise of Capitalism.* London: John Murray Publishers, Ltd., 1926, p. 226 (**627**).

Taylor, A. E. *Aristotle.* New York: Dover Publications, Inc., 1955, pp. 90-91 (**120**).

Taylor, H. O. *The Medieval Mind,* 4th ed. London: Macmillan & Co., Ltd., 1925, Vol. I, p. 89 (**313**); Vol. II, p. 583 (**272**).

Valency, Maurice. *In Praise of Love.* New York: The Macmillan Company, 1958, pp. 206, 216, 226-227 (**343**).

Van Doren, Mark. *Mark Van Doren on Great Poems of Western Literature.* New York: P. F. Collier, Inc., 1962, pp. 125, 128 (**152**).

Vincentius Lirinensis, St. Cited in "Introductory Note," by Peter Holmes, in *The Ante-Nicene Fathers,* Vol. III, eds. Alexander Roberts and James Donaldson. Grand Rapids, Mich.: Wm. B. Eerdmans Publishing Co., 1956, pp. 7-8 (**250**).

Voigt, Georg. Cited in *The Renaissance in Historical Thought,* by Wallace K. Ferguson. Boston: Houghton Mifflin Company, 1948, p. 162 (**420**).

Volgin, Vyacheslav. "Sir Thomas More," in *News, A Review of World Events,* XXXIX (February 15, 1953), 15 (**551-552**).

Voltaire. Cited in "Introduction," by Max Lerner, in *The Prince and the Discourses,* by Niccolò Machiavelli. New York: Modern Library, Inc., 1940, p. xli (**483**).

Vossler, Karl. *Medieval Culture: An Introduction to Dante and His Times,* Vol. I. New York: Harcourt, Brace & World, Inc., 1929, pp. 136-137 (**336**); 159, 163 (**367**); 264-265 (**388-389**).

Weber, Max. *The Protestant Ethic and the Spirit of Capitalism.* New York: Charles Scribner's Sons, 1958, p. 172 (**627**).

Wenley, R. M. *Stoicism and Its Influence.* New York: Cooper Square Publishers, Inc., 1963, pp. 68 (**203**), 75 (**166**).

Wilkins, E. H. *A History of Italian Literature.* Cambridge: Harvard University Press, 1954, p. 57 (**387**).

Zeller, Eduard. *Outlines of the History of Greek Philosophy.* New York: Meridian Books, 1955, pp. 40 (**77**), 160 (**93**).